SOMETHING ABOUT THE AUTHOR®

Something about
the Author *was named
an "**Outstanding
Reference Source,**"
the highest honor given
by the American
Library Association
Reference and Adult
Services Division.*

ISSN 0276-816X

sOMEThING ABOUT ThE AUThOR®

**Facts and Pictures about Authors
and Illustrators of Books for Young People**

volume 142

GALE®

THOMSON
★ ™
GALE

Detroit • New York • San Diego • San Francisco • Cleveland • New Haven, Conn. • Waterville, Maine • London • Munich

Something About the Author, Volume 142

Project Editor
Scot Peacock

Editorial
Katy Balcer, Shavon Burden, Sara Constantakis, Anna Marie Dahn, Alana Joli Foster, Natalie Fulkerson, Arlene M. Johnson, Michelle Kazensky, Julie Keppen, Joshua Kondek, Thomas McMahon, Jenai A. Mynatt, Judith L. Pyko, Mary Ruby, Lemma Shomali, Susan Strickland, Maikue Vang, Tracey Watson, Thomas Wiloch, Emiene Shija Wright

Research
Michelle Campbell, Sarah Genik, Barbara McNeil, Tamara C. Nott, Gary J. Oudersluys, Tracie A. Richardson, Cheryl L. Warnock

Permissions
Margaret Chamberlain

Imaging and Multimedia
Dean Dauphinais, Robert Duncan, Leitha Etheridge-Sims, Mary K. Grimes, Lezlie Light, Dan Newell, David G. Oblender, Christine O'Bryan, Kelly A. Quin, Luke Rademacher

Composition and Electronic Capture
Carolyn A. Roney

Manufacturing
Stacy L. Melson

LIBRARY OF CONGRESS CATALOG CARD NUMBER 62-52046

ISBN 0-7876-5214-8
ISSN 0276-816X

Printed in the United States of America
10 9 8 7 6 5 4 3 2 1

Contents

Authors in Forthcoming Volumes

Below are some of the authors and illustrators that will be featured in upcoming volumes of *SATA*. These include new entries on the swiftly rising stars of the field, as well as completely revised and updated entries (indicated with *) on some of the most notable and best-loved creators of books for children.

*Alma Flor Ada ❚ Ada is not only a prolific storyteller, but a prime mover in the bilingual education movement. Many of her picture books, including *Mediopollito/Half-Chicken,* are available in bilingual Spanish and English editions that promote literacy in both tongues. With F. Isabel Campoy, Ada has also translated into Spanish a significant number of picture books written in English, including Lois Ehlert's *Día de mercado,* originally published as *Market Day.*

*Sharleen Collicott ❚ Collicott has been illustrating children's picture books since the early 1970s, but she didn't publish her first self-illustrated work, *Seeing Stars,* until 1996. Her pictures—colorful, detailed paintings that range from intimate views to double-page spreads—characteristically feature fantastic animals and have been compared to such artists as Hieronymous Bosch for their imaginative quality and attention to detail. In 2002, Collicott published the self-illustrated work *Toestomper and the Caterpillars*; a sequel, *Toestomper and the Bad Butterflies,* was released in 2003.

*Greg Evans ❚ Evans is the creative talent behind the popular comic strip "Luann," featuring the trials and traumas of an American high school student. Evans has twice been nominated for the Reuben Award's Cartoonist of the Year. Collections of Evans's "Luann" strip can be found in such books as *If Confusion Were a Class I'd Get an A* and *My Bedroom and Other Environmental Hazards.*

Michael Kusugak ❚ Kusugak is a Canadian author who has broadened the spectrum of children's literature through his contribution of stories focusing on his Inuit heritage. Many of his titles, among them *Hide and Sneak, Baseball Bats for Christmas* and the collection *Arctic Stories,* engage early elementary-grade readers with their crisp prose and unique subject matter.

Meg Greene Malvasi ❚ Malvasi, who often publishes under the name Meg Greene, has penned biographies of such contemporary celebrities as actors Matt Damon and Will Smith, as well as such historical figures as Pope John Paul II, explorer Jacques Cartier, and American Revolutionary war hero Thaddeus Kosciuzko. She is also a frequent contributor to the renowned children's history magazine *Cobblestone.* Her 2001 work *Buttons, Bones, and the Organ Grinder's Monkey: Tales of Historical Archaeology,* was named a Best Book for Teens by the New York Public Library.

*Michael Morpurgo ❚ Morpurgo blends adventure, fantasy and moral drama in his lyrical yet always understated prose. Consistent themes for Morpurgo are the conquest of evil by good and the vindication of virtues such as loyalty, hard work and determi-

nation. Much of Morpurgo's fiction is historical, set in the recent past, and in such exotic locales as the Scilly Islands, China, Renaissance Venice, and the Pyrenees. His subjects range from war to rural life, from the sea to the boarding school, and his writing combines stark realism with touches of fancy and magic. Morpurgo released three works in 2003: *Sleeping Sword, Gentle Giant,* and *Mairi's Mermaid.*

*Garth Nix ❚ An award-winning Australian writer, Nix has, according to critics, created amazing and intricate worlds, a cast of characters that stick in the imagination, and lessons of friendship and loyalty that resonate. He is best known for his fantasy novels in the "Old Kingdom" trilogy, including *Sabriel, Lirael,* and the 2003 work *Abhorsen.* Writing for a slightly younger audience, he has also penned a six-novel cycle, "The Seventh Tower" series.

Tamara L. Roleff ❚ Roleff is a book editor and author who specializes in nonfiction titles. In her job for Greenhaven Press, she has edited titles for several book series, among them "Opposing Viewpoints," "History Firsthand," and "Current Controversies." In 2003 Roleff published *The World Trade Center* from the "History Firsthand" series and *Police Corruption* from the "At Issue" series.

Sarah Stewart ❚ Stewart is the author of four books, *The Money Tree, The Library, The Gardener,* and *The Journey,* all done in collaboration with her husband, illustrator David Small. *The Gardener* and *The Journey* are both told in epistolary form, and both deal with a young girl's experiences in the city. In *The Gardener,* a young girl is sent to live with her uncle during the Great Depression, while *The Journey* recounts an Amish child's trip to Chicago.

Kevin Yagher ❚ Yagher is a creator of special effects makeup and a creature designer in the motion picture industry. He has worked on such films as *Master of Disguise, Mission Impossible II,* and *Face Off,* and has directed television presentations, including episodes of the Home Box Office series *Tales from the Crypt.* Yagher's Hollywood experience as a master of special effects and his long association with the fantasy/science fiction film genre provided a foundation for his first book. *Heverly* is the story of an elf, Prince Eli, who must save his homeland of Heverly.

*Paul Yee ❚ Yee is a Canadian author whose Chinese heritage and experiences growing up in the Chinatown district of Vancouver, British Columbia have inspired many of his highly acclaimed books for younger readers. While writing primarily for Canadian children of Chinese ancestry who desire to learn about themselves and their heritage, his books have found audiences with children of many backgrounds from both Canada and the United States. Among Yee's titles are the short-story collections *Tales from Gold Mountain: Stories of the Chinese in the New World* and *Dead Man's Gold and Other Tales,* as well as the novels *Breakaway* and *The Curses of Third Uncle.* in 2002 Yee published *The Jade Necklace,* a picture book.

Introduction

Something about the Author (*SATA*) is an ongoing reference series that examines the lives and works of authors and illustrators of books for children. *SATA* includes not only well-known writers and artists but also less prominent individuals whose works are just coming to be recognized. This series is often the only readily available information source on emerging authors and illustrators. You'll find *SATA* informative and entertaining, whether you are a student, a librarian, an English teacher, a parent, or simply an adult who enjoys children's literature.

What's Inside *SATA*

SATA provides detailed information about authors and illustrators who span the full time range of children's literature, from early figures like John Newbery and L. Frank Baum to contemporary figures like Judy Blume and Richard Peck. Authors in the series represent primarily English-speaking countries, particularly the United States, Canada, and the United Kingdom. Also included, however, are authors from around the world whose works are available in English translation. The writings represented in *SATA* include those created intentionally for children and young adults as well as those written for a general audience and known to interest younger readers. These writings cover the entire spectrum of children's literature, including picture books, humor, folk and fairy tales, animal stories, mystery and adventure, science fiction and fantasy, historical fiction, poetry and nonsense verse, drama, biography, and nonfiction. Obituaries are also included in *SATA* and are intended not only as death notices but also as concise overviews of people's lives and work. Additionally, each edition features newly revised and updated entries for a selection of *SATA* listees who remain of interest to today's readers and who have been active enough to require extensive revisions of their earlier biographies.

Autobiography Feature

Beginning with Volume 103, *SATA* features two or more specially commissioned autobiographical essays in each volume. These unique essays, averaging about ten thousand words in length and illustrated with an abundance of personal photos, present an entertaining and informative first-person perspective on the lives and careers of prominent authors and illustrators profiled in *SATA*.

Two Convenient Indexes

In response to suggestions from librarians, *SATA* indexes no longer appear in every volume but are included in alternate (odd-numbered) volumes of the series, beginning with Volume 57.

SATA continues to include two indexes that cumulate with each alternate volume: the Illustrations Index, arranged by the name of the illustrator, gives the number of the volume and page where the illustrator's work appears in the current volume as well as all preceding volumes in the series; the Author Index gives the number of the volume in which a person's biographical sketch, autobiographical essay, or obituary appears in the current volume as well as all preceding volumes in the series.

These indexes also include references to authors and illustrators who appear in *Gale's Yesterday's Authors of Books for Children, Children's Literature Review,* and *Something about the Author Autobiography Series.*

Easy-to-Use Entry Format

Whether you're already familiar with the *SATA* series or just getting acquainted, you will want to be aware of the kind of information that an entry provides. In every *SATA* entry the editors attempt to give as complete a picture of the person's life and work as possible. A typical entry in *SATA* includes the following clearly labeled information sections:

PERSONAL: date and place of birth and death, parents' names and occupations, name of spouse, date of marriage, names of children, educational institutions attended, degrees received, religious and political affiliations, hobbies and other interests.

ADDRESSES: complete home, office, electronic mail, and agent addresses, whenever available.

CAREER: name of employer, position, and dates for each career post; art exhibitions; military service; memberships and offices held in professional and civic organizations.

AWARDS, HONORS: literary and professional awards received.

WRITINGS: title-by-title chronological bibliography of books written and/or illustrated, listed by genre when known; lists of other notable publications, such as plays, screenplays, and periodical contributions.

ADAPTATIONS: a list of films, television programs, plays, CD-ROMs, recordings, and other media presentations that have been adapted from the author's work.

WORK IN PROGRESS: description of projects in progress.

SIDELIGHTS: a biographical portrait of the author or illustrator's development, either directly from the biographee—and often written specifically for the *SATA* entry—or gathered from diaries, letters, interviews, or other published sources.

BIOGRAPHICAL AND CRITICAL SOURCES: cites sources quoted in "Sidelights" along with references for further reading.

EXTENSIVE ILLUSTRATIONS: photographs, movie stills, book illustrations, and other interesting visual materials supplement the text.

How a *SATA* Entry Is Compiled

A *SATA* entry progresses through a series of steps. If the biographee is living, the *SATA* editors try to secure information directly from him or her through a questionnaire. From the information that the biographee supplies, the editors prepare an entry, filling in any essential missing details with research and/or telephone interviews. If possible, the author or illustra-

tor is sent a copy of the entry to check for accuracy and completeness.

If the biographee is deceased or cannot be reached by questionnaire, the *SATA* editors examine a wide variety of published sources to gather information for an entry. Biographical and bibliographic sources are consulted, as are book reviews, feature articles, published interviews, and material sometimes obtained from the biographee's family, publishers, agent, or other associates.

Entries that have not been verified by the biographees or their representatives are marked with an asterisk (*).

Contact the Editor

We encourage our readers to examine the entire *SATA* series. Please write and tell us if we can make *SATA* even more helpful to you. Give your comments and suggestions to the editor:

Editor
Something about the Author
The Gale Group
27500 Drake Rd.
Farmington Hills MI 48331-3535

Toll-free: 800-877-GALE
Fax: 248-699-8054

Something about the Author Product Advisory Board

The editors of *Something about the Author* are dedicated to maintaining a high standard of excellence by publishing comprehensive, accurate, and highly readable entries on a wide array of writers for children and young adults. In addition to the quality of the content, the editors take pride in the graphic design of the series, which is intended to be orderly yet inviting, allowing readers to utilize the pages of *SATA* easily and with efficiency. Despite the longevity of the *SATA* print series, and the success of its format, we are mindful that the vitality of a literary reference product is dependent on its ability to serve its users over time. As literature, and attitudes about literature, constantly evolve, so do the reference needs of students, teachers, scholars, journalists, researchers, and book club members. To be certain that we continue to keep pace with the expectations of our customers, the editors of *SATA* listen carefully to their comments regarding the value, utility, and quality of the series. Librarians, who have firsthand knowledge of the needs of library users, are a valuable resource for us. The *Something about the Author* Product Advisory Board, made up of school, public, and academic librarians, is a forum to promote focused feedback about *SATA* on a regular basis. The nine-member advisory board includes the following individuals, whom the editors wish to thank for sharing their expertise:

Eva M. Davis
Youth Department Manager,
Ann Arbor District Library,
Ann Arbor, Michigan

Joan B. Eisenberg
Lower School Librarian,
Milton Academy,
Milton, Massachusetts

Francisca Goldsmith
Teen Services Librarian,
Berkeley Public Library,
Berkeley, California

Harriet Hagenbruch
Curriculum Materials Center/Education Librarian,
Axinn Library,
Hofstra University,
Hempstead, New York

Monica F. Irlbacher
Young Adult Librarian,
Middletown Thrall Library,
Middletown, New York

Robyn Lupa
Head of Children's Services,
Jefferson County Public Library,
Lakewood, Colorado

Eric Norton
Head of Children's Services,
McMillan Memorial Library,
Wisconsin Rapids, Wisconsin

Victor L. Schill
Assistant Branch Librarian/Children's Librarian,
Harris County Public Library/Fairbanks Branch,
Houston, Texas

Caryn Sipos
Community Librarian,
Three Creeks Community Library,
Vancouver, Washington

Acknowledgments

Grateful acknowledgment is made to the following publishers, authors, and artists whose works appear in this volume.

ARRIGAN, MARY ▌ Arrigan, Mary, photograph. Reproduced by permission.

BECKER, HELAINE ▌ From an illustration in *Frederick Douglass,* by Helaine Becker. Blackbirch Press, Inc., 2001. Illustration © North Wind Picture Archives. Reproduced by permission.

BLUME, JUDY (SUSSMAN) ▌ Doty, Roy, illustrator. From an illustration in *Tales of a Fourth Grade Nothing,* by Judy Blume. Dutton Children's Books, 1972. Illustrations copyright © 1972 by E. P. Dutton, Inc. All rights reserved. Reproduced by permission of the publisher, E. P. Dutton, an imprint of New American Library, a division of Penguin USA./ Klee, Jutta, photographer. From a cover of *Here's to You, Rachel Robinson,* by Judy Blume. Laurel-Leaf Books, 1995. Reproduced by permission of Dell Publishing, a division of Random House, Inc./ From a cover of *Summer Sisters,* by Judy Blume. Dell Publishing, 1998. Used by permission of Dell Publishing, a division of Random House, Inc./ Reynolds, Peter, illustrator. From a jacket of *Double Fudge,* by Judy Blume. Copyright © 2002 by Peter Reynolds. Reproduced by permission of Dutton Children's Books, a division of Penguin Young Readers Group, a member of Penguin Group (USA) Inc., 345 Hudson ST., New York, NY 10014. All rights reserved./ Blume, Judy, photograph. AP/Wide World Photos. Reproduced by permission.

BULLARD, LISA ▌ Bullard, Lisa, photograph. Reproduced by permission.

CAPEK, MICHAEL ▌ Mays, Buddy, photographer. From a photograph in *A Personal Tour of a Shaker Village,* by Michael Capek. Lerner Publications Company, 2001. Reproduced by permission./ Capek, Michael, photograph. © 2000 Michael Capek. Reproduced by permission.

CHANG, RAYMOND ▌ McElrath-Eslick, Lori, illustrator. From an illustration in *Da Wei's Treasure: A Chinese Tale. Retold* by Margaret and Raymond Chang. Margaret K. McElderry Books, 1999. Illustrations © 1999 by Lori McElrath-Eslick. Reproduced by permission of Margaret K. McElderry Books, an imprint of Simon & Schuster Children's Publishing Division./ Chang, Raymond, photograph. © copyright 2003 Raymond Chang. Reproduced by permission.

COBURN, ANN ▌ From a cover of *Get Up and Tie Your Fingers,* by Ann Coburn. Oberon Books, 2001. Reproduced by permission./ From a cover of *Worm Songs,* by Ann Coburn. The Bodley Head. Reproduced by permission of The Random House Group Limited.

CONDON, BILL ▌ From a cover of *Dogs,* by Bill Condon. Hodder Headline Australia Pty Limited, 2000. Reproduced by permission./ Condon, Bill, photograph. Reproduced by permission.

DASH, JOAN ▌ Dash, Joan, photograph. Reproduced by permission.

DENSLOW, SHARON PHILLIPS ▌ Denslow, Sharon Phillips, photograph. © 2002 Sharon Denslow. Reproduced by permission.

DODD, MARTY ▌ Dodd, Marty, photograph. Reproduced by permission.

FISSCHER, CATHARINA G. M. ▌ Fisscher, Catharina G. M., photograph. © 2001 Catharina G. M. (Tiny) Fisscher. Reproduced by permission.

GARDNER, MARTIN ▌ Enik, Ted, illustrator. From an illustration in *Visitors from Oz,* by Martin Gardner. St. Martin's Press, 1998. Copyright © 1998 by Ted Enik. Reprinted by permission of St. Martin's Press, LLC./ Myers, V. G., illustrator. From an illustration in *Mind-Boggling Word Puzzles,* by Martin Gardner. Sterling Publishing Co., Inc., 2002. Reproduced by permission./ Gardner, Martin, photograph © by Martin Gardner. Reproduced by permission.

GEARY, RICK ▌ Geary, Rick, illustrator. From an illustration in *The Borden Tragedy: A Memoir of the Infamous Double Murder at Fall River, Mass., 1892,* by Rick Geary. Nantier, Beall, Minoustchine Publishing Inc., 1997. © 1997 by Rick Geary. Reproduced by permission./ Geary, Rick, illustration (self-portrait). Reproduced by permission.

GERSTEIN, MORDICAI ▌ From an illustration in *Fox Eyes,* by Mordicai Gerstein. Copyright © 2001 by Mordicai Gerstein. Used by permission of Random House Children's Books, a division of Random House, Inc./ From an illustration in *What Charlie Heard,* by Mordicai Gerstein. Frances Foster Books, 2002. © 2002 by Mordicai Gerstein. Reproduced by permission of Farrar, Straus and Giroux, LLC./ Gerstein, Mordicai, photograph by Stephen Petagorsky. © 1998 Mordicai Gerstein. Reproduced by permission.

GLEESON, LIBBY ▌ All photographs reproduced by permission of Libby Gleeson.

GREENSPUN, ADELE ARON ▌ Greenspun, Adele Aron, photograph by Joanie Schwarz. © 2000 Adele Aron Greenspun. Reproduced by permission.

HULL, MAUREEN ▌ Hull, Maureen, photograph by Findlay Muir. Reproduced by permission of Maureen Hull.

KACER, KATHY ▌ Kacer, Kathy, photograph. Reproduced by permission.

KIEFER, KATHLEEN BALMES ▌ Kiefer, Kathleen, photograph by John Kiefer. © 2002 Kathleen Kiefer. Reproduced by permission.

KLASS, DAVID ▌ Benny, Mike, illustrator. From a jacket of *Danger Zone,* by David Klass. Scholastic Inc., 1996. Jacket painting © 1996 by Scholastic Inc. Reproduced by permission./ Fisher, Jeffrey, illustrator. From a jacket of *Home of the Braves,* by David Klass. Copyright © 2002 by David Klass. Frances Foster Books, 2002. Reproduced by permission of Farrar, Straus and Giroux, LLC.

KVASNOSKY, LAURA MCGEE ∎ Schachner, Judith Byron, illustrator. From an illustration in *What Shall I Dream?,* by Laura McGee Kvasnosky. Dutton, 1996. Illustrations copyright © 1996 by Judith Byron Schachner. Reproduced by permission of Dutton Children's Books, a division of Penguin Books USA Inc./ From an illustration in *Zelda and Ivy,* by Laura McGee Kvasnosky. Candlewick Press, 1998. © 1998 by Laura McGee Kvasnosky. Reproduced by permission of the publisher Candlewick Press, Inc., Cambridge, MA.

LITTLETON, MARK R. ∎ Burkhart, Bruce, Melissa A. Burkhart and Dennis Hengeveld, illustrators. From a cover of *What's in the Bible for . . . Teens,* by Mark Littleton and Jeanette Gardner Littleton. Starburst Publishers, 2000. Reproduced by permission./ Greule Jr., Otto, photographer. From a photograph in Baseball, by Mark Littleton. Zonderkidz, 2002. Allsport/Getty Images. Reproduced by permission.

LOURIE, PETER (KING) ∎ Lourie, Peter, photographer. From a photograph in *Rio Grande: From the Rocky Mountains to the Gulf of Mexico,* by Peter Lourie. Caroline House, Boyds Mills Press, Inc. Copyright © 1999 by Peter Lourie Reproduced by permission./ Lourie, Peter, photograph. Copyright © 1999 by Peter Lourie. Reproduced by permission of Boyds Mills Press.

LYONS, MARY E(VELYN) ∎ Vlach, John Michael, photographer. From a photograph in *Catching the Fire: Philip Simmons, Blacksmith,* by Mary E. Lyons. Houghton Mifflin Company, 1997. Reproduced by permission of the Phillip Simmons Foundation, Inc., and the photographer./ Tauss, Marc, photographer. From a jacket of *Dear Ellen Bee: A Civil War Scrapbook of Two Union Spies,* by Mary E. Lyons and Muriel M. Branch. Atheneum Books for Young Readers, 2000. Jacket photograph © 2000 by Marc Tauss. Reproduced by permission./ Lyons, Mary E., photograph. © 2003 Mary E. Lyons. Reproduced by permission.

MACGRORY, YVONNE ∎ MacGrory, Yvonne, photograph. Reproduced by permission.

MEYER, CAROLYN (MAE) ∎ Meyer, Carolyn Mae, smiling, wearing a striped top, photograph. © Diane J. Schmidt. Reproduced by permission of Carolyn Mae Meyer./ All other photographs reproduced by permission of Carolyn Mae Meyer.

MITCHELL, JOYCE SLAYTON ∎ Borns, Steven, photographer. From a photograph in *Tractor-Trailer Trucker: A Powerful Truck Book,* by Joyce Slayton Mitchell. Tricycle Press, 2000. Copyright © 2000 by Joyce Slayton Mitchell and Steven Borns. Reproduced by permission of Tricycle Press. www.tenspeed.com./ From a cover of *Winning the Heart of the College Admissions Dean: An Expert's Advice for Getting into College,* by Joyce Slayton Mitchell. Ten Speed Press, 2001. Copyright © 2001 by Joyce Slayton Mitchell, Ten Speed Press, Berkeley, CA. www.tenspeed.com.

MORAY WILLIAMS, URSULA ∎ Howard, Paul, illustrator. From an illustration in *Adventures of the Little Wooden Horse,* by Ursula Moray Williams. Kingfisher, 2001. Illustrations © 2001 by Paul Howard. All rights reserved. Reproduced by permission of Kingfisher Publications PLC./ Howard, Paul, illustrator. From an illustration in *Gobbolino the Witch's Cat,* by Ursula Moray Williams. Kingfisher, 2001. Illustrations © Paul Howard 2001. Reproduced by permission of Kingfisher Publications PLC. All rights reserved.

MURPHY, JILL (FRANCES) ∎ From an illustration in *A Piece of Cake,* by Jill Murphy. Candlewick Press, 1989. © 1989 by Jill Murphy. Reproduced by permission of the publisher Candlewick Press, Inc., Cambridge, MA, on behalf of Walker Books Ltd., London./ From an illustration in *The Last Noo-Noo,* by Jill Murphy. Candlewick Press, 1998. © 1995 by Jill Murphy. Reproduced by permission of the publisher Candlewick Press, Inc., Cambridge, MA, on behalf of Walker Books Ltd., London.

NEWBERY, LINDA ∎ Newbery, Linda, photograph by Woodward's Photographic Studios, Oxfordshire, England. Reproduced by permission.

NIEUWSMA, MILTON J(OHN) ∎ Nieuwsma, Milton J., photograph by Marilee Nieuwsma. © 2003 Milton Nieuwsma. Reproduced by permission.

NUMEROFF, LAURA JOFFE ∎ Munsinger, Lynn, illustrator. From an illustration in *What Grandmas Do Best/What Grandpas Do Best,* by Laura Numeroff. Simon & Schuster, London, 2000. Illustrations © 2000 by Lynn Munsinger. Reproduced by permission of Simon & Schuster Books for Young Readers, an imprint of Simon & Schuster Children's Publishing Division./ Numeroff, Laura J., photograph. Reproduced by permission.

PARKER, TONI TRENT ∎ Parker, Toni Trent, photograph. Reproduced by permission.

PFEFFER, WENDY ∎ Brickman, Robin, illustrator. From an illustration in *A Log's Life,* by Wendy Pfeffer. Simon & Schuster Books for Young Readers, 1997. Illustrations © 1997 by Robin Brickman. Reproduced by permission of Simon & Schuster Books for Young Readers, an imprint of Simon & Schuster Children's Publishing Division./ Lubach, Vanessa, illustrator. From an illustration in *The Big Flood,* by Wendy Pfeffer. Millbrook, 2001. Illustrations © 2001 by Vanessa Lubach. Reproduced by permission./ Pfeffer, Wendy, photograph. Reproduced by permission.

PIELICHATY, HELENA ∎ Pielichaty, Helena, photograph. Reproduced by permission.

PROVENZO, EUGENE (F. JR.) ∎ Zorn Jr., Peter A., illustrator. From an illustration in *Favorite Board Games You Can Make and Play,* by Asterie Baker Provenzo and Eugene F. Provenzo, Jr. Dover Publications, Inc., 1990. Reproduced by permission./ From a cover of *The Internet and the World Wide Web for Preservice Teachers,* by Eugene F. Provenzo, Jr. Allyn & Bacon, 1999. Copyright © 1999 by Pearson Education. Reproduced by permission of the publisher./ Provenzo, Eugene, photograph. © Eugene F. Provenzo, Jr. Reproduced by permission.

REUTER, BJARNE (B.) ∎ McPheeters, Neal, illustrator. From an illustration in *The Boys from St. Petri,* by Bjarne Reuter. Translated by Anthea Bell. Cover illustration © Neal McPheeters, 1996. Reproduced by permission of Puffin Books, a division of Penguin Young Readers Group, a member of Penguin Group (USA) Inc., 345 Hudson St., New York, NY 10014. All rights reserved.

ROPER, ROBERT ∎ Spring, Bob and Ira, photographers. From a photograph in *Fatal Mountaineer: The High-Altitude Life and Death of Willi Unsoeld,* American Himalayan Legend, by Robert Roper. St. Martin's Press, 2002. Reproduced by permission.

RUE, LEONARD LEE III ∎ Rue, Leonard Lee III, photographer. From a photograph in *Leonard Lee Rue III's Way of the Whitetail,* by Leonard Lee Rue III. Voyageur Press, 2000. Photographs © 2000 by Leonard Rue Enterprises. Reproduced by permission./ Rue, Leonard Lee III, photograph by Uschi Rue. Reproduced by permission of Voyageur Press.

SAVAGE, CANDACE (M.) ∎ From an illustration in *Born to Be a Cowgirl,* by Candace Savage. Tricycle Press, 2001. Poster courtesy of the Library of Congress./ Savage, Candace, photograph. Reproduced by permission.

SHIPPEY, T(HOMAS) A(LAN) ∎ Webb, Lanny, illustrator. From a cover of *Fiction 2000: Cyberpunk and the Future of Narrative.* Edited by George Slusser and Tom Shippey. University of Georgia Press, 1992. © 1992 by the University of Georgia Press. Reproduced by permission.

SINYKIN, SHERI(L TERRI) COOPER ∎ All photographs reproduced by permission of Sheri Cooper Sinykin.

SMITH, HELENE ∎ Smith, Helene, photograph by Geoff Smith. Reproduced by permission.

STOOPS, ERIK D(ANIEL) ∎ Smultea, Mari A., photographer. From a photograph in *Dolphins,* by Erik D. Stoops, Jeffrey L. Martin and Debbie Lynne Stone. Sterling Publishing Co., Inc., 1998. Reproduced by permission./ Todd, Frank S. Photographer. From a photograph in *The Banded Penguins,* by Kimberly Joan Williams and Erik D. Stoops. Faulkner's Publishing Group, 2001. Photographs © 2001 by Frank S. Todd (EcoCepts). Reproduced by permission.

STRICKLAND, (WILLIAM) BRAD(LEY) ∎ Helquist, Brett, illustrator. From a cover of *The Beast Under the Wizard's Bridge,* by Brad Strickland. Cover illustration © Brett Helquist, 2001. Reproduced by permission of Puffin Books, a division of Penguin Young Readers Group, a member of Penguin Group (USA) Inc., 345 Hudson St., New York, NY 10014. All rights reserved./ Gorey, Edward, illustrator. From a cover of *The Wrath of the Grinning Ghost,* by Brad Strickland. Puffin Books, 2002. Reproduced by permission of Dial Books for Young Readers, a division of Penguin Young Readers Group. A member of Penguin Group (USA)./ Strickland, Brad, photograph by Barbara Strickland. © 2003 Brad Strickland. Reproduced by permission.

TOLAN, STEPHANIE S. ∎ Tolan, Stephanie S., photograph by Judy Owen. Reproduced by permission of Stephanie S. Tolan.

VAGIN, VLADIMIR (VASILEVICH) ∎ Vagin, Vladimir, illustrator. An illustration titled "Baba Yaga." Reproduced by permission./ Vagin, Vladimir, photograph. Reproduced by permission.

WALDMAN, NEIL ∎ From an illustration in *The Starry Night,* by Neil Waldman. Caroline House, Boyds Mills Press, Inc. Copyright © 1999 by Neil Waldman. Reproduced by permission./ From an illustration in *They Came from the Bronx: How the Buffalo Were Saved from Extinction,* by Neil Waldman. Caroline House, Boyds Mills Press, Inc. Copyright © 2001 by Neil Waldman. Reproduced by permission./ Waldman, Neil, photograph. Reproduced by permission of Neil Waldman.

WATSON, WENDY (MCLEOD) ∎ Watson, Wendy, illustrator. From an illustration in *Happy Easter Day!,* by Wendy Watson. Clarion Books, 1993. Illustrations © 1993 by Wendy Watson. Reproduced by permission.

WILSON, SARAH ∎ Sweet, Melissa, illustrator. From an illustration in *Love and Kisses,* by Sarah Wilson. Candlewick Press, 2002. Illustrations © 2002 by Melissa Sweet. Text © 2002 by Sarah Wilson. Reproduced by permission of the publisher Candlewick Press Inc., Cambridge, MA.

something about the author

ALLEN, Betsy
  See HARRISON, Elizabeth Cavanna

* * *

ARRIGAN, Mary 1943-

Personal

Born February 15, 1943, in Newbridge, County Kildare, Ireland; daughter of Brendan Nolan (a health inspector) and Marian Maher; married Emmet Arrigan (an English teacher), August 17, 1968; children: Emmett, Conor, Caoimhe. *Education:* Attended Holy Family Convent, National College of Art and Design, and University College (Dublin, Ireland).

Addresses

Home—Abbey Lodge, Roscrea, County Tipperary, Ireland. *Agent*—Ed Victor, 6 Bayley St., Bedford Square, London WC1B 3HB, England. *E-mail*—earrigan@eircom.net.

Career

Taught art at the secondary level for twenty years; retired in 1994 to write full time.

Mary Arrigan

Member

Irish Writers Union, Children's Books Ireland.

Awards, Honors

Sunday Times/CWA Short Story Award, 1991; Hennessy Literary Award, 1993; Bisto Award shortlist, Children's Book Ireland, 1994, for *Lá le mamó;* Readers' Association Award shortlist, 1995, for *Mamó cois trá*; White Raven Title, International Youth Library, 1997, for *The Dwellers Beneath*; Bisto Merit Award, Children's Book Ireland, 2000, for *Siúlóid bhreá.*

Writings

FOR CHILDREN

Andy, Zeph and the Flying Cottage, illustrated by Jennifer Bell, Hamish Hamilton (London, England), 1994.

Searching for the Green, Attic Press (Dublin, Ireland), 1995.

Dead Monks and Shady Deals, illustrated by Terry Myler, Children's Press (Dublin, Ireland), 1995.

Saving the Dark Planet, Attic Press (Dublin, Ireland), 1995.

Landscape with Cracked Sheep, illustrated by Terry Myler, Children's Press (Dublin, Ireland, and Chester Springs, PA), 1996.

The Dwellers Beneath, Attic Press (Dublin, Ireland), 1996.

Seascape with Barber's Harp, illustrated by Terry Myler, Children's Press (Dublin, Ireland, and Chester Springs, PA), 1997.

The Spirits of the Bog, Children's Press (Dublin, Ireland, and Chester Springs, PA), 1998.

(And illustrator) *Nutty Knut,* Poolbeg Press (Dublin, Ireland), 1999.

Maeve and the Long-Arm Folly, illustrated by Terry Myler, Children's Press (Dublin, Ireland, and Chester Springs, PA), 1999.

Grimstone's Ghost, Collins (London, England), 2000.

(And illustrator) *Knut and Freya in Wales,* Poolbeg (Dublin, Ireland), 2000.

The Spirits of the Attic, Children's Press (Dublin, Ireland, and Chester Springs, PA), 2000.

Ghost Bird, Red Fox (London, England), 2001.

Baldur's Bones, Collins (London, England), 2001.

Pa Jinglebob: The Fastest Knitter in the West, illustrated by Korky Paul, Egmont (London, England), 2002.

Lawlor's Revenge, Collins (London, England), 2002.

Larkspur and the Grand March, illustrated by Debbie Boon, Egmont (London, England), 2003.

Contributor of short stories to *Scream,* Poolbeg (Dublin, Ireland), 1998, and *Mirrors,* Collins (London, England), 2001. Arrigan's works have been translated into German, Dutch, Polish, Swedish, and Danish.

IN GAELIC

(Self-illustrated) *Lá le mamó* (title means "A Day with Gran"), An Gúm (Dublin, Ireland), 1993.

(Illustrator) Caitlín Uí Anluain, *Mac Dathó agus a chú,* An Gúm (Dublin, Ireland), 1994.

(Self-illustrated) *Mamó cois trá* (title means "Gran at the Seaside"), An Gúm (Dublin, Ireland), 1994.

(Self-illustrated) *An maicín cliste* (title means "The Clever Nephew"), An Gúm (Dublin, Ireland), 1995.

(Self-illustrated) *An scáth báistí* (title means "The Umbrella"), An Gúm (Dublin, Ireland), 1995.

(Self-illustrated) *An bhó fhionn* (title means "The White Cow"), An Gúm (Dublin, Ireland), 1996.

(Self-illustrated) *Mamó ar an fheirm* (title means "Gran on the Farm"), An Gúm (Dublin, Ireland), 1996.

(Illustrator) Emmett Arrigan and Elisabeth Monkhouse, *Daisy Bates,* An Gúm (Dublin, Ireland), 1996.

(Self-illustrated) *Mamó ag an sorcas* (title means "Gran at the Circus"), An Gúm (Dublin, Ireland), 1997.

(Illustrator) Bram Stoker, *Dracula* (adapted for children by Emmett Arrigan), An Gúm (Dublin, Ireland), 1997.

(Self-illustrated) *Siúlóid bhreá* (title means "A Grand Walk"), An Gúm (Dublin, Ireland), 1999.

(Translator) Marcus Pfister, *An t-iasc ildathach,* North South Books (New York, NY), 2001.

Also author and illustrator of *Mamó ag an zú* (title means "Gran at the Zoo"), An Gúm (Dublin, Ireland); illustrator of *Gearóidín gabhar* (title means "Geraldine the Goat"), An Gúm (Dublin, Ireland).

Sidelights

Mary Arrigan's ghost stories for young people have earned praise for their fine prose and thrilling suspense. Although she works with the materials of traditional horror, such as haunted houses, curses, and the undead, her novels also feature well-drawn and evocative settings as well as strong characterizations and humor, according to reviewers. In *Ghost Bird,* the curiosity of three children leads them into terror when they investigate the haunting of the Old Garvan House. Another haunted house is at the center of Arrigan's novel, *Grimstone's Ghost,* in which a twelve year old travels with his mother and sister to inherit the family mansion. Brother and sister are at the mercy of Captain Grimstone, the ghost of their ancestor's worst enemy, when they are left alone one night at the house and must find a golden goblet in order to free the family from the terrible curse.

The undead rise again in Arrigan's novel *Baldur's Bones,* in which fourteen-year-old Finn goes to live with relatives in remote Ireland after being orphaned. There, he finds not only a true friend but also the skull of an ancient Viking warrior in a nearby graveyard. Taking possession of the skull, however, Finn unwittingly unleashes the power of its original possessor, and the teenager finds himself caught between two ancient spirits, one evil and one that needs his help. As in reviews of Arrigan's earlier novels, critics found much to praise about this book, including a highly suspenseful plot, likable characters whose emotional lives are well explored, and welcome dashes of puckish humor that lighten the tension. Robert Dunbar, writing in *Books for Keeps,* called *Baldur's Bones* a "skillfully structured and extremely atmospheric novel." *School Librarian* reviewer Sarah Merrett offered similar laudatory comments, calling *Baldur's Bones* "more than just a ghost story." While still "being a fast-paced thriller," the novel, according to Merrett, "deals sensitively with deep emotions."

Arrigan told *SATA:* "As children growing up in a small Irish town in the 1950s, our highlight of the week was the visit to the library. The children's section (which opened only on Saturdays) was tucked under the stairs. We were allowed two books—one fiction and one non-fiction. I can still smell the wet raincoats as we crowded to reach for the well-thumbed Enid Blytons. The two-book allowance would, of course, be read by Monday. Thus was born a sister/brotherhood of wheeling and dealing amidst the unlawful swapping of books. The best known gangsters must have cut their teeth in libraries like ours—who else but a knobbly-kneed godfather with adenoids and patchy haircut could allocate book-swaps for a penny and have all the books back to the original borrowers before the following Saturday?

"But I had a secret stash. My father was a health inspector. As such he was obliged to remove and burn library books from houses struck down with tuberculosis, polio, and other contagious diseases, to prevent the spread of same. But my father, a scholarly book lover and sometime creative writer himself, could never bring himself to destroy books. So my brother Gabriel and I had the choice of all these disease-ridden books. Mighty. There's nothing like the threat of a throat-gurgling death to make a book more exciting and fire the imagination.

"My brother became more interested in the diseases rather than the books and went on to become a doctor. Me? My imagination is still on fire, and I still think fondly of those wet raincoats as I write for the child who never quite leaves that special part of our minds."

Biographical and Critical Sources

PERIODICALS

Books for Keeps, September, 2001, Rudolf Loewenstein, review of *Ghost Bird,* p. 24; November, 2001, Robert Dunbar, review of *Baldur's Bones,* pp. 29-30.
School Librarian, spring, 2001, Peter Hollindale, review of *Grimstone's Ghost,* p. 24; autumn, 2001, Deepa Earnshaw, review of *Ghost Bird,* p. 135; winter, 2001, Sarah Merrett, review of *Baldur's Bones,* p. 210.

*　　*　　*

BACHEL, Beverly K. 1957-

Personal

Born August 29, 1957, in Minneapolis, MN. *Education:* Attended Drake University.

Addresses

Home and office—722 Seventh St. S.E., Minneapolis, MN 55414. *E-mail*—bbachel@qwest.net.

Career

Writer, artist, and consultant. Idea Girls, founder; also founder of a communications consulting firm.

Writings

What Do You Really Want? How to Set a Goal and Go for It! A Guide for Teens, Free Spirit Publishing (Minneapolis, MN), 2001.

Contributor to periodicals.

Sidelights

Beverly K. Bachel told *SATA:* "I attribute my success to my ability to set goals, a skill I learned the summer I sold my first pitcher of lemonade. As the founder of a communications consulting firm, I have written for dozens of Fortune 500 companies and numerous publications. In addition, I am the founder of Idea Girls, a group of entrepreneurs dedicated to developing products that inspire others to pursue their dreams and use their talents to make positive changes in the world."

Biographical and Critical Sources

PERIODICALS

Booklist, May 15, 2001, Roger Leslie, review of *What Do You Really Want? How to Set a Goal and Go for It! A Guide for Teens,* p. 1741.

ONLINE

Idea Girls, http://www.ideagirls.com/ (March 16, 2003).

*　　*　　*

BALMES, Kathy
See KIEFER, Kathleen Balmes

*　　*　　*

BECKER, Helaine 1961-

Personal

Born August 9, 1961, in Plainview, NY; daughter of Aaron (a science publisher) and Arlene (a teacher; maiden name, Eber) Becker; married Karl Szasz (a chief executive officer), June 29, 1986; children: Michael Szasz, Andrew Szasz. *Ethnicity:* "Human." *Education:* Duke University, B.Sc. (history; cum laude), 1983. *Hobbies and other interests:* Swimming, ice dancing, running, cycling, karate, cooking, reading, gardening, "a profound interest in an active, involved, committed life!"

Addresses

Home—252 Snowdon Ave., Toronto, Ontario M4N 2B3, Canada. *E-mail*—helbeck@earthlink.net.

Career

Edusource/Concepts in Learning, Toronto, Ontario, Canada, owner, 1986-96; McClelland & Stewart (publishers), Toronto, Ontario, Canada, copywriter, 1988-90; Renaissance Solutions, Toronto, Ontario, Canada, consultant, 1996-2001; Louise Kool & Galt, Toronto, Ontario, Canada, director of sales and marketing, 2001-02.

Member

Canadian Association of Children's Authors, Illustrators, and Performers.

Awards, Honors

Recommended Reading selection, Ontario Elementary Teachers' Federation, and Our Choice selection, Canadian Children's Book Centre, 2002, both for *Mama Likes to Mambo.*

Writings

Spelling Puzzlers for Grade 1 (professional edition), Rigby (Barrington, IL), 2000.
Mama Likes to Mambo (verse), illustrated by John Beder, Stoddart (Toronto, Ontario, Canada), 2001.
John Brown (biography), Blackbirch (Woodbridge, CT), 2001.
Frederick Douglass (biography), Blackbirch (Woodbridge, CT), 2001.

Contributor of educational material to publishers, including Scott Resources, Spectrum Publishers, and Mad Science, Inc., and to *Chirp* magazine.

Adaptations

"Ode to Underwear" was recorded as a zydeco tune by The Irish Descendants.

Sidelights

Helaine Becker has published two young adult biographies and a collection of poems, in addition to numerous works of educational material for students and teachers. Her biography of Frederick Douglass covers

In Frederick Douglass, *Helaine Becker offers a portrait of the preeminent African-American abolitionist and famous orator of the nineteenth century.*

the entirety of the influential man's life, devoting half of its pages to his young life as a slave, his escape to freedom, and the development of his career as a leader of the antislavery movement. The latter part of the volume places Douglass' political activism in the context of his time and place.

Becker's collection of poems, *Mama Likes to Mambo,* contains sixteen unrelated, humorous poems. "The poems are funny, and Becker obviously enjoyed writing them," remarked Kathy Broderick in *Booklist.* The author plays with language effectively, reviewers noted, including inventing evocative words in order to achieve a rhyme and creating poems whose shape reflects the subject of the poem. The poems are portrayed by illustrator John Beder with animal characters. "If Helaine Becker continues writing poetry," *Canadian Materials* contributor Ian Stewart predicted, "she will surely join the ranks of Canada's most popular and important children's authors."

Becker told *SATA:* "I've been a writer since the age of five, when I wrote my first poem. It was terrible. My second poem, at the age of six, was not much better.

But it remains in my mind chiefly because my grade one teacher *corrected* it! That bugged me.

"By grade five, my favourite song was The Beatles' 'I Wanna Be a Paperback Writer.' In the next few years, I had a few poems published in the Nassau County Public Library's Literary Journal, and I wrote my first 'chapter book,' which received thundering acclaim from the kid next door. After that, I experienced a long literary dearth, while I embarked on the more 'sensible' path of chasing boys, finishing school, and doing lots of travel with a smelly old backpack.

"Many years, a husband, two kids, and a dog later, I realized I could as much give up writing as give up chocolate. Ideas for stories and poems would come to me at the dinner table, in the office, while driving, or on the Stairmaster. I started writing again and now know that whether or not my poems or books are published, I am a writer, a *real* writer, down to my toes. It's who I am, not what I do.

"*Why* do I write? Because I can't help it. Ideas pop into my head from some outer cosmos, and I have to write them down or bust. *What* do I write? In general, stuff that makes me laugh, stuff that celebrates the incredible joyfulness of existence. I find life to be a fascinating, exciting box of candy to be explored, grabbed with two hands, and gobbled down whole. 'No shame, no pride' is my motto. This way of thinking has enabled me to tackle a wide variety of new challenges such as learning how to mambo and ice dance in my thirties, getting my orange belt in karate the year I turned forty, and going from a determined couch rat to a ten-kilometer runner. It's also taught me to persist in the face of failure, such as 101 rejection letters from publishers. I now know that the only kind of true failure is the failure to try. So—pardon the pun—I'm a trying kind of gal!

"An unexpected reward from returning to writing has been the pleasure I get from reading and performing for children. I am a regular presenter to schools and have 'performed' at Toronto's Children's Museum. I have so much fun with the kids and adore sharing my joy in words and in life with them."

Biographical and Critical Sources

PERIODICALS

Booklist, September 15, 2002, Kathy Broderick, review of *Mama Likes to Mambo,* p. 236.
Canadian Materials, March 15, 2002, Ian Stewart, review of *Mama Likes to Mambo.*
Resource Links, February, 2002, Valerie Pollock, review of *Mama Likes to Mambo,* p. 2.
School Library Journal, April, 2002, Starr E. Smith, review of *Frederick Douglass,* p. 163; May, 2002, Marian Creamer, review of *Mama Likes to Mambo,* p. 134.

ONLINE

Canadian Association of Children's Authors, Illustrators, and Performers, http://www.canscaip.org/ (May 16, 2003), biography of Helaine Becker.

*　　　*　　　*

BLUME, Judy (Sussman) 1938-

Personal

Born February 12, 1938, in Elizabeth, NJ; daughter of Rudolph (a dentist) and Esther (Rosenfeld) Sussman; married John M. Blume (an attorney), August 15, 1959 (divorced, 1975); married George Cooper (a writer), June 6, 1987; children: (first marriage) Randy Lee (daughter), Lawrence Andrew; Amanda (stepdaughter). *Education:* New York University, B.A., 1961. *Religion:* Jewish.

Addresses

Agent—Owen Laster, William Morris Agency, 1325 Avenue of the Americas, New York, NY 10019.

Career

Writer of juvenile and adult fiction. Founder of KIDS Fund, 1981.

Member

Society of Children's Book Writers and Illustrators (member of board), Authors Guild (member of council), National Coalition against Censorship (council of advisors).

Awards, Honors

Best Books for Children selection, *New York Times,* 1970, Nene Award, Hawaii Association of School Librarians and the Hawaii Library Association, 1975, Young Hoosier Book Award, Association for Indiana Media Educators, 1976, and North Dakota Children's Choice Award, Children's Round Table of the North Dakota Library Association, 1979, all for *Are You There God? It's Me, Margaret;* Charlie May Swann Children's Book Award, Arkansas Elementary School Council, 1972, Young Readers Choice Award, Pacific Northwest Library Association, and Sequoyah Children's Book Award, Oklahoma Library Association, both 1975, Arizona Young Readers Award, Arizona State University and University of Arizona—Tempe, Massachusetts Children's Book Award, Education Department of Salem State College, Georgia Children's Book Award, College of Education of the University of Georgia, and South Carolina Children's Book Award, South Carolina Association of School Librarians, all 1977, Rhode Island Library Association Award, 1978, North Dakota Children's Choice Award, Children's Round Table of the North Dakota Library Association, and West Austra-

Judy Blume

lian Young Readers' Book Award, Library Association of Australia, both 1980, United States Army in Europe Kinderbuch Award and Great Stone Face Award, New Hampshire Library Council, both 1981, all for *Tales of a Fourth Grade Nothing;* Outstanding Books of the Year selection, *New York Times,* 1974, Arizona Young Readers Award, Arizona State University and University of Arizona—Tempe, and Young Readers Choice Award, Pacific Northwest Library Association, both 1977, and North Dakota Children's Choice Award, Children's Round Table of the North Dakota Library Association, 1983, all for *Blubber;* South Carolina Children's Book Award, South Carolina Association of School Librarians, 1978, for *Otherwise Known as Sheila the Great;* Michigan Young Reader's Award, Michigan Council of Teachers, 1980, for *Freckle Juice;* Texas Bluebonnet list, 1980, CRABery Award, Michigan Young Reader's Award, Michigan Council of Teachers, and International Reading Association Children's Choice Award, all 1981, Buckeye Children's Book Award, State Library of Ohio, Nene Award, Hawaii Association of School Librarians and Hawaii Library Association, Sue Hefley Book Award, Louisiana Association of School Libraries, United States Army in Europe Kinderbuch Award, West Australian Young Readers' Book Award, Library Association of Australia, North Dakota Children's Choice Award, Children's Round Table of the North Dakota Library Association, Colorado Children's Book Award, University of Colorado, Georgia Children's Book Award, College of Education of the University of Georgia, Tennessee Children's Choice Book Award, Texas Bluebonnet Award, Texas Association of School Librarians and the Children's

Round Table, and Utah Children's Book Award, Children's Literature Association of Utah, all 1982, Northern Territory Young Readers' Book Award, Young Readers Choice Award, Pacific Northwest Library Association, Garden State Children's Book Award, New Jersey Library Association, Iowa Children's Choice Award, Iowa Educational Media Association, Arizona Young Readers' Award, Arizona State University and University of Arizona—Tempe, Young Reader Medal, California Reading Association, and Young Hoosier Book Award, Association for Indiana Media Educators, all 1983, Land of Enchantment Book Award, New Mexico Library Association and New Mexico State International Reading Association, 1984, and Sunshine State Young Reader's Award, Florida Association for Media in Education, 1985, all for *Superfudge;* CRABery Award, 1982, Dorothy Canfield Fisher Children's Book Award, Vermont Department of Libraries and the Vermont Congress of Parents and Teachers, Buckeye Children's Book Award, State Library of Ohio, Young Reader Medal, California Reading Association, and American Book Award finalist, Association of American Publishers, all 1983, Blue Spruce Colorado Young Adult Book Award, Colorado Library Association, and Iowa Children's Choice Award, Iowa Educational Media Association, both 1985, all for *Tiger Eyes;* Children's Books of the Year selection, Child Study Association of America, 1985, for *The Pain and the Great One;* Best Books for Young Adults selection, American Library Association, 1986, for *Letters to Judy;* Young Reader Medal, California Reading Association, Iowa Children's Choice Award, Iowa Educational Media Association, Nene Award, Hawaii Association of School Librarians and the Hawaii Library Association, Nevada Young Readers Award, Nevada Library Association, Sunshine State Young Reader's Award, Florida Association for Media in Education, Pennsylvania Young Reader's Award, Pennsylvania School Librarians Association, Michigan Readers Choice Award, Michigan Reading Association, all 1993, all for *Fudge-a-Mania;* Parent's Choice Award, 1993, for *Here's to You, Rachel Robinson.* Golden Archer Award, 1974; Today's Woman Award, Council of Cerebral Palsy Auxiliary, Nassau County, 1981; Outstanding Mother Award, 1982; Eleanor Roosevelt Humanitarian Award, Favorite Author—Children's Choice Award, Milner Award, Friends of the Atlanta Public Library, for children's favorite living author, and Jeremiah Ludington Memorial Award, all 1983; Carl Sandburg Freedom to Read Award, Chicago Public Library, 1984; Civil Liberties Award, Atlanta American Civil Liberties Union, and John Rock Award, Center for Population Options, both 1986; D.H.L., Kean College, 1987; Excellence in the Field of Literature Award, New Jersey Education Association, 1987; South Australian Youth Media Award for Best Author, South Australian Association for Media Education, 1988; Most Admired Author, Heroes of Young America Poll, 1989; National Hero Award, Big Brothers/Big Sisters, 1992; Dean's Award, Columbia University College of Physicians and Surgeons, 1993; Margaret A. Edwards Award for Outstanding Literature for Young Adults, American Library Association, 1996, for lifetime achievement writing for teens; honorary degree from Mount Holyoke College, Doctor of Fine Arts, 2003.

Writings

CHILDREN'S FICTION; EXCEPT AS NOTED

The One in the Middle Is the Green Kangaroo, illustrated by Lois Axeman, Reilly & Lee (Chicago, IL), 1969, revised edition, illustrated by Amy Aitken, Bradbury (Scarsdale, NY), 1981, revised edition, illustrated by Irene Trivas, 1991.

Iggie's House, Bradbury (Englewood Cliffs, NJ), 1970.

Are You There God? It's Me, Margaret, Bradbury (Englewood Cliffs, NJ), 1970.

Then Again, Maybe I Won't, Bradbury (Scarsdale, NY), 1971.

Freckle Juice, Four Winds (New York, NY), 1971.

Tales of a Fourth Grade Nothing, illustrated by Roy Doty, Dutton (New York, NY), 1972.

Fourth-grader Peter must endure his three-year-old brother Fudge, considered cute by everyone else but a grand annoyance to Peter, in Blume's humorous first book from her wildly popular series about the boys. (From Tales of a Fourth Grade Nothing, *illustrated by Roy Doty.)*

Otherwise Known as Sheila the Great, Dutton (New York, NY), 1972.

It's Not the End of the World, Bradbury (Scarsdale, NY), 1972.

Deenie, Bradbury (Scarsdale, NY), 1973.

Blubber, Bradbury (Scarsdale, NY), 1974.

Forever . . ., (young adult novel), Bradbury (Scarsdale, NY), 1975.

Starring Sally J. Freedman as Herself, Bradbury (Scarsdale, NY), 1977.

Superfudge, Dutton (New York, NY), 1980.

Tiger Eyes (for young adults), Bradbury (Scarsdale, NY), 1981.

The Pain and the Great One, Bradbury (Scarsdale, NY), 1984.

Just as Long as We're Together, Orchard Books (New York, NY), 1987.

Fudge-a-Mania, Dutton (New York, NY), 1990.

Here's to You, Rachel Robinson, Orchard Books (New York, NY), 1993.

Double Fudge, Scholastic (New York, NY), 2002.

OTHER

Wifey (adult novel), Putnam (New York, NY), 1978.

Smart Women (adult novel), Putnam (New York, NY), 1983.

Letters to Judy: What Your Kids Wish They Could Tell You (nonfiction), Putnam (New York, NY), 1986.

The Judy Blume Memory Book (limited edition), Dell (New York, NY), 1988.

(And producer with son, Lawrence Blume) *Otherwise Known as Sheila the Great* (screenplay; adapted from her novel), Barr Films, 1988.

Summer Sisters (adult novel), Delacorte (New York, NY), 1998.

(Editor) *Places I Never Meant to Be: Original Stories by Censored Writers,* Simon & Schuster (New York, NY), 1999.

Contributor to *Author Talk: Conversations with Judy Blume (and others),* Simon & Schuster (New York, NY), 2000. Some of Blume's works are housed in the Kerlan Collection at the University of Minnesota.

Adaptations

Forever . . . was adapted as a television film broadcast by Columbia Broadcasting System (CBS), 1978; *Freckle Juice* was adapted as an animated film by Barr Films, 1987; the "Fudge" books were adapted by American Broadcasting Companies (ABC) as a television series, 1994-96, and on CBS, 1997; *Tales of a Fourth Grade Nothing* was adapted as a play; *Wifey* was produced by Audio Book in 1979. Listening Library has adapted various Blume books along with teacher's guides, including *Freckle Juice,* 1982; *Blubber,* 1983; *The One in the Middle Is the Green Kangaroo,* 1983; and *Deenie,* 1983. Audiobooks adapted by Listening Library include *Are You There God? It's Me, Margaret,* 1985; *It's Not the End of the World,* 1985; and *The Pain and the Great One,* 1985. Blume books adapted for audio by Ingram

Straight-A student Rachel is finding it very stressful trying to be perfect and the complications of middle school are abounding as she finishes seventh grade. (Cover photo by Jutta Klee.)

include *Superfudge,* 1992; *Fudge-a-Mania,* 1993; *Tales of a Fourth Grade Nothing,* 1996; *Are You There God? It's Me, Margaret,* 1997; and *Otherwise Known as Sheila the Great,* 1997.

Sidelights

"For several generations of former adolescents, Judy Blume is the reason flashlights were invented," wrote *Entertainment Weekly*'s Rebecca Ascher Walsh in a 2002 review of *Double Fudge.* "From the 'Fudge' books to *Are You There God? It's Me, Margaret* to *Forever . . .,* Blume has expertly guided huddling insomniac masses through the confusion of childhood and teenage hell into young adulthood." Since she published her first book in 1969, Blume has become one of the most popular and controversial authors for children. Her accessible, humorous style and direct, sometimes explicit treatment of youthful concerns have won her many fans—as well as critics who sometimes seek to

censor her work. Nevertheless, Blume has continued to produce works that are, according to critics, both entertaining and thought-provoking. "Judy Blume has a knack for knowing what children think about and an honest, highly amusing way of writing about it," Jean Van Leeuwen stated in the *New York Times Book Review.* Mark Oppenheimer summed up her achievement in the same periodical, writing "Judy Blume's willingness to recognize children's serious thoughts about sex, religion, and class made her a figure of controversy twenty-five years ago. Blume became an icon, as famous for those who tried to cleanse libraries of her books as for the books themselves."

Many critics attribute Blume's popularity to her ability to discuss openly, realistically, and compassionately the subjects that concern her readers. Her books for younger children, such as *Tales of a Fourth Grade Nothing, Blubber,* and *Otherwise Known as Sheila the Great,* deal with problems of sibling rivalry, establishing self-confidence, and social ostracism. Books for older readers, such as *Are You There God? It's Me, Margaret, Deenie,* and *Just as Long as We're Together* consider matters of divorce, friendship, family breakups, and sexual development (including menstruation and masturbation), while *Forever . . .* specifically deals with a young woman's first love and first sexual experience. But whatever the situation, Blume's characters confront their feelings of confusion as a start to resolving their problems. In *Are You There God? It's Me, Margaret,* for instance, the young protagonist examines her thoughts about religion and speculates about becoming a woman. The result is a book that uses "sensitivity and humor" in capturing "the joys, fears, and uncertainty that surround a young girl approaching adolescence," Lavinia Russ wrote in *Publishers Weekly.*

"Blume's books reflect a general cultural concern with feelings about self and body, interpersonal relationships, and family problems," Alice Phoebe Naylor and Carol Wintercorn remarked in the *Dictionary of Literary Biography.* But Blume has taken this general concern further, the critics continue, for "her portrayal of feelings of sexuality as normal, and not rightfully subject to punishment, [has] revolutionized realistic fiction for children." Blume's highlighting of sexuality reflects her ability to target the issues that most interest young people; when she first began writing, she "knew intuitively what kids wanted to know because I remembered what I wanted to know," she explained to John Neary of *People.* "I think I write about sexuality because it was uppermost in my mind when I was a kid: the need to know, and not knowing how to find out. My father delivered these little lectures to me, the last one when I was ten, on how babies are made. But questions about what I was feeling, and how my body could feel, I *never* asked my parents."

Born in New Jersey, in 1938, Blume and her older brother grew up in a home full of books. Her father, a dentist, "nurtured her vivid imagination and love of game-playing," according to a contributor for *Newsmakers 1998.* Her mother, quieter and more introspective, encouraged her young daughter in a growing love of books and reading. Beginning in the third grade, Blume, her mother, and her brother went to live in Florida for two years in hopes of improving her brother's heath, and she was separated from her father during this time. The outgoing Blume began taking dance classes as a young child and generally excelled at school, attending an all-girls high school where she sang in the chorus and worked on the school newspaper as a features editor. Graduating from high school, she went on to Boston University for a year until a bout of mononucleosis forced her to drop out. She subsequently enrolled at New York University, where she graduated in 1961, majoring in early childhood education. During her sophomore year of college, she met her first husband, John M. Blume, a lawyer, and the couple was married during Blume's junior year. Shortly after graduation, Blume had her first child, Randy Lee, and then two years later had a son, Lawrence Andrew.

The life of a mother in the suburbs was not, however, one for the active Blume. Deciding she needed a creative outlet, Blume began making up children's stories as she went about her housework, even illustrating them in crayon. Her early stories were rejected by magazines, and then, coming upon a brochure for a New York University class in writing for children and young adults, she enrolled. As part of the coursework, she wrote what became her first publication, *The One in the Middle Is the Green Kangaroo,* a picture book about an in-between child. The following semester, Blume took the class once more time, writing the initial draft for her second publication, *Iggie's House,* a children's novel about racial prejudice. *The One in the Middle* was published in 1969, and was called "satisfying" by Zena Sutherland in a review for *Bulletin of the Center for Children's Books.*

Blume's first two books did not give, however, any indication of the direction she would go with her third, *Are You There God? It's Me, Margaret.* In 1967, S. E. Hinton, a schoolgirl herself at the time, revolutionized the world of young-adult literature with her hard-hitting and gritty *The Outsiders,* a novel about class rivalry in an Oklahoma high school. But until Blume's 1970 publication of *Are You There God?,* the literature for younger adolescents had generally gone along its well-worn pathway of simplistic plots and happy endings. With *Are You There God?,* Blume broke publishing taboos by speaking about such unmentionables as a girl's period and first bra. Based on many of Blume's own adolescent experiences, the novel tells the tale of Margaret Simon and her family, who move to the suburbs in New Jersey. There she has to make new friends, and she is beset by worries about getting her period and the size of her breasts. She is also concerned about religion; born to a Christian mother and Jewish father, she is confused where she fits and thus starts visiting different churches and talking directly with God. Most re-

Two very different adolescent girls—one flamboyant and talented, one quiet and conservative—spend six summers together and share numerous life-altering experiences as they become intimate friends.

viewers praised the book's humor but decried Blume's focus on what were once unmentionables. Ann Evans, writing in the *Times Literary Supplement,* for example, found that Blume focused too much on Margaret's body and that her "private talks with God are insufferably self-conscious and arch." A critic for *Kirkus Reviews* also complained that "there's danger in the preoccupation with the physical signs of puberty." Children did not read the reviews; they read the book. And read it and read it. When it appeared in paperback in 1974, it attracted readers in the hundreds of thousands, and Blume began getting the deluge of letters from young readers that has persisted over the decades, thanking her for letting them know they were not alone in such thoughts.

Blume repeated the favor for young male readers with *Then Again, Maybe I Won't,* published in 1971, and featuring young Vic, who, like Margaret, has just moved to a new town. He is also worried about the changes that are taking place with his body; he has uncontrollable erections and worries about wet dreams. His family has also undergone a change, recently becoming more affluent. This book was not as popular as *Are You There God?*, but it broke similar ground in juvenile literature, making formerly taboo topics part of the subject matter of children's literature.

More problem books from Blume's early career include *It's Not the End of the World*, in which the twelve-year-old protagonist learns to cope with her parents' separation and divorce; *Deenie*, in which a beautiful thirteen-year-old girl, whose mother desperately wants her to become a model, is diagnosed with the spinal disease scoliosis; and *Blubber*, about childhood cruelty as expressed in taunting an overweight girl. Blume's work continued to stir up the critics and invite parental condemnation if not outright attempts—in many schools successful—at censorship. In *Deenie*, for example, the young girl thinks at first that her disease has been brought on by her masturbation. Despite such concerns, *School Library Journal*'s Melinda Schroeder called *Deenie* a "compelling" novel.

Blume's least controversial and perhaps one of her most popular series are the "Fudge" books, five interrelated stories that span thirty years of writing, starting off with *Tales of a Fourth Grade Nothing*. That book details the trials and tribulations of Peter Warren Hatcher and his younger brother, Fudge. The brothers live in an apartment in Manhattan and undergo the usual sibling rivalry. At one point, young Fudge—rambunctious and often in trouble—swallows his older brother's turtle. This book became the third best-selling children's book of all time, with over six million copies sold. *Otherwise Known as Sheila the Great*, a spin-off of this first title, focuses on Peter's nemesis as she tries to deal with summer camp.

Blume returned to the brothers in the 1980 tale *Superfudge*, in which the family is joined by a baby sister, Tootsie, who complicates the boy's lives. The family has also moved to Princeton, New Jersey, in this title, and Fudge is ready to enter kindergarten. That book became Blume's best selling hardcover edition, receiving much praise by critics. Writing in *Washington Post Book World*, Brigitte Weeks lauded Blume's ability to create "good clean fun," while *School Library Journal*'s Pamela D. Pollack commented that "no one knows the byways of the under-twelves better than Blume." *Fudge-a-Mania*, from 1990, continues the saga, with a reunion of all the characters in a summer house in Maine. Even when Blume returns to familiar characters, as she does in this novel and others in the series, her sequels "expand on the original and enrich it, so that [the] stories . . . add up to one long and much more wonderful story," Van Leeuwen remarked in her *New York Times Book Review* article about *Fudge-a-Mania*.

Then, in 2002, to satisfy the wishes of her grandchild, Blume returned once again to Peter and Fudge in *Double Fudge*. In this installment, Fudge is about to begin school and is obsessed with money. His parents take him to visit the Bureau of Engraving and Printing in Washington, D.C., where the family accidentally runs into distant cousins from Hawaii, the Howie Hatcher clan with their twin daughters, Fauna and Flora, and their younger brother who has the same name as Fudge: Farley Drexel Hatcher. These Hawaiian cousins follow the Hatchers back to Manhattan and end up camping out on their floor and then renting an apartment in the same building for a time, much to the dismay of Peter, who is mightily embarrassed by their presence. "Peter's wry reactions to the sometimes outsize goings-on, Fudge's inimitable antics and the characters' rousing repartee contribute to the sprightly clip of this cheerful read," wrote a reviewer for *Publishers Weekly*. Terrie Dorio, reviewing the book in *School Library Journal*, found it to be "a worthy successor" to earlier titles in the series, but a critic for *Kirkus Reviews* was less impressed, calling it a "surprisingly unfunny book." *Booklist*'s Gillian Engberg, on the other hand, commended Blume on her "humor and pitch-perfect ear for sibling rivalry and family dynamics [that] will have readers giggling with recognition." Likewise, Michael Thorn, reviewing the book in *Times Educational Supplement*, found it to be a "model of comic pace and tone."

In fact, note reviewers, this "pitch-perfect ear" as well as Blume's insight into character is nowhere more apparent than in her fiction for pre-adolescents, who are undeniably her most loyal and attentive audience. As Naomi Decter observed in *Commentary*, "there is, indeed, scarcely a literate girl of novel-reading age who has not read one or more Blume books." Not only does Blume address sensitive themes, she "is a careful observer of the everyday details of children's lives and she has a feel for the little power struggles and shifting alliances of their social relationships," R. A. Siegal commented in the *Lion and the Unicorn*. Claim critics, this realism enhances the appeal of her books.

Blume reflected on her ability to communicate with her readers in a *Publishers Weekly* interview with Sybil Steinberg: "I have a capacity for total recall. That's my talent, if there's a talent involved. I have this gift, this memory, so it's easy to project myself back to certain stages in my life. And I write about what I know is true of kids going through those same stages." In addition, Blume enjoys writing for and about this age group. "When you're twelve, you're on the brink of adulthood," the author told Joyce Maynard in the *New York Times Magazine*, "but everything is still in front of you, and you still have the chance to be almost anyone you want. That seemed so appealing to me. I wasn't even thirty when I started writing, but already I didn't feel I had much chance myself." As a result, "whether she is writing about female or male sexual awakening, and whatever other adolescent problems, Judy Blume is on target," Dorothy M. Broderick asserted in the *New York Times Book Review*. "Her understanding of young people is sympathetic and psychologically sound; her skill engages the reader in human drama without melodrama."

Blume's style also plays a major role in her popularity; as Adele Geras remarked in *New Statesman,* Blume's books "are liked because they are accessible, warm hearted, often funny, and because in them her readers can identify with children like themselves in difficult situations, which may seem silly to the world at large but which are nevertheless very real to the sufferer." "It's hard not to like Judy Blume," Carolyn Banks elaborated in the *Washington Post Book World.* "Her style is so open, so honest, so direct. Each of her books reads as though she's not so much writing as kaffee klatsching with you." In addition, Siegal observed that Blume's works are structured simply, making them easy to follow. "Her plots are loose and episodic: they accumulate rather than develop," the critic states. "They are not complicated or demanding."

Another way in which Blume achieves such a close affinity with her readers is through her consistent use of first-person narratives. As Siegal explained: "Through this technique she succeeds in establishing intimacy and identification between character and audience. All her books read like diaries or journals and the reader is drawn in by the narrator's self-revelations." "Given the sophistication of Miss Blume's material, her style is surprisingly simple," Decter similarly commented. "She writes for the most part in the first person: her vocabulary, grammar, and syntax are colloquial; her tone, consciously or perhaps not, evokes the awkwardness of a fifth grader's diary." In *Just as Long as We're Together,* for instance, the twelve-year-old heroine "tells her story in simple, real kid language," noted Mitzi Myers in the *Los Angeles Times,* "inviting readers to identify with her dilemmas over girlfriends and boyfriends and that most basic of all teen problems: 'Sometimes I feel grown up and other times I feel like a little kid.'" Stephanie, Alison, and Rachel are the three characters of that title, but Stephanie takes center stage, as her parents split up and she begins to put on weight. More problems ensue as she starts to have problems with her friends, partly because of a new friendship Stephanie is forming with Alison. The girls make a return engagement—this time with the focus on Rachel—in the 1993 *Here's to You, Rachel Robinson,* a book "filled with intelligence and humor and real understanding of the human condition," according to Claire Rosser in *Kliatt.* In this novel, Rachel's brother, Charles, is expelled from boarding school, much to the chagrin of Rachel's mother, a newly appointed judge. Reviewing both novels, *Kliatt*'s Sherri Forgash Ginsberg concluded that "they are truly pure enjoyment."

Although Blume's work is consistently in favor with readers, it has frequently been the target of criticism. Some commentators have charged that the author's readable style, with its focus on mundane detail, lacks the depth to deal with the complex issues that she raises. In a *Times Literary Supplement* review of *Just as Long as We're Together,* for example, Jan Dalley claimed that Blume's work "is all very professionally achieved, as one would expect from this highly successful author,

but Blume's concoctions are unvaryingly smooth, bland, and glutinous." But Beryl Lieff Benderly noted that the author's readability sometimes masks what the critic calls her "enormous skill as a novelist," as she wrote in a *Washington Post Book World* review of the same book. "While apparently presenting the bright, slangy, surface details of life in an upper-middle class suburban junior high school, she's really plumbing the meaning of honesty, friendship, loyalty, secrecy, individuality, and the painful, puzzling question of what we owe those we love."

Other reviewers have taken exception to Blume's tendency to avoid resolving her fictional dilemmas in a straightforward fashion, for her protagonists rarely finish dealing with all their difficulties by the end of the book. Many critics, however, think that it is to Blume's credit that she does not settle every problem for her readers. One such critic, Robert Lipsyte of *Nation,* maintained that "Blume explores the feelings of children in a nonjudgmental way. The immediate resolution of a problem is never as important as what the protagonist . . . will learn about herself by confronting her life." Lipsyte explained that "the young reader gains from the emotional adventure story both by observing another youngster in a realistic situation and by finding a reference from which to start a discussion with a friend or parent or teacher. For many children, talking about a Blume story is a way to expose their own fears about menstruation or masturbation or death." Countering other criticisms that by not answering the questions they raise Blume's books fail to educate their readers, Siegal likewise suggested: "It does not seem that Blume's books . . . ought to be discussed and evaluated on the basis of what they teach children about handling specific social or personal problems. Though books of this type may sometimes be useful in giving children a vehicle for recognizing and ventilating their feelings, they are, after all, works of fiction and not self-help manuals."

Even more disturbing to some adults is Blume's treatment of mature issues and her use of frank language. "Menstruation, wet dreams, masturbation, all the things that are whispered about in real school halls" are the subjects of Blume's books, related interviewer Sandy Rovner in the *Washington Post.* As a result, Blume's works have frequently been the targets of censorship, and Blume herself has become an active crusader for freedom of expression. To answer those who would censor her work for its explicitness, Blume replied: "The way to instill values in children is to talk about difficult issues and bring them out in the open, not to restrict their access to books that may help them deal with their problems and concerns," she said in a Toronto *Globe and Mail* interview with Isabel Vincent. And, as she revealed to Peter Gorner in the *Chicago Tribune,* she never intended her work to inspire protest in the first place: "I wrote these books a long time ago when there wasn't anything near the censorship that there is now," she told Gorner. "I wasn't aware at the time that I was writing anything controversial. I just know what these books would have meant to me when I was a kid."

Others similarly defend Blume's choice of subject matter. For example, Natalie Babbitt asserted in the *New York Times Book Review:* "Some parents and librarians have come down hard on Judy Blume for the occasional vulgarities in her stories. Blume's vulgarities, however, exist in real life and are presented in her books with honesty and full acceptance." And those who focus only on the explicit aspects of Blume's books are missing their essence, Judith M. Goldberger proposed in the *Newsletter on Intellectual Freedom.* "Ironically, concerned parents and critics read Judy Blume out of context, and label the books while children and young adults read the whole books to find out what they are really about and to hear another voice talking about a host of matters with which they are concerned in their daily lives. The grownups, it seems, are the ones who read for the 'good' parts, more so than the children."

What started the controversy for Blume was her 1975 young adult novel, *Forever . . .,* a frank exploration of one young woman's first sexual relationship. So explicit was the text, that her publishers initially published it as an adult novel, though its teenage protagonist and exploration of the topic clearly put it into the young-adult category. The book was taken out of many school libraries at the request of outraged parents, but Blume was ultimately vindicated for her candor in 1996 with the presentation of the Margaret A. Edwards Award for Outstanding Literature for Young Adults for her body of work.

Blume realizes that the controversial nature of her work receives the most attention, and that causes concern for her beyond any censorship attempts. As the author explained to Maynard: "What I worry about is that an awful lot of people, looking at my example, have gotten the idea that what sells is teenage sex, and they'll exploit it. I don't believe that sex is why kids like my books. The impression I get, from letter after letter [I receive], is that a great many kids don't communicate with their parents. They feel alone in the world. Sometimes, reading books that deal with other kids who feel the same things they do makes them feel less alone." The volume of Blume's fan mail seems to reinforce the fact that her readers are looking for contact with an understanding adult. Hundreds of letters arrive each week not only praising her books but also asking her for advice or information. As Blume remarked to Steinberg in *Publishers Weekly,* "I have a wonderful, intimate relationship with kids. It's rare and lovely. They feel that they know me and that I know them."

In 1986, Blume collected a number of these letters from her readers and published them, along with some of her own comments, as *Letters to Judy: What Your Kids Wish They Could Tell You.* The resulting book, aimed at

both children and adults, "is an effort to break the silence, to show parents that they can talk without looking foolish, to show children that parents are human and remember what things were like when they were young, and to show everyone that however trivial the problem may seem it's worth trying to sort it out," wrote Geras. "If parents and children alike read 'Letters to Judy,'" advice columnist Elizabeth Winship likewise observed in the *New York Times Book Review,* "it might well help them to ease into genuine conversation. The book is not a how-to manual, but one compassionate and popular author's way to help parents see life through their children's eyes, and feel it through their hearts and souls." Blume feels so strongly about the lack of communication between children and their parents that she uses the royalties from *Letters to Judy,* among other projects, to help endow the KIDS Fund, which she established in 1981. Each year, the fund contributes its income to various nonprofit organizations set up to help young people communicate with their parents.

As Peter heads into seventh grade, he faces more frustrations dealing with his active little brother Fudge and his newly-discovered twin cousins in Blume's comical novel from her well-loved series. (Cover illustration by Peter Reynolds.)

Over the years, Blume's writing has matured and her audience has expanded with each new book. Blume is reluctant to classify her works according to age group, as she disclosed in her interview with Steinberg: "I hate to categorize books. . . . I wish that older readers would read my books about young people, and I hope that younger readers will grow up to read what I have to say about adult life. . . . I think that my appeal has to do with feelings and with character identification. Things like that don't change from generation to generation. That's what I really know." "I love family life," the author added in her interview with Gorner. "I love kids. I think divorce is a tragedy, traumatic, and horribly painful for everybody. That's why I wrote *Smart Women.* I want kids to read that and to think what life might be like for their parents. And I want parents to think about what life is like for their kids."

Banks commended Blume not only for her honest approach to issues, but for her "artistic integrity": "She's never content to rest on her laurels, writing the same book over and over as so many successful writers do." For instance, *Tiger Eyes,* the story of Davey, a girl whose father is killed in a robbery, is "a lesson on how the conventions of a genre can best be put to use," Lipsyte claimed. While the author uses familiar situations and characters, showing Davey dealing with an annoying younger sibling, a move far from home, and a new family situation, "the story deepens, takes turns," the critic continued, particularly when Davey's family moves in with an uncle who works for a nuclear weapons plant. The result, Lipsyte stated, is Blume's "finest book—ambitious, absorbing, smoothly written, emotionally engaging and subtly political." Walter Clemons noted in a *Newsweek* review of *Tiger Eyes:* "No wonder teen-agers love Judy Blume's novels: She's very good. . . . Blume's delicate sense of character, eye for social detail and clear access to feelings touches even a hardened older reader. Her intended younger audience gets a first-rate novel written directly to them."

Her 1998 adult novel, *Summer Sisters,* does not deal with such hard-hitting themes as *Tiger Eyes,* but in it she proves that she remains, as *Booklist*'s Ilene Cooper put it, a "pithy writer." The book, like her 1978 *Wifey* and 1983 *Smart Women,* was published as an adult title. However, as most of the action focuses on a pair of friends in the adolescence and teenage years, it "could just as easily have been on a YA list," according to Cooper. Set during a series of summers on Martha's Vineyard, the book follows the fortunes of Vix Weaver and Caitlin Somers through the 1970s and 1980s. Vix is the daughter of middle-class parents from Santa Fe, New Mexico, while Caitlin moves in a more upscale crowd. One summer Caitlin invites her friend Vix to share her house on the Vineyard, and during the summer of their sixth-grade year and subsequent summers spent together, the two form a strong bond through shared adventures and sexual awakenings. A reviewer for *Publishers Weekly* felt that this "portrait of an unlikely yet enduring friendship as it changes over

time . . . will remind readers why they read Blume's books when they were young: she finds a provocative theme and spins an involving story." Similarly, Michele Leber, writing in *Library Journal,* noted that the strength of this "relentlessly readable book" is its "vivid portrait of teens in the 1980s." More praise came for this bestselling novel from Mary Alice Giarda in *School Library Journal.* Giarda felt that Blume's "perceptive treatment" of childhood experience and the wonders of summertime "make this an entertaining read."

"Judy Blume is concerned [with describing] characters surviving, finding themselves, growing in understanding, coming to terms with life," John Gough noted in *School Librarian.* While the solutions her characters find and the conclusions they make "may not be original or profound," the critic continues, ". . . neither are they trivial. The high sales of Blume's books are testimony to the fact that what she has to say is said well and is well worth saying." "Many of today's children have found a source of learning in Judy Blume," Goldberger contended. "She speaks to children, and, in spite of loud protests, her voice is clear to them." As Faith McNulty similarly concluded in the *New Yorker:* "I find much in Blume to be thankful for. She writes clean, swift, unadorned prose. She has convinced millions of young people that truth can be found in a book and that reading is fun. At a time that many believe may be the twilight of the written word, those are things to be grateful for." Blume herself, after over three decades of publishing and seventy-five million books sold, is characteristically ironic about her achievement as well as the possibilities of her continued writing. As she told Walsh in *Entertainment Weekly,* "'Happiness has ruined my career! . . . All right, it hasn't ruined it, but I don't have the same need. I don't have the same angst. And I think that good writing comes from that kind of angst.'"

Biographical and Critical Sources

BOOKS

Authors and Artists for Young Adults, Volume 26, Gale (Detroit, MI), 1999.
Children's Literature Review, Gale (Detroit, MI), Volume 2, 1976, Volume 15, 1988, Volume 69, 2001.
Contemporary Literary Criticism, Gale (Detroit, MI), Volume 12, 1980, Volume 30, 1984.
Dictionary of Literary Biography, Volume 52: *American Writers for Children since 1960: Fiction,* Gale (Detroit, MI), 1986, pp. 30-38.
Fisher, Emma and Justin Wintle, *The Pied Pipers,* Paddington Press (New York, NY), 1975.
Gleasner, Diana, *Breakthrough: Women in Writing,* Walker (New York, NY), 1980.
Lee, Betsey, *Judy Blume's Story,* Dillon Press (Minneapolis, MN), 1981.
Newsmakers 1998, Issue 4, Gale (Detroit, MI), 1998.
St. James Guide to Young Adult Writers, 2nd edition, St. James Press (Detroit, MI), 1999.

Weidt, Maryann, *Presenting Judy Blume,* Twayne (Boston, MI), 1989.

Wheeler, Jill C., *Judy Blume,* Abdo & Daughters (Edina, MN), 1996.

PERIODICALS

Booklist, March 15, 1998, Ilene Cooper, review of *Summer Sisters,* p. 1179; June 1, 1999, Sally Estes, review of *Places I Never Meant to Be,* p. 1812; September 15, 2002, Gillian Engberg, "Fudge Is Back!," p. 235.

Bulletin of the Center for Children's Books, April, 1970, Zena Sutherland, review of *The One in the Middle Is the Green Kangaroo,* p. 125; May, 1975, Zena Sutherland, review of *Blubber,* p. 142; October, 1993, Roger Sutton, review of *Here's To You, Rachel Robinson,* p. 39.

Chicago Tribune, September 24, 1978; March 15, 1985, Peter Gorner, interview with Judy Blume, section 2, pp. 1-2.

Christian Science Monitor, May 14, 1979; March 14, 1984.

Commentary, March, 1980, Naomi Decter, "Judy Blume's Children," pp. 65-67.

Commonweal, July 4, 1980.

Detroit Free Press, February 26, 1984.

Detroit News, February 15, 1985.

Detroit News Magazine, February 4, 1979.

English Journal, September, 1972; March, 1976.

Entertainment Weekly, October 11, 2002, Rebecca Ascher Walsh, "The 'Fudge' Report," p. 77.

Globe and Mail (Toronto, Canada), November 17, 1990, Isabel Vincent, "A Heroine for Children," p. C10.

Kirkus Reviews, October 1, 1970, review of *Are You There God? It's Me, Margaret,* p. 1093; September 1, 2002, review of *Double Fudge,* p. 1304.

Kliatt, January, 1995, Sherri Forgash Ginsberg, review of *Just as Long as We're Together* and *Here's to You, Rachel Robinson,* p. 4; January, 1996, Claire Rosser, review of *Here's to You, Rachel Robinson,* p. 4.

Knight Ridder/Tribune News Service, October 9, 2002, Mary Ann Grossman, "Blume Doesn't Sound Too Convincing When She Talks about Retiring," p. K7522.

Library Journal, April 15, 1998, Michele Leber, review of *Summer Sisters,* p. 111.

Lion and the Unicorn, fall, 1978, R. A. Siegal, "Are You There God? It's Me, Me, Me!," pp. 72-77.

Los Angeles Times, December 26, 1987, Mitzi Myers, "An Optimistic World According to Blume."

Los Angeles Times Book Review, October 5, 1980; February 26, 1984; August 31, 1986.

Ms., July-August, 1998, Carolyn Mackler, "Judy Blume on Sex, the Suburbs, and 'Summer Sisters,'" pp. 89-90.

Nation, November 21, 1981, Robert Lipsyte, "A Bridge of Words," pp. 551-553.

Newsletter on Intellectual Freedom, May, 1981, Judith M. Goldberger, "Judy Blume: Target of the Censor," pp. 57, 61-62, 81-82.

New Statesman, November 5, 1976; November 14, 1980; October 24, 1986, Adele Geras, "Help!," pp. 28-29.

Newsweek, October 9, 1978, Linda Bird Francke, "Growing up with Judy," pp. 99-101; December 7, 1981,

Walter Clemons, review of *Tiger Eyes,* pp. 101-104; August 23, 1982.

New Yorker, December 5, 1983, Faith McNulty, "Children's Books for Christmas," pp. 191-201.

New York Times, October 3, 1982; February 21, 1984.

New York Times Book Review, May 24, 1970; November 8, 1970; December 9, 1970; January 16, 1972, Dorothy M. Broderick, "Growing Time," p. 8; September 3, 1972; November 3, 1974; December 28, 1975; May 25, 1976; May 1, 1977; November 23, 1980, Natalie Babbitt, review of *Superfudge,* pp. 36-37; November 15, 1981; February 19, 1984; June 8, 1986, Elizabeth Winship, "Taking Adolescents Seriously," p. 12; November 11, 1990, Jean Van Leeuwen, "Peter's Pesky Little Brother," p. 29; November 16, 1997, Mark Oppenheimer, "Why Judy Bloom Endures," pp. 44-45.

New York Times Magazine, December 3, 1978, Joyce Maynard, "Coming of Age with Judy Blume!," p. 80; August 23, 1982.

People, John Neary, interview with Judy Blume, October 16, 1978, pp. 47-48; August 16, 1982; March 19, 1984; December 28, 1998, "Judy Blume: The Queen of Preteen Fiction Hits Home with Her Grown-Up Fans," p. 80.

Publishers Weekly, January 11, 1971, Lavinia Russ, review of *Are You There God? It's Me, Margaret,* pp. 62-63; April 17, 1978, Sybil Steinberg, "PW Interviews: Judy Blume," pp. 6-7; March 30, 1998, review of *Summer Sisters,* p. 66; August, 1999, review of *Places I Never Meant to Be,* p. 152; March 4, 2002, "In Full Blume," p. 82; March 18, 2002, John F. Baker, "Judy Blume Moves 'Fudge,'" p. 16; June 24, 2002, review of *Double Fudge,* p. 57; August 12, 2002, Sally Lodge, "The Return of Fudge," p. 150.

Saturday Review, September 18, 1971.

School Librarian, May, 1987, John Gough, "Growth, Survival and Style in the Novels of Judy Blume," pp. 100-106; November, 1991, p. 143.

School Library Journal, January, 1972, Alice Adkins, review of *Freckle Juice,* p. 50; August, 1980, Pamela D. Pollack, review of *Superfudge,* pp. 60-61; December, 1990; May, 1974, Melinda Schroeder, review of *Deenie,* p. 53; June, 1996, Carolyn Caywood, "Deja Views," p. 62; June, 1998, Mary Alice Giarda, review of *Summer Sisters,* p. 175; August, 1999, Cindy Darling Codell, review of *Places I Never Meant to Be,* p. 152; September, 2002, Terrie Dorio, review of *Double Fudge,* p. 181.

Time, August 23, 1982.

Times Educational Supplement, September 20, 2002, Michael Thorn, "Whizz-Kids Revisited," p. 14.

Times Literary Supplement, October 1, 1976; April 7, 1978, Ann Evans, review of *Are You There God? It's Me, Margaret,* p. 383; January 29-February 4, 1988, Jan Dalley, "The Great American Feast," p. 119.

U.S. News and World Report, October 14, 2002, Vicky Hallett, "She Can't Say Farewell to Fudge," p. 12.

Washington Post, August 14, 1977; October 8, 1978; November 9, 1980; September 13, 1981; November 3, 1981, Sandy Rovner, interview with Judy Blume.

Washington Post Book World, November 9, 1982, Brigitte Weeks, "The Return of Peter Hatcher," p. 12; February 12, 1984, Carolyn Banks, "A Hot Time in the Hot Tub Tonight," p. 3; April 27, 1986, Phyllis Theroux, "Judy Blume Listens to Her Young Readers," pp. 3-4; November 8, 1987, Beryl Lieff Benderly, "Judy Blume: Junior High Blues," p. 19.

Writer's Digest, November, 2001, Karen Struckel Brogan, "Judy Blume," pp. 30-31.

ONLINE

Judy Blume Web Site, http://www.judyblume.com/ (April 19, 2003).

*   *   *

BRADLEY, Will
See STRICKLAND, (William) Brad(ley)

*   *   *

BULLARD, Lisa 1961-

Personal

Born August 10, 1961, in Waco, TX; daughter of James E. and Blenda J. Bullard. *Education:* Concordia College (Moorhead, MN), B.A. (summa cum laude), 1982; University of Denver Publishing Institute, graduated 1985.

Addresses

Office—c/o Carolrhoda Books, 241 First Ave. N., Minneapolis, MN 55401. *E-mail*—bullardlm@msn.com.

Career

Lerner Publications, Minneapolis, MN, member of marketing department, 1985-91; Coffee House Press, Minneapolis, MN, marketing director, 1992-95; Graywolf Press, Saint Paul, MN, marketing director, 1995-2000; New Rivers Press, Minneapolis, MN, interim executive director, 2000-01; freelance writer, 2001—. Loft Literary Center, Minneapolis, MN, writing teacher, 1998—, member of Education Committee, 2003—. Minnesota Book Publishers Roundtable, member of board of directors, 1995-99, president, 1997-99; Upper Midwest Booksellers Association, member of board of directors, 1995-98. Cohost of "Write on Radio," KFAI, Minneapolis, MN, 1995-99.

Member

Society of Children's Book Writers and Illustrators, Children's Literature Network, Loft Literary Center.

Awards, Honors

Children's Resources Silver Award, National Parenting Publications, 2001, Honor Title, Storytelling World Awards, and Children's Choice Award, International Reading Association/Children's Book Council, both 2002, all for *Trick-or-Treat on Milton Street;* Career Initiative Grant, Loft Literary Center, 2002.

Lisa Bullard

Writings

Not Enough Beds! A Christmas Alphabet Book, illustrated by Joni Oeltjenbruns, Carolrhoda Books (Minneapolis, MN), 1999.

Trick-or-Treat on Milton Street, illustrated by Joni Oeltjenbruns, Carolrhoda Books (Minneapolis, MN), 2001.

Marvelous Me: Inside and Out, illustrated by Brandon Reibeling, Picture Window Books (Minneapolis, MN), 2003.

My Body: Head to Toe, illustrated by Brandon Reibeling, Picture Window Books (Minneapolis, MN), 2003.

My Day: Morning, Noon, and Night, Picture Window Books (Minneapolis, MN), 2003.

My Family: Love and Care, Give and Share, illustrated by Brandon Reibeling, Picture Window Books (Minneapolis, MN), 2003.

My Home: Walls, Floors, Ceilings, and Doors, illustrated by Brandon Reibeling, Picture Window Books (Minneapolis, MN), 2003.

My Neighborhood: Places and Faces, illustrated by Brandon Reibeling, Picture Window Books (Minneapolis, MN), 2003.

Powerboats, Lerner Publications (Minneapolis, MN), 2004.

Stock Cars, Lerner Publications (Minneapolis, MN), 2004.

Contributor of book reviews to the *Ruminator Review.*

Sidelights

Lisa Bullard's first children's book, *Not Enough Beds! A Christmas Alphabet Book,* is a jaunty rhyme told by Zachary about the wonderful muddle that happens every year when the house overflows with relatives visiting for the holidays. Relatives with names beginning with every letter of the alphabet from A to Z cheerfully bed down in chairs, on the porch, or under a table because there just are not enough beds to fit them all. A contributor to the *New York Times Book Review* called this "engaging, cluttered fun," while Helen Rosenberg, writing in *Booklist,* described *Not Enough Beds!* as a "lively Christmas tale."

Another popular holiday with children of all ages sets the stage for Bullard's next book, *Trick-or-Treat on Milton Street.* In this story, Charley is sure that Halloween will be dull this year because he, his mother, and his new stepfather have just moved to a new neighborhood, one with very few children. Then, when Charley's mom gets sick on Halloween and cannot take him trick-or-treating, he has to go with his new stepfather, another disappointment. But behind every door in the neighborhood, Charley finds a friendly adult dressed in a funny costume, and when he arrives home, his new neighbors are waiting for him to join in a party in his honor. A critic from *Kirkus Reviews* noted that the story contains "an important lesson about giving new things and new people a chance." A contributor to *Publishers Weekly* argued, however, that while there are some scenes that Bullard gets "just right," others seem overly sweet, as sweet as "a gooey caramel apple." Young readers will find Oeltjenbruns' illustrations reward careful examinations, according to Maryann H. Owen in *School Library Journal,* who concluded that "though the story is a bit wordy in places, it is a warm and fuzzy holiday tale."

Bullard told *SATA:* "One of the best critiques I received came through an anecdote. Someone was telling me that their five-year-old granddaughter enjoyed my first picture book so much that she had memorized the entire text and could 'read' the story out loud by herself (all 224 words). Halfway through one of her recitations, the little girl stopped cold. 'But Grandma,' she asked, 'just what *is* a hubbub?' 'Hubbub' is the word I worked hardest for as a writer, the one for which second-best wouldn't do: a celebration-dazed, noisy, overfull, lovely-to-say-aloud word that few contemporary children have heard. It works with the story's rhyme and meter, perfectly describes that moment in the story's action, and is a word with all sorts of wonderful possibilities. I'm delighted to have introduced it to at least one young reader.

"I write for children in an attempt to share with them some of my foundational beliefs, the ones that made me a writer in the first place: that words have an 'awful' power (in the old-fashioned sense of 'commanding awe'), and that we help shape our lives through the stories we tell and the words we choose to tell them. I

have heard many writers whose books are packaged in a child-friendly format add a disclaimer that they aren't really 'children's writers' at all but rather all-purpose writers whom children might happen to read. I write books with children in mind as my intentional audience—if adults enjoy the books too, that's all to the good since they usually serve as the vehicle through which younger children hear a story. But I am mostly interested in converting children to lovers of language, in delighting them with word-play, and helping to turn them into lifelong book-lovers. That is one of the reasons that I was so proud to win an International Reading Association/Children's Book Council Children's Choice Award for *Trick-or-Treat on Milton Street* since it is one of the few awards actually chosen by children themselves.

"I begin with the subjects kids find the most compelling: families, friends, special holidays, the rituals of life. I believe children are most likely to respond to something that entertains them, and I have found humor to be especially appealing. If you can surprise a child with something just a little oddball or unexpected, you will have their complete attention, and their own imaginations will be immediately engaged. Rhyme and some of the other tools of the poets help to give language a playful feel. Picture books are meant to be read out loud, so the sound of the words is as important as the way they interact with the art on the page. At the same time, the story must provide a strong visual sense but leave room for the illustrator to have creative sway with their artistic enhancement. Altogether, I try to find an entree to the world children occupy, and use language and stories to draw them a little bit outside or beyond themselves."

Biographical and Critical Sources

PERIODICALS

Booklist, September 15, 1999, Helen Rosenberg, review of *Not Enough Beds! A Christmas Alphabet Book,* p. 266.

Horn Book Guide, July-December, 2001, review of *Trick-or-Treat on Milton Street.*

Kirkus Reviews, July 15, 2001, review of *Trick-or-Treat on Milton Street,* p. 1022.

New York Times Book Review, December 19, 1999, review of *Not Enough Beds!,* p. 30.

Publishers Weekly, September 27, 1999, review of *Not Enough Beds!,* p. 60; September 24, 2001, review of *Trick-or-Treat on Milton Street,* p. 42.

School Library Journal, October, 1999, Tracy Taylor, review of *Not Enough Beds!,* p. 66; September, 2001, Maryann H. Owen, review of *Trick-or-Treat on Milton Street,* p. 184.

ONLINE

Lisa Bullard Home Page, http://www.lisabullard.com/ (May 28, 2003).

C

CAPEK, Michael 1947-

Personal

Born September 19, 1947, in Covington, KY; son of Harold (in business) and Naomi (Larken) Capek; married Terri Richardson (a teacher), June 14, 1969; children: Christopher, Kari Jo. *Education:* Cumberland College, B.A., 1969; Eastern Kentucky University, M.A., 1976. *Hobbies and other interests:* Photography, nature.

Addresses

Home—5965 Tipp Dr., Taylor Mill, KY 41015. *E-mail*—mcapek@goodnews.net.

Career

Walton-Verona High School, Walton, KY, teacher of English, 1969-96.

Member

Society of Children's Book Writers and Illustrators.

Awards, Honors

Merit Honor Award, Society of Children's Book Writers and Illustrators, 1993, for article in *Cricket* magazine; Young Readers Book Award, *Scientific America,* 1996, for *Murals: Cave, Cathedral, to Street.*

Writings

Artistic Trickery: The Tradition of Trompe L'Oeil Art, Lerner Publications (Minneapolis, MN), 1995.

Murals: Cave, Cathedral, to Street, Lerner Publications (Minneapolis, MN), 1996.

A Ticket to Jamaica, Carolrhoda Books (Minneapolis, MN), 1998.

Jamaica ("Globe-Trotters Club" series), Carolrhoda Books (Minneapolis, MN), 1999.

Michael Capek

A Personal Tour of a Shaker Village, Lerner Publications (Minneapolis, MN), 2001.

Lively Stones: A Narrative History of Belleview Baptist Church, Tennessee Valley Publishers (Knoxville, TN), 2002.

Contributor to *Heath Middle Level Literature: Grade 8,* D.C. Heath, 1994, and to other textbooks. Contributor of numerous stories and articles to periodicals, including *Highlights for Children, Ranger Rick, Short Story Digest, Images, Cricket,* and *Adventure;* contributor of devotionals to *Encounter!* and *Essential Connection.*

By describing the daily routine of four Shakers, Capek takes young readers back to 1849 and describes how Pleasant Hill, Kentucky, functioned as an industrious town as well as a religious community in **A Personal Tour of a Shaker Village.** *(Photo by Buddy Mays.)*

Work in Progress

A young adult biography of artist/animator Winsor Mc-Cay; a young adult historical novel about the U.S. Camel Corps experiment of 1855.

Sidelights

A former educator, author Michael Capek has contributed numerous stories, poems, devotionals, and articles to children's magazines. In addition, he has penned several nonfiction titles for young readers, among them *Artistic Trickery: The Tradition of Trompe L'Oeil Art* and the award-winning *Murals: Cave, Cathedral, to Street,* both of which educate young people about art styles and history. A high school teacher who taught in his home state of Kentucky for almost thirty years, Capek once cited a "need to instruct, which I've always felt," as his main motivation for writing.

Capek's first book, 1995's *Artistic Trickery,* written for readers aged ten and above, is an overview of the decorative art style known as *trompe l'oeil* (meaning "fool the eye") and of the artists who created it, from the Roman Empire to the present day. Trompe l'oeil, pronounced "tromp-loy," is a technique painters employ to achieve a result that is so realistic that it appears to be the actual subject depicted or a photograph of it. As

Capek's title implies, many trompe l'oeil artists have used their talents to create visual tricks that amuse and fool the eye. In his book, Capek includes reproductions of trompe l'oeil artworks, profiles of artists working in the tradition, and a discussion of the various categories of this type of artwork, such as food, doors, people, and money. *Artistic Trickery* was generally well received by critics, among them a *Publishers Weekly* reviewer who praised Capek's "clear, comprehensive text." The reviewer remarked that in this book "one of the more oddball traditions in art gets a well-deserved spotlight." Julie Yates Walton of *Booklist* lauded Capek for writing so "engagingly" and "appreciatively of his subject."

Capek takes on another form of art in *Murals: Cave, Cathedral, to Street.* According to Carolyn Phelan of *Booklist,* he compiles a "well written" and "informative history" of an art form that dates as far back as prehistorical man. Capek begins by discussing modern-day murals that can be found on buildings and works backward to explore the works of important twentieth-century muralists such as Diego Rivera and Wendell Jones, classical works such as Leonardo da Vinci's *The Last Supper,* murals of the Aztecs, Toltecs, Mayans, Egyptians, Romans, Christians, and others in the ancient world, and the prehistoric cave paintings discovered in France. By providing information on how artistic styles have changed over the years, Capek has written a book that serves as "a good starting point for the student who wants to learn more about art," Jeanne M. McGlinn noted in *Voice of Youth Advocates.*

In addition to books on art, Capek has also authored several books that take young readers to unusual locations he himself has found of interest. In *Jamaica,* part of Carolrhoda's "Globe-Trotters Club" series, readers gain an in-depth knowledge of Jamaica, including the island's topography, weather, language, holidays, religions, folktales, and sports. Capek stays closer to his Kentucky home in two nonfiction titles: *A Personal Tour of a Shaker Village* and *Lively Stones: A Narrative History of Belleview Baptist Church.* Bringing his audience back in time to the mid-nineteenth century, Capek recreates for readers the thriving Shaker community of Pleasant Hill, Kentucky, through stories, photographs, maps, and descriptions of day-to-day life there. In her review of *A Personal Tour of a Shaker Village* for *Horn Book Guide,* Anne St. John praised the book for presenting young people with "a personalized picture of the past." The 200th anniversary of one of Boone County, Kentucky's first churches was the inspiration for *Lively Stones,* which includes profiles of ten of the church's most noted parishioners. Capek said of the book, "Though it's naturally aimed at a serious, adult audience, I ultimately wrote *Lively Stones* for that same inquisitive child for whom I write all my books."

Capek once commented: "My main motivation in writing for children is always to excite and influence readers' thinking in some way, the way I was aroused and influenced as a child by the books I read. Invariably, when I write, it's for the child-self that hides deep inside me. It's hard to please that child and even harder to move him. He's incredibly innocent, but brutally honest. And unless I'm quick about it, I'll lose him. He's got better things to do than listen to some adult ramble on. If I can make him laugh or make him think or make him care, I've succeeded. My entire writing life is dedicated to pleasing that child.

"I've written a lot of fiction," Capek continued, "but for sheer challenge there's nothing like nonfiction. I love it—to paraphrase John F. Kennedy—not because it's easy, but because it's hard to do well. To write fact that compels like fiction, that's a lofty goal, in my opinion."

Biographical and Critical Sources

PERIODICALS

Booklist, June 1 and 15, 1995, Julie Yates Walton, review of *Artistic Trickery: The Tradition of Trompe L'Oeil Art,* p. 1758; June 1 and 15, 1996, Carolyn Phelan, review of *Murals: Cave, Cathedral, to Street,* p. 1687.
Bulletin of the Center for Children's Books, July-August, 1995, p. 379.
Horn Book Guide, fall, 2001, Anne St. John, review of *A Personal Tour of a Shaker Village,* p. 330.
Kirkus Reviews, April 1, 1996, p. 527.
Publishers Weekly, May 8, 1995, review of *Artistic Trickery,* p. 298.
School Library Journal, July, 1995, p. 84; October, 1996, p. 154; August, 2001, Wendy Lukehart, review of *A Personal Tour of a Shaker Village,* p. 192.
Scientific American, December, 1996, p. 120.
Voice of Youth Advocates, October, 1996, Jeanne M. McGlinn, review of *Murals,* pp. 226-227.

ONLINE

Michael Capek Home Page, http://www.homestead.com/kidswriter/ (March 15, 2003).

*　　*　　*

CAVANNA, Betty
See HARRISON, Elizabeth Cavanna

*　　*　　*

CAVANNA, Elizabeth
See HARRISON, Elizabeth Cavanna

*　　*　　*

CAVANNA, Elizabeth Allen
See HARRISON, Elizabeth Cavanna

CHANG, Raymond 1939-

Personal

Born March 6, 1939, in Hong Kong; naturalized U.S. citizen; son of Junsheng (a banker) and Ju-fen (a homemaker; maiden name, Li) Chang; married Margaret A. Scrogin (a librarian and writer), August 3, 1968; children: Elizabeth Hope. *Ethnicity:* "Chinese." *Education:* University of London, B.S. (with first class honours), 1962; Yale University, M.S., 1963, Ph.D., 1966.

Addresses

Home—146 Forest Rd., Williamstown, MA 01267. *Office*—Department of Chemistry, Williams College, Williamstown, MA 01267-2682.

Career

Washington University, St. Louis, MO, postdoctoral research fellow, 1966-67; Hunter College of the City University of New York, New York, NY, assistant professor of chemistry, 1967-68; Williams College, Williamstown, MA, assistant professor, 1968-73, associate professor, 1974-78, professor of chemistry, 1978—, Halford R. Clark Professor of Natural Sciences, 1989—, chair of department, 1993-95. University of California, Lawrence Radiation Laboratory, visiting scientist at Laboratory of Chemical Biodynamics, 1972-73; Stanford University, visiting professor, 1977-78; Amherst College, visiting scientist, 1981. Olympiad Examinations Task Force, member, 1989-91, Graduate Record Examination Committee, 1994-99.

Member

American Chemical Society (member of examination committees for physical chemistry, 1979-83, and general chemistry, 1983-85), American Association for the Advancement of Science, Sigma Xi.

Awards, Honors

Books for the Teen Age selection, New York Public Library, 1980, 1981, and 1982, all for *Speaking of Chinese;* Parents' Choice Honor Book award, 1990, for *In the Eye of War,* and 1999, for *Da Wei's Treasure;* outstanding children's book citation, *Parenting* magazine, 1994, for *The Cricket Warrior: A Chinese Tale;* Selectors' Choice, *Elementary School Library Collection,* 2000, for *The Beggar's Magic: A Chinese Tale.*

Writings

WITH WIFE, MARGARET SCROGIN CHANG

Speaking of Chinese, W. W. Norton (New York, NY), 1978, updated edition, 2001.
In the Eye of War, Margaret K. McElderry Books (New York, NY), 1990.

Raymond Chang

(Retellers) *The Cricket Warrior: A Chinese Tale,* illustrated by Warwick Hutton, Margaret K. McElderry Books (New York, NY), 1994.

(Retellers) *The Beggar's Magic: A Chinese Tale,* illustrated by David Johnson, Margaret K. McElderry Books (New York, NY), 1997.

(Retellers) *Da Wei's Treasure: A Chinese Tale,* illustrated by Lori McElrath-Eslick, Margaret K. McElderry Books (New York, NY), 1999.

Chang's books have been published in Braille editions.

OTHER

Basic Principles of Spectroscopy, McGraw-Hill (New York, NY), 1971.

Physical Chemistry with Applications to Biological Systems, Macmillan (New York, NY), 1977, 3rd edition published as *Physical Chemistry for the Chemical and Biological Sciences,* University Science Books (Sausalito, CA), 2000.

Chemistry, Random House (New York, NY), 1981, 7th edition, McGraw-Hill (Boston, MA), 2002.

General Chemistry, Random House (New York, NY), 1986, 3rd edition published as *General Chemistry: The Essential Concepts,* McGraw-Hill (Dubuque, IA), 2003.

(With Wayne Tikkanen) *The Top Fifty Industrial Chemicals,* Random House (New York, NY), 1988.

(With Jerry S. Faughn and Jon Turk) *Physical Science,* 2nd edition, Saunders College Publishing (Philadelphia, PA), 1995.

Essential Chemistry, McGraw Hill (New York, NY), 1996, 2nd edition, 2000.

Contributor of articles to chemistry journals. Member of editorial board, *Chemical Educator.* Contributor to instructor's manuals, workbooks, and study guides to his chemistry texts.

Sidelights

Chemistry professor Raymond Chang lives a dual life as an author. Not only has he written several highly praised chemistry textbooks for college students, but he also draws on his memories growing up in China in the books he has coauthored for children. Together with his wife, Margaret Scrogin Chang, Chang has written *In the Eye of War,* a novel for children about a Chinese family living in occupied Shanghai. Also with his wife, he has created the texts for several picture books based on traditional Chinese tales, among them *The Cricket Warrior: A Chinese Tale* and *The Beggar's Magic: A Chinese Tale.*

In *The Cricket Warrior,* the Changs update a traditional Chinese folktale first written down by seventeenth-century author Pu Songling. When a poor farmer and his son Wei nian trap a healthy fighting cricket, the farmer promises the insect to the emperor, a man who loves cricket fights and has imposed a "cricket tax" on each family in his domain in order to keep himself well supplied. After the curious young Wei nian accidentally frees the insect, he quickly realizes that he has put his family's humble farm in jeopardy and seeks the aid of his ancestor's spirit in transforming himself into a cricket. Winning many matches for the emperor, he preserves his father's commitment and makes his family wealthy before regaining his human form. *The Cricket Warrior* contains what *School Library Journal* reviewer John Philbrook described as a "brisk, colloquial narrative," through which the Changs "skillfully render . . . each turn of plot." Praising the Chang's retelling in a review of *The Cricket Warrior,* a *Publishers Weekly* contributor noted that their "dynamic retelling" of the traditional Chinese tale "emphasizes Wei nian's concern with honor . . . and the strength of the familial bond." Recommending the story for reading aloud, *Booklist* contributor Carolyn Phelan praised the Changs' style, which she described as "fluid" and "spiced with dramatic dialogue."

Also based on a traditional Chinese tale first set down centuries ago by Pu Songling, *The Beggar's Magic* draws young listeners to a small village where a mysterious elderly stranger has captured the interest of young Fu Nan and his friends through the unknown man's ability to perform magic. The entire village benefits from the stranger's talents after he creates, almost overnight, a bountiful pear tree with fruit enough for all in

Da Wei, a young Chinese fisherman, escapes the clutches of an evil landlord and finds love and happiness when he inherits a magic rock from his father in Margaret and Raymond Chang's retelling of an adventurous folktale. (From Da Wei's Treasure, *illustrated by Lori McElrath-Eslick.)*

the village to share. Only after the stranger leaves does Fu Nan realize that the stranger had created this "tree" by magically transporting pears from a cache hoarded by stingy and greedy Farmer Wu. Calling *The Beggar's Magic* a "delightful cautionary tale on avarice and selfishness," *School Library Journal* contributor Philbrook added that the earth-toned ink-and-watercolor illustrations by David Johnson combine effectively with the Changs' "simple and elegant" prose to create "a perfect gem of a book that will linger in the mind long after a first reading." *Horn Book* reviewer Ann A. Flowers found *The Beggar's Magic* to be "a gentle and delicate tale" that would serve young listeners as a "quiet lesson in sharing," while in *Booklist*, Phelan praised the Changs' retelling as one done "with simplicity and elegance."

Published in 1999, Chang's retelling of *Da Wei's Treasure: A Chinese Tale* comes from a more personal source than *The Cricket Warrior* and *The Beggar's Magic:* it is based on a story Chang's mother told him while he was growing up in Shanghai. Da Wei is the son of a poor man who ekes out a meager living in the barren lands of northern China. The only thing of value to his father is a rock shaped like a mountain in miniature, on top of which is perched a carved miniature house. After Da Wei's father dies, the miniature scene generates a magical cart, which leads young Da Wei to a magical land that yields him not only a beautiful wife

and great wealth, but also a certain amount of problems that only magic can make right. In her *Booklist* review of *Da Wei's Treasure*, GraceAnne A. DeCandido praised it as a "heartwarming story," and a *Publishers Weekly* contributor wrote that "the Changs' . . . eloquent retelling weaves together familiar strands of classic tales" in creating an uplifting read-aloud. Also commenting that Chang's mother may have drawn from a number of traditional tales, such as the classic "The Crane's Wife," in her own bedside tale, *School Library Journal* reviewer Nina Lindsay maintained that "the narrative is long and involved but never ceases to be intriguing."

Chang's wife once explained to *SATA* that her husband's family "moved to Hong Kong from their home in Shanghai to escape the 1937 Japanese invasion of China. Chang was born in the British Crown Colony, the youngest son of a family that already included seven children. Not long after the Japanese marched into Hong Kong on Christmas Day, 1941, the Changs moved back to Shanghai, where they lived under Japanese occupation. In 1949, they returned to Hong Kong, leaving Shanghai for good.

"Because of his family's background and the many relocations, Chang became fluent in several Chinese dialects. At home he heard his mother's dialect, Sichuanese. He talked with his playmates in Shanghainese, while in school they all learned Beijing Mandarin, the national standard for spoken language. In Hong Kong, he had to learn a completely different spoken language, the Cantonese dialect of southern China. Fortunately for him, the same written language unites all of China.

"At the age of seventeen, Chang followed his sister to London for what he thought would be a few years of study in the West. He did not return to Hong Kong for seventeen years, and then it was only for a brief visit. On the boat that took him to England, Chang soon realized that the English he had learned as a Chinese schoolboy was inadequate for everyday communication and totally useless for reading the dinner menu, which was all in French! Once in London, he set about improving his English and now speaks so fluently that most people assume he was born in the United States.

"After a couple of years in preparatory school, Chang entered the University of London to study chemistry, and he graduated with first-class honours. Partly because three of his sisters had married and moved to the United States, he decided to continue his education in the United States of America. He earned his Ph.D., married an American, and moved to a scenic corner of New England to become a chemistry professor at Williams College.

"Since for many years he was the only Asian on the faculty, Chang often went outside his field of chemistry to explain Chinese language and culture to curious students. For several years he taught a popular winter study course, a one-month introduction to Chinese language and calligraphy. When he tried to gather background materials for his course, he found no book on the Chinese language that was written for the general reader, the layman without a background in linguistics or Sinology.

"Though he was already the author of two chemistry books, he asked me to help him write a popular introduction to the Chinese language, one that people interested in China could read in bed without a pencil. *Speaking of Chinese* was the result. Chang drew on his boyhood experiences to select the proverbs, describe Chinese grammar, and write the calligraphy used in the text.

"In 1982, Chang led a group of Williams College students and alumni on a winter study tour of the People's Republic of China. It was his first trip home in more than thirty years. In Shanghai, he was amazed by the vast numbers of people, all so healthy and well clothed. His old neighborhood looked far more crowded than he remembered. His childhood home, shabby but still standing, housed three families.

"Like many Chinese professionals who have returned to their native land for a visit, he found the territory familiar, but he knew that the country of his childhood was no longer his."

Biographical and Critical Sources

PERIODICALS

Booklist, November 1, 1994, Carolyn Phelan, review of *The Cricket Warrior: A Chinese Tale,* p. 502; October 15, 1997, Carolyn Phelan, review of *The Beggar's Magic: A Chinese Tale,* p. 407; May 15, 1999, GraceAnne A. DeCandido, review of *Da Wei's Treasure: A Chinese Tale,* p. 1699.

Focus on Asian Studies, autumn, 1978, review of *Speaking of Chinese,* p. 40.

Horn Book, June, 1979, review of *Speaking of Chinese;* November-December, 1997, Ann A. Flowers, review of *The Beggar's Magic,* p. 690.

Journal of Chemical Education, November, 1994, Michael S. Bradley, review of *Chemistry,* p. A289; October, 1996, Howard D. Dewalt, review of *Essential Chemistry,* pp. A240-241; May, 2001, Andrew Pounds, review of *Physical Chemistry for the Chemical and Biological Sciences,* pp. 594-595.

Publishers Weekly, September 5, 1994, review of *The Cricket Warrior,* p. 110; June 14, 1999, review of *Da Wei's Treasure,* p. 70.

School Library Journal, January, 1995, John Philbrook, review of *The Cricket Warrior,* p. 102; December, 1997, John Philbrook, review of *The Beggar's Magic,* p. 107; June, 1999, Nina Lindsay, review of *Da Wei's Treasure,* p. 112.

Scientific American, December, 1978, review of *Speaking of Chinese.*

COBURN, Ann

Personal

Born in Northumberland, England; children: two.

Addresses

Home—Northumberland, England. *Agent*—c/o Nicki Stoddart, PFD, Drury House, 34-43 Russell St., London WC2B 5HA, England.

Career

Freelance writer, 1991—. Also writes for television.

Awards, Honors

Wriets Award, Arts Council of England, 1996; John Whiting Award, 1997, for *Get Up and Tie Your Fingers.*

Writings

Get Up and Tie Your Fingers (play), performed in Edinburgh, Scotland, 1997, Theatre Communications Group (New York, NY), 2001.

Also author of the plays *The Devil's Ground, Safe,* and *Daytime.*

JUVENILE NOVELS

The Granite Beast, Bodley Head (London, England), 1991.
Welcome to the Real World, Bodley Head (London, England), 1992.
The Domino Effect, Bodley Head (London, England), 1994.

"BORDERLANDS" SERIES

Worm Songs, Bodley Head (London, England), 1996.
Web Weaver, Bodley Head (London, England), 1997.
Dark Water, Bodley Head (London, England), 1998.

Sidelights

British author Ann Coburn has been writing novels for young readers since her first book, *The Granite Beast,* was published in 1991. Her other titles include *Welcome to the Real World* and *The Domino Effect.* Coburn is also the author of the "Borderlands" series of novels, including *Worm Songs, Web Weaver,* and *Dark Water,* which features plots involving time travel and the supernatural. Additionally, Coburn is the author of several plays, among them *Get Up and Tie Your Fingers,* which played at the Edinburgh Festival Fringe and won the John Whiting Award for new theater writing.

Born in Northumberland, Coburn grew up in northeast England and lives again in her native Northumberland where she writes children's books, plays, and television scripts. Her book career was jump-started with *The Granite Beast,* in which readers become acquainted with Ruth, a thirteen-year-old girl who has just lost her father. Her mother is determined to carry out her deceased husband's dream of owning a shop in Cornwall, and so Ruth is uprooted from her home and school in Coventry. Her new Cornish classmates—and even her teachers—are unaccepting of her, forcing the girl to rely upon the town outcast, a seventeen-year-old car mechanic named Ben. Ben is the one who comforts her when she begins having terrible nightmares; together they piece together the meaning of her dark dreams to figure out the nature of an impending disaster that will take place in a nearby abandoned tin mine. When Ruth's history teacher plans a field trip to that very mine, she is unable either to prevent the expedition or stay away herself. As a critic for *Junior Bookshelf* put it: "What happens in the tin-mine makes the exciting climax to this horror story." Reviewers of *The Granite Beast* were predominantly positive, though David Self in the *Times Educational Supplement* felt that "it has a middle section in which the plot rather awkwardly fails to

In this work by Ann Coburn, four young people work out the mystery surrounding a dragon in an attempt to save a friend from accusations of witchcraft.

progress." Self did concede though that the novel "successfully marries school realism with fantasy." The contributor for the *Junior Bookshelf* predicted that "Young readers will be loath to put the book down once they have started to read it." And Graham Case in the *School Librarian* hailed it as a "really good read and well crafted."

Welcome to the Real World became available to readers in England in 1992. This novel tells the story of five different adolescents who are being bullied and blackmailed about embarrassing secrets by Andrew, the son of their school's caretaker. At first the victims are unaware of each other, but eventually they realize they are not alone and come together to deal with their mutual problem in what a *Junior Bookshelf* reviewer called "a denouement which would have done credit to *The Avengers.*" Though this same critic regarded *Welcome to the Real World* a "rather worrying story" and seemed concerned that Coburn had not explored the probability that Andrew's bullying behavior was actually "a cry for help," the reviewer did applaud the author's understanding of the characters' age group. Writing in *School Librarian,* Maggie Bignell, by contrast, considered *Welcome to the Real World* "well worth buying for the library" and also recommended it for classroom study by secondary students. She lauded the novel for exposing adolescents to several different forms of narrative, "from stream of consciousness to formally written school records," and also including "third-person narration."

Coburn's *The Domino Effect* has been widely praised for dealing with the controversial subject matter of sexual harassment and attempted rape. The novel concerns sixteen-year-old Rowan, whose mother is the target of a boss's campaign to ruin her career. The final step in his plan to humiliate her is to rape her at a business seminar he has asked her to lead. Rowan's mother only accepts this invitation because she believes her boss intends it as a step towards improving their hostile working relationship. Fortunately, she manages to escape short of full-scale brutalization. Rowan's mother is at first immobilized by shock after the experience but eventually recovers and decides to bring justice upon her former employer. When the matter becomes public knowledge, the entire town takes sides, and Rowan loses both her boyfriend and the girl she thought was her best friend because of it. A *Junior Bookshelf* contributor paired *The Domino Effect* with another young adult novel about sexual abuse and noted that both deal with "themes which forty years ago would not have been considered seriously by any British publisher, ten years ago would have been given far less explicit treatment." Linda Saunders, writing in *School Librarian,* cited the "humanity and realism" present in *The Domino Effect,* urging that it "should be read by younger as well as older teenagers." Val Bierman, writing in *Books for Keeps,* also had praise for *The Domino Effect,* declaring it "thoughtful" and "provocative." The *Junior Bookshelf* critic, like Saunders, concluded that the novel "deserve[s] to be read."

Oberon Modern Plays

Ann Coburn

GET UP AND TIE YOUR FINGERS SAFE

Two plays by Coburn cover very different topics: lives of the women in a nineteenth-century Scottish fishing town and modern-day relationships between parents and children.

After *The Domino Effect,* Coburn began work on a group of young adult novels known as the "Borderlands" series. The first of this series, set in the area where England borders upon Scotland, is titled *Worm Songs. Worm Songs* introduces the four main characters: Alice, Frankie, David, and Michael. Alice is concerned about her relationship with her stepfather and stepbrothers, while Frankie (who is female) is worried that her move from the United States to the Borderlands signals her parents' impending divorce. All four young people are members of a photography club, and it is through photography that they are able to travel to different time periods. In *Worm Songs,* they meet Martha, a midwife and healer of the sixteenth century who is about to be burned as a witch on the authority of Sir Robert, Lord of the East March. She is reconciled to the prospect of her own death but asks the four friends to ensure the survival of her infant daughter. "The carrying out of this task," according to a contributor for *Junior Bookshelf,* "makes for fascinating reading." Gaye

Hicyilmaz, discussing *Worm Songs* (as well as the second "Borderlands" novel, *Web Weaver*) in the *Times Educational Supplement,* compared Coburn favorably with prolific and popular British children's writer Enid Blyton and labeled *Worm Songs* a "delight." Similarly, the *Junior Bookshelf* reviewer remarked that "When the last pieces of this cleverly contrived jigsaw are slipped neatly into their places, a most satisfactory picture is revealed." He further proclaimed that "Coburn's economy of style ensures that every word contributes to the storyline."

Web Weaver finds the four friends involved in a mystery surrounding an antique Victorian camera, which Hicyilmaz described as having "a life of its own." She reported that this plot device "forces" the protagonists "to consider the question of whether 'seeing is believing,'" and further commented that "Coburn understands that most paradoxical of childhood yearnings: the dream of a safe adventure." Coburn continued the "Borderlands" series with *Dark Water,* which takes the time-traveling characters on a historic sailing trip. Alice's father, a geo-scientist, decides to take his daughter and her three friends along with him on a survey of a region known as the Devil's Hole, a sort of Bermuda triangle of the British Isles. The captain they hire to sail them into the region is reluctant to do so, having lost a grandfather to this treacherous bit of sea. When they finally enter the region, their navigation equipment fails and they are suddenly swept onto a collision course with an oncoming green blob on the radar screen. A reviewer for the *Sunday Times Book Shop* lauded this effort as "a suspenseful and elegant combination of the scientific and the spooky," while Griselda Greaves, writing in *School Librarian* praised Coburn's "clearly defined" characters, as well as the "honestly written" style of the novel which could draw young readers away from more commercial supernatural fiction such as the "Goosebumps" books and instead allow them to appreciate "better written and more scientifically challenging examples of the genre."

Biographical and Critical Sources

PERIODICALS

Books for Keeps, March, 1995, Val Bierman, review of *The Domino Effect,* p. 16.

Junior Bookshelf, August, 1991, review of *The Granite Beast,* 171; February, 1993, review of *Welcome to the Real World,* p. 28; February, 1995, review of *The Domino Effect,* p. 48, 49; December, 1996, review of *Worm Songs,* p. 264.

School Librarian, August, 1991, Graham Case, review of *The Granite Beast,* p. 113; February, 1993, Maggie Bignell, review of *Welcome to the Real World,* p. 29; May, 1995, Linda Saunders, review of *The Domino Effect,* p. 76; autumn, 1998, Griselda Greaves, review of *Dark Water,* p. 135.

Sunday Times Book Shop, June 21, 1998, review of *Dark Water.*

Times Educational Supplement, September 6, 1991, David Self, review of *The Granite Beast,* p. 30; April 4, 1997, Gaye Hicyilmaz, review of *Worm Songs* and *Web Weaver,* section 2, p. 8.*

*   *   *

COIT, Margaret Louise 1919-2003

OBITUARY NOTICE—See index for *SATA* sketch: Born May 30, 1919, in Norwich, CT; died March 15, 2003, in Amesbury, MA. Educator and author. Coit is best remembered as the Pulitzer-prize winning author of a biography on John C. Calhoun. She was a graduate of the University of North Carolina, where she received her A.B. in 1941, and after completing her education she worked as a correspondent for the *Lawrence Daily Eagle* in Massachusetts until 1955. She joined the faculty at Fairleigh Dickinson University in 1956, becoming a full professor of history in 1971, and retiring in 1984. Although she was born in Connecticut, Coit was raised in North Carolina and became interested in Calhoun, a hero to many Southerners, while growing up there. She made the former U.S. secretary of state and vice president, who is sometimes remembered for his defense of slavery, the subject of her first book, *John C. Calhoun: American Portrait* (1950), which was hailed for revealing the complex, real man behind the image of a cold and forbidding politician. She continued to write biographies, including *Mr. Baruch* (1957), about the financier Bernard Baruch, and *Andrew Jackson* (1965), a biography for younger readers. Her authoritative biography on Calhoun gave her the opportunity to edit a later biography, *Calhoun: Great Lives Observed* (1970).

OBITUARIES AND OTHER SOURCES:

BOOKS

American Women Writers, second edition, St. James (Detroit, MI), 2000.
Brennan, Elizabeth A., and Elizabeth C. Clarage, *Who's Who of Pulitzer Prize Winners,* Oryx (Phoenix, AZ), 1999.

PERIODICALS

Boston Globe, March 19, 2003, p. D12.
Los Angeles Times, March 22, 2003, p. B19.
Washington Post, March 23, 2003, p. C10.

*   *   *

COLLEDGE, Anne 1939-

Personal

Born May 24, 1939, in Ruabon, Denbighshire, Wales; daughter of Frederick (a railway carriage and wagon examiner) and Margaret (a nanny; maiden name, Griffiths) Davies; divorced; children: Helen Margaret, Jennifer Anne. *Education:* Homerton College, teaching certificate, 1958; Royal School for the Deaf, teacher for the deaf certificate, 1959; Sunderland University, B.A. (psychology and English; with honors), 1985. *Politics:* Labour. *Religion:* Church of England.

Addresses

Home—26 Sunningdale Dr., Washington, Tyne and Wear NE37 2LL, England. *E-mail*—Anne.Colledge@ btinternet.com.

Career

Teacher of the deaf at various locations in the United Kingdom, 1959-99; writer, 1999—.

Member

British Association for Teachers of the Deaf.

Writings

Northern Lights, Pipers' Ash (Chippenham, England), 1999.

Contributor of short stories and articles to British periodicals, including *Guardian.*

Work in Progress

Secret Places, a children's novel about "a deaf girl who goes back in history to find answers to her problems, including her mother's illness;" research on the history of the area surrounding Hadrian's Wall, for use in a novel.

Sidelights

Anne Colledge told *SATA:* "I have always needed to write from childhood. In my work as a teacher of deaf children, I found people knew little about deafness. I hope to help this situation with my books.

"I like David Almond's books for children and Terry Deary's. It is important to persevere when writing as the competition is severe."

Biographical and Critical Sources

ONLINE

Anne Colledge Web Site, http://www.annecol.co.uk/ (June 18, 2003).

*   *   *

CONDON, Bill 1949-

Personal

Born April 21, 1949, in Sydney, Australia; married Dianne Bates (a writer). *Hobbies and other interests:* Scrabble, tennis, films, playing with his dog.

Bill Condon

Addresses

Home—20 Kulgoa Rd., Woonona, New South Wales, Australia. *E-mail*—billcondon@bigpond.com.

Career

Children's book author, poet, and playwright. Formerly worked as a journalist, truck driver, greyhound trainer, punter, and factory worker.

Awards, Honors

Children's Book of the Year honour book for older readers, Children's Book Council of Australia, 2001, for *Dogs;* Kids Own Australian Literature Award (KOALA) for Younger Readers, 2001, for *Miss Wolf and the Porkers.*

Writings

FICTION

(With wife, Dianne Bates) *The Slacky Flat Gang,* Brooks Waterloo (South Melbourne, Australia), 1988.

That Smell Is My Brother, Pascal Press (Glebe, Australia), 1990.

What a Stinker! (stories), illustrated by Stephen Francis, Heinemann Australia (Sydney, Australia), 1992.

Auntie Spells Trouble, illustrated by Rex W. Turnbull, Angus & Robertson (Pymble, Australia), 1992.

The Jolly Green Monster, illustrated by Stephen Axelsen, Heinemann Australia (Sydney, Australia), 1992.

Hooked on Bananas, illustrated by Simon Bosch, Angus & Robertson (Pymble, Australia), 1995.

(With Dianne Bates) *The Case of the Kidnapped Brat,* Mammoth (Dingley, Australia), 1995.

The Princess and the Martians, illustrated by Mervyn Pywell, Heinemann Australia (Port Melbourne, Australia), 1996.

(With Dianne Bates) *Bushranger Bob and the Nude Olympics* ("Bushrangers" series), Hodder Headline (Rydalmere, Australia), 1999.

(With Dianne Bates) *No Nickers and the Christmas Day Hold-Up* ("Bushrangers" series), Hodder Headline (Rydalmere, Australia), 1999.

(With Dianne Bates) *Ned the Nong and the Kelly Kids* ("Bushrangers" series), Hodder Headline (Rydalmere, Australia), 1999.

Top That! ("Spin Out" series), Longman (South Melbourne, Australia), 1999.

Poor Jason! ("Spin Out" series), Longman (South Melbourne, Australia), 1999.

Master of Disaster ("Trend" series), Longman (South Melbourne, Australia), 1999.

Bonkers Conquers ("Trend" series), Longman (South Melbourne, Australia), 1999.

Frizz, illustrated by Coral Tulloch, Longman (South Melbourne, Australia), 1999.

Miss Wolf and the Porkers ("Aussie Bites" series), illustrated by Caroline Magerl, Penguin Books Australia (Victoria, Australia), 2001.

FOR YOUNG CHILDREN

Alike and Different, Rigby (Port Melbourne, Australia), 1995.

You Know Who, Rigby (Port Melbourne, Australia), 1996.

It Could Be Worse, illustrated by Mark Sofilas, Rigby (Port Melbourne, Australia), 1996, Rigby (Crystal Lake, IL), 1998.

We're Okay, Rigby (Port Melbourne, Australia), 1996.

Can I Do That?, Rigby (Port Melbourne, Australia), 1996.

Can Topsy Talk?, Rigby (Port Melbourne, Australia), 1996.

I Wonder What That Means, Rigby (Port Melbourne, Australia), 1996.

Depending on Each Other, Rigby (Port Melbourne, Australia), 1996.

Airport Adventure, Rigby (Port Melbourne, Australia), 1997.

Max and Mintie, illustrated by Edward Crosby, Rigby (Port Melbourne, Australia), 1997, Rigby (Crystal Lake, IL), 1998.

The Wacky Machines, Rigby (Port Melbourne, Australia), 1997, Rigby (Crystal Lake, IL), 1998.

Our Canteen, Rigby (Port Melbourne, Australia), 1997, Rigby (Crystal Lake, IL), 1998.

"CREEPERS" SERIES

(With Robert Hood) *Loco-Zombies,* illustrated by Hood, Hodder Headline (Rydalmere, Australia), 1996.

(With Robert Hood) *Slime Zone,* illustrated by Hood, Hodder Headline (Rydalmere, Australia), 1996.

(With Robert Hood) *Freak Out!,* illustrated by Hood, Hodder Headline (Rydalmere, Australia), 1996.

(With Robert Hood) *Bone Screamers,* illustrated by Hood, Hodder Headline (Rydalmere, Australia), 1996.

(With Robert Hood) *Ghoul Man,* illustrated by Hood, Hodder Headline (Rydalmere, Australia), 1996.

(With Robert Hood) *Rat Heads,* illustrated by Hood, Hodder Headline (Rydalmere, Australia), 1997.

(With Robert Hood) *Feeding Frenzy,* illustrated by Hood, Hodder Headline (Rydalmere, Australia), 1997.

(With Robert Hood) *Brain Sucker,* illustrated by Hood, Hodder Headline (Rydalmere, Australia), 1997.

(With Robert Hood) *Humungoid,* illustrated by Hood, Hodder Headline (Rydalmere, Australia), 1997.

"SUPA DOOPERS" SERIES

Holly and Mac, illustrated by Gus Gordon, Longman (South Melbourne, Australia), 1997, Sundance (Littleton, MA), 1999.

Snow Bright and the Seven Sumos, illustrated by Ian Forss, Longman (South Melbourne, Australia), 1997, Sundance (Littleton, MA), 1999.

Snow Bright and the Tooth Magician, illustrated by Ian Forss, Longman (South Melbourne, Australia), 1998, Sundance (Littleton, MA), 1999.

A Waste of Space, illustrated by Coral Tulloch, Longman (South Melbourne, Australia), 1998, Sundance (Littleton, MA), 1999.

King Arthur and the Square Table, illustrated by Ian Forss, Longman (South Melbourne, Australia), 1999.

"TWISTED TALES" SERIES

Chunderella, illustrated by Terry Denton, Hodder Headline (Rydalmere, Australia), 1998.

Bumplestiltskin, illustrated by Terry Denton, Hodder Headline (Rydalmere, Australia), 1998.

Pop-Eyed Piper, illustrated by Terry Denton, Hodder Headline (Rydalmere, Australia), 1998.

Jack and the Magic Baked Beans, illustrated by Terry Denton, Hodder Headline (Rydalmere, Australia), 1998.

OTHER

(With Dianne Bates) *Madcap Café and Other Humorous Plays,* Brooks Waterloo (South Melbourne, Australia), 1986.

(With Dianne Bates) *Operation Lily-Liver: A Shadow Play,* illustrated by Geoff Hook, Macmillan (South Melbourne, Australia), 1987.

Wonkyzap and the Timetwister (play), Macmillan (Sydney, Australia), 1987.

Starring Samuel Snodgrass: A Collection of Plays, illustrated by Randy Glusac, Nelson (Melbourne, Australia), 1988.

Jerry the Jerk (poetry), Pascal Press (Glebe, Australia), 1990.

(With Dianne Bates) *Stagestruck: A Collection of Plays,* illustrated by Kathryn Pentecost, Harcourt Brace Jovanvich (Sydney, Australia), 1992.

A wrenching story of two boys at odds with their fiercely competitive fathers, Condon's **Dogs** *describes the potentially destructive forces behind the sport of dog racing.*

Don't Throw Rocks at Chicken Pox (poetry), Angus & Robertson (Pymble, Australia), 1992.

A Feast of Funny Plays, Reed Library (Port Melbourne, Australia), 1993.

Plays to Entertain, Heinemann Australia (Port Melbourne, Australia), 1994.

Villains (nonfiction), Cardigan Street (Carlton, Victoria, Australia), 1996.

Heroes (nonfiction), Reed Library (Port Melbourne, Australia), 1996.

Far Out and Funny Plays, two volumes, Longman (Melbourne, Australia), 1997.

Those Who Dared (nonfiction), Heinemann Australia (Port Melbourne, Victoria, Australia), 1998.

Billy Drake's Cake (reader), Macmillan (South Yarra, Australia), 2000, illustrated by Philip Webb, Wright Group (Bothell, WA), 2000.

Dogs (young-adult novel), Hodder Headline (Sydney, Australia), 2000.

Work in Progress

More books for children; a young-adult novel.

Sidelights

Prolific Australian children's author Bill Condon has written more than seventy children's books since beginning his writing career in the early 1980s. "Nearly all of my work is humorous," Condon told *SATA*, "though in 2000, I wrote a serious young-adult novel titled *Dogs*, which is about teenage boys and their fathers, all set in the world of greyhound racing." A book about overcoming intergenerational differences, *Dogs* was named a Children's Book Council of Australia honour book for older readers in 2001.

Born in Sydney, Australia, in 1949, Condon was not the most enthusiastic student; as was noted on a biographical essay posted on his Web site, he "left school at the first chance he got" and worked in a succession of jobs that included training greyhounds for the racetrack, doing yard work, working in a milk factory, and driving a truck. He stumbled into a temporary job as a journalist with a small-town weekly newspaper that lasted ten years, then branched into his successful career as a children's book author. Writing is, for Condon, "the only vocation he [ever] felt an affinity for."

Most of Condon's books are designed to capture the interest of reluctant elementary school-aged readers, and his many fans can attest to his success. In addition, Condon's 2001 book *Miss Wolf and the Porkers* received a coveted Kids Own Australian Literature Award (KOALA). A *Magpies* contributor was quick to point out that *Miss Wolf and the Porkers* "certainly puts a different spin" on the familiar story about the three little pigs. In Condon's humorous version of the story, the wolf is an elementary school librarian who has three young and rambunctious pigs forced upon her in the form of not-so-willing library assistants. The three piglets decide that the library is much too dull a place, and their efforts to liven things up prompt Miss Wolf to regress to her wolfish roots and plan a lunch menu that includes a few pork tenderloins. Fortunately for the piggies, school principal Mr. Kidney intervenes just in time to save the hairs on all three piggy chinny-chin-chins.

Other books by Condon include a number of installments in the "Creepers" series—which includes titles such as *Slime Zone, Ghoul Man,* and *Brain Sucker*—that provide school-aged readers a dollop of spine-tingling horror. The "Creepers" series was a collaboration between Condon and illustrator and friend Robert Hood; the two passed chapters back and forth via fax during the writing process. Toddlers also become an enthusiastic audience for a selection of books by Condon featuring simple texts designed for the very young. Particularly attractive to reluctant readers, the author's "Twisted Tales" series features titles based loosely on traditional fairy tales, but any moralizing in the original is replaced by a healthy dose of gross-out fun. *Chunderella,* for example, finds a hefty princess with a healthy appetite attracted to an equally rotund Prince Percival, and readers witness a match made in the kitchen as the portly pair fall in love over plates of Brussels sprouts doused with chocolate sauce. *Jack and the Magic Baked Beans* similarly sets the time-honored "Jack and the Beanstalk" on its edge as Condon adds a bald emu and a giant with a sore backside to the story's cast of characters.

Supplementing his collection of fiction for children, Condon has also authored several plays designed for young audiences, as well as volumes of children's poetry. A full-time writer, he lives with his wife near the city of Sydney, New South Wales, on the Australian coast.

Biographical and Critical Sources

PERIODICALS

Magpies, July, 2001, review of *Miss Wolf and the Porkers,* p. 20.

ONLINE

Bill Condon Home Page, http://www.users.bigpond.com/ billcondon/bill.html (April 5, 2003).

D

DASH, Joan 1925-

Personal

Born July 18, 1925, in New York, NY; daughter of Samuel (a lawyer) and Louise (a lawyer; maiden name, Sachs) Zeiger; married J. Gregory Dash (a physicist), June 23, 1945; children: Michael, Elizabeth, Anthony. *Education:* Barnard College, B.A., 1946. *Politics:* "Progressive." *Religion:* Jewish.

Addresses

Home—3900 Second Ave. NE, Seattle, WA 98105. *Agent*—Raines & Raines, 103 Kenyon Rd., Medusa, NY 12120.

Career

Writer.

Awards, Honors

Boston Globe/Horn Book Award for Nonfiction, and Sibert Honor Book, American Library Association, both 2001, both for *The Longitude Prize.*

Joan Dash

Writings

A Life of One's Own: Three Gifted Women and the Men They Married (for adults), Harper & Row (New York, NY), 1973, reprinted, Paragon House (New York, NY), 1988.

Summoned to Jerusalem: The Life of Henrietta Szold, Harper & Row (New York, NY), 1979.

The Triumph of Discovery: Women Scientists Who Won the Nobel Prize, Julian Messner (Englewood Cliffs, NJ), 1991.

We Shall Not Be Moved: The Women's Factory Strike of 1909, Scholastic (New York, NY), 1996.

The Longitude Prize, illustrated by Dusan Petricic, Farrar, Straus and Giroux (New York, NY), 2000.

The World at Her Fingertips: The Story of Helen Keller, Scholastic (New York, NY), 2001.

Sidelights

Joan Dash is a prizewinning author of biographies for young adults. Her early works, including *A Life of One's Own: Three Gifted Women and the Men They Married,* *Summoned to Jerusalem: The Life of Henrietta Szold,* and *The Triumph of Discovery: Women Scientists Who Won the Nobel Prize,* participate in the growing movement to bring to light the achievements of notable women in history. In *The Triumph of Discovery,* for example, Dash puts the spotlight on four women who have won the Nobel Prize since 1960; at the time of the book's creation, only ten Nobels had ever been awarded to women, including two to Marie Curie. Dash was praised for clearly elucidating the nature of these scientists' contributions, as well as placing their personal and professional life experiences in the context of their times. Perhaps most importantly, "the author communicates the excitement and satisfaction of a life in science," remarked Zena Sutherland in *Bulletin of the Center for Children's Books.*

Another group of unsung heroines is at the center of Dash's *We Shall Not Be Moved: The Women's Factory Strike of 1909.* Here, the author provides an affecting account of conditions for workers in New York City's garment district, many of whom were predominantly Jewish women who had recently immigrated to the United States. In gathering to protest their working and living conditions, the women confronted bigotry as well as stereotypes about the nature of women and of the working classes. Dash also portrays the society women who marched with and funded the strike, which was the first ever by women workers. "This is strong feminist history," praised Hazel Rochman in *Booklist,* who complained only about the lack of attribution of facts and quotes to the sources listed in the bibliography.

Returning to the world of science biography for *The Longitude Prize,* Dash offers a "rousing history" of the invention of a device used to measure longitude at sea, according to Steven Engelfried in *School Library Journal.* The Longitude Prize was offered by the British Parliament in 1714, after the tragic loss of British ships and sailors due to unreliable maps as there was no accurate instrument for measuring longitude at sea. For forty years, British clockmaker John Harrison pursued the prize, succeeding in the end by dint of sheer will and obstinacy as well as expertise, according to Dash's account, and overcoming not only the technical difficulties of creating a timepiece accurate enough to determine longitude, but also the class prejudices of those who offered the prize. "Rich anecdotes pepper her account of the difficult, often irascible Harris, but [Dash] never attempts to invent," remarked Susan P. Bloom in the *Horn Book.*

Other critics similarly noted Dash's straightforward approach to relaying what is certainly known about John Harrison, and carefully delineating what may be surmised from the historical record and what may only be guessed at. This is an issue that Dash addressed in her acceptance speech for the *Boston Globe/Horn Book* Award for Nonfiction, which she won in 2001 for *The Longitude Prize.* After working on the book that would become *The Longitude Prize* for several years, Dash explained, her editor gently pointed out that the spirit of the person at its center, John Harrison, seemed not to have made it into the book. "Maybe we could present a

history of the search for longitude—making no secret of the fact that John Harrison was the lead character—and at the same time bring the reader face-to-face with the problem," Dash recalled thinking. "That is, we don't know much about him, but we can guess here, we can estimate there, we stand on firm ground here, here, and here, and this is why the ground is firm. In other words, discussing how we know the things we know—the artifacts we call history." Indeed, this aspect of the biography is one often noted by reviewers as a positive contribution to the book's accomplishment. "The piecing together of data by historians becomes a fascinating element of the book," remarked Engelfried. For others, Dash's greatest accomplishment in this biography is her ability to infuse the biography of a scientist and his three-hundred-year-old invention with energy and excitement. "Fans of science, history and invention and anyone who roots for the underdog will enjoy this prize of a story," concluded a contributor to *Publishers Weekly.*

Dash is also the author of *The World at Her Fingertips: The Story of Helen Keller,* a biography noted for taking young readers beyond the story of Keller's famous first encounter with language at the water pump. Here, Dash focuses on the life of the courageous woman whose fierce pursuit of independence took her to college and a career as a public speaker. Throughout, Dash emphasizes that this quest made Keller peculiarly dependent on those around her, especially her teachers, who taught her to speak by allowing the blind and deaf woman to put her hand in their mouths in order to determine placement and movement of tongue, jaw, and palate. In tribute to these kinds of details, *Booklist* reviewer Carolyn Phelan observed that Dash's account of Keller's life "seems closer to reality than the more idealized stories sometimes offered to children." For *School Library Journal* critic Jennifer Ralston, Dash's reliance on Keller's own autobiographies "brings the subject's vibrant personality, intelligence, and sensitivity to life in a way no narrative alone could." "Overall, readers will come away from this biography realizing how extraordinary Helen Keller was and, just as importantly, how she was a lot like everybody else," concluded a contributor to *Horn Book.*

Dash told *SATA:* "I've come to believe that the writer's job is to tell a story, and that this is true for writers of nonfiction as well as fiction. The difference is that in fiction, the writer has to make up the story she's telling. With nonfiction, the writer must find the story within the material. Is there always story in the material? Of course there is. That's why a newspaperman is told to 'go out there and get the story.' Find the facts, then find the story within them."

Biographical and Critical Sources

PERIODICALS

Booklist, January 1, 1996, Hazel Rochman, review of *We Shall Not Be Moved: The Women's Factory Strike of*

1909, p. 804; January 1, 2001, Gillian Engberg, review of *The Longitude Prize,* p. 930; February 15,
2001, Carolyn Phelan, review of *The World at Her
Fingertips: The Story of Helen Keller,* p. 1129; December 1, 2001, Stephanie Zvirin, review of *The Longitude Prize,* p. 658.

Book Report, January-February, 1992, Eldorado Yoder, review of *The Triumph of Discovery: Women Scientists
Who Won the Nobel Prize,* p. 51; September-October,
1996, Julie Burwinekl, review of *We Shall Not Be
Moved,* p. 53.

Bulletin of the Center for Children's Books, September,
1991, Zena Sutherland, review of *The Triumph of Discovery,* p. 6.

Horn Book, November, 2000, Susan P. Bloom, review of
The Longitude Prize, p. 767; March, 2001, review of
The World at Her Fingertips, p. 227; January-
February, 2002, Joan Dash, transcript of acceptance
speech for the 2001 *Boston Globe/Horn Book* Award
for nonfiction, p. 35.

Kirkus Reviews, January 1, 1991, review of *The Triumph
of Discovery,* p. 44.

New York Times Book Review, August 25, 1996, review of
We Shall Not Be Moved, p. 23.

Publishers Weekly, October 23, 2000, review of *The Longitude Prize,* p. 77.

School Library Journal, February, 1996, Ruth K. Mac-
Donald, review of *We Shall Not Be Moved,* p. 116;
November, 2000, Steven Engelfried, review of *The
Longitude Prize,* p. 168; April, 2001, Jennifer Ralston,
review of *The World at Her Fingertips,* p. 157.

Voice of Youth Advocates, August, 1997, review of *We
Shall Not Be Moved,* p. 163.

* * *

DENSLOW, Sharon Phillips 1947-

Personal

Born August 25, 1947, in Murray, KY; daughter of Joe
Hilton (a printer) and Mary Elizabeth (Riley) Phillips;
married Leroy Allen Denslow (a newspaper editor),
June 13, 1969; children: Erin, Kate. *Education:* Murray
State University, B.S., 1969.

Addresses

Home—130 Villanova Circle, Elyria, OH 44035.
Agent—c/o Author Mail, 7th Fl., Greenwillow Books,
10 East Fifty-third St., New York, NY 10022.

Career

Porter Public Library, Westlake, OH, children's librarian, 1970-88, head of children's service, 1988-2000;
writer.

Awards, Honors

First place Juvenile Merit Award, Friends of American
Writers, 1991, for *Night Owls*; Oppenheim Toy Portfolio Gold Award, 2000, for *Big Wolf and Little Wolf*;

Sharon Phillips Denslow

American Library Association (ALA) notable book citation, 2001, among the best books of the year citations
from Capitol Choices, 2002, New York Public Library,
2002, and Bank Street College, all for *Georgie Lee.*

Writings

Night Owls, illustrated by Jill Kastner, Bradbury Press
(New York, NY), 1990.
At Taylor's Place, illustrated by Nancy Carpenter, Brad-
bury Press (New York, NY), 1990.
Riding with Aunt Lucy, illustrated by Nancy Carpenter,
Bradbury Press (New York, NY), 1991.
Hazel's Circle, illustrated by Sharon McGinley-Nally,
Bradbury Press (New York, NY), 1992.
Bus Riders, illustrated by Nancy Carpenter, Four Winds
Press (New York, NY), 1993.
Radio Boy, illustrated by Alec Gillman, Simon & Schuster
(New York, NY), 1994.
Woollybear Good-Bye, illustrated by Nancy Cote, Four
Winds Press (New York, NY), 1994.
On the Trail with Miss Pace, illustrated by G. Brian Karas,
Simon & Schuster (New York, NY), 1995.
Big Wolf and Little Wolf, illustrated by Cathie Felstead,
Greenwillow (New York, NY), 2000.
Georgie Lee, illustrated by Lynne Rae Perkins, Greenwil-
low (New York, NY), 2002.
All Their Names Were Courage, Greenwillow (New York,
NY), 2003.

Contributor to *Country Living.*

Work in Progress

In the Snow, with illustrations by Nancy Tafuri, and
Seven Nights a Week, a collection of lullabies and
rhymes, both for Greenwillow.

Sidelights

Sharon Phillips Denslow is the author of a number of picture-book texts that have been praised for their gentle texts and positive portrayals of families. In titles such as *At Taylor's Place, Riding with Aunt Lucy,* and *Georgie Lee,* Denslow portrays affectionate, supportive relationships between grandparents and other elderly individuals whose lives touch those of young people in some special way. In each of these books, note critics, Denslow illustrates with words that such love and support flow both ways, from old to young and vice versa.

Denslow was born in Murray, Kentucky, grew up in a small town, and spent much time on her grandparents' farms. "Everyone in the family was a wonderful storyteller," she once recalled, "and in small towns everything has its own story." During high school, she discovered a talent for writing, going on to major in English and journalism in college. After graduation, Denslow married, moved with her husband to Ohio, and found a job as a children's librarian. "I read children's books by day and wrote stories at night," she once recalled of her first attempts at being a published writer. "Once I got so discouraged, I burned up hundreds of my stories and poems. But I went back to writing. . . . Finally, at age thirty-eight, I decided it was now or never and began writing seriously."

Two years later, in 1988, Denslow had her book *Night Owls* accepted for publication. The story of an elderly woman and her nephew and their enjoyment of staying up late, *Night Owls* "is about everyone who has ever been reluctant to go inside and miss the magic of the night," its author once explained. "No matter how many books I write, *Night Owls* will always be my favorite." According to a *Horn Book* critic, Denslow's text is "brief, low-key, and conversational in tone," while *School Library Journal* contributor Kathy Piehl wrote that *Night Owls* celebrates life and "rejoices in night's beauty."

Denslow has gone on to see several more picture books published, their illustrations completed by a variety of talented artists. 1990's *At Taylor's Place* finds a craftsman willing to share his knowledge with an eager young apprentice in "a warm, gentle story of affection across the generations," according to *School Library Journal* contributor Joan McGrath. In a review for *Booklist,* Deborah Abbott had special praise for the everyday farm activities portrayed, as well as Denslow's depiction of a close-knit intergenerational relationship in this "quiet story." Also focusing on farm life, *Georgie Lee* features Grandmother and nine-year-old grandson J. D. working, playing, and exploring the family farm, with many of their activities prompted by the antics of the mischievous family cow. Denslow once wrote that the setting for *Georgie Lee* is based on her own grandmother's farm. According to a *Kirkus Reviews* critic, "country and city kids alike" will enjoy the pair's adventures—which involve sudden summer storms, a haunted house, and encounters with critters ranging from goats to catfish—in a book the critic dubbed a "deceptively simple first chapter book." Noting that the story "unfolds smoothly," *Booklist* contributor Denise Wilms added that *Georgie Lee* contains a "gentle humor [that] will go over well with younger children." Christine Alfano of *Riverbank Review* praised, "*Georgie Lee* offers a magic combination of simplicity, substantial characters, and humor. . . . Denslow understands that sometimes it's not so much what's at the center of our lives, but what pokes in from the sidelights, that truly and most beautifully shapes our days."

Riding with Aunt Lucy focuses on an elderly woman who only recently earned her first driver's license so she can go on trips with her great-nephew Leonard. The book is particularly special to its author. As Denslow once explained, *Riding with Aunt Lucy* is "dedicated to my grandmothers who never learned to drive and who always had to wait for someone to take them wherever they needed to go. I wish they could have enjoyed the fun of the road like Lucy." In another story about traveling, *Bus Riders* depicts the friendship that develops between an elderly school bus driver and two elementary school-aged children on his route, a friendship that the children become aware of when the driver must leave work for several weeks to have minor surgery. Praise for *Bus Riders* came from *Horn Book* contributor Margaret A. Bush, who enjoyed Denslow's story that "celebrates the special community that develops among regular riders," while a *Kirkus Reviews* contributor commended the humorous text and the "ebullient, witty art" contributed by illustrator Nancy Carpenter.

Denslow's continuing focus on the elderly comes from her own childhood. She once explained: "My grandparents were very important to me when I was growing up. . . . Perhaps I hope my books will be a way for kids everywhere to feel the closeness I had. I believe that every child needs someone who thinks they're wonderful just the way they are, and I think children need to feel they have something important to do. In my stories, I try to capture small flashes of friendship children will enjoy and remember. I hope to capture something so truly that the story comes to life."

Denslow shared her advice on why reading is important with *SATA*: "You have to read before you can do almost everything else in life. Math, computers, writing, composing, athletics, making up secret codes, deciphering treasure maps, filling out the forms for your dog's license, and learning about things so you can make up your own mind about them for starters. That's just knowing how to read. Real reading (reading more than you're absolutely required to) gives you something extra—the chance to be some other place, some other time, with people who don't live next door—the chance to share in the wonderful stories (real and imagined) everywhere around you—the chance to learn and know and appreciate what you didn't know before."

Biographical and Critical Sources

PERIODICALS

Booklist, October 1, 1990, Deborah Abbott, review of *At Taylor's Place,* p. 338; October 1, 1991, Hazel Rochman, review of *Riding with Aunt Lucy,* p. 336; May 1, 1992, Kay Weisman, review of *Hazel's Circle,* p. 1606; March 15, 1993, Sheilamae O'Hara, review of *Bus Riders,* p. 1358; June 1, 1995, Kay Weisman, review of *On the Trail with Miss Pace,* p. 1784; October 1, 1995, Lauren Peterson, review of *Radio Boy,* p. 325; May 1, 2000, Carolyn Phelan, review of *Big Wolf and Little Wolf,* p. 1676; July, 2002, Denise Wilms, review of *Georgie Lee,* p. 1856.
Five Owls, May, 1993, Kathie Krieger Cerra, review of *Bus Riders,* pp. 112-113.
Horn Book, May, 1990, review of *Night Owls,* pp. 321-322; November, 1990, Ann A. Flowers, review of *At Taylor's Place,* p. 725; May, 1993, Margaret A. Bush, review of *Bus Riders,* p. 315; July-August, 2002, Joanna Rudge Long, review of *Georgie Lee,* p. 458.
Kirkus Reviews, March 1, 1993, review of *Bus Riders,* p. 298; May 1, 1995, review of *On the Trail with Miss Pace,* p. 632; April 15, 2002, review of *Georgie Lee,* p. 566.
Publishers Weekly, February 9, 1990, review of *Night Owls,* p. 59; May 22, 1995, review of *On the Trail with Miss Pace,* p. 59; May 15, 2000, review of *Big Wolf and Little Wolf,* p. 116.
Riverbank Review, fall, 2002, Christine Alfano, review of *Georgie Lee.*
School Library Journal, March, 1990, Kathy Piehl, review of *Night Owls,* pp. 189-190; November, 1990, Joan McGrath, review of *At Taylor's Place,* p. 91; November, 1991, Christine A. Moesch, review of *Riding with Aunt Lucy,* pp. 92, 94; July, 1993, Lisa Dennis, review of *Bus Riders,* p. 59; December, 1994, Ruth Semrau, review of *Woollybear Good-Bye,* p. 73; June, 1995, Ruth Semrau, review of *On the Trail with Miss Pace,* p. 80; September, 1995, Louise L. Sherman, review of *Radio Boy,* p. 168; May, 2000, Laura Santoro, review of *Big Wolf and Little Wolf,* p. 140; May, 2002, Terrie Dorio, review of *Georgie Lee,* p. 111.

ONLINE

Westlake Porter Public Library, http://www.westlakelibrary.org (May 28, 2003), "Youth Services Coordinator Sharon Denslow to Retire."

* * *

DODD, Marty 1921-

Personal

Born July 30, 1921, in Todmorden Station, South Australia, Australia; son of Tjundaga "Tommy" (a stockman, road maker, and surveyor) and Rosie (a homemaker) Dodd; married Rita Lang; children:

Marty Dodd

Johnny, Glenys, Kevin, Rosemarie, Raelene, Robert, Christopher. *Ethnicity:* "Aboriginal Australian (language group Antikirinya)." *Religion:* Christian. *Hobbies and other interests:* "Family interests—many grandchildren, great-grandchildren, occasional opal noodling with family."

Addresses

Home—c/o P.O. Box 347, Umoona Community, Coober Pedy, South Australia 5723, Australia. *Agent*—Michele Madigan, 11 Burdekin Ave., Murray Bridge, South Australia 5723, Australia.

Career

Worked as a stockman, horse breaker, and race horse trainer in the outback of South Australia, c. 1935-75. Worked as an opal gouger and opal checker concurrently with primary career, from the 1940s to the mid 1970s, then full time, 1975-c.1999; worked on Aboriginal cultural sites during the 1980s and 1990s. Chairperson, Umoona Aged Care, Inc., 1999-2000.

Member

Antikirinya, Inc., Kokatha Mula, Inc.

Writings

They Liked Me, the Horses, Straightaway, Ginninderra Press (Charnwood, Australian Capital Territory, Australia), 2000.

Adaptations

They Liked Me, the Horses, Straightaway is being adapted for audiotape by the Queensland Narrating Service, to be broadcast on National Indigenous Radio Service by the Central Australian Aboriginal Media Service (Alice Springs, Northern Territory, Australia).

Sidelights

Marty Dodd told *SATA:* "In my mind, I'm just an ordinary stockman, but people said it would be good to hear how I was a racehorse trainer in the days when Anangu—Aboriginal people—weren't even allowed to go in the races themselves. So that's how I came to make my book. I could do what they could—train the horses to win. Not many people can win the Kingoonya and Oodnadatta Cups by getting the horses there walking two hundred miles each way—like I did.

"The horses used to like me. Horses respond to kindness. My boss found out my horses weren't restless. They wouldn't run away from me. Mine were calm. That's just my way. So he got me to break in all the horses. It turned out all right for me and for all the horses as well.

"In the fields, looking for opal, I enjoyed that too. Yes, I had many years with the opal—digging it out, checking behind the bulldozers, noodling on the dumps. But what I really am is a stockman. When you've lived among animals—you know them.

"As to my early life, I was only four or five, only young, when they broke up our family—even though the family wants you. We never went back to our own mothers and fathers. No, they just took us. The father wanted us, but they sent us to [the Colebrook] Home.

"Then I had my own family, and later on my wife left me. Left me with all the kids. Seven kids! I had fifteen years of growing them up in between going for opal. Some of the time living on Umoona, on the reserve, living in a little humpy. Some of the time living up on the hill, in the bushes, camping with the kids. We didn't have a house.

"I just had to be there all those years. The kids are part of you. I was mother and father. I grew up those kids from when she left. In my mind, everyone is free in the world. They can do what they want to do. That's why I never worried about nothing much. I just take it in my stride. This is the way things are."

Biographical and Critical Sources

PERIODICALS

Magpies, March, 2001, Alison Gregg, "Being There: Stories to Bring History to Life for Young Readers," p. 42.

F-G

FISSCHER, Catharina G. M. 1958-
(Tiny Fisscher)

Personal

Born June 11, 1958, in Castricum, The Netherlands; daughter of Harry Fisscher (a teacher) and Truus Buurman (a homemaker); married Alex Mous (an actor), March 21, 1985; children: Dorith. *Education:* Pedagogische Academie, 1976, received primary school teaching degree; STIVAS A & B, 1981, certificate for beauty and skin-care specialist; attended International School for Aromatherapy, 1993.

Addresses

Office—c/o Kane/Miller Book Publishers, P.O. Box 8518, La Jolla, CA 92038-8515.

Career

Writer and primary school teacher. Has worked as a tour leader, hostess, secretary, teacher in a beauty school, and as an aerobics and Pilates instructor; former owner of skin care and aromatherapy shop.

Writings

Kristalkinderen (novel; title means "Crystal Children"), illustrated by Wilbert van der Steen, Akasha (Eeserveen, The Netherlands), 2002.

AS TINY FISSCHER

En dan was ik de prinses, illustrated by Barbara de Wolf, Van Goor (Amsterdam, The Netherlands), 1999, translation published as *The Four Princesses,* Kane/Miller (La Jolla, CA), 2001.

Floep! (picture book), illustrated by Wilbert van der Steen, Van Goor (Amsterdam, The Netherlands), 2000.

Catharina G. M. Fisscher

En dan was ik de ridder (picture book; title means "If I Were a Knight"), illustrated by Wilbert van der Steen, Van Goor (Amsterdam, The Netherlands), 2002.

Loek, de blindengeleidehond (novel; title means "Luke, the Guide Dog"), illustrated by Wilbert van der Steen, Van Goor (Amsterdam, The Netherlands), 2002.

Sidelights

Catharina G. M. Fisscher, who writes under the pseudonym Tiny Fisscher, told *SATA:* "From early childhood on, I wanted to be a writer. It took a long time before I actually started writing.

"First I studied to be a teacher, but at that time I was still very young and I didn't want to work with children yet. I did my education to become a beautician and in the years after attended numerous courses and training in aromatherapy, massage, alternative medicine, etc. Also, I had several jobs in between all of this. I worked in Switzerland and Corsica as a salesperson and a hostess, and toured across Europe as a tour leader.

"After all that, I ended up in a school, teaching girls to be beauticians. I got married, had a child (now seventeen), and started my own practice. At that time, I started to write poems and short stories for children. It took a couple of years before I sent them to publishers. In 1997, [an editor] from Van Goor saw my talent and asked me to write the princess book. That's how everything began.

"Four years ago, I sold my practice and had to stop [teaching] at school because of burnout. Two years ago, I started a new career as an aerobics and Pilates teacher, and this year I finally [began] my profession as a teacher in primary school.

"I probably could not write without having these other professions. In order to write, I have to meet people, both adults and children, and hear their stories. Inspiration for my stories/books always comes unexpectedly, while walking my dog, or during the night, waking up suddenly with an idea. Sometimes I don't write for months, other times I am sitting behind my computer every free moment I've got (at those times it would be great not having these extra jobs). I hope to be able to write books for the rest of my life and that people all over the world will enjoy them!"

Biographical and Critical Sources

PERIODICALS

Publishers Weekly, January 14, 2002, "Princess Power," p. 62.

*   *   *

FISSCHER, Tiny
See FISSCHER, Catharina G. M.

FURLONG, Monica (Mavis) 1930-2003

OBITUARY NOTICE—See index for *SATA* sketch: Born January 17, 1930, in Harrow (some sources cite Kenton), Middlesex, England; died of cancer, January 14, 2003, in Umberleigh, Devon (some sources cite in London), England. Novelist, journalist, and author. Furlong was a leading advocate for the ordination of women as priests of the Church of England. A journalist by profession, most notably for the *Daily Mail* in the 1960s, she used the written word to communicate her spirituality, feminism, and deep commitment to the church. She was also an activist. In the early 1980s, Furlong presented a one-day Festival of Women. In 1982 she was appointed moderator of the Movement for the Ordination of Women. A few years later she helped to establish the Saint Hilda's Community, a weekly religious gathering led by ordained female clergy from the United States. In 1992 the General Synod of the Church of England finally extended the right of ordination to women, but Furlong objected to the compromise provisions attached to the decision. She responded with the books *Act of Synod—Act of Folly* and *The Church of England: The State It's In.* Furlong's writings extended beyond journalism and nonfiction on ecumenical matters. She wrote novels for young adults, including *Wise Child* and *A Year and a Day,* mystical fantasies set in Dark-Age England, and fiction and poetry for adults, including the novel *The Cat's Eye.* She was also credited with several biographies, notably of Thomas Merton and Therese of Lisieux, and another titled *Zen Effects: The Life of Alan Watts.*

OBITUARIES AND OTHER SOURCES:

BOOKS

Furlong, Monica, *Bird of Paradise,* Mowbray, 1995.
Furlong, Monica, *Our Childhood's Pattern: Memoirs of Growing Up Christian,* Morehouse, 1995.

PERIODICALS

Independent (London, England), January 18, 2003, obituary by Ruth McCurry, p. 20.
Los Angeles Times, January 30, 2003, p. B13.
Times (London, England), January 16, 2003, p. 36.

*   *   *

GARDNER, Martin 1914-

Personal

Born October 21, 1914, in Tulsa, OK; son of James Henry and Willie (Spiers) Gardner; married Charlotte Creenwald, October 17, 1952; children: James Emmett, Thomas Owen. *Education:* University of Chicago, B.A., 1936. *Hobbies and other interests:* Magic, chess, musical saw.

Martin Gardner

Addresses

Home—3001 Chestnut Rd., Hendersonville, NC 28792.

Career

Journalist and writer. Reporter for *Tulsa Tribune;* public relations staffer for University of Chicago; *Humpty Dumpty's Magazine,* New York, NY, contributing editor, 1952-62; *Scientific American,* New York, NY, writer of mathematical games, 1957-82. *Military service:* U.S. Naval Reserve, 1942-46.

Member

Mathematical Association of America (honorary life member); American Mathematical Society (honorary life member).

Awards, Honors

Professional Achievement Award, University of Chicago, 1971; annual award of the Academy of Magic Arts, California, 1975; honorary doctorate, Bucknell University, 1978; asteroid discovered in 1980 named "Gardner" by the Anderson Mesa Station of Lowell Observatory, 1982; U.S. Steel Foundation Prize for Science Writing, American Institute of Physics, 1983; Steele Prize for Mathematical Writing, American Mathematical Society, 1987; annual David Hilbert International Award (Australia) for mathematics, 1992; honorary doctorate, Furman University, 1993.

Writings

Twelve Tricks with a Borrowed Deck, illustrated by Tarbell, L. L. Ireland (Chicago, IL), 1940.

In the Name of Science, Putnam (New York, NY), 1952, revised edition published as *Fads and Fallacies in the Name of Science,* Dover (Mineola, NY), 1957.

Mathematics, Magic, and Mystery, Dover (Mineola, NY), 1956.

Logic Machines and Diagrams, McGraw (New York, NY), 1958, revised edition published as *Logic Machines, Diagrams, and Boulean Algebra,* Dover (Mineola, NY), 1968, further revised edition, University of Chicago Press (Chicago, IL), 1982.

The Scientific American Book of Mathematical Puzzles and Diversions, Simon & Schuster (New York, NY), 1959, revised edition published as *Hexaflexagons and Other Mathematical Diversions: The First Scientific American Book of Puzzles and Games,* University of Chicago Press (Chicago, IL), 1988.

The Arrow Book of Brain Teasers, Scholastic (Chicago, IL), 1959.

Science Puzzlers, illustrated by Anthony Ravielli, Viking (New York, NY), 1960, published as *Entertaining Science Experiments with Everyday Objects,* Dover (Mineola, NY), 1981.

The Second Scientific American Book of Mathematical Puzzles and Diversions, Simon & Schuster (New York, NY), 1961, revised edition, University of Chicago Press (Chicago, IL), 1987.

Mathematical Puzzles, illustrated by Anthony Ravielli, Crowell (New York, NY), 1961, reprinted as *Entertaining Mathematical Puzzles,* Dover (Mineola, NY), 1986.

Relativity for the Millions, illustrated by Anthony Ravielli, Macmillan (New York, NY), 1962, revised edition published as *The Relativity Explosion,* Random House (Chicago, IL), 1976, published as *Relativitiy Simply Explained,* Dover (Mineola, NY), 1997.

The Ambidextrous Universe, illustrated by John Mackey, Basic Books (New York, NY), 1964, revised edition, New American Library (New York, NY), 1979, further revised edition published as *The New Ambidextrous Universe: Symmetry and Asymmetry from Mirror Reflections to Superstrings,* W. H. Freeman (New York, NY), 1990.

Archimedes, Mathematician and Inventor, illustrated by Leonard E. Fisher, Macmillan (New York, NY), 1965.

New Mathematical Diversions from Scientific American, Simon & Schuster (New York, NY), 1966.

The Numerology of Dr. Matrix, Simon & Schuster (New York, NY), 1967, revised edition published as *The Incredible Dr. Matrix,* Scribner (New York, NY), 1975, further revised edition published as *The Magic Numbers of Dr. Matrix,* Prometheus (Amherst, NY), 1985.

The Unexpected Hanging, and Other Mathematical Diversions, Simon & Schuster (New York, NY), 1969, revised edition, University of Chicago Press (Chicago, IL), 1991.

Perplexing Puzzles and Tantalizing Teasers, illustrated by Laszlo Kubinyi, Simon & Schuster (New York, NY), 1969, reprinted under the same title with the addition of *More Perplexing Puzzles and Tantalizing Teasers,* Dover (New York, NY), 1988.

Never Make Fun of a Turtle, My Son, illustrated by John Alcorn, Simon & Schuster (New York, NY), 1969.

Space Puzzles, illustrated by Ted Schroeder, Simon & Schuster (New York, NY), 1971, reprinted as *Puzzling Questions about the Solar System,* Dover (Mineola, NY), 1997.

The Sixth Book of Mathematical Games from Scientific American, W. H. Freeman (New York, NY), 1971, revised edition published as *The Sixth Book of Mathematical Diversions from Scientific American,* University of Chicago Press (Chicago, IL), 1983.

Codes, Ciphers, and Secret Writing, Simon & Schuster (New York, NY), 1972.

The Flight of Peter Fromm, William Kaufmann (Los Altos, CA), 1973.

The Snark Puzzle Book, illustrated by Henry Holiday and John Tenniel, Simon & Schuster (New York, NY), 1973.

Mathematical Carnival, Knopf (New York, NY), 1975, revised edition, Mathematical Association of America (Washington, DC), 1992.

Mathematical Magic Show, Knopf (New York, NY), 1977, revised edition, Mathematical Association of America (Washington, DC), 1990.

More Perplexing Puzzles and Tantalizing Teasers (also see above), illustrated by Laszlo Kubinyi, Pocket Books (New York, NY), 1977.

The Encyclopedia of Impromptu Magic, Magic, Inc. (Chicago, IL), 1978.

Aha! Insight, W. H. Freeman (New York, NY), 1978.

Mathematical Circus, Knopf (New York, NY), 1979, revised edition, Mathematical Association of America (Washington, DC), 1992.

Science: Good, Bad, and Bogus, Prometheus (Amherst, NY), 1981.

How Not to Test a Psychic: A Study of the Unusual Experiments with Renowned Clairvoyant Pavel Stepanek, Prometheus (Amherst, NY), 1981.

Aha, Gotcha! Paradoxes to Puzzle and Delight, W. H. Freeman (New York, NY), 1982.

Order and Surprise, Prometheus (Amherst, NY), 1983.

Science Fiction Puzzle Tales, Clarkson N. Potter (New York, NY), 1983.

Wheels, Life, and Other Mathematical Amusements, W. H. Freeman (New York, NY), 1983.

The Whys of a Philosophical Scrivener, Morrow (New York, NY), 1983.

Puzzles from Other Worlds, Vintage (New York, NY), 1984.

Knotted Doughnuts and Other Mathematical Entertainments, W. H. Freeman (New York, NY), 1986.

Riddles of the Sphinx and Other Mathematical Puzzle Tales, Mathematical Association of America (Washington, DC), 1987.

The No-Sided Professor and Other Tales of Fantasy, Humor, Mystery, and Philosophy, Prometheus (Amherst, NY), 1987.

The New Age: Notes of a Fringe-Watcher, Prometheus (Amherst, NY), 1988.

Time Travel and Other Mathematical Bewilderments, W. H. Freeman (New York, NY), 1988.

Penrose Tiles to Trapdoor Ciphers: Essays on Recreational Mathematics, W. H. Freeman (New York, NY), 1989, expanded edition published as *Penrose Tiles to Trapdoor Ciphers, . . . and The Return of Dr. Matrix,* Mathematical Association of America (Washington, DC), 1997.

Gardner's Whys and Wherefores, University of Chicago Press (Chicago, IL), 1989.

(With Bart Whaley and Jeff Busby) *The Man Who Was Erdnase,* Jeff Busby Magic (Oakland, CA), 1991.

On the Wild Side: The Big Bang, ESP, the Beast 666, Levitation, Rain Making, Trance-Channeling, Seances and Ghosts, and More, Prometheus (Amherst, NY), 1992.

Fractal Music, Hypercards, and More: Mathematical Recreations from Scientific American, W. H. Freeman (New York, NY), 1992.

The Healing Revelations of Mary Baker Eddy: The Rise and Fall of Christian Science, Prometheus (Amherst, NY), 1993.

Martin Gardner Presents, Richard Kaufman (Silver Spring, MD), 1993.

Classic Brainteasers, Sterling (New York, NY), 1994.

My Best Mathematical and Logic Puzzles, Dover (New York, NY), 1994.

Urantia: The Great Cult Mystery, Prometheus Books (Amherst, NY), 1995.

The Night Is Large: Collected Essays, 1938-1995, St. Martin's Press (New York, NY), 1996.

Weird Water and Fuzzy Logic: More Notes of a Fringe Watcher, Prometheus Books (Amherst, NY), 1996.

The Universe in a Handkerchief: Lewis Carroll's Mathematical Recreations, Games, Puzzles, and Word Plays, Copernicus (New York, NY), 1996.

Science Magic: Martin Gardner's Tricks and Puzzles, illustrated by Tom Jorgenson, Sterling Publishing (New York, NY), 1997.

The Last Recreations: Hydras, Eggs, and Other Mathematical Mystifications, Copernicus (New York, NY), 1997.

Martin Gardner's Table Magic, Dover (Mineola, NY), 1998.

Visitors from Oz: The Wild Adventures of Dorothy, the Scarecrow, and the Tin Woodman (novel), illustrated by Ted Enik, St. Martin's Press (New York, NY), 1998.

Mental Magic: Surefire Tricks to Amaze Your Friends, illustrated by Jeff Sinclair, Sterling (New York, NY), 1999.

Match Magic: More than Seventy Impromptu Tricks with Matches, Piccadilly Books (Colorado Springs, CO), 1999.

Did Adam and Eve Have Navels?: Discourses on Reflexology, Numerology, Urine Therapy & Other Dubious Subjects, W. W. Norton (New York, NY), 2000.

From the Wandering Jew to William F. Buckley, Jr.: On Science, Literature, and Religion, Prometheus Books (Amherst, NY), 2000.

Mathematical Puzzle Tales, Mathematical Association of America (Washington, DC), 2000.

In Gardner's book, influenced by the "Oz" tales of L. Frank Baum, Dorothy, the Tin Woodman, and the Scarecrow are transported to New York City in the 1990s and have wild escapades eluding two murderous mobsters. (From Visitors from Oz, *illustrated by Ted Enik.)*

The Colossal Book of Mathematics: Classic Puzzles, Paradoxes, and Problems, Norton (New York, NY), 2001.

A Gardner's Workout: Training the Mind and the Spirit, A. K. Peters (Natick, MA), 2001.

Mind-Boggling Word Puzzles, illustrated by V. G. Myers, Sterling (New York, NY), 2001.

Are Universes Thicker than Blackberries? Discourses on Gödel, Magic Hexagrams, Little Red Riding Hood, and Other Mathematical and Pseudoscience Topics, W. W. Norton (New York, NY), 2003.

EDITOR

(With Russel B. Nye) *The Wizard of Oz and Who He Was,* Michigan State University Press (East Lansing, MI), 1957.

Great Essays in Science, Pocket Books (New York, NY), 1957, revised edition published as *The Sacred Beetle and Other Great Essays in Science,* Prometheus (Amherst, NY), 1984.

Sam Loyd, *Best Mathematical Puzzles of Sam Loyd,* Dover (Mineola, NY), Volume I, 1957, Volume II, 1960.

Lewis Carroll, *The Annotated Alice: Alice's Adventures in Wonderland and Through the Looking Glass,* Clarkson N. Potter (New York, NY), 1960, reprinted under the same name with the addition of *More Annotated Alice,* W. W. Norton (New York, NY), 2000.

Charles C. Bombaugh, *Oddities and Curiosities of Words and Literature,* Dover (Mineola, NY), 1961.

Lewis Carroll, *The Annotated Snark,* Simon & Schuster (New York, NY), 1962.

Samuel Taylor Coleridge, *The Annotated Ancient Mariner,* Clarkson N. Potter (New York, NY), 1965.

Lewis Carroll, *The Nursery "Alice,"* McGraw (New York, NY), 1966.

Rudolf Carnap, *Philosophical Foundations of Physics,* Basic Books (New York, NY), 1966, revised edition published as *An Introduction to the Philosophy of Science,* 1974.

E. L. Thayer, *The Annotated Casey at the Bat: A Collection of Ballads about the Mighty Casey,* Clarkson N. Potter (New York, NY), 1967.

Henry E. Dudeney, *Five Hundred Thirty-six Puzzles and Curious Problems,* Scribner (New York, NY), 1967.

Boris Kordemski, *Moscow Puzzles,* Scribner (New York, NY), 1971.

Koban Fujimura, *The Tokyo Puzzles,* Scribner (New York, NY), 1978.

Lewis Carroll, *The Wasp in a Wig,* Clarkson N. Potter (New York, NY), 1978.

The Wreck of the Titanic Foretold?, Prometheus (Amherst, NY), 1986.

Gilbert K. Chesterton, *The Annotated Innocence of Father Brown,* Oxford University Press (New York, NY), 1987.

Lewis Carroll, *More Annotated Alice* (also see above), Random House (Chicago, IL), 1990.

Clement Clarke Moore, *The Annotated Night before Christmas,* Summit (New York, NY), 1991.

Best Remembered Poems, Dover (Mineola, NY), 1992.

Famous Poems from Bygone Days, Dover (Mineola, NY), 1995.

H. G. Wells, *"The Country of the Blind" and Other Science-Fiction Stories,* Dover Publications (Mineola, NY), 1997.

Silvanus P. Thompson, *Calculus Made Easy: Being a Very-Simplest Introduction to Those Beautiful Methods of Reckoning Which Are Generally Called by the Terrifying Names of the Differential Calculus and the Integral Calculus,* with new material by Gardner, St. Martin's Press (New York, NY), 1998.

Gilbert K. Chesterton, *The Annotated Thursday: G. K. Chesterton's Masterpiece, The Man Who Was Thursday,* Ignatius Press (San Francisco, CA), 1999.

Martin Gardner's Favorite Poetic Parodies, Prometheus (Amherst, NY), 2001.

Sidelights

"Over his several decades of writing, [Martin] Gardner has accomplished so much it's hard to believe there's just one of him," wrote a critic for *Publishers Weekly* in a review of Gardner's year 2000 title *From the Wandering Jew to William F. Buckley Jr.: On Science, Literature, and Religion.* That eclectic title stands as a representation of Gardner's sixty-plus books on topics from a debunking of UFOs and pseudoscience, to complex math and science topics and games, to annotations of *Alice in Wonderland* and the authoring of children's books. "Careers in modern society are largely predictable," wrote Dennis Flanagan in *American Scientist.* "Lawyer, doctor, businessman, scientist—so it goes. But who could possibly have predicted the career of Martin Gardner? Even Gardner couldn't have, although in time he invented it himself. And what an invention!"

Gardner is a polymath, a one-of-a-kind in American publishing, say reviewers. Kendrick Frazier, in an interview with Gardner for the *Skeptical Inquirer,* noted that Gardner's mind is "highly philosophical, at home with the most abstract concepts, yet his thinking and writing crackle with clarity—lively, crisp, vivid. He achieved worldwide fame and respect for the three decades of his highly popular mathematical games column for *Scientific American,* yet he is not a mathematician. He is by every standard an eminent intellectual, yet he has no Ph.D. or academic position." Despite not having studied science or mathematics, Gardner has written widely on both subjects, in such popular books as *The Ambidextrous Universe* and *The Relativity Explosion,* and his columns from the *Scientific American* have been collected in numerous books.

Additionally, Gardner is, according to Frazier, "the leading light of the modern skeptical movement," pioneering the field of debunking pseudoscience with his 1952 publication *In the Name of Science.* Since then he has gone on to author numerous other titles in the same vein, such as *Science: Good, Bad, and Bogus* and *The New Age: Notes of a Fringe Watcher.* Beyond such science and mathematics titles, Gardner is best known for his work on annotated texts, especially for his *The Annotated Alice: Alice's Adventures in Wonderland and Through the Looking Glass.* According to Morton N. Cohen, writing in *Victorian Studies,* Gardner "deserves credit for establishing the 'annotated text' as we know it today." With over a million copies sold, *The Annotated Alice* has given birth to an entire genre of such annotated texts, by Gardner and others. Lastly, the energetic and prolific Gardner has also written children's poetry and novels, including the 1998 homage to L. Frank Baum, *Visitors from Oz: The Wild Adventures of Dorothy, the Scarecrow, and the Tin Woodman.* Gardner, however, is humble about his achievements. Speaking with Frazier, he labeled himself "a journalist who writes mainly about math and science, and a few other fields of interest." Michael Dirda, writing in *Skeptical Inquirer,* saw it differently. "If Edmund Wilson was, as they say, the principal American man of letters in our time," Dirda wrote, "then Martin Gardner must be our leading man of numbers."

Born in Tulsa, Oklahoma, in 1914, Gardner grew up with a profound love of books. Gardner once told *SATA,* "As a small child my greatest reading experiences were books of L. Frank Baum. I have tried to repay him by writing about him in books and magazines, and doing the introductions for a continuing series of Dover paperback reprints that now includes Baum's first two Oz books and five of his early non-Oz fantasies. There is no question that Baum was our country's greatest writer of juvenile fantasy, and it is one of the scandals of American letters that only in recent decades has this been recognized by critics and librarians. I am proud to have played a role in hastening this inevitable recognition." When not reading, young Gardner was busy learning magic tricks, playing chess, or playing tennis. Of the three, Gardner has continued with magic throughout his life.

Gardner entered the University of Chicago in 1932, intending to transfer to California Institute of Technology later on and study to become a physicist. However, the intellectually rigorous and varied curriculum he studied at Chicago changed all this. Reading the great works from Plato to Freud, Gardner soon found his home in philosophy, losing in the process, as he noted in his *The Whys of a Philosophical Scrivener,* an "ugly Protestant fundamentalism" which he had inherited from his mother. Gardner was a staunch believer in creationism when he entered college; reading modern geology helped him to put that belief in doubt. By the time he graduated, he had lost his faith in Christianity. After graduation, Gardner stayed on at the university for a time but had no intention of studying for an advanced degree. By this time he had already made up his mind that he wanted to be a writer, not an academic. A short sojourn as a reporter took him back to Oklahoma, where he worked for the *Tulsa Tribune,* but then he returned to the University of Chicago to work in the press relations office. During World War II, he served in the U.S. Naval Reserve for four years.

Gardner began his freelance writing career after the war, selling his first story to *Esquire.* For two years, he supported himself on the sale of humorous pieces to that magazine, including "The No-Side Professor," a take-off on topology. He also continued to study, taking a course from the Viennese logical positivist Rudolf Carnap, who taught that metaphysical questions were in fact meaningless; that is, there was no scientific proof for such questions, and they could only be debated on an emotional level. Many years later, Gardner helped to transcribe Carnap's lecture notes in *An Introduction to the Philosophy of Science.* Such rigorous training in what could and could not be done with language was to prove invaluable in Gardner's later work.

Meanwhile, however, the ever-flexible Gardner became a contributing editor to the children's periodical *Humpty*

Gardner, a master at puzzles, draws together a collection of unusual and challenging word games in Mind-Boggling Word Puzzles, *illustrated by V. G. Myers.*

Dumpty's Magazine for nearly a decade, providing not only stories but also poems for each issue. His poetry was collected in the 1969 *Never Make Fun of a Turtle, My Son,* twenty pieces of verse dealing with moral advice to young readers. A reviewer for *Bulletin of the Center for Children's Books* felt that the poems have a "swinging quality" appropriate for "the light-hearted, chiding messages." Gardner advises on themes from sharing to shopping to watching television.

During his tenure at *Humpty Dumpty's Magazine,* Gardner also began a career as a science writer. In 1952, he published *In the Name of Science,* which proved so unpopular at first that it was almost immediately remaindered. Five years later, Dover reprinted the book under the title *Fads and Fallacies in the Name of Science,* in which Gardner attacked such pseudoscience as UFOs and L. Ron Hubbard's Scientology. Under its new title, the book attracted a faithful readership and has remained in print ever since. In 1956, Gardner sold his first article to the *Scientific American,* and by the next year, he was editing the "Mathematical Games" column for the magazine, a position he held for the next quarter of a century, despite the fact that he had not formally studied mathematics since high school. "Had I known I would be writing some day a column on math, I would have taken some math courses [at university]," Gardner told Frazier. "If you look over my

Scientific American columns you will see that they get progressively more sophisticated as I began reading math books and learning more about the subject. There is no better way to learn anything than to write about it."

Gardner's tenure at *Scientific American* led not only to books of mathematics games, puzzles, and teasers reprinted from the pages of the magazine but also to a career in writing science books. The collections of his columns were awaited eagerly by recreational mathematicians. Books such as *Mathematical Carnival, Knotted Doughnuts and Other Mathematical Entertainments, Time Travel and Other Mathematical Bewilderments,* and *Fractal Music, Hypercards, and More* attracted thousands of loyal readers to Gardner's puzzles. Accompanied by diagrams, sketches, and, of course, answers, such puzzles inspired many young readers to enter mathematics as a career. Critics were as charmed by the books as was the public. A reviewer for *Library Journal* called his *Mathematical Carnival* "a delightful book," and a contributor for *Publishers Weekly* felt that same book "can stretch even the most intelligent reader's mind." Another reviewer for *Publishers Weekly* called Gardner's *Mathematical Magic Show* "a heady romp." A contributor for *Choice* felt that *Wheels, Life, and Other Mathematical Amusements* "matches the high standards of his other books." A *Booklist* writer also had praise for this title, noting that Gardner's "excitement and enjoyment are irresistibly infectious." Reviewing his *Knotted Doughnuts* in *Science Books and Films,* Matthias F. Reese noted that the book "provides insights to mathematics together with entertainments." *Time Travel,* according to a *Booklist* contributor, features Gardner's "usual sharp wit and self-deprecating humor amid mathematical brainteasers."

Gardner also compiled columns about a fictional Dr. Matrix from his *Scientific American* columns in books such as *The Numerology of Dr. Matrix,* later revised and reprinted as *The Incredible Dr. Matrix.* Reviewing the latter title in the *New York Times Book Review,* Harry Schwartz noted that the book contained "more fun and mind-stretching than this reviewer has space to suggest or sample." And J. Johnson, reviewing the 1997 *The Last Recreations: Hydras, Eggs, and Other Mathematical Mystifications* in *Choice,* thought the book was "a welcome addition to the series," but was also saddened by the book's appearance, as it was to be the last of the series. "Martin Gardner, you will be greatly missed!" Johnson concluded. But not for long. Gardner collected fifty of the best puzzles from his column for the 2001 omnibus volume, *The Colossal Book of Mathematics: Classic Puzzles, Paradoxes, and Problems.* A reviewer for *Publishers Weekly* commented that Gardner's "elegant style could draw in new aficionados," and claimed that the author remains "a model of clear prose, understated wit, and intellectual honesty."

Gardner has also written puzzle books with a specifically young audience in mind. Some of these books were collections of columns Gardner contributed to *Isaac Asimov's Science Fiction Magazine,* brain-teasers employing a science fiction story format. *Science Fiction Puzzle Tales* was one product of these contributions, puzzles that are "fun for the recreational logician or amateur detective," according to a reviewer for the *Washington Post Book World.* A contributor to *School Library Journal* found the puzzles in that same title "challenging," while Wain Saeger, writing in *Voice of Youth Advocates,* thought that math teachers would be "delighted" with the book, incorporating such puzzles in "lesson plans to enliven their classes." *Puzzles from Other Worlds* is also sci-fi based, a collection of puzzles and teasers that "will exercise even the brainiest," according to a *Washington Post Book World* reviewer. Ellen M. Funkhouser, writing in *Voice of Youth Advocates,* similarly found the title "an excellent selection of brain teasers." Gardner presents other puzzles for younger readers in *Perplexing Puzzles and Tantalizing Teasers* and *Puzzling Questions about the Solar System.* Reviewing *Perplexing Puzzles* in *Library Journal,* Lina Daukas found the book "stimulating," and a contributor for *Publishers Weekly* thought it was "the perfect solution for" stimulating children's minds in the summer. In 2001, Gardner brought out *Mind-Boggling Word Puzzles,* a book that will "challenge children to think more playfully about language," according to *Booklist*'s Carolyn Phelan.

Gardner has also written on various science topics, from relativity to the nature of the universe. *The Ambidextrous Universe* has gone through several editions and become a "classic," according to *Library Journal*'s Gregg Sapp. Theodore W. Munch, writing in *Science Books and Films,* also had praise for the book, noting that it "will provide interesting and sometimes exciting reading." Reviewing the third edition of the book in *Science Books and Films,* John L. Hubisz found the text both "entertaining and humorous," and in a *New Yorker* review of the second edition, Jeremy Bernstein remarked that the book is filled with "wit and elegance." Further titles in the sciences from Gardner include *Logic Machines and Diagrams* and *The Relativity Explosion,* a layperson's guide to the theories of Albert Einstein.

Some of Gardner's most popular science writing is in the debunking of pseudoscience. In his first foray into the genre, *In the Name of Science,* he takes on topics from the flat-earth theory to the mystical powers of the Great Pyramids and extra sensory perception. Michael Shermer, writing in *Scientific American* fifty years after the original publication of that book, noted that it "is arguably the skeptic classic of the past half a century." Gardner tackles UFOs and the theories of Imanuel Velikovsky in *Science,* a book that helps young readers "differentiate between real science and fake," according to Valentin R. Livada in *Kliatt.* Gardner has also written the column "Fringe Watcher" for many years in the journal *Skeptical Inquirer,* and his columns are collected in several book-length editions, as well. In *The New Age,* he does battle with topics from biorhythms to

psychic surgery and other favorites of New Age thinkers. However, in so doing, according to a reviewer for *Publishers Weekly,* Gardner "ignores the fact that some of today's mainstream science was yesterday's 'fringe' science." More of his *Skeptical Inquirer* columns are served up in *Did Adam and Eve Have Navels?: Discourses on Reflexology, Numerology, Urine Therapy & Other Dubious Subjects,* and Gardner also attempts to expose religious fakery in titles such as *Urantia: The Great Cult Mystery.*

For most writers, such an assortment of writings would be enough for one career, but Gardner has written in other, non-science fields, as well. His first foray into the genre of annotated books was with his beloved L. Frank Baum in *The Wizard of Oz and Who He Was.* A long-time fan of Lewis Carroll's *Alice's Adventures in Wonderland* and *Through the Looking Glass,* Gardner also realized that much of the best writing in those books would not be understood by modern readers or readers unfamiliar with the particular part of England in which they are set. He determined to right that wrong, and the result was several annotated books about Alice, the first being *The Annotated Alice: Alice's Adventures in Wonderland and Through the Looking Glass.* That book, according to Benny Green, writing in the *Spectator,* was a "reckless . . . gamble," for with such annotations Gardner risked over-explaining the text. But to Green, the gamble was also "completely successful," and Gardner's annotations were "the perfect demonstration of the art." Gardner went on to other Carroll titles, including *The Annotated Snark* and *The Wasp in the Wig.* In 1990, a new edition entitled *More Annotated Alice* appeared, and in 2000 an even fuller edition appeared, *The Annotated Alice: The Definitive Edition,* combining the first two books. Reviewing that edition in *Library Journal,* Thomas L. Cooksey remarked that Gardner's "commentary is sufficiently detailed to be informative without burdening Alice with excessive pedantic baggage." Gardner has gone on to annotate other writers, from Gilbert K. Chesterton and his "Father Brown," to Samuel Taylor Coleridge in *The Annotated Ancient Mariner* and E. L. Thayer's poem in *The Annotated Casey at the Bat.*

In addition to such annotated editions, Gardner has proved himself a well-regarded essayist in collections such as *The Night Is Large: Collected Essays, 1938-1995.* He is also the author of an early novel, *The Flight of Peter Fromm,* a book that in part explains his own rejection of religion. In 1998, Gardner published a sequel to Baum's Oz tale with *Visitors from Oz,* a "winner," according to a critic for *Kirkus Reviews.* The book deals with the machinations of movie producer Samuel Gold to film "The Emerald City of Oz," an animated movie. Believing Oz is real, Gold sends off an e-mail to Glinda inviting Dorothy and her friends back to Earth to visit. But there are problems with this, for Oz has been removed to a parallel universe and Dorothy must figure out—with the help of Professor Wogglebug—how to get to Earth and back to Oz again. The professor advises the use of a topological structure called a Klein bottle (its one-sided surface has neither an inside or outside) to help in the adventure. At one point Dorothy and company find an entrance to Wonderland and encounter the White Rabbit and other characters from the Carroll tale. Sally Estes, writing in *Booklist,* felt that Gardner "charmingly sustains the Oz tradition" with this novel.

"Gardner has an old-fashioned, almost nineteenth-century, Oliver Wendell Holmes kind of mind," wrote Adam Gopnik in the *New York Times Book Review.* He is, Gopnik continued, "self-educated, opinionated, cranky, and utterly unafraid of embarrassment." These qualities, along with an ever-inquisitive mind, have helped to make Gardner the prolific author he is, claim critics. Gardner concluded in his interview with Frazier, "I consider myself lucky in being able to earn a living doing what I like best. As my wife long ago realized, I really don't do any *work.* I just *play* and get paid for it."

Biographical and Critical Sources

BOOKS

Dictionary of the Avant-Gardes, A Capella Press (Chicago, IL), 1993.
The Encyclopedia of Science Fiction, edited by John Clute and Peter Nicholls, St. Martin's Press (New York, NY), 1993.
Gardner, Martin, *Whys of a Philosophical Scrivener,* Morrow (New York, NY), 1983.
Science Fiction & Fantasy Literature, 1975-1991, Gale (Detroit, MI), 1992.
Ward, Martha, et al, *Authors of Books for Young People,* 3rd edition, Scarecrow Press (Metuchen, NJ), 1990.

PERIODICALS

American Scientist, January-February, 1997, Thomas Banchoff, review of *The Universe in a Handkerchief: Lewis Carroll's Mathematical Recreations, Games, Puzzles, and Word Plays,* pp. 86-87; January-February, 2002, Dennis Flanagan, review of *The Colossal Book of Mathematics: Classic Puzzles, Paradoxes, and Problems,* pp. 74-76.
Booklist, June 15, 1969, review of *Perplexing Puzzles and Tantalizing Teasers,* p. 1174; February 15, 1984, review of *Wheels, Life, and Other Mathematical Amusements,* p. 839; January 15, 1988, review of *Time Travel and Other Mathematical Bewilderments,* p. 822; July, 1996, Benjamin Segedin, review of *The Night Is Large: Collected Essays, 1938-1995,* p. 1796; September 15, 1998, Sally Estes, review of *Visitors from Oz: The Wild Adventures of Dorothy, the Scarecrow, and the Tin Woodman,* p. 206; September 15, 2000, Gilbert Taylor, review of *Did Adam and Eve Have Navels?: Discourses on Reflexology, Numerology,*

Urine Therapy & Other Dubious Subjects, p. 196; September 1, 2001, Carolyn Phelan, review of *Mind-Boggling Word Puzzles,* p. 99.
Bulletin of the Center for Children's Books, May, 1969, review of *Never Make Fun of a Turtle, My Son,* p. 142.
Choice, February, 1984, review of *Wheels, Life, and Other Mathematical Amusements,* p. 853; May, 1998, J. Johnson, review of *The Last Recreations: Hydras, Eggs, and Other Mathematical Mystifications,* p. 1566.
Insight on the News, January 10, 2000, Rex Roberts, "Explicating Alice," p. 32.
Kirkus Reviews, May 1, 1996, review of *The Night Is Large,* p. 663; September 15, 1998, review of *Visitors from Oz,* p. 1310.
Kliatt, spring, 1983, Valentin R. Livada, review of *Science: Good, Bad, and Bogus,* p. 54.
Library Journal, September 15, 1969, Susan R. Morris, review of *Never Make Fun of a Turtle, My Son,* p. 3204; October 15, 1969, Lina Daukas, review of *Perplexing Puzzles and Tantalizing Teasers,* p. 3820; March 1, 1976, Edith S. Crockett, review of *Mathematical Carnival,* p. 665; March 1, 1991, Gregg Sapp, review of *The New Ambidextrous Universe,* p. 63; April 15, 1995, Sandra Collins, review of *Urantia,* p. 81; June 15, 1995, Harry Frumerman, review of *The Night Is Large,* pp. 65-66; December, 1999, Thomas L. Cooksey, review of *The Annotated Alice: Alice's Adventures in Wonderland and Through the Looking Glass,* p. 130; November 15, 2000, Lloyd Davidson, review of *Did Adam and Eve Have Navels?,* p. 93.
New Yorker, October 8, 1979, Jeremy Bernstein, review of *The Ambidextrous Universe,* pp. 169-174, 177.
New York Times Book Review, November 7, 1976, Harry Schwartz, review of *The Incredible Dr. Matrix,* pp. 6-7; December 5, 1999, Adam Gopnik, review of *The Annotated Alice,* pp. 62, 64.
Odyssey, October, 2003, Barbara Krasner-Khait, "Martin Gardner: Recreational Math Master," p. 22.
Publishers Weekly, June 2, 1969, review of *Perplexing Puzzles and Tantalizing Teasers,* p. 136; September 15, 1975, review of *Mathematical Carnival,* p. 50; August 8, 1977, review of *Mathematical Magic Show,* pp. 61-62; March 11, 1988, review of *The New Age,* p. 91; August 19, 1996, review of *Weird Water and Fuzzy Logic,* p. 47; August 24, 1998, review of *Visitors from Oz,* p. 47; December 20, 1999, review of *The Annotated Alice,* p. 18; August 28, 2000, review of *Did Adam and Eve Have Navels?,* p. 63; August 28, 2000, review of *From the Wandering Jew to William F. Buckley Jr.: On Science, Literature, and Religion* p. 63; July 30, 2002, review of *The Colossal Book of Mathematics,* p. 76; June 2, 2003, review of *Are Universes Thicker than Blackberries? Discourses on Gödel, Magic Hexagrams, Little Red Riding Hood, and Other Mathematical and Pseudoscience Topics,* p. 45.
School Library Journal, October, 1981, review of *Science Fiction Puzzle Tales,* p. 165.
Science Books and Films, January, 1981, Theodore W. Munch, review of *The Ambidextrous Universe,* p. 129; May, 1987, Matthias F. Reese, review of *Knotted Doughnuts and Other Mathematical Entertainments,*

pp. 302-303; January, 1991, John L. Hubisz, review of *The New Ambidextrous Universe,* p. 6.

Scientific American, March, 2002, Michael Shermer, "Hermits and Cranks," pp. 36-37.

Skeptical Inquirer, November-December, 1996, Michael Dirda, review of *The Night Is Large,* pp. 47-48; March-April, 1998, Kendrick Frazier, "A Mind at Play: An Interview with Martin Gardner," pp. 34-39; November-December, 2001, Mark Durm, "Lucid Commentaries with Something to Say," p. 62.

Spectator, October 5, 1974, Benny Green, review of *The Annotated Alice,* p. 439.

Victorian Studies, spring, 2001, Morton N. Cohen, review of *The Annotated Alice,* p. 473.

Voice of Youth Advocates, October, 1981, Wain Saeger, review of *Science Fiction Puzzle Tales,* p. 42; February, 1985, Ellen M. Funkhouser, review of *Puzzles from Other Worlds,* p. 344.

Washington Post Book World, July 26, 1981, review of *Science Fiction Puzzle Tales,* p. 8; August 26, 1984, review of *Puzzles from Other Worlds,* p. 12; December 1, 1991, review of *The Annotated Night before Christmas,* p. 14; January 3, 1998, Michele Slung, review of *Visitors from Oz,* pp. 11, 13; December 24, 2000, Michael Dirda, review of *Did Adam and Eve Have Navels?,* p. 15.

*   *   *

GEARY, Rick 1946-

Personal

Born February 25, 1946, in Kansas City, MO; son of Edward V. (a banker) and Helen Louise (a homemaker; maiden name, Brooks) Geary; married Deborah Lee Chester (a teacher), January 11, 1987. *Education:* University of Kansas, B.F.A., 1968, M.A., 1971.

Addresses

Home and office—1166 24th St., San Diego, CA 92102. *E-mail*—rickdeborahgeary@cox.net.

Career

Freelance cartoonist and illustrator, 1977—.

Member

National Cartoonists Society, Graphic Artists Guild.

Awards, Honors

National Cartoonists Society Award for Magazine and Book Illustration, 1995; Quick Picks for Reluctant Young Adult Readers selection, American Library Association Young Adult Services Division, 1996, for *Jack the Ripper.*

Rick Geary

Writings

Spider-Man: Ghosts, Ghouls, and the Hobgoblin, illustrated by Ken Steacy, Fun Works (Burbank, CA), 1996.

ILLUSTRATOR

Donna Z. Meilach, *Plant Hangers,* Crown (New York, NY), 1977.

J. Arthur Campbell, *Chemistry: The Unending Frontier,* Goodyear Publishing (Santa Monica, CA), 1978.

Donna Z. Meilach, *Macrame Gnomes and Puppets,* Crown (New York, NY), 1980.

Byron Preiss and Michael Sorkin, *Not the Webster's Dictionary,* Simon & Schuster (New York, NY), 1983.

Robert M. Gorodess, *How to Sell Remodeling,* Craftsman Book Co. (Carlsbad, CA), 1985.

Mark Davies, *Inside the Airport,* Contemporary Books (Chicago, IL), 1990.

David Keller, *Great Disasters: The Most Shocking Moments in History,* Avon (New York, NY), 1990.

Charles Dickens, *Great Expectations,* Berkley Publishing Group (New York, NY), 1990.

Emily Brontë, *Wuthering Heights,* Berkley Publishing Group (New York, NY), 1990.

H. G. Wells, *The Invisible Man,* Berkley Publishing Group (New York, NY), 1991.

Jerry Prosser, *Cyberantics: A Little Adventure,* Dark Horse Comics (Milwaukie, OR), 1992.

Ilene Rosenzweig, *The I Hate Madonna Handbook,* St. Martin's Press (New York, NY), 1994.

Francis L. Fennell, _Collegiate English Handbook,_ Collegiate Press (San Diego, CA), 1998.

Katia E. Moritz and Jennifer Jablonsky, _Blink, Blink, Clop, Clop: Why Do We Do Things We Can't Stop?: An OCD Storybook,_ Childswork, Childsplay (Secaucus, NJ), 1998.

Patricia Lakin, _Harry Houdini: Escape Artist,_ Aladdin (New York, NY), 2002.

CARTOON BOOKS

Television, Schanes & Schanes (San Diego, CA), 1978.

Hello from San Diego, Schanes & Schanes (San Diego, CA), 1978.

Byting Back: A Compendium of TechnoWhimsy, Valleyware Publishing (Solana Beach, CA), 1983.

COLLECTIONS

U-Comix Sonderband 28, Volksverlag (Linden, West Germany), 1980.

At Home with Rick Geary, Fantagraphics Books (Agoura, CA), 1985.

Rick Geary's Wonders & Oddities, Dark Horse Comics (Milwaukie, OR), 1988.

Housebound with Rick Geary, Fantagraphics Books (Seattle, WA), 1991.

Prairie Moon and Other Stories, Dark Horse Comics (Milwaukie, OR), 1992.

GRAPHIC NOVELS

A Treasury of Victorian Murder, Nantier Beall Minoustchine Publishing (New York, NY), 1987, new edition, 2002.

Jack the Ripper: A Journal of the Whitechapel Murders, 1888-1889, NBM Publishing (New York, NY), 1995.

The Borden Tragedy: A Memoir of the Infamous Double Murder at Fall River, Mass., 1892, NBM Publishing (New York, NY), 1997.

The Fatal Bullet: A True Account of the Assassination, Lingering Pain, Death, and Burial of James A. Garfield, Twentieth President of the United States; Also Including the Inglorious Life and Career of the Despised Assassin Guiteau, NBM Publishing (New York, NY), 1999, published as _The Fatal Bullet: The Assassination of President James A. Garfield,_ 2001.

The Mystery of Mary Rogers, NBM Publishing (New York, NY), 2001.

COMICS

The Exploits of the Junior Carrot Patrol: "The Unbelievable Journey," Dark Horse Comics (Milwaukie, OR), 1989.

The Exploits of the Junior Carrot Patrol: "The Backwards Machine," Dark Horse Comics (Milwaukie, OR), 1990.

Blanche Goes to New York, Dark Horse Comics (Milwaukie, OR), 1992.

Blanche Goes to Hollywood, Dark Horse Comics (Milwaukie, OR), 1993.

Blanche Goes to Paris, Headless Shakespeare Press (Seattle, WA), 2001.

SELF-ILLUSTRATED CHILDREN'S BOOKS

The Night before Christmask, Dark Horse Comics (Milwaukie, OR), 1994.

The Mask Summer Vacation, Dark Horse Comics (Milwaukie, OR), 1995.

The Mask in School Spirits, Dark Horse Comics (Milwaukie, OR), 1995.

Spider-Man: Chase for the Blue Tiger, YES! Entertainment (Pleasanton, CA), 1995.

Spider-Man: Lights, Camera, Danger!, XYZ Distributors (Wauwatosa, WI), 1996.

Regular contributor of illustrations to periodicals, including _San Diego Reader,_ 1975—, _National Lampoon,_ 1979-92, _Copley News Service,_ 1985-97, _New York Times Book Review,_ 1988-92, and _Mad_ magazine, 1996-2000. Also contributor of illustrations to _San Diego Union-Tribune, Spy, Old Farmer's Almanac, American Libraries, PULSE_ (Tower Records), _Wood and Steel_ (Taylor Guitars), _Rolling Stone, Computoredge, Roadstar, California Lawyer, Los Angeles_ magazine, _San Diego_ magazine, and _Los Angeles Times._ Contributor of writings and illustrations to "Treasury of Victorian Murder" series, NBM Publishing, 1987—, and "Society of Horrors," in _Disney Adventures_ magazine, 1999—.

Work in Progress

The Beast of Chicago, a graphic novel in "Victorian Murder Series," for publication in 2003.

Sidelights

Rick Geary is a prominent cartoonist whose drawings have illustrated such well-known venues as the _New York Times_ and the _Los Angeles Times_ as well as _National Lampoon_ and _Mad,_ magazines long loved for their comics. Young adults may know Geary's work through his contributions to these periodicals, or for his graphic novels, notably his contributions to the "Treasury of Victorian Murder" series published by NBM Publishers. Reviewers have found Geary's additions to the series meticulously researched and intriguingly illustrated with unusual points of view and details that add to the tone as well as to the historical veracity of the stories. His _Jack the Ripper: A Journal of the Whitechapel Murders, 1888-1889_ was selected for the Quick Picks for Reluctant Young Adult Readers List by the American Library Association's Young Adult Services Division, and _The Mystery of Mary Rogers, The Fatal Bullet,_ and _The Borden Tragedy_ were each also noted by reviewers for their likely appeal to reluctant readers.

In *Jack the Ripper*, Geary details the murders of five London prostitutes in 1888 in police-procedural style, sifting through the evidence, including coroner's reports, witnesses' accounts, and clues. His artwork and a "deadpan pulp narrative" create a haunting volume in which the hypocrisy of Victorian society is highlighted, according to a contributor to *Publishers Weekly*. Another famous unsolved murder inspired *The Borden Tragedy: A Memoir of the Infamous Double Murder at Fall River, Mass., 1892,* in which Geary goes over the murder of Abby and Andrew Borden, head of a prominent Massachusetts family, and the trial and acquittal of Andrew's daughter, Lizzy, who was never exonerated in the public eye. "It's Geary's artfully precise reconstruction of turn-of-the-century Fall River that makes this work so haunting, and such a delight," observed a contributor to *Publishers Weekly*, who compared it favorably to his *Jack the Ripper*. Like the earlier case, much has already been written about the Borden case, remarked Ray Olson in *Booklist*, who added that "the comics medium arguably communicates the facts more

Part of his series of books on Victorian era murders, Geary's graphic novel outlines a factual, detailed account of the notorious but unsolved killing of Abby and Andrew Borden, often blamed on their daughter Lizzie. (From The Borden Tragedy, *written and illustrated by Geary.)*

forcefully and memorably than any of the many other works about the crimes."

In *The Fatal Bullet: A True Account of the Assassination, Lingering Pain, Death, and Burial of James A. Garfield, Twentieth President of the United States; Also Including the Inglorious Life and Career of the Despised Assassin Guiteau*, Geary tells the parallel stories of American president Garfield and Charles Guiteau, the man who shot him in the back of the head while he was boarding a train six months into his presidency. The two were strangely similar in background and interests—both studied law and politics—and Geary plays the two off each other, alternating the story of Garfield's rise to the rank of general during the Civil War and then on to the presidency with Guiteau's descent into madness. Geary's text and illustrations also reveal historical details such as the relative dearth of security around the president and the dismal state of medicine, which caused Garfield to suffer for months before dying of his bullet wound. *Booklist*'s Ray Olson compared *The Fatal Bullet* favorably to *The Borden Tragedy*, remarking that here Geary "surpasses his own bravura" in the earlier book's illustrations, singling out "subtly expressive facial drawing, and skillful juxtaposition of frames" for special praise.

In *The Mystery of Mary Rogers*, Geary offers his own true-crime comic "take" on another famous nineteenth-century murder, following in the footsteps of Edgar Allan Poe to tell the tale of the popular cigar girl who was abused and thrown to her death in the Hudson River in 1841. When Mary Rogers was found dead in the river, a quick burial and the proximity of the victim to the Manhattan elite provoked rumors of a botched abortion and a cover-up. Speculation about the perpetrator was rampant. As in his earlier entries in this series, Geary does not attempt to solve the crime, but presents again all the evidence and uses his illustrations to offer the variety of possible suspects and outcomes. Geary's illustrations "capture the spirit of a booming and boisterous New York City in the 1840s," remarked a contributor to *Publishers Weekly*. Christine C. Menefee made a similar point in her review in *School Library Journal*, and concluded that "with its commendable historical accuracy, [*The Mystery of Mary Rogers*] would also enliven studies of U.S. history."

Geary told *SATA:* "At first, my only ambition was to be a freelance cartoonist and illustrator. In time, I found that there was a certain kind of illustrated storytelling I wanted to pursue, which I did initially in a series of self-published mini-books. This led to twelve years of contributing comic stories to *National Lampoon,* and thence to more or less continuous work in the comic book industry.

"My interest in the strange and unusual corners of history, particularly true crime, led me to the continuing series 'A Treasury of Victorian Murder,' for NBM Publishing, the latest volume of which is *The Mystery of Mary Rogers.* My goal in these books is clarity and accuracy, above all, along with a certain deadpan humor."

"I work in a studio at my home near downtown San Diego. Though I value the freedom of working at home, my days are necessarily highly structured in order to complete the half-dozen or so projects I have going at one time. Self-employment, it took me years to learn, requires self-discipline.

"There are many artists and writers whose work I enjoy and appreciate, but the most influential, as both artist and writer, is probably the late Edward Gorey."

Biographical and Critical Sources

PERIODICALS

Booklist, December 1, 1997, Ray Olson, review of *The Borden Tragedy: A Memoir of the Infamous Double Murder at Fall River, Mass., 1892,* p. 604; July, 1999, Ray Olson, review of *The Fatal Bullet: A True Account of the Assassination, Lingering Pain, Death, and Burial of James A. Garfield, Twentieth President of the United States; Also Including the Inglorious Life and Career of the Despised Assassin Guiteau,* p. 1919; April 15, 2001, Ray Olson, review of *The Mystery of Mary Rogers,* p. 1514.
Publishers Weekly, April 17, 1995, review of *Jack the Ripper: A Journal of the Whitechapel Murders, 1888-1889,* p. 42; January 19, 1998, review of *The Borden Tragedy,* p. 364; July 12, 1999, review of *The Fatal Bullet,* p. 86; May 28, 2001, review of *The Mystery of Mary Rogers,* p. 52.
School Library Journal, September, 1990, Sylvia S. Marantz, review of *Inside the Airport,* p. 215; March, 1998, Francisca Goldsmith, review of *The Borden Tragedy,* p. 249; August, 2001, Christine C. Menefee, review of *The Mystery of Mary Rogers,* p. 213; December, 2002, Edith Ching, review of *Harry Houdini: Escape Artist,* p. 124.

OTHER

Rick Geary Home Page, http://www.rickgeary.com/ (January 15, 2003).*

*   *   *

GERSTEIN, Mordicai 1935-

Personal

Born November 24, 1935, in Los Angeles, CA; son of Samuel (a playwright) and Fay (a homemaker; maiden name, Chornow) Gerstein; married Sandra MacDonald

Mordicai Gerstein

(a painter), 1957 (divorced, 1969); married Susan Yard Harris (an artist and illustrator of children's books), May, 1984; children: (first marriage) Jesse, Aram; (second marriage) Risa Faye. *Education:* Attended Chouinard Art Institute, 1953-56. *Hobbies and other interests:* Painting, drawing, reading, occasionally playing the banjo and mandolin, cooking, eating, running, and traveling.

Addresses

Home—Northampton, MA. *Agent*—Raines & Raines, 71 Park Ave., New York, NY 10016.

Career

Writer, designer, and illustrator of books for children; animated film writer, director, and producer; painter. United Productions of America, artist-designer at studio in Los Angeles, CA, 1956-57, and at studio in New York, NY, beginning in 1957; freelance animation designer in New York, NY; Summer Star Productions (animation company), New York, NY, founding owner, 1969-79.

Awards, Honors

Award of the Film Clubs of France, 1966, for film *The Room;* CINE Golden Eagle Award, International Film and Television Festival of New York (IFTFNY), 1967, for film *The Magic Ring;* Outstanding Books of the Year citation, *New York Times,* 1983, for *Arnold of the Ducks;* Parents' Choice Award, 1986, for *Tales of Pan;* Ten Best-Illustrated Children's Books and Notable Book citations, both from *New York Times Book Review,* 1987, for *The Mountains of Tibet;* CINE Golden Eagle Award, IFTFNY, Gold Medal, first prize for children's entertainment, American Film Institute Video Awards, first prize for short video, Chicago International Festival of Children's films, and Parents' Choice Award, all 1989, all for film *Beauty and the Beast;* Best Illustrated Book of the Year citation, *New York Times,* "The Best of 1998" citation, School Library Society, Fanfare List, *Horn Book,* Editors' Choice Award, *Booklist,* and Parents' Choice Award, all 1998, all for *The Wild Boy;* Notable Book of the Year citation, *New York Times,* 1998, for *Victor: A Novel Based on the Life of the Savage of Aveyron;* Parents' Choice Award, and Notable Book selections, *Horn Book* and American Library Association, all 2002, all for *What Charlie Heard.*

Writings

SELF-ILLUSTRATED, EXCEPT WHERE NOTED

Arnold of the Ducks, Harper (New York, NY), 1983.
Follow Me!, Morrow (New York, NY), 1983.
Prince Sparrow, Four Winds (New York, NY), 1984.
Roll Over!, Crown (New York, NY), 1984.
The Room (adapted from his film of the same title), Harper (New York, NY), 1984.
William, Where Are You?, Crown (New York, NY), 1985.
Tales of Pan, Harper (New York, NY), 1986.
The Seal Mother, Dial (New York, NY), 1986.
The Mountains of Tibet, Harper (New York, NY), 1987.
The Sun's Day, Harper (New York, NY), 1989.
(Reteller) Madame Leprince de Beaumont, *Beauty and the Beast,* Dutton (New York, NY), 1989.
Anytime Mapleson and the Hungry Bears, illustrated by wife Susan Yard Harris, Harper (New York, NY), 1990.
The New Creatures, Harper (New York, NY), 1991.
The Gigantic Baby, illustrated by Arnie Levin, Harper (New York, NY), 1991.
(With Susan Yard Harris) *Guess What?,* Crown (New York, NY), 1991.
The Story of May, HarperCollins (New York, NY), 1993.
The Shadow of a Flying Bird: A Legend of the Kurdistani Jews, Hyperion (New York, NY), 1994.
(With Susan Yard Harris) *Daisy's Garden,* Hyperion (New York, NY), 1995.
The Giant, Hyperion (New York, NY), 1995.
Bedtime, Everybody!, Hyperion (New York, NY), 1996.
Behind the Couch, Hyperion (New York, NY), 1996.
Jonah and the Two Great Fish, Simon & Schuster (New York, NY), 1997.

Stop Those Pants!, Harcourt (San Diego, CA), 1998.
Victor: A Novel Based on the Life of the Savage of Aveyron, Farrar, Straus (New York, NY), 1998.
The Wild Boy, Farrar, Straus (New York, NY), 1998.
The Absolutely Awful Alphabet, Harcourt (San Diego, CA), 1999.
Noah and the Great Flood, Simon and Schuster (New York, NY), 1999.
Queen Esther the Morning Star: The Story of Purim, Simon and Schuster (New York, NY), 2000.
Fox Eyes, Golden Books (New York, NY), 2001.
What Charlie Heard, Farrar, Straus and Giroux (New York, NY), 2002.
Sparrow Jack, Farrar, Straus and Giroux (New York, NY), 2003.
The Man Who Walked Between the Towers, Roaring Brook Press (Brookfield, CT), 2003.

ILLUSTRATOR

Elizabeth Levy, *Nice Little Girls,* Delacorte (New York, NY), 1974.
Elizabeth Levy, *Frankenstein Moved In on the Fourth Floor,* Harper (New York, NY), 1979.
Patricia Thomas, *"There Are Rocks in My Socks!" Said the Ox to the Fox,* Lothrop (New York, NY), 1979.
Elizabeth Levy, *Dracula Is a Pain in the Neck,* Harper (New York, NY), 1983.
Elizabeth Levy, *The Shadow Nose* (mystery), Morrow (New York, NY), 1983.
Rosalie Silver, *David's First Bicycle,* Golden Press (New York, NY), 1983.
Robert Southey, *The Cataract of Lodore,* Dial (New York, NY), 1991.
Leslie Norris, *Albert and the Angels,* Farrar, Straus and Giroux (New York, NY), 2000.
Eric A. Kimmel, *The Jar of Fools: Eight Hanukkah Stories from Chelm,* Holiday House (New York, NY), 2000.
Elizabeth Spires, *I Am Arachne: Fifteen Greek and Roman Myths,* Frances Foster Books (New York, NY), 2001.
Eric A. Kimmel, *Three Samurai Cats: A Story from Japan,* Holiday House (New York, NY), 2002.
Erica Silverman, *Sholem's Treasure: How Sholem Aleichem Became a Writer,* Farrar, Straus and Giroux (New York, NY), 2004.

ILLUSTRATOR; "SOMETHING QUEER IS GOING ON" MYSTERY SERIES

Elizabeth Levy, *Something Queer Is Going On,* Delacorte (New York, NY), 1973.
Elizabeth Levy, *Something Queer at the Ballpark,* Delacorte (New York, NY), 1975.
Elizabeth Levy, *Something Queer at the Library,* Delacorte (New York, NY), 1977.
Elizabeth Levy, *Something Queer on Vacation,* Delacorte (New York, NY), 1980.
Elizabeth Levy, *Something Queer at the Haunted School,* Delacorte (New York, NY), 1982.
Elizabeth Levy, *Something Queer at the Lemonade Stand,* Delacorte (New York, NY), 1982.

Elizabeth Levy, *Something Queer in Rock 'n' Roll,* Delacorte (New York, NY), 1987.

Elizabeth Levy, *Something Queer at the Birthday Party,* Delacorte (New York, NY), 1990.

Elizabeth Levy, *Something Queer in Outer Space,* Hyperion (New York, NY), 1993.

Elizabeth Levy, *Something Queer in the Cafeteria,* Hyperion (New York, NY), 1994.

Elizabeth Levy, *Something Queer at the Scary Movie,* Hyperion (New York, NY), 1995.

Elizabeth Levy, *Something Queer in the Wild West,* Hyperion (New York, NY), 1997.

ILLUSTRATOR; "FLETCHER MYSTERY" SERIES

Elizabeth Levy, *A Hare-Raising Tail,* Aladdin (New York, NY), 2002.

Elizabeth Levy, *The Principal's on the Roof,* Aladdin (New York, NY), 2002.

Elizabeth Levy, *The Mixed-Up Mask Mystery,* Aladdin (New York, NY), 2003.

Elizabeth Levy, *The Mystery of Too Many Elvises,* Aladdin (New York, NY), 2003.

Elizabeth Levy, *The Cool Ghoul Mystery,* Aladdin (New York, NY), 2003.

OTHER

Creator of "The Inner Man," editorial cartoons for periodicals such as *Village Voice* and *Oui;* author of children's films *The Room,* 1965, and *The Magic Ring,* 1966; adapter of the children's film *The Nose,* 1965. *The Room* is available in Braille.

Adaptations

Arnold of the Ducks was adapted for an animated film and broadcast as a Columbia Broadcasting System (CBS-TV) *Storybreak,* 1985; *Beauty and the Beast* was adapted for film and released by Stories to Remember, 1989, and has been recorded on audio cassette and released by Dutton; *The Seal Mother* and *Prince Sparrow* were adapted for filmstrips by McGraw-Hill.

Sidelights

Mordicai Gerstein is the author/illustrator of more than thirty books for young readers, including picture books, chapter books, and novels. Illustrating the work of other writers, especially that of Elizabeth Levy, he has over two dozen more book credits. Gerstein also worked for many years in animation, but since the early 1980s, he has devoted his time to children's books.

Born in 1935, in Los Angeles, Gerstein grew up in East Los Angeles and the San Fernando Valley and was introduced to literature and art at an early age by his parents. His mother loved painting and books, and his father, Samuel Gerstein, was a playwright who also made his living in business. Deeply influenced by the stories and books he read as a youngster, Gerstein began drawing illustrations for his favorites even as a

In Gerstein's self-illustrated Fox Eyes, *young Martin defies his wise aunt and looks into the eyes of a mysterious red fox, then discovers he has to live as the fox for a day.*

child. After high school, he studied painting privately in New Mexico and then attended the Chouinard Art Institute in California. Leaving the Chouinard Art Institute in 1956, he worked for the animation studio United Productions of America, painting in his spare time. Married for the first time, he moved to New York, continued painting, and also began making his own animated films, earning a living from animated films, commercial animation, and a weekly cartoon he drew for the *Village Voice.* In 1973, he first turned to book animation, entering an ongoing working partnership with children's writer Elizabeth Levy and providing illustrations as well as ideas for her children's books.

This collaboration continues, with Gerstein providing the illustrations for Levy's popular "Something Queer Is Going On" mystery series, as well as the "Fletcher Mystery" series, a spin-off of the "Queer" works. The books in the first series trace the adventures of best friends Gwen and Jill, while the books in the second series feature Jill's canine, Fletcher, as he solves comical mysteries in books intended for children just beginning chapter books. Reviewing *Something Queer at the Ballpark,* a contributor for *Publishers Weekly* claimed

Gerstein's "tongue-in-cheek asides . . . move the action right along." Judy Greenfield, reviewing *Something Queer in Rock 'n' Roll* for *School Library Journal,* praised Gerstein's "hilarious cartoon-like illustrations." Anne Connor, writing for *School Library Journal,* also found Gerstein's illustrations for *Something Queer in Outer Space* to be "full of humor," while Sharon R. Pearce, writing in the same periodical, praised Gerstein's artwork for the 1997 *Something Queer in the Wild West,* noting that his "detailed" gouache and black-line illustrations add "tidbits of information and a lighthearted tone."

Gerstein's first children's books were for other writers, but soon he began to see that picture books are an especially creative medium, and he began to write and illustrate his own stories, even as he continued to illustrate the work of others. Gerstein, who taught himself the technique called color separation, uses a wide range of media in his illustrations, which critics have generally praised for their ability to communicate, to show detail, and to capture the sense of movement.

Gerstein wrote his first book, *Arnold of the Ducks,* combining memories of his childhood with the boy-raised-by-wild-animals theme borrowed from stories such as *Tarzan* by Edgar Rice Burroughs and Rudyard Kipling's *The Jungle Book.* In Gerstein's whimsical fantasy, the young Arnold is plucked from a shallow pool by a pelican with bad eyesight who deposits him into a nest of recently hatched ducklings. Accepted by the mother duck, the human child is raised along with her offspring, first learning to swim and then to fly. Eventually, through a mishap with a flying kite, Arnold is returned to his natural parents via the family dog. Years after he has readjusted to being human again, the sound of familiar quacking passing overhead causes him to vainly try to follow the soaring ducks. But like Arnold's innocence, that part of his life is forever gone.

In *The Room,* a 1984 adaptation of his film by the same name, Gerstein provides a history of all the tenants who lived in a small New York apartment. The odd assortment of renters includes twin bank robbers, a magician, and a dentist who keeps a throng of ducks. While his theme concerns the passage of time, Gerstein's story focuses on the events of everyday life. Commenting on *The Room* in the *New York Times Book Review,* Martha Saxton praised "its richly detailed illustrations . . . full of vivid people and fascinating objects." Like a friend "whose good qualities emerge slowly," Saxton further remarked, "one wants to keep this book around for a long time."

Tales of Pan features the antics of Pan, the mischievous half-man/half-goat god of Greek mythology. During the course of this story, Gerstein introduces his readers to a number of Pan's relatives, whose adventures are presented along with the behavior of the prankish deity. Entertained by Gerstein's depiction of feats involving the supernatural changes of gods into various animals,

New York Times Book Review contributor Jacques d'Amboise wrote that Pan's death comes "too soon. I want to know more." Affirming, too, that *Tales of Pan* "succeeds in pleasing," the reviewer expressed disappointment in Gerstein's encouragement to merely "watch for Pan. . . . You might see him, close by and up to his old tricks"—and called instead for a sequel on the mythical being's return.

Gerstein's 1987 work *The Mountains of Tibet* was inspired by the ancient volumes collectively known as the *Tibetan Book of the Dead.* When recited properly, the *Book of the Dead* was meant to deliver the deceased's soul through a safe journey to the plane of death, thus avoiding the hazards associated with afterlife. Addressing the issue of souls returning to Earth to live another life, Gerstein's story chronicles a small boy's passage into manhood, where he learns the trade of woodcutting, and finally old age. After death, the elderly woodcutter is mysteriously given a choice between experiencing another life and going to heaven. The man opts for rebirth, hoping to see another part of the world, but ironically he is reborn in the same Tibetan valley of his former home. Discussing *The Mountains of Tibet* in the *New York Times Book Review,* John Bierhorst noted that "a charming surprise" is revealed at the story's end. The reviewer added that Gerstein's colorful pictures present some features of Tibetan art and make a classic picture book.

In 1993, Gerstein produced *The Story of May,* a fanciful tale about the girlish month and her efforts to meet her father, December. She travels throughout the year, meeting up with various relatives such as Uncle July and Aunt February, and learns from them how the months came to be ordered and why her mother, April, was separated from her father. "What could easily be coy becomes touching," a *Publishers Weekly* reviewer noted, due to May's quest to discover her roots. Ruth K. MacDonald, writing in *School Library Journal,* observed that "the story is both light and serious, given its mythic roots and the general silliness of the stereotypical characters." Gerstein's illustrations colorfully portray each distinct month; "each is a dazzling embodiment of the month for which he or she is named," *New York Times Book Review* critic Janet Maslin observed. Praising the "inspired playfulness" of the book's pictures and prose, the critic concluded that young readers will "embrace Mr. Gerstein's enchanting calendar and make it a permanent memory."

Throughout the 1990s, picture books continued to be Gerstein's primary endeavor. These books took their inspiration from many quarters, including myth and the Bible, as well as from contemporary events. His father's passing in 1991 led to *The Shadow of a Flying Bird: A Legend of the Kurdistani Jews,* a story dealing with the theme of death. In this tale, Moses, 120 years old, grouses when God tells him it is finally time for him to die. His prayers for continued life are barred from heaven, and the sun and moon turn a deaf ear to his pleas for more life so that he can finally reach the land of milk and honey. When God must finally take the soul of Moses himself, he sits down and weeps. John Crowley, writing in the *New York Times Book Review,* found Gerstein's book, illustrated with oil paintings, "both intriguing and visually compelling enough to last a long time." Crowley commended the fact that Gerstein's treatment of death "does not diminish the toughness of the matter." *Booklist*'s Ilene Cooper called the picture book "a moving fable," and dubbed his artwork "Chagall-like" and "full of magic." Hanna B. Zeiger lauded Gerstein's oil paintings in a *Horn Book* review, noting that they "convey the magnitude of the heavenly debate," and adding that "this Biblical legend leaves a powerful image of death as the inevitable partner of life."

Further biblical legends from the Old Testament are served up in *Jonah and the Two Great Fish* and *Noah and the Great Flood.* In a review of the first book, Janice M. DelNegro commented in *Bulletin of the Center for Children's Books* that "in simple prose Gerstein retells the story of the reluctant prophet, Jonah, enriching the Biblical account with details from Jewish legend." Patricia Pearl Dole also had praise for *Jonah* in a *School Library Journal* review, calling it "a delightful version" that will make "a lively and colorful read-aloud." Gerstein tackles the story of the Ark in *Noah and the Great Flood,* an "exuberant picture book," according to a reviewer for *Publishers Weekly.* Again combining Jewish legend with a Biblical tale, Gerstein comes up with a product that both "children and adults will marvel at," according to the same critic, who went on to laud the "bold energy" of the oil-painting illustrations. *Horn Book*'s Jennifer M. Brabander was pleased that Gerstein did not feel compelled to invest his *Noah* with "a trendy environmental or moralistic slant," instead treating the tale as the "blockbuster of a story" it is. DelNegro concluded in *Bulletin of the Center for Children's Books,* "Gerstein's gift for retelling Bible stories is evident," with his text and pictures providing "a cheerful reverence to this familiar tale."

With *Queen Esther the Morning Star,* Gerstein retells the Biblical story of Esther, the young Jewish girl who saved her people by becoming the Queen of Persia. "He has followed the Old Testament tale closely," noted Susan Scheps in *School Library Journal,* who further praised Gerstein's cartoon artwork which gives "a strong Persian flavor" to this "appealing" retelling. Writing in a starred *Publishers Weekly* review, a critic found the same title to be a "dynamic, evocatively-illustrated retelling" whose writing "proceeds at a masterly pace."

Turning to more everyday and contemporary concerns of young readers, Gerstein spins two tales around young Daisy: *Daisy's Garden* and *Bedtime, Everybody!* In collaboration with his wife Susan Yard Harris, Gerstein takes young readers through the growing season of a garden in the first tale, from early spring to late fall. On each page Daisy and her animal friends complete some

garden task, from tilling to planting to harvesting. The text is in simple rhyme accompanied with watercolor illustration. Jane Marino, reviewing the title in *School Library Journal,* called it "a soft, appealing book," while Leone McDermott, writing in *Booklist,* praised the "cheery rhymes and sweetly detailed drawings." In *Bedtime, Everybody!,* Daisy tries to get her stuffed animals ready for bed, but they are not cooperating. Only after Daisy herself nods off does her animal entourage get tired eyes. A critic for *Kirkus Reviews* dubbed this story "an amiable bedtime tale," though Cynthia K. Richey, reviewing the same title in *School Library Journal,* found it a "bland fantasy." Richey, however, thought that Gerstein's "stylized, cartoonlike characters are well realized."

The versatile Gerstein also serves up humor in several of his picture books, including *Stop Those Pants!* and *The Absolutely Awful Alphabet.* In the first title, Gerstein takes a "witty look at unexpected delays in getting dressed," according to *Booklist*'s Shelle Rosenfeld. Getting up in the morning, young Murray can not find his pants; they have gotten bored and gone into hiding in hopes of finding some adventure. Murray and the missing pants play hide and seek until they finally come to an interesting compromise. Rosenfeld also noted that the story demonstrates the virtues of "being brave, persistent, and sharp." A reviewer for *Publishers Weekly* called the same book a "surreal escapade," and Susan Pine, writing in *School Library Journal,* similarly referred to the book as "an entertaining look at morning mayhem." More chaos is served up in *The Absolutely Awful Alphabet,* in which each letter stands for some dreadful monster or demon. A contributor for *Kirkus Reviews* noted that "fiends and ghouls abound in a tongue-in-cheek take on standard alphabet fare."

Gerstein has also tackled longer works such as chapter books and beginning novels. Zachary discovers a magical world behind the couch in search of his stuffed purple pig, Wallace, in *Behind the Couch,* a "delight" and a "fast-paced romp," according to Christina Dorr writing in *School Library Journal.* A boy and a wily fox change places in *Fox Eyes,* a chapter book recounting an amazing month that Martin spends with his aunt, including the day he spends inside the body of Sharpnose the fox. "Gerstein's easy chapter book opens with whimsy," noted Janice M. DelNegro of this title in a *Bulletin of the Center for Children's Books* review, "but the matter-of-factness of the prose . . . anchors the fantasy." Similar praise came from a critic for *Kirkus Reviews* who concluded, "New chapter book readers will be won over by the episode's engaging cast and well-tuned sense of wonder."

Gerstein devoted both a novel and a picture book to the story of the so-called Savage of Aveyron, a boy found naked and abandoned in the woods of the south of France in 1800. With no language and barely any human social attributes, the boy had clearly been living wild with the animals. Under the tutelage of a doctor,

Gerstein's biography depicts Charles Ives, who composed music early in the twentieth century, basing his works on the natural sounds around him. (From What Charlie Heard, *written and illustrated by Gerstein.)*

the boy subsequently was force-fed civilization and re-named Victor. The boy, however, never really lost his wild ways, did not learn to speak, and his short life "was spent on the cusp of a society that could neither fully form nor accept him," according to Kathryn Harrison, writing in the *New York Times Book Review.* Gerstein produced both the picture book *The Wild Boy* and the novel *Victor: A Novel Based on the Life of the Savage of Aveyron* to explore this fascinating tale. A *Publishers Review* critic, in a review of the novel, noted that Gerstein gives an "arresting account" of the doctor's attempts at socializing the boy in this "compelling intellectual and social history." Roger Leslie, writing in *Booklist,* remarked on an "emotional remoteness" in the novel, but also commented that the book "remains intriguing thanks to well-researched details." Jennifer A. Fakolt, reviewing *Victor* in *School Library Journal,* found it to be a "dark, often complex novel for older readers that is well worth the time, effort, and thought." Reviewing *The Wild Boy,* a critic for *Publishers Weekly* noted that "nature and civilization collide in this thought-provoking picture book." The same re-

viewer also praised Gerstein's "smoothly-paced writing." DelNegro, writing in *Bulletin of the Center for Children's Books,* found the story "much simplified in text but beautifully evoked in watercolor illustrations." *Horn Book*'s Mary M. Burns also lauded the picture book, noting that it "has a haunting, wistful charm captured in a minimal space through a well-honed poetic text accompanied by delicately limned, impressionistic illustrations." And a critic for *Kirkus Reviews,* while writing about the picture book, also captured the essence of the novel's appeal. Noting that the boy never really gives up the wildness at his center, the reviewer concluded that was "a fact that will rivet children."

Gerstein has also turned his hand to biography in his picture books, as in the title *What Charlie Heard,* about the American composer Charles Ives, and *Sparrow Jack,* about English immigrant John Bardsley. Reviewing *What Charlie Heard,* a critic for *Publishers Weekly* felt that Gerstein "plies an artistic style as densely and consciously layered as one of Ives's compositions" in his profile. Gerstein provides details such as the sounds Ives might have heard as a child, his efforts in high school to compose, and the competing needs of his job as an insurance agent and his desire to create music in this "inspired picture-book biography," as the same critic typified it. A critic for *Kirkus Reviews* also lauded Gerstein's effort, calling his book an "unusual and joyful treatment of an unusual and joyful subject." John Peters, writing in *Booklist,* had further praise: "Not only a fine book about following one's own star, this is also a glimpse at a composer many children won't know about."

Sparrow Jack features the little-known story of John Bardsley, an Englishman who settled in Philadelphia during the middle of the nineteenth century. When the greenery in his adopted city was being devoured by an invasion of leaf-eating inchworms, Bardlsey devised a simple solution that, despite the skepticism of the other citizens in the city of brotherly love, proved to be effective. A lover of sparrows in his native country, Bardlsey returned to England and captured one thousand of these birds, transporting them back to America by ship and tending to them in his house throughout the winter. The next spring, as all the sparrows sought food for their newly-hatched offspring, the abundant supply of inchworms turned out to be an excellent source, thereby ridding the city of the pest. Describing the book as "an enjoyable and unusual bit of history," *School Library Journal* critic Steven Englefried called *Sparrow Jack* a "pleasing blend of history and legend." "In Gerstein's skilled hands," according to a critic in *Publishers Weekly,* "this odd historical tidbit . . . shapes up into a funny and engrossing tale."

Gerstein once told *SATA,* "For me, picture books are little theaters one holds in the hand and operates by turning the pages. I make my books for everyone, not just children. All of us are either children or have been children, so that childhood is an experience we all have in common." The author wants his books to communicate to readers on more than one level of understanding, "so to speak to everyone."

He continued, "Until I began writing, I had no idea of what I wanted to say, or what stories I might tell. I find writing to be a very exciting and mysterious process, a direct connection to the place where dreams are made. Before I began writing, I thought I had to know the story I was going to tell; now I write to discover the story, to let it tell itself. I write to find out what I have to say and what I'm made of; my nature and content. I'm always surprised."

Biographical and Critical Sources

BOOKS

Ward, Martha E., et al., *Authors of Books for Young People,* 3rd edition, Scarecrow Press (Metuchen, NJ), 1990.

PERIODICALS

Booklist, October 1, 1994, Ilene Cooper, review of *The Shadow of a Flying Bird: A Legend of the Kurdistani Jews,* p. 330; July 15, 1995, Leone McDermott, review of *Daisy's Garden,* pp. 1882-1883; June 1, 1996, Susan Dove Lempke, review of *Bedtime, Everybody!,* p. 1731; April 15, 1997, Kay Weisman, review of *Something Queer in the Wild West,* p. 1429; October 1, 1997, Susan Dove Lempke, review of *Jonah and the Two Great Fish,* p. 322; July, 1998, Shelle Rosenfeld, review of *Stop Those Pants!,* pp. 1885-1886; October 1, 1998, Roger Leslie, review of *Victor: A Novel Based on the Life of the Savage of Aveyron,* p. 324; January 1, 1999, GraceAnne A. DeCandido, review of *Noah and the Great Flood,* p. 881; April 1, 1999, Hazel Rochman, review of *The Absolutely Awful Alphabet,* p. 1416; December 15, 1999, Ellen Mandel, review of *Queen Esther the Morning Star,* p. 787; April 1, 2002, John Peters, review of *What Charlie Heard,* p. 1338; April 1, 2003, Michael Cart, review of *Sparrow Jack,* p. 1402.

Bulletin of the Center for Children's Books, November, 1985; July-August, 1986; November, 1986; January, 1988; April, 1993, pp. 248-49; November, 1997, Janice M. DelNegro, review of *Jonah and the Two Great Fish,* pp. 84-85; December, 1998, Janice M. DelNegro, review of *The Wild Boy,* p. 131; February, 1999, Janice M. DelNegro, review of *Noah and the Great Flood,* pp. 200-201; September, 2001, Janice M. DelNegro, review of *Fox Eyes,* p. 14.

Horn Book, March-April, 1995, Hanna B. Zeiger, review of *The Shadow of a Flying Bird,* pp. 205-206; November-December, 1998, Mary M. Burns, review of *Victor* and *The Wild Boy,* p. 714; March-April, 1999, Jennifer M. Brabander, review of *Noah and the Great Flood,* p. 222.

Horn Book Guide, spring, 1995, Hanna B. Zeiger, review of *The Shadow of a Flying Bird,* p. 94; fall, 1995, Amy Quigley, review of *Daisy's Garden,* p. 265.

Kirkus Reviews, February 1, 1996, review of *Bedtime, Everybody!,* p. 226; August 1, 1998, review of *The Wild Boy,* p. 1117; March 1, 1999, review of *The Absolutely Awful Alphabet,* p. 375; June 1, 2001, review of *Fox Eyes,* p. 801; January 15, 2002, review of *What Charlie Heard,* p. 104.

New York Times Book Review, April 10, 1983; June 10, 1984, Martha Saxton, "Children's Books: *The Room,* Written and Illustrated by Mordicai Gerstein," p. 35; August 10, 1986, Jacques d'Amboise, review of *Tales of Pan,* p. 25; November 8, 1987, John Bierhorst, "Going around Once—Or Twice," p. 44; June 6, 1993, Janet Maslin, review of *The Story of May,* p. 32; November 20, 1994, John Crowley, review of *The Shadow of a Flying Bird,* p. 30; November 15, 1998, Kathryn Harrison, "Who Is the Real Savage?," p. 50.

Publishers Weekly, July 6, 1984, review of *Something Queer at the Ballpark,* p. 65; April 12, 1993, review of *The Story of May,* p. 62; August 15, 1994, review of *The Shadow of a Flying Bird,* pp. 95-96; April 27, 1998, review of *Stop Those Pants!,* pp. 65-66; July 13, 1998, review of *Victor,* p. 79; July 13, 1998, review of *The Wild Boy,* p. 77; February 22, 1999, review of *Noah and the Great Flood,* p. 86; March 15, 1999, review of *The Absolutely Awful Alphabet,* p. 57; February 21, 2000, review of *Queen Esther the Morning Star,* p. 53; January 27, 2002, review of *What Charlie Heard,* p. 290; January 27, 2003, review of *Sparrow Jack,* p. 258; March 17, 2003, review of *Three Samurai Cats: A Story from Japan,* p. 76.

School Library Journal, January, 1988, Judy Greenfield, review of *Something Queer in Rock 'n' Roll,* p. 67; April, 1993, Ruth K. MacDonald, review of *The Story of May,* p. 96; February, 1994, Anne Connor, review of *Something Queer in Outer Space,* p. 88; September, 1994, pp. 207-208; April, 1995, Jane Marino, review of *Daisy's Garden,* pp. 101-102; June, 1996, Cynthia K. Richey, review of *Bedtime, Everybody!,* p. 100; July, 1996, Christina Dorr, review of *Behind the Couch,* p. 65; May, 1997, Sharon R. Pearce, review of *Something Queer in the Wild West,* p. 104; August, 1997, Patricia Pearl Dole, review of *Jonah and the Two Great Fish,* pp. 147-148; June, 1998, Susan Pine, review of *Stop Those Pants!,* p. 103; October, 1998, Jennifer A. Fakolt, review of *Victor,* p. 135; April, 1999, Torrie Hodgson, review of *Noah and the Great Flood,* p. 113; May, 1999, Robin L. Gibson, review of *The Absolutely Awful Alphabet,* p. 106; April, 2000, Susan Scheps, review of *Queen Esther the Morning Star,* p. 119; November, 2001, Blair Christolon, review of *Fox Eyes,* pp. 123-124; March, 2002, Lisa Mulvenna, review of *What Charlie Heard,* p. 214; June, 2003, Steven Englefried, review of *Sparrow Jack,* p. 99; June, 2003, Miriam Lang Budin, review of *Three Samurai Cats,* p. 129.

Time, December 14, 1987, p. 79.

Voice of Youth Advocates, February, 1999, Megan Isaac, review of *Victor,* p. 433.

*   *   *

GLEESON, Libby 1950-

Personal

Born September 19, 1950, in Young, New South Wales, Australia; daughter of Norman John (a teacher) and Gwynneth (a homemaker; maiden name, Whitten) Gleeson; married Euan Tovey (a scientist); children: Amelia, Josephine, Jessica. *Education:* University of Sydney, B.A., 1973; New South Wales Department of Education, teaching certification, 1975. *Hobbies and other interests:* Family, reading, swimming, tennis, community arts.

Addresses

Home—11 Oxford St., Petersham, New South Wales 2049, Australia. *Agent*—Curtis Brown, P.O. Box 19, Paddington, New South Wales 2021, Australia.

Career

Instructor in secondary school and university, 1974-86; visiting lecturer at various universities, 1985—; full-time writer, 1989—. Has also been a consultant for

teaching English as a second language, 1986-90. Authors' representative on Public Lending Right Committee of Australia. Chair of judging committee, New South Wales Premier's Literary Award, 2003.

Member

Australian Society of Authors (chair, 1999-2001).

Awards, Honors

Angus & Robertson Award for Writers for Young Readers, 1984, Honor Book, Children's Book Council of Australia, 1985, shortlisted for New South Wales Premier's Award, 1985, South Australia Premier's Award, 1985, and Guardian Newspaper's Award for Children, all for *Eleanor, Elizabeth;* Honor Book, Australian Children's Book of the Year, 1988, and shortlisted for Victorian Premier's Award, 1988, both for *I Am Susannah;* Children's Literature Peace Prize, 1991, and International Board on Books for Young People (IBBY) Award, 1992, both for *Dodger;* Prime Minister's Multicultural Award, 1991, for *Big Dog;* Honor Book, CBC Picture Book of the Year, 1993, for *Where's Mum?;* shortlisted for Children's Book of the Year from Children's Book Council of Australia, 1994, for *Love Me, Love Me Not;* Lady Cutler Award for services to children's literature, 1997; Book of the Year citation from Children's Book Council of Australia, 1997, for *Hannah Plus One;* shortlisted for Children's Book of the Year from Children's Book Council of Australia, 1998, for *Queen of the Universe;* Honor Book citation from Children's Book Council of Australia, and shortlisted for New South Wales Premier's Literary Award, both 2000, both for *Hannah and the Tomorrow Room;* Bologna Ragazzi Award in fiction (infants category), and shortlisted for Children's Book of the Year from Children's Book Council of Australia, both 2000, both for *The Great Bear;* Picture Book of the Year award from Children's Book Council of Australia, 2002, for *An Ordinary Day;* Young Australian Readers Award, 2002, for *Dear Writer.*

Writings

FICTION

Eleanor, Elizabeth, Angus & Robertson (Sydney, Australia), 1984, Holiday House (New York, NY), 1990.

I Am Susannah, Angus & Robertson (Sydney, Australia), 1987, Holiday House (New York, NY), 1989.

One Sunday, illustrated by John Winch, Angus & Robertson (Sydney, Australia), 1988.

Big Dog, illustrated by Armin Greder, Ashton Scholastic (Sydney, Australia), 1991, published as *The Great Big Scary Dog,* Tambourine Books (New York, NY), 1994.

Dodger, Turton & Chambers, 1991, Puffin (New York, NY), 1996.

Hurry Up!, illustrated by Mitch Vane, SRA School Group (Santa Rosa, CA), 1992.

Uncle David, illustrated by Armin Greder, Ashton Scholastic (Sydney, Australia), 1991, Tambourine (New York, NY), 1993.

Where's Mum?, illustrated by Craig Smith, Omnibus Books (Norwood, South Australia), 1993, published as *Where's Mom?,* Scholastic (New York, NY), 1996.

Mum Goes to Work, illustrated by Penny Azar, Ashton Scholastic (Sydney, Australia), 1992, published as *Mom Goes to Work,* Scholastic (New York, NY), 1995.

Love Me, Love Me Not, Viking (New York, NY), 1993.

Sleeptime, Ashton Scholastic, 1993.

Walking to School, illustrated by Linda McClelland, SRA School Group (Santa Rosa, CA), 1994.

Skating on Sand, illustrated by Ann James, Viking (Sydney, Australia), 1994.

The Princess and the Perfect Dish, illustrated by Armin Greder, Ashton Scholastic (Sydney, Australia), 1995.

Hannah Plus One, illustrated by Ann James, Puffin (Sydney, Australia), 1996.

Refuge, Puffin (Ringwood, Victoria, Australia), 1998.

Queen of the Universe, illustrated by David Cox, Omnibus Books (Norwood, South Australia), 1998.

Hannah and the Tomorrow Room, illustrated by Ann James, Puffin (Sydney, Australia), 1999.

The Great Bear, illustrated by Armin Greder, Scholastic (Sydney, Australia), 1999.

Dear Writer, illustrated by David Cox, Puffin (Sydney, Australia), 2000.

An Ordinary Day, illustrated by Armin Greder, Scholastic (Sydney, Australia), 2001.

The Rum Rebellion: The Diary of David Bellamy ("My Story" series), Scholastic (Sydney, Australia), 2001.

Shutting the Chooks In, illustrated by Ann James, Scholastic (Sydney, Australia), 2003.

Cuddle Time, illustrated by Julie Vivas, Walker Books, 2003.

CONTRIBUTOR TO ANTHOLOGIES

Bizarre, Omnibus Books (Norwood, South Australia), 1989.

Stay Loose Mother Goose, Omnibus Books (Norwood, South Australia), 1990.

The Blue Dress, Heinemann (London, England), 1991.

Landmarks, Turton & Chambers, 1991.

Goodbye and Hello, Viking (New York, NY), 1992.

Top Drawer, Phoenix, 1992.

Family, Heinemann (London, England), 1994.

Out of the Box: Red Book, Phoenix, 1994.

The Phone Book, Random House (New York, NY), 1995.

The Champion and Other Stories, Phoenix, 1996.

Personal Best, Mammoth, 1996.

Blasters: Animal Tales, Heinemann (London, England), 1997.

Storykeepers, Duffy & Snellgrove, 2001.

OTHER

The Libby Gleeson Video, Insight Profile, 1995.

Writing Hannah: On Writing for Children (nonfiction), Hale & Ironmonger, 1999.

Making Picture Books (nonfiction), Scholastic (Sydney, Australia), 2003.

Also author of numerous short stories, including "The Boy Who Wouldn't Get Out of Bed," "Bedtime Story," "Farewell," "In the Swim," and "Her Room." Gleeson's works have been translated into Swedish, Dutch, German, Korean, and Italian.

Sidelights

Award-winning Australian children's author Libby Gleeson is equally at home writing picture books for young children and realistic novels for older readers. The author draws upon her own imagination, her experiences raising three daughters, and her childhood to craft stories about family, friendship, and facing adversity. Although all of her books are set in Australia, their appeal is universal, and they have been translated into several foreign languages. *Horn Book* contributor Karen Jameyson cited Gleeson for "an impressive array" of children's books in which "the influences of family swoop through the pages."

Gleeson began her first novel, *Eleanor, Elizabeth,* while living in England. She based the work on aspects of her own childhood in Western New South Wales, Australia. The story centers around a young girl named Eleanor who has just moved to a new town. In the course of the move, Eleanor discovers her grandmother's diary, written in 1895 when her grandmother was twelve. The diary helps Eleanor come to terms with her new home, and, as Connie Tyrrell Burns wrote in *School Library Journal,* "to appreciate her own concerns in the light of her grandmother's." The diary also helps save the lives of Eleanor, her brother, and a friend when they escape from a raging bushfire by finding her grandmother's secret cave.

In *I Am Susannah,* it is the main character's best friend who moves away, leaving Susannah to deal with her self-involved mother, making new friends, and her first encounter with adolescent kissing games. At the same time, a mysterious woman with a supposedly tragic past, known as the "Blue Lady," moves into her best friend's old house. When Susannah, an aspiring artist, spies the Blue Lady's artistic talents, the two begin a friendship of their own. Nancy Vasilakis praised *I Am Susannah* in *Horn Book* for its "excellent characterizations and an exploration of pertinent contemporary themes."

In 1991, Gleeson published two works of very different natures, *The Great Big Scary Dog* and *Dodger.* The first, called an "unusual and engaging book" by *School Library Journal* reviewer Lisa Dennis, moved Gleeson's focus from adolescent angst to the typical fears of a preschooler. *The Great Big Scary Dog* is the story of how three young children, using their imaginations and a very colorful costume, help a little girl overcome her fear of a neighborhood dog. *Horn Book* correspondent Ann A. Flowers praised *The Great Big Scary Dog* for portraying "a common childhood trauma brought to a satisfying resolution." Because that resolution involves a Chinese friend and a New Year dragon, the book won the Prime Minister's Multicultural Award.

Dodger returns to themes of adolescent anxieties and adjustments. Mick Jamieson, the central character, is a troubled student of thirteen. Since his mother's recent death, Mick has had to move from a small Australian country town to suburban Campbelltown to live with his grandmother. His father, a truck driver, is away all the time, although Mick is constantly hoping for his return. *Dodger* is also the story of Penny, a first-year teacher who sees enough in Mick to cast him as the Artful Dodger in the school production of *Oliver,* despite the resistance of several other teachers. In a review for *Magpies,* Stephanie Owen Reeder noted the sensitive handling of the relationship between the two characters, as well as Gleeson's portrayal of "young adolescents dealing with life in believable settings, and in a way which captures the emotions of the reader."

Following *Dodger,* Gleeson returned to books for younger children, including *Uncle David,* about a young child's tendency to exaggerate, *Mum Goes to Work,* which compares mothers' work with that of their children's in the day-care center, and *Great Bear,* an award-winning fable about the creation of Ursa Major as a constellation. Both *Uncle David* and *Great Bear* are illustrated by Armin Greder, who has worked closely with Gleeson for more than a decade. As a team, Geeson and Greder won the prestigious Bologna Ragazzi Award for the fanciful story and drawings that comprise *Great Bear.*

Gleeson's three children have had considerable influence on her work. "I am constantly observing them and being reminded of my own experiences as a child," she told *SATA.* "I try to bring to the reader the feelings of those real experiences so that they can identify with the characters—whether they be kids from the bush as in *Eleanor, Elizabeth,* the city as in *I Am Susannah,* or suburbia as in *Dodger.*" Now that her daughters have grown, the author also finds inspiration from children she meets when she visits schools to talk about her writing. Everything Gleeson writes, however, is filtered through her imagination and her wider experience—as Jameyson put it in *Horn Book,* "like all taking from reality it has to be fictionalized." Jameyson credited Gleeson for creating books that "have sprung from a rich, wonderful, and typically turbulent family life. . . . And the dialogue is so authentic that you'd swear you had your ear to a cup on the wall instead of your eyes on a page."

Biographical and Critical Sources

PERIODICALS

Booklist, April 1, 1994, Hazel Rochman, review of *The Great Big Scary Dog,* p. 1458.
Horn Book, September, 1989, Nancy Vasilakis, review of *I Am Susannah,* pp. 628-629; April, 1991, p. 65; July-August, 1993, review of *Uncle David,* pp. 443, 496; September-October, 1994, Ann A. Flowers, review of *The Great Big Scary Dog,* p. 576; March-April, 1997, Karen Jameyson, "Typical Turbulence: Writing and Raising a Family," p. 225.
Magpies, March, 1991, Stephanie Owen Reeder, review of *Dodger,* p. 4.
Publishers Weekly, April 11, 1994, review of *The Great Big Scary Dog,* p. 63.
School Library Journal, June, 1989, p. 108; June, 1990, Connie Tyrrell Burns, review of *Eleanor, Elizabeth,* pp. 121-122; September, 1993, p. 208; May, 1994, Lisa Dennis, review of *The Great Big Scary Dog,* p. 94.
Voice of Youth Advocates, October, 1989, p. 212; August, 1990, p. 160.

ONLINE

Libby Gleeson Home Page, http://www.libbygleeson.com/ (May 5, 2003).

Autobiography Feature

Libby Gleeson

I was born in 1950 in Young, a small country town, in New South Wales, Australia. It's a farming community, famous for its stone fruit, but I must admit I remember it only from the black-and-white photos in my parents' collection. We left when I was four years old. My father was a high school teacher, and promotion came from regularly moving. From Young, we went to another small town on the new South Wales Tableland,

Libby Gleeson

Glen Innes. This one I do remember, because we stayed there for six years. I started school, along with my two older sisters and one younger brother. Later another sister and brother were born. We lived in a new area of town in a street with lots of children. We had the freedom to roam around, playing wild games in the semi-cleared bushland and coming back home for meals and to fall asleep.

This move brought us close to my mother's family. Her grandparents, of Irish stock, were early settlers in a region south of Glen Innes, and the farm they owned was now worked by her brothers. We often visited them and her mother who had moved from the farm into the town of Quirindi. There, over endless cups of tea, my mother, my aunts, and my grandmother would talk. I observed and listened intently to the dramatic stories of the life in the mid- to late-nineteenth and early-twentieth centuries. I was fascinated and moved by tales of isolation and of physical hardship and of the fragility of life. In particular stories of the children on isolated farms being educated by itinerant teachers in "schoolrooms" on the farm stuck in my mind.

What also stuck in my mind from a very early age was the notion that education was the most valuable inheritance my parents could give me. My mother pressed upon her daughters the need for training and career. She often said that she had married very young, with nothing to fall back on if anything ever happened to our father. She is a resourceful woman, and I'm sure she would have provided for us had the need arisen, but her words impressed me deeply and, I believe, prepared me well for the women's movement which became a political force in my early adulthood.

Glen Innes in the 1950s did not have a public library, and one of the men's clubs approached my fa-

ther, as the senior English teacher in the town, and invited him to set up a small library for children. Of course he accepted and became the buyer and the cataloguer of the collection of children's books that resulted. We got to read the books before anyone else in town, and we even got to paint the little black squares on the spines and copy the relevant Dewey number on in white ink. My two elder sisters were allowed to work behind the counter, issuing the books, but I was too young and stayed curled up on the floor, reading.

When I was ten, we were on the move again. This time we went west, out onto the plains, the hot, dry wheat belt town of Dubbo. Its name means "red earth" in the local Aboriginal language, and in the early months of dust storms and drought, we came to know why the name had been chosen. Some members of my family remain there to this day, and so this is the town I think of as the most memorable and formative in my own thinking. At the time I saw the move as an adventure, but years later when I began writing fiction, it was to this move that my mind turned. In my first novel, *Eleanor, Elizabeth*, the family is journeying to their new home in the west of the state. They will be living on a farm, loosely based on the farms in the area where I grew up. The children in the back of the car are playing I Spy . . .

> B for burn and B for blister. B for Brunswick Heads. But not this time. No wet swimmers, fish and chips for tea. No home, back up the mountains, past Grafton and Tenterfield, high in the crisp, cool air. Not this time.
>
> West. Out West. You'll burn up out West. It's a hundred in the shade. Earth's red, rivers are slow. Flat as a board. B for board. Go West young man. Great-great-grandfather Walters had. Drove sheep from Bathurst. B for Bathurst. Three weeks on the road. Three hours in the car. So far.

(Extract from *Eleanor, Elizabeth,* Chapter 1)

Television had arrived, but our family chose not to buy one, and instead, evenings were spent in conversation or reading. We haunted the library—this new town was large enough for a good public library—and I regularly brought home the maximum number of books allowed, only to return three or four days later to repeat the process. I read whatever books I could get my hands on. Although I enjoyed fairy tales and gothic fantasy, it was realistic fiction that satisfied me most. The works of L. M. Montgomery and the school stories of British publishing transported me from my hot, dry, slow country existence to other worlds. I discovered snow, boarding school, class structures, and European history. Like many of my, and former, generations, I thought that life was something that happened and was written about in the northern hemisphere.

I dreamt of escape. I did well at school, studying hard, writing bad poetry, and fantasizing about traveling the world. There was an assumption that when high

The author with her siblings, 1957. Left to right: Jenny, Jill, Libby, John, Margaret

school ended, I would leave, as my sisters had done. There were few job opportunities in the town and no form of higher education. I set my sights on the University of Sydney, and in 1969 I left home.

At this stage I was unsure of my future career. I knew I wanted to study history and literature, but the period beyond University was a blank space. It was only during my last two years studying that I decided that teaching was a profession that I admired and wanted to be part of.

It was an exhilarating time to be studying at the University. There was ferment on the streets in opposition to the Vietnam War. There was ferment in the University about traditional courses and teaching and methods of assessment. And there was the women's movement. I became involved in all of these.

One course that influenced me greatly was a course in children's literature that I studied during my final year. The young lecturer was a passionate believer in introducing the writers of our own country. Many of his students were like me—avid readers in our childhood, but raised on a reading diet of largely British and American books. Stories were not about children like us or places that we knew. I had never read a story set in contemporary Sydney or in a regional area, nor had I read a historical novel about the settlement of my own country. Yet many books I had read had transported me to the American War of Independence or the civil war in Britain or into contemporary United States and British environments.

At the time I was determined that when I began to work in a school, I would teach my students using whatever Australian titles I could find. I didn't realize that I was also nurturing ideas of creating those very works myself.

I taught English and history for two years in a small town south of Sydney. I really loved teaching and became very involved with my students in performing plays, coaching sporting teams, and becoming part of the community. But I was also young and wanting to travel. I was unattached, and many of my friends from University days had gone traveling—usually to London. In 1976 I followed them. I wanted to experience the world. I wanted to get a job in a country where English was not the language and immerse myself in another culture, and I planned to stay away for at least two years.

After traveling in Western Europe for the summer, I got a job teaching English in a northern Italian industrial town near Milan. Here in Crema I taught school students and adults. I spoke no Italian, and for the first three months, when Italian sounded like a jumble of sounds, I felt very lonely. Like many travelers, I consoled myself by keeping a diary. I also found myself thinking more and more about writing fiction. I did experiment with writing about the life I was leading, but it was too close and I think too difficult. It was self-indulgent. Instead I found myself writing about the time when I had last moved as a child, the time when I was ten.

At first I thought I wanted to write short stories, and one focused on the first day at a new school for a girl in fourth class. There were images of her standing alone on the verandah watching all the other students playing with their friends. It wasn't long before this form failed to satisfy me. I wanted to know what happened before and after that moment. I knew this idea had the making of a novel. Up from my unconscious mind came so many ideas and connections between other ideas that I had been thinking about for some time. I wanted to write about a strong young girl, one who didn't fall back on the boy characters to solve her problems or give approval. Research I had read in my final year at University had detailed the paucity of strong roles for girls in much of our children's fiction; she was to be a kid like I believed I had been—independent and resourceful.

Those family stories came back to me, and I resolved to draw a connection between this young girl and her grandmother, now dead, but a woman who had had her own dilemmas as she had grown up in her isolated, country world. I wasn't confident that I could handle a time-slip novel, so I settled for a diary that the grandmother has written and which the young girl finds and reads. The name Eleanor popped into my head—I had no idea why, and so I named my young girl Eleanor and called her grandmother Elizabeth. I decided that young Eleanor would use the old family schoolhouse as her private space and retreat, and it would be there that she would find the diary.

Years later when asked about my early reading, I recalled the book *A Girl of the Limberlost* by Gene Stratton Porter. I loved that story of the young girl who had defied her mother and struggled to get, through her own efforts, the education that she so passionately wanted. Written at the turn of the nineteenth century, the book was unlike any other I had read in its intensity, its commitment to conservation, and its honesty about family relationships. The young girl's name was Elnora.

By the time many of these ideas had settled, I had finished my contract in Italy, and I had decided to return to London. This was largely to immerse myself in my own language. My Italian had progressed to the point where I was finding it felt a little strange to be speaking one language in the day and writing in another at night.

Back in London a number of fortunate events happened. First, I decided to maintain the Italian that I had learnt and so went along to an adult education institution to enroll in a weekly conversation class. I saw a sign advertising a "writers' workshop." I had never heard of a writers' workshop, had no idea what it meant, but on the spur of the moment decided that it was for me. Then began an intensive period of sharing my work with the group, taking on board criticism, and then rewriting. I learnt so much about the process of writing—about how stories work, about the need for detail to create authentic characters, about writing dialogue, about how to be self-critical. . . . The list goes on. For two years I attended that group, and my work developed from an over-written, sentimental collection of chapters in an exercise book to a publishable manuscript.

Second, I met my husband. Like me, Euan was a traveler from the other side of the world. He comes from the South Island of New Zealand, where his family, originally from Scotland and Cornwall, settled three generations ago. He is a scientist, and after twelve months traveling was about to return home. Together we decided to stay a little longer—me to finish the book, and he to work with a leading laboratory in allergic disease research. We lived in a household of other young travelers from France, Italy, and Iran. Some of our housemates were filmmakers, and the environment was full of creative energy. Someone always had an idea for a film or a production, and there were visitors and friends dropping in from all over the world. By 1980 Euan and I decided to return to Australia. I had finished my novel, and he had decided to finish his Ph. D., and that meant reenrolling at the University of Sydney. We took our time holidaying in Italy and making a leisurely trip home through Pakistan and India, arriving in time for Christmas.

I was pregnant with my first child by the time I got around to submitting the novel. I read all the information in writers' journals about how one needs to prepare

The author (seated in chair) celebrating her twenty-first birthday with her siblings, 1971

a list of publishers and not get despondent until you have been rejected by every one. The first publisher I sent it to engaged me for some time in conversations about making some changes to the work. Finally it was rejected, largely on the grounds that it was too complex a novel for its intended readership. This was because of the different types of text—straightforward narrative, nineteenth-century diary, interior monologue, as well as the assertive nature of the main character (this was 1981), and a number of language issues. Into the bottom drawer went the manuscript, and I concentrated on mothering. Some months later Euan badgered me into taking it out and submitting it to the oldest publisher in Australia, Angus and Robertson. The phone rang one Saturday night. He and I were babysitting the child of some friends, and this child and our own toddler daughter, Amy, were squabbling in the playpen. The voice on the end of the phone told me that she was the commissioning editor of the publishing house, she had just finished my book and would I come in and sign a contract on Monday. Euan and I opened a bottle of champagne, climbed into the playpen with the children, and toasted success. *Eleanor, Elizabeth* won the Angus and Robertson award for new writing for young people and went on to be short-listed for a number of other awards. It was an Honour book in the Children's Book Council of Australia Awards, 1985.

The rest of that decade was a mixture of working and writing and having babies. I was working at the University of New South Wales training teachers in TESOL: the Teaching of English as a Second Language. I had an idea for my second novel, and I applied to the Australia Council for a fellowship, which would give me enough money so that I could reduce my paid work hours. I was unsuccessful the first time I applied, but the following year brought success. And following Amy in 1982 came Josephine in 1985 and Jessica in 1987.

Libby and Euan, Hampstead Heath, London, 1979

We were living in Newtown, the heart of the inner city in a tiny old workers' cottage, which we renovated. One block away was the St. Stephen's Church and graveyard, one of the oldest in Sydney. Its peace and quiet contrasted with the noise and chaos of the busy shopping strip two blocks away, and I found I used to take the children there to sit under the trees and to play on the headstones. Ideas circulated. I wasn't finished with my thoughts of strong independent girls and of connecting relationships across generations. I imagined the life of a city child whose best friend leaves and who frequents the graveyard for its peace and solitude. There she meets an old woman, and that woman's life becomes an inspiration to her to travel and to resist convention. I was confident that my idea was strong, but when I began to write, I found I could not capture the voice of the old woman. Every time I tried to write her, I felt bored, and if I felt that way, why should not a reader feel the same way? After many months of trying, I discovered my solution. I removed the old woman's voice from the text until the last chapters. Instead the reader, and indeed the main character, learns about her by observation and from the gossip of other women in the community. Not only did this solve my problem, it gave me a whole new level for the story: truth and fiction and the role of hearsay.

When that novel was finished and successfully published, I faced a decision time in my life. I was now gaining some success as a writer, and I was the busy mother of three young children. I was also successful in my work at the University and faced with pressure to gain further qualifications and seek promotion. Should I enroll for a Ph.D. in linguistics or in education? Or should I quit my day job and write? Writing won. I have never regretted that decision. For a couple of years I consulted back in my old job, but by 1991 I cut loose. Now I had to earn my share of family income solely from writing and associated activities. And there were other activities. From the time of my first publication, I was receiving invitations to visit schools and universities to talk about my work and to run writing workshops. I enjoyed this very much as a way of keeping in touch with the readership and also as a way to use the skills I had developed as a teacher.

I wanted to grow as a writer and try different styles or genres. The first came with the decision to write the third novel in the voice of a young boy. I was keen that I wasn't typecast as always writing in the story of a twelve-year-old girl, and so I wrote a novel based on events that happened during my secondary school teaching years. The book, *Dodger*, is strongly fictionalized and tells the story of Penny, a first-year-out teacher, and Mick, a boy of thirteen whom she casts as the Artful Dodger in the school's production of *Oliver*. Because of Mick's behaviour, other teachers tell Penny that she is being foolish, and that he will only let her and the show down. She, however, is determined to give Mick this opportunity, to challenge him to live up to her expectations. Of course, not everything runs smoothly, and through the straight narrative text and Penny's letters to one of her friends, we follow the year to the final performance. It was a challenge to get inside the head of a young boy, and it was also an opportunity to express my own ideas of the role of drama and activities outside the classroom in education.

The next experiment was in writing short stories. A number of teachers and librarians had asked me why I didn't write love stories when that was what so many of their students wanted to read. I had written one story, about the kissing games at a young teen party and the outcome the next day, and I decided to build on the characters in that work. In all there are ten characters and nine stories. Each story, a love story, is told through the eyes of one of the characters except for the last story, which is told by two young people. Each story is focused on a different stage of love—friendship and acceptance, infatuation, being the object of a school friend's crush, falling for your best friend, until the final story is of the young couple in the class who are actually involved in their first relationship. I saw the book, titled *Love Me, Love Me Not*, as a collection of stories, but one of the reviewers said that for her it read as a novel with a constantly evolving and changing main character.

While my children were babies and until they were all independent readers at school, their father and I were constantly at the local library with them, borrowing the beautiful picture books that had begun to appear from the mid-1970s. I had known nothing of these books before, as in my own childhood there was not the technology for the four-colour printing. We had illustrated stories—most often in black and white—but the new printing techniques allowed for a much richer colour in the books.

I had always thought of myself as a novelist, but suddenly I was reading many of these much shorter works every day. The first idea I had for a work seemed ridiculously simple. One morning I waved my husband and our daughter off to take a load of rubbish to the city dump. We had been renovating the house, and they had a truckload of builder's rubble. What would happen, I thought, if Amy finds objects at the dump that she likes and wants to bring home to play with? And what if Euan lets her do this, and they come home with as much junk as they have thrown away? I decided to write the story as a simple account of the father's actions and to leave the behaviour of the daughter to the illustrator. That way the illustrations become integral to the reading of the book. Without the contribution about the child, there is no story.

My experience with this book, *One Sunday*, was absolutely formative in my understanding of the process of collaboration between writer and illustrator. I imagined the way the pages would look and I told the illustrator. I wanted the truck in the middle of the page and the two characters on either side respectively throwing away or gathering up the objects. The illustrator, John Winch, was most tolerant. He pointed out that a sequence of pages looking exactly the same would be boring in the extreme. I pulled back and, in the process, discovered that an illustrator is a creative artist who must be given space to respond to the text. He or she will have ideas that you have never imagined. I do not think well in visual terms, but all the illustrators I have worked with do, and I have learnt so much about making picture books from them.

More ideas for picture books followed. I call this time in my creative life my *Mum period,* because I seemed forever to be around little children, at home or in play centres or in their kindergarten classes. I loved it. I was so humbled by how beautiful, creative, and imaginative they were and what fun one could have with them. Their growing and learning was astounding. I was also exhausted by them. Books like *Where's Mum?, Mum Goes to Work, Big Dog, Uncle David,* and *Sleeptime* grew straight from moments at home.

The feminist ideas that permeate the early novels were instrumental in writing *Mum Goes to Work.* At the time my eldest daughter was four and in her final year of child care prior to going to school. In a discussion about work, her teacher discovered that the children had an idea of their fathers' occupations, but all spoke of their mothers as having no jobs outside the home. All the mothers were in full-time work or study. I surveyed the mothers and then wrote the text, which follows through the day looking at the activities that the children are doing in care and the mothers are doing at work.

The same ideas are present in another picture book written when my daughters were just a little older. In the mid-1990s as the mother of growing daughters, I was very aware of anorexia. Girls were surrounded by images of ultraslim young women, and I resolved to subvert this with my fairy tale *The Princess and the Perfect Dish.* I wanted a story that followed the conventions and used the language and motifs of a tradi-

The author at the time of the publication of her first novel, **Eleanor, Elizabeth,** *1984*

tional tale, but which celebrated a big, fat, beautiful woman. I had a wonderful time immersing myself in the fairy tales of Western culture, discovering that there were many where princesses and queens set tasks for their suitors. The task I chose as the pivotal force in the story is that of making for the heroine the perfect dish.

> "If I am to marry," the Princess said, "then it will be to someone I choose.
>
> "I will marry the one who is able to prepare for me the most wonderful, mouthwatering, tastetempting dishes imaginable. The one whose cooking is absolutely irresistible. He will be the one with whom I can live happily ever after."
>
> So it was announced.
>
> (Extract from *The Princess and the Perfect Dish*)

Perhaps the excellent cooking of my own partner, Euan, influenced the ideas that found their way into this work!

By this stage I was working very closely with the Swiss-Australian illustrator Armin Greder. His work on *The Princess and the Perfect Dish* showed a strong European sensibility that has persisted as we continue to make books together.

In working on that book, I was not only interested in the ideas it contained but in all aspects of creating the story. The language and the structure of the story are very different from a modern picture book text. From my very first novel, I have been deeply interested in the ways that a writer manipulates language and form to achieve a certain result. Often words or phrases pop into our heads, and we write intuitively, but the craft of writing comes in knowing what we want to get from a passage of text and then shaping it to achieve that end. Of course there are often results from our work that we haven't predicted. All readers bring their own lives and experiences to what they read, and we have no control over that. Sometimes readers point out something in a story that I was unaware of, but in general, I write and rewrite until I feel confident that I have done my utmost to make the story the best possible piece that I can.

Just as the lives of my young children brought me to picture books, so too did they bring me to novels for young readers. Although my girls were accomplished, independent readers quite early in their school careers, I was still very aware of what they were reading and curious to know the works and their authors. Slapstick comedy and pseudo horror works dominated the shelves of the bookshops, but I thought there could be a place for serious works that focused on a child of six or seven. Serious but not earnest: there would be no place for moralizing or preaching.

It was Easter 1990 when the thoughts crystallized for me. We were on a family holiday, camping in a beachside national park three hours south of Sydney. The day before our departure from home, Josephine, aged six, had announced that she wanted to take her roller skates and learn to skate over the holiday period. I had said no, because there was no place either to learn or to practise skating. Needless to say, Jo hid the skates in her sleeping bag and produced them on the first morning. The skates were put on and did not come off except to swim for the whole ten days. Despite a rocky and stumbling beginning, Jo learnt to skate, and I was very proud of her initiative and her determination. On the way home from that holiday, as we were driving up a mountain pass, reflecting on the past weeks, her Dad said to her, "Did you enjoy skating on sand?" I knew it was a title. Within a week I had a notebook filling with ideas of all the possible things that could happen on a holiday such as ours. I wrote down all I could remember of our time there but also every memory from every beach or camping holiday I could dredge up from my own past.

In shaping *Skating on Sand*, I wanted to vary the novel form that I had used to date. I decided to write in the present tense. I find that brings immediacy to the work that suggests confidences being shared. I thought of writing in the first person, but after some experimenting decided against it. Instead, I began the book with a one-page piece in the first person and then moved into a third person narrative, albeit one where the central character, Hannah, is always the focus. The book begins:

We're going camping.

We're going camping in the bush by the sea.

Mum says we can go bushwalking and fishing and swimming in the sea all by ourselves. Dad says there will be kangaroos that eat out of your hands and possums and rosellas and kookaburras that come down from the trees and aren't even scared of you.

Lena and Sue can't wait. They're busting to go. They reckon they can remember how we used to go camping when I was a baby but that was six years ago and I think they're just making it up.

"You wouldn't know, Hannah," Sue says. "You weren't even one. You used to let your nappy fall off and you crawled round in the dirt eating leaves and snails."

Lena says I can't take my skates.

(Extract from *Skating on Sand*, prologue)

I think the book captures some of the feeling of that holiday, which was its inspiration, even though it is not a straightforward account of those days. One scene in the book is directly taken. While on holiday I heard a group of children playing a game where each one spells his or her name backwards, and that is what they are called throughout the game. I decided to use that game, with my central character having a name which is a palindrome, a name spelt the same backwards as forwards: Hannah.

The author with her family, 1990. Clockwise from top left: Libby, husband Euan, daughters Josephine, Jessica, and Amy

It is the dynamics of families that fascinate me, and so in *Skating on Sand* I am interested not only in Hannah's determination to skate, but also in the way her life is affected by her relationships with her sisters and her parents. Ours is a three-child family, and I watch my children, even now in late adolescence, constantly shifting allegiance and creating and resolving conflict along the way. Two against one is the constant pattern, and I decided to exaggerate the problem by giving Hannah twin sisters a few years older than she is. Mum and Dad are practical and resourceful and frequently stand back to force their offspring to search out solutions to resolve whatever is the day's conflict.

Whenever I finished an earlier work, a long novel, I was determined never to write that character again. With Hannah, it was different. The novel was shorter, and I felt there was a lot about her to explore and discover. So soon after *Skating on Sand* was published, I began notes on what other stories might be possible. I decided on the imminent birth of another child. This is an extremely important and difficult experience for small children, and one where they find their fears almost impossible to articulate. I imagined that Hannah might fear the birth of yet more twins, and so she would remain the odd one out, stuck in a family with twins older and twins younger than she is. Like many young children, Hannah has an imaginary friend, Megan, in whom she confides and to whom she resorts when the circumstances she is dealing with become too difficult. But imaginary friends belong in the world of home, and Hannah is now at school. When one of her classmates discovers Megan's existence, Hannah's response leads her into serious trouble.

When this second novel, *Hannah Plus One*, was finished, I still felt the need to say more. That novel had looked at birth and its effects on Hannah and on her family. I reasoned that the next volume should look at death and the way in which a young child responds. The writing of the third Hannah novel coincided with an invitation from a publisher to write a book about the process of writing fiction for young people. I have conducted a course for aspiring children's writers at the University of Sydney, for a number of years and there was an assumption that this involved lectures that could be easily written up as a book. The course, however, consists of workshops that follow the interests and the writing progress of the students rather than lectures, so a book of the kind envisaged, was impossible.

Instead, I proposed that I keep a diary during a writing of the book that became *Hannah and the Tomorrow Room,* and then that diary could be easily reworked as an account of the writing of one particular novel. That book, *Writing Hannah: On Writing for Children,* became an intensely recorded account of the dilemmas faced when writing fiction. I conceived *Hannah and the Tomorrow Room* as a story about Hannah's growth as she and her baby sister Megan are about to move into their new room and establish their very separate identities from the older girls. But Hannah's grandfather has been very ill, and now he is to come and stay in what was to be the new bedroom. Hannah is devastated, and her friends encourage her to get rid of him.

> Annie takes charge. "Maybe you should get him to leave."
>
> "How?"
>
> "Either you make him better and he goes home or . . ."
>
> "I can't do that. I'm not a doctor or a nurse."
>
> "Or you make everything so horrible that he goes anyway. He doesn't want to stay."
>
> Hannah feels uncomfortable. She's never set out to be bad before. She doesn't know what to do.
>
> "My grandma only stays a few days when she comes to our place," says Tui, "She says we drive her mad 'cause we make too much noise and we leave our stuff everywhere and we want to watch television all the time. She fights with Mum about us and she says she goes back to her place for peace and quiet."
>
> (Extract from *Hannah and the Tomorrow Room,* Chapter 3)

Hannah proceeds to carry out a number of actions designed to convince Grandpa that he doesn't want to stay. I had planned that Grandpa would gradually sicken and die. After a number of months' work, it became very clear to me that I could not write the book the way I had planned. As I wrote in *Writing Hannah*:

> In the world I have established, the world of Hannah and her family and friends, I am considering a fairly dastardly act. I am setting up a narrative line whereby Hannah schemes to get rid of her grandfather and then I am going to kill him off. That will be dramatic and emotional at the level off action. But the novel is more than the sum of the action in it. It is also its own moral universe. Each work of fiction has not only its text, but also its sub-text, its ideology . . . in *Hannah and the Tomorrow Room,* family is valued and responsibility for the older family member is acknowledged. The children have the right to speak up and be heard, but Hannah's behaviour cannot be condoned. It subverts the dominant family ethic of loving and caring for each family member.
>
> Grandpa's death, although not attributable to Hannah, will somehow fulfill her fantasy and legitimize her actions on one level. At another level his death can be attributable to her. Her sense of guilt will be overwhelming. And I plan to leave her there at the end of the novel.
>
> It isn't that I am squeamish about writing about death. Far from it. Death can and does belong in contemporary writing for this, as for every, age group. But not in this book. I can't do it. Not to Hannah. Grandpa can't die.
>
> (Extract from *Writing Hannah, On Writing for Children,* Chapter 9)

At the launch of **The Princess and the Perfect Dish,**
*1995. Left to right: Libby, publisher David Harris, il-
lustrator Armin Greder, editor Donna Rawlins, author
Marion Halligan, publicist Sandy Campbell*

I had to find another way to resolve the story, to allow Grandpa to leave with dignity and Hannah to
achieve her desire, her room. Hannah needed to be the
agent of the resolution, a difficult, although not impossible, task, given that she is only eight years old.

Writing the Hannah books has been an absolute
delight. They have allowed me to ponder the world
through the eyes of a very young child. I believe I have
taken her feelings, concerns, and ideas seriously without any moralizing or preaching. Foremost in my mind
has been an attempt to find the truth in Hannah's reality
and to entertain the reader without resorting to glib
humour.

I am often asked if I write more than one book at a
time. The answer is usually no. One book is hard
enough without confusing the mind with the intense
thinking needed about different sets of characters and
story ideas. But while writing the Hannah stories in the
1990s, I was also working on a novel for older adolescents called *Refuge*. As with many of my books, family
was at its centre.

I feel young people have to break with their family
in order to establish themselves as individuals. I don't
mean a hostile or violent break, but, rather, they have to
become aware of their own ideas and thinking, and the
parent has also to let the young person go, to accept
that they are not simply extensions of the parent, but individuals in their own right. For one generation it might
be political or religious ideas, for another ideas about
personal morality or lifestyle. I wanted to explore the
situation of a loving family where parents are accepting
of their children's growing up and away from them.
What kind of conflict might arise between the members
of such a family?

One day in September 1996, I opened *The Sydney
Morning Herald,* the quality newspaper in my city, and
was stunned by a particular photograph. It was of a
Catholic nun, a large woman, with her arm held protec-
tively around the shoulders of a young man. He was
East Timorese, an asylum-seeker in Australia.

In 1975, Indonesia invaded East Timor, a small island nation between Indonesia and Australia. Resistance
continued for over twenty years, and in that time many
East Timorese families sent their children to Australia
for education and to protect them from the brutality of
the occupying forces. Now the Australian government
was saying that these seekers of asylum were in no way
refugees and should return to their homeland or to Por-
tugal, the colonial power that had most recently gov-
erned East Timor. Like many Australians, I was deeply
ashamed of the inhuman way our policy on immigra-
tion was being carried out. The Catholic nun and many
other Australians had decided to create a network of
safe houses so that asylum-seekers who received orders
to leave Australia could disappear, go underground, and
be protected. Many ex-servicemen who had been hidden by the East Timorese during the Second World War
were part of this plan.

This real-life drama being played out in the Australian courts and community became the heart of my
novel. I asked the question: what would the parents,
who had been radicals during the Vietnam War days, do
if their children wanted to use their home as a safe
house for an asylum-seeker? Here is how the mother responds when Anna, her student daughter, makes the
suggestion:

> "Hang on. You want us to be a safe house for
> asylum seekers from East Timor?"
>
> "Yes."
>
> "You, who until today have not shown the slight-
> est sympathy with this cause."
>
> "Yes."
>
> "And have you actually told anyone that this is
> going to happen?"
>
> "Well . . . no . . . not yet."
>
> "Well don't. Because it isn't."
>
> "Mu-um."
>
> "No. You listen to me. You don't have any idea
> of what you're letting yourself—and us—into.
> You don't know the dangers or the possibility that
> you will be breaking the law. Probability, in
> fact. . . . have you forgotten for a moment what
> my job is? I'm a lawyer, Anna. I can't break the
> law."

(Extract from *Refuge,* Chapter 5)

The arguments continue, and Anna and her younger
brother decide that they will act without their parents'
knowledge and hide a young woman, Rosa. Their house
is large, and their parents lead busy lives, but the secret
cannot be kept forever. The novel introduces other characters, Kim, a Cambodian Australian and Tyr, a Greek
Australian, both of whom had come to Australia as
refugees and are now settled.

Refuge isn't a novel about refugees. There are refugees in the work, and issues concerning refugee policy
are raised but it is primarily a character-driven work

Visiting a local school during Children's Book Week, 1997

looking at the relationships between the young people Anna and Andrew, their family, and their friends through an interesting and difficult moment in our history. In many ways, it was my own response to living in a household of young teenagers who were beginning to realize the injustices of the world and who wanted to know what they, and we their parents, were doing about it.

For my next novel, *The Rum Rebellion: The Diary of David Bellamy*, I went back almost two hundred years to a moment in Australian history when a coup took place. In 1808, Australia, as a white settlement, was only twenty years old. The non-Aboriginal population was primarily convicts and their guards, members of the New South Wales Regiment. There were a handful of free settlers farming the rivers about twenty miles inland of Sydney. Captain William Bligh, better known from the events of the mutiny on the *Bounty,* was the governor of the colony. There were conflicting views about the way the new society should develop. Should the colony grow with small farms, worked by free settlers and a few convict labourers, or should a smaller number of free men have very large farms with many convicts assigned to them? These wealthy landowners would also play an important role in developing trade with Europe, India, and America. Governor Bligh was a firm supporter of the small farmers. One such small farmer was George Suttor, a free settler. He had come to the colony in 1800 to establish himself as a small farmer and nurseryman. He brought with him his wife and one son, and his family grew rapidly in the next eight years. George believed in the vision that Governor

Bligh had for the new land. He also felt that the colony needed to move from a prison to a community where free men had the same rights as they did in England. That did not mean a democratically elected parliament. It meant trial by a jury of other free men, not soldiers, and it meant limiting the power of the military.

In those early, disorganized years, there was no single system of money in the colony. You could receive your wages or the payment for your maize crop in goods—food or farm tools. The most common payment was in rum, alcohol, and every writer of the period talks of the drunkenness of the population. The officers bought rum off the trading ships at one price and then sold it to others in the colony for much, much more. They made such high profits that every governor did his best to control the trade. Governor Bligh was no exception. On 26th January 1808, a wealthy ex-soldier, John Macarthur led the men of the New South Wales Regiment in a rebellion. They imprisoned the governor and ruled the colony, serving their own interests until a new governor arrived a year later. The ringleaders were then returned to England to face trial. Under the military administration, men like George Suttor were tried and imprisoned for their opposition.

I had been invited to write a novel in the series "My Story," published by Scholastic and similar to the American "My America" series. I chose the rebellion of 1808, because it is little known in this country. In many history books written for young people, John Macarthur is better known for his development of the wool industry than for his leading of the rebellion. Governor Bligh is better known for his surviving the mutiny on his ship the *Bounty* than for his vision and struggle in the early years of Australia. Much of his poor reputation has come from the unsympathetic depictions of him in a number of Hollywood feature films of the mutiny.

Writing a historical novel was fascinating. I began with primary sources: the correspondence of the administration in the early years. The governors of the colony wrote regularly to the bureaucrats in London detailing the difficulties of the new settlement. Those letters are held in the Mitchell Library, part of the State Library of New South Wales here in Sydney. From there I moved to the newspapers of the times that had accounts of the rebellion and then to various secondary sources, histories written in recent times. These included accounts of the lives of children, details of a farm labourer's life, as well as biographies and general histories of Sydney in the nineteenth century.

Early in my research I came across George Suttor. He was part of a group that petitioned the governor in 1807 for more freedoms and then, after the rebellion, he protested to the new administration and to the colonial secretary's office back in London. Because his family firmly supported the governor, I decided to use him in my work. His children at the time were quite young so I created a nephew, David Bellamy, and brought him to live with George and his family.

The book was to be written in diary form, which imposed restrictions. In a modern novel, the writer can leap around in time. Flashbacks can quickly bring the reader up to date with the reasons for action or for results. In a diary, however, there must be more adherence to a time sequence, one cannot shape action to suit the plot, and there is no room for anachronistic invention. Many diaries contain banal detail of the trivia of everyday life.

To create an authentic voice for David, I spent time immersing myself in Victorian novels. Dickens, although not exactly of the period, provided a model for much of the language. I also had to imagine ways to involve my twelve-year-old hero in the action.

The events that led to the rebellion were largely economic, political, and constitutional. I had to try to find those elements accessible both to the young boy in the story and to my young readers. By connecting David to one of the protesting families, I was able to follow the fortunes of the family as first they supported the governor and then faced a period when the father was jailed for his views. David may not be party to the constitutional niceties, but he did know the fear of becoming the man of the family when his uncle was removed and his aunt was ill.

In the late 1990s I became very involved in the main national writers' organization: the Australian Society of Authors. This society gives advice to its members about everything to do with the business of writing: contracts, rates of payment, literary agents, and so on. It also lobbies the government about national policy on copyright law, trade in published works, cultural policy, and support for the creative arts. For three years, I chaired the organization and spent much time with my head full of politics rather than fiction.

I didn't, however, stop writing. I found I only had "headspace" for very short, finely focused work and the result has been a number of picture books created with Armin Greder. I use that form of words deliberately. The earlier picture books, mentioned above, were all written first as stories and then were illustrated. Now, when working with Armin, the process is different.

The first of these books is *The Great Bear*, published in 1999. It began, four years prior to that, as a dream where I woke up with such a vivid impression of what had been in my mind, and so curious about what it might mean, that I wrote it down.

The sequence of images was a huge dancing bear in a medieval village, somewhere in mountainous Central Europe. The bear was tormented and tormented and finally broke free. She ran to the centre of the village square, climbed the flagpole, and balanced on the top. I knew she could never climb down, but I was unafraid for her. Then she launched herself into the stars, and I thought of Ursa Major, the Great Bear constellation. It felt very satisfying. I knew there was a story there and

so wrote out the sequence of events. This was an aid to memory, not even a first draft. The next step was to relate the dream to Armin. He immediately related to the story (which had not yet been written) and began drawing. Through the mail I received images of bears and brutal-looking villagers. I struggled to write the tale to accompany the pictures he was sending me. It was prosaic to begin with, a simple story relating the events as dreamt. It was not "good" enough. It needed to be lifted to a level of intensity. I wanted the reader to feel the bear's anguish and to understand the desire to break free. I wanted drama and poetry. I wanted the levels of psychological and mythological insight to be available to very young readers. I talked at length with Armin and then went back to my desk and struggled with the ideas, with the structure of the story, with the language, with every word, every nuance of meaning. He kept drawing. We discussed the role of the sky and how to show it as a character in the story, a potential place of freedom. How could he draw those stars to depict them as vital and inviting? The action takes place at night, how could we use colour to alleviate the overarching evil of the villagers?

What perspectives could draw the reader into the story? Armin Greder believes strongly that his role is to draw in the spaces between and beyond the words. He doesn't decorate texts or draw to give a visual rendition of the words. The illustrations are there to create the visual narrative that takes you beyond the words, that helps the reader to construct meaning from the whole.

We were nearing completion of this book when Armin told me that in the last third of the text, he could

"Celebrating my fiftieth birthday with the publication of 'A Genuine Redhead,' 2000"

find no place to illustrate. There were no "spaces be-tween the words," and he felt he could create nothing but a visual rendition of my text. Would I consider dropping the words? I barely hesitated. By the time the reader arrives at the point where the written text ceases, the story line is so powerful that there is no danger of a lack of understanding developing. In fact, some readers have suggested that the silence of the last section of the work renders the first sections of written text all the louder and more powerful. We also decided at this point to add star charts as endpapers. We felt these added a layer of suggestion to the reader that the mythical ele-ment, the origin of Ursa Major, was there in the story. We took the book to our publisher at Scholastic, aware that he would have to really understand and like what we had done and be prepared to champion it through the process of evaluation by his colleagues in sales and marketing. He did.

Illustrators like Armin Greder invite readers to think beyond the words, to ask questions of the story. His im-ages in *The Great Bear* are varied from the small crayon drawings of the bear on the lower, left-hand page to the brooding, menacing dark images that dominate the cen-tre of the book. In them he shifts perspective, drawing the reader into thinking they are the bear. You cannot read this work without feeling as the bear feels, identi-fying with her suffering, celebrating her liberation. As such it is a book that encourages contemplation and discussion.

I had no idea where this story had come from. The book was launched at Sydney Writers' Festival and the speaker was a man of very deep religious conviction. He said he felt the book was about human suffering and the need to set oneself free and drew our attention to the events happening in the world at the time. When he mentioned East Timor and the persecution of its people, I knew that the research I had done for the novel *Ref-uge* had somehow been transformed by my subcon-scious into the allegorical tale of the bear.

The tale of the bear is dark and uncompromising. We have been delighted at its success, winning the Bo-logna Ragazzi, the premier picture book award, at the International Book Fair in Bologna, 2000.

Since then, Armin and I have collaborated on an-other project, *An Ordinary Day.* It is a far gentler story, a whimsical tale of a small boy in a huge metropolis who sets out for school along a busy, car-filled street. The words of the story drop away after the first third of the story, and the reader is left with only visual language. Small pictures across the double page spread take the reader on the same journey as the boy, Jack. There are reappearing images of fish: on a calendar, the breakfast plate, in a bowl on the table, and then on a sign on a van. The huge sea of traffic begins to trans-form into a pod of whales. Jack's imagination trans-forms the cars, vans and trucks until they are the huge, glorious sea creatures soaring skywards. Jack soars with them, until his bus appears and he becomes earthbound again. The final image in the book, however, suggests that his imagination is still free ranging.

Making books such as these two has not only been wonderfully satisfying, but it has also led me to ponder the nature of the art form. I am particularly keen to work more in the area of full collaboration where an idea can be realised by both word and image, each one contributing to the meaning. At the same time, I con-tinue to work with other illustrators in a more conven-tional way, with a written story that then requires illustration.

My interest in the picture book and its potential has led me to create a book, *Making Picture Books,* that will be published in October 2003. In it I follow my own practice from first idea to the struggle through many drafts until I am satisfied with a story. I have tried to identify the questions I ask myself whenever I am stuck on a story or unable to resolve a particular problem. I interviewed a number of successful writers in the field to present the variety of ways of working that exist. Then I did the same for illustrators. Many of Armin Greder's ideas and processes are there as are those of other successful Australian illustrators. I also detail the close collaboration that comes from those in the industry who have worked together for a long time. The interviews conducted for this book have exposed me to the many different ways writers and illustrators think about their art. I have learnt much about my own process and that of my peers, and I find I now look at story and at illustration with even more respect than before.

Writing about writing satisfies the part of me that is interested in analyzing process and in thinking critically about what we do. It is never, however, a substitute for the real thing. I have felt frustrated through this past year, wanting to feel myself back in that creative mode. I have a bit of a manuscript, discarded some years ago, that may turn into a fourth book about Hannah. I have ideas for stories that focus on young people in Australia today, fearful of the international situation. And over lunch last weekend, someone told me a story from his childhood that with a bit of tweaking around the edges just might turn into another picture book.

In 2000 I turned fifty and was overwhelmed when my husband and children organized many of my friends to write, and illustrate, stories about my life so far. There are tales from my childhood, written by my broth-ers and sisters, tales of travel from very old friends, and tales of books and publishing and writing activism from those who have known me more recently. Called "A Genuine Redhead" (I am), it was kept secret from me and launched at a wonderful party.

When writing this autobiographical essay, I won-dered whether some theme would emerge. Is all of my work linked in some way? Are there consistent ideas or styles of writing? If so, they haven't immediately pre-sented themselves. Family is important. Character and relationships are important. Social justice and compas-sionate treatment of each other is important. And I know I care about precision in language and form. But deep down I want to tell a good story. I want to move my reader and take them somewhere other than the chair they are sitting in. I want them to care about what and whomever they are reading about. I want them to know that through language and ideas, through character and story, they can imagine places and people they have never known but that they just might visit or become.

GREENSPUN, Adele Aron 1938-
(Adele Aron Schwarz)

Personal

Born December 22, 1938, in Philadelphia, PA; daughter of Samuel and Eva (maiden name, Stern) Aron; married Steven Schwarz (divorced); married Bertram Greenspun (a physician), January 18, 1987; children: (first marriage) Erica, Joanie. *Education:* Attended University of Arts, International Center for Photography, The New School, and Wilkes College; University of Pennsylvania, B.S., 1960. *Hobbies and other interests:* Cross-country skiing, Pilates, taking photographs, reading memoirs.

Addresses

Home and office—1900 Rittenhouse Sq., #9, Philadelphia, PA 19103.

Career

Freelance and portrait photographer. Worked variously as a teacher, a sculptor, a documentary photographer, and a financial account executive. *Exhibitions:* Under the Northeastern Pennsylvania Art Alliance, Greenspun's photograph exhibit toured twelve towns, colleges, and art museums, 1979-81. Also exhibited works at The Art Gallery, College Miseracordia, Dallas, PA, 1981; The Art Institute, Philadelphia, PA, 1990; American Society of Media Photographers and University of the Arts, both 1992-93; Philadelphia Inquirer Exhibition, Philadelphia, PA, 1995; and American Society of Magazine Photographers, 1996.

Member

Authors Guild, American Association of Media Photographers, Society of Children's Book Writers and Illustrators, Young Author's Day, Philadelphia Children's Reading Roundtable.

Awards, Honors

Wilkes College poetry prize, 1977; Silver Award, Art Directors Club, 1992; Philadelphia Children's Reading Round Table Book of the Month Selection, Free Library of Philadelphia, 1992; *Daddies* was named one of the one hundred most noteworthy children's books published in 1992 by Children's Literature Center, Library of Congress.

Writings

SELF-PHOTOGRAPHED

Daddies, Philomel Books (New York, NY), 1991.
(With daughter Joanie Schwarz) *Bunny and Me*, Scholastic (New York, NY), 2000.
(With daughter Joanie Schwarz) *Ariel and Emily*, Dutton (New York, NY), 2003.
(With daughter Joanie Schwarz) *Grandparents Are the Greatest Because . . .*, Dutton (New York, NY), 2003.

Also contributor of fiction and nonfiction to books, including *Encounter with Family Realities*, West Publishing (St. Paul, MN), 1977, and *Stories for Free Children*, McGraw-Hill (New York, NY), 1985. Contributor of photographs to books including *Ten Thousand Eyes: ASMP's Celebration of the 150th Anniversary of Photography*, 1991, and *Philadelphia Images*, University of the Art Press (Philadelphia, PA), 1990. Contributor of fiction and nonfiction to periodicals, including *Ladies Home Journal, McCall's*, and *Ms*. Contributor of photographs to periodicals, including *Parents, U.S. News and World Report, Moment*, and *Self*. Contributor to periodicals under the name Adele Aron Schwarz, ending 1991.

Daddies is available as an e-book. *Bunny and Me* has been published in Hebrew.

Work in Progress

Judianne, a young adult novel set in the early 1950s during the Korean War; *My Baby Brother*, a picture book.

Sidelights

When Adele Aron Greenspun was nine years old, her father gave her a Kodak Brownie Box camera, and she has been taking pictures ever since. Her interest in combining words and illustrations began in sixth grade, when she wrote and drew pictures for a book project on Ancient Egyptians. "The interaction between the written word and images fascinated me," she told *SATA*. "But it would be decades before that wish was fulfilled."

When Greenspun was eleven, her father, to whom she was devoted, died. Greenspun was on her way to summer camp the day he died, and her mother did not tell her. She spent the summer writing letters to her father and crafting a beautiful blue box she planned to give him at summer's end. "My father's death left a big hole

Adele Aron Greenspun

in my heart," Greenspun told *SATA*. "When I was nineteen, my mother died, leaving me to care for my brother who was two and a half years younger. It is not surprising that I write about loss and the importance of family."

More than fifty black and white photographs of fathers with children under the age of twelve capture what Greenspun, in a publicity release, has called "emotional, dramatic, loving and joyous moments" of fathers and their sons and daughters, sharing everyday occasions such as a visit to the zoo, a piano lesson, and the disappointment of a lost baseball game. She traveled to places as far away as St. Croix and as nearby as the house next door in Philadelphia, and took over ten thousand photographs before the book was done.

Although Greenspun has worked as a financial consultant as well as a portrait photographer specializing in families, children, and teenagers, "the voice inside me to do a book never was quieted," she remarked in the publicity release for *Daddies*. "By the end of 1988 . . ., the book *Daddies* took hold as an idea and catapulted me throughout the United States to witness and document children and their fathers."

"The book has settled things for me in a lot of ways," Greenspun told Ruth Rovner of the *Jewish Times*. "The blue box I could never give to my own father I'm finally giving to my readers and their fathers."

It was nearly ten years after the appearance of the award-winning *Daddies* before another picture book by Greenspun was published. Greenspun told *SATA*, "I was told 'Black-and-white photography is old fashioned.' Illustrations for my next three books were made by digitally coloring my black and white photographs on the computer." *Bunny and Me*, featuring artwork that represents a collaborative effort between Greenspun and daughter Joanie Schwarz, shares some of the strengths

of Greenspun's first effort. Here is a simple story told primarily through photographic illustrations that reviewers deemed would be entirely attractive to very young children. Using simple text, *Bunny and Me* tells the story of the friendship that blossoms between a baby and a bunny as they blow bubbles, play dress-up, and engage in other games. Then bunny disappears, chasing after a ball, and a tearful baby searches for the rabbit, becoming happy again when the bunny is found. "The interplay between this sweet duo will engage youngsters," observed Rosalyn Pierini in *School Library Journal*, who added that young children should be warned against approaching animals unknown to them.

Bunny and Me is illustrated with photographs taken by the author and altered with computer technology to create the illusion that baby and bunny are playing together. Each photo is then set against a painted background and framed to give the appearance of a quiet outdoor scene. "The trompe l'oeil images will delight toddlers and engage their caregivers," predicted GraceAnne A. DeCandido in *Booklist*. The result is "a perfectly delicious picture book," DeCandido concluded.

Greenspun told *SATA*, "*Bunny and Me* is especially meaningful to me because it is a family project. The models for the baby are my two granddaughters, Ariel and Frances. The baby's outfit was knitted by their mother, my daughter Erica. *Bunny and Me* is satisfying to younger readers because the disappearance of the rabbit taps into their fears of separation. The baby, after searching for the rabbit, behind trees, under benches, inside bushes, feels triumphant [when she] reunites with the bunny. Although all of us have losses, it is what we do with those losses that is important."

Greenspun and Schwarz have also collaborated on two other picture books, *Grandparents Are the Greatest Because . . .*, which is similar in format to *Daddies*, and *Ariel and Emily*, the story of best friends playing at the park. A reviewer for *Kirkus Reviews* noted that the photograps are "made magical by the collage and hand-coloring technique." Greenspun told *SATA*, "The inspiration for *Ariel and Emily* came from noticing that when a one year old has her tower of blocks knocked down by her friend, they both laugh. The fallen heap of blocks only serves to create possibilities for another creative tower. Their friendship continues as they crawl off in the star-spangled grass to their next adventure."

Of *Grandparents Are the Greatest Because . . .*, Greenspun explained to *SATA* that the book began "when my first grandchild was born. I wanted to change the image of grandparents in children's picture books. Today's grandparents are fortunate to be alive in an era, thanks to medical science, when many live longer, are healthier, and are given the opportunity to pursue athletic endeavors. They may run marathons, play tennis, cross-country ski, bike, kayak, jog, [and] climb mountains. In addition many grandparents continue to enjoy their intellectual pursuits." Four of Greenspun's grandchildren, as well as her husband, appear in the photographs of *Grandparents Are the Greatest Because . . .*

Biographical and Critical Sources

PERIODICALS

Booklist, March 15, 2000, GraceAnne A. DeCandido, review of *Bunny and Me,* p. 1386.

Jewish Times, June 18, 1992, Ruth Rovner, "Greenspun No Longer Finds Father's Day Depressing."

Kirkus Reviews, December 1, 2002, review of *Ariel and Emily.*

School Library Journal, April, 2000, Rosalyn Pierini, review of *Bunny and Me,* p. 105; March, 2003, Martha Topol, review of *Ariel and Emily,* p. 193.

OTHER

Publicity Packet, Putnam and Grosset, c. 1991, "Adele Greenspun."*

*   *   *

GULBIS, Stephen 1959-

Personal

Born January 7, 1959, in Radstock, England; son of Reinis and Gillian Gulbis; married, 1992; wife's name, Judith (a musician); children: Laura, Rosie. *Education:* Bath Academy of Art, B.A. (graphic design; with honors), 1981.

Addresses

Home—2 Church Furlong, Tadmarton, Banbury, Oxfordshire OX15 5SG, England.

Career

Freelance illustrator, 1981-99; writer and illustrator, 1999—.

Writings

(And illustrator) *Cowgirl Rosie and Her Five Baby Bison,* Little, Brown (New York, NY), 2001.

(Illustrator) *I Know an Old Lady Who Swallowed a Fly,* Scholastic (New York, NY), 2001.

(And illustrator) *Lily and the Magical Moonbeam,* Orchard Books (London, England), 2003.

(And illustrator) *Old Macdonald Had a Barn,* David Bennett Books (London, England), 2003.

(And illustrator) *The Wheels on the Bus,* David Bennett Books (London, England), 2003.

Work in Progress

Tiger Tom, for Orchard Books (London, England), completion expected in 2004.

Sidelights

Stephen Gulbis told *SATA:* "Writing and illustrating children's books involves me in creating something new—which is the best fun you can have. I love picture books because usually the words and pictures have equal weight. However, I think the best picture books demand repeated readings, and the key to this is a good story. Not even the most brilliant artwork can disguise a poor text. I must admit I find writing harder than illustrating—those bright shiny new ideas are so elusive!"

Biographical and Critical Sources

PERIODICALS

Booklist, May 15, 2001, Ilene Cooper, review of *Cowgirl Rosie and Her Five Baby Bison,* p. 1757.

Publishers Weekly, February 12, 2001, review of *Cowgirl Rosie and Her Five Baby Bison,* p. 211.

School Library Journal, May, 2001, Piper L. Nyman, review of *Cowgirl Rosie and Her Five Baby Bison,* p. 122.

H

HARRISON, Elizabeth Cavanna 1909-2001 (Betsy Allen, Betty Cavanna, Elizabeth Cavanna, Elizabeth Allen Cavanna, Elizabeth Headley)

Personal

Born June 24, 1909, in Camden, NJ; died August 13, 2001, in Vezelay, France; daughter of Walter and Emily (Allen) Cavanna; married Edward Headley, August 5, 1940 (died, 1952); married George Russell Harrison (a university dean of science), March 9, 1957 (died, July 27, 1979); children: (first marriage) Stephen. *Education:* Douglass College (now part of Rutgers, The State University—New Brunswick Campus), A.B., 1929. *Religion:* Protestant. *Hobbies and other interests:* Art, antiques.

Career

Bayonne Times, Bayonne, NJ, reporter, 1929-31; *Westminster Press,* Philadelphia, PA, began as advertising manager, became art director, 1931-41; full-time writer, beginning 1941.

Member

Writers Guild, Boston Museum of Fine Arts, Philadelphia Art Alliance, Technology Matrons (program chair, 1961-62), Phi Beta Kappa, Women's Travel Club of Boston (second vice president, 1972-73), Cosmopolitan Club (New York, NY).

Awards, Honors

Spring Book Festival's honor book, 1946, for *Going on Sixteen,* and 1947, for *Secret Passage;* New Jersey Institute of Technology citation, and English Teachers Association of New Jersey citation, 1966, both for *Mystery at Love's Creek;* Edgar Allan Poe Award runner-up, 1970, for *Spice Island Mystery,* and 1972, for *The Ghost of Ballyhooly;* New Jersey Institute of Technology citation, 1976, for *Catchpenny Street.*

Writings

UNDER NAME BETTY CAVANNA

Puppy Stakes, Westminster (Philadelphia, PA), 1943.
The Black Spaniel Mystery, Westminster (Philadelphia, PA), 1945.
Secret Passage, John C. Winston (Philadelphia, PA), 1946.
Going on Sixteen, Westminster (Philadelphia, PA), 1946, revised edition, Morrow (New York, NY), 1985.
Spurs for Suzanna, Westminster (Philadelphia, PA), 1947.
A Girl Can Dream, Westminster (Philadelphia, PA), 1948.
Paintbox Summer, Westminster (Philadelphia, PA), 1949.
Spring Comes Riding, Westminster (Philadelphia, PA), 1950.
Two's Company, Westminster (Philadelphia, PA), 1951.
(Compiler) *Pick of the Litter: Favorite Dog Stories,* Westminster (Philadelphia, PA), 1952.
Lasso Your Heart, Westminster (Philadelphia, PA), 1952.
Love, Laurie, Westminster (Philadelphia, PA), 1953.
Six on Easy Street, Westminster (Philadelphia, PA), 1954.
The First Book of Seashells, F. Watts (New York, NY), 1955.
Passport to Romance, Morrow (New York, NY), 1955.
The Boy Next Door, Morrow (New York, NY), 1956.
Angel on Skis, Morrow (New York, NY), 1957.
Stars in Her Eyes, Morrow (New York, NY), 1958.
The Scarlet Sail, Morrow (New York, NY), 1959.
Accent on April, Morrow (New York, NY), 1960.
A Touch of Magic, Westminster (Philadelphia, PA), 1961.
Fancy Free, Morrow (New York, NY), 1961.
The First Book of Wildflowers, F. Watts (New York, NY), 1961.
A Time for Tenderness, Morrow (New York, NY), 1962.
Almost Like Sisters, Morrow (New York, NY), 1963.
Jenny Kimura, Morrow (New York, NY), 1964.
Mystery at Love's Creek, Morrow (New York, NY), 1965.
A Breath of Fresh Air, Morrow (New York, NY), 1966.
The First Book of Wool, photographs by husband George Russell Harrison, F. Watts (New York, NY), 1966, published in England as *Wool,* F. Watts (London, England), 1972.
The Country Cousin, Morrow (New York, NY), 1967.

Mystery in Marrakech, Morrow (New York, NY), 1968.

Spice Island Mystery, Morrow (New York, NY), 1969.

The First Book of Fiji, photographs by George Russell Harrison, F. Watts (New York, NY), 1969, published in England as *Fiji,* F. Watts (London, England), 1972.

The First Book of Morocco, photographs by George Russell Harrison, F. Watts (New York, NY), 1970.

Mystery on Safari, Morrow (New York, NY), 1971.

The Ghost of Ballyhooly, Morrow (New York, NY), 1971.

Mystery in the Museum, Morrow (New York, NY), 1972.

Petey, Westminster (Philadelphia, PA), 1973.

Joyride, Morrow (New York, NY), 1974.

Ruffles and Drums, Morrow (New York, NY), 1975.

Mystery of the Emerald Buddha, Morrow (New York, NY), 1976.

Runaway Voyage, Morrow (New York, NY), 1978.

Stamp Twice for Murder, Morrow (New York, NY), 1981.

The Surfer and the City Girl, Westminster (Philadelphia, PA), 1981.

Storm in Her Heart, Westminster (Philadelphia, PA), 1983.

Romance on Trial, Westminster (Philadelphia, PA), 1984.

Wanted: A Girl for the Horses, Morrow (New York, NY), 1984.

Banner Year, Morrow (New York, NY), 1987.

UNDER NAME ELIZABETH HEADLEY

A Date for Diane (also see below), Macrae Smith (Philadelphia, PA), 1946.

Take a Call, Topsy!, Macrae Smith (Philadelphia, PA), 1947, reprinted under name Betty Cavanna as *Ballet Fever,* Westminster (Philadelphia, PA), 1978.

She's My Girl!, Macrae Smith (Philadelphia, PA), 1949, reprinted under name Betty Cavanna as *You Can't Take Twenty Dogs on a Date,* Westminster (Philadelphia, PA), 1979.

Catchpenny Street, Macrae Smith (Philadelphia, PA), 1951, reprinted under name Betty Cavanna, Westminster (Philadelphia, PA), 1975.

Diane's New Love (also see below), Macrae Smith (Philadelphia, PA), 1955.

Toujours Diane (also see below), Macrae Smith (Philadelphia, PA), 1957.

The Diane Stories: All about America's Favorite Girl Next Door (contains *A Date for Diane, Diane's New Love,* and *Toujours Diane*), Macrae Smith (Philadelphia, PA), 1964.

"AROUND THE WORLD TODAY" SERIES; UNDER NAME BETTY CAVANNA

Arne of Norway, photographs by George Russell Harrison, F. Watts (New York, NY), 1960.

Lucho of Peru, photographs by George Russell Harrison, F. Watts (New York, NY), 1961.

Paulo of Brazil, photographs George Russell Harrison, F. Watts (New York, NY), 1962.

Pepe of Argentina, photographs by George Russell Harrison, F. Watts (New York, NY), 1962.

Lo Chau of Hong Kong, photographs by George Russell Harrison, F. Watts (New York, NY), 1963.

Chico of Guatemala, photographs by George Russell Harrison, F. Watts (New York, NY), 1963.

Noko of Japan, photographs by George Russell Harrison, F. Watts (New York, NY), 1964.

Carlos of Mexico, photographs by George Russell Harrison, F. Watts (New York, NY), 1964.

Tavi of the South Seas, photographs by George Russell Harrison, F. Watts (New York, NY), 1965.

Doug of Australia, photographs by George Russell Harrison, F. Watts (New York, NY), 1965.

Ali of Egypt, photographs by George Russell Harrison, F. Watts (New York, NY), 1966.

Demetrios of Greece, photographs by George Russell Harrison, F. Watts (New York, NY), 1966.

"CONNIE BLAIR MYSTERY" SERIES; UNDER PSEUDONYM BETSY ALLEN

Puzzle in Purple, Grosset (New York, NY), 1948.

The Secret of Black Cat Gulch, Grosset (New York, NY), 1948.

The Riddle in Red, Grosset (New York, NY), 1948.

The Clue in Blue, Grosset (New York, NY), 1948.

The Green Island Mystery, Grosset (New York, NY), 1949.

The Ghost Wore White, Grosset (New York, NY), 1950.

The Yellow Warning, Grosset (New York, NY), 1951.

The Gray Menace, Grosset (New York, NY), 1953.

The Brown Satchel Mystery, Grosset (New York, NY), 1954.

Peril in Pink, Grosset (New York, NY), 1955.

The Silver Secret, Grosset (New York, NY), 1956.

The Mystery of the Ruby Queen, Grosset (New York, NY), 1958.

OTHER

Contributor of serials to *American Girl* and other magazines. Some writings appear under the names Elizabeth Cavanna and Elizabeth Allen Cavanna.

A collection of Harrison's manuscripts are held at the University of Southern Mississippi, in the de Grummond Collection.

Sidelights

Books by Elizabeth Cavanna Harrison (best known as Betty Cavanna) often concern junior high school girls. Cavanna explained this, as she once recalled, as the result of "an almost total emotional recall for this particular period of my own life, which made it possible for me to identify with a teenage heroine. Fashions in clothes and speech change, but the hopes, dreams, and fears of the young remain fairly constant, and over the years I have explored all sorts of youthful problems—among them loneliness, shyness, jealousy, social maladjustment, and the destructiveness of alcoholism, divorce, race prejudice, and mother-daughter rivalry within family situations." Her books are known for their popularity with younger high school readers.

Dwight L. Burton of *English Journal* used *Going on Sixteen* to describe why Cavanna's books have appeal. The novel, Burton explained, "rests upon its genuineness and sincerity rather than upon melodrama. Julie, the heroine, is a somewhat shy, nondescript girl who lives on a farm with her father." Burton noted that as the story follows Julie's progress through three years of high school, Cavanna "avoids the easy assumptions present in many books with a similar theme. . . . There is realistic evolution of character brought about by Julie's own efforts and recognition of her faults and by the sympathetic guidance of a teacher." In 1985, Morrow published a revised edition of *Going on Sixteen* as a "Morrow Junior Classic."

In addition to novels for adolescent girls, Cavanna also has written several series. Under the "Betsy Allen" pseudonym, she wrote a mystery series, which includes *The Clue in Blue, The Riddle in Red, The Secret of Black Cat Gulch, The Green Island Mystery,* and *The Ghost Wore White.* Her husband provided the photography for her "Around the World Today" series, in which each book tells the story of a young person from a different part of the world. Books in this series include *Arne of Norway, Pepe of Argentina, Ali of Egypt,* and *Demetrios of Greece.* Cavanna also has written a number of nonfiction titles such as *The First Book of Seashells, The First Book of Wildflowers, The First Book of Fiji,* and *The First Book of Morocco.*

Biographical and Critical Sources

BOOKS

Contemporary Literary Criticism, Volume 12, Gale (Detroit, MI), 1980.
St. James Guide to Young Adult Writers, 2nd edition, St. James Press (Detroit, MI), 1999.
Something about the Author Autobiography Series, Volume 4, Gale (Detroit, MI), 1987.
Thomison, Dennis, editor, *Readings about Adolescent Literature,* Scarecrow (Metuchen, NY), 1970.

PERIODICALS

Atlantic, December, 1946.
Book Week, November 29, 1964.
Christian Science Monitor, November 4, 1965.
English Journal, September, 1951, Dwight L. Burton, review of *Going on Sixteen.*
New York Herald Tribune Book Review, June 10, 1945; May 5, 1946; April 11, 1948; June 17, 1951.
New York Times Book Review, January 5, 1947; July 20, 1947; May 15, 1949; November 15, 1953; December 15, 1957.
Saturday Review, August 13, 1949.

Obituaries

PERIODICALS

Chicago Tribune, August 14, 2001, section 2, p. 9.
Los Angeles Times, August 15, 2001, p. B10.
New York Times, August 15, 2001, p. A25.
Washington Post, August 14, 2001, p. B5.*

HEADLEY, Elizabeth
See HARRISON, Elizabeth Cavanna

*   *   *

HULL, Maureen 1949-

Personal

Born August 28, 1949, in Cape Breton Island, Nova Scotia, Canada; daughter of Charlotte Morrison Hull; married David B. Harding, October 1, 1979; children: Amy Harding, Moira Harding. *Ethnicity:* "Scots/ English." *Education:* Attended Nova Scotia College of Art and Design, Dalhousie University, and Pictou Fisheries School.

Addresses

Home and office—1 Harding Ln., Pictou Island, Nova Scotia B0K 1JO, Canada.

Career

Held various positions in the wardrobe department of the Neptune Theatre, Halifax, Nova Scotia, Canada, 1970-75; fisher, Pictou Island, Nova Scotia, Canada, 1977-2000; writer, 1992—.

Member

Writers' Union of Canada, Writers' Federation of Nova Scotia, Canadian Society of Children's Authors, Illustrators, and Performers, Pictou Island Community Association (past president and vice president).

Awards, Honors

Winner, Atlantic Writers' Competition, for poetry and short fiction; awarded several grants from Canada Council and Nova Scotia Arts Council.

Writings

Righteous Living: Stories, Turnstone Press (Winnipeg, Manitoba, Canada), 1999.
Wild Cameron Women (picture book), illustrated by Judith Christine Mills, Stoddart Kids (Toronto, Canada), 2000.

Work in Progress

A young adult novel, *The View from a Kite;* picture books, *The Best Way Home, Rainy Days with Bear, The Guinness Book of World Records Birthday Cake,* and *Anemone;* an early reader novel, *Exotic Pets;* an adult novel, *Clearing by Dawn,* due for publication in 2005.

Maureen Hull

Sidelights

"I was born and grew up on Cape Breton Island," Maureen Hull told *SATA*. "I subsequently moved to Halifax where I attended the Nova Scotia College of Art and Design and Dalhousie University, and worked in the costume department of Neptune Theatre.

"In 1976, I moved again, to another, smaller, island off the coast of Nova Scotia, in the Northumberland Strait (present population: twenty-one). Here, on Pictou Island, I fished lobster with my husband, and we raised two daughters.

"My writing for children grew out of my years of home-schooling my daughters. We wrote stories together as part of the learning process and, when they moved on to correspondence courses, I continued writing, both adult and children's work. As a member of the Writers' Federation of Nova Scotia, I have participated in the Writers in the Schools program for the past five years, reading and conducting workshops in schools around the province. My daughters, now at university, remain my best and most reliable critics."

Canadian history plays a small but crucial role in Hull's first children's book, *Wild Cameron Women*. In this picture book story about a child's irrational fear of bears coming out of the closet in the dark of the night, a grandmother invokes the history of Canada, which long ago proved a haven to Scots driven from their lands. Nana Cameron tells young Kate Cameron, her granddaughter, about another young Kate who lived two hundred years before, and who, with the aid of the family tartan and some choice Gaelic words, was able to frighten off a bear. With the story Nana delivers three nightgowns made from the family tartan, and young Kate gathers her courage and her Gaelic words to frighten away the beasties. While Susan Marie Pitard, who reviewed *Wild Cameron Women* for *School Library Journal*, found "the story-within-a story construct . . . a bit muddled," Patricia Morley, a reviewer for the *Canadian Book Review Annual*, asserted that "Maureen Hull's witty, reassuring tale . . . is a delightfully clever way of calming" the fears of young children in the night.

Biographical and Critical Sources

PERIODICALS

Canadian Book Review Annual, 2000, Patricia Morley, review of *Wild Cameron Women*, pp. 6072-6073.
School Library Journal, December, 2000, Susan Marie Pitard, review of *Wild Cameron Women*, p. 111.

K

KACER, Kathy 1954-

Personal

Born September 6, 1954, in Toronto, Canada; daughter of Arthur and Gabriela (Offenberg) Kacer; married Ian Epstein (a lawyer), December 19, 1981; children: Gabi Epstein, Jake Epstein. *Education:* University of Toronto, B.Sc., 1976; University of New Brunswick, M.A. (clinical psychology), 1978. *Religion:* Jewish.

Addresses

Home—50 Beechwood Ave., Toronto, Ontario M2L 1J3 Canada. *E-mail*—kathy_kacer@yahoo.com

Career

The Griffin Centre (children's mental health center), Toronto, Ontario, Canada, clinical director, 1989-95; consultant in organizational development to social service agencies and government, Toronto, Ontario, Canada, 1995—; writer, 1996—.

Member

Canadian Society of Children's Authors, Illustrators, and Performers (recording secretary), Writers Union of Canada.

Awards, Honors

Geoffrey Bilson Award for Historical Fiction for Young People shortlist, and Reader's Choice Award, Canadian Children's Book Center, both 1999, Silver Birch Award, Ontario Library Association, and Canadian Jewish Book Award, young adult fiction category, both 2000, Hackmatack Children's Choice Award, Maritime Library Association, 2001, and Red Cedar Book Award shortlist, Young Readers' Choice Association of British Columbia, 2002, all for *The Secret of Gabi's Dresser;* Sydney Taylor Book Award Honorable Mention, American Association of Jewish Libraries, 2001, Book of the Year

Kathy Kacer

shortlist, Canadian Library Association, and Red Maple Award, Ontario Library Association, both 2002, all for *Clara's War.*

Writings

The Secret of Gabi's Dresser, Second Story Press (Toronto, Ontario, Canada), 1999.

Clara's War, Second Story Press (Toronto, Ontario, Canada), 2001.

Home Free: Margit, Book 1, Penguin Canada (Toronto, Ontario, Canada), 2002.

The Night Spies, Second Story Press (Toronto, Ontario, Canada), 2003.

Work in Progress

A play based on *The Secret of Gabi's Dresser.*

Sidelights

Kathy Kacer's first book for children, *The Secret of Gabi's Dresser,* is a first-person fictionalized account of Kacer's mother's escape from the Nazis in Slovakia during World War II. Starting in 1940, the story traces the encroaching Nazification of a country that would later become the Czech Republic, where ten-year-old Gabi and her family face increasing restrictions on their freedoms. In 1943, when the Nazis come to take her away at age thirteen, Gabi hides in a dresser while her mother manages to distract the soldiers from the hiding place, saving her daughter's life so that they both can go into hiding until the end of the war. Although Kacer's use of a child-narrator makes her rendering of some aspects of the story awkward, according to *Canadian Children's Literature* critic Marjorie Gann, the story itself is undeniably "gripping," this critic allowed. Writing in *Quill & Quire,* Patty Lawlor, on the other hand, thought that Kacer had successfully rendered "a reader-friendly, simply-told story about a Jewish girl during the Second World War," recommending the book for children not yet ready for Anne Frank's diary.

The Secret of Gabi's Dresser was shortly followed by *Clara's War,* which offers another view of the Holocaust and the effect of the Nazi plan for the Jews on a family in Czechoslovakia. Like her first, Kacer's second young-adult novel draws upon historical events for the basis of a fictional story. In *Clara's War,* thirteen-year-old Clara is a less fortunate Czechoslovakian girl than Gabi for she and her family have been captured by the Nazis and transported to Theresienstadt, a concentration camp that acts as a way-station before the final destination of Auschwitz. There, amazingly, a children's opera was secretly staged and performed fifty times between 1943 and liberation in 1945, according to Jeffrey Canton in *Quill & Quire.* Thus, along with the terror and suffering that are part of every day life for young Clara, there is also schoolwork, growing friendships, and participation in an artistic endeavor. While the novel is explicit about the horrors of camp life, Kacer's focus on this artistic venture transforms her novel into "a story of hope, courage, and humanity in the face of overwhelming suffering and adversity," Canton asserted. Although Paula J. LaRue complained in *School Library Journal* that the book ends on an ambiguous note, leaving Clara in Theresienstadt with the war yet to end, another critic, Lynne Remick, writing in *Kliatt,* commented favorably on the inclusion of historical photographs and information about child survivors of the death camp at the book's end. As a character who represents a survivor of the camp, Clara's "story offers enlightenment and still allows the reader to grasp some hope for humanity and its future," Remick concluded.

"I am an author who has chosen to write stories about the Holocaust, that are geared to a young readership," Kacer told *SATA.* "And given this quest, I am often asked the question of how to bring this sensitive material to young children in a way that won't terrify them.

"I have spoken to children in dozens of schools and libraries about the Holocaust in the context of my two novels: *The Secret of Gabi's Dresser* and *Clara's War.* So much of my belief in the ability to present Holocaust material to young children is based on my own personal childhood experiences. From an early age, my parents shared with me their experiences of being survivors of the Holocaust.

"I have a fundamental belief in the ability and in fact, the responsibility, to teach the Holocaust to children. In doing so, one has to be sensitive to the age and stage of development of the child, and create an atmosphere of trust and openness, encouraging full dialogue.

"I remain determined to share these stories with children, and in so doing, ensure that these stories will not be lost."

Biographical and Critical Sources

PERIODICALS

Canadian Children's Literature, fall, 1999, Marjorie Gann, review of *The Secret of Gabi's Dresser,* pp. 167-173.

Kliatt, November, 2001, Lynne Remick, review of *Clara's War,* p. 16.

Quill & Quire, July, 1999, Patty Lawlor, review of *The Secret of Gabi's Dresser,* p. 49; May, 2001, Jeffrey Canton, review of *Clara's War,* p. 34.

School Library Journal, February, 2002, Paula J. LaRue, review of *Clara's War,* p. 134.

*   *   *

KIEFER, Kathleen Balmes 1957-
(Kathy Balmes)

Personal

Born November 9, 1957, in Ohio; daughter of Vernon (a lawyer) and Pat (a writer) Balmes; married John Kiefer (an engineer), August 29, 1987; children: Caitlin, Molly. *Education:* University of California—Berkeley, B.A. (economics), 1980; University of Washington, M.B.A., 1982. *Politics:* Democrat. *Religion:* "Raised Catholic."

Kathleen Balmes Kiefer

Addresses
Home—290 North Almenar Dr., Greenbrae, CA 94904.

Career
Pacific Gas and Electric Company, San Francisco, CA, assistant economic analyst, 1982-84, financial analyst, 1984-89; Astor Investment Management, Larkspur, CA, account administrator, 1990-93; Silver Moon Press, New York, NY, California marketing representative. Author.

Writings

(Under name Kathy Balmes) *Thunder on the Sierra,* illustrated by Vicki Catapano, Silver Moon Press (New York, NY), 2001.

Work in Progress
A middle-grade authorized biography of California senator Barbara Boxer; researching a Hispanic woman, Bernarda Ruiz, "who was important in stopping the Mexican-American war in early California."

Biographical and Critical Sources

PERIODICALS

Marin Independent Journal, September 11, 2001, Beth Ashley, "Writing for the Kids: Three Marin Women Recently Released New Books Written for and about Children," p. C1.
School Library Journal, August, 2001, Carol A. Edwards, review of *Thunder on the Sierra,* p. 175.

*   *   *

KLASS, David 1960-

Personal
Born March 8, 1960, in VT; son of Morton (an anthropology professor) and Sheila (a writer and English professor; maiden name, Solomon) Klass; married Giselle Benatar; children: Gabriel. *Education:* Yale University, B.A., 1982; University of Southern California, School of Cinema-Television, M.A., 1989.

Addresses
Home—New York, NY. *Agent*—Aaron M. Priest Literary Agency, 708 Third Ave., 23rd Floor, New York, NY 10017.

Career
Novelist and screenwriter. Director of *Shelter in the Storm,* 1987. Worked as an English teacher.

Member
Writers Guild of America West.

Awards, Honors
Outstanding Works of Fiction for Young Adults Award, Southern California Council, One Hundred "Best of the Best" selection, American Library Association (ALA), both 1990, both for *Wrestling with Honor;* Notable Children's Trade Book in the Field of Social Studies, Children's Book Council/National Council for the Social Studies, Best Book for Young Adults selection, ALA, and runner-up, Bank Street College Annual Children's Book Award, all 1994, all for *California Blue;* Best Book for Young Adults selection, ALA, 1995, for *Danger Zone.*

Writings

FOR YOUNG ADULTS

The Atami Dragons, Scribner (New York, NY), 1984.
Breakaway Run, E. P. Dutton (New York, NY), 1986.
A Different Season, E. P. Dutton (New York, NY), 1988.

Wrestling with Honor, E. P. Dutton (New York, NY), 1989.
California Blue, Scholastic (New York, NY), 1994.
Danger Zone, Scholastic (New York, NY), 1995.
Screen Test, Scholastic, (New York, NY), 1997.
You Don't Know Me: A Novel, Frances Foster Books (New York, NY), 2001.
Home of the Braves, Farrar, Straus (New York, NY), 2002.

OTHER

Night of the Tyger (adult novel), St. Martin's Press (New York, NY), 1990.
Samuri, Inc. (adult novel), Fawcett (New York, NY), 1992.

Also contributor of short stories to anthologies.

SCREENPLAYS

Kiss the Girls, Paramount Pictures Corporation (Hollywood, CA), 1997.
Desperate Measures, Columbia TriStar (Culver City, CA), 1998.
Runaway Virus, American Broadcasting Companies, Inc. (New York, NY), 2000.
(With sister Judy Klass) *In the Time of Butterflies* (based on the novel of the same name by Julia Alvarez), Showtime (New York, NY), 2001.
Walking Tall, Metro Goldwyn Meyer (Century City, CA), 2004.

Adaptations

Desperate Measures was adapted into a novel by Robert Tine, Berkley Boulevard Books (New York, NY), 1998.

Sidelights

A *Kirkus Reviews* critic described David Klass's contribution to young adult literature as sports fiction "enriched" with "perceptive explorations of character and social themes." Klass's characters find themselves confronting the implications of issues ranging from feminism to environmentalism, in contexts that are very familiar to many young adults—the playing field or competitive arena. While critics have lauded Klass's attention to detail and the evocative narratives in his sports scenes, many have also noted his complex presentation of social issues and his ability to avoid sentimentality in discussing personal traumas like divorce, child abuse, or the loss of a parent. Perhaps the key to Klass's success has been the philosophy he once declared: "I don't believe novels should be about 'issues'—I think they should be about people."

The son of Morton Klass, an anthropology professor, and Shelia Solomon Klass, a prominent young-adult writer, Klass grew up in a Leonia, New Jersey, home surrounded by a strong love for literature. "I came from a family of readers and writers," Klass told *Authors and*

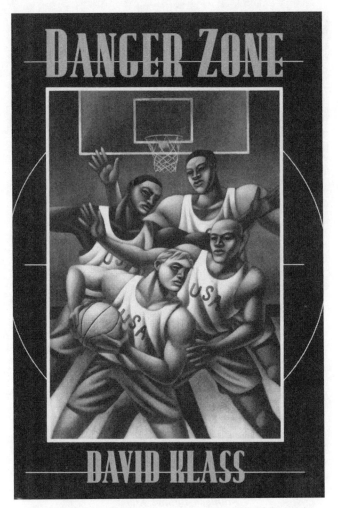

Jimmy Doyle is chosen to represent the United States in an international basketball tournament in Rome, but while there he learns as much about prejudice and hatred as he does about the sport. *(Cover illustration by Mike Benny.)*

Artists for Young Adults (*AAYA*). "I can't imagine a family where more emphasis and love was given to literature. My family reads ferociously." Both Klass's younger and older sisters, Judy and Perri, are novelists, and an uncle writes science fiction novels. "Growing up in this family, it was almost impossible not to become a writer," Klass noted.

An avid athlete in high school, Klass realized in college that professional athletics would not be a realistic goal for him, and instead he increased his efforts at Yale, winning an award for best creative writing as an undergraduate. After graduation, Klass decided to try his hand in the world of law, interning at a law office for one year. At the end of that year, Klass told *AAYA,* "I knew two things: one, that I did not want to be a lawyer, and two, that I wanted to have an adventure." For this adventure, Klass took a job as a teacher in Japan, instructing students in conversational English. He realized that if he was going to write a book, this would be the place.

The inspiration for this first young-adult novel came from his immersion in a new culture, experiencing all the sights and sounds in a provincial Japanese town. "The book just flew off my fingers," Klass told *AAYA*. "From the outset I determined to write a young adult title. It just seemed right for me. I was twenty-three at the time, and in many ways still had the maturity level of a seventeen-year-old. The voice of a high school kid came naturally to me—it still does. And I was not ready to tackle the length and complexity of an adult novel."

The resulting work, *The Atami Dragons,* features a young male protagonist who leaves trouble at home when he goes to Japan. Jerry Sanders has just lost his mother, and he decides to accompany his father and sister on a business trip to Japan for the summer. As he sacrifices the opportunity to play baseball in the United States when he leaves for Japan, Jerry jumps at the chance to play baseball in Japan. He makes new friends, experiences baseball in another culture, and begins to come to terms with his mother's death. As *Booklist* critic Zvirin noted, Klass brings "equal shares of humor, sports, and sentiment" to this story of loss and recovery.

Breakaway Run, Klass's next novel, was written with the insight he gained as an English teacher working in this Japanese high school. It begins when Tony Ross leaves his quarreling parents to study for five months in Atami, Japan, the same town the author taught in. Tony initially finds adjusting to the ways of his host family and Japanese culture difficult; he is frustrated by his inability to communicate with others and disturbed by the way he is treated as an outsider. Gradually, however, Tony's personal qualities and his athletic abilities (especially in soccer) earn him the respect and affection of his host family and schoolmates. He even manages to cope with and adjust to the news that his parents are divorcing. According to *Booklist*'s Stephanie Zvirin, Klass includes details about the sports Tony plays, and his "portrayal of Japanese culture and customs" demonstrates "obvious respect and knowledge."

While writing *Breakaway Run,* Klass received some exciting news. His first novel had been optioned by the movies, and a Hollywood producer came to Atami to visit Klass and view the possible location. At the time, Klass was still toying with the idea of going to law school once he was back in the United States, but this producer convinced him that his real future lay in Hollywood as a screenwriter. "So I went to Hollywood," Klass told *AAYA*, "and of course the movie deal fell through, as so many do. I found myself in Los Angeles, one of a million other young screenwriters, alone, broke, and with no sense of how to break through as a screenwriter." For the next seven years, Klass lived close to the bone economically, working at various odd jobs, doing treatments for producers that earned a meager living, and also studying for a master's degree at the University of Southern California, putting himself through college by working as a teacher's assistant in

English composition sections. "During this time my work on YA novels was about the only thing that kept me sane, that made me believe I really was a writer," Klass recalled. "I didn't much like L.A., I missed the seasons, and I found the whole entertainment business and social life surrounding it slightly surreal."

During his time in Hollywood, however, Klass published three more successful young-adult titles: *A Different Season, Wrestling with Honor,* and *California Blue.* According to a *Kirkus Reviews* critic, Klass presents "another thoughtful, expertly crafted story" with *A Different Season.* In this novel, the protagonist does not enjoy baseball in another culture, but he does experience cultural pressure to transform his favorite sport. Jim Roark, known to everyone as "Streak," is a talented pitcher who finds himself attracted to Jennifer Douglas, another outstanding athlete. When Jennifer attempts to join the baseball team, however, Jim insists that girls and women have no business playing baseball, and the teens' relationship suffers.

As critics have noted, Klass uses the debate between Jim and Jennifer, and the public debate that ensues, to present arguments for and against the integration of sports teams. Jennifer is finally allowed to join the team, and although their team loses the final game, Jennifer and Jim learn to respect their differences of opinion. "Klass writes with precision and grace about baseball," asserted Hazel Rochman in *Booklist*. A *Publishers Weekly* critic appreciated Klass's decision not to "resolve the book's central conflict," instead letting readers "draw their own conclusions."

Wrestling with Honor takes up the issue of drug testing. Ron Woods, an honor student, Eagle Scout, and captain of the wrestling team, never expected that the mandatory drug test he had to take would demonstrate positive for marijuana use. Although Ron is not a drug user and realizes that the test results must be a mistake, he refuses to take another test to clear his name because he believes the tests violate his right to privacy. Ron is subsequently banned from his team, and his relationships with his teammates, family, and girlfriend deteriorate. Before the novel ends, however, he explores his feelings about the death of his father in the Vietnam war, discovers why his drug test was positive, and confronts his fiercest wrestling competitor. Readers "will be cheering all the way through [the novel's] exciting—if manipulated—final scene," concluded a critic in *Publishers Weekly*.

Klass focuses on environmentalism in *California Blue,* a novel that a *Kirkus Reviews* critic suggested is Klass's "best yet." Klass once explained the development of this novel: "I tried to write *California Blue* several times, in different genres: as an adult novel, as a screenplay, and even as a stage play. Each of these attempts failed miserably because all I had to work with was the issue of loggers versus environmentalists. Finally, I hit upon a way of personalizing the story. For some reason, nearly all of my novels turn out to be father-son stories. I came up with the idea of telling this story from the point of view of a teenage boy whose father has always worked for the town's lumber mill. When the boy finds a rare butterfly whose existence threatens the future operation of the mill, he and his father are drawn into direct conflict." This conflict between John and his father is intensified by the fact that each has always disagreed with the other about the relative merits of athleticism and intellectualism, and John's father may be dying from leukemia.

Although a *Publishers Weekly* critic stated that Klass has written a "beautifully rendered novel" and "handles [the] complex situations with grace and subtlety," Klass reported that other critics did not agree with his decision to portray one rarely discussed situation in his novel. "I've been very surprised that the romantic attraction between John and his teacher in *California Blue* has drawn criticism from some quarters. He's such an honest, moral person, and for that matter so is she. Do people think that such things don't happen, or that writers shouldn't address them responsibly but honestly?"

High school senior Joe Brickman wants to be the captain of his soccer team and date his neighbor, but unpredictable and unsettling things get in the way of Joe's simple dreams. (Cover illustration by Jeffrey Fisher.)

As critics began to favorably notice the works of Klass, the author's screenwriting career also began taking off, with successes such as *Kiss the Girls,* a thriller starring Morgan Freeman and Ashley Judd, and *Desperate Measures,* featuring Michael Keaton and Andy Garcia. Klass was able to leave Hollywood for the East Coast, settling in Manhattan, where he could write for the movies at a distance and continue with his YA novels.

Klass finds a balance between writing screenplays and YA novels. "I love the freedom that YA novels provide me," Klass told *AAYA.* "Hollywood wants to know what they're going to get in a script. I present them with a detailed, ten-page, scene-by-scene outline, and then follow that closely as I write the screenplay. I am always aware of audience reaction when writing for Hollywood. It is a constant exercise in calculation. You can make your hero a drunkard, but never a coward, for example. Viewers wouldn't allow that. But with YA novels I've never written a page that was calculating. I am one with the characters, not separate enough to figure out what the audience wants or needs. I have a general idea where the story begins and where it ends up. Then I have to find the voice of the narrator—I generally write these novels in first person. Once I find the voice, I just let my character take me through the story and stay out of the way. It's wonderfully freeing not to have to work from a detailed outline for my YA novels."

Klass usually writes very quickly: two titles, *Danger Zone* and *Screen Test,* were written in an energetic three-month period after moving from Hollywood. With *Danger Zone,* Klass turned to basketball and a high school "Teen Dream Team" which competes in Europe in an international tournament. Jimmy Doyle, a star guard from Minnesota, finds that he is distrusted by much of the rest of the team, largely made up of inner-city African-American players. Doyle must win their respect, battling against rivalry and racism to do so. But once in Europe, a new form of racism appears. German skinheads threaten the team, and in the final game, Jimmy takes a terrorist bullet just as he sinks the winning shot. A *Kirkus Reviews* contributor thought that Klass embroidered the plot with "frank, thoughtful observations about fathers and sons, city versus small-town values, race, friendship, and courage," while Tom S. Hurlburt noted in *School Library Journal* that "the racial tension throughout the book rings true, and readers seeking lots of hoop action will be thoroughly satisfied." Nancy Zachary, writing in *Voice of Youth Advocates,* called the book a "fast-paced adventure that deals realistically with pressure, racism, and terrorism."

Screen Test is Klass's take on Hollywood. "I don't think I've ever sat down to write a novel with a conscious message I wanted to impart—with the possible exception of *Screen Test,*" Klass explained to *AAYA.* "Rather than impart a message, I try to create a difficult situation with lots of conflict and let any message grow out of the characters' response to the situation." The situation in *Screen Test* involves sixteen-year-old Liz, who is discovered by a big-shot Hollywood producer when she takes part in a student film. Offered a starring role in a feature film, Liz leaves her New Jersey home for a summer in Hollywood and a possible film career. But Liz soon learns painful truths about "Tinsel Town" and her seductive male co-star; she eventually learns to value her parents and the East Coast more than the flaky values of Hollywood. Writing in *Booklist,* Ilene Cooper found that Klass offers "some good lessons here on finding your own way."

Critics noted a marked change with the author's literary techniques in the 2001 novel *You Don't Know Me,* with *School Library Journal* reviewer Joel Schumaker remarking "Klass blazes past his previous efforts stylistically." Faced with abuse from his mother's violent live-in boyfriend, pressure from his teachers at school, and confusion over the girl of his dreams, fourteen-year-old John creates a detailed conversation in his head, the only place where he can escape the absurdity of the world he lives in. As readers discover the thoughts in the young protagonist's head, they come to understand John's desperation as he feels no one understands him. After a near-fatal beating at the hands of his soon-to-be stepfather, John's world opens up, and he learns how well regarded he is by not only his teachers and classmates but, perhaps most importantly, his mother. According to a *Publishers Weekly* contributor, "the hero's underlying sense of isolation and thread of hope will strike a chord with nearly every adolescent." Describing the book as "vivid and original" with "a strange, hopeful ending," *Horn Book*'s Anita L. Burkam found John "a genuinely sympathetic character whose pathos may dip into self-pity but never into self-indulgence." *Journal of Adolescent and Adult Literacy* reviewer Tshegofatso Mmolawa offered high marks for Klass's richly-woven novel. "*You Don't Know Me* is multilayered," observed Mmolawa, "but presents the complex life of an understandably angst-ridden adolescent in an enlightening and humorous way."

Klass returns to an athletic-themed book in *Home of the Braves,* a story about high-school senior Joe Brickman. A star soccer player, Joe expects to be the popular boy in school and finally find the courage to ask his long-time crush out on a date. However, a Brazilian transfer student, nicknamed "Phenom," pushes the young narrator out of his top dog status, upsetting his imagined plans for the school year. But more important problems arise when conflicts between students from different parts of town turn violent and Joe must stand up to the ringleader of the tension, a football player whose gang pummels Joe's best friend. *School Library Journal* reviewer Joanne K. Cecere found Klass's "multilayered" story offers young-adult readers "characters [that] are, for the most part, believable teens searching for answers to complex societal and individual issues." The author's "strong doses of realism and grittiness" enhances the book's setting, claimed *Booklist*'s Todd Morning, who went on to call *Home of the Braves* "a winning novel with many elements that will ring true for older readers."

Continuing to work both writing screenplays and novels, Klass believes his books fill an important space on the young-adult shelves. As he concluded in his *AAYA* interview, "Everybody tells you that it is very hard to publish books for boys between the ages of thirteen and eighteen. But my feeling is that if there are no books out there for them, that will become a self-fulfilling prophecy. If you write exciting, true, meaningful stories, they will read them. And reading is important. As someone who works in Hollywood, I know there is something unique and almost mystical about the experience of reading. It's an older form than the visual of movies, and despite all the money spent to make movies, I think that written words are an infinitely more powerful way to tell a story."

Biographical and Critical Sources

BOOKS

Klass, David, in an interview with J. Sydney Jones for *Authors and Artists for Young Adults,* Volume 26, Gale (Detroit, MI), 1999.
St. James Guide to Young Adult Writers, 2nd edition, St. James Press (Detroit, MI), 1999.

PERIODICALS

Booklist, December 1, 1984, Stephanie Zvirin, review of *The Atami Dragons,* p. 518; August, 1987, Stephanie Zvirin, review of *Breakaway Run,* pp. 1737-1738; January 1, 1988, Hazel Rochman, review of *A Different Season,* p. 775; November 15, 1988, p. 567; July, 1992, p. 1933; March 1, 1994, p. 1252; December 1, 1997, Ilene Cooper, review of *Screen Test,* p. 615; September 1, 2002, Todd Morning, review of *Home of the Braves,* p. 127.
Bulletin of the Center for Children's Books, December, 1984; December, 1987.
Horn Book, July, 2001, Anita L. Burkam, review of *You Don't Know Me,* p. 455.
Journal of Adolescent and Adult Literacy, October, 2001, Tshegofatso Mmolawa, review of *You Don't Know Me,* p. 172.
Kirkus Reviews, November 1, 1987, review of *A Different Season,* p. 1576; February 15, 1994, review of *California Blue;* November 15, 1995, review of *Danger Zone;* July 15, 1997, review of *Screen Test.*
Publishers Weekly, November 27, 1987, review of *A Different Season,* p. 86; September 30, 1988, review of *Wrestling with Honor,* p. 71; February 14, 1994, review of *California Blue,* p. 90; March 12, 2001, review of *You Don't Know Me,* p. 92.
School Library Journal, March, 1996, Tom S. Hurlburt, review of *Danger Zone,* p. 218; March, 2001, Joel Shoemaker, review of *You Don't Know Me,* p. 252; September, 2002, Joanne K. Cecere, review of *Home of the Braves,* p. 226.
Voice of Youth Advocates, April, 1996, Nancy Zachary, review of *Danger Zone,* p. 27.*

KVASNOSKY, Laura McGee 1951-

Personal

Born January 27, 1951, in Sacramento, CA; daughter of Harvey C. (a newspaper publisher) and Helen (a comptroller; maiden name, McDonald) McGee; married John Kvasnosky (a public relations executive), December 16, 1972; children: Timothy John, Noelle Helen. *Education:* Occidental College, B.A., 1973, studied writing with Jane Yolen at Centrum (Port Townsend, WA), 1994; studied illustration with Keith Baker at School of Visual Concepts (Seattle, WA). *Religion:* "Northwest pantheist." *Hobbies and other interests:* Gardening, cross-country skiing, hiking.

Addresses

Home and office—4425 51st Ave., Seattle, WA, 98105. *E-mail*—kvasjl@mindspring.com.

Career

Writer and illustrator. Graphic designer and proprietor of one-person design shop, Seattle, WA, 1980—. Society of Children's Book Writers and Illustrators, edited regional newsletter, 1992-94.

Member

Society of Children's Book Writers and Illustrators (Washington region board member); Authors Guild; NW Girlchoir (member of board of directors, 1992-96).

Awards, Honors

Best Books selection, *Parents* magazine, and Children's Book of the Month Club selection, both 1995, both for *See You Later, Alligator;* "Pick of the Lists" selection, American Booksellers Association, 1996, for *A Red Wagon Year* (written by Kathi Appelt); Notable Book selection, American Library Association, 1999, for *Zelda and Ivy.*

Writings

SELF-ILLUSTRATED

Pink, Red, Blue, What Are You?, Dutton (New York, NY), 1994.

One, Two, Three, Play with Me, Dutton (New York, NY), 1994.

See You Later, Alligator, Harcourt (San Diego, CA), 1995.

Mr. Chips!, Farrar, Straus, and Giroux (New York, NY), 1996.

Zelda and Ivy, Candlewick Press (New York, NY), 1998.

Zelda and Ivy and the Boy Next Door, Candlewick Press (New York, NY), 1999.

Zelda and Ivy One Christmas, Candlewick Press (New York, NY), 2000.

When Prince Alexander frets about what to dream at night, his royal parents summon experts to the task in Laura McGee Kvasnosky's work **What Shall I Dream?,** illustrated by Judith Byron Schachner.

ILLUSTRATOR

Florence Page Jaques, *There Once Was a Puffin,* Dutton (New York, NY), 1995.

Kathi Appelt, *A Red Wagon Year,* Harcourt (San Diego, CA), 1996.

Libby Hough, *If Somebody Lived Next Door,* Dutton (New York, NY), 1997.

OTHER

What Shall I Dream?, illustrated by Judith Byron Schachner, Dutton (New York, NY), 1996.

One Lucky Summer (chapter book), Dutton (New York, NY), 2002.

Sidelights

The author and/or illustrator of a dozen books for children, Laura McGee Kvasnosky is known for her gentle humor both in text and illustrations. Particularly popular are her "Zelda and Ivy" books about a couple of "true-to-life little fox sisters," as Ilene Cooper described the fictional siblings in *Booklist.* Blending text with vibrant gouache illustrations, Kvasnosky delights and entertains, according to critics. Though most of her solo work and collaborative efforts have been in picture books, Kvasnosky is also the author of a chapter book, *One Lucky Summer,* in which a pair of ten-year-olds are brought together by a flying squirrel.

"I come from a long line of California newspaper writers," Kvasnosky once told *SATA.* "Perhaps we feel a genetic urge to organize a story as a way to understand life. Being part of [a larger] family also affects what I choose to write about. I'm the middle of five kids. In many ways my childhood was like growing up in a summer camp. My mother even put name tags in our underwear.

"Three things happened in third grade that led me to become a writer and illustrator. First, we moved, so I was a new kid at school. As an outsider looking in, I developed observation skills. Second, I made up tremendous stories in hopes of attracting friends, thus developing a keen understanding of the blend of fact and fiction that a good, 'believable' story requires. Third, my reading improved to the point where I could really read. I became (and still am) a bookworm.

"I began my work career at the age of eight, sharpening pencils for my editor-father. Over the years, I contributed in the advertising and editorial departments of his newspaper, too. When my children were small, I created over 10,000 Christmas ornaments in my kitchen. Then, in 1980, I started my own graphic design firm. I decided to go for a lifelong dream of publishing a children's book when I turned forty."

Kvasnosky's first published works for children were the self-illustrated board books *One, Two, Three, Play with Me* and *Pink, Red, Blue, What Are You?,* published in 1994. Using short, rhyming phrases and bright pictures to introduce colors and numbers, these works also employ various groupings of multiethnic children to illustrate learning concepts. In *Pink, Red, Blue, What Are You?,* animals define themselves by their color, temperament, and sometimes their olfactory qualities: "We're pink, we stink," proclaim a group of pigs; "We're green, we're mean," warn the alligators. A *Publishers Weekly* reviewer found these board books "simple, fun and effective," while *School Library Journal* contributor Linda Wicher praised Kvasnosky's illustrations, asserting that "the sketched figures are full of movement and wit."

Another of Kvasnosky's self-illustrated books for preschoolers, *See You Later, Alligator,* features a group of young reptiles whose parents begin the day by dropping them off at River Bottom School. Reptilian variations of the title phrase, including "In a shake, garter snake" and "In a blizzard, little lizard," attempt to convey the book's emphasis on "upbeat separations," according to *School Library Journal* contributor Nancy Seiner. *Booklist*'s April Judge concluded that though "slight, the book will tickle the funny bones of young listeners."

Kvasnosky has also written picture books for independent readers, including the stories *What Shall I Dream?*

Ivy finds herself drawn into the schemes of her older sibling, Zelda, in Kvasnosky's three short tales that comprise **Zelda and Ivy.** *(Written and illustrated by Kvasnosky.)*

and her self-illustrated *Mr. Chips! What Shall I Dream?,* described as "a lovely bedtime story" by *School Library Journal* contributor Judith Constantinides, takes readers into the world of young Prince Alexander, who worries over what to dream. His royal family uses their power and influence to summon Dream Brewers, Dream Weavers, and Dream Sweepers to assist him; but when the dreams these masters concoct prove unsatisfying, it is the shrewd observation of the humble nursemaid that saves the day. *Mr. Chips!,* on the other hand, is a simple story of the affectionate bond between a dog and a child. In this instance, the dog, Mr. Chips, is away for days and does not return home before his little companion Ellie and her family move to a new town. "Stories about lost pets who manage to find their families despite vast distances are always touching, and this one is no exception," asserted a *Kirkus Reviews* critic. *School Library Journal* contributor Marianne Saccardi called *Mr. Chips!* "a heartwarming story," adding: "Kvasnosky's cartoon art is bright and appropriately childlike as well." Lauren Peterson, reviewing the same title in *Booklist,* called the book "a heartwarming story."

By far Kvasnosky's most popular titles are the "Zelda and Ivy" books. The fox sisters start their zany adventures in *Zelda and Ivy* in which older sister Zelda tries to boss around younger sister Ivy in three humorous chapters. Ivy goes along with Zelda's schemes in these stories, even though they seem a bit scary. In the first chapter, the sisters are playing circus and Zelda convinces Ivy to be the girl on the flying trapeze, with less than pleasant results. A second chapter finds Ivy with a blue tail, which is more of Zelda's doing, having convinced her younger sibling that it is the cool thing to do. And in the final episode of the sisters' debut, it looks as if Ivy is finally going to get the upper hand when Zelda convinces her that dust under her pillow will grant her a wish. However, at the last moment, Zelda figures a way to reassume her role as head fox. This picture book received much critical praise when published in 1998. *Booklist*'s Ilene Cooper noted that Kvasnosky "not only has a way with words; her illustrations are delightful, too." Cooper further commented that the book was "fun with some bite." A reviewer for *Publishers Weekly* praised "this insightful look at sisterhood," noting that it "reach[es] out to readers regardless of their birth order." Many of the critics compared the expressiveness of Kvasnosky's illustrations to those of Kevin Henke. *Horn Book*'s Martha V. Parravano lauded the illustrations for their "gift for communicating a wealth of emotion through the dot of an eye or the angle of a tail." Janice M. DelNegro, reviewing *Zelda and Ivy* in *Bulletin of the Center for Children's Books,* predicted the text would "elicit groans and chuckles of recognition" and commended the illustrations as "engagingly fresh and lively." And *School Library Journal*'s Luann Toth thought that young readers "will recognize and relate to these three stories that take a gentle, humorous look at sibling dynamics."

The sisters make a return performance in *Zelda and Ivy and the Boy Next Door.* In this second book in the series, the sisters are happy when Eugene moves in next door, thinking they will have a new playmate. However, the triangular nature of the new friendship presents difficulties when two gang up on one, and loyalties shift and change. Drama ensues when the trio attempt to set up a lemonade stand and play a game of pirates. Competition between the sisters especially becomes intense when both sisters decide to have a romantic crush on Eugene. Originally smitten by Zelda, Eugene becomes tired of the way she teases him and instead turns his attentions to Ivy. Cooper found this second installment in the fox sisters' lives to be "delightfully droll and at the same time awfully sweet." Writing in *School Library Journal,* Toth enthused, "Encore Zelda and Ivy!"

Kvasnosky served up that encore in the year 2000 with *Zelda and Ivy One Christmas.* With the holidays coming, the sisters have high hopes and many wishes. Zelda wants a fancy gown while Ivy desires a Princess Mimi doll and the ballet accouterments to go with it. These dreams come out one day while they are helping their elderly neighbor, Mrs. Brownlie, make gingerbread cookies. Hearing these wishes, the woman tells the sisters how she once went to a ball with her now dead husband. On the way home that day, Ivy suggests making the woman a bracelet to cheer her up on Christmas, and older sister Zelda agrees, acting as if it were her idea in the first place. When the big day comes, Santa disappoints the sisters with matching bathrobes, but

when the sisters open up gifts from a mysterious "Christmas Elf," they are delighted to find the doll and the desired gown. "As always, humor pervades the situations and the dialogue," noted Martha V. Parravano in a starred *Horn Book* review. Parravano also lauded Kvasnosky's "illustrations, with their heavy but vibrant lines . . . full of energy and movement." Ellen Mandel also praised the tale in *Booklist,* calling it an "engaging return" for the sisters, and one that depicts the joy of giving: "companionship, affection, and memories, priceless rewards for any season." And a reviewer for *School Library Journal* concluded that the book is a "must for everyone's Christmas list."

Kvasnosky turned her hand to longer fiction in the 2002 chapter book *One Lucky Summer.* Steven Bennett is having a bad summer, forced to move away from his Santa Cruz, California, home and its breezy beach weather, his best friend, and his Little League team, and go to the state capital at humid Sacramento where he knows no one. He has also temporarily lost his best playing-catch buddy as his photographer father is on assignment in Peru, and his mother offers little consolation, being busy authoring a cook book. His bad luck continues when he discovers that his new next door neighbor is a girl, and not just any regular girl, but one with dreams of becoming a ballerina. Even worse, Lucinda, the ballerina, does not take kindly to Steven's pet lizard, Godzilla, especially when the creature ruins her favorite tutu. Steven's mother, however, soon makes friends with Lucinda's mother who invites the newcomers to their cabin by the lake for a week. The scene is set for disaster as tension continues to grow between the two youngsters. When Godzilla escapes from his cage, though, the two set out to find it and discover a baby flying squirrel instead. Their shared determination to keep the squirrel, dubbed Lucky, alive brings Steven and Lucinda closer together, and soon Steven is faced with a difficult decision: to let his pet lizard go or keep the squirrel. He knows that if he does not take the baby squirrel back with him, it will surely die, but he cannot keep both lizard and squirrel. Critics felt that Kvasnosky made a smooth transition from picture book to chapter book with *One Lucky Summer.* Writing in *School Library Journal,* Alison Grant noted that the "novel should prove to be a lucky choice for girls and boys alike." Similarly, *Booklist*'s Kay Weisman praised Kvasnosky's "strong, believable characters and . . . good ear for dialogue," while a reviewer for *Publishers Weekly* called the book a "tightly written, affecting tale about adjustment and friendship."

"The seeds that grow into future books are often planted in young children," Kvasnosky once told *SATA.* "I know that because it is my experience. It is one reason I enjoy working with young writers and artists. Creating children's books is my dream job. The experiences I value most—nurturing a family, writing, graphic design, reading—all meet in this one enterprise."

Biographical and Critical Sources

BOOKS

Kvasnosky, Laura McGee, *Pink, Red, Blue, What Are You?,* Dutton (New York, NY), 1994.
Kvasnosky, Laura McGee, *See You Later, Alligator,* Harcourt (San Diego, CA), 1995.

PERIODICALS

Booklist, September 15, 1995, April Judge, review of *See You Later, Alligator,* p. 175; July, 1996, Lauren Peterson, review of *Mr. Chips!,* p. 1830; October 1, 1996, Julie Corsaro, review of *A Red Wagon Year,* pp. 356-357; June 1, 1997, Carolyn Phelan, review of *If Somebody Lived Next Door,* p. 1719; April, 1998, Ilene Cooper, review of *Zelda and Ivy,* p. 1324; May 1, 1999, Ilene Cooper, review of *Zelda and Ivy and the Boy Next Door,* p. 1599; November 15, 2000, Ellen Mandel, review of *Zelda and Ivy One Christmas,* p. 648; March 1, 2002, Kay Weisman, review of *One Lucky Summer,* p. 1137.
Bulletin of the Center for Children's Books, November, 1996, p. 105; January, 1997, Amy E. Brandt, review of *What Shall I Dream?,* pp. 177-178; April, 1998, Janice M. DelNegro, review of *Zelda and Ivy,* p. 285.
Horn Book, July-August, 1998, Martha V. Parravano, review of *Zelda and Ivy,* pp. 475-476; November-December, 2000, Martha V. Parravano, review of *Zelda and Ivy One Christmas,* p. 747.

Horn Book Guide, spring, 1997, Lolly Robinson, review of *Mr. Chips!,* p. 35, and Tanya Auger, review of *What Shall I Dream?,* p. 35.
Kirkus Reviews, July 1, 1996, review of *Mr. Chips!,* p. 970.
Publishers Weekly, May 2, 1994, review of *Pink, Red, Blue, What Are You?* and *One, Two, Three, Play with Me!,* p. 305; May 15, 1995, p. 71; June 24, 1996, review of *Mr. Chips!,* p. 58; Mary 12, 1997, review of *If Somebody Lived Next Door,* p. 75; May 11, 1998, review of *Zelda and Ivy,* p. 67; April 8, 2002, review of *One Lucky Summer,* p. 228.
School Library Journal, August, 1994, Linda Wicher, review of *Pink, Red, Blue, What Are You?* and *One, Two, Three, Play with Me!,* p. 139; November, 1995, Nancy Seiner, review of *See You Later, Alligator!,* p. 74; August, 1996, Marianne Saccardi, review of *Mr. Chips!,* p. 126; September, 1996, Judith Constantinides, review of *What Shall I Dream?,* p. 182; July, 1997, Christy Norris, review of *If Somebody Lived Next Door,* p. 69; June, 1998, Luann Toth, review of *Zelda and Ivy,* p. 113; May, 1999, Luann Toth, review of *Zelda and Ivy and the Boy Next Door,* p. 92; October, 2000, review of *Zelda and Ivy One Christmas,* p. 60; April, 2002, Alison Grant, review of *One Lucky Summer,* p. 114.

ONLINE

Laura McGee Kvasnosky Home Page, http://www.lmk books.com/ (December 19, 2002).*

L

LITTLETON, Mark R. 1950-

Personal

Born September 25, 1950, in Camden, NJ; son of H. Richard and Elizabeth T. (a homemaker) Littleton; married Valerie, February 14, 1983 (divorced, July 23, 1993); married Jeanette Gardner; children: Nicole, Alisha. *Education:* Colgate University, B.A., 1972, Dallas Theological Seminary, graduated 1977. *Politics:* Republican. *Religion:* Independent.

Addresses

Agent—c/o Author Mail, Thomas Nelson, 501 Nelson Pl., Nashville, TN 37214.

Career

Author of fiction and nonfiction books for children and adults; Annapolis Fellowship of Christian Writers, Annapolis, MD, leader, beginning 1984. Has also worked as a pastor.

Awards, Honors

Award of Merit, *Campus Life,* 1987, for *A Place to Stand: When Life Throws You Off Balance,* and 1992, for *Tales of the Neverending;* Gold Medallion Award nominee, 1989, for *Beefin' Up: Daily Feed for Amazing Grazing,* and 1995, for *Pairin' Up.*

Writings

A Place to Stand: When Life Throws You Off Balance (nonfiction), Multnomah Press (Portland, OR), 1986.
When God Seems Far Away: Biblical Insight for Common Depression (nonfiction), H. Shaw (Wheaton, IL), 1987.
Lies We Like to Hear: Satan's Everyday Strategies (nonfiction), H. Shaw (Wheaton, IL), 1988.
Submission Is for Husbands, Too (adult nonfiction), Accent Books (Denver, CO), 1988.

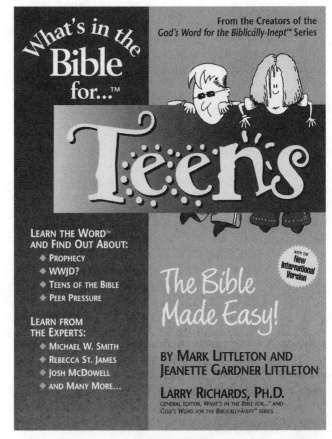

Mark R. Littleton and Jeanette Gardner Littleton offer insight into biblical text that examines subjects of relevance to teens. *(Cover illustration by Bruce Burkhardt, Melissa A. Burkhardt and Dennis Hengeveld.)*

Cool Characters with Sweaty Palms, Victor Books (Wheaton, IL), 1989.
What to Do When God Doesn't Follow Your Plan, Accent Books (Denver, CO), 1989.
The Terrible Plight of Oliver B., illustrated by Ron Wheeler, Bayside Press (Pacific, MO), 1990.
Tales of the Neverending (adult fiction), Moody Press (Chicago, IL), 1990.

Delighted by Discipline (nonfiction), Victor Books (Wheaton, IL), 1990.

Escaping the Time Crunch (nonfiction), Moody Press (Chicago, IL), 1990.

Battle Ready: Winning the War with Temptation, Victor Books (Wheaton, IL), 1992.

Death Trip (adult novel), Moody Press (Chicago, IL), 1992.

When They Invited Me to Fellowship . . . I Thought They Meant a Cruise (young-adult nonfiction), Christian Publications (Camp Hill, PA), 1992.

(With Brian and Alsie Kelley) *Stasia's Gift* (nonfiction), Crossway (Wheaton, IL), 1993.

The Storm Within (nonfiction), Tyndale House (Wheaton, IL), 1994.

(With Frank Minirth) *You Can!* (nonfiction), Thomas Nelson (Nashville, TN), 1994.

The Basics: Nailing Down What Builds You Up (young adult nonfiction), Christian Publications (Camp Hill, PA), 1994.

Before Eden (adult fiction), Thomas Nelson (Nashville, TN), 1995.

God Is!, Starburst (Lancaster, PA), 1997.

(With Jeanette Gardner Littleton) *Light the Torch, Pass the Flame: Lessons from Our Fathers,* Beacon Hill Press (Kansas City, MO), 1998.

NIrV Kids' Book of Devotions: A 365-Day Adventure in God's Word, Zondervan (Grand Rapids, MI), 1998.

Conversations with God the Father: Encounters with One True God, StarBurst Publications (Lancaster, PA), 1998.

(With Steve Peters) *Truth about Rock,* Bethany House (Minneapolis, MN), 1998.

Jesus: Everything You Need to Know to Figure Him Out, Westminister John Knox Press (Louisville, KY), 2001.

(Adaptor) *Leading as a Friend* (based on *Developing the Leader within You* by John C. Maxwell), Tommy Nelson (Nashville, TN), 2001.

(Adaptor) *Leading in Your Youth Group* (based on *Developing the Leader within You* by John C. Maxwell), Tommy Nelson (Nashville, TN), 2001.

(Adaptor) *Leading Your Sports Team* (based on *Developing the Leader within You* by John C. Maxwell), Tommy Nelson (Nashville, TN), 2001.

(With Jeanette Gardner Littleton) *What's in the Bible for . . . Teens,* Starburst (Lancaster, PA), 2002.

Getting Honest with God: Praying as If God Really Listens, InterVarsity Press (Downers Grove, IL), 2003.

(Author of notes; with Sandy Silverthorne and Marnie Wooding) *The Edge Devotional Bible: New International Version,* Zonderkidz (Grand Rapids, MI), 2003.

"ALLY O'CONNOR ADVENTURES"

Tracks in the Sand, Baker Books (Grand Rapids, MI), 2001.

Sarah's Secret, Baker Books (Grand Rapids, MI), 2001.

Hoofbeats on the Trail, Baker Books (Grand Rapids, MI), 2002.

"UP" SERIES; YOUNG ADULT NONFICTION

Beefin' Up: Daily Feed for Amazing Grazing, Multnomah Press (Portland, OR), 1989.

Tunin' Up: Daily Jammin' for Tight Relationships, Multnomah Press (Portland, OR), 1991.

Fillin' Up, illustrated by Graci Evans, Multnomah Press (Portland, OR), 1993.

Pairin' Up, Multnomah Press (Portland, OR), 1995.

"ROCKY CREEK ADVENTURES" SERIES; YOUNG ADULT FICTION

The Adventure at Rocky Creek, Cook (Elgin, IL), 1993.

Tree Fort Wars, Cook (Elgin, IL), 1993.

Trouble down the Creek, Cook (Elgin, IL), 1994.

"CRISTA CHRONICLES"; YOUNG ADULT FICTION

Secrets of Moonlight Mountain, Harvest House (Eugene, OR), 1992.

Winter Thunder, Harvest House (Eugene, OR), 1992.

Robbers on Rock Road, Harvest House (Eugene, OR), 1993.

Escape of the Grizzly, Harvest House (Eugene, OR), 1994.

Danger on Midnight Trail, Harvest House (Eugene, OR), 1994.

Friends No Matter What, Harvest House (Eugene, OR), 1994.

"SPORTS HEROES" SERIES

Baseball, Zondervan (Grand Rapids MI), 1995.

Basketball, Zondervan (Grand Rapids MI), 1995.

Football, Zondervan (Grand Rapids MI), 1995.

Track and Field, Zondervan (Grand Rapids MI), 1995.

Soccer, Zondervan (Grand Rapids MI), 1996.

Summer Olympics, Zondervan (Grand Rapids MI), 1996.

Baseball Two, Zondervan (Grand Rapids MI), 1996.

Basketball Two, Zondervan (Grand Rapids MI), 1996.

Olympics 2002, Zondervan (Grand Rapids MI), 2002.

Extreme Sports, Zondervan (Grand Rapids MI), 2002.

Auto Racing, Zondervan (Grand Rapids, MI), 2002.

Baseball Three, Zondervan (Grand Rapids, MI), 2002.

Sidelights

Mark R. Littleton has established a successful career as a writer whose Christian beliefs figure strongly in his work. In addition to writing novels and nonfiction geared to audiences ranging from middle-schoolers to adults, Littleton has also devoted much time to creating inspirational books such as *A Place to Stand: When Life Throws You Off Balance* and *Getting Honest with God: Praying as If God Really Listens.* His "Sports Heroes" series, designed to appeal to school-aged reluctant readers, illustrates the role faith plays in the lives of notable baseball, basketball, and football stars, and serves as a counterweight to the many newspaper accounts of athletes whose lives have been marred by drugs, alcohol, and other negative factors. Reviewing Littleton's youth group guide *When They Invited Me to Fellowship . . . I Thought They Meant a Cruise* for *Voice of Youth Advocates,* contributor Denise Roberts recommended the work for giving teen readers sound advice on forming

In Baseball, *Littleton focuses on Christian players and outlines their commitment to focus on their faith.* (Photo by Otto Greule, Jr.)

"true friendships and [maintaining] loyalty" within a close-knit group setting where personalities, emotions, and opinions often clash.

On the fiction front, Littleton has penned several adult and young adult novels, and has also created two fiction series for middle-grade readers. Beginning with *Secrets of Moonlight Mountain* in 1992, his six-part "Crista Chronicles" focus on twelve-year-old Crista Mayfield as she attempts to fill the void left by the death of her mother while also finding time to solve a few local mysteries. Although noting that the storylines in the first few installments of the series were slow to unfold, *Voice of Youth Advocates* reviewer Libby Bergstrom, in a review of *Secrets of Moonlight Mountain, Winter Thunder,* and *Robbers on Rock Road,* added that Crista's "Christian values . . . are a natural part of her life, and are not presented in a preachy manner." Other series by Littleton include the "Ally O'Connor Adventures" and the "Rocky Creek Adventures." Designed to appeal to horse-lovers, the "Ally O'Connor" books find fourteen-year-old Ally and boyfriend Nick confronted with a neighborhood thief in *Hoofbeats on the Trail* and deter-

mined to thwart the thief's efforts to harm a herd of wild mustangs in North Carolina.

Littleton once explained to *SATA:* "I became a Christian after graduation from college in August, 1972. Since then I have been a youth pastor, pastor, and writer. I like writing for kids because such writing is always fast-paced, interesting, and touching. I hope someday to write a bestseller and then keep on writing more."

Biographical and Critical Sources

PERIODICALS

Library Journal, February 1, 1995, Henry Carrigan, Jr., review of *Before Eden,* p. 65.
Publishers Weekly, November 13, 2000, review of *What's in the Bible for . . . Teens,* p. 102.
Voice of Youth Advocates, April, 1994, Libby Bergstrom, review of *Secrets of Moonlight Mountain, Winter Thunder,* and *Robbers on Rock Road,* p. 28; February, 1997, Denise Roberts, review of *When They Invited Me to Fellowship . . . I Thought They Meant a Cruise,* pp. 319-320.*

*   *   *

LOURIE, Peter (King) 1952-

Personal

Born February 3, 1952, in Ann Arbor, MI; son of Donold King (a lawyer and writer) and Nancy Groves (maiden name, Clement; present surname, Stout) Lourie; married Melissa Stern (an actress and producer), May 2, 1988; children: Suzanna, Walker. *Education:* New York University, B.A., 1975; University of Maine—Orono, M.A., 1978; attended Cuernavaca Language School, 1978; Columbia University, M.F.A., 1989.

Addresses

Home—Middlebury, VT. *Agent*—Virginia Knowlton, Curtis Brown Associates, 10 Astor Pl., New York, NY 10003. *E-mail*—peter@peterlourie.com.

Career

Educator, lecturer, and author of nonfiction. Nairobi National Museum, Nairobi, Kenya, assistant to Margaret Leakey at Centre for Prehistory, 1971; American Museum of Natural History, New York, NY, guide in Hall of the American Indian, 1971; British Museum, London, England, assistant to curator of Greek coins, 1974; Colegio Americano, Quito, Ecuador, instructor in English as a second language, 1979-80; Dutchess Community College, Poughkeepsie, NY, adjunct lecturer in English composition and literature, 1984-89; Masters

Peter Lourie

School, Dobbs Ferry, CT, writing teacher and director of Dobbs Writers Conference, 1989-91; University of Vermont, Burlington, VT, instructor in travel writing, 1992, director of summer writing program, 1994-95.

Member

Authors Guild, Authors League of America, Society of Children's Book Writers and Illustrators.

Awards, Honors

Magazine Merit Award, Honor Certificate for nonfiction, Society of Children's Book Writers and Illustrators, 1990; Best Books for the Teen Age selection, New York Public Library, 1993, for *Yukon River: An Adventure to the Gold Fields of the Klondike;* John Burroughs Nature Book for Young Readers selection, John Burroughs Association, 1994, for *Everglades: Buffalo Tiger and the River of Grass;* Notable Children's Trade Book in the Field of Social Studies, Children's Book Council/National Council for the Social Studies, 1995, for *Everglades,* and 2002, for *Rio Grande: From the Rocky Mountains to the Gulf of Mexico.*

Writings

FOR CHILDREN

Amazon: A Young Reader's Look at the Last Frontier, illustrated by Marcos Santilli, Caroline House (Honesdale, PA), 1991.

(And illustrator) *Hudson River: An Adventure from the Mountains to the Sea,* Caroline House (Honesdale, PA), 1992.

(And illustrator) *Yukon River: An Adventure to the Gold Fields of the Klondike,* Caroline House (Honesdale, PA), 1992.

Everglades: Buffalo Tiger and the River of Grass, Boyds Mills Press (Honesdale, PA), 1994.

Erie Canal: Canoeing America's Great Waterway, Boyds Mills Press (Honesdale, PA), 1994.

The Lost Treasure of Captain Kidd (novel), illustrated by Michael Chandler, Shawangunk Press (Wappingers Falls, NY), 1996.

In the Path of Lewis and Clark: Traveling the Missouri, Silver Burdett Press (Parsippany, NJ), 1997.

Lost Treasure of the Inca, Boyds Mills Press (Honesdale, PA), 1999.

Rio Grande: From the Rocky Mountains to the Gulf of Mexico, Boyds Mills Press (Honesdale, PA), 1999.

Mississippi River: A Journey down the Father of Waters, Boyds Mills Press (Honesdale, PA), 2000.

The Mystery of the Maya: Uncovering the Lost City of Palenque, Boyds Mills Press (Honesdale, PA), 2001.

On the Trail of Sacagawea, Boyds Mills Press (Honesdale, PA), 2001.

On the Trail of Lewis and Clark: A Journey up the Missouri River, Boyds Mills Press (Honesdale, PA), 2002.

Tierra del Fuego: A Journey to the End of the World, Boyds Mills Press (Honesdale, PA), 2002.

The Lost World of the Anasazi: Exploring the Mysteries of Chaco Canyon, Boyds Mills Press (Honesdale, PA), 2003.

OTHER

Sweat of the Sun, Tears of the Moon: A Chronicle of an Incan Treasure (for adults), Atheneum (New York, NY), 1991.

River of Mountains: A Canoe Journey down the Hudson (for adults), Syracuse University Press (Syracuse, NY), 1995.

Contributor of articles to magazines, including *Highlights for Children, Parenting, Diversion, Treasure, South American Explorer,* and *American Photographer.* Contributor of weekly column to *Putnam County News and Recorder,* 1985-87.

Sidelights

Peter Lourie's nonfiction books, based on his fascination with waterways, his many travels, and his training as an anthropologist, frequently highlight his concern for the environment, his love of nature, and his fascination with the history of exploration. Several of his books for young readers, including *In the Path of Lewis and Clark: Traveling the Missouri* and *On the Trail of Sacagawea,* present Lourie's personal experiences while following the trail of the eighteenth-century explorers who first ventured into the northwestern United States. Interested readers can also explore the history and panorama of the Hudson, Mississippi, and Rio Grande rivers as they join the canoeist author along these major North American waterways. In another work taken from the perspective of someone at water level, *Erie Canal: Canoeing America's Great Waterway* focuses on the results of early nineteenth-century efforts to engineer an artificial river connecting Lake Erie with the Hudson River.

Enhanced by his stunning photographs, Lourie's book about the magnificent Rio Grande traces a journey along the river from Colorado to the Gulf of Mexico. (*From* Rio Grande.)

A longtime traveler, Lourie began his career as the author of book-length travelogues with 1991's *Sweat of the Sun, Tears of the Moon: A Chronicle of an Incan Treasure.* While a graduate student working in Ecuador during the 1980s, Lourie had become fascinated by local legends about caches of Inca treasure supposedly hidden by persecuted natives from the invading Spanish conquistadors during the 1500s. Intrigued by stories of a cache of gold intended by the Incas to ransom their leader Atahualpa but instead hidden in the Llanganita mountains following Atahualpa's murder at the hands of Francisco Pizarro, Lourie let gold fever get the better of him and began his own hunt for treasure. His account of this failed effort makes for "not only intriguing history, but [also] a great read that both parent and child should enjoy," according to *Knight-Ridder/Tribune News Service* writer Sue Corbett. John Maxwell Hamilton wrote in the *New York Times Book Review* that although Lourie "captures the discomfort, dreams, and despair of treasure hunting," his first book is diminished by a prose style Hamilton characterized as "often purple." Other reviewers found much more to praise in *Sweat of the Sun, Tears of the Moon,* with a *Publishers*

Weekly contributor calling the journal "a captivating, if meandering adventure."

After publishing *Sweat of the Sun, Tears of the Moon,* Lourie decided to adapt his adventures in the Andes for younger readers. The resulting volume, *Lost Treasure of the Inca,* is a "fascinating . . . Indiana Jones-mix of history, lost treasure, and visions of wealth," according to *School Library Journal* contributor Patricia Manning. Lourie's quest for Atahualpa's gold, made in the company of three guides and marred by swarming mosquitos, red ants, and a map of dubious accuracy, is transformed in this book into what *Bulletin of the Center for Children's Books* contributor Elizabeth Bush called "a ripping good yarn." Praising the author's inclusion of photographs taken on his failed treasure hunt, as well as a copy of the actual map used, a *Kirkus Reviews* critic added that "so powerful is his narrative style," Lourie will convince readers he will uncover the gold.

Lourie returns to the jungles of South America in *Amazon: A Young Reader's Look at the Last Frontier.* Traversing the heart of the Amazon basin by canoe, Lourie describes for readers the clash between the traditional hunter-gatherer culture and the interests of those who burn the ancient rain forest in order to farm the land. "The entire book creates an indelible picture of this endangered system," observed Frances E. Millhouser in *School Library Journal. Bulletin of the Center for Children's Books* contributor Roger Sutton praised the "you-are-there immediacy" of *Amazon,* and Mary Harris Veeder, writing in Chicago's *Tribune Books,* singled out Lourie's "winningly direct prose." Although a *Publishers Weekly* contributor claimed the work "lacks immediacy and focus," several critics praised Lourie's efforts to deal with the environmental destruction in that area without lecturing to his audience.

Closer to home, Lourie has explored many of the major rivers of North America by canoe, and he shares his experiences in several books for young armchair travelers. In *Hudson River: An Adventure from the Mountains to the Sea,* he recounts the history of and the current conditions along the 315-mile-long Hudson River. Though in her *School Library Journal* critique Kate Hegarty Bouman found the author's photographs of his journey more impressive than his narrative, Karen Hutt wrote in *Booklist* that Lourie's "straightforward account will appeal to canoe enthusiasts and to readers with a particular interest" in the history of the Hudson River. Intended for older readers, Lourie's *River of Mountains: A Canoe Journey down the Hudson* expands this account. He remarks upon environmental concerns, the effects of industrialization and development on both the river and its shores, and the Hudson's role as a waterway for Viking explorers, sixteenth-century French fur traders, and pirates such as Captain William Kidd. The role of the river during the American Revolution is also covered, in a book that presents what *A. B. Bookman Weekly* contributor Jeffrey R. Jones described as "a trace history of eastern America."

Lourie's *Yukon River: An Adventure to the Gold Fields of the Klondike* recounts his nearly 500-mile canoe trip in which he follows the path turn-of-the-twentieth-century gold prospectors took to access the Klondike. A *Kirkus Reviews* critic called *Yukon River* "powerful and beautifully presented." *Everglades: Buffalo Tiger and the River of Grass* finds Lourie in the company of a Miccosukee chief as they glide down the Florida river that was once home to that Native American tribe, while a 1,885-mile trek through lands once home to Pancho Villa and Billy the Kid is recounted in *Rio Grande: From the Rocky Mountains to the Gulf of Mexico.* Lourie leaves his favored canoe for the more modern riverboat in *In the Path of Lewis and Clark: Traveling the Missouri.* The 1,700-mile trip along the river in 1804-06 by Meriwether Lewis and William Clark was undertaken in 1995 by Lourie and Native-American novelist William Least Heat-Moon. Noting the author's inclusion of passages from the journals recounting that historic nineteenth-century trip, *School Library Journal* contributor David A. Lindsey praised Lourie's account for its "easy, relaxed manner" and the author's inclu-

sion of "fascinating historical information." Although *Booklist* contributor Susan Dove Lempke pointed out that the 128-page *In the Path of Lewis and Clark* might not be appropriate for "children who snooze through slide shows," Lourie's abridged version of the trip, published in 2002 as *On the Trail of Lewis and Clark: A Journey up the Missouri River,* is designed for younger readers or those with less-extensive attention spans.

In addition to nonfiction titles, Lourie has also penned a novel for middle-grade readers that draws on his fascination with history and missing gold. In *The Lost Treasure of Captain Kidd,* Manhattan native Alex moves with his parents to the Hudson River valley, where he finds a new best friend in Gillian. Gillian inspires Alex with his dreams of finding a hoard of gold doubloons that, legend holds, were buried by buccaneer Captain Kidd in the 1600s. Stealing a map to the pirate treasure from the mentally unbalanced Cruger, Gillian puts both boys in danger in his desire for gold. Called "an intriguing look at the effect of greed upon friendship" by *Booklist* contributor Frances Bradburn, *The Lost Treasure of Captain Kidd* was cited by Elaine E. Knight in her *School Library Journal* review as a work "with regional appeal for readers who like lots of historical detail."

Biographical and Critical Sources

PERIODICALS

A. B. Bookman Weekly, July 15, 1996, Jeffrey R. Jones, review of *River of Mountains: A Canoe Journey down the Hudson,* pp. 208-209.

Appraisal, spring, 1999, Karin Proskey and Nick Gawel, review of *Amazon: A Young Reader's Look at the Last Frontier, Hudson River: An Adventure from the Mountains to the Sea,* and *Everglades: Buffalo Tiger and the River of Grass,* pp. 51-52.

Booklist, April 1, 1992, Karen Hutt, review of *Hudson River,* p. 1442: February 15, 1996, Frances Bradburn, review of *The Lost Treasure of Captain Kidd,* p. 1021; February 15, 1997, Susan Dove Lempke, review of *In the Path of Lewis and Clark: Traveling the Missouri,* p. 1013; July, 1997, Stephanie Zvirin, review of *Erie Canal: Canoeing America's Great Waterway,* p. 1815; February 15, 1999, John Peters, review of *Rio Grande: From the Rocky Mountains to the Gulf of Mexico,* p. 1065; October 15, 1999, Randy Meyer, review of *Lost Treasure of the Inca,* p. 438; October 1, 2000, Carolyn Phelan, review of *Mississippi: A Journey down the Father of Waters,* p. 334; May 1, 2001, Helen Rosenberg, review of *On the Trail of Sacagawea,* p. 1677; September 15, 2001, Randy Meyer, review of *The Mystery of the Maya: Uncovering the Lost City of Palenque,* p. 220; April 1, 2002, Carolyn Phelan, review of *On the Trail of Lewis and Clark,* p. 1322; October 15, 2002, Kay Weisman, review of *Tierra del Fuego: A Journey to the End of the Earth,* p. 403.

Bulletin of the Center for Children's Books, November, 1991, Roger Sutton, review of *Amazon,* pp. 68-69; November, 1999, Elizabeth Bush, review of *Lost Treasure of the Inca,* p. 98.

Catholic Library World, September, 1998, Mary Luke Mulraney, review of *Hudson River,* p. 90.

Kirkus Reviews, February 1, 1991, review of *Sweat of the Sun, Tears of the Moon: A Chronicle of an Incan Treasure,* p. 157; August 1, 1992, review of *Yukon River: An Adventure to the Gold Fields of the Klondike,* p. 997; December 15, 1995, review of *The Lost Treasure of Captain Kidd,* p. 1722; February 1, 1999, review of *Rio Grande,* p. 224; October 15, 1999, review of *Lost Treasure of the Inca,* p. 1646; September 1, 2001, review of *The Mystery of the Maya,* p. 1295.

Knight-Ridder/Tribune News Service, June 15, 2000, Sue Corbett, "Two Tales of the Inca: One on Lost Gold, the Other on a Lost Life," p. K362.

Library Journal, July, 1995, Nancy Moeckel, review of *River of Mountains,* p. 109.

New York Times Book Review, June 9, 1991, John Maxwell Hamilton, review of *Sweat of the Sun, Tears of the Moon,* p. 48; June 11, 1995, Ted Conover, review of *River of Mountains,* p. 9.

Publishers Weekly, February 1, 1991, review of *Sweat of the Sun, Tears of the Moon,* p. 75; August 30, 1991, review of *Amazon,* p. 86.

School Library Journal, January, 1992, Frances E. Millhouser, review of *Amazon,* p. 130; June, 1992, Kate Hegarty Bouman, review of *Hudson River,* pp. 109-110; June, 1996, Elaine E. Knight, review of *The Lost Treasure of Captain Kidd,* p. 122; April, 1997, David A. Lindsey, review of *In the Path of Lewis and Clark,* pp. 151-152; September, 1997, Joan Soulliere, review of *Erie Canal,* p. 204; November, 1999, Patricia Manning, review of *Lost Treasure of the Inca,* pp. 172-173; October, 2000, Kathleen Simonetta, review of *Mississippi River,* p. 188; April, 2001, Nancy Collins-Warner, review of *On the Trail of Sacagawea,* p. 164; November, 2001, Daryl Grabarek, review of *The Mystery of the Maya,* p. 180; June, 2002, Nancy Collins-Warner, review of *On the Trail of Lewis and Clark,* p. 164; September, 2002, Eva Elizabeth Von-Ancken, review of *Tierra del Fuego,* p. 249.

Tribune Books (Chicago, IL), October 13, 1991, Mary Harris Veeder, review of *Amazon,* p. 6.

ONLINE

Peter Lourie Web site, http://www.peterlourie.com/ (June 7, 2003).*

*　　*　　*

LYONS, Mary E(velyn) 1947-

Personal

Born November 28, 1947, in Macon, GA; daughter of Joseph and Evelyn Lyons; married Paul Collinge (an owner of a used and rare bookstore). *Education:* Appalachian State University, B.S., 1970, M.S., 1972; Uni-

Mary E. Lyons

versity of Virginia, doctoral study. *Hobbies and other interests:* Playing Irish penny whistle and banjo, performing with the group Virgil and the Chicken Heads.

Addresses

Home—Charlottesville, VA. *Agent*—William Reiss, John Hawkins Associates, Suite 1600, 71 West 23rd St., New York, NY, 10010.

Career

Writer. Has worked as a reading teacher at elementary and middle schools in North Carolina and in Charlottesville, VA, and as a school librarian at elementary, middle, and high schools, Charlottesville, VA.

Awards, Honors

Best Books for Young Adults, American Library Association (ALA), and Carter G. Woodson Book Award, National Council for the Social Studies (NCSS), both 1991, both for *Sorrow's Kitchen: The Life and Folklore of Zora Neale Hurston;* Notable Children's Trade Book in the Field of Social Studies, National Council for the Social Studies and Children's Book Council (NCSS/CBC), 1992, for *Raw Head, Bloody Bones: African-*

American Tales of the Supernatural, and 1996, for *Keeping Secrets: The Girlhood Diaries of Seven Working Writers;* Best Books for Young Adults, ALA, Golden Kite Award for fiction, Society of Children's Book Writers and Illustrators, both 1992, Honor Book, Jane Addams Children's Book Award, 1993, and Parents' Choice Award, 1996, all for *Letters from a Slave Girl: The Story of Harriet Jacobs;* Notable Book designation, ALA, 1993, and Carter G. Woodson Award, NCSS, 1994, both for *Starting Home: The Story of Horace Pippin, Painter;* Notable Children's Trade Book in the Field of Social Studies, NCSS/CBC, 1994, for *Stitching Stars: The Story Quilts of Harriet Powers;* Books for the Teen Age, New York Public Library, 1995, for *Deep Blues: Bill Traylor, Self-Taught Artist;* Carter G. Woodson Elementary Merit Book, NCSS, 1995, for *Master of Mahogany: Tom Day, Free Black Cabinetmaker;* Jefferson Cup Series Award, Virginia Library Association, 1996, for the "African-American Artists and Artisans" series; Best Science Fiction and Fantasy List, *Voice of Youth Advocates,* 2001, for *Knockabeg: A Famine Tale;* Best Books selection, *Bulletin of the Center for Children's Books,* 2001, for *Feed the Children First: Irish Memories of the Great Hunger.* Three fellowships from the Virginia Foundation for the Humanities; Teacher Scholar Award, National Endowment for the Humanities, 1991-92.

Writings

FOR YOUNG PEOPLE

Sorrow's Kitchen: The Life and Folklore of Zora Neale Hurston, Scribner (New York, NY), 1990.

(Editor) *Raw Head, Bloody Bones: African-American Tales of the Supernatural,* Scribner (New York, NY), 1991.

Letters from a Slave Girl: The Story of Harriet Jacobs, Scribner (New York, NY), 1992.

The Butter Tree: Tales of Bruh Rabbit, illustrated by Mireille Vautier, Holt (New York, NY), 1995.

Keeping Secrets: The Girlhood Diaries of Seven Working Writers, Holt (New York, NY), 1995.

The Poison Place: A Novel, Atheneum Books for Young Readers (New York, NY), 1997.

(With Muriel M. Branch) *Dear Ellen Bee: A Civil War Scrapbook of Two Union Spies,* Atheneum Books for Young Readers (New York, NY), 2000.

Knockabeg: A Famine Tale, Houghton Mifflin (Boston, MA), 2001.

(Editor) *Feed the Children First: Irish Memories of the Great Hunger,* Atheneum Books for Young Readers (New York, NY), 2002.

"AFRICAN-AMERICAN ARTISTS AND ARTISANS" SERIES

Starting Home: The Story of Horace Pippin, Painter, Scribner (New York, NY), 1993.

Stitching Stars: The Story Quilts of Harriet Powers, Scribner (New York, NY), 1993.

Master of Mahogany: Tom Day, Free Black Cabinetmaker, Scribner (New York, NY), 1994.

Deep Blues: Bill Traylor, Self-Taught Artist, Scribner (New York, NY), 1994.

Painting Dreams: Minnie Evans, Visionary Artist, Houghton (Boston, MA), 1996.

Catching the Fire: Philip Simmons, Blacksmith, Houghton Mifflin (Boston, MA), 1997.

(Editor) *Talking with Tebé: Clementine Hunter, Memory Artist,* Houghton Mifflin (Boston, MA), 1998.

FOR ADULTS

A Story of Her Own: A Resource Guide to Teaching Literature by Women, National Women's History Project, 1985.

Sidelights

Mary E. Lyons is Southern born and her Southern sensibility is clearly evident in her many award-winning historical and biographical works for children. In her fiction and nonfiction titles, Lyons explores the lives of marginalized people in history, from women to African Americans to impoverished Irish during the potato famine. Among her nonfiction works is the "African-American Artists and Artisans" series, geared for middle grade readers. For older nonfiction readers, Lyons has penned a biography of Zora Neale Hurston, as well as the letters of young working girls in *Keeping Secrets:*

In Catching the Fire, *her biography of blacksmith Philip Simmons, Mary E. Lyons pays tribute to the African-American artist whose wrought iron pieces grace the city of Charleston, South Carolina. (Photo by John Michael Vlach.)*

The Girlhood Diaries of Seven Working Writers, writings of a young slave girl in *Letters from a Slave Girl: The Story of Harriet Jacobs,* and first-hand accounts of the potato famine in *Feed the Children First: Irish Memories of the Great Hunger.* Lyons has also published fiction for young adults, including *The Poison Place: A Novel* and *Knockabeg: A Famine Tale.*

Lyons was born in Macon, Georgia, on November 28, 1947, the daughter of Joseph and Evelyn Lyons. "We moved a lot when I was a child," Lyons once commented. "We followed my father in his work, and by the time I was eleven, I had already lived in five Southern states and eight Southern towns." It was this somewhat rootless childhood, Lyons contends, that made her later search for Southern roots in her writing. "Moving around was hard for a little girl," Lyons once commented. "I didn't know it at the time, but reading provided an instant escape. If I felt uncomfortable in a strange neighborhood or new school, I glued myself to a book and forgot it all."

As a youth, Lyons liked the idea of being a writer, but aside from school assignments did not write much on her own. She and a friend spent lazy afternoons thinking up possible titles to romance novels, and as a ninth grader, she began keeping a diary. However, it was not until she was a freshman in college that she discovered she had a talent with words that most of her classmates did not have. "Though writing was not a skill I thought about much, I discovered I was able to organize my thoughts and put them down on paper with fluency," Lyons commented. "To my surprise, I did well with my writing, so well that one of my teachers once accused me of plagiarizing a paper. I was innocent. It was my work, but she just couldn't believe that I could write that well. Though I laugh about it now, it was discouraging at the time."

Another revelation was of a more universal sort but no less influential in her life. A pivotal experience during college was the assassination of Martin Luther King, Jr. "A few months after the assassination, I began working part-time in an employment agency," Lyons recalled. "I was the only white there, and the experience just changed my life. I began to see the way blacks were treated." The civil rights movement in the South was more than a historical backdrop for Lyons's coming of age. She slowly began to identify with the dispossessed and "invisible" members of society.

Out of college, Lyons's first teaching job was in an inner-city school, primarily black. The school was situated in the middle of a housing project; the doors were locked most of the time for security. Lyons, who was a mediocre science student, was assigned science classes, and learned firsthand the difficulties of teaching under such adverse circumstances. After this first year, Lyons returned to college to get a master's degree in reading, a subject she taught in public schools for the next seventeen years. Then, burning out as a reading teacher,

Lyons again returned to college and retrained as a school librarian, a job which led directly to writing her first publication. It was while helping students choose books that she noticed how popular the gathered folktales of Zora Neale Hurston were. Finding that there were no biographies of this black writer, Lyons decided to write one herself.

Sorrow's Kitchen vividly presents Hurston as an eccentric and often misinterpreted intellectual. Associated with the Harlem Renaissance in the 1920s and 1930s, Hurston's reputation suffered through the middle of the century, but she has since become the subject of much critical attention. Lyons's succinct biography, directed to young readers, speaks with a laudatory but objective tone as it recounts Hurston's accomplishments and follows her life, from her birth in Florida to her literary activities in Harlem. Praised by critics for its careful and precise documentation, the book records Hurston's anthropological work, especially in the preservation of African-American folktales and legends. Called "fascinating, enlightening, stimulating, and satisfying" by Elizabeth S. Watson of *Horn Book, Sorrow's Kitchen* also features Lyons's brilliant use of eye-catching excerpts from Hurston's own writings.

Several of the stories that Zora Neale Hurston discovered and preserved appear in Lyons's second book, *Raw Head, Bloody Bones: African-American Tales of the Supernatural.* In this collection are fifteen tales of ghosts, demons, and other monsters, many of them retold by Lyons in their original Gullah dialect, a speech pattern used by some African Americans living in the coastal regions of South Carolina. According to Lyons's introduction to these scary tales, most were originally unearthed by the Federal Writer's Project and were designed to teach moral lessons as well as to frighten and entertain listeners. Once again critics have noted that Lyons's excellent notes and bibliography make this a valuable work for children interested in the history of African-American folklore.

After the publication of *Sorrow's Kitchen* and *Raw Head, Bloody Bones,* Lyons began to focus full-time attention on writing for children. Assisted by several honors and awards, including a National Endowment for the Humanities Teacher Scholar Award, Lyons has centered many of her efforts on important figures in African-American culture, many of whom have been otherwise overlooked. *Letters from a Slave Girl* is an account of the life of Harriet Ann Jacobs. Depicting Jacobs's story through a series of fictionalized letters based upon her autobiography, Lyons recreates Jacobs's struggle with sexual harassment and the indifference of whites in the South to her plight. Lyons's book carries the reader through seven years that Jacobs spent in hiding, and to her eventual escape north in this tale that a *Kirkus Reviews* critic called "a moving evocation of the tragedies inflicted by slavery."

Several of Lyons's next projects were undertaken as part of the "African-American Artists and Artisans" series. Focusing on the rich African cultural heritage in American art, Lyons has produced a well-regarded collection of biographical sketches, stories, and images concerning some typically overlooked individuals in nineteenth and early twentieth-century American history. *Starting Home: The Story of Horace Pippin, Painter* renders the life of this self-taught painter. A soldier in World War I, Pippin produced several haunting works of folk-art, many of which depict his involvement in the Great War. Lyons's second volume for the series, *Stitching Stars: The Story Quilts of Harriet Powers,* recounts the life of this talented former slave whose quilts are considered valuable pieces of American social history. Reviewing *Stitching Stars* for the *Bulletin of the Center for Children's Books,* Deborah Stevenson observed that "Lyons's lively writing stitches concepts together with smoothness and clarity. . . . [This] is both an unusual take on history and a reminder of the democratic possibilities of art."

Master of Mahogany: Tom Day, Free Black Cabinetmaker, Deep Blues: Bill Traylor, Self-Taught Artist, and *Painting Dreams: Minnie Evans, Visionary Artist* are three more of Lyons's books in the "Artists and Artisans" series. Her story of Thomas Day offers insights into the life of a free black man in the era of slavery. A successful businessman, Day used his carpentry skills to become an individual of considerable wealth, overcoming the suspicions of many whites in the pre-war South. *Deep Blues* and *Painting Dreams* are both portraits of untutored artists who created their work under very unusual circumstances. Born into slavery in 1856, Bill Traylor did not begin painting until he was eighty years old. A talented folk-artist, he went on to earn a measure of fame when his works were "discovered" in 1939. Lyons's presentation of Minnie Evans's life investigates the work of this deeply religious woman haunted by dreams that provided the inspiration for her art that was made from scrap materials. As with her other books, Lyons has been praised for her careful documentation and meticulous scholarship in these works.

Entries in the "Artists and Artisans" series continue with *Catching the Fire: Philip Simmons, Blacksmith* and *Talking with Tebé: Clementine Hunter, Memory Artist.* In *Catching the Fire,* Lyons presents the life and work of Philip Simmons, a blacksmith whose gates, fences, and railings decorate the city of Charleston, South Carolina, where Simmons has lived most of his life. Based on personal interviews with Simmons and those who have worked with him, the book was dubbed "an engrossing biography" by a *Kirkus Review* critic and "engaging" by a reviewer for *Horn Book.* Stevenson concluded in *Bulletin of the Center for Children's Books* that *Catching the Fire* would be "useful not only as an introduction to a gifted professional craftsman, but also a reminder of how unexpected things can become art when executed with authority." In the final book in the series, *Talking with Tebé,* Lyons presents the work of Clementine Hunter, called Tebé, whose

paintings portray the life of a Southern laborer. This story is told through Hunter's own words in magazine and newspaper articles and in tape-recorded interviews. A contributor for *Kirkus Reviews* applauded Lyons's "expertly edited interviews" that manage to develop a "glowing portrait of the hard-working, outspoken woman."

Lyons's writings also include her versions of six African-American trickster tales in *The Butter Tree: Tales of Bruh Rabbit.* These retellings have been praised by critics for their simplicity and accessibility to young people. *Horn Book* reviewer Maeve Visser Knoth commented: "Lyon's skilled retellings are brief and uncluttered, recalling the oral tradition. She uses few adjectives, yet her language is colorful and evokes regional flavor."

Lyons has also written an important volume of literary scholarship titled *Keeping Secrets.* Focusing on the biographies of such individuals as Louisa May Alcott, Kate Chopin, Ida B. Wells, and Charlotte Perkins Gilman, *Keeping Secrets* combines enlightening excerpts from the writings of these famous women with an analysis of questions pertaining to women's identity and freedom in modern American society.

The Poison Place is, by Lyons's accounts, the most difficult of her books thus far—difficult in terms of researching and writing. Begun in 1989 as a scrap of an idea, Lyons finally got back to the book years later. The book uses historical fact as its background, detailing the lives of two men. One is Charles Willson Peale, the eighteenth-century portraitist and founder of the first public museum in the United States, the Peale Museum in Philadelphia. The other is Moses Williams, Peale's former slave who became a silhouette cutter and the first black professional artist in post-revolutionary America. Research took Lyons to Philadelphia to visit the Peale Museum, now known as Independence Hall. The novel is told through the voice of Williams on a night-time tour with his young daughter through the museum. Williams's own struggle for survival is contrasted to Peale's story and that of his museum. As Rachelle M. Bilz noted in *Voice of Youth Advocates,* "Moses' lifelong quest for freedom is intertwined with the Peale family's success and failure." Through the narrator's revelations, the reader is led to wonder how much responsibility Peale himself had in the eventual poisoning of his own son, a taxidermist in the museum who died from the arsenic he used in his work. Bilz concluded that the novel was "Fast paced and well written . . . sure to appeal to historical fiction fans," while a *Kirkus Reviews* critic called the novel "a riveting work of historical fiction."

Teaming up with Muriel M. Branch, Lyon next turned to a novel in the form of a scrapbook, related through photos, stories from newspapers of the time, and personal letters. *Dear Ellen Bee: A Civil War Scrapbook of Two Union Spies,* tells the tale of a rich white woman,

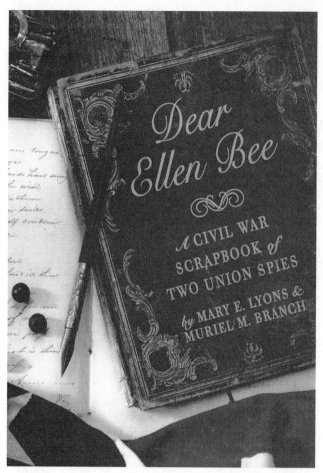

A fictionalized account of two women who lived during the Civil War, Dear Ellen Bee *is the tale of a wealthy Southern white woman and her black servant who together smuggled information from the Confederate camp to the generals of the Union army. (Cover photo by Marc Tauss.)*

Miss Bet, and her freed slave, Liza, who operated as spies for the Union in Virginia, working under the joint alias of Ellen Bee. Based on actual historical characters, the novel was described as "meticulously researched" by a reviewer for *Publishers Weekly.* Covering the decade from 1856 to 1865, the book follows Liza as she is sent to Philadelphia to be educated. Returning to Richmond, Virginia, the former slave is married, and there is a new and uncomfortable distance between her and Miss Bet as the two begin to gather information for the North, reluctantly working together. The *Publishers Weekly* reviewer found the book to be "a well-informed account of daring women." Patricia B. McGee, writing in *School Library Journal,* felt that the use of the scrapbook technique, including tickets and facsimiles of documents seemingly pasted onto the pages, "functions brilliantly," and *Booklist*'s Carolyn Phelan similarly praised the book as "an original presentation of intriguing historical material." Nancy Zachary, writing in *Voice of Youth Advocates* also commended the book, concluding that "terrific research provides a fascinating portrait of these real heroines."

Lyons focuses on Ireland in two further books, the novel *Knockabeg* and the nonfiction anthology *Feed the Children First.* Lyons's novel *Knockabeg* presents a departure for the writer, a fantasy set during the Irish potato famine with strange creatures and faeries. The Trooping Faeries, good wee folk, do battle with their nemesis, the Nuckelavees, who are planning to spread blight on the potato crop in Ireland. This would have disastrous results for the human inhabitants of the island as well as for the Trooping Faeries, as the humans will not be able to leave food out for the faeries as they usually do. Thus the Nuckelavees will be able to take the land once the humans are forced to abandon it. The faeries are obliged to fight with a human at their side, and young Eamon fills that role. Things are made more complicated, however, with the presence of Sticky, an evil Solitary One who is serving out a punishment sentence with the Trooping Faeries, and it is unclear whose side she is on. The tale is narrated by an Irish storyteller, or "seanchai," and the book has, as a result, a large number of colloquial expressions, for which Lyons supplies a glossary. Kit Vaughan, writing in *School Library Journal,* cautioned readers not to expect "a light tale of magic" or "an entirely happy ending." A *Publishers Weekly* critic lauded the "clever embellishments" of the faery elements in Lyons's tale, but also noted that "the author develops too many characters, settings, and story lines to keep straight." A contributor for *Kirkus Reviews* was more positive, however, commenting that "lovers of historical fiction or fantasy" would take to the novel.

With *Feed the Children First,* Lyons takes a nonfiction approach to the same subject, presenting first-person accounts, gathered in the 1940s by the Irish Folklore Commission, of the mid-nineteenth century potato famine. With no photographic record to work from, Lyons used Irish letters, paintings, and sketches of the period to accompany her edited text. A reviewer for *Kirkus Reviews* thought this would be "a useful volume," while a critic for *Publishers Weekly* found it a "somber anecdotal account." Hazel Rochman, writing in *Booklist,* felt the book could be used in conjunction with other, more in-depth studies of the potato famine, for the "personal voices and images . . . bring the horror . . . very close." Lyons remarked to *SATA* "that American children have few ways to learn about the Irish famine of 1845-52. The subject is rarely mentioned in textbooks, and even publicly-funded Web sites such as the Library of Congress American memory site offer little or no information. *Feed the Children First* is only forty-eight pages long. It's for kids who want an introduction to the famine but who don't want to tackle a 200-page book."

A socially-active author, Lyons presents one constant theme in her writing: the importance and value of the various underrepresented members of society, in America and other countries, particularly the contributions of women and African Americans. Lyons intends to continue with historical fiction in the future, and to write for young readers. "I can't imagine writing for anyone besides young people," Lyons once commented. "They really like to be told the truth and can handle complexities that adults can't."

Biographical and Critical Sources

BOOKS

Authors and Artists for Young Adults, Volume 26, Gale (Detroit, MI), 1999.
St. James Guide to Children's Writers, 5th edition, St. James Press (Detroit, MI), 1999.

PERIODICALS

Booklist, December 15, 1990, p. 816; January 1, 1992, p. 830; November, 1992, p. 79; November 15, 1993, p. 618; October 1, 1994, p. 322; November 15, 1994, p. 598; June 1, 1995, pp. 1744-1745; July, 1996, p. 1852; September 1, 1997, Carolyn Phelan, review of *Catching the Fire: Philip Simmons, Blacksmith,* p. 117; December 1, 1997, Randy Meyer, review of *The Poison Place: A Novel,* p. 616; November 1, 2000, Carolyn Phelan, review of *Dear Ellen Bee: A Civil War Scrapbook of Two Union Spies,* p. 540; December 15, 2001, Hazel Rochman, review of *Feed the Children First: Irish Memories of the Great Hunger,* pp. 725-726.
Bulletin of the Center for Children's Books, January, 1991, p. 124; February, 1992, p. 162; December, 1993, Deborah Stevenson, review of *Stitching Stars: The Story Quilts of Harriet Powers,* p. 128; December, 1994, p. 136; October, 1997, Deborah Stevenson, review of *Catching the Fire,* p. 57; January, 1998, Janice M. DelNegro, review of *The Poison Place,* p. 166.
Horn Book, March-April, 1991, Elizabeth S. Watson, review of *Sorrow's Kitchen: The Life and Folklore of Zora Neale Hurston,* p. 216; January-February, 1992, pp. 81-82; November-December, 1992, pp. 729-730; March-April, 1994, pp. 219-220; March-April, 1995, p. 221; September-October, 1995, Maeve Visser Knoth, review of *The Butter Tree: Tales of Bruh Rabbit,* p. 614; September-October, 1997, Susan P. Bloom, review of *Catching the Fire,* pp. 592-593; September-October, 1998, Susan P. Bloom, review of *Talking with Tebé: Clementine Hunter, Memory Artist,* pp. 620-621.
Horn Book Guide, spring, 1998, Susan P. Bloom, review of *Catching the Fire,* p. 145; spring, 2001, Frieda F. Bostian, review of *Dear Ellen Bee,* p. 76.
Kirkus Reviews, November 1, 1992, review of *Letters from a Slave Girl: The Story of Harriet Jacobs,* p. 1380; May 15, 1996, p. 747; July 1, 1998, review of *Catching the Fire;* October 1, 1997, review of *The Poison Place;* July 1, 1998, review of *Talking with Tebé,* pp. 968-969; August 1, 2001, review of *Knockabeg: A Famine Tale,* p. 1127; December 1, 2001, review of *Feed the Children First,* p. 1687.
Publishers Weekly, October 25, 1991, p. 69; February 20, 1995, p. 206; September 18, 2000, review of *Dear Ellen Bee,* p. 112; July 23, 2001, review of *Knockabeg,* p. 78; December 10, 2001, review of *Feed the Children First,* pp. 71-72.
Reading Today, April, 2001, Lynne T. Burke, review of *Dear Ellen Bee,* p. 32.
School Library Journal, January, 1991, p. 119; December, 1992, p. 113; May, 1994, p. 113; October, 1994, p. 136; January, 1995, p. 127; June, 1995, p. 103; July, 1995, p. 100; July, 1996, p. 93; September, 1997, Margaret C. Howell, review of *Catching the Fire,* p. 233; November, 1997, Sally Margolis, review of *The Poison Place,* pp. 120-121; September, 1998, Judith Constantinides, review of *Talking with Tebé,* p. 221; October, 2000, Patricia B. McGee, review of *Dear Ellen Bee,* p. 164; September, 2001, Kit Vaughan, review of *Knockabeg,* p. 226.
Voice of Youth Advocates, February, 1991, p. 378; December, 1992, p. 282; October, 1995, pp. 252, 254; December, 1997, Rachelle M. Bilz, review of *The Poison Place,* p. 318; February, 2001, Nancy Zachary, review of *Dear Ellen Bee,* p. 425.

ONLINE

Lyons Den Books for Young Readers, http://www.lyons denbooks.com/ (June 21, 2003).

M

MacGRORY, Yvonne 1948-

Personal
Born November 16, 1948, in Ireland; daughter of Alexander Joseph (a foreman fitter) and Brigid (a homemaker; maiden name, Moore) McDyer; married Eamon MacGrory (a cabinetmaker), July 24, 1971; children: Jane, Donna, Mark. *Religion:* Roman Catholic.

Addresses
Home—Kilraine, Glenties, County Donegal, Ireland. *Agent*—Rena Dardis, 45 Palmerston Rd., Dublin 6, Ireland.

Career
Has worked as a state registered nurse in London, England, and Dublin, Ireland; became a full-time homemaker in 1976. Writer.

Member
Irish Writers' Union, Irish Nurses Organization.

Awards, Honors
Bisto Award for First Children's Novel, Children's Books Ireland, 1991, for *The Secret of the Ruby Ring.*

Writings

The Secret of the Ruby Ring, illustrated by Terry Myler, Children's Press (Dublin, Ireland), 1991, Milkweed Editions (Minneapolis, MN), 1994.
Martha and the Ruby Ring, illustrated by Terry Myler, Children's Press (Dublin, Ireland), 1993.
The Ghost of Susannah Parry, illustrated by Terry Myler, Children's Press (Dublin, Ireland), 1995.
The Quest of the Ruby Ring, illustrated by Terry Myler, Children's Press (Dublin, Ireland), 1999, published as *Emma and the Ruby Ring,* Milkweed Editions (Minneapolis, MN), 2002.

Yvonne MacGrory

Adaptations

The Secret of the Ruby Ring has been made into a film for television by Hallmark.

Work in Progress

"A children's book set during the civil war in Ireland, 1922."

Sidelights

Yvonne MacGrory's time-slip novels for young adults are firmly grounded in Irish political and social history, and include details of daily life during the period. In her first book, *The Secret of the Ruby Ring,* eleven-year-old Lucy receives a ruby ring as a present from her grandmother. The ring comes with two wishes, the first of which avaricious Lucy spends on a wish to live in a much larger house. She immediately finds herself walking down a country road outside a castle. It is 1885, and when the foolish girl discovers she has lost the magic ring, she goes to work as a nursemaid in the castle, desperately trying to wish herself back into her own time again. *Booklist* reviewer Carolyn Phelan praised MacGrory's "intriguing and convincing . . . depiction of the historical era," which shows, among other details, the ways in which nineteenth-century rural Ireland was a place of few creature comforts, especially for the working classes. While Roger Sutton of the *Bulletin of the Center for Children's Books* remarked that experienced fans of the time-slip genre might prefer a story with more complexity, particularly in the arena of plot, which is focused entirely on the search for Lucy's lost ring, "it is, though, a simple, straightforward tale, and . . . neophytes can just sit back and enjoy the search," Sutton concluded. Joanne Kelleher, a contributor to *School Library Journal,* on the other hand, focused instead on aspects of style and content in her comments, praising the author's descriptive prose and effective use of historical detail to tell her tale. "A definite purchase to answer requests for 'a book set in a foreign country,' time travel, or historical fiction," Kelleher concluded.

"I worked part-time as a state registered nurse in London after my first child was born," MacGrory told *SATA,* "but when we returned to live in Ireland, I became a full-time housewife.

"When my children got older, I began to consider some form of employment again—ideally I wanted to work from the home.

"One day I heard a woman author being interviewed on radio, and she told how she had written her first book as a wager and had since gone on to write a bestseller. I was fascinated by the interview and wondered if I too could write a book. The thought continued to nag at me, but it was not until my two daughters had an argument about sharing a bedroom and we had a discussion about magic wands and wishes that I got my inspiration for my first book, *The Secret of the Ruby Ring.* I did not tell my family about it until I had been accepted by a publisher. I wrote the first draft in long hand, and this book has since been made into a film for television by Hallmark of Los Angeles."

Biographical and Critical Sources

PERIODICALS

Booklist, March 1, 1994, Carolyn Phelan, review of *The Secret of the Ruby Ring,* p. 1262.

Bulletin of the Center for Children's Books, May, 1994, Roger Sutton, review of *The Secret of the Ruby Ring,* p. 294.

School Library Journal, March, 1994, Joanne Kelleher, review of *The Secret of the Ruby Ring,* p. 222; May, 2002, Heather Dieffenbach, review of *Emma and the Ruby Ring,* p. 156.

*　　*　　*

McAVOY, Jim 1972-

Personal

Surname is pronounced "*Mack*-a-voy;" born 1972, in Philadelphia, PA. *Education:* St. Joseph's University, B.A. (English), 1994.

Addresses

Agent—c/o Author Mail, Chelsea House Publishers, 1974 Sproul Rd., Suite 400, Broomall, PA 19008.

Career

Writer.

Writings

Tom Hanks, Chelsea House Publishers (Philadelphia, PA), 2000.

Aretha Franklin, Chelsea House Publishers (Philadelphia, PA), 2002.

Mel Gibson, Lucent Books (San Diego, CA), 2002.

*　　*　　*

MEYER, Carolyn (Mae) 1935-

Personal

Born June 8, 1935, in Lewistown, PA; daughter of H. Victor (in business) and Sara (maiden name, Knepp) Meyer; married Joseph Smrcka, June 4, 1960 (divorced, 1973); married E. A. Mares (an author and educator), May 30, 1987; children: (first marriage) Alan, John, Christopher; (second marriage) Vered (stepdaughter). *Education:* Bucknell University, B.A. (cum laude), 1957. *Politics:* Liberal. *Religion:* Episcopalian.

Addresses

Home—Albuquerque, NM. *Office*—202 Edith Blvd. N.E., Albuquerque, NM 87102. *Agent*—Amy Berkower, Writers House Inc., 21 W. 26th St., New York, NY 10010. *E-mail*—meyerwrite@earthlink.net.

Career

Worked as a secretary, late 1950s; freelance writer, 1963—. Institute of Children's Literature, instructor, 1973-79; Bucknell University, Alpha Lambda Delta Lecturer, 1974, guest lecturer in children's literature, 1976-78. Presenter at workshops in high schools and colleges.

Member

Authors Guild, Phi Beta Kappa.

Awards, Honors

Notable Book citation, American Library Association (ALA), 1971, for *The Bread Book*, 1976, for *Amish People*, and 1979, for *C. C. Poindexter*; Children's Book Showcase award, Children's Book Council, 1977, for *Amish People*; Best Books citation, *New York Times*, 1977, for *Eskimos: Growing Up in a Changing Culture*; Best Book for Young Adults citation, ALA, 1979, for *C. C. Poindexter*, 1980, for *The Center: From a Troubled Past to a New Life*, 1985, for *The Mystery of the Ancient Maya*, 1986, for *Voices of South Africa* and *Denny's Tapes*, 1992, for *Where the Broken Heart Still Beats*, 1993, for *White Lilacs*; YASD Best Books citation, *Voice of Youth Advocates*, 1988, for *Denny's Tapes* and *Voices of South Africa*; Author of the Year Award, Pennsylvania School Librarians Association, 1990; Northwest Librarians Association Readers' Choice Award, 2000, for *Mary, Bloody Mary*.

Writings

NONFICTION FOR YOUNG PEOPLE

Miss Patch's Learn-to-Sew Book, illustrated by Mary Suzuki, Harcourt (New York, NY), 1969.

(Self-illustrated) *Stitch by Stitch: Needlework for Beginners*, Harcourt (New York, NY), 1970.

The Bread Book: All about Bread and How to Make It, illustrated by Trina Schart Hyman, Harcourt (New York, NY), 1971.

Yarn: The Things It Makes and How to Make Them, illustrated by Jennifer Perrott, Harcourt (New York, NY), 1972.

Saw, Hammer, and Paint: Woodworking and Finishing for Beginners, illustrated by Toni Martignoni, Morrow (New York, NY), 1973.

Christmas Crafts: Things to Make the 24 Days before Christmas, illustrated by Anita Lobel, Harper (New York, NY), 1974.

Milk, Butter, and Cheese: The Story of Dairy Products, illustrated by Giulio Maestro, Morrow (New York, NY), 1974.

The Needlework Book of Bible Stories, illustrated by Janet McCaffery, Harcourt (New York, NY), 1975.

People Who Make Things: How American Craftsmen Live and Work, Atheneum (New York, NY), 1975.

Rock Tumbling: From Stones to Gems to Jewelry, photographs by Jerome Wexler, Morrow (New York, NY), 1975.

Amish People: Plain Living in a Complex World, photographs by Michael Ramsey, Gerald Dodds, and the author, Atheneum (New York, NY), 1976.

Coconut: The Tree of Life, illustrated by Lynne Cherry, Morrow (New York, NY), 1976.

Lots and Lots of Candy, illustrated by Laura Jean Allen, Harcourt (New York, NY), 1976.

(With research assistance from Bernadine Larsen) *Eskimos: Growing Up in a Changing Culture*, photographs by John McDonald, Atheneum (New York, NY), 1977.

Being Beautiful: The Story of Cosmetics from Ancient Art to Modern Science, illustrated by Marika, Morrow (New York, NY), 1977.

Mask Magic, illustrated by Melanie Gaines Arwin, Harcourt (New York, NY), 1978.

The Center: From a Troubled Past to a New Life, Atheneum (New York, NY), 1980.

Rock Band: Big Men in a Great Big Town, Atheneum (New York, NY), 1980.

(With Charles Gallenkamp) *The Mystery of the Ancient Maya*, Atheneum (New York, NY), 1985, revised edition, Simon & Schuster (New York, NY), 1995.

Voices of South Africa: Growing Up in a Troubled Land, Harcourt (New York, NY), 1986.

Voices of Northern Ireland: Growing Up in a Troubled Land, Harcourt (New York, NY), 1987.

A Voice from Japan: An Outsider Looks In, Harcourt (New York, NY), 1988.

In a Different Light: Growing Up in a Yup'ik Eskimo Village in Alaska, photographs by John McDonald, Simon & Schuster (New York, NY), 1996.

FICTION FOR YOUNG PEOPLE

C. C. Poindexter, Atheneum (New York, NY), 1979.

Eulalia's Island, Atheneum (New York, NY), 1982.

The Summer I Learned about Life, Atheneum (New York, NY), 1983.

The Luck of Texas McCoy, Atheneum (New York, NY), 1984.

Elliott & Win, Atheneum (New York, NY), 1986.

Denny's Tapes, McElderry (New York, NY), 1987.

Wild Rover, McElderry (New York, NY), 1989.

Killing the Kudu, McElderry (New York, NY), 1990.

Japan—How Do Hands Make Peace? Earth Inspectors No. 10, McGraw (New York, NY), 1990.

Where the Broken Heart Still Beats: The Story of Cynthia Ann Parker, Harcourt (New York, NY), 1992.

White Lilacs, Harcourt (New York, NY), 1993.

Rio Grande Stories, Harcourt (New York, NY), 1994.

Drummers of Jericho, Harcourt (New York, NY), 1995.

Gideon's People, Harcourt (New York, NY), 1996.

Jubilee Journey, Harcourt (New York, NY), 1997.

"ROYAL DIARIES" SERIES

Isabel: Jewel of Castilla, Scholastic (New York, NY), 2000.
Anastasia: The Last Grand Duchess, Scholastic (New York, NY), 2000.
Kristina: The Girl King, Scholastic (New York, NY), 2003.

"YOUNG ROYALS" SERIES

Mary, Bloody Mary, Harcourt (New York, NY), 1999.
Beware, Princess Elizabeth, Harcourt (New York, NY), 2001.
Doomed Queen Anne, Harcourt (New York, NY), 2002.

"HOTLINE" SERIES; NOVELS FOR YOUNG ADULTS

Because of Lissa, Bantam (New York, NY), 1990.
The Problem with Sidney, Bantam (New York, NY), 1990.
Gillian's Choice, Bantam (New York, NY), 1991.
The Two Faces of Adam, Bantam (New York, NY), 1991.

FOR ADULTS

Brown Eyes Blue (novel), Bridge Works (Bridgehampton, NY), 2003.

OTHER

McCall's (magazine), author of columns "Cheers and Jeers," 1967-68, and "Chiefly for Children," 1968-72, and of multi-part series on crafts and women, and consulting editor for "Right Now" section, 1972. Contributor of articles and book reviews to periodicals, including *Family Circle, Redbook, Golf Digest, Los Angeles Times, Accent on Leisure, Town and Country, Publishers Weekly,* and *Americana.*

Sidelights

The author of approximately fifty books for young readers, Carolyn Meyer has achieved notable success in both nonfiction and fiction. She has written numerous well-received books based on her encounters with Yup'ik Eskimos, members of Amish religious groups, rock and roll bands, and the peoples of South Africa, Northern Ireland, and Japan. Additionally, she has also produced a score of young adult novels, including award-winners such as *C. C. Poindexter, Denny's Tapes, Where the Broken Heart Still Beats,* and *White Lilacs.* Meyer is also the author of the Bantam "Hotline" series about high schoolers who staff a counseling hotline and confront such strong issues as teen suicide and drug abuse, and she has introduced younger readers to such important historical figures as England's Queen Elizabeth I, Isabel of Castile, and Anne Boleyn. A widely traveled author, Meyer has sometimes taken on projects

that challenge her both physically and emotionally. Her approach to writing is pragmatic and disciplined. She told the *Albuquerque Journal:* "I know how to do these (young reader) books and do them well."

Meyer's career falls into roughly three segments. In her early years as a published author, she wrote many "how-to" craft books for younger readers. She then accepted the challenge of writing about different cultures, from the Pennsylvania Amish to the citizens of South Africa and Northern Ireland. More recently she has penned a number of historical novels, some in diary form and others in first person. Interspersed throughout, she has created fiction from the events of her personal life and from the experiences of her sons and stepdaughter. Inspiration is found in moments of everyday life or from the suggestions of editors, friends, and even strangers. Like many another author for youngsters, Meyer often puts herself in a challenged child's shoes in order to understand the special pressures that child feels during his or her most troubling formative years.

One day while visiting her mother in her old hometown of Lewistown, Pennsylvania, Meyer passed an Amish family—one of many in the general area—riding in their horse-drawn buggy. Members of Amish religious groups typically shun much of the technology that has been invented since the original Amish congregations were founded in Germany and Switzerland centuries ago. Meyer, a German American, realized that she had grown up in their presence without ever trying to get to know them. Her curiosity sparked *Amish People: Plain Living in a Complex World.* Writing in the *New York Times Book Review,* Edward Hoagland called Meyer's book "an excellent introduction to Amishism." Soon thereafter she encountered a white woman who had married into a Yup'ik Eskimo family in Alaska, and the two worked together to describe the woman's new way of life for the book *Eskimos: Growing Up in a Changing Culture.* Almost twenty years later, Meyer returned to the fictionalized Yup'ik village of that book to take a look at what changes the years had wrought for the next generation in the book, *In a Different Light: Growing Up in a Yup'ik Eskimo Village in Alaska. Booklist* reviewer Chris Sherman remarked that in *In a Different Light,* the author "provides a vivid and thoughtful portrait of a culture in transition."

Meyer's ability to explain different cultures drew the attention of an editor at the Harcourt publishing house, who brought her a challenging project: travel to South Africa—a scene of great racial tension between an oppressed black majority and the ruling white minority—and gather material for a book that would show young people what it was like to grow up there. The book became *Voices of South Africa: Growing Up in a Troubled Land.* Billing herself simply as a children's author, Meyer toured South Africa and spoke to as many different kinds of people as she could, although she found that white people were sometimes defensive, children were sometimes afraid to speak freely in the presence of their teachers, and black people were difficult for any white writer to meet. Despite such obstacles, as Cathi MacRae wrote in *Wilson Library Bulletin,* "Meyer still manages to offer an engrossing personal account of one American's effort to understand. She smoothly combines travelogue, conversations, and historical background." A writer for *Kirkus Reviews* called the work a "brilliant study" and declared: "Readers who seek understanding, rather than easy answers, will find it here."

Meyer repeated the formula from *Voices of South Africa* to create additional books in the same format. A visit to Northern Ireland resulted in *Voices of Northern Ireland: Growing Up in a Troubled Land,* a record of her journey and of the interviews she conducted with Protestants and Catholics alike. *Horn Book*'s Ethel R. Twichell commented, "Meyer is a shrewd observer and appears to have had the gift of encouraging the young to talk to her." A visit to Japan, however, was much different than the other journeys. Faced with a language and cultural barrier, the author decided to emphasize her own perplexed response to Japanese customs. The resulting book was appropriately entitled *A Voice from Japan: An Outsider Looks In.* Rosie Peasley, writing in *School Library Journal,* suggested that Meyer's honest voice would keep readers "turning pages happily" because of "[f]ascinating details about Japanese homes, bedding, food, education, and customs."

Meyer's first published novel, *C. C. Poindexter,* is somewhat autobiographical. C. C., a fifteen-year-old girl who is six-foot-one and getting taller, tries to find a sense of direction for her life while watching her parents struggle through the aftermath of divorce. The book is almost painfully accurate in its depiction of a teenager who feels alienated from her peers and equally alone at home. This debut novel earned Meyer a "Best Books for Young Adults" citation from the American Library Association and convinced her that her writing could go in nonfiction and fiction directions, both of which she has continued to follow.

One of Meyer's sons helped inspire her second novel. One summer Meyer took her children with her to the Caribbean island of St. Lucia. There, as she researched a fairly conventional book about coconuts, her son had a more eye-opening experience when he became friends with a black family that lived permanently on the island. Meyer adapted her son's adventure for *Eulalia's Island,* in which thirteen-year-old Sam, a morose boy from Pennsylvania, goes along on a family vacation to the Caribbean, meets fourteen-year-old island native Eulalia, and gains a new appreciation of life and himself.

Meanwhile Meyer, who had spent a dozen years living as a homemaker in suburban Connecticut, looked around for a new place to live as part of her new life as a professional writer. She finally settled in New Mexico, and then later, with her second husband, moved to Texas. In the years since Meyer went west, many of her young adult novels—including *The Luck of Texas McCoy, Elliott & Win,* and *Wild Rover*—have been set in the region and have been inspired by people she met there. The title character of *Texas McCoy* is a sixteen-year-old girl who inherits a New Mexico ranch and battles successfully to keep it running. "Meyer writes with storytelling flair," said Trev Jones in *School Library Journal,* "and young readers will sense immediately the importance of Texas' inheritance to her."

Elliott & Win tells the story of fourteen-year-old Win who hopes to receive some adult guidance in a Big Brother sort of program, but when he is paired with opera-loving Elliott, he is disappointed. Disappointment soon turns to distrust when a buddy tells Win that Elliott is probably homosexual; however, Win eventually comes to appreciate his new friend. David Gale, writing in *School Library Journal,* called this a "well-crafted story of human concerns."

Another award-winning fiction title from Meyer is the 1987 *Denny's Tapes,* in which the seventeen-year-old boy of the title, the child of a black father and white mother, is caught in the middle of a new marriage. When his mother remarries, Denny finds himself falling in love with his new white stepsister. Thrown out of the house, he drives cross-country in search of his father and his roots. *Booklist* contributor Hazel Rochman felt that teens would be interested in "the gritty details of Denny's journey," and "moved by the search for a father which is also a struggle for identity."

Never one to shy away from difficult subjects, Meyer deals with physical disability in *Killing the Kudu.* Eighteen-year-old Alex, a paraplegic, learns to deal with his life, coming to terms with the cousin who caused his disability and finding his first love. Dislocation is the theme of *Where the Broken Heart Still Beats,* a fictionalized account of Cynthia Ann Parker, who was kidnapped as a child by Comanches and reunited with her biological family twenty-five years later. But once forcibly rejoined with her white relatives, Cynthia feels lost and longs for her Indian life. The only friend she finds in her new life is her adolescent cousin, Lucy, who narrates the tale. Betsy Hearne, writing in *Bulletin of the Center for Children's Books,* dubbed this a "thoughtful and thought-provoking book," while *School Library Journal* correspondent Ann W. Moore called it a "fascinating look at the Comanche and their captives."

More Texas history is served up in the novels *White Lilacs* and *Jubilee Journey,* both of which deal with race relations in a small town. In the first of these companion volumes, the year is 1921 and twelve-year-old Rose Lee watches as her black community is threatened by the whites in the town of Dillon. The white towns-people, wanting to create a park out of a stretch of land where blacks have settled, try to move them to a miser-able tract of land outside of town. "Perfectly evoking time and place, Meyer carefully layers detail upon de-tail," noted Cindy Darling Codell in a *School Library Journal* review of the novel. Codell concluded: "Thoughtful readers will hope for an encore." In 1997, Meyer continued the story in *Jubilee Journey*. This time, many years have passed and Rose Lee's granddaughter and great-grandchildren come south to Dillon from their northern home. Emily Rose, one of these great-grandchildren and one who has always felt comfortable in her enlightened Connecticut community, learns some new and painful truths about the history of her family and about the history of race relations in America.

In 1999 Meyer shifted her focus to European royals with *Mary, Bloody Mary*. This book takes readers back into the sixteenth century, where Meyer provides a "riv-eting slice of fictional royal history" which "paints a sympathetic portrait of Henry VIII's oldest daughter, before she earns the title Bloody Mary," according to a reviewer for *Publishers Weekly*. More such historical fiction followed, including *Isabel: Jewel of Castilla*, the story of the Queen of Spain's early years, *Anastasia, the Last Grand Duchess*, an account of the daughter of the last emperor of Russia, *Beware, Princess Elizabeth*, about Bloody Mary's younger sister, and *Doomed Queen Anne*, the second wife of Henry VIII. In *School Library Journal*, Cheri Estes called *Beware, Princess Elizabeth* a "gripping historical drama" of a real histori-cal figure whose "intelligence, drive, and independence will appeal to today's readers." Carolyn Phelan in *Booklist* praised *Doomed Queen Anne* as "an involving narrative that offers a believable portrait of a flawed, even unsympathetic, woman."

Meyer has also written a four-volume series for Ban-tam, "Hotline," about a group of high school kids oper-ating an emergency phone service. Teen suicide is dealt with in the first of these, *Because of Lissa*, in which the phone service is inaugurated as a response to Lissa's death. "YAs will welcome this book, as it offers a solu-tion with sensitivity and understanding," commented Linda Zoppa in a *School Library Journal* review. Sub-sequent volumes continue with the adventures and en-counters of this hotline group, dealing with sex, run-aways, and alcohol and drug abuse. In order to research these books, Meyer herself volunteered at an emer-gency hotline for several months.

Meyer began her career trying to write for adults, with little success. After more than thirty years as a children's book author, she finally published her first adult novel, *Brown Eyes Blue*, in 2003. The book is a multi-generational portrait of a grandmother, mother, and daughter, all of whom conceal secrets from one another despite their close ties. Set in the Pennsylvania country-side, the story begins with grandmother Lavinia's deci-sion to paint graphic male nudes rather than the bucolic Amish scenes for which she has become noted. Facing a turning point of her own, Lavinia's daughter Dorcas returns home and opens a bed and breakfast inn. Sasha, Dorcas's daughter, comes onto the scene with her own life-altering decisions already made. *Library Journal* correspondent Sheila Riley noted of the book: "Most of the characters are fully and interestingly drawn," and Danise Hoover in *Booklist* commended the piece for its "three very interesting women who take turns narrating." A reviewer for *Publishers Weekly* praised, Meyer "makes a charming adult debut with this novel. . . . Meyer weaves the story of three generations of women who, with their distinctive voices, will endear them-selves to readers."

Whether writing about distant cultures, gawky adoles-cents, or teenagers at risk, Meyer "eschews the easy plotline and delves into the uncomfortable realities of our world," according to M. Jean Greenlaw and Eliza-beth D. Schafer writing in the *St. James Guide to Young Adult Writers*. Green and Schafer concluded that a reader "awaits her new works with a sense of anticipation."

Biographical and Critical Sources

BOOKS

Authors of Books for Young People, 3rd edition, Scare-crow (Metuchen, NJ), 1990.
St. James Guide to Young Adult Writers, 2nd edition, Gale (Detroit, MI), 1999.

PERIODICALS

Albuquerque Journal, June 10, 2001, David Steinberg, "Author Turns Out Reams for Young Readers," p. F8.
Booklist, November 1, 1987, Hazel Rochman, review of *Denny's Tapes*, pp. 466-467; November 15, 1990, p. 655; October 1, 1994, p. 328; June 1, 1995, p. 1753; March 15, 1996, p. 1282; May 1, 1996, Chris Sher-man, review of *In a Different Light*, p. 1496; Septem-ber 1, 1997, Kay Weisman, review of *Jubilee Journey*, p. 126; March 1, 2001, GraceAnne A. DeCandido, re-view of *Beware, Princess Elizabeth*, p. 1278; Septem-ber 15, 2002, Carolyn Phelan, review of *Doomed Queen Anne*, p. 222; March 15, 2003, Danise Hoover, review of *Brown Eyes Blue*, p. 1275.
Bulletin of the Center for Children's Books, April, 1978, p. 131; November, 1978, p. 48; December, 1979, p. 75; October, 1984, p. 32; May, 1986, p. 174; No-vember, 1986, p. 55; November, 1987, p. 52; Novem-ber, 1988, p. 80; January, 1991, pp. 125-26; Novem-ber, 1992, Betsy Hearne, review of *Where the Broken Heart Still Beats*, pp. 117-118; September, 1994, p. 19; April, 1995, p. 282; May, 1996, p. 309; September, 1997, p. 19.

Horn Book, August, 1975, p. 391; August, 1976, p. 415; February, 1978, p. 61; December, 1978, p. 646; October, 1982, p. 520; May, 1987, p. 358; January-February, 1988, Ethel R. Twichell, review of *Voices of Northern Ireland,* p. 87; September-October, 1996, Margaret A. Bush, review of *In a Different Light,* p. 622.

Kirkus Reviews, January 1, 1986, p. 215; September 1, 1986, review of *Voices of South Africa,* p. 1377; September 1, 1987, p. 1323; October 1, 1992, p. 1258; July 15, 1993, p. 937; June 15, 1994, p. 849; April 15, 1996, p. 604.

Library Journal, April 1, 2003, Sheila Riley, review of *Brown Eyes Blue,* p. 130.

New York Times Book Review, May 9, 1976, Edward Hoagland, review of *Amish People,* p. 14; December 18, 1977, p. 23; January 20, 1980, p. 30; July 16, 1995, p. 27.

Publishers Weekly, May 30, 1994, p. 57; May 8, 1995, p. 296; September 27, 1999, review of *Mary, Bloody Mary,* p. 106; May 19, 2003, review of *Brown Eyes Blue,* p. 54.

School Library Journal, September, 1982, p. 141; February, 1985, Trev Jones, review of *The Luck of Texas McCoy,* p. 86; March, 1986, David Gale, review of *Elliott & Win,* p. 178; November, 1988, Rosie Peas-ley, review of *A Voice from Japan,* p. 138; November, 1990, p. 50; January, 1991, Linda Zoppa, review of *Because of Lissa,* p. 114; July, 1991, p. 88; September, 1992, Ann W. Moore, review of *Where the Broken Heart Still Beats,* pp. 278-279; October, 1993, Cindy Darling Codell, review of *White Lilacs,* p. 152; September, 1995, pp. 219, 227; June, 1996, Mollie Bunum, review of *In a Different Light,* p. 162; January, 1998, p. 114; October, 1999, p. 154; July, 2000, Ann W. Moore, review of *Isabel: Jewel of Castile,* p. 108; October, 2000, Susan Shaver, review of *Anastasia: The Last Grand Duchess,* p. 166; May, 2001, Cheri Estes, review of *Beware, Princess Elizabeth,* p. 156; August, 2002, Mercedes Smith, review of *Isabel: Jewel of Castilla,* p. 559; October, 2002, Bruce Anne Shook, review of *Doomed Queen Anne,* p. 168.

Voice of Youth Advocates, February, 1991, p. 354; April, 1993, p. 27; June, 1995, p. 96; June, 1996, p. 98; August, 1996, p. 150.

Wilson Library Bulletin, December, 1988, Cathi MacRae, "The Young Adult Perplex," p. 92.

ONLINE

Carolyn Meyer Home Page, http://www.readcarolyn.com/ (May 6, 2003).

Autobiography Feature

Carolyn Meyer

Early signs of talent: I was only six months old when I began my first book, ghost-written by my adoring father who must have thought it would be awfully cute if his first (and, as it turned out, only) child kept a diary of her earliest days.

I still have that leather-bound volume in which my father recorded a daily account of my activities--what time I woke my parents in the morning, what I ate, what time I had my bath, when my grandparents came to visit, and what my parents did after I had been put to bed in the evening (listened to the radio; played Monopoly).

That book was never published, of course, but it does provide a good picture of what my parents' lives were like in 1935, the year I was born, in Lewistown, Pennsylvania, where my father worked for the telephone company and my mother gave piano lessons to a few pupils.

We lived in a neighborhood where there were few playmates, and I looked forward to kindergarten, a step toward being grown up. But I hated it almost from the first day. I had begun to wear glasses, thick lenses mounted in round gold frames. Nobody else had glasses, and I was quickly labeled as odd (which may not have had anything to do with the glasses). I didn't know how to play with other kids, and I looked funny. Not a good combination.

The first major event in kindergarten was the Halloween parade. I didn't like dressing up, especially in the funny clown suit my mother bought me, but it was even worse because of Jane. Jane, the daughter of my mother's friend, was decked out in shining stars and big satin bows, the costume of a fairy princess, who got to lead the parade around Miss Keller's classroom. The funny-looking clown was assigned to bring up the rear.

After that I figured out a foolproof way to avoid doing things I didn't want to do. I learned that you

Carolyn Meyer

don't have to go anywhere or do much of anything when you are the only child and—get this—the ONLY GRANDCHILD in a loving but over-protective family if you happen to mention that you don't feel well. As a matter of fact, I seldom felt well after that, and I managed to spend the rest of my kindergarten year and the first couple of years of grade school at home in bed, surrounded by my books, a little radio my grandfather brought me, and a lot of hovering attention from my mother.

Eventually I learned to be selective: I wasn't sick *all* the time—just when there were things that made me nervous or insecure, like birthday parties and school picnics where I would not be able to rely on intellect but would be expected to participate in all kinds of games I thought were stupid and a waste of time. My social skills were not improving.

*

A Sunday afternoon radio announcement on December 7, 1941, altered the rest of my childhood. I remember the news of the bombing of Pearl Harbor over the Philco in our living room and my parents' excited response. Six months later my daddy took me for a

walk and explained that he was going away to the war, that he might be gone for a long time, and it was up to me to take care of Mummy.

That was the summer of 1942. I was seven years old. I can still picture my father in his Air Corps uniform, standing on the platform between the passenger cars, waving and waving as the train rounded a curve and disappeared. It was three years until we saw him again, and I missed him terribly.

We were all caught up in the war. We saved tin cans and flattened them and sold stamps for war bonds. I got a little cardboard kit for identifying enemy aircraft that might fly over the farms and small factories of central Pennsylvania. I declared myself a leader of the Junior Commandos, sponsored by a Philadelphia newspaper to inspire patriotism in young kids, and I got an arm band to wear over the sleeve of my snowsuit. (A leader without any followers, I think.)

I rarely missed a daily episode of "Hop Harrigan, Ace of the Airways." Whenever I could corral some kids to play with me, I cast myself in the leading role of Hop himself, assigning to others the parts of Hop's girlfriend, the virtuous nurse Gail Nolan, of his loyal but less intelligent sidekick, Tank Tinker, and of his perennial enemy, the Gray Ghost. Once in a while I would take the villain's role, but mostly I saw myself as the calm, capable, heroic Hop Harrigan. My mother worried that I always took the male role when I played out fantasies. I explained that I didn't want to be a man—I just wanted to be in charge. That was no comfort to her.

Meanwhile, I was busy trying to be a good student—and succeeding. I went to the same small country school my mother had attended: four rooms, six grades, forty children in a room with the teacher kept busy shifting back and forth between two grades. I easily won all the spelling bees, and I was lightning quick with the answers to the arithmetic flashcards, although the drill always made me half sick with nervousness.

The teachers soon found that I could be a big help and sent me to the cloakroom, a big closet with a window and a water fountain and all our woolen coats, to tutor kids who were having trouble reading. I had already done all the assignments from my own grade plus whatever other grade was sharing the room, and I was glad to have something to do. This gave me some status, but status in the classroom wasn't my problem. Status on the playground was another matter.

I couldn't do ANYTHING, like catching a ball or hitting it, or running fast enough to beat anybody anywhere. We played softball, and I was a failure, even when they gave me six strikes to compensate the team that had to take me. "Russia," which involved complicated ball bouncing and catching (failure), "Red Rover," in which people tried to break through the line you were in (failure), skinning the cat and other feats of skill on the monkey bars (failure). Most of the time I managed to bring an excuse from my mother so I wouldn't have to go outside at recess, and since I lived only a block from school, I waited at the end of our driveway until the janitor appeared on the front steps of the school to ring his big brass bell before I left for school in the morning.

I couldn't even clap together the erasers outside the school building after school, because my mother was afraid I was allergic to chalk dust, and I wasn't allowed to wash the blackboards because the water was cold and might give me a chill. Who knows if any of these things were real? They seemed real enough at the time, real enough to keep my mother frantically taking me from one doctor to another, first in Lewistown and then in Philadelphia, trying to find out why I was so fragile and what could be done about it.

Rotha, a girl with dirty hair and badly rotted teeth, may have come closest to the truth. She called me "Professor Pisspot," figuring there wasn't a thing wrong with me except that I was too smart for my own good. I was certainly a misfit. Being sick was the only way I knew how to deal with the isolation of not fitting in with a bunch of healthy, normal, outgoing kids who liked to play games and raise a little hell and weren't much concerned with the academic life. With the basic ingredients of being an only child, a homely child, and an intelligent child, I learned to live a rich inner life. It was probably an excellent way for any writer to begin.

By the time I started junior high school, things had changed. My father had returned from his three-year stint in the service, and we seemed like a real fam-

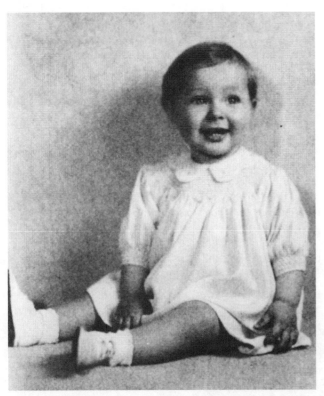

The author, age one: "My first book, ghostwritten by my father, was already under way when I posed for this formal portrait."

ily again. I was bored with being sick at all the critical times, and mysteriously and miraculously all the illnesses, whether real or imaginary, simply disappeared. My parents decided that I should attend the town high school, rather than the rural school nearer our home. My father dropped me off there on his way to the office in the morning (he was selling insurance and real estate then), and I took a bus home at night, or my mother picked me up.

Getting braces on my teeth was a milestone. I was hopeful that my looks would improve, that the ugly duckling would turn into a swan, and that I would be popular and happy, sought after by those creatures I had just discovered: boys!

It didn't work. The dreams didn't come true, not for many years. I was still Professor Pisspot in thick glasses, although a few years older and a few inches taller. I still enjoyed my studies and got almost all *A*s; a *B* was a near-tragedy. I had good, demanding teachers who insisted that we read and understand, that we become good spellers (I already was), that we master the most obscure points of grammar. I discovered the fun of working on the school newspaper, and I sang in the school chorus and took part regularly in school assemblies and plays. I also took piano lessons, although it was clear that I didn't have my mother's talent.

I enjoyed all my subjects and was good at them, with the glaring exception of physical education. Somebody had told me that in order to graduate from high school I would have to stand on my head. For six years I worried that I would be the only straight-A student in the history of the high school to be denied a diploma because I couldn't perform that feat. I never thought to ask anybody if it were true.

At the end of ninth grade, the last year of junior high, the principal called a group of us into his office, to tell us who would receive an award at the special assembly. The award I coveted and which I thought was a cinch was the Most Useful Girl Award. I was sure I was the most useful girl in the ninth grade, that I had appeared in the most assemblies, written the most articles for the school paper, and done other useful things. But Mr. Snyder announced that the winner of the Most Useful Girl Award was Jane, the girl in the silver stars and satin bows who led the Halloween parade ten years earlier. Jane tap danced and played the piano, and I did not. She was more Useful than I.

Instead, I won the Mathematics Award, which was probably a greater achievement than tap dancing, but at the time I was inconsolable. That was also the end of my enjoyment of math. I suffered through another required year of algebra and one of plane geometry, but I never took solid geometry or trigonometry, and I signed up for only the barest minimum of science, enough to get into college.

I did a little writing in those years, but not much—only what was required in my classes and for the school paper, which I edited in my junior year. As a senior I moved on to edit the *Lore,* the yearbook. Under my pic-

The author at age four, with her parents, Sara and Vic Meyer, 1939

ture was a list of my accomplishments and my ambition: to be a radio scriptwriter. Television in 1953 was not yet a part of our lives or our dreams. My ambition was the result of a series of interesting summer jobs.

I had learned to type the summer I was fifteen and to drive the summer after that, when I was hired as a typist by the local radio station. My boss discovered that I had a talent for writing commercials, and I began preparing one-minute ads for furniture stores, dress shops, and other advertisers.

The summer before I left for college I went to work for a new station that was opening out in the country, twenty miles from town, where both transmitter and broadcasting studio were in a little cement block building in the middle of a cow pasture. The audience was mostly farmers, and the advertisers were mostly dealers in farm products, like egg washers and manure spreaders. That was the advertising copy I wrote that summer, for which I was paid minimum wage—fifty cents an hour.

I graduated from high school at the head of my class with a pocketful of awards, including the senior

high school version of the Most Useful Girl Award. This would have been all pretty heady stuff, except that I was still a social misfit. I didn't have a date for the senior dinner dance; I went by myself, sat by myself, and went home by myself. My date for the senior prom materialized, only at the last minute, after the efforts of some of my friends to corner some poor soul who didn't want to go in the first place and certainly didn't want to go with me any more than I wanted to go with him. After the graduation exercises, still high from the valedictory address I had just given, I left with my parents, while everyone else went off to have a good time. At least it *seemed* that way.

All of this was hard enough to take, and I didn't take it in good grace. But it was made even harder by my mother in whose footsteps I was supposed to follow. My mother was also an only child and also a graduate of Lewistown High School. She had also been the valedictorian of her class and the editor of the *Lore*. Some of my teachers had been her teachers, and they remembered Sara Knepp as a phenomenon, a talented pianist with a photographic memory.

The problem for me was that she was also very pretty—beautiful, in fact. And she was popular: she had had dates for all the parties and dances, more adoring beaux than anyone needed. Nobody had ever, ever called her Professor Pisspot. It was undoubtedly hard on her to have such a plain daughter (she used to say that I was probably a late bloomer), but it was MUCH harder on me to have a beautiful, talented, popular mother.

My mother had definite ideas of how a young lady should dress. She didn't believe in fads or passing fashions; she believed in classic clothes. She had a point, but the clothes she picked out for me would have been classic for a forty-year-old woman; on me they were simply old-ladyish and unattractive. I have blue eyes— the same as my mother's blue eyes, in fact—but instead of buying me clothes to make the most of those eyes, she bought me a horrible green party dress, a dreadful yellow blouse and skirt, a suit with an orange jacket, colors she would never wear.

Then there were the shoes. I had terrible feet, she decided, and so I was never allowed to wear loafers, as everyone else did, or heaven forbid, sandals or sneakers. I had to wear brown orthopedic oxfords with white socks. Recently I saw a bumper sticker that said, "You're ugly, and your mother dresses you funny," and I felt like crying. After all these years.

*

I had no trouble deciding where I would go to college: Bucknell University, my father's school. My mother pressed for Vassar or Smith or Mount Holyoke, one of the prestigious women's colleges. I would have none of it. Bucknell it was, only fifty-five miles from home, in the same rolling Pennsylvania hills.

Although there wasn't much change in physical landscape, Bucknell introduced me to a new landscape of ideas. Naturally I signed up for all the English literature and writing classes I could—English was my major—and escaped anything that had to do with math and science, a choice I regret today. I wish I knew more about science, but I find that even now I have to force myself to learn anything scientific. I took some French, but not enough to speak it well. I studied philosophy and religion because they interested me, but I gave scant attention to history and sociology, although I later learned about those areas on my own. I got involved with the radio station, the newspaper, and the literary magazine, and I was editor of *L'Agenda,* the yearbook, during my senior year.

I was still on my track of being a superachiever with excellent grades and election to Phi Beta Kappa. But these were the 1950s, and my options after graduation seemed very narrow. Those were the days when young women were expected to marry when they graduated, or to work for a year or two at most and then to marry. The idea of having a career was considered radical, and I was no radical. I wanted what everybody else wanted.

My father, a sensible man, insisted that if I were going to major in English, I needed to get a teaching certificate or learn typing and shorthand. Since I had no desire to teach high-school English and was not interested in going on to graduate school, a secretarial course seemed to be the solution. During a summer class in Boston, I learned enough to be employable, and that's what concerned my dad.

I talked about being a writer, but even I didn't take that seriously. Instead I managed to meet a boy at the beginning of my senior year, convince myself that I was in love, acquire his fraternity pin by Christmas and a diamond engagement ring by Easter—so that I got my college diploma with all the right credentials. When the engagement fell through shortly before the wedding, it was no particular disaster; I think I was relieved. The problem then, since I wasn't getting married, was that I had no idea what else to do with myself.

I went to New York, which I knew nothing about, stayed with a friend in the suburbs, and started job hunting. Prospects were not brilliant for young female college graduates. The boys went into executive training programs, sometimes starting in the mailroom, but at least on a career path; the girls got jobs as secretaries. The myth was that persistent girls who didn't get sidetracked into marriage and family could eventually work their way into interesting jobs—but not as interesting as the jobs the boys got, and probably not as interesting as marriage. I took a secretarial job which I disliked from the first day, and at the earliest opportunity, I allowed myself to get sidetracked.

Within a few years I had a husband, Joseph Smrcka; three sons—Alan, John, and Christopher; a home in the suburbs; and an office in the basement, where I

"In my grandparents' backyard just before we saw my father off to World War II"

had begun to put in several hours a day writing. I thought it was important to be a perfect housewife and mother, and so I spent my mornings—my best and most productive hours—doing household chores. In the afternoons, when everything was in order and the kids were taking naps, I wrote, ready to drop everything as soon as somebody woke up or came home from school or work.

I tried writing all kinds of things, and I approached writing with the same zeal and determination and discipline with which I had approached my courses in high school and college. I wrote short stories and sent them to the *New Yorker,* which sent them right back. I wrote a novel; it still molders in a box labeled "inactive." Then I sent a short story to a secretarial magazine that bought it for twenty-five dollars and published it *in shorthand.* None of my friends or family could read it.

I tried other articles and short stories for specialized magazines, sold a few pieces, gradually gaining confidence, learning my craft. By the time I was expecting my third child, I had acquired an agent who thought my idea of writing a sewing book for little girls was probably salable. With Chris a newborn just home from the hospital, I put the finishing touches on *Miss*

Patch's Learn-to-Sew Book; it was sold at once to Margaret McElderry, then editor at Harcourt, Brace & World.

By the time that first book was published, my middle son, John, was in second grade. Every week during library period he checked *Miss Patch* out of the school library and brought it home. To the best of my knowledge, he never actually read it; he'd just take it back when it was due and check it out again. When I pointed out to him that we already had a shelf full of *Miss Patch* books at home, he informed me that every time a book was checked out of his school library, it was marked with a date stamp. A page full of date stamps showed that the book was popular, and he wanted everybody to know that his mother's book was in demand.

Miss Patch was the first of several "how to" books that tied in with my interest in cooking and needlework, plus a growing interest in history. *The Bread Book,* for instance, is as much about the history and myths of bread as it is about baking it.

As my children grew older, I became less interested in "how to do it" and more interested in the people who did it. *People Who Make Things: How American Craftsmen Live and Work* was a transitional book, the first to take me further than the local library. In 1973, I had been divorced for a couple of years and was just beginning to test my self-reliance. I traveled around the country, visiting people who worked in crafts that interested me—pottery, weaving, woodworking, blacksmithing, glassblowing—to learn what their lives and their work were like.

(Published in 1975, that book is a reminder that we had not yet become sensitized to sexist language. It's no longer appropriate to refer to "craftsmen." Although I had definite feminist leanings, it took me a while to catch on to non-sexist ways of saying things.)

One September on a visit to my mother in Pennsylvania, I encountered an Amish family, clip-clopping along a country road in their horse-drawn buggy. I waved, and they waved back; at that moment I decided to do a book about the Amish and their historical roots.

The summer of 1975, a friend and I and my three boys rented a beach house on the Caribbean island of St. Lucia for two months. At that time I was teaching a correspondence course for people who wanted to learn to write for kids, The Institute of Children's Literature. One of my students, a former nun who had married an Eskimo, lived in an Eskimo village in Alaska. We were writing to each other regularly, and one day, in the shade of a coconut palm on a tropical island, I had the idea of writing about the lives of Alaskan Eskimos. Letters flew back and forth from the tropics to the Arctic as we made plans for our joint research and my visit to Alaska the following spring.

While I was on St. Lucia I began my first novel for young adults: *C. C. Poindexter.* A major shift from the nonfiction I had been writing to the fiction I wanted to

write, it's the story of a fifteen-year-old girl who is six feet one inch tall and still growing. But it's really the story of a misfit—C. C.'s height is what separates her from others—and I had plenty of personal experience in that area.

It was an unusually productive summer. I gathered all the material I needed for a book about coconuts, of all things, as well as for my next novel: *Eulalia's Island.* My twelve-year-old son John, the one who had widened the circulation of *Miss Patch* five years earlier, was befriended by a black St. Lucian family. Soon this blond, hazel-eyed boy was spending virtually all his time with them, learning about the island and its culture, and passing some of what he learned on to the rest of us.

My sons have always been a source of ideas for me, sometimes more than I wished. That same middle son had what might be politely termed a difficult adolescence—so much so that he was eventually sent to a therapeutic community for troubled kids. It was a rough time for him, and for all of us. One way I dealt with the pain of that period was to write a book about it, titled *The Center: From A Troubled Past to A New Life.* The book ends on an optimistic note, and although our lives were not exactly peaceful even after that episode, John eventually received his bachelor's degree in psychology and is going on for graduate work.

*

My father had died in 1965, and when my mother died in 1979, I, the only child, went back to Lewistown to arrange her funeral. While cleaning out the attic, I found two slim, gray notebooks, diaries my father had kept in 1928, the summer he was twenty-one, a college student home from Bucknell. He lived with his conservative parents near Philadelphia and worked for the telephone company, checking the underground cables beneath the streets of the city.

That was the summer Vic Meyer was madly in love with a girl named Peg, who was at home with her family in Pittsburgh, on the other side of the state. Every night he would come home tired and dirty, have dinner with his family, write to his sweetheart and fill a page or two in his diary before he fell into bed. But few letters arrived for him from Pittsburgh. When he did receive one, it was usually something flip. He wrote that he wanted to announce their engagement, even though he knew it would be a long time until they could marry. She wrote back, refusing. All through the summer of 1928 he suffered at the hands of Peg, until at last they were both back at Bucknell. And then one night she returned his fraternity pin, breaking his heart once and for all.

This was, for me, a totally unknown side of my father. I had the diaries he kept when he was overseas during World War II, in Corsica and Italy, but they were obviously written for others to read. The diaries from 1928 were utterly personal. I forgot all about cleaning out the attic of my parents' home and sat down to read those diaries, laughing at his descriptions of some of the relatives and crying over his heartache.

After the funeral I went home to Santa Fe, New Mexico, where I then lived, and wrote to the Bucknell Alumni Office, asking if they had any record of this Peg. I was sent her married name and current address in Florida. I composed a careful letter, introducing myself as the daughter of Vic Meyer, a "friend" from Bucknell days, and then quoted the most heartrending of the paragraphs from Dad's diary, a description of that crisp October evening on the banks of the Susquehanna River when she returned his fraternity pin and he believed his life was over.

A couple of weeks later I received a gracious reply. Of course she remembered Vic Meyer, she wrote: "He was serious and sincere, and I was giddy and badly spoiled." She described her grown children and her husband, a doctor who had graduated from the University of Pittsburgh. (Aha! I thought; *that's* who she was seeing that summer while my father ate his heart out.) She and "Bunny," as she called him, were now retired and spending winters in Florida. It was nice to hear from me, she said, and if I ever found myself in her part of Florida, she would be happy to have me visit.

"All dressed up for the senior prom," 1953

That was all I needed. I wrote back immediately that by incredible coincidence I happened to be planning a business trip to Florida in a few weeks, and I would indeed stop to see her. Then I made hasty arrangements to take my youngest son, Chris, to Disney World, during his winter break—my "business trip."

I had a head full of fantasies of how wonderful it would be. Peg would probably invite me to stay for dinner, and we would reminisce about my father. If "Bunny" weren't within earshot, she might confess that she had never really forgotten Vic Meyer. She would probably invite me to spend the night, and we would sit up late, sipping hot chocolate and exchanging anecdotes.

I took along my father's old album filled with old photographs. Peg had been quite a beauty, and my father had collected pages of snapshots and formal portraits of her, and some of the two of them. I also packed a couple of pictures of the woman he had eventually married—my mother—including a fine picture taken of them the year before he died.

Peg was still a lovely woman, white-haired and elegantly dressed, in many ways reminding me of my mother. She led me to a sun porch and invited me to sit down. Then she waited. I tried to make conversation. Nothing caught fire. She offered me a cigarette; I don't smoke. She offered me none of the things I wanted—not even a cup of tea, let alone dinner and a bed for the night; no personal remembrance, no glimpse of the past. She was not interested in the photographs.

I had not bothered to reserve a motel room at the height of the tourist season, and there were NO VACANCY signs hung out everywhere I looked. The temperature had plunged to well below freezing. I had visions of shivering all night in some orange grove. Miserably disappointed, I drove until I found a depressing room in a lonely motel, and the next day I flew home.

It took several years after that until I was able to convert the rich material of those diaries into a novel that succeeded as fiction, although I made several attempts. Finally I hit upon the idea of creating Teddie, a younger sister for "Rob." The background was all there: I knew these characters well and I knew the setting. Now I had Teddie (very much like me) to find her brother's diary and discover his unhappiness; in my invented story, she tries to fix it. The result was *The Summer I Learned about Life.*

The move to Santa Fe had come about after twelve years in Norwalk, Connecticut, followed by a couple of experiments. The first was a nostalgic year in a pretty rural Pennsylvania town not far from where I grew up; there I learned that small town life doesn't suit me. Next, in the fall of 1977, I tried New York, a city with which I had been having a love/hate relationship for a long time. It had been exactly twenty years earlier that I first arrived in Manhattan fresh from college and a broken engagement. That experience had not been a happy one for me: I didn't have the skills for big-city living, and my job possibilities seemed depressingly limited.

But in 1977 I was a different person than I had been in 1957. I was grown up. I was a moderately successful writer, selling books regularly, writing magazines articles, and piecing out my income by working for the Institute of Children's Literature. I had mothered three children (the youngest, Chris, had gone to live with his father in Connecticut), survived a divorce, and done some traveling around the country. This time, I thought, I was ready for New York. I knew how to do it.

It didn't work. Alone, isolated, knowing few people, I spent most of my time shut up in a tiny subleased apartment on the West Side, writing all day long. And I couldn't afford the things that appealed to me in New York; plays, ballet, opera, concerts, all were expensive. It was a long, lonely winter. I was miserable.

But in the spring of 1978 I left for the Helene Wurlitzer Colony in Taos, New Mexico. I had never been west of the Mississippi, except for a short flying visit to San Francisco and a longer one to Alaska. I drove alone across the country, an exhilarating trip. I settled into the writer's colony and did what I had come to do: I wrote and wrote. And when my time was up, I could not face the idea of going back East again, to the isolation of New York and the suffocation of the little town in Pennsylvania.

I decided to stay in New Mexico and found a tiny house in Santa Fe. Then I went back East long enough to make the necessary arrangements and to pack up a few pieces of furniture and the rest of my clothes and books. I hitched a U-Haul trailer to the back of my car and drove across the country for the third time.

Moves like that are always traumatic, even when they're interesting and stimulating. I settled into Santa Fe and for a while enjoyed the art scene there. But after a few years I realized that Santa Fe, too, was just another small town. I had made good friends, but I felt stifled. I had a habit, it seemed, of falling in love with charming places, and then finding out too late that they weren't the right place for me after all.

In the winter of 1984, after five years in Santa Fe, I decided to move again, this time to Albuquerque, sixty miles to the south. Albuquerque is nothing like Santa Fe. It's a sprawling city, or maybe just an overgrown small town, mountains on one side, high desert on the other. It has none of Santa Fe's trendy art scene, none of its beauty or sophistication or chic. It's not charming, but it's real. It suits me just fine.

*

I continued to write fiction, of course. There's something enormously satisfying about seizing on some incident, a snatch of conversation, some fragment of

"In 1969 Chris, almost three, sat on my lap for a story while Alan, ten, and John, six, pretended to listen for the photographer's benefit"

one's own experience, and shaping it into a story. (Sometimes, of course, the fragment is quite large, like the diary; but even that large chunk is still just a piece of a much larger whole that must be invented around it.)

While I was still living in Santa Fe, I looked out my window one day and saw a horse nibbling at the shrubbery. I went out to investigate, and within fifteen minutes I had agreed to take riding lessons from the horse's owner, despite my fears. During the weeks that I suffered through those lessons, I learned something about life on her family's ranch. Her stories became the nucleus of *The Luck of Texas McCoy.*

When a friend of mine got involved in the Big Brother program in Santa Fe, I listened to his stories, too. George was and is a cultured bachelor, classic cook, and passionate lover of the arts. I began to wonder what it must be like for his Little Brother to eat gourmet meals instead of fast-food burgers and fries and attend the opera instead of baseball games and horror movies. That was the fragment around which I wove the story of *Elliott & Win.* My friend Joan's worries about her two biracial sons gave me the idea for *Denny's Tapes.* And an acquaintance with a man who had served time in the state penitentiary coincided with the escape of several convicts from the pen—and that started me off on *Wild Rover.*

I enjoy writing fiction, but the lure of nonfiction remains strong. Sometimes I think the two kinds of writing come from different parts of the brain—one from the imaginative, childlike side, the other from the intellectual, rational, disciplined adult half of the brain.

In the past I had always come up with ideas for my nonfiction books, arguing that if they weren't my ideas in the first place, I might have trouble working up a genuine passion for somebody else's inspiration. Then one day I was contacted by an editor I didn't know who had read *The Mystery of the Ancient Maya,* a nonfiction collaboration with an archaeologist. The editor liked the way I wrote about early explorers who had gone to Mexico and Central America to study the civilization of the Maya Indians. And she had an idea.

That was in the spring of 1985, when South Africa was much in the news, the problems of apartheid a part of our national consciousness. Willa Tupper (now Penman) wanted to publish a book for teenagers about what it was like to grow up in South Africa, with black and white so fiercely set against one another. I knew nothing about South Africa, but ignorance can be cured. My interest aroused, I agreed to do the book and began making plans to go to South Africa. By then I was completely free to travel: Alan was in graduate school in Arizona, John was in college in Colorado, Chris was bumming around California.

Initially I hadn't the slightest notion of how I was going to make contacts there. I also had no idea how explosive the situation would become in the weeks before I was to leave at the end of August. I knew the official route was not the one to take. I did not want to identify myself as a journalist; that would make me immediately suspect. But I was lucky from the start: inquiring about a plane ticket in the travel agent's office, I met a man from South Africa and told him about the book I planned to write. He invited me home for tea. He and his wife offered to arrange introductions to several of their friends in South Africa: whites, of course, but of both English and Afrikaner background. Then it was up to me to parlay those contacts into something more.

The South African government has no sympathy for American journalists, and so when anyone asked, I explained that I was writing a book for children. That seemed harmless enough—but not always. Suspicious Afrikaners did not want me in their government-run schools. It was hard to meet blacks, and sometimes illegal to visit them. I was variously considered a bloody Yank, a communist agitator, and a CIA agent. But most of the time I got along well, people were kind, and although I disagreed with their politics, I tried to be fair. Being fair usually offends everyone. Whites thought I didn't understand, blacks thought I was much too soft on whites. I was in a no-win situation, like nearly everyone there.

When *Voices of South Africa: Growing Up in a Troubled Land* was published a year later in the fall of 1986, I took a copy around to my South African friends who had been so helpful. I haven't heard from them since. I probably offended them, too.

Within a few months I had another idea: if it is hard to grow up in South Africa, where neither blacks nor whites have any idea what their future holds, it must be just as hard to grow up in Northern Ireland, where violence is a daily fact of life. I called Willa.

"I've got an idea," I said. "Belfast."

"You're on," she said.

And so in the spring of 1986, I went to Northern Ireland. Once again I had managed to put together a short list of contacts, and even when I arrived there, I wasn't quite sure where to start. But once again I was lucky. People showed up when I needed them. They were kind. I liked them, even when I deplored their politics. But I found it depressing. South Africa had been an intensely emotional experience; I felt that the country would eventually end in a bloodbath, the huge and very angry black majority overrunning the white minority. In Northern Ireland I believed that the hatred and the violence would go on for hundreds of years more, as it has in the past. I was glad to go home.

A new editor, Elinor Williams, took over for Willa on *Voices of Northern Ireland* (with the same depressing subtitle, "Growing Up in a Troubled Land,") and it was to Elinor that I pitched my next idea: Japan. Once again the situation was entirely different, the rules had changed, and I had to figure them out as I went along.

There was the usual panic of trying to find people who would be helpful, but I managed to round up a sheaf of letters of introduction. The Japanese aren't amenable to the seat-of-the-pants, go-with-the-flow kind of research that had worked well in South Africa and Northern Ireland. They are much more formal, and they wanted things worked out according to a schedule, but with enough flexibility to change direction if it seemed advisable later on.

By the time I left for Japan at the end of August 1987, my life had changed dramatically in another direction. After sixteen years of living alone, I had married E. A. "Tony" Mares, poet, playwright, historian, and teacher, and I was not anxious to be away from my husband of three months. In the past my research trips had been adventures: this one was a chore, and I yearned to be home. The other trips had often been lonely, as traveling alone usually is, but I had understood the language and most of the time I could grasp the customs, even when cultural differences were subtle.

In both South Africa and Northern Ireland women are not "liberated," rarely travel independently, seldom pursue professional careers, and are not regarded as free agents. I was considered a curiosity, and often seen as very strange—especially when I rented a car and took off for places women rarely went alone. Even with those differences I could usually find people to talk to, to spend time with. In Japan, however, I was up against a language barrier. I spoke no Japanese beyond a few polite phrases, and although many Japanese study English assiduously and can read rather well, few actually speak English. Beyond language lay the culture barrier.

"Smiling in 1978 because I'm leaving New York for New Mexico"

In all three countries I divided my time between hotels and people's homes. Hotels offered privacy, a chance to catch up on laundry, and freedom to come and go as I pleased; families provided windows into the lives of real people, but the stress of being someone's guest runs high—and never higher than in Japan, where there are even rules for what may be worn into the toilet. I was never quite sure what was expected of me, never confident of the polite thing to do in all kinds of circumstances.

That kind of research—spending time with the people about whom I am planning to write—is fascinating and challenging. It is the culmination of months of study and library research, learning as much as I can about the country and the people I will visit, reading about their history, reading their novels, reading what others have written about them, trying to understand their culture, trying to figure out what makes them tick. It's only when I'm thoroughly informed that I'm ready to plunge into the actual situation.

I never take notes or use a tape recorder when I am with people, because I don't do formal interviews. I usually carry a small notebook in my purse, in case someone gives me the name of someone to contact, or I need to note a particular phrase or fact. I pay close at-

tention, and then, as soon as I can, I rush back to wherever I'm staying and make notes of everything I can remember.

After South Africa and Northern Ireland I ended up with several large notebooks completely filled, field notes to supplement my research notes. But I tried something different in Japan: I took along a miniature tape recorder and a bunch of tiny tapes, and every day I would talk my notes into the willing little machine. At the end of the trip I had hours and hours and *hours* of tapes that I then had to transcribe when I got home. There was proof of what I had always suspected—I talk too much!

No matter which way I chose to record my observations, I was faced with the tremendous task of sorting and organizing and integrating all that material and then writing it in a form that would be readable and interesting, as well as informative. Each time the process took me several months, which really isn't very long, considering the amount of material to be dealt with. When I finished the book about Japan, I knew that it needed a new title. *A Voice from Japan: An Outsider Looks In* reflects my problems with the language and cultural barriers of Japan that made that trip so different from the other two.

I have heard of writers who work through each sentence before going on to the next, each paragraph, each page, a constant striving for perfection in the process. I have never been able to work that way, mostly because too much happens in the actual process of writing. As I go along, I think of things that I had not thought of earlier; new directions are always opening up. If I were convinced that those first paragraphs and pages were truly perfect, I'm not sure I'd be willing to go back and revise the whole works when a new idea suddenly pops into my head, changing everything that went before.

And so I blast through the first draft, whether it's nonfiction or fiction, as fast as I can. It's almost stream of consciousness; certainly it's rough, ragged, repetitive, and often doesn't make sense at all. Sometimes I forget the name I gave a character in the last chapter, or a meal eaten several pages back gets eaten again, or I decide suddenly that a male character really should be a female. No matter. Everything I'm thinking about at that moment pours out. Sometimes it pours rather slowly. Other times it gushes.

That's the first draft, like mixing the raw clay. I occasionally worry that I will be run over by a trolley before I have a chance to put it all together in a second draft, and that one of my sons, going through my desk as I went through my mother's attic, will find this wretched first draft, glance at it, and say to his brothers, "Poor Ma. She really lost it there at the end. This isn't even readable."

Because it's in the second draft that the shaping takes place, that the mound of clay takes on form. I go through the second draft punching it this way and that,

"Alan, John, and Chris in Arizona," 1983

shifting things around, deciding more or less definitely what the names are to be, what sex they're to be, and when they are to eat that meal. I know very well by now who my characters are, what is to be included and what is not. The material is organized: I know what the chapters are to be and what's in each one (although this might change again later). I know where I'm going and how to get there. It's a slower process than the first draft, and there can be no evasion of the basic problems.

Then, in the third draft, I pay attention to language and to fine detail. I read aloud to myself, listening to the vocabulary, the rhythm of the sentences. I polish, polish, polish, until I'm satisfied. Then, with my heart in my throat and a vague sense of disappointment that the finished manuscript doesn't come even close to the brilliance of that first flash of inspiration, I send it off to my editor. And wait.

I wait to hear if this "child" of mine is lovable. Because even when an editor says "I love it!," that really means *"I love it, but it needs more work."* Always there are requests for changes—sometimes major changes. Most of the time I'm able to make those changes without much trouble, although it's not always quite so easy to get reinvolved with a piece of work that in my mind is finished.

One of the pleasures of working with a good editor is mutual respect—my respect for the editor's judgment, the editor's respect for my abilities.

Such an editor is Margaret McElderry, who helped me believe that I could write fiction as well as nonfiction. Once I had told a story in present tense— "Sam *sits* at the table"—and Margaret felt it would be a better story if it were told in past tense. It was not just a simple matter of changing it to "Sam *sat* at the table." The whole tone changed.

Another time I used a third-person narrator—*"Sam* sat at the table"—but Margaret felt I was too emotionally distant from Sam, that I had not really gotten under his skin. Margaret believed—and she was right—that I didn't seem to know Sam very well. So I rewrote the novel twice—first translating it into first-person narrator (*"I* sat at the table"), which forced me to know a great deal more about what Sam was actually thinking and feeling. And then, because I still believed that, for other reasons, the story needed to be third-person narration, I rewrote it in third person (*"Sam* sat at the table"). This time I knew exactly how Sam felt as he sat there, and the feeling came through in the telling.

*

When I began to write, I did everything first in longhand, ballpoint pen on lined yellow paper, and re-typed it on my portable typewriter. Later I taught myself to write directly on that portable, resorting to pen and paper only when I needed to work out an opening paragraph or some tricky passage. Then I would make all my editing changes on the typed page and retype it. If it got too messy with subsequent editing, I'd retype it once more, until I had a clean copy to send to an editor.

Eventually I changed to an electric typewriter. It drove me crazy at first, sitting there *humming*. That was nothing compared to my reluctant switch to a computer several years ago, having given up the argument that I didn't really need one. It took me a couple of months to get used to it, during which I did a lot of yelling and muttering. Now, of course, I'm addicted to it; I don't know how I ever lived without it. But once in a while I'm *forced* to live without it, and that's not such a bad thing.

The first draft of this piece, for instance, was written on an old electric typewriter that I borrow once a week when I'm on duty at a crisis intervention hotline at the mental health center. I'm at the center because I'm doing research for a new series of books for young adults called "Hotline," to be published by Bantam. Built around a group of high-school students who respond to the suicide of one of their friends by forming a hotline, the series follows the stories of four students, their families, their friends, and the people who call the hotline. In order to write the series, I enrolled for the training program at the mental health center and agreed to do four hours a week of volunteer work.

Fortunately, the phone doesn't ring often, but when it does, I have to be ready, to deal not only with suicide calls—there are actually few of those—but with all kinds of other crises, unhappy people who desperately need to talk to somebody. For several weeks during the long, dull periods between calls, I turned on the ancient electric and told my own story. Eventually I retyped that barely legible draft on my computer, making a few changes, additions and subtractions, as I went along. Then I printed it out, and for the next few Wednesday afternoons between calls, I tore it apart and reworked it.

I've always believed that I can write anywhere. Generally, of course, there's no place like home. I've had my own office at home since my children were babies. But those "babies" are long gone now, off living lives of their own. I've relocated my office from time to time, always choosing the best room in the house for my work space. And once my children were grown, I began to take the best *time* for my work, as well. Mornings are most productive, but I've learned to take a mid-day break, usually swimming laps for a half hour or so, and then going back to work. But no matter what I do, I can't seem to get anything done in the evenings. That's the time for reading, and even that ends early. My husband Tony, on the other hand, doesn't really come alive until around noon, and his best working time is late at night.

In the summer of 1988 we spent a month in Mexico in the lovely colonial city of Morelia where Tony was teaching a course in Spanish. I went along for the fun of it—but the first of the "Hotline" manuscripts was due the first of August, and it had taken me all of the spring to write the first draft. To make that deadline (and there is no question of *not* making a deadline), I had a lot of work to do in Mexico.

I took with me a printed copy of the manuscript—and remember, that first draft is rough! I also took along pencils, scissors, and Scotch tape. We stayed in a funky old hotel with one naked light bulb suspended over the bed—no desk, no chair, no reading lamp. Every morning when Tony went off to teach, I spread out the pages of my manuscript on the bed, and worked away, pulling that first draft apart and then stitching it together in different ways, rewriting sections that didn't seem right, molding and shaping. When the chambermaid came to clean the room, I moved down to the dining room. When they wanted to mop the dining room floor, I carried everything back upstairs again. The reworked pages that I brought home early in July were a mess; I hoped I could make sense of them. It took a week to feed all those changes into my computer and to print out a clean copy. Then for two more weeks I hovered over it, refining, polishing, changing, and then sometimes changing back to the way it was in the first place.

I made the deadline, of course, but then I went through the same symptoms of withdrawal that always follow completion of a manuscript. What had seemed to me exciting and elegantly written while I was working on it suddenly appeared leaden and dull. I lost faith in it. It was not until the call came, "We love it!" (meaning, "We love it, but . . .") that I could relax—and begin the second book of the series and then, a few weeks later, deal with rewrites of the first one.

Although there are inevitably disappointments in a writer's life when ideas are turned down, manuscripts rejected, and books are subjected to unfavorable reviews or don't sell and seem to drop out of sight, there is nothing more devastating in the life of a writer than having no ideas at all.

I thought I was immune. From the time I first began writing in 1963, I always had plenty of ideas. The problems then were (1) finding time to write and mental peace in the midst of a hectic family life and (2) finding someone to publish my work. As time went on, the pressures of the family gradually diminished until that was no longer an issue. Publishers were eager for my books. The larger issue then was: What do I really want to write about? Always I had a project in the works and at least two more in the early stages of thinking and planning. Being human, I did sometimes fret that some day I might run out of ideas. I joked about it; friends laughed.

And then, one day I *did* run out. In 1984, the year I moved from Santa Fe to Albuquerque, I had undergone some fairly serious surgery. Physically I recovered quickly; although I was an unhealthy child, I've been a remarkably healthy adult and take good care of myself. Emotionally I seemed to be in good shape, too. But something happened. I would face that blank computer screen, every bit as intimidating as a blank piece of paper, and nothing would happen. Nothing.

So I would force myself to do *something*. I am an extremely disciplined writer, and I've always written even when I really didn't feel like it, even when my world was falling apart all around me. But in those black days in the winter of 1984 and 1985, whatever I forced myself to write simply didn't work. After more than twenty years of writing almost every day, I seemed to have nothing more to say. I came to the conclusion that I might not be a writer after all and that I would have to find something else to do with my life. This called for a complete redefinition of who I am, and it was very painful, one of the most depressing periods of my life.

Fortunately it didn't last long. First, I went to see a psychotherapist, who helped me to affirm that I was still a writer. About that time someone came along with the idea for a book about South Africa. The weight lifted from my spirit, and I was off and running again. I had learned that my body was vulnerable; then I learned that the creative part of me was vulnerable too. These lessons learned, I became more deeply grateful for whatever gifts of time and talent I've received.

In many circles it's not chic to be religious, to speak of one's religious and spiritual life, but I've never been much concerned with chic. As a child I went to church with my parents, but when I went away to college I began to question *everything,* including what I had been taught in Sunday school. For several years I went through a cycle of turning away, re-examining, and finally turning back in a new way.

My relationship to God the Creator is so fundamental to my life as a writer that I can't avoid mentioning it. I believe that my talent, small as it may be, is a gift from God, and that by using it for good, I participate in

"On our wedding day." Carolyn and E. A. "Tony" Mares at home in New Mexico, 1987

the on-going Creation. Such a belief will keep me doing the best I can do, writing the best I can write, even through the dry spells, for as long as I live.

POSTSCRIPT

Carolyn Meyer contributed the following update to *SATA* in 2003:

It's morning, not yet nine o'clock (I do my best writing early in the day), and it suddenly occurs to me that I have spent most mornings for the past forty years *at this very same desk:* a sheet of plywood covered with Formica (now chipped around the edges), one end resting on a two-drawer filing cabinet, the other supported by two wooden legs.

An idea floats by. I start thinking about the long succession of offices in which this desk has been set up, beginning in the gloomy basement in Queens (a baby bawling upstairs, his nap finished), through a parade of houses in a series of towns and cities, and finally ending up in this sunny room that was once the front porch of a Victorian house in an old Albuquerque neighborhood.

That might be an interesting way to tell a story, I think, and I interrupt what I'd been working on to jot some notes in my journal with the heading *Places I've put my gypsy shoes under this same desk.* The Queens basement; a spare bedroom in a rambling house in Connecticut; a former sun porch in Pennsylvania; an attic dormer overlooking a pear tree in Texas; five different houses in Santa Fe and Albuquerque, New Mexico—I list them all, at least a dozen. I've probably missed a couple.

After a second cup of tea I manage to pull myself back to this morning's task: describing what I've been writing for the past fifteen years. *Where was this desk fifteen years ago? What was I thinking about then? What was I writing?*

Soon after I'd wrapped up the fourth book in the "Hotline" series, my major project at the time I wrote the first part of this autobiographical article, we moved the desk to Texas. My husband, Tony, a historian, was offered a teaching job at the University of North Texas in Denton, a pleasant college town north of Dallas. We sold our lovingly restored home in Albuquerque and bought another old house in need of work. (I have a penchant for falling in love with houses with loads of charm, a leaky roof, and a bad furnace; 1120 North Locust was no exception.) The summer of 1990 we packed up and moved, Tony began teaching, and I tried to figure out where I fit into this new scene.

At first we were desperately homesick. But it was six hundred long miles from Denton to Albuquerque, across the Texas Panhandle, the bleak monotony broken by little towns along the way, each with a Dairy Queen. In one of them, in Quanah, Texas, I picked up a pamphlet placed there by the Quanah Historical Society. While waiting for my Blizzard to be delivered, I read about the origins of the town, named for Quanah Parker, the last of the nineteenth-century Comanche chiefs.

One short paragraph described Quanah's mother, Cynthia Ann Parker, kidnapped as a nine-year-old from her white family by marauding Comanches and taken to live with the nomadic tribe. She learned their ways, eventually married a Comanche man, and bore three children—the eldest was Quanah. After living for twenty-five years with the Comanches, Cynthia Ann was kidnapped *again,* this time by the Texas Rangers, who dragged her unwillingly back to the Parker family.

I had scarcely finished my Blizzard when the question had begun to haunt me: *What must it have been like to be that child, that young woman, a captive not once but twice?* I was already on my way to my next book, an important one for me, because it was the first novel in which I had to do considerable research before I could even begin to tell the story.

Although I made good friends in Denton, I always felt very much the outsider: I didn't talk like a Texan (that Yankee twang always marked me), and I didn't dress like one (high-fashion Dallas was just down the road). This state of affairs, of course, was nothing new for me—I sometimes felt like the little girl in the clown suit again. But I found that being an outsider put me in the position of being an observer.

In the spring of 1991, while I was working on *Where the Broken Heart Still Beats: The Story of Cynthia Ann Parker* (one of my favorite titles), I read an item in the local newspaper about the dedication of a historic plaque, scheduled to take place in a city park

Tony and Carolyn with Vered, who provided the inspiration for Drummers of Jericho, *at her wedding in 2000*

only a few blocks from our house. According to the article, the land that had been made into a park had once been occupied by a thriving African-American community known as Quakertown, settled in the middle of white Denton by freed slaves at the end of the Civil War. Then, in the 1920s, a number of Denton's civic leaders decided that this piece of prime real estate could be put to much better use as a public park—public for whites, of course; blacks were not welcome.

Interested in this bit of local history and ready for a break from writing, I attended the dedication. I listened as one elderly African American after another described memories of growing up in Quakertown and of what happened when the white folks of Denton decided it was theirs to take.

What must it have been like, I wondered as I walked home afterwards, *to be a young girl growing up in a tight-knit community and finding out that your home and your community were about to be destroyed?*

Rose Lee Jefferson and her family began to take shape in my imagination. The result was *White Lilacs.*

About this time I found myself in the Mom role again, when my fifteen-year-old step-daughter, Vered (a Hebrew name), came to live with us. Vered's Israeli-born mother had sent her to school in Israel. When the first Gulf War broke out and missiles began flying into Tel Aviv, Vered returned to the United States and elected to move in with her father and me. That fall she entered high school.

Vered signed up for the marching band, which had a reputation for taking the top prizes in state competition, and was working on this year's half-time presentation. She brought home the music she was to play: Christian hymns, to be played as the band marched down the field in the form of a cross. Vered objected; she's Jewish, and she didn't want to participate in a Christian program. Her father and I also objected; this was a public high school, and we believed this thoroughly religious program was unconstitutional. I called the ACLU; a judge ordered the band director to change the program. The kids at school were outraged. They knew who the "snitch" was, and revenge was swift. It got very ugly—both in the high school and on "Letters" pages of the local newspaper.

When the furor finally died down, I wrote *Drummers of Jericho,* a novel that has turned out to be nearly as controversial as the situation that inspired it.

"Where do you get your ideas?" It's a question I'm asked so often that I've grown grumpy, because there is no simple reply. The answer is different for each book. Ideas are everywhere. They blow by like wind-borne seeds; sometimes they land on fertile ground and take root and flourish and bloom, and sometimes they wither and die. It all depends.

One summer I returned for a visit to my hometown of Lewistown, Pennsylvania, and ran into an old friend of my parents. Over lunch, Mr. S. happened to mention that his grandfather had once been a peddler in Lancaster County. A Jew who had escaped the pogroms in Russia, the peddler's customers were mostly Amish, who spoke a German dialect similar to Yiddish. I was immediately curious, and while Stanley tried to eat his sandwich, I peppered him with questions. Soon I was deeply involved in creating the story of a friendship that could have developed between an Amish boy and a Jewish boy growing up in Lancaster about 1911. The result was *Gideon's People.*

*

Meanwhile, I was getting a lot of questions about *White Lilacs:* Whatever happened to Rose Lee Jefferson? Frankly, I had never thought beyond the end of the book, until an event in my own family focused my attention on that young African-American girl. My oldest son, Alan, had married Amanda, a beautiful black woman from England, and in February of 1993 they presented me with my first grandchild, Erin. Luckily, they were living in nearby Dallas so that I could often visit this beautiful little girl. But I recognized, even then, that life would not always be blissful for a biracial child born into a "mixed marriage." And I began to imagine Erin entering her teens and wondering who she was and where she fit in. It's a process we all go through in our lives, but one that can be complicated when identity lies outside what is viewed as traditional.

Idly then, I, too, began to wonder, *Whatever happened to Rose Lee Jefferson?* She'd be in her eighties, a great-grandmother. Suppose she had a granddaughter who'd married a white man, and far away in another part of the country were great-grandchildren she'd never met. What if they came to visit? What would *that* have been like? The story began to take shape in my imagination. I called it *Jubilee Journey* and dedicated it to Erin and her younger brother, Joe.

*

We had been living in Texas for a couple of years, we had friends, we had a good life—but how we did still yearn for things New Mexican! For green *chile,* an absolutely fundamental part of our favorite cuisine; for the Sandia Mountains turning lavender pink at sunset; for Indian pots, adobe houses, *luminarias* at Christmas, low-riders cruising the back roads.

One evening as I slouched on the sofa with a magazine that obviously didn't have much of a grip on my attention, the idea came into my head, fully formed, of a collection of linked stories that would be put together by a fictional bunch of New Mexican kids working on a fictional Heritage Class project; they'd call their book *Rio Grande Stories;* I'd call my book *Rio Grande Stories.* How clever!

The next morning I sketched out the entire structure. Easiest book I'd ever thought up! But that's all that came easily; creating a dozen unique characters plus a dozen separate but related stories and then doing all the research for each proved daunting: Exactly how is an Indian pot made? What does it take to transform a Chevy into a work of art? I thought I'd never finish. The odd thing is that a lot of readers thought the book was nonfiction, that all those kids I worked so hard to invent were actually *real.*

*

This would seem to be the right place to introduce the woman I call "the archeditor," Liz Van Doren. Liz and I first worked together on *Where the Broken Heart Still Beats;* we're now on our tenth book. And in many ways it is "our" book, because the editorial process is so tightly woven with the writing process. Never was this more intense than when I was clawing my way through *Rio Grande Stories.*

My usual method is to do tons of research (more about that later) while I'm still thinking about the characters. When I feel I know enough to begin, I start a first draft, letting the story unfold. After two or three chapters, I often need to start over, or at least to reconsider the direction in which the story is headed: Is this really where I want to go? This process, with lots of false starts and floundering, continues for some months, until I have what feels like a workable story. I revise it and polish it until I'm convinced it's wonderful—or *almost* wonderful. And then I send it to Liz.

For weeks after that I worry—*Does she like it? Does she hate it? Has she ripped it to shreds?* The answer lies somewhere in the middle, and after what

seems like a very long time, the manuscript comes back, sloshed with purple marker, or sometimes green, and accompanied by a *very* long letter that always begins in the same way: "Dear Carolyn, I have just read the manuscript for [*fill in any title here*] and I love most of what you have written. However . . . ." And then for eight or ten pages, single spaced, Liz carefully (and diplomatically) explains exactly what it is she doesn't love and details ways in which it might be improved.

I throw a fit, of course, no matter how gently the criticism is phrased, but once I've recovered from the shock of discovery that my book is not perfect—far from it!—I settle down and begin working on those suggestions. Sometimes Liz and I go through this process more than once, until we're both satisfied and can honestly say that we both love *all* of it.

Liz was there when my life went through another tectonic shift. In 1995, after five years in Texas, Tony and I decided to move back to New Mexico. I'd wept when we moved to Denton, and I wept when we left—I had made friends, and Texas had furnished me with a lot of interesting ideas. But Tony had accepted a new position, and it was time for me, too, to try something new, although I wasn't sure what that was going to be. I thought I might write some adult fiction—I'd never really put that dream away completely, since the days when I sent short stories to the *New Yorker,* and the *New Yorker* sent them right back.

But the adult fiction path proved as rocky as ever. One day Liz called—we hadn't talked in awhile—to ask how things were going. (Not particularly well, to be honest.) Then, gingerly, she made a suggestion: Had I ever thought of writing about the Tudor princesses?— that is, if I were to consider writing another book for young adults.

I reacted unenthusiastically. I knew little about English history and even less about the Tudors, although I did remember that King Henry VIII had a number of wives—I just wasn't sure how many.

"Think about it," Liz said; I promised I would and headed for the library. My interest was quickly caught by the life of Henry's unfortunate elder daughter, Mary, who later became known—unfairly, I thought—as "Bloody Mary." *What must it have been like to grow up as the daughter of a man like Henry VIII?* Once again, there was the question that always set the wheels of my imagination spinning. Once again, I was hooked.

History was never my favorite subject in school— all that stuff about generals, battles, and treaties bored me silly. But when I began writing books for young readers, I discovered the side of history I had somehow never noticed before: it's not just dates and who conquered what; it's also about people and how they lived their lives. My most recent books, beginning with the Cynthia Ann Parker story, all involved considerable historical research. But when the Tudor family took over

The author with her grandchildren, (left to right) Sophie, Erin, and Joe, 2002

my life, I was really into it—not just the details—the difference between a kirtle and a petticoat, a saraband and a galliard, how to bring that roast peacock to the banquet table with all feathers intact—but trying to show how an eleven-year-old princess living five hundred years ago might have reacted to becoming betrothed to a French king three times her age. How would she feel? How would she show her feelings? And to whom? To her hot-tempered father? To a gossipy servant? How would she think? And, even more challenging, how would she express her thoughts as she told her story to today's young readers?

These were the questions with which I struggled as I wrote *Mary, Bloody Mary;* a later book about Mary's half-sister, in *Beware, Princess Elizabeth;* a portrait of Henry's second wife, Anne Boleyn, in *Doomed Queen Anne;* and a fourth book in what has become the "Young Royals" series, about Henry's first wife, Catherine of Aragon. Now, as I write this, I'm awaiting a letter from the archeditor that will begin, "I've just read the manuscript for *Yield, Princess Catherine,* and I love most of what you have written. However . . ."

*

The characters and the situations changed in each of the four books. Although some details remained the same (the petticoats, the peacocks), each became another complex research project. When I first began to write books involving historical research, a trip or two to the local public library usually sufficed, and that is still my starting point. Travel is often a pleasant option, whether it's to the cabin in Fort Worth, Texas, where Cynthia Ann Parker once lived or to the Tower of London where Elizabeth was held prisoner by her sister, Mary, and where Anne Boleyn was beheaded.

Certainly the tool that has most radically changed my research is the Internet. In 1999, I bought a faster computer and went online; since then I've made two major discoveries:

1. The great thing about the Internet is *there's so much stuff out there.*

2. The bad thing about the Internet is *there's so much stuff out there.*

But here's the catch: *How do you tell which is which?*

When I check out a book on Tudor life, I am fairly confident that the author has taken the trouble to provide accurate facts based on more than whim or guesswork. But anybody at all can put up a website; some are accurate, and some are simply wrong. (My own website, www.readcarolyn.com, is meant to be entertaining as well as a source of information.) I'm inclined to base my story on scholarship that I know I can trust and to fill in the gaps with details gleaned from any interesting source that I think will enhance the story.

I have learned that even the most diligent scholars sometimes do get it wrong or disagree among themselves on even the most basic facts. When I was researching *Where the Broken Heart Still Beats,* I could not find agreement on the year of Cynthia Ann's death—experts placed it anywhere from 1864 to 1874. And when I was researching *Doomed Queen Anne,* I found disparities on the year of her birth—was it 1501? 1507? Somewhere in between? In the end, I went with the dates that worked best for the story I wanted to tell.

The question often comes up: Is it history or is it fiction? Is it true or did you make it up? My answer is that historical fiction is a mix of both. I don't change facts that seem irrefutable—the date on which Anne Boleyn died, for example—but I often invent characters to help in the story, such as Mary's ladies-in-waiting and Cynthia Ann's cousin, Lucy. Major historical events are factual and accurate, but day-to-day incidents are almost always the product of my own imagining of what might-have-been.

This kind of day-to-day invention was certainly the case in the three books I've written for Scholastic's "Royal Diaries" series. Very little is known of the daily life of the young Spanish princess in *Isabel: Jewel of Castilla.* In fact, it's unlikely that she ever kept a diary. But we do know that Isabel was deeply religious and that her confessor, or spiritual guide, was Tomás Torquemada, who later became the infamous Grand Inquisitor responsible for the torture and death of many innocent people during the Spanish Inquisition. It wasn't hard to imagine him giving the princess a blank book and assigning her the task of keeping a list of her sins as a spiritual exercise.

On the other hand, Anastasia Romanov, of *Anastasia: The Last Grand Duchess,* did keep records of her life as daughter of the Tsar of Russia. Some of her journals and albums survive, a gold mine of rich detail enabling me to visualize nearly every aspect of her life. Swedish monarch Kristina Vasa began late in life to write a memoir of her early years, which provided material for *Kristina: The Girl King.* Unfortunately, the memoir stops long before Kristina reached the age of twelve, when my "diary" for her begins, leaving me to piece together her teenage years from meager scraps.

Writing "diaries" of historical figures turned out to be challenging in ways I had not anticipated. The diarist is always innocent of her own future. In *Doomed Queen Anne,* which is not in dairy form, Anne narrates her own story, right up to the morning of her death, knowing how it will turn out. Contrast this with Anastasia, who tells her story through her diary entries, day by day, unaware of what will happen next. Creating a story in this form is tricky, especially when a great deal of historical information must be slipped in so that the reader can understand the events in the "diary."

Once again the trail has grown faint. After a dozen novels based on historical events with imagined characters, like *White Lilacs,* or historical persons with both actual and fictional events, like *Beware, Princess Elizabeth,* I'm ready once again to strike out in a new direction, to explore different territory.

One new path is already marked out: as I write this, I'm awaiting publication of my first novel for adult readers, *Brown Eyes Blue.* After many years and many disappointments (Take that, *New Yorker!*), I'm excited— and, yes, nervous, too.

But I also want to continue doing what I've been doing for forty years: writing for young readers. About what? Well, I don't know yet. But I expect that one of these days I will, and that it will be another grand adventure, begun at this same old desk with the chipped Formica top.

MITCHELL, Joyce Slayton 1933-

Personal

Born August 13, 1933, in Hardwick, VT; daughter of George Dix (an automobile dealer) and Sarah (Arkin) Slayton; married William E. Mitchell (an anthropologist), July 4, 1959; children: Edward Slayton, Elizabeth Dix. *Education:* Denison University, A.B., 1955; University of Bridgeport, M.S., 1958; Columbia University, further graduate study, 1960-62. *Politics:* Republican. *Religion:* Presbyterian. *Hobbies and other interests:* Tennis, skiing, jogging, biking, studying French, theatre, movies, living in Paris every August.

Addresses

Home—150 East 93rd St., New York, NY 10128.

Career

West Rocks Junior High School, Norwalk, CT, teacher of physical education, 1955-58; Amity Regional High School, Woodbridge, CT, counselor, 1958-59; Greenwich High School, Greenwich, CT, counselor, 1959-62; consultant in education, 1962—; author, 1965—. Visiting lecturer at Johnson State College, 1975. Member of advisory council of Harvard University's Divinity School, 1974-75.

Member

American Personnel and Guidance Association (member of board of directors of Women's Caucus, 1976), National Vocational Guidance Association (professional member), American School Counselor Association, Na-

tional Association of College Admissions Counselors, National Organization for Women (founder and coordinator of Vermont chapter, 1973-74), Vermont Guidance Association.

Awards, Honors

Books for the Teen Age selections, New York Public Library, 1980, for *Free to Choose: Decision Making for Young Men,* 1981, for *Be a Mother and More: Career and Life Planning for Young Women,* and 1982, for *See Me More Clearly: Career and Life Planning for Teens with Physical Disabilities.*

Writings

The Guide to College Life, Prentice-Hall (Englewood Cliffs, NJ), 1968.

The Guide to Canadian Universities, Simon & Schuster (New York, NY), 1970.

(Editor) *Other Choices for Becoming a Woman: A Handbook to Help High School Women Make Decisions,* Know, Inc. (Pittsburgh, PA), 1974, revised edition, Delacorte (New York, NY), 1975.

I Can Be Anything: Careers and Colleges for Young Women, College Entrance Examination Board (New York, NY), 1975, 3rd edition, 1982.

(Editor) *Free to Choose: Decision Making for Young Men,* Delacorte (New York, NY), 1976.

Tokenism: The Opiate of the Oppressed, Know, Inc. (Pittsburgh, PA), 1976.

Stopout!: Working Ways to Learn, Garrett Park Press (Garrett Park, MD), 1978.

The Work Book: A Guide to Skilled Jobs, Sterling Publishing (New York, NY), 1978.

Young readers can gather important information about big rig trucks from the detailed story of a driver who prepares for a road trip. (From Tractor-Trailer Trucker, *written by Joyce Slayton Mitchell and illustrated with photos by Steven Borns.)*

The Classroom Teacher's Workbook for Career Education, Avon (New York, NY), 1979.

What's Where: The Official Guide to College Majors, Avon (New York, NY), 1979.

The Men's Career Book: Work and Life Planning for a New Age, Bantam (New York, NY), 1979.

See Me More Clearly: Career and Life Planning for Teens with Physical Disabilities, Harcourt (New York, NY), 1980.

Be a Mother and More: Career and Life Planning for Young Women, Bantam (New York, NY), 1980.

Taking on the World: Empowering Strategies for Parents of Children with Disabilities, Harcourt (New York, NY), 1982.

Choices and Changes: A Career Book for Men, College Entrance Examination Board (New York, NY), 1982.

Your Job in the Computer Age: The Complete Guide to the Computer Skills You Need to Get the Job You Want, Scribner (New York, NY), 1984.

College to Career: The Guide to Job Opportunities, College Entrance Examination Board (New York, NY), 1986, revised edition published as *The College Board Guide to Jobs and Career Planning,* College Entrance Examination Board (New York, NY), 1990, 2nd edition, 1994.

Making More Money: Fifty-five Special Job-Hunting Strategies for Retirees, Prentice Hall (Englewood Cliffs, NJ), 1986.

Winning the Chemo Battle, Norton (New York, NY), 1988.

The Best Guide to the Top Colleges: How to Get into the Ivy's or Nearly Ivy's, Garrett Park Press (Garrett Park, MD), 1991.

College Smarts: The Official Freshman Handbook, Garrett Park Press (Garrett Park, MD), 1991.

Mitchell Express: The Fast Track to the Top Colleges, Garrett Park Press (Garrett Park, MD), 1993.

(With daughter, Elizabeth Dix Mitchell) *A Special Delivery: Mother-Daughter Letters from Afar,* Equilibrium Press (Culver City, CA), 2000.

Winning the Heart of the College Admissions Dean: An Expert's Advice for Getting into College, Ten Speed Press (Berkeley, CA), 2001.

Contributor to education, counseling, and feminist journals, and to *Seventeen.* Contributor to *N.O.W. Anthology,* edited by Mordica Pollack, Know, Inc. (Pittsburgh, PA), 1973. Member of editorial board of *School Counselor,* 1975-78.

PICTURE BOOKS

My Mommy Makes Money, illustrated by True Kelly, Little, Brown (Boston, MA), 1984.

Tractor-Trailer Trucker: A Powerful Truck Book, illustrated by Steven Borns, Tricycle Press (Berkeley, CA), 2000.

Crashed, Smashed, and Mashed: A Trip to Junkyard Heaven, illustrated by Steven Borns, Tricycle Press (Berkeley, CA), 2001.

Knuckleboom Loaders Load Logs, illustrated by Steven Borns, Overlook Press (Woodstock, NY), 2003.

Sidelights

Career counselor and educator Joyce Slayton Mitchell has devoted much of her career as a writer to counseling young adults in making intelligent college and career choices. Helping high school students make wise college selections has been one of her major goals, and she has published books such as 1991's *The Best Guide to the Top Colleges: How to Get into the Ivy's or Nearly Ivy's* and *Winning the Heart of the College Admissions Dean: An Expert's Advice for Getting into College.* Calling the latter book "a fine combination of solid advice and good sense," *Booklist* contributor Stephanie Zvirin also praised Mitchell's approach as "upbeat" and "well-organized." One of her most widely used books, *The College Board Guide to Jobs and Career Planning* is published under the auspices of the highly respected College Entrance Examination Board, which runs the widely used Scholastic Aptitude Test (SAT) program.

Born in 1933, Mitchell grew up in a small town in northern New England and attended college in the Midwest. Earning her master's degree in 1958, she moved to Connecticut and worked as a school counselor before getting married and moving with her anthropologist husband back to Vermont. "The only thing I could think to do was to write," she once recalled to *SATA* of her period raising her family in a rural Vermont town. "To write about the questions students had when I was a counselor. 'What's it like in college?' 'What's it like in a city, in a village, in the suburbs?' 'What's it like to go to an intellectual college, a collegiate college, a business college, an artistic or community-centered college?' 'What's it like to be a banker? a promotion manager? a stockbroker? a computer graphics technician?' After all the surprises I got in college and working and marriage and motherhood, the main question I want to write about for young people is: 'What's it like?'"

Mitchell's *The College Board Guide to Jobs and Career Planning,* which was initially published in 1986 as *College to Career: The Guide to Job Opportunities,* is similar in content to the U.S. Department of Labor's *Occupational Outlook Handbook* or *OOH,* in its discussion of the salary, educational and vocational requirements, and employment prospects for the one hundred most common jobs in the United States. However, Mitchell includes such things as the computer skills necessary for each job, the number of minorities and women in each field, and quotes regarding relative job satisfaction from men and women who have worked in each particular field five years or less. Dubbing Mitchell's job descriptions "peppy," Denise Perry Donavin noted in *Booklist* that *The College Board Guide to Jobs and Career Planning* provides high school and college students "a good place to start, par-

"Joyce Mitchell was my daughter's college advisor. I have checked with my daughter, and we agree: Pay attention to whatever Joyce Mitchell says."
—*Peter Jennings, ABC News and parent*

Winning the Heart of the College Admissions Dean

An Expert's Advice for Getting into College

Joyce Slayton Mitchell

Mitchell covers the most crucial aspects of college application and offers young readers advice on facing the competition for seats at demanding universities.

ticularly since definitive instructions are given" for young people at a variety of educational levels. *Voice of Youth Advocates* contributor Elaine Mersol dubbed Mitchell's book a "smaller, friendlier version" of the government's *OOH,* and praised in particular the author's "emphasis on decision making by young adults."

Mitchell is keenly aware of the differences in the adult path followed by men and women, and consequently she has authored books organized along gender lines. Addressing the special concerns of young women— such as the so-called glass ceiling, whether to work and raise children, and when to start a family—are such books as *I Can Be Anything: Careers and Colleges for Young Women, Other Choices for Becoming a Woman: A Handbook to Help High School Women Make Decisions,* and *Be a Mother and More: Career and Life Planning for Young Women.* Noting the praise given Mitchell's books, *Kliatt* contributor Kathleen J. Bognanni commented that *Be a Mother and More* "continues her tradition of sensible advice."

Young men are given equal treatment by Mitchell in a sequence of books devoted to their unique career and lifestyle concerns. In 1976's *Free to Choose: Decision Making for Young Men,* the author prompts young men to view drug use, sex, and religion as lifestyle choices for which they can then take responsibility, and includes military service among the career choices available. Job descriptions serve as the bulk of *The Men's Career Book: Work and Life Planning for a New Age,* which includes advice to help men "avoid the cultural pressures to become . . . a person who is measured by his earning power," in the words of a *Kliatt* contributor. And in *Choices and Changes: A Career Book for Men,* both young men new to the job market and those seeking to change careers are helped through the in-depth overviews of numerous jobs. A *Kliatt* reviewer called *Choices and Changes* "a good starting place for a future job seeker," while in *Booklist* Stephanie Zvirin dubbed Mitchell's text "enthusiastic yet thoroughly realistic counsel," adding that the author "wastes no time getting to the point." As Mitchell once noted of her nonfiction guides: "As a feminist and an educator, my work all reflects the importance of decision-making on the basis of a student's abilities and interests rather than from a stereotypic expectation of what 'girls should do' or what 'boys should do.' My books are designed to help high school students understand the many choices open in developing all facets of their lives, so that they are not bound by traditional views of women and men."

In addition to her many works of nonfiction, Mitchell has also ventured into fiction writing with *Crashed, Smashed, and Mashed: A Trip to Junkyard Heaven,* a picture book using what a *Kirkus Reviews* critic termed "sharp, artfully angled" photographs by Steven Borns to introduce youngsters to the afterlife of broken-down or otherwise wrecked cars. A companion volume, *Tractor-*

Trailer Trucker: A Powerful Truck Book satisfies children's' curiosity about the big rigs rolling along the nation's highways, and includes a guide to "trucker talk" and other facts that *Booklist* contributor Gillian Engberg maintained would "satisfy truck fanatics."

Biographical and Critical Sources

PERIODICALS

American Reference Book Annual, 1980, Peggy Clossey Boone, review of *The Men's Career Book: Work and Life Planning for a New Age,* pp. 294-295, and Peggy Sullivan, review of *The Work Book: A Guide to Skilled Jobs,* p. 295; 1981, Leonard Grundt, review of *What's Where? The Official Guide to College Majors,* pp. 305-306; 1995, Christine E. King, review of *Mitchell Express: The Fast Track to the Top Colleges,* p. 166, and Barbara Conroy, review of *The College Board Guide to Jobs and Career Planning,* p. 173.

Booklist, January 1, 1977, review of *Free to Choose: Decision Making for Young Men,* p. 661; June 1, 1978, review of *I Can Be Anything: Careers and Colleges for Young Women,* pp. 1545-1546; June 1, 1979, review of *The Men's Career Book,* p. 1486; September 1, 1979, review of *Stopout! Working Ways to Learn,* p. 28; February 1, 1982, review of *Taking on the World: Empowering Strategies for Parents of Children with Disabilities,* p. 687; January 15, 1983, review of *Choices and Changes: A Career Book for Men,* p. 645; February 15, 1983, review of *I Can Be Anything,* p. 750; April 15, 1988, review of *Winning the Chemo Battle,* p. 1379; November 1, 1990, Denise Perry Donavin, review of *The College Board Guide to Jobs and Career Planning,* p. 486; April 1, 2000, Gillian Engberg, review of *Tractor-Trailer Trucker: A Powerful Truck Book,* p. 1459; March 15, 2001, Stephanie Zvirin, review of *Crashed, Smashed, and Mashed: A Trip to Junkyard Heaven,* p. 1399; August, 2001, Stephanie Zvirin, review of *Winning the Heart of the College Admissions Dean: An Expert's Advice for Getting into College,* p. 2059.

Bulletin of the Center for Children's Books, December, 1980, review of *See Me More Clearly,* p. 76; June, 1984, review of *My Mommy Makes Money,* p. 189.

Kirkus Reviews, November 15, 1976, review of *Other Choices for Becoming a Woman: A Handbook to Help High School Women Make Decisions,* and *Free to Choose,* p. 1229; July 1, 1980, review of *See Me More Clearly,* p. 843; March 1, 2001, review of *Crashed, Smashed, and Mashed,* p. 335.

Kliatt, fall, 1979, review of *The Men's Career Book,* pp. 34-35; winter, 1979, review of *I Can Be Anything,* p. 34; winter, 1980, Elaine R. Goldberg, review of *The Classroom Teacher's Workbook for Career Education,* p. 36; spring, 1981, Kathleen J. Bognanni, review of *Be a Mother and More: Career and Life Planning for Young Women,* pp. 31-32; winter, 1983, review of *Choices and Changes,* p. 41, and *I Can Be Anything,* p. 42; January, 1991, Kathryn L. Harris, review of *The College Board Guide to Jobs and Career Planning,* p. 36; September, 1991, review of *The Best Guide to the Top Colleges,* pp. 42-43.

Library Journal, December 15, 1978, Stanley P. Lyle, review of *The Work Book,* p. 2515, and Barbara Green Ashdown, review of *Stopout!,* p. 2506; May 15, 1979, Stanley P. Lyle, review of *The Men's Career Book,* p. 1136; February 15, 1983, Barbara Carow, review of *Choices and Changes,* p. 394; November 15, 1986, Wendy Allex, review of *College to Career,* p. 92.

Publishers Weekly, March 13, 2000, review of *Tractor-Trailer Trucker,* p. 86; August 13, 2001, review of *Winning the Heart of the College Admissions Dean,* p. 305.

School Library Journal, November, 1975, Marlayne Morgan, review of *I Can Be Anything,* p. 98; December, 1976, Joan Scherer Brewer, review of *Other Choices for Becoming a Woman,* p. 62; January, 1977, Joan Scherer Brewer, review of *Free to Choose,* p. 103; February, 1979, Mickey Moskowitz, review of *The Work Book,* pp. 68-69; April, 1983, Deanna J. McDaniel, review of *I Can Be Anything,* p. 126; August, 1984, Audrey Conant, review of *My Mommy Makes Money,* p. 63; August, 2000, Edith Ching, review of *Tractor-Trailer Trucker,* pp. 172-173; June, 2001, Pamela K. Bomboy, review of *Crashed, Smashed, and Mashed,* p. 177; December, 2001, review of *Winning the Heart of the College Dean,* p. 168.

Voice of Youth Advocates, April, 1981, Deborah Grimes, review of *See Me More Clearly,* p. 46; February, 1985, Nancy Clark, review of *Your Job in the Computer Age,* p. 341; December, 1990, Elaine Mersol, review of *The College Board Guide to Jobs and Career Planning,* p. 317; October, 1994, Jennifer A. Long, review of *The College Board Guide to Jobs and Career Planning,* p. 245.*

*   *   *

MORAY WILLIAMS, Ursula 1911-

Personal

Born April 19, 1911, in Petersfield, Hampshire, England; daughter of Arthur (an archeologist and tutor in classics) and Mabel Lizzie (a teacher; maiden name, Unwin) Moray Williams; married Conrad (Peter) Southey John (an aircraft engineer), September 28, 1935 (died, 1974); children: Andrew, Hugh, Robin, James. *Education:* Educated privately at home by a governess; attended finishing school in Annecy, France, 1927-28, and the Winchester College of Art (Winchester, England), 1928-29. *Religion:* Church of England. *Hobbies and other interests:* Gardening, sewing, traveling.

Addresses

Home—Pearcroft Cottage, Conderton, Gloucestershire, England. *Agent*—Curtis Brown Ltd., 162-168 Regent St., London, W1R 5TA England.

Career

Author and illustrator of books for children. Magistrate and Justice of the Peace, Worchestershire-Evesham bench, 1958-81; chairman of Evesham Juvenile Panel, 1972-75; deputy chairman of Adult Bench, 1975-81. Former governor of County High School, Evesham, England; former governor of Vale of Evesham School for Educationally Subnormal Children; former manager of Beckford Junior School. President of Women's Royal British Legion, 1974—. Former presiding member of Mother's Union. Founder of children's writing competitions in Cheltenham, England; the Outer Hebrides; and New Zealand. Has given book talks at school libraries in Australia, New Zealand, and the United Kingdom.

Member

National Book League, West of England Writers Association, PEN (London, England), Cheltenham Literary Festival Society.

Awards, Honors

Spring Book Festival Award middle honor, *New York Herald Tribune*, 1971, for *The Three Toymakers; Gobbolino the Witch's Cat* was buried in a time capsule, 1978, in Harmondsworth, England, for the children of 2078 to discover.

Writings

SELF-ILLUSTRATED CHILDREN'S BOOKS

Jean-Pierre, A. and C. Black (London, England), 1931.

For Brownies: Stories and Games for the Pack and Everybody Else, Harrap (London, England), 1933.

Grandfather (verse), Allen and Unwin (London, England), 1933.

The Pettabomination (also see below), Archer Press (London, England), 1933, revised edition, Lane (London, England), 1948.

More for Brownies, Harrap (London, England), 1934.

(Illustrated with sister, Barbara Moray Williams) *Kelpie, the Gipsies' Pony*, Harrap (London, England), 1934, Lippincott (Philadelphia, PA), 1935.

Anders and Marta, Harrap (London, England), 1935.

Adventures of Anne, Harrap (London, England), 1935.

The Twins and Their Ponies, Harrap (London, England), 1936.

Sandy-on-the-Shore, Harrap (London, England), 1936.

Tales for the Sixes and Sevens, Harrap (London, England), 1936.

Dumpling: The Story of a Pony, Harrap (London, England), 1937.

(Illustrated with sister, Barbara Moray Williams) *Elaine of La Signe*, Harrap (London, England), 1937, published as *Elaine of the Mountains*, Lippincott (Philadelphia, PA), 1939.

The Good Little Christmas Tree (also see below), Harrap (London, England), 1943, illustrated by Jane Paton, Hamish Hamilton (London, England), 1970, illustrated by Gillian Tyler, Knopf (New York, NY), 1991.

The Three Toymakers, Harrap (London, England), 1945, revised edition, illustrated by Shirley Hughes, Hamish Hamilton (London, England), 1970, Thomas Nelson (Camden, NJ), 1971.

The House of Happiness (also see below), Harrap (London, England), 1946.

Malkin's Mountain, Harrap (London, England), 1948, revised edition, illustrated by Shirley Hughes, Hamish Hamilton (London, England), 1970, Thomas Nelson (New York, NY), 1972.

The Story of Laughing Dandino, Harrap (London, England), 1948.

The Binklebys at Home, Harrap (London, England), 1951.

The Binklebys on the Farm, Harrap (London, England), 1953.

The Secrets of the Wood, Harrap (London, England), 1955.

Grumpa, Brockhampton Press (Leicester, England), 1955.

Goodbody's Puppet Show, Hamish Hamilton (London, England), 1956.

Golden Horse with a Silver Tail, Hamish Hamilton (London, England), 1957.

Hobbie, Brockhampton Press (Leicester, England), 1958.

The Moonball, Hamish Hamilton (London, England), 1958, illustrated by Jane Paton, Meredith Press (New York, NY), 1967.

O for a Mouseless House!, Chatto and Windus (London, England), 1964.

OTHER CHILDREN'S BOOKS

(With husband C. S. John, as Peter John) *The Adventures of Boss and Dingbatt*, photographs by John, Harrap (London, England), 1937.

Adventures of the Little Wooden Horse, illustrated by Joyce Lankester Brisley, Harrap (London, England), 1938, Lippincott (Philadelphia, PA), 1939, illustrated by Peggy Fortnum, Penguin (Baltimore, MD), 1959, illustrated by Paul Howard, Kingfisher (New York, NY), 2001.

Adventures of Puffin, illustrated by Mary Shillabeer, Harrap (London, England), 1939.

Peter and the Wanderlust, illustrated by Jack Matthew, Harrap (London, England), 1939, illustrated by Henry C. Pitz, Lippincott (Philadelphia, PA), 1940, revised edition published as *Peter on the Road*, Hamish Hamilton (London, England), 1963.

Pretenders' Island, illustrated by Joyce Lankester Brisley, Harrap (London, England), 1940, Knopf (New York, NY), 1942.

A Castle for John-Peter, illustrated by Eileen A. Soper, Harrap (London, England), 1941.

Gobbolino the Witch's Cat, Harrap (London, England), 1942, illustrated by Paul Howard, Kingfisher (New York, NY), 2001.

Jockin the Jester, illustrated by Barbara Moray Williams, Chatto and Windus (London, England), 1951, Thomas Nelson (Nashville, TN), 1973.

The Noble Hawks, Hamish Hamilton (London, England), 1959, published as *The Earl's Falconer*, illustrated by Charles Geer, Morrow (New York, NY), 1961.

The Nine Lives of Island Mackenzie, illustrated by Edward Ardizzone, Chatto and Windus (London, England),

1959, published as *Island Mackenzie,* Morrow (New York, NY), 1960.

Beware of This Animal, illustrated by Jane Paton, Hamish Hamilton (London, England), 1964, Dial Press (New York, NY), 1965.

Johnnie Tigerskin, illustrated by Diana Johns, Harrap (London, England), 1964, Duell, Sloan, and Pearce (New York, NY), 1966.

High Adventure, illustrated by Prudence Seward, Thomas Nelson (London, England), 1965.

The Cruise of the "Happy-Go-Gay," illustrated by Gunvor Edwards, Hamish Hamilton (London, England), 1967, published as *The Cruise of the Happy-Go-Gay,* Meredith Press (New York, NY), 1968.

A Crown for a Queen, illustrated by Shirley Hughes, Meredith Press (New York, NY), 1968.

The Toymaker's Daughter, illustrated by Shirley Hughes, Hamish Hamilton (London, England), 1968, Meredith Press (New York, NY), 1969.

Mog, illustrated by Faith Jaques, Allen and Unwin (London, England), 1969.

Boy in a Barn, illustrated by Terence Dalley, Nelson (New York, NY), 1970.

Johnnie Golightly and His Crocodile, illustrated by Faith Jaques, Chatto, Boyd, and Oliver (London, England), 1970, Harvey House (Irvington-on-Hudson, NY), 1971.

Traffic Jam, illustrated by Robert Hales, Chatto and Windus (London, England), 1971.

Man on a Steeple, illustrated by Mary Dinsdale, Chatto and Windus (London, England), 1971.

Mrs. Townsend's Robber, illustrated by Gavin Rowe, Chatto and Windus (London, England), 1971.

Out of the Shadows, illustrated by Gavin Rowe, Chatto and Windus (London, England), 1971.

Castle Merlin, Allen and Unwin (London, England), Thomas Nelson (Nashville, TN), 1972.

Children's Parties and Games for a Rainy Day, Corgi Books (London, England), 1972.

A Picnic with the Aunts, illustrated by Faith Jaques, Chatto and Windus (London, England), 1972.

The Kidnapping of My Grandmother, illustrated by Mike Jackson, Heinemann (London, England), 1972.

Tiger-Nanny, illustrated by Gunvor Edwards, Brockhampton Press (Leicester, England), 1973, Thomas Nelson (Nashville, TN), 1974.

Grandpapa's Folly and the Woodworm-Bookworm, illustrated by Faith Jaques, Chatto and Windus (London, England), 1974.

The Line, illustrated by Barry Wilkinson, Penguin (London, England), 1974.

No Ponies for Miss Pobjoy, illustrated by Pat Marriott, Chatto and Windus (London, England), 1975, Thomas Nelson (Nashville, TN), 1976.

Bogwoppit, illustrated by Shirley Hughes, Thomas Nelson (Nashville, TN), 1978.

Jeffy the Burglar's Cat, illustrated by David McKee, Andersen Press (London, England), 1981.

Bellabelinda and the No-Good Angel, illustrated by Glenys Ambrus, Chatto and Windus (London, England), 1982.

The Further Adventures of Gobbolino and the Little Wooden Horse, illustrated by Pauline Baynes, Penguin (London, England), 1984, illustrated by Paul Howard, Kingfisher (New York, NY), 2002.

Spid, illustrated by David McKee, Andersen Press (London, England), 1985.

Grandma and the Ghowlies, illustrated by Susan Varley, Andersen Press (London, England), 1986.

Paddy on the Island, illustrated by Tor Morisse, Andersen Press (London, England), 1987.

Also author of stories for reluctant readers. Contributor to numerous anthologies and to magazines, including *Cricket, Lady, Marshall Cavendish Storyteller,* and *Puffin Post.* Moray Williams's books have been translated into over thirteen languages, including Icelandic, Japanese, and Romanish.

PLAYS FOR CHILDREN

(Self-illustrated) *The Autumn Sweepers and Other Plays* (includes *Mother Josephine Bakes Bread, Forfeits, Tavi of Gold, The Organ Grinder: A Mime,* and *A Sea Ballet*), A. and C. Black (London, England), 1933.

The Good Little Christmas Tree (adapted from her play of the same name), Samuel French (London, England), 1951.

The House of Happiness (adapted from her play of the same name), Samuel French (London, England), 1951.

The Pettabomination: A Play in One Act (adapted from her play of the same name), Samuel French (London, England), 1951.

Adaptations

Gobbolino the Witch's Cat was recorded on Delyse Records, 1967, on Storyteller Cassettes, 1982-83, and as an audiobook by Chivers Audiobooks, 1995, and BBC Audiobooks, 1996; *Spid* was released on audio cassette by Chivers Children's Audio Books, 1990; *Grandma and the Ghowlies* was released on audio cassette by Chivers Audio Books, 1991, and BBC Audio Books, 1997; *Bogwoppit* was released on audio cassette by Chivers Children's Audio Books, 1994; *Adventures of the Little Wooden Horse* was released on audio cassette by Chivers Audio Books, 1996, and BBC Audiobooks in 1999; *Jeffy the Burglar's Cat* was released on audio cassette by Chivers Audio Books, 1998; *The Further Adventures of Gobbolino and the Little Wooden Horse* was released on audio cassette by Chivers Children's Audio Books, 1998; *The Good Little Christmas Tree* was released on audio cassette, 2000, and CD, 2001, both by BBC Audiobooks; *Bogwoppit, Gobbolino the Witch's Cat, Jeffy the Burglar's Cat, The Nine Lives of Island Mackenzie, Paddy on the Island,* and *The Three Toymakers* were adapted for television by the British Broadcasting Company and were presented on the children's program *Jackanory.*

Sidelights

An English author and illustrator of books for children, Ursula Moray Williams has been popular with the young for over seventy years. She has created approximately

A sweet kitten who longs to leave his witch mistress sets out on an adventurous journey to find a family to adopt him in Gobbolino the Witch's Cat, *written by Ursula Moray Williams and illustrated by Paul Howard.*

seventy titles that are noted for their variety, imagination, charm, and incisive observations of human nature. Moray Williams has written genre books—school stories, ghost stories, and adventure tales, among others—as well as humorous stories, historical fiction, realistic fiction, picture books, fantasies, plays, verse, and books that combine fantasy and realism. She fills her works with things that appeal to children, such as animals, both real and anthropomorphic; toys; exotic settings, such as the Bavarian Alps and tropical desert islands; and the supernatural. The author perhaps is best noted as the creator of *Adventures of the Little Wooden Horse,* the story of a toy pony who goes into the world to earn money to support his beloved maker; originally published in 1938, the book now is considered a classic. Thematically, Moray Williams blends fantasy, humor, and adventure to address the relationship of good and evil. Her protagonists—child, toy, and animal alike—are loving and generous personages, say critics, who encounter danger, deception, violence, discrimination, and rejection. However, the characters surmount these obstacles through their courage, compassion, loyalty, and kindness.

As a literary stylist, Moray Williams is praised for writing clear, graceful prose that features interesting plot twists and cliffhanger chapter endings; she also is noted for adding witty, satiric undertones to several of her stories and for creating works that are perfect for reading aloud. As an illustrator, Moray Williams has provided line drawings and collage cut-outs for about a third of her works; her books also have been illustrated by artists such as Edward Ardizzone, Shirley Hughes, Gunvor Edwards, Faith Jaques, David McKee, and the author's twin sister, Barbara Moray Williams. Although she occasionally is criticized by reviewers for writing stories that are too long, too sentimental, or too old-fashioned, Moray Williams generally is considered an author whose long and remarkable career demonstrates her keen understanding of children and what appeals to them. Writing in *St. James Guide to Children's Writers,* Winifred Whitehead commented that Moray Williams "is an inventive as well as a prolific writer, and in their different ways her books are well-written, pleasantly intriguing, and occasionally achieve a haunting power and a delightfully sharp and witty observation of the foibles of mankind." Joanne Lewis Sears, writing in *Dictionary of Literary Biography,* stated that Moray Williams "has given children readable, absorbing tales, both fanciful and realistic, for more than half a century. . . . She writes in so many modes and to such varied age levels that her work occupies no fixed niche in the history of children's literature. . . . Her simple, forthright values and amusingly unrepentant protagonists please children far removed from the sunshine world she once shared with her twin sister, Barbara." Writing in *Books for Your Children,* Anne Wood concluded that the author's "quick response to everything positive, creative, beautiful, and amusing is reflected in her writing. And yet what makes her work for children stand out from the common run is the way in which her characters . . . overcome adversity, wickedness, and, above all, rejection."

Born in Petersfield, Hampshire, England, Moray Williams came into the world just ten minutes after her identical twin sister, Barbara. Their parents, Arthur and Mabel Lizzie Moray Williams, had lost their first child, a boy, to pneumonia; the twins were born on his second birthday. Writing in *Something about the Author Autobiography Series (SAAS),* Moray Williams recalled that her parents "often told us how they would look on the pair of us and laugh for joy at the thought of having two babies given back to them for the one they had lost." Arthur Moray Williams was an archeologist who also tutored students in Greek and Latin, and Mabel Lizzie Moray Williams was a teacher who had trained in the Froebel method in Germany. The author wrote, "My mother gave us our first lessons, and taught us very early to read. I still remember the excitement of finding out that H-O-T spelt 'hot' and not 'hat' or 'hut' or 'hit.'"

Despite the onset of World War I, Moray recalled, "Our childhood was a happy one." At the time that war was declared, the twins had joined the Girl Guides, the British version of the Girl Scouts, and had learned to ride. Moray Williams noted that although she and Barbara "loved the Guides and worshipped our captain, nothing took the places of horses in our hearts." The author remembered that she and her sister "became horse mad, like many another girl of our age. . . . Years later I wrote a book called *The Twins and Their Ponies* which described those happy days, but inevitably we grew out of that excitement, though the smell and sound of a horse still gets into my blood at times."

After the end of the war, Ursula, Barbara, and their younger brother, Alan, were told suddenly that they were going to move to an old "folly," as their parents described it, on the other side of Hampshire. While the move took place, the twins and their brother stayed with their maternal grandparents in Bromley, Kent. Moray Williams recalled that, though she and Barbara were upset about leaving their old life, they had developed something special from which they could not be parted: "One thing that the Move and the Grown-Up World could not take away from us was our drawing and our storytelling. For years we had to go to bed so early that of course we could not sleep, so we used those precious hours for telling stories, breaking off in turn to toss the thread to one another: 'Now you!' 'Now you!' I can't remember any occasion when the other twin changed the plot too violently.

"We told about three families in turn, and later, when we stayed up longer, we wrote these stories down. . . always new ones, of course, working at a long table with a screen of books stretched across the middle, and a lot of pictures in colour to make them more interesting. These books took about three months to finish, and were presented to each other on Christmas morning, and first thing on our birthdays." Moray Williams recalled writing her first full-length book, the story of a bad little boy, at the age of seven. She gave it to a twenty-year-old man who had just finished giving the fledgling author her first ride on a horse; Moray Williams mused that the young man, who was quite embarrassed by her gift, probably fed her book to the horse.

Moray Williams and her family moved into the "Folly," a house in North Stoneham that was located between Southampton and Winchester. Built in the mid-1700s, the home originally was owned by a man who, according to Moray Williams, "wanted to parade his affluence and his self-importance, but he had not enough money to pay for the best materials, nor anything but rather shoddy workmanship." The house was enormous, filled with huge, high rooms; long, dark corridors; and a glass ceiling on which was painted a copy of Michelangelo's "Transfiguration." The house also had a huge library; however, the twins were disappointed to find that it was just a sham. Moray Williams noted, "When we rushed into the room and tore at the volumes on the shelves, there was not one book we could take down to read. Titles, yes. Beautiful bindings, maybe, and dozens of

them, hundreds really. But of absolutely no use for reading. The whole library had been constructed to impress the original owner's friends. . . . Long afterwards I brought it to partial life in *Grandpapa's Folly and the Woodworm-Bookworm,* and I also built round it *A Castle for John-Peter.*"

Since they lived on a large, wild park, the twins were permitted to have a pony of their own. They worked to earn the money for it by selling goat's milk, flowers, nuts, blackberries, and other things. Finally, they made enough money to buy their first pony, Puss, which Moray Williams called "the gentlest thing we ever met. In time we had larger ponies, one after another, and we were given a pony cart by a generous friend, which gave us hours of pleasure."

Arthur Moray Williams decided that his children should have a governess, and so the family hired Miss Rattray, a woman of Scottish descent whom they called Tchat. Of Tchat, the author wrote, "She taught us a lot. . . Tchat taught us to love English and French classics. . . . In 'lessons' Tchat added Jane Austen, [Alexandre] Dumas, Victor Hugo, and set us subjects for English essays that we found entrancing. We also drew and painted with her, and continued writing our anniversary books that went on for years and years." The twins' parents gave them many books that they had owned as children as well as more contemporary books for Christmas and their birthdays. Their mother also read aloud to the girls from such authors as Charles Dickens, Rudyard Kipling, and Mark Twain. At a children's party, Ursula received a copy of Frances Hodgson Burnett's story *The Secret Garden,* which, she confided in *SAAS,* "became my favorite book of all time." She continued, "I remain so grateful to Tchat and my parents for their emphasis on books and reading aloud. I am sure I would not have become a writer without their encouragement."

When the twins were almost seventeen, they were sent to live with a French pastor and his family, the Noyers, in Annecy, Haute-Savoie, France. The pair spent what Moray Williams called "an idyllic year," where they attended school, swam in the lake, rowed, hiked, skied, climbed mountains, played tennis, and did many other things that previously they had only read about. Moray Williams noted, "The scenery and countryside were so beautiful they made a great impression on me, and I slowly began to write independently." Later, Moray Williams would use the background of Annecy for several of her books, including three volumes of her "Toymaker" series, *The Three Toymakers, Malkin's Mountain,* and *The Toymaker's Daughter.*

After returning home from France, the twins went to the Winchester College of Art, a school nine miles from the "Folly." Moray Williams commented, "My sister enjoyed this, but I did not. After a year, I broke away to write books for children, while Barbara went on to London to study at the Royal College of Art under Sir William Rothenstein. My parents very generously allowed me to stay at home and write." In 1931, twenty-year-old Moray Williams produced her first book, *Jean-Pierre,* a story set in the mountains of Annecy. In this work, which the author illustrated with bright colors on a black background, a small boy and his goat are forbidden to climb alone in the mountains, but do so anyway. Her second and fourth books, *For Brownies: Stories and Games for the Pack and Everybody Else* and *More for Brownies,* were inspired by the author's experience as Brown Owl, or den mother, to a Brownie troop in the village where she lived. Moray Williams's uncle, Sir Stanley Unwin, headed the prestigious publishing firm of Allen and Unwin. He helped his niece to get her early books published but, when he began to complain that he was her unpaid agent, she soon found herself a professional.

In 1935, Moray Williams married Conrad Southey John, called Peter, an aircraft engineer and former Royal Air Force pilot who was the great-grandson of Robert Southey, a Poet Laureate of England. The couple had four sons, Andrew, Hugh, Robin, and James. As Peter John, John collaborated with his wife on and provided the photographs for *The Adventures of Boss and Dingbatt;* he passed away in 1974.

The first of Moray Williams's books to win her international acclaim was *Adventures of the Little Wooden Horse.* While pregnant with her first son, Andrew, she crafted the tale of a quiet but brave horse, a carved push-along toy on wheels, whose unconditional love for Uncle Peder, an old toy maker, inspires him to leave home in order to save his master from poverty. The horse finds work with a cruel farmer before escaping on a canal barge. Taken across the sea on a trading ship, he works in a coal mine, takes the place of a royal coach horse, walks the high-wire in a circus, and rescues ponies that are trapped in a mine, among other adventures. Finally, the horse swims home across the ocean with the money that he has earned tucked inside his hollow body. Since the publication of this story, which has never been out of print, critics generally have called *Adventures of the Little Wooden Horse* an exciting and moving tale.

Writing in *Books for Keeps,* Margery Fisher remarked that the author's "shrewd understanding of the way people treat outsiders gives depth to a nursery tale with an abiding faith in the values of courage and loyalty." Fisher concluded that *Adventures of the Little Wooden Horse* "is as fresh as it ever was." Writing in her *Who's Who in Children's Books: A Treasury of the Familiar Characters of Childhood,* Fisher stated, "Beside familiar characters like [Rachel Field's] Hitty and [Richard Henry Horne's] Maria Poppet, the Little Wooden Horse must take his place as one of those seemingly simple characters whose behaviour and exploits carry deeper meanings and touch unexpected depths of feeling in the reader. Staunch, loyal, unselfish, the Little Wooden Horse is all the more appealing because he is a reluc-

tant hero. . . . Affection and security are as important to the character, and the story, as the variety and colour of the adventures which the little horse survives." Describing the books as "Highly moral and deeply emotional," Victor Watson, writing in *The Cambridge Guide to Children's Books in English,* called *Adventures of the Little Wooden Horse* "a heartbreaking but happily resolved episodic tale."

In 1942, Moray Williams created another of her most popular works with *Gobbolino the Witch's Cat.* In this story, which she wrote for two of her sons, a kitten that is the son of Graymalkin, the famous witch's cat from William Shakespeare's play *Macbeth,* wants only to be a kitchen cat. Rather than being all black, as witch's cats are supposed to be, Gobbolino is a tabby, with blue eyes and a white paw. Deserted by his mother and sister, and despised for his goodness by the witch whom he serves, Gobbolino sets out to find a place with a warm fire and a kind family to take care of him. However, Gobbolino's ability to do magic brings him trouble, and his reputation as a witch's cat follows him on his adventures, which include acting as Dog Toby in a Punch and Judy puppet show. More than once, he is betrayed by people whom he thought were his friends. Despite his disappointments, Gobbolino eventually finds the home that he has dreamed of: a farm full of children. Writing in *Books for Your Children* Anne Wood remarked, "Of all Ursula's creations, it is probably Gobbolino the Witch's Cat who is her best known character. He is certainly endearing, wishing only for a quiet fireside life but despite himself, beset at every turn by his inherited magic powers."

In 1984, Moray Williams brought her two most popular characters together in *The Further Adventures of Gobbolino and the Little Wooden Horse.* In this work, Gobbolino answers a desperate cry for help from his sister Sootica, who begs him to rescue her from the witch who owns her. On his journey, Gobbolino meets the little wooden horse, who offers to accompany him. After arriving at the home of the old witch in the Hurricane Mountains, Gobbolino is asked by his sister, a crafty kitty, to take her place with the witch so that she can escape, a plan to which he agrees. In order for the witch to believe this ruse, Gobbolino must hide his tabby markings and white paw. When the witch discovers his true identity, she casts a spell that prevents the cat and horse from leaving the Hurricane Mountains. At great personal risk, the two friends finally get the village priest to break the witch's spell with a blessing. The pair escape, but the horse loses an ear. He and the cat travel towards home but go back to the witch when they hear that she has become ill. Gobbolino nurses the witch back to health. Finally, both she and Sootica, who has returned after being mistreated in the outside world for her status as a witch's cat, vow that they will stop casting spells. As her last hurrah as a sorcerer, the witch allows Gobbolino and the little wooden horse to fly home, where they are met by both Uncle Peder and the children from Gobbolino's farm.

Calling *The Further Adventures of Gobbolino and the Little Wooden Horse* "a pleasantly alarming and adventurous sequel," Winifred Whitehead of *St. James Guide to Children's Writers* noted that the title characters demonstrate "the values of a kind heart and faithfulness and that even witches deserve loyalty and compassion." Fisher of *Growing Point* stated that this sequel to "two well-loved stories . . . will be welcomed with pleasurable anticipation by two generations. Nobody will be disappointed. Ursula Moray Williams writes in the tradition of George MacDonald and E. Nesbit, using a measure of unalarming, even homely magic to carry to the young the essential message that conflicts of good and evil rests partly in their hands." Fisher concluded that "this third book worthily extends the exploits of two inimitable nursery heroes." In her foreword to *The Further Adventures of Gobbolino and the Little Wooden Horse,* Philippa Pearce called the coming together of the main characters a "rarity in literature, I believe, and, in this instance, a treasure." Calling the two friends equals, "or rather, complementaries," Pearce continued, "A nearer approximation might be the first encounter of [Kenneth Grahame's] Ratty and Mole on the riverbank." Pearce concluded, "The enterprise to which our two heroes dedicate themselves leads to frightening adventures, and so the two of them—how like us!—are often frightened. But they never, ever give up. . . . Above all, they both believe—they *know*—that they are doing the right thing, the good thing."

Moray Williams's series of "Toymaker" books, a multivolume set of fantasies set in Drussl in the Bavarian Alps, are considered among her best works. These stories feature Marta, a beautiful, ageless mechanical doll that possesses both magical powers and a malicious nature. The series, which began in 1935 with *Anders and Marta* and was published out of sequence, uses the form of the traditional folktale to examine the nature of evil. In *The Three Toymakers,* a volume published in 1945, the author introduces Marta, who is made by the amoral toy maker Malkin as an entry in a contest with wood-carvers from around the world. The artisans are competing for a thousand gold pieces, awarded by the king to the craftsman who can create the most perfect toy. Malkin, who previously has created ugly, scowling playthings, fashions Marta, a doll with white skin, black hair, and silky lashes. Though lovely to look at, Marta is endowed with her maker's nasty streak. Her bad behavior causes Malkin to lose the contest, and he takes Marta and moves to the dark side of the mountain. Writing in *Horn Book,* Virginia Haviland commented, "Told with swiftness, the story rises in suspense through the final hours when all is set straight in fine folk-tale manner." A critic in *Publishers Weekly* noted that "justice triumphs in a most satisfying ending."

In *Malkin's Mountain,* a volume published in 1948, Malkin tries to prevent his chief rival, Peter the Toymaker, from harvesting the wood that he needs to create his marvelous toys. Malkin uses magic to move the mountain where Peter harvests his wood, and he pro-

tects himself with an army of corrupt wooden soldiers, who threaten to destroy the people of Peter's village. Peter's protégé Rudi and his twins try to save the toy maker and are captured by Malkin and Marta, who is now Malkin's queen. Marta tries to seduce Rudi and his sons with offers of power; however, their faith and persistence come to the fore, and eventually they defeat the evil toy maker and his doll-queen.

In 1968, Moray Williams completed her "Toymaker" series with *The Toymaker's Daughter.* In this work, Marta, who remembers the kindness shown to her by Rudi and his younger brother Anders, escapes from Malkin and goes to live with Anders and his family. Marta longs to be a real girl, and for a while it looks as though she might achieve her goal. Although she tries hard to be good, Marta cannot help herself, and she uses her magic to play mean-spirited tricks. Finally, she decides that it is better to be known as Malkin's most wonderful creation than to remain a half-doll, half-child. She returns to the dark side of the mountain to take care of Malkin, who has been trying to get her to come back. Writing in *Library Journal,* Arlene Ruthenberg commented that "the well-developed plot . . . and appealing story will win this title fans among girls not yet solidly into the mystery story phase." Ruth Hill

In Moray Williams's **Adventures of the Little Wooden Horse,** *a toy horse goes off to seek his fortune but never wavers from his determination to return to his beloved toymaker. (Illustrated by Paul Howard.)*

Viguers of *Horn Book* noted, "The book has the mountain atmosphere so much loved in *Heidi* and will give delight to little girls who enjoy tales of dolls who come alive." Writing in *Saturday Review,* Zena Sutherland remarked, "The characters live and breathe, both real and doll-girl being made of spice as well as sugar." In assessing the series, Sears wrote in *Dictionary of Literary Biography* that the "Toymaker" books "represent Williams's most complex and thematically interesting work." Sears concluded that, to Williams's credit, the series "engages problems of absolute evil through an unself-conscious, absorbing narrative—one that retains shades of moral complexity without damaging the pace of the plot."

In addition to her works for younger children, Moray Williams has written well-received titles for young people. One of the most well received is *The Noble Hawks,* a book that was published in 1959, appearing in the United States as *The Earl's Falconer.* Historical fiction set in medieval times, the story outlines what happens when young Dickon, the son of a yeoman, rescues an injured falcon from the top of a tree. Although only those of noble birth were allowed to own or to fly falcons in those days, Dickon's bravery and his genuine love for the birds impress his liege lord, the Earl of Alden, who allows him to become a falconer. Calling the book "a most valuable work," a reviewer in the *Times Literary Supplement* stated, "Accuracy in an unfamiliar subject is the hallmark of *The Noble Hawks.*" Writing in the *Spectator* about the same book, Geoffrey Nicholson commented, "The conversation is a little precious, but the action is tense and vigorous enough." Ruth Hill Viguers of *Horn Book* concluded in a review of *The Earl's Falconer,* "Boys and girls interested in falconry will find almost everything to satisfy them in this well-written story."

Also among Moray Williams's most popular works is *Bogwoppit,* a humorous fantasy for middle-graders. Published in 1978, the story describes how Samantha Millett, an eleven-year-old orphan, goes to live with her reclusive, cranky aunt, Daisy Clandorris. Aunt Daisy, who lives in a mansion on a country estate called the Park, does not like children; in fact, she intends to let Samantha stay with her only until she can make other arrangements. The Park is overrun with bogwoppits, rat-like creatures with short wings and long tails that are thought to be extinct. The bogwoppits have infested the house through its drains. When Samantha arrives at the manor, Daisy is attempting to disinfect it in order to destroy the bogwoppits; however, Samantha becomes fond of one of the creatures, even taking it to school with her. When an army of bogwoppits kidnap Daisy to prevent their extermination, Samantha goes under the house to find her. Daisy is rescued, though reluctantly as she has found the bogwoppits to be less irritating than people. When Daisy's husband, the long-absent Lord Ernest Clandorris, turns up suddenly, he announces that he has been in South America studying bogwoppits. Finally, Daisy decides to accompany her husband back

to the jungle; before she leaves, she bequeaths the Park, which will be turned into a bogwoppit sanctuary, to Samantha, whom she has learned to love. Calling the tale "suspenseful and fantastic," a reviewer in *Publishers Weekly* admitted that Moray Williams imbued her imaginary creatures "with so much personality that one hates to think that they are only make-believe." Victor Watson, writing in *The Cambridge Guide to Children's Books in English* called *Bogwoppit* "deliciously absurd."

Moray Williams once told *Something about the Author,* "My ideas just come. I never plan them, and always find something inside me trying to get out! I still write better when time is just a little short! And [I] still deeply love the country and the isolation bred of our early life in that strange old house we lived in." Regarding her writing, she told Anne Wood of *Books for Your Children,* "It's very exciting. I have no idea in the morning what will happen to it when I sit down to write at five o'clock that evening." She once remarked, "Children's books have changed a bit since the 1930s in that violence, divorce, and, to a certain extent, sex are now tolerated—but children respond eternally to sincerity, a proportion of emotion or sentiment, excitement, and kindness—which makes them feel less vulnerable!" In assessing her career, Moray Williams wrote in *St. James Guide to Children's Writers,* "I've no idea why I write or wrote what I did. Ask a hen why it lays an egg."

Biographical and Critical Sources

BOOKS

Dictionary of Literary Biography, Volume 160: *British Children's Writers, 1914-1960,* Gale (Detroit, MI), 1995.
Doyle, Brian, editor, *The Who's Who of Children's Literature,* Schocken Books (New York, NY), 1971.
Fisher, Margery, *Who's Who in Children's Books: A Treasury of the Familiar Characters of Childhood,* Holt, Rinehart, and Winston (New York, NY), 1975.
St. James Guide to Children's Writers, 5th edition, St. James Press (Detroit, MI), 1999.
Something about the Author Autobiography Series, Volume 9, Gale (Detroit, MI), 1990.
Watson, Victor, *The Cambridge Guide to Children's Books in English,* Cambridge University Press (Cambridge, England), 2001.
Williams, Ursula Moray, *The Further Adventures of Gobbolino and the Little Wooden Horse,* foreword by Philippa Pearce, Kingfisher (New York, NY), 2002.

PERIODICALS

Books for Keeps, November, 1991, Margery Fisher, review of *Adventures of the Little Wooden Horse,* p. 30.
Books for Your Children, autumn, 1986, Anne Wood, "A Taste for a Feeling Book?," p. 2.
Growing Point, January, 1985, Margery Fisher, review of *The Further Adventures of Gobbolino and the Little Wooden Horse,* pp. 4358-4359.

Horn Book, June, 1961, Ruth Hill Viguers, review of *The Earl's Falconer,* p. 267; October, 1969, Ruth Hill Viguers, review of *The Toymaker's Daughter,* p. 638; August, 1971, Virginia Haviland, review of *The Three Toymakers,* p. 387.

Library Journal, September 18, 1969, Arlene Ruthenberg, review of *The Toymaker's Daughter,* pp. 3209-3210.

Publishers Weekly, May 31, 1971, review of *The Three Toymakers,* p. 135; May 8, 1978, review of *Bogwoppit,* p. 75.

Saturday Review, August 16, 1969, Zena Sutherland, review of *The Toymaker's Daughter,* p. 37.

Spectator, June 12, 1959, Geoffrey Nicholson, review of *The Noble Hawks,* p. 849.

Times Literary Supplement, May 29, 1959, review of *The Noble Hawks,* p. xi.*

*   *   *

MURPHY, Jill (Frances) 1949-

Personal

Born July 5, 1949, in London, England; daughter of Eric Edwin (an engineer) and Irene (Lewis) Murphy; children: Charles. *Education:* Attended Chelsea, Croydon, and Camberwell art schools.

Addresses

Home—London, England. *Agent*—c/o Author Mail, Candlewick Press, 2067 Massachusetts Ave., Cambridge, MA 02140.

Career

Writer and illustrator, 1976—. Worked in a children's home for four years and as a nanny for one year.

Awards, Honors

Kate Greenaway Award nomination, British Library Association (BLA), 1981, and Children's Choice Book of 1981, Children's Book Council and International Reading Association, both for *Peace at Last; Parents* Best Books for Babies award, 1987, for *Five Minutes' Peace;* Kate Greenaway Award nominations, BLA, 1989, for *All in One Piece,* and 1994, for *A Quiet Night In.*

Writings

SELF-ILLUSTRATED; FOR CHILDREN

The Worst Witch (also see below), Allison & Busby (London, England), 1974, Schocken (New York, NY), 1980.

The Worst Witch Strikes Again (also see below), Allison & Busby (London, England), 1980, Viking Kestrel (New York, NY), 1988.

Peace at Last, Macmillan (London, England), Dial (New York, NY), 1980, published as *Peace at Last—In Miniature!,* Macmillan (New York, NY), 1987.

A Bad Spell for the Worst Witch (also see below), Kestrel (London, England), 1982, Viking Kestrel (New York, NY), 1988.

On the Way Home, Macmillan (London, England), 1982.

Whatever Next!, Macmillan (London, England), 1983, published as *What Next, Baby Bear!,* Dial (New York, NY), 1984.

Mrs Bear ("Bear Cut-Out Books" series), Macmillan (London, England), 1985.

Baby Bear ("Bear Cut-Out Books" series), Macmillan (London, England), 1985.

Mr Bear ("Bear Cut-Out Books" series), Macmillan (London, England), 1985.

Five Minutes' Peace (also see below), Walker (London, England), Putnam (New York, NY), 1986.

All in One Piece (also see below), Walker (London, England), Putnam (New York, NY), 1987.

Worlds Apart, Walker (London, England), 1988, Putnam (New York, NY), 1988.

A Piece of Cake (also see below), Walker (London, England), Putnam (New York, NY), 1989.

Geoffrey Strangeways, Walker (London, England), 1990, published as *Jeffrey Strangeways,* Candlewick Press (Cambridge, MA), 1992.

A Quiet Night In (also see below), Walker (London, England), 1993, Candlewick Press (Cambridge, MA), 1994.

The Last Noo-Noo, Walker (London, England), Candlewick Press (Cambridge, MA), 1995.

The Worst Witch at Sea, Viking (London, England), 1993, Candlewick Press (Cambridge, MA), 1995.

(With Rose Griffiths) *The Worst Witch's Spelling Book,* Puffin (London, England), 1995.

Adventures of the Worst Witch (includes *The Worst Witch, The Worst Witch Strikes Again,* and *A Bad Spell for the Worst Witch*), Viking (London, England), 1996.

All for One, Walker (London, England), 2000, Candlewick Press (Cambridge, MA), 2002.

The Large Family Collection (includes *Five Minutes' Peace, All in One Piece, A Piece of Cake,* and *A Quiet Night In*), Walker (London, England), 2000.

OTHER

(Illustrator) Fiona Macdonald, *The Duke Who Had Too Many Giraffes, and Other Stories,* Allison & Busby (London, England), 1977.

(Illustrator) Brian Ball, *The Witch in Our Attic,* British Broadcasting Corp. (London, England), 1979.

Murphy's writings have been translated into Welsh, Bengali, Chinese, Gujarati, Urdu, and Vietnamese.

Adaptations

The Worst Witch and *Peace at Last* were adapted for television in 1978 and 1984, respectively. *The Worst Witch, A Bad Spell for the Worst Witch, Geoffrey Strangeways,* and *Peace at Last* have all been adapted to audio; the "Worst Witch" books were again adapted for a television series on England's ITV, as *Worst Witch,* from 1998-2001, and as *Weirdsister College,* from 2001-2002.

Sidelights

Two decades before the "Harry Potter" books—about a British schoolboy at an academy for wizards—became a publishing sensation on both sides of the Atlantic, Jill Murphy had already conceived of and begun a series about a young British schoolgirl and her trials and tribulations at a school for witches. Murphy's "Worst Witch" books, the first of which was published in 1974, include *The Worst Witch, The Worst Witch Strikes Again, A Bad Spell for Worst Witch,* and *The Worst Witch at Sea.* In addition to this popular series, Murphy has also written and illustrated several warm and humorous picture books featuring the Larges, a family of pachyderms, two titles about the Bear family, and a duet of books about a loveable little monster named Marlon. Critics say these books for preschoolers and primary grade

readers deal with domestic and school situations in a light, even-handed, and reinforcing manner. Murphy has also penned juvenile novels, including *Worlds Apart,* about a young girl who rediscovers her missing father, as well as a spoof of a medieval quest tale in *Geoffrey Strangeways.* Recipient of several Kate Greenaway Award nominations for her illustrations, Murphy is considered both a droll humorist and reassuring explicator of family situations in her text, and a spirited illustrator. Reviewing Murphy's artwork for *Peace at Last,* for example, a contributor for *Publishers Weekly* commended the "exuberant spirit of her remarkable paintings," which "leap with jovial surprise."

Born in London, England, in 1949, Murphy has "always drawn since I can remember," as she remarked in the *St. James Guide to Children's Writers,* "and written stories from an early age (four to be exact): the two skills were automatically linked. I still feel more comfortable in the company of children, so it's natural I should like to write about things they appreciate." Mur-

An elephant mother starts a family diet but relents when Grandma's cake proves too irresistible in **A Piece of Cake,** *written and illustrated by Jill Murphy.*

phy once told *SATA:* "I inherited the ability to draw from my father [an engineer] and I had a mother who *liked* being a mother. She encouraged me to be observant and to write from the age of three." Murphy began her writing ventures with small stapled books which she both authored and illustrated. She also confessed to having a difficult time at school because the only thing she wanted to do was "write stories and draw pictures." For Murphy, there was never any doubt that she would become an author and illustrator.

Attending art schools in Chelsea, Croydon, and Camberwell, Murphy, by the age of eighteen, had written and illustrated what would become her first published book, the middle grade novel *The Worst Witch.* However, a drawer full of rejection slips would be collected before she found a publisher for that title, and meanwhile, she had a living to make, as a book jacket illustrator, a nanny, and as an assistant in a children's home, a position that inspired her first picture book, *Peace at Last.*

Murphy's first "Witch" book, *The Worst Witch,* appeared in 1974. Responding to a question by a group of young interviewers on the *Young Writer* Web site, Murphy noted the inspiration for these books. "My two friends and I used to come home [from school] in our dark uniforms, looking very scruffy at the end of the day. . . . My Mum used to say 'Look at you all. You look like the three witches!,' and it gave me the idea for a witch's school—so that it was exactly like my school, but with a subtle touch of magic."

In this first tale and in subsequent titles in the series, Murphy employs the usual motif of the girl's school story, including the typical girl who is good at everything, the one who is miserable at everything, and the mean headmistress, blending them with one magical element: the school happens to be Miss Cackle's Academy for Witches. In her first year at the Academy, Mildred Hubble is the bumbling sort who always messes up her copybook. She manages to brew up bad potions, turn a fellow student into a pig quite by mistake, and make a mess of broomstick exercises for Halloween. But when she runs away from school only to stumble upon and undo the evil plotting of a rival coven of witches who are planning to take over the Academy, Mildred suddenly finds her place in the scheme of things.

This first book was widely praised by critics both in England and the United States. Leon Garfield, reviewing *Worst Witch* in *Spectator,* felt that Murphy's debut novel "is more in the nature of a romp, but it comes off beautifully." Accompanied by line drawings by the author, this tale is a "brisk, tongue-in-cheek version of doings at a British academy for young ladies," according to a reviewer for *Publishers Weekly.* Zena Sutherland, writing in the *Bulletin of the Center for Children's Books,* found that the real appeal of the book was to be found "in the small disasters that beset the hapless Mildred's path."

Further adventures are presented in *The Worst Witch Strikes Again,* in which Mildred is put in charge of a new girl, Enid, who gets up to even more mischief than Mildred while appearing quiet and demure. "The racy humour of the book is supported by vigorous drawings that lend personality to the characters in terms of gentle caricature," wrote Margery Fisher in a *Growing Point* review. Also reviewing the second title, *School Library Journal* contributor Susan Cain thought that while the story was lacking, Murphy's artwork was "numerous and humorous."

The third title in the series, *A Bad Spell for the Worst Witch,* finds Mildred in her second year at Miss Cackle's Academy for Witches, returning to Enid and Maud, her best friends. Things are not rosy back at the Academy, however, and soon Mildred gets on the wrong side of the teacher, Miss Hardbroom, once again. And then things get even worse after she is turned into a frog by her old nemesis, Ethel Hallow. Yet Mildred is able to once again turn adversity into victory, coming to the aid of a magician who has also been turned into a frog in this "beautifully cosy book," as Rodie Sudbery described it in *School Librarian.* A. Thatcher, writing in *Junior Bookshelf,* added further praise by calling the book "funny, very original, and fast-moving."

Mildred's 1993 outing, *The Worst Witch at Sea,* finds her and a party of second-year girls invited to the seaside home of Mr. Rowan-Webb, the magician whom she saved in *A Bad Spell for the Worst Witch.* Mildred, however, cannot make the trip without her beloved cat, Tabby, but she must figure out where to hide the feline at the magician's castle. Elaine E. Knight, writing in *School Library Journal,* found this a "pleasant, undemanding story," and additionally commended Murphy's "humorous, gently eerie black-and-white drawings." R. Baines, writing in *Junior Bookshelf,* also lauded Murphy's "lively" drawings. This popular series has inspired both a dramatized version, starring Diana Rigg, as well as a series on England's ITV that began in 1998.

Murphy has also proven herself adept at picture books, writing in several highly popular and critically acclaimed series. With her 1980 *Peace at Last,* she introduces the Bear family, in particular Papa Bear who is desperately trying to get away from all the noise that is keeping him awake at night. Mrs. Bear's snoring is the biggest enemy to his tranquility, and he tries to find a place where he will not hear it. Kristi L. Thomas, writing in *School Library Journal,* praised Murphy's text and especially her illustrations, describing them as "richly colored scenes glowing with inner lights." Elaine Moss, reviewing the picture book in the *Times Literary Supplement,* noted that Murphy's illustrations of the Bear family "are full of good old-fashioned domestic humour." And Zena Sutherland, writing in *Bulletin of the Center for Children's Books,* found the book to be "an engaging vignette of family life," while Frances Ball, in a *Books for Your Children* review, called the same title "beautifully simple, beautifully illustrated."

The Bears make a return in *Whatever Next!*, a book that focuses on the youngest member of the clan on his evening picnic trip to the moon in a cardboard rocket. After having adventures with an owl, he returns home, landing through the chimney, but when he tries to tell his mother about the wonderful trip, she does not listen. Instead she just puts him in the bath to wash away the soot. Fisher, writing in *Growing Point*, found this a "gentle tale, which reconciles domestic security and imagination." Tessa Rose Chester also commented on this theme of "the security of family life" in a *Times Educational Supplement* review, while *Booklist*'s Ilene Cooper focused on the artwork in her review of the American edition, *What Next, Baby Bear!*, praising the "charming full-page pictures in jewel-like colors."

Murphy introduces the Large family in the 1986 title, *Five Minutes' Peace*. In this first title about the elephant family, Mama Large is trying to get a few moments of quiet on her own, but her young children manage to ruin her every attempt. They climb into her bubble bath and then follow her back to the kitchen to see what she is up to. A critic for *Publishers Weekly* thought this book "is pure joy," and that "Murphy's frazzled mom will find a soft spot in every reader." M. Hobbs, writing in *Junior Bookshelf*, found this picture book "splendid," and Betsy Hearne, writing in *Bulletin of the Center for Children's Books*, claimed that the book would "appeal to young listeners; adults will love every minute of it." Reviewing the book in *School Librarian*, Graham Nutbrown drew attention to Murphy's "delightful, detailed, whole-page illustrations."

The misadventures of the Large family continue in *All in One Piece*, in which Granny comes to baby-sit while Mr. and Mrs. Large go to the office party together. Again Mrs. Large has trouble getting any time on her own in this "endearing picture book," as Marcus Crouch dubbed it in *Junior Bookshelf*. Judith Sherman of *Books for Keeps* praised Murphy's "winning formula" of making picture books that are as interesting to kids as they are to parents, and a reviewer for *Publishers Weekly* added to the chorus of approval by concluding that "this continuing saga of the beleaguered Mrs. Large and her boisterous offspring is still a delight."

With *A Piece of Cake*, Mrs. Large decides she is a tad too elephantine and puts herself as well as the entire family on a draconian diet which is spoiled by the arrival of a tempting cake from Granny. "Murphy's drawings are both delicate and droll," declared a reviewer for *Publishers Weekly*, who also felt that the message of liking and accepting yourself as you are "will strike a universal chord in readers." A critic for *Kirkus Reviews* also appreciated the "winsome good humor" of this book, while Virginia E. Jeschelnig, writing in *School Library Journal*, concluded, "This book won't win the battle of the bulge, and readers may enjoy it all the more for that reason."

The Large family also make a 1994 appearance in *A Quiet Night In*, a book that finds Mrs. Large attempting

Small monster Marlon fights all attempts to get him to give up his pacifier in **The Last Noo-Noo,** *written and illustrated by Murphy.*

to enjoy a quiet birthday for her husband at home with a romantic dinner. But once again, the children make things difficult, this time, however, quite innocently. They demand a reward for going to bed early, and the subsequent bedtime story leaves both parents exhausted, without dinner, and sleeping soundly on the sofa. Judy Constantinides, writing in *School Library Journal*, felt this tale was a "definite winner" and "not to be missed," while *Booklist*'s Mary Harris Veeder lauded Murphy's artwork which has the "same affectionate feel for children's daily lives as her text." Jo Goodman, reviewing the title in *Magpies*, noted that again Murphy has created a book "both for children and a therapeutic laugh for parents." And a contributor for *Publishers Weekly* praised the artwork for its "droll particulars," adding that such illustrations are "an ideal match for [Murphy's] cleverly understated text."

Murphy has also tried her hand at stand-alone novels for juvenile readers. In *Worlds Apart*, she presents an "exercise in adolescent wish-fulfillment," according to a contributor for *Publishers Weekly*. Twelve-year-old Susan Hunter lives with her mother Petunia just outside of London with little material wealth but also with very few real problems. Susan has, however, always been curious about the identity of her father; her mother will not talk about him. Finally, however, one day she manages to get some information out of her mother only to discover that her father is the famous actor Lloyd Hunter, who only recently returned to the London stage after making it big on American television. Susan manages to get into his dressing room, make contact, and even effect a reconciliation between him and her mother. In the end, they all move into a big house together, and she even gets her own dog, finally. The reviewer for *Publishers Weekly* further noted that "this is more fairy tale than novel." Bill Boyle, writing in the *School Librarian,* observed, however, that "this is not nearly so contrived in the development of the story," calling the novel a "well-written, highly relevant tale." *Booklist*'s Ilene Cooper similarly noted that the "happily-ever-after factor may be just the thing kids will like about the story."

Murphy's *Geoffrey Strangeways* features the tale of an eleven-year-old, fatherless boy in a medieval world who longs to be a knight. The only problem with this dream is that he is a commoner and that means there is no chance for him in the realm of knights. But Jeffrey keeps on dreaming and finally gets his chance when he rescues a real knight errant after trying to find work at Free Lance Rescue Services Ltd. A contributor for *Kirkus Reviews* found this tale, published as *Jeffrey Strangeways* in the United States, to be "throughly British" but also "entirely accessible." The same reviewer praised the text and dubbed the work "a witty, wonderfully entertaining spoof/adventure." Julie Corsaro, writing in *Booklist,* thought the book would be "a natural read-aloud for primary-grade children," and *School Library Journal* reviewer Michael Cart also praised the "cheerful anachronisms" in this "lightherarted tale." Similarly, in a review of *Geoffrey Strangeways,* Margaret Banerjee of *School Librarian* called this tale of a would-be knight errant "hilarious."

Murphy returns to the picture book format with two stories about Marlon, a crocodile-like little monster, in *The Last Noo-Noo* and *All for One.* In the first story, Marlon is still hooked on his noo-noo, his family's nickname for a pacifier. When his grandmother says it is time for him to get rid of these remnants of babyhood, his mother agrees and trashes all the noo-noos in the house. Or so she thinks. Marlon hides a stash of pacifiers and even plants one in the garden. Finally his monster friends talk Marlon into getting rid of his hidden noo-noos, but in the spring, a big surprise greets the family. Jill Bennett, reviewing this title in *School Librarian,* found it to be "a story which will have a monster appeal." A *Publishers Weekly* contributor noted that *The Last Noo-Noo* was "an appropriately light-hearted look at a situation that will hit close to home for many toddlers," while *Booklist*'s Stephanie Zvirin lauded Murphy's "precise illustrations" as well as "the dialogue and situation [which] are straight out of real life."

In the 2000 title, *All for One,* Marlon returns in "a heartfelt and ultimately triumphant tale about being excluded," according to a critic for *Kirkus Reviews.* When Marlon gets bored playing all on his own, he attempts to join in the games of the neighborhood kids. However, every time he tries to become part of their play, they change the game, leaving Marlon out. Finally Marlon decides to make his own game at his swimming pool, and the tables are quickly turned. It is Marlon who is in charge now when they all come around. This second monster tale was also met with approval by

critics. A contributor for *Publishers Weekly* dubbed it "a satisfying tale," while *Booklist*'s Cooper felt "Murphy gets the sentiments just right."

Over the years, reviewers have noted how Murphy has repeatedly gotten childhood sentiments and feelings "just right." Perhaps this may be more surprising in that she did not have her own child until the mid-1990s. But for Murphy, childhood is a realm which she still keeps alive inside of her. And for her, writing and drawing is also as natural as walking, as she once related to *SATA.* "I can't think of a more satisfying career and feel very fortunate that I am able to do it."

Biographical and Critical Sources

BOOKS

Children's Literature Review, Volume 39, Gale (Detroit, MI), 1996.

St. James Guide to Children's Writers, 5th edition, St. James Press (Detroit, MI), 1999.

PERIODICALS

Booklist, May 1, 1984, Ilene Cooper, review of *What Next, Baby Bear!,* p. 1252; December 1, 1987, Barbara Elleman, review of *All in One Piece,* p. 636; February 1, 1989, Ilene Cooper, review of *Worlds Apart,* pp. 940-941; June 15, 1992, Julie Corsaro, review of *Jeffrey Strangeways,* p. 1840; May 1, 1994, Mary Harris Veeder, review of *A Quiet Night In,* p. 1609; November 1, 1995, Stephanie Zvirin, review of *The Last Noo-Noo,* p. 478; October 1, 2002, Ilene Cooper, review of *All for One,* p. 337.

Books for Keeps, September, 1989, Judith Sherman, review of *All in One Piece,* p. 11.

Books for Your Children, spring, 1981, Frances Ball, review of *Peace at Last,* p. 10; summer, 1986, Margaret Carter, "Jill Murphy," p. 12; summer, 1990, S. Williams, review of *A Piece of Cake,* p. 7.

Bulletin of the Center for Children's Books, October, 1980, Zena Sutherland, review of *The Worst Witch,* p. 38; April, 1981, Zena Sutherland, review of *Peace at Last,* p. 157; January, 1987, Betsy Hearne, review of *Five Minutes' Peace,* p. 93; March, 1989, Zena Sutherland, review of *Worlds Apart,* p. 177; September, 1992, Kathryn Jennings, review of *Jeffrey Strangeways,* p. 20.

Growing Point, September, 1980, Margery Fisher, review of *The Worst Witch Strikes Again,* p. 3744; January, 1984, Margery Fisher, review of *Whatever Next!,* p. 4203.

Horn Book Guide, spring, 1999, Maeve Visser Knoth, review of *A Piece of Cake,* p. 38.

Junior Bookshelf, October, 1982, A. Thatcher, review of *A Bad Spell for the Worst Witch,* p. 192; October, 1982, p. 180; April, 1984, M. Hobbs, review of *Whatever Next!,* p. 62; December, 1986, M. Hobbs, review of *Five Minutes' Peace,* p. 220; February, 1988, Marcus

Crouch, review of *All in One Piece,* p. 24; February, 1991, Marcus Crouch, review of *Geoffrey Strangeways,* p. 36; February, 1994, R. Baines, review of *The Worst Witch at Sea,* p. 25.

Kirkus Reviews, December 1, 1988, review of *Worlds Apart,* pp. 1742-1743; December 1, 1989, review of *A Piece of Cake,* p. 1751; May 15, 1992, review of *Jeffrey Strangeways,* p. 673; June 15, 2002, review of *All for One,* pp. 885-886.

Los Angeles Times Book Review, June 13, 1982, p. 8.

Magpies, July, 1994, Jo Goodman, review of *A Quiet Night In,* p. 26.

New Statesman, December 3, 1982, p. 22.

Newsweek, December 1, 1980, p. 103.

New Yorker, December 1, 1980, pp. 103-104, 220; December 1, 1986, p. 123.

New York Times, December 28, 1986, p. 20; December 3, 1987.

New York Times Book Review, December 30, 1984, p. 19; December 28, 1986, p. 20.

Observer, December 7, 1980, p. 31.

Publishers Weekly, June 13, 1980, review of *The Worst Witch,* p. 73; October 17, 1980, review of *Peace at Last,* p. 65; August 22, 1986, review of *Five Minutes' Peace,* p. 92; August 14, 1987, review of *All in One Piece,* p. 101; December 9, 1988, review of *Worlds Apart,* p. 65; October 27, 1989, review of *A Piece of Cake,* p. 66; February 7, 1994, review of *A Quiet Night In,* pp. 86-87; October 9, 1995, review of *The Last Noo-Noo,* pp. 85-86; June 17, 2002, review of *All for One,* p. 67.

School Librarian, December, 1982, Rodie Sudbery, review of *A Bad Spell for the Worst Witch,* p. 343; February, 1987, Graham Nutbrown, review of *Five Minutes' Peace,* p. 36; February, 1989, Bill Boyle, review of *Worlds Apart,* p. 22; May, 1990, Angela Redfern, review of *A Piece of Cake,* p. 60; February, 1991, Margaret Banerjee, review of *Geoffrey Strangeways,* p. 24; February, 1996, Jill Bennett, review of *The Last Noo-Noo,* p. 16.

School Library Journal, September, 1980, Susan Cain, review of *The Worst Witch* and *The Worst Witch Strikes Again,* p. 62; December, 1980, Kristi L. Thomas, review of *Peace at Last,* p. 54; September, 1984, Judith Gloyer, review of *What Next, Baby Bear!,* pp. 107-108; January, 1988, p. 68; March, 1989, Trev Jones, review of *Worlds Apart,* p. 178; January, 1990, Virginia E. Jeschelnig, review of *A Piece of Cake,* pp. 86-87; May, 1992, Michael Cart, review of *Jeffrey Strangeways,* pp. 114, 116; May, 1994, Judy Constantinides, review of *A Quiet Night In,* pp. 100, 102; October, 1995, Elaine E. Knight, review of *The Worst Witch at Sea,* p. 138; January, 1996, Kathy Piehl, review of *The Last Noo-Noo,* p. 91.

Spectator, April 12, 1975, Leon Garfield, review of *The Worst Witch,* pp. 440-441.

Times (London, England), March 16, 1991.

Times Educational Supplement, December 19, 1980, Mary James, review of *Peace at Last,* p. 21; January 14, 1983, p. 34; January 13, 1984, Tessa Rose Chester, review of *Whatever Next!,* p. 44; November 2, 1984, p. 26; April 4, 1997, Victoria Neumark, review of *Worlds Apart,* p. 8.

Times Literary Supplement, November 21, 1980, p. 1328; March 27, 1981, Elaine Moss, review of *Peace at Last,* p. 342; September 17, 1982, p. 1003; November 20, 1987, Kate Flint, review of *All in One Piece,* p. 1284; June 9-15, 1989, Linda Taylor, review of *Worlds Apart,* p. 648.

Tribune Books (Chicago, IL), September 21, 1986, p. 9.

Voice Literary Supplement, December, 1989, p. 34.

Washington Post Book World, February 14, 1982, p. 12.

ONLINE

Young Writer, http://www.mystworld.com/youngwriter/ (March 25, 2003), "Issue 1: Jill Murphy."*

N

NEUBERGER, Julia (Babette Sarah) 1950-

Personal

Born February 27, 1950, in London, England; daughter of Walter Manfred (a civil servant) and Alice (an art critic; maiden name, Rosenthal) Schwab; married Anthony John Neuberger (an academic), September 17, 1973; children: Harriet Elinor Clare, Matthew Benedick Robert. *Education:* Newnham College, Cambridge, B.A. (with honors), 1973, M.A. (with honors), 1975; attended Leo Baeck College (London, England), Rabbinic diploma. *Politics:* Liberal Democrat. *Religion:* Jewish.

Addresses

Office—King's Fund, 11-13 Cavendish Sq., London W1G 0AN, England.

Career

Ordained rabbi, 1977; South London Liberal Synagogue, London, England, rabbi, 1977-89; Leo Baeck College, London, England, lecturer and associate fellow, 1979-97; Newnham College, Cambridge, Cambridge, England, associate fellow, 1983-96; King's Fund College, London, England, associate fellow, 1993-97; University of Ulster, Coleraine, Northern Ireland, chancellor, 1994-2000; King's Fund Institute (heath-care organization), London, England, chief executive, 1997—. Harvard Medical School, Boston, MA, visiting fellow, 1991-92. Has served as chair for numerous institutions and events, including the Rabbinic Conference, Union of Liberal and Progressive Synagogues, 1983-85, and Camden and Islington Community Health Sciences, National Health Service Trust, 1993-97. Trustee for numerous organizations, including the Imperial War Museum, 1999—.

Member

Royal Society of Arts (fellow), Patients Association (chair, 1988-91), Groucho Club.

Awards, Honors

Harkness fellow, Commonwealth Club of New York, 1991-92; recipient of eight honorary doctorates; honorary fellow, Mansfield College, Oxford, 1998.

Writings

Judaism (for children), Dinosaur, 1986, published as *The Story of the Jews,* illustrated by Chris and Hilary Evans, Cambridge University Press (New York, NY), 1986.

FOR ADULTS

Caring for Dying People of Different Faiths, Lisa Sainsbury Foundation (London, England), 1987.

(Editor) *Days of Decision,* four volumes, Macmillan (London, England), 1987.

Whatever's Happening to Women?: Promises, Practices, and Pay Offs, Kyle Cathie (London, England), 1991.

Liberating the Legacy: The Battles Women Still Have to Win, Kyle Cathie (London, England), 1991.

(Editor, with Canon John A. White) *A Necessary End: Attitudes to Death,* Macmillan (London, England), 1991.

(Editor) *The Things That Matter: An Anthology of Women's Spiritual Poetry,* Kyle Cathie (London, England), 1992, St. Martin's Press (New York, NY), 1995.

Ethics and Healthcare: The Role of Research Ethics Committees in the United Kingdom, King's Fund Institute (London, England), 1992.

On Being Jewish, Heinemann (London, England), 1996.

(With Stephen Webster) *The End or Merely the Beginning: The Place of Belief and Ideology in Later Life: Implications for Practice in Caring for Older People,* Counsel & Care (London, England), 1996.

Dying Well: A Guide to Enabling a Good Death, Hochland & Hochland (Cheshire, England), 1999.

(With Bill New) *Hidden Assets: Values and Decision-Making in the NHS,* King's Fund Institute (London, England), 2002.

Contributor to *Holy Show: Irish Artists and the Old Testament* (exhibition catalogue), Graphic Studio (Dublin, Ireland), 2002; contributor of articles and reviews to professional journals and newspapers.

Sidelights

Rabbi, writer, and educator Julia Neuberger is the chief executive of the King's Fund, the most well-known health-care think-tank in Great Britain. Known for her intellect and her commitment to the promotion of ethical care under Britain's National Health Care system, as well as for being the first female rabbi in the world to have her own congregation, Neuberger is also an editor and the author of a book for children that profiles her Jewish faith. *Judaism,* published in 1986 as *The Story of the Jews* and illustrated by Chris and Hilary Evans, focuses on the history and customs of the Jewish people. Neuberger also expands her discussion of what it means to be Jewish for an adult audience in her 1996 work *On Being Jewish,* which was praised as an "intelligent and reflective book" by London *Observer* contributor Anthony Julius.

In *The Things That Matter: An Anthology of Women's Spiritual Poetry,* Neuberger combines her spirituality with her equally strong feminist beliefs. A gathering of English and American poets who wrote from the eighteenth through the twentieth century, the volume includes the work of Charlotte Mew, H. D., Anne Morrow Lindbergh, and Stevie Smith among its sixty-seven contributors. Reviewing the collection for *Booklist,* Donna Seaman explained that Neuberger "compiled this volume . . . because she believes that women's spirituality and role in religion" have been largely ignored. While noting that most of the poems are conventional in rhyme and somewhat "outmoded" stylistically, *Library Journal* contributor Judy Clarence added that readers of *The Things That Matter* would nonetheless make "some wonderful discoveries."

Biographical and Critical Sources

PERIODICALS

Booklist, March 1, 1995, Donna Seaman, review of *The Things That Matter: An Anthology of Women's Spiritual Poetry,* p. 1175.
Library Journal, February 15, 1995, Judy Clarence, review of *The Things That Matter,* p. 159.
New Statesman, December 5, 1997, p. 30; June 24, 2002, p. 8.
Observer (London, England), October 13, 1996, Anthony Julius, review of *On Being Jewish,* p. 15.
School Librarian, February, 1987, p. 76.
Times Literary Supplement, February 2, 1996, Monica Furlong, review of *On Being Jewish,* p. 32.

ONLINE

King's Fund, http://194.66.253.160/ (May 18, 2003), brief biography of Julia Neuberger.*

NEWBERY, Linda 1952-

Personal

Born December 8, 1952, in London, England; married. *Hobbies and other interests:* "Reading, gardening, swimming, going to the cinema and theatre, and walking" in mountainous areas.

Addresses

Home—Northamptonshire, England. *Agent*—Maggie Noach, 22 Dorville Cr., London W6 0HJ, England. *E-mail*—L.newbery@btinternet.com.

Career

Worked as a teacher in an Oxfordshire comprehensive school until 2000. Writer and reviewer.

Awards, Honors

Writers' Guild Award nomination, for *The Wearing of the Green;* Carnegie Medal nomination, Birmingham Book Award shortlist, and Pick of the Year selection, Federation of Children's Book Groups, 1995, all for *The Shouting Wind;* Carnegie Medal nomination, for *From E to You; Guardian* Children's Fiction Prize shortlist, for *The Shell House.*

Writings

YOUNG ADULT NOVELS

Run with the Hare, Armada (London, England), 1988.
Hard and Fast, Armada (London, England), 1989.
Some Other War, Armada (London, England), 1990.
The Kind Ghosts, Lions (London, England), 1991.
The Wearing of the Green, Lions (London, England), 1992.
Riddle Me This, Lions (London, England), 1993.
The Shouting Wind, Collins (London, England), 1995.
The Cliff Path, Collins (London, England), 1995.
A Fear of Heights, Collins (London, England), 1996.
The Nowhere Girl, Adlib (London, England), 1997.
Flightsend, Scholastic (London, England), 1999.
(With Chris d'Lacey) *From E to You,* Scholastic (London, England), 2000.
The Damage Done, Scholastic (London, England), 2001.
No Way Back, Orchard (London, England), 2001.
Break Time, Orchard (London, England), 2001.
The Shell House, D. Fickling Book (Oxford, England, and New York, NY), 2002.
Windfall, Orchard (London, England), 2002.

FOR CHILDREN

The Marmalade Pony, Hippo (London, England), 1994, reprinted in *The Big Animal Magic Book,* Hippo (London, England), 1998.
Smoke Cat, illustrated by Anne Sharp, Hippo (London, England), 1995, reprinted in *The Big Animal Ghost Book,* Scholastic (London, England), 1999.

Linda Newbery

Ice Cat, illustrated by Peter Kavanaugh, Scholastic (London, England), 1997.
Whistling Jack, illustrated by Anthony Lewis, Collins (London, England), 1997.
Star's Turn, Corgi Pups (London, England), 1999.
The Cat with Two Names, Hippo (London, England), 2000.
Blitz Boys, A & C Black (London, England), 2000.
(Reteller) Hans Christian Andersen, *The Little Mermaid,* illustrated by Bee Willey, Scholastic (London, England), 2001.

OTHER

Contributor to short story and poetry anthologies.

Sidelights

Linda Newbery has been writing for British children and young adults since 1988, but her first book to be widely reviewed in the United States is 2002's *The Shell House,* an intertwining tale of two stories, both centered on Graveney Hall. In 1917, the time-setting for one of the stories, it was a beautiful English country home, but by the early twenty-first century, the setting for the other story, it is the burned-out shell of the title. Both stories center on a young man's quest for identity. Greg, at the center of the contemporary plot, is a seventeen-year-old student whose attraction to one of his fellow students, a beautiful young athlete named Jordan, has him confused. Greg meets Faith, a young Christian teenager, on the grounds of the burned-out estate, and the two challenge each other on spiritual matters. Greg eventually connects with Jordan, who is more comfortable with his homosexuality, and Greg reveals his sexual preferences to his parents. This story is intertwined with scenes from an earlier era, centered on Edmund, who is destined to inherit Graveney Hall. Edmund is a soldier in World War I when he meets Alex, another soldier, and falls in love. The feeling is mutual, and the two form a relationship that is ended with Alex's death on the battlefield. Edmund returns home to Graveney Hall utterly changed by the war, and his attempts to return to normality, by becoming engaged or seeking solace from the church vicar, end in disaster.

While Newbery was often praised for her sensitive yet evocative handling of the quest for sexual identity among young men past and present, a few aspects of the book were not universally admired. A contributor to *Publishers Weekly,* for example, dubbed Greg's story "a pitch perfect tale of contemporary teenage life," but faulted the parallel story of Edmund in 1917 as "overly dramatic if occasionally moving." For a contributor to *Kirkus Reviews,* on the other hand, "the parallel stories play off each other perfectly." And the occasionally awkward rendering of the issues at hand, especially faith in God and sexual orientation, are easily overlooked in relation to the book's overall accomplishment: "flaws aside, it stands as an ambitious, multilayered, and above all literary contribution to a literature that all too often seeks to dodge complexity," this reviewer concluded. *Booklist* reviewer Michelle Kaske offered a similar opinion of the book's two narratives, claiming "Woven together, the strands coalesce into a dramatic, if not complex, combination of both contemporary and historical fiction."

An earlier book, *From E to You,* coauthored by Chris d'Lacey, made a brief appearance in the United States. The book tells the story of the friendship that grows between Guy and Annabelle through their frequent e-mails. In the beginning, both teens closely guard their feelings, as they have been thrown together by their fathers, but as they gradually reveal painful events of the present and recent past, the two build trust in each other and the friendship blossoms. A contributor to *Publishers Weekly,* who noted that the male coauthor contributed the female character's missives while Newbery created the voice of the character Guy, concluded that the authors had "shaped two very distinct and likable characters and a cleverly composite tale."

Newbery told *SATA:* "When I started at secondary school, the strict headmistress took my form for a weekly lesson. One week, she asked us all what we wanted to be when we grew up. My answer, without hesitation, was: 'I want to be a writer, and have lots of cats.' Everyone laughed at this, and the headmistress looked rather disapproving. Not a real job, evidently.

"My writing was then kept secret. I spent hours in my bedroom filling exercise books with stories. In my twenties I switched to poetry and wrote a lot of it, all very bad. Some of it is still in my wardrobe, where it had better stay.

"Books for teenagers weren't around when I was a teenager, so I went through a Black Magic phase when I devoured Dennis Wheatley and scared myself silly, and on to A-Level English Literature. I didn't discover teenage fiction until I was in my twenties and training to be a teacher. As soon as I came across marvelous writers like Robert Cormier, Jill Paton Walsh, K. M. Peyton, and Aidan Cambers, the urge to write fiction returned.

"The first teenage novel I had published was *Run with the Hare,* based partly on my experiences in an animal rights group. Since then, I've written for younger children, but I keep returning to young adult fiction because I love the scope it offers. I always enjoy learning or doing something new while I write; besides a great deal of background reading, I've traveled for research purposes to Dublin, Normandy, Berlin, and the First World War battlefields in France and Belgium. My most exciting research activities so far have been boarding a wartime Lancaster bomber, negotiating Striding Edge and Jack's Rake in the Lake District, and jumping out of a Cessna aeroplane at two thousand feet.

"Apart from writing, I like to spend my time reading, gardening, swimming, going to the cinema and theatre, and walking, especially in mountainous places like Wales, the Lake District, and the West of Ireland. I live with my husband and three cats in Northamptonshire.

"I've worked as a secretary, riding instructor, counselor on a USA summer camp, and English teacher, gradually working part-time as I did more and more writing. It's taken a long time, but at last I'm a full-time writer with lots of cats. I wonder if my old headmistress would be interested?"

Biographical and Critical Sources

PERIODICALS

Booklist, August, 2002, Michelle Kaske, review of *The Shell House,* p. 1946.

Kirkus Reviews, July 1, 2002, review of *The Shell House,* p. 960.

Publishers Weekly, June 25, 2001, review of *From E to You,* p. 73; June 24, 2002, review of *The Shell House,* p. 59.

School Librarian, summer, 2001, Chris Brown, review of *The Cat with Two Names,* p. 90.

School Library Journal, August, 2002, Joanne K. Cecere, review of *The Shell House,* p. 196.

ONLINE

ACHUKA, http://www.achuka.com/ (May 16, 2003), interview with Linda Newbery.

Guardian Unlimited, http://books.guardian.co.uk/ September 28, 2002, Jan Mark, review of *The Shell House,* (January 7, 2003).

Linda Newbery Web site, http://www.btinternet.com/~L. Newbery/ (May 16, 2003).

* * *

NIEUWSMA, Milton J(ohn) 1941-

Personal

Born September 5, 1941, in Sioux Falls, SD; son of John (a minister) and Jeanne (a teacher) Nieuwsma; married Marilee (a teacher), February 1, 1964; children: Jonathan, Gregory, Elizabeth. *Ethnicity:* "Dutch/German." *Education:* Hope College, B.A., 1963; University of Illinois—Springfield, M.A., 1978. *Politics:* Independent. *Religion:* Protestant.

Addresses

Agent—Jeff Herman Agency, 332 Bleecker St., New York, NY 10014. *E-mail*—mnieuwsma@macatawa.com.

Career

Contributing editor to the *Chicago Tribune* and the *Los Angeles Times,* 1978-98; TransAmerican Syndicate, Chicago, IL, president, 1988-97. Visiting professor, Rutgers University, 1992-96, St. Xavier University, 1996-97. Has worked as a consultant to the Amicus Group, and president of the Idlewood Beach Association; a former governor of the Chicago Zoological Society, and a chair of the Riverside United Fun Campaign.

Member

Society of Midland Authors.

Awards, Honors

Best Books for Teen Age selection, New York Public Library, 1999, and Top Ten Books about the Holocaust selection, Institute of Higher European Studies (The Hague, Netherlands), 2001, both for *Kinderlager: An Oral History of Young Holocaust Survivors.*

Writings

(Editor) *Kinderlager: An Oral History of Young Holocaust Survivors,* Holiday House (New York, NY), 1998.

Also author of *Our America,* a documentary film for television, airing on WTVS-TV (a Public Broadcasting System affiliate in Detroit, MI), 1968, and *Thomas Jefferson: The Reluctant Rebel,* 1978. Author of hundreds of feature articles published in newspapers.

Work in Progress

Children of the Shoah, a documentary for WGVU-TV (a Public Broadcasting System affiliate in Grand Rapids, MI).

Milton J. Nieuwsma

Sidelights

Milton J. Nieuwsma is an editor whose book *Kinderlager: An Oral History of Young Holocaust Survivors* brings to light the experience of three young Polish girls who survived deportation to the Auschwitz death camp during World War II. An oral history, *Kinderlager* features each woman retelling her own story as a child in the camp in her own voice. Tova Friedman, aged five when she was shipped to Auschwitz, Frieda Tennenbaum, aged nine, and Rachel Hyams, aged six, were all from the same small Polish town. Each experienced an initial move to a Jewish ghetto with their families before their final deportation to the camp, where they eventually met again in the Kinderlager, as the children's portion of Auschwitz was called. In each of the narratives, the women recall the efforts of their mothers to save them from the gas chambers. Nieuwsma frames the accounts with a prologue and epilogue, but otherwise does not intercede between the narrators and the reader. "Indeed, the lucid narrative style is that of memory itself," commented Serena J. Leigh in *Voice of Youth Advocates,* continuing, "the three 'books' seem like collections of snapshots."

These children were some of the youngest survivors of Hitler's plan to erase the Jews from the planet, and as the older generation of survivors begins to pass away, "this account . . . comes as a powerful witness to the

Holocaust," remarked a contributor to the *Horn Book.* Their narratives overlap once they reach the camps and reunite, but otherwise, the stories are both individualized and representative, commentators noted. Each concludes with an account of the postwar years, first in displaced persons camps, searching for lost relatives and friends, and later, emigrating, but never leaving behind the memory of the atrocities they witnessed or its toll on their hearts and minds. "Nieuwsma . . . has done an impressive job of capturing their voices and presenting coherent accounts of their experiences," claimed a reviewer in *Publishers Weekly.* However, this reviewer did fault the author for failing to provide a more complete context for the narrator's stories. While Betsy Hearne, a contributor to *Bulletin of the Center for Children's Books,* found that the journalistic style of the narrator's accounts prevented audiences from becoming emotionally involved with them, "nevertheless, this collective narrative will contribute to a young reader's understanding the weight of systematic destruction of children younger than themselves during the Holocaust," Hearne concluded.

Biographical and Critical Sources

PERIODICALS

Booklist, November 1, 1998, Hazel Rochman, review of *Kinderlager: An Oral History of Young Holocaust Survivors,* p. 480.
Bulletin of the Center for Children's Books, January, 1999, Betsy Hearne, review of *Kinderlager,* p. 177.
Horn Book, January, 1999, review of *Kinderlager,* p. 83.
Publishers Weekly, November 23, 1998, review of *Kinderlager,* p. 68.
School Library Journal, December, 1998, Yapha Nussbaum Mason, review of *Kinderlager,* p. 141.
Voice of Youth Advocates, Serena J. Leigh, review of *Kinderlager,* p. 381.

*   *   *

NUMEROFF, Laura Joffe 1953-

Personal

Born July 14, 1953, in Brooklyn, NY; daughter of William (an artist) and Florence (a teacher; maiden name, Joffe) Numeroff. *Education:* Pratt Institute, B.F.A. (with honors), 1975; attended Parsons College, 1975. *Religion:* Jewish. *Hobbies and other interests:* Collecting children's books, watching movies.

Addresses

Home—San Francisco, CA. *Agent*—c/o Author Mail, HarperCollins, 10 East 53rd St., New York, NY 10022.

Career

Author and illustrator of children's books. Lecturer at schools in California; has worked at jobs including running a merry-go-round and doing private investigation.

Laura Joffe Numeroff

Awards, Honors

California Young Reader Award, Colorado Children's Book Award, and Georgia Children's Picture Storybook award, all 1988, and Buckeye Medal, 1989, all for *If You Give a Mouse a Cookie;* Parents' Choice Award, 1991, for *If You Give a Moose a Muffin.*

Writings

If You Give a Mouse a Cookie, illustrated by Felicia Bond, Harper (New York, NY), 1985.

If You Give a Moose a Muffin, illustrated by Felicia Bond, HarperCollins (New York, NY), 1991.

Dogs Don't Wear Sneakers, illustrated by Joseph Mathieu, Simon & Schuster (New York, NY), 1993.

Why a Disguise?, illustrated by David McPhail, Simon & Schuster (New York, NY), 1994.

Chimps Don't Wear Glasses, illustrated by Joseph Mathieu, Simon & Schuster (New York, NY), 1995.

Mouse Cookies: Ten Easy-to-Make Cookie Recipes, illustrated by Felicia Bond, HarperCollins (New York, NY), 1995.

(With Barney Saltzberg) *Two for Stew,* illustrated by Sal Murdocca, Simon & Schuster (New York, NY), 1996.

The Chicken Sisters, illustrated by Sharleen Collicott, HarperCollins (New York, NY), 1997.

What Mommies Do Best/What Daddies Do Best, illustrated by Lynn Munsinger, Simon & Schuster (New York, NY), 1998, published separately as *What Daddies Do Best,* Simon & Schuster (New York, NY), 2001, and *What Mommies Do Best,* Simon & Schuster (New York, NY), 2002.

Monster Munchies, illustrated by Nate Evans, Random House (New York, NY), 1998.

If You Give a Pig a Pancake, illustrated by Felicia Bond, Laura Geringer Books (New York, NY), 1998.

Sometimes I Wonder If Poodles Like Noodles, illustrated by Tim Bowers, Simon & Schuster (New York, NY), 1999.

The Best Mouse Cookie, illustrated by Felicia Bond, Laura Geringer Books (New York, NY), 1999.

(With Wendy S. Harpham) *The Hope Tree: Kids Talk about Breast Cancer,* illustrated by David McPhail, Simon & Schuster (New York, NY), 1999.

If You Take a Mouse to the Movies, illustrated by Felicia Bond, Laura Geringer Books (New York, NY), 2000.

What Grandmas Do Best/What Grandpas Do Best, illustrated by Lynn Munsinger, Simon & Schuster (New York, NY), 2000, published separately as *What Grandmas Do Best* and *What Grandpas Do Best,* Simon & Schuster (New York, NY), 2001.

If You Take a Mouse to School, illustrated by Felicia Bond, Laura Geringer Books (New York, NY), 2002.

If You Give an Author a Pencil (autobiography), photographs by Sherry Shahan, Richard C. Owen Publishers (Katonah, NY), 2002.

Laura Numeroff's Ten-Step Guide to Living with Your Monster, illustrated by Nate Evans, Laura Geringer Books (New York, NY), 2002.

What Sisters Do Best/What Brothers Do Best, illustrated by Lynn Munsinger, Simon & Schuster (New York, NY), 2003.

(With Nate Evans) *Sherman Crunchley,* illustrated by Tim Bowers, Dutton (New York, NY), 2003.

If You Give a Pig a Party, illustrated by Felicia Bond, Laura Geringer Books (New York, NY), in press.

SELF-ILLUSTRATED

Amy for Short, Macmillan (New York, NY), 1976.

Phoebe Dexter Has Harriet Peterson's Sniffles, Greenwillow (New York, NY), 1977.

Walter, Macmillan (New York, NY), 1978.

(With Alice Richter) *Emily's Bunch,* Macmillan (New York, NY), 1978.

(With Alice Richter) *You Can't Put Braces on Spaces,* Greenwillow (New York, NY), 1979.

The Ugliest Sweater, F. Watts (New York, NY), 1980.

Doesn't Grandma Have an Elmo Elephant Jungle Kit?, Greenwillow (New York, NY), 1980.

Beatrice Doesn't Want To, F. Watts (New York, NY), 1981, revised edition, illustrated by Lynn Munsinger, Candlewick Press (Cambridge, MA), 2004.

Digger, Dutton (New York, NY), 1983.

OTHER

Many of Numeroff's works have been translated into other languages, including Spanish, Hebrew, French, Korean, Afrikaans, Italian, Japanese, and German.

Adaptations

You Can't Put Braces on Spaces and *The Ugliest Sweater* have been made into educational filmstrips by Westport Communications Group; *If You Give a Mouse a Cookie* has been adapted into an interactive CD-ROM book, HarperCollins, 1995, and has been recorded as an audiotape cassette. Many of Numeroff's other books have been recorded on audiocassette, including *If You Give a Moose a Muffin,* HarperAudio, 1997, *If You Give a Pig a Pancake,* HarperAudio, 1999, *The Chicken Sisters,* Live Oak Media, 2002, and *If You Take a Mouse to School,* Laura Geringer Books, 2003.

Work in Progress

Picture books, including *Camp Pooch-a-Mooch, What Aunts Do Best/What Uncles Do Best,* and *What Puppies Do Best/What Kittens Do Best.*

Sidelights

Author and illustrator Laura Joffe Numeroff has created numerous humorous—if not downright goofy—picture books, playing with language and twisting tongues with her playful rhymes and syncopated rhythms, and pleasing eyes with her bright and bold artwork. The success of her 1985 children's story *If You Give a Mouse a Cookie* has made Numeroff well-known among the read-aloud set, a popularity that has increased with the related titles *If You Give a Moose a Muffin, If You Give a Pig a Pancake, If You Take a Mouse to the Movies, If You Take a Mouse to School,* and *If You Give a Pig a Party.* With a wry humor that has become characteristic of her writing for children, Numeroff depicts the relationship between a helpful young boy and a demanding young mouse in an engaging, lyrical manner. Her stories about spunky female characters and unusual childhood situations continue to engage nonsense lovers of all ages.

"I grew up in a world of books, music, and art," Numeroff once told *SATA.* "I was a voracious reader and read six books every week." Favorite books included those by Beverly Cleary, Marguerite Henry, the "Dr. Doolittle" series of animal books, *Eloise* by Kay Thompson and illustrated by Hilary Knight, *Stuart Little* by E. B. White and illustrated by Garth Williams, and *The Cat in the Hat* by Dr. Seuss. "I've also been drawing pictures since I was old enough to hold a crayon, and writing came soon after. Doing children's books combines the two things I love the most." The youngest of three daughters, Numeroff was encouraged in her reading and artwork by her father, a staff member of New York's *World Telegram and Sun,* as well as her mother, a junior high school economics teacher. As Numeroff noted on her author's Web site, she started writing her own stories and drawing pictures to go along with them at an early age. "I would make a book cover for them and write down the name of a publisher." At age fifteen, Numeroff had a short change of heart regarding her career plans. She decided to follow in the footsteps of her older sister Emily, who was a fashion designer. "I thought that sounded like a great job," she remarked on her author Web site. Thus she applied to and was accepted by New York's Pratt Institute but disliked everything about the fashion department. "I couldn't sew to save my life," she lamented on her Web

In her two-in-one picture book, Numeroff pays tribute to the special qualities of grandparents. (From What Grandmas Do Best/What Grandpas Do Best, *illustrated by Lynn Munsinger.)*

site. Instead, she decided to take only classes that appealed to her, and one of these was a class taught by Barbara Bottner called "Writing and Illustrating for Children's Books." Her first book, *Amy for Short,* was one of her homework assignments.

With illustrations by the author, *Amy for Short* describes the friendship between Mark and Amy, who are brought together because they stand out from the rest of their classmates due to their height. As the tallest kid in the class, Amy is destined to have the coveted role of a tree in her school play and act the part of Abraham Lincoln in a summer camp performance. When Amy suddenly shoots past Mark in stature, she worries that he will no longer be her pal, but he proves his friendship by bowing out of the most important Little League game of the year to show up at her birthday party.

Emily's Bunch introduces readers to a determined young girl who wants to find the most original Halloween costume ever to wear to the annual Halloween party. She remains undaunted by her older brother's insistence that one person cannot appear in costume as a bunch of grapes. When her friends arrive at the Halloween party and gather around her, each with purple sacks over their heads, Emily proves her cleverness.

A brother and sister who butt heads is again the focus of *Beatrice Doesn't Want To.* When Henry has to take his stubborn little sister to the library while he does his homework, she makes studying impossible until he drags her into the children's room where a story hour is in progress. Resistant at first, she soon becomes caught up in the magic of reading. By the end of Numeroff's humorous easy reader, stubborn Beatrice has to be dragged out of the library through the same door she did not want to enter in the first place.

1983's *Digger* provides a new twist to the story of a child who wants a pet. Described by a *Kirkus Reviews* critic as "agreeably off-track without being all that far-fetched," the story features a young boy who tries to help his dad find a solution to the man's wish for a pet. Their landlord will not allow animals though, and a book of dog pictures just cannot replace Digger, the dog Daddy had when he was a boy. Fortunately for father and son, the pro-pet policy of a new landlady affords the answer to their dilemma.

If You Give a Mouse a Cookie was Numeroff's break-through title and has become a childhood favorite, appearing in an interactive CD-ROM version and in several book editions since it was first published in 1985. A "what if" story about an insistent young mouse and the increasingly bewildered young boy who tries to help him out, Numeroff's tale lets its readers follow the chain of numerous activities, until they leave the polite young protagonist fast asleep. "If you give a mouse a cookie, he's going to ask for a glass of milk," the tale begins, winding its way to a close with lighthearted humor. "The similarities between mouse and child won't be lost on observant youngsters," noted a *Booklist* reviewer. *If You Give a Moose a Muffin* provided a humorous sequel, as "the complexities that can follow a simple act of kindness are played out with the same rampant silliness," according to a reviewer in *Publishers Weekly*. From jam to go on top, to more muffins, to a trip to the store, the demands of a moose on the loose add an even greater element of absurdity to Numeroff's circular plot.

Numeroff has continued to provide youngsters with stories that showcase her wacky inventiveness. In *Dogs Don't Wear Sneakers*, as well as its sequel, *Chimps Don't Wear Glasses*, the title gives readers a hint of what is to come, as the book serves up a full plate of nonsense rhymes. "Dogs don't wear sneakers/And pigs don't wear hats/And dresses look silly/On Siamese cats," the poem goes, while illustrations by Joseph Mathieu show exactly the opposite: dapper hounds and lavishly costumed cats and pigs add to the general lunacy. A *Kirkus Reviews* critic deemed that the "deliciously silly text" of *Dogs Don't Wear Sneakers* is presented in "a spirited, comical style."

The 1996 publication, *Two for Stew,* features a matronly woman who simply will not believe her waiter at Chez Nous when he claims the restaurant is out of its specialty, stew. The story is told through a conversation between the woman and the waiter; a critic in *Publishers Weekly* applauded the "lilting stanzas" created by Numeroff and coauthor Barney Saltzberg, calling the work a "giddy and sometimes campy salute to stew." Betty Teague, writing in *School Library Journal*, also had praise for this title, commenting favorably on the "toe-tapping rhythm . . . of this lilting text," and further claiming that the book "has all the trappings of a Broadway musical."

With the 1997 *The Chicken Sisters*, Numeroff presents a "loony story [that] gently pokes fun at three eccentric sisters," as a reviewer for *Publishers Weekly* remarked. In this case the siblings are also chickens, all of whom have somewhat bothersome hobbies. One bakes terrible sweets; another sings off-tune; and the third knits everything with pom-poms. While such hobbies do not bother the sisters, they are a plague to the neighbors, until one day a wolf moves into the neighborhood and the sisters are able to use these skills to a new advantage. The same *Publishers Weekly* contributor called this book "off-the-wall fun," while *Booklist*'s Ilene Cooper found it to be "a snappy story in every way." Jane Marino, writing in *School Library Journal,* also had praise for this title, dubbing it "a winner sure to please at story time."

Numeroff returns to the what-if formula of *If You Give a Mouse a Cookie* in *If You Give a Pig a Pancake.* The sweet little pig would, of course, need syrup, which in turn would make her all sticky. Then she would need to clean up. And with this little piggy there is more: she tap dances, sends photos to all of her friends, builds a treehouse, and then asks for more pancakes. Critics responded warmly to this title, with a contributor for *Publishers Weekly* noting that "if you give a child this book, chances are, they'll devour it eagerly." Shirley Lewis, writing in *Teacher Librarian,* called it a "charmer," and a critic for *Kirkus Reviews* lauded "the funny, clever formula [that] creates just the right amount of anticipation." Diane Janoff concluded in *School Library Journal,* "The humor and quick pace of Numeroff's engaging narrative make this book an excellent choice for reading aloud."

More of the same kind of silliness appears in *If You Take a Mouse to the Movies* and *If You Take a Mouse to School,* both again illustrated by Felicia Bond and featuring the same mouse from *If You Give a Mouse a Cookie.* In *If You Take a Mouse to the Movies,* the little mouse wishes to go the movies along with the patient little boy from the first title. But at the movies the popcorn reminds him of stringing the white stuff to put on the Christmas tree, and then on to other thoughts about the Christmas season, including snowmen and caroling, and then back to the movies again. Once again, fans and critics were pleased with the result. A critic writing in *Publishers Weekly* commended Numeroff's "playful what-if scenario," and *Booklist*'s Gillian Engberg similarly lauded this "lively cause-and-effect romp," further noting that it was "a charmer that's sure to get plenty of circulation." Janice M. DelNegro, reviewing the title in *Bulletin of the Center for Children's Books,* remarked on Numeroff's "understated humor [that] is reinforced by the cumulative effect of the events." And a reviewer for *School Library Journal* summed up the book by calling it a "wonderfully silly story." Mouse and boy make a further return in the 2002 *If You Take a Mouse to School,* "a rollicking romp," according to a contributor for *Publishers Weekly.* In this instance, mouse asks for his own lunchbox, a snack, a notebook, and pencils—and all this before he even hops into the little boy's backpack and sets off for school. At school, the mouse runs around from activity to activity, spelling out words on the blackboard, building a tiny house with building blocks, and making mouse-sized furniture from clay. The same reviewer form *Publishers Weekly* called this title a "winner." A critic for *Kirkus Reviews* was also pleasantly amused, dubbing the book "a giggle-fest," and Maryann H. Owen, reviewing the book in *School Library Journal,* felt it was "a lively experience for mouse and boy."

Numeroff explores family roles in *What Mommies Do Best/What Daddies Do Best,* and in a sequel, *What Grandmas Do Best/What Grandpas Do Best. Booklist*'s Stephanie Zvirin called the former title a "sweet picture book," and one that works against stereotypes. Animal mothers and fathers are featured in the book, with the mother's activities—reading to the children or playing ball in the park—told with the book right side up; the father's activities, exactly the same as the mother's, are told with the book held upside down. Zvirin also described the book as "soothing . . . [and] comforting." Writing in the *New York Times Book Review,* Scott Veale found the same book to be a "lighthearted catalogue" of activities, while Susan Hepler wrote in *School Library Journal* that the book was a "perfect cuddly bedtime or storytime read-aloud." Numeroff's sequel, *What Grandmas Do Best/What Grandpas Do Best,* is a "charming flip-flop book," according to a critic for *Kirkus Reviews.* Once again Numeroff proves that what each does best is the same as the other, just that they do the activities in different ways. Catherine T. Quattlebaum, reviewing the companion book in *School Library Journal,* felt it was "wonderful for quiet lap-sit storytimes," as well as a "charming introduction to the special times shared with grandparents."

Dealing with a more serious topic, *The Hope Tree: Kids Talk about Breast Cancer* attempts to instruct and comfort children about what happens when their mother has cancer. Employing cuddly animal characters, Numeroff uses a fictional support group of kids talking about their mothers' breast cancer to discuss issues many families face while fighting the illness. Mary R. Hoffman, writing in *School Library Journal,* felt that this title was "a comforting picture book." Similarly, a contributor for *Publishers Weekly* called it "a comforting and compassionate volume."

Numeroff returns to sillier territory with the picture books *Sometimes I Wonder If Poodles Like Noodles* and *Laura Numeroff's Ten-Step Guide to Living with Your Monster,* both of which celebrate the world of pets. The former title presents twenty-one simple rhyming poems told from a girl's point of view, all with a "light, playful tone," according to a reviewer for *Horn Book Guide. Numeroff's Ten-Step Guide* is a tongue-in-cheek affirmation of the dos and don'ts of pet raising, albeit in the guise of training a monster. John Sigwald of *School Library Journal* found this to be a "silly picture book," and a reviewer for *Publishers Weekly* thought it was a "comically outlandish outline to the parameters of monster (a.k.a. pet) ownership."

As well as possessing an offbeat sense of humor, Numeroff has always been an avid reader. She once told *SATA,* "I prefer biographies, nonfiction, and stories dealing with 'real-life' dramas—never did like fairy tales all that much. I guess that's why my children's stories tend to be based on things kids actually go through, like wearing braces, being too tall for your age, being a daydreamer, having to wear something your grandmother gave you even though you think it's hideous. The best reviews come from kids who write me—that makes it all worth it!"

Numeroff collects children's books and can usually be found in the library or bookstore. "My work is my life," she once commented to *SATA.* "I can draw no distinction between the words 'work' and 'spare time.' I love what I'm doing and the only time it becomes work is when there's re-writing." While she plans to attempt screenplays and adult fiction, "I'll always have a first love for children's books. I hope to be writing until my last days."

Biographical and Critical Sources

BOOKS

Numeroff, Laura Joffe, *If You Give a Mouse a Cookie,* Harper (New York, NY), 1985.
Numeroff, Laura Joffe, *Dogs Don't Wear Sneakers,* Simon & Schuster (New York, NY), 1993.

PERIODICALS

Booklist, June 1, 1985, review of *If You Give a Mouse a Cookie,* p. 1404; May 1, 1997, Ilene Cooper, review of *The Chicken Sisters,* p. 1497; April, 1998, Stephanie Zvirin, review of *What Mommies Do Best/What Daddies Do Best,* p. 1333; May 15, 1998, Carolyn Phelan, review of *If You Give a Pig a Pancake,* p. 1633; November 15, 2000, Hazel Rochman, review of *What Grandmas Do Best/What Grandpas Do Best,* p. 649; December 1, 2000, Gillian Engberg, review of *If You Take a Mouse to the Movies,* p. 722.
Bulletin of the Center for Children's Books, June, 1978, p. 165; January, 1979, p. 85; January, 1982; September, 1991, p. 17; December, 2000, Janice M. DelNegro, review of *If You Take a Mouse to the Movies,* p. 157.
Horn Book Guide, spring, 1997, review of *Two for Stew,* p. 41; fall, 1998, review of *If You Give a Pig a Pancake,* p. 302; spring, 1999, review of *What Mommies Do Best/What Daddies Do Best,* p. 15, and review of *Monster Munchies,* p. 51; fall, 1999, review of *Sometimes I Wonder If Poodles Like Noodles,* p. 375.
Kirkus Reviews, February 15, 1983, review of *Digger,* p. 182; July 1, 1993, review of *Dogs Don't Wear Sneakers,* p. 864; August 1, 1995, review of *Chimps Don't Wear Glasses,* p. 1115; May 1, 1998, review of *If You Give a Pig a Pancake,* p. 663; September 1,

2000, review of *What Grandmas Do Best/What Grandpas Do Best,* p. 1288; June 15, 2002, review of *If You Take a Mouse to School,* p. 886.

New York Times Book Review, May 17, 1998, Scott Veale, review of *What Mommies Do Best/What Daddies Do Best,* p. 31.

Publishers Weekly, September 18, 1978, p. 167; June 28, 1991, review of *If You Give a Moose a Muffin,* p. 100; August 30, 1993, p. 94; July 29, 1996, review of *Two for Stew,* p. 87; April 7, 1997, review of *The Chicken Sisters,* p. 90; March 16, 1998, review of *If You Give a Pig a Pancake,* p. 62; November 9, 1998, review of *Chimps Don't Wear Glasses,* p. 80; June 14, 1999, review of *Sometimes I Wonder If Poodles Like Noodles,* p. 69; August 21, 2000, review of *What Grandmas Do Best/What Grandpas Do Best,* p. 72; September 25, 2000, review of *If You Take a Mouse to the Movies,* p. 69; October 15, 2001, review of *What Grandmas Do Best* and *What Grandpas Do Best,* p. 73; December 10, 2001, review of *The Hope Tree: Kids Talk about Breast Cancer,* p. 73; February 25, 2002, review of *Laura Numeroff's Ten-Step Guide to Living with Your Monster,* p. 65; June 24, 2002, review of *If You Take a Mouse to School,* pp. 54-55.

School Library Journal, December, 1978, p. 45; May, 1983, p. 65; May, 1985, p. 80; January, 1994, p. 96; December, 1996, Betty Teague, review of *Two for Stew,* pp. 102-103; May, 1997, Jane Marino, review of *The Chicken Sisters,* p. 109; April, 1998, Susan Hepler, review of *What Mommies Do Best/What Daddies Do Best,* p. 106; July, 1998, Diane Janoff, review of *If You Give a Pig a Pancake,* p. 81; May, 1999, Nina Lindsay, review of *Sometimes I Wonder If Poodles Like Noodles,* p. 111; October, 2000, review of *If You Take a Mouse to the Movies,* p. 62, and Catherine T. Quattlebaum, review of *What Grandmas Do Best/ What Grandpas Do Best,* p. 132; October, 2001, Mary R. Hoffman, review of *The Hope Tree,* p. 127; June, 2002, John Sigwald, review of *Laura Numeroff's Ten-Step Guide to Living with Your Monster,* p. 106; September, 2002, Maryann H. Owen, review of *If You Take a Mouse to School,* p. 202.

Teacher Librarian, September, 1998, Shirley Lewis, review of *If You Give a Pig a Pancake,* p. 47.

ONLINE

Laura Numeroff's Web Site, http://www.lauranumeroff.com/ (March 17, 2003).*

P

PARKER, Toni Trent 1947-

Personal
Born July 10, 1947, in Winston-Salem, NC; daughter of William J., Jr. (an executive director of the United Negro College Fund) and Viola Scales (a homemaker) Trent; married Barrington D. Parker, Jr. (a federal judge); children: Christine, Kathleen, Jennifer. *Education:* Oberlin College, B.A., 1970; attended University of California—Berkeley, graduate studies in African-American history. *Hobbies and other interests:* Gardening.

Addresses
Office—Black Books Galore!, 65 High Ridge Rd., Stamford, CT 06905. *E-mail*—TParker275@aol.com.

Career
Writer. Black Books Galore!, Stamford, CT, cofounder, 1993—. Publisher of *Blackberry Express,* a quarterly newsletter about African-American children's books. Formerly worked for an education fund in New York, NY.

Awards, Honors
Parenting Leaders Award, *Parents* magazine, 1998; National Association for the Advancement of Colored People Image Award nominee (children's literature category), for *Black Books Galore! Guide to Great African American Children's Books.*

Writings

FOR CHILDREN

Hugs and Hearts, illustrated with photographs by Earl Anderson, Scholastic (New York, NY), 2002.

Toni Trent Parker

Painted Eggs and Chocolate Bunnies, illustrated with photographs by Earl Anderson, Scholastic (New York, NY), 2002.

Sweets and Treats, illustrated with photographs by Earl Anderson, Scholastic (New York, NY), 2002.

Snowflake Kisses and Gingerbread Smiles, illustrated with photographs by Earl Anderson, Scholastic (New York, NY), 2002.

Being Me: A Keepsake Scrapbook for African American Girls, illustrated by Meryl Treatner, Scholastic (New York, NY), 2002.

OTHER

(Compiler) *Annotated Bibliography of Books, Reports, and Papers Published, Written, or Sponsored by the Phelps-Stokes Fund,* Phelps-Stokes Fund (New York, NY), 1976.

(With Donna Rand and Sheila Foster) *Black Books Galore! Guide to Great African American Children's Books,* John Wiley & Sons (New York, NY), 1998.

(With Donna Rand) *Black Books Galore! Guide to Great African American Children's Books about Boys,* John Wiley & Sons (New York, NY), 2001.

(With Donna Rand) *Black Books Galore! Guide to Great African American Children's Books about Girls,* John Wiley & Sons (New York, NY), 2001.

(With Donna Rand) *Black Books Galore! Guide to More Great African American Children's Books,* John Wiley & Sons (New York, NY), 2001.

Sidelights

Toni Trent Parker and her coauthors have provided an invaluable service, according to critics, to parents, teachers, and librarians in preparing a series of reference books listing, describing, and recommending books for children about prominent African Americans. Beginning with *Black Books Galore! Guide to Great African American Children's Books,* and continuing with *Black Books Galore! Guide to Great African American Children's Books about Boys* and *Black Books Galore! Guide to Great African American Children's Books about Girls*, Parker and two women she met in a children's play group put together the materials they had gathered for their own benefit when seeking out children's books about notable African Americans. In their introduction to these volumes, the authors stipulate that they are not children's literature experts or librarians but concerned parents looking to help others fill a gap they themselves had felt as parents. The response from reviewers, however, has emphasized the utility of these volumes for those who work with, as well as live with, children. "Their choices and comments seem quite well made, and 'professionals' as well as parents should find the book quite helpful," remarked Phyllis Holman Weisbard in a review of *Black Books Galore! Guide to Great African American Children's Books about Girls* published in *Feminist Collections*.

The volumes present lists of recommended titles divided by age-level of audience; a listing by subject matter is included in an index at the back. Each entry includes relevant bibliographic information as well as a description of the book; these are "lively and informative," according to *Booklist* contributor Hazel Rochman in a review of *Black Books Galore! Guide to Great African American Children's Books about Girls.* Sprinkled throughout the volumes are helpful bits of information about specific titles. Quotes from books, book covers, anecdotes from authors and illustrators, and first-person recommendations round out the additional offerings in these volumes. In a review of the two-volume set, which separates books for boys and girls, "the authors . . .

have compiled two fantastic new resources for children, young adults, parents and educators," wrote Khafre K. Abif in *Black Issues Book Review.*

Sensing another gap in literature for youngsters, Parker set about writing a series of picture books for toddlers featuring African-American children. Illustrated with photographs by Earl Anderson and narrated with simply-worded lyrics, *Painted Eggs and Chocolate Bunnies* (about Easter), *Hugs and Hearts* (about Valentine's Day), *Sweets and Treats* (about Halloween), and *Snowflake Kisses and Gingerbread Smiles* (about Christmas), are considered by reviewers to be charming additions to the youngest children's bookshelves.

Parker told *SATA:* "I started out as a bookseller, specializing in African-American children's books. I organize African-American children's book festivals. And then I noticed there were no toddler books for the holidays featuring cute black children, so I wrote, and Scholastic published!"

Biographical and Critical Sources

PERIODICALS

Black Enterprise, February, 1999, Sonja Brown Stokely, review of *Black Books Galore! Guide to Great African American Children's Books* p. 211.

Black Issues Book Review, July, 2001, Khafre K. Abif, review of *Black Books Galore! Guide to Great African American Children's Books about Girls* and *Black Books Galore! Guide to Great African American Children's Books about Boys,* p. 73.

Booklist, December 15, 2000, Hazel Rochman, review of *Black Books Galore! Guide to Great African American Children's Books about Girls,* p. 830.

Ebony, April, 2001, review of *Black Books Galore! Guide to Great African American Children's Books about Girls* and *Black Books Galore! Guide to Great African American Children's Books about Boys,* p. 16.

Feminist Collections, winter, 2002, Phyllis Holman Weisbard, review of *Black Books Galore! Guide to Great African American Children's Books about Girls,* p. 24.

Living in Stamford, November-December, 2000, Abby West, "Black Books Galore! Works to Expand Children's Literary Horizons One Book at a Time," pp. 81-82.

Philadelphia Inquirer, February 27, 2002, Lucia Herndon, "Mothers Created a Special Book Fair."

Publishers Weekly, January 1, 2001, review of *Black Books Galore! Guide to Great African American Children's Books about Girls* and *Black Books Galore! Guide to Great African American Children's Books about Boys,* p. 94; December 3, 2001, review of *Hugs and Hearts,* p. 62; December 24, 2001, review of *Painted Eggs and Chocolate Bunnies,* p. 66.

School Library Journal, September, 1999, Marie Wright, review of *Black Books Galore! Guide to Great African American Children's Books,* p. 249; March, 2001,

Eunice Weech, review of *Black Books Galore! Guide to Great African American Children's Books about Boys,* p. 289; May, 2002, Mary Lankford, review of *Black Books Galore! Guide to More Great African American Children's Books,* p. 183; September, 2002, Be Astengo, review of *Sweets and Treats,* p. 204; October, 2002, Linda Israelson, review of *Snowflake Kisses and Gingerbread Smiles,* p. 62.

*   *   *

PFEFFER, Wendy 1929-

Personal

Surname is pronounced *Pef*-er; born August 27, 1929, in Upper Darby, PA; daughter of Wendell (a high school principal and college professor) and Margaret (a homemaker; maiden name, Nelson) Sooy; married Thomas Pfeffer (a naval aeronautical engineer), March 17, 1951; children: Steven T., Diane Kianka. *Education:* Glassboro State College (now Rowan University), B.S., 1950. *Hobbies and other interests:* Sailing, playing bridge, traveling, reading, collecting antiques, cross country skiing, walking.

Addresses

Home—3 Timberlane Dr., Pennington, NJ 08534.

Career

First grade teacher in Pitman, NJ, 1950-53; Pennington Presbyterian Nursery School, cofounder, director, and early childhood specialist, 1961-91; freelance writer, 1981—. Jointure for Community Adult Education, workshop teacher for writing children's books, 1986; member of focus group for Mercer County libraries, 1993; speaker and instructor at creative writing workshops.

Member

Society of Children's Book Writers and Illustrators, Garden State Writers, Authors of Bucks County, Authors Guild, Savy Marketeers.

Awards, Honors

Best Book for Elementary Schools, *Booklist* and *School Library Journal,* 1994, for *Popcorn Park Zoo: A Haven with a Heart;* Best Children's Science Books, *Science Books and Films,* 1994, and Pick of the List, American Booksellers Association (ABA), 1996, both for *From Tadpole to Frog;* Outstanding Science Trade Book for Children, National Science Teachers Association/Children's Book Council (NSTA/CBC), and inclusion in "Children's Books Mean Business" exhibit, ABA and CBC, both 1996, both for *Marta's Magnets;* Pick of the List, ABA, 1996, and Children's Books of the Year list, Bank Street College of Education, 1997, both for *What's It Like to Be a Fish?;* Junior Library Guild selection,

Wendy Pfeffer

Pick of the List, ABA, John Burroughs List of Nature Books for Young Readers, all 1997, Outstanding Science Trade Book for Children, NSTA/CBC, 1998, and Giverny Award for Best Children's Science Picture Book, Louisiana State University, 2000, all for *A Log's Life;* Outstanding Science Trade Book for Children, NSTA/CBC, for *Mute Swans;* Best Children's Books of the Year selection, Bank Street College of Education, for *The Big Flood.*

Writings

Writing Children's Books: A Home Study Course (with audio cassette), Fruition Publications (Blawenburg, NJ), 1985, Drew Publications (New York, NY), 2002.

Starting a Child Care Business, a Rewarding Career: A Home Study Course, Fruition Publications (Blawenburg, NJ), 1989, reprinted as *Starting a Child Care Business in Your Home, a Rewarding Career: A Home Study Course,* 1992.

The Gooney War, illustrated by Mari Goering, Shoe Tree Press (White Hall, VA), 1990.

All About Me: Developing Self-Image and Self-Esteem with Hands-On Learning Activities, First Teacher (Bridgeport, CT), 1990.

The World of Nature: Exploring Nature with Hands-On Learning Activities, First Teacher (Bridgeport, CT), 1990.

(Coauthor) *The Sandbox,* Child's Play, 1991.

After an oak tree is felled by lightning, it becomes home to woodland creatures, rots and disintegrates, then nourishes an acorn into a new sapling, a cycle depicted in **A Log's Life,** *written by Wendy Pfeffer and illustrated by Robin Brickman.*

Popcorn Park Zoo: A Haven with a Heart, photographs by J. Gerard Smith, Messner (Englewood Cliffs, NJ), 1992.

Marta's Magnets, illustrated by Gail Piazza, Silver Burdett Press (Parsippany, NJ), 1995.

A Log's Life, illustrated by Robin Brickman, Simon and Schuster (New York, NY), 1997.

The Big Flood, illustrated by Vanessa Lubach, Millbrook Press (Brookfield, CT), 2001.

Mallard Duck at Meadow View Pond, illustrated by Taylor Oughton, Smithsonian/Soundprints (Norwalk, CT), 2001.

Puppy Power, Celebration Press (Parsippany, NJ), 2001.

Thunder and Lightning, Scholastic (New York, NY), 2002.

The Shortest Day: Celebrating the Winter Solstice, illustrated by Jesse Reisch, Dutton (New York, NY), 2003.

Firefly at Stony Brook Farm, illustrated by Larry Mikec, Smithsonian/Soundprints (Norwalk, CT), 2004.

Life on a Coral Reef, HarperCollins (New York, NY), in press.

Contributor to *Past and Promise: Lives of New Jersey Women,* 1990. Also author of numerous stories and articles for periodicals, including *Grade Teacher, Friend, Children's Digest, Instructor, National Association of Young Writers News,* and *First Teacher.*

"CREATURES IN WHITE" SERIES

Mute Swans, Silver Burdett Press (Parsippany, NJ), 1996.
Polar Bears, Silver Burdett Press (Parsippany, NJ), 1996.
Arctic Wolves, Silver Burdett Press (Parsippany, NJ), 1997.
Snowy Owls, Silver Burdett Press (Parsippany, NJ), 1997.

"LIVING ON THE EDGE" SERIES

Deep Oceans, Benchmark Books (New York, NY), 2002.
Arctic Frozen Reaches, Benchmark Books (New York, NY), 2002.
Antarctic Icy Waters, Benchmark Books (New York, NY), 2002.

Hot Deserts, Benchmark Books (New York, NY), 2002.
High Mountains, Benchmark Books (New York, NY), 2002.

"LET'S-READ-AND-FIND-OUT SCIENCE" SERIES

From Tadpole to Frog, illustrated by Holly Keller, HarperCollins (New York, NY), 1994.
What's It Like to Be a Fish?, illustrated by Holly Keller, HarperCollins (New York, NY), 1996.
Sounds All Around, illustrated by Holly Keller, HarperCollins (New York, NY), 1999.
Dolphin Talk: Whistles, Clicks, and Clapping Jaws, illustrated by Helen Davie, HarperCollins (New York, NY), 2003.
From Seed to Pumpkin, illustrated by James Graham Hale, HarperCollins (New York, NY), 2004.
Wiggling Worms, illustrated by Steve Jenkins, HarperCollins (New York, NY), 2004.

Work in Progress

A picture book, *Light So Bright,* for HarperCollins, publication expected in 2005.

Sidelights

Wendy Pfeffer is the award-winning author of twenty-six picture books for young readers that are mainly introductions to the sciences. Combining clear and simple language with bright and bold illustrations, Pfeffer produces works, according to reviewers, which take beginning readers into the life cycle of the frog, or which describe the cycle of nature in the decay of a fallen log. Working in several series, she introduces hardy animals that adapt and survive in the harshest environments in her "Living on the Edge" series as well as those that are colored white in the "Creatures in White" series. Subjects from an explication of thunder and lightning to a description of sound production have all found their way into Pfeffer's books. In addition to her writing, Pfeffer is a frequent visitor at elementary schools, leading writing workshops and giving interactive presentations.

Pfeffer once told *SATA:* "I grew up in a household of mathematics and language. My father, a professor of mathematics, was in demand as a speaker on 'Magical Mathematics' as well as 'The Origin of Words and Phrases.' Two brief examples of his thousands are: 'COP' being short for 'Constabulary of Police,' and 'TIP' which stood for 'To Insure Promptness.' I was also introduced to the Latin derivatives of words at a very early age.

"Despite all this introduction into the world of words, my love of language probably came from my grandfather who was a medical doctor but had a great desire to write as well as practice medicine. He did find time to pen one novel and spent many pleasant hours dramatizing stories for his spellbound grandchildren." Pfeffer also formed an early love of writing, as she once told

SATA: "From the time I was very young I wanted to write. When I learned to print, the first thing I did was to compose a story like *Hansel and Gretel.* In fact, it was *Hansel and Gretel.* When I was a little older, I kept a diary, then was editor of both the high school newspaper and yearbook. Years later, as I read and dramatized books while teaching young children, I felt that gnawing urge to write again. In fact, I knew I had to write."

After attending Glassboro State College and earning a bachelor's degree in 1950, Pfeffer began a career as an elementary school teacher, nursery school director, and early childhood specialist. Since 1981, she has been a freelance writer. "I have always loved to read and dramatize stories for young children," Pfeffer once told *SATA.* "Even though not all of my publications are specifically for children, they all deal with children directly or indirectly. Working with children has helped me to write for children, but just working with children doesn't provide all the insight necessary to know what makes a good children's book. A fine writing teacher once told me, 'To write for children, you must find the child in you.'"

After contributing stories and articles for several years to magazines such as *Children's Digest* and *Grade Teacher,* attending writers' conferences, and taking writing courses, Pfeffer published her first book, a home study course on how to write for children, *Writing Children's Books: A Home Study Course.* First published in 1985, this how-to volume appeared in a new edition in 2002. Over the years, Pfeffer has conducted numerous workshops that take participants through the process of creating a children's book, from getting ideas to submitting the finished manuscript. Her first picture book for children, *The Gooney War,* appeared in 1990, and since that time, she has brought out one or more titles a year. "The majority of my work is nonfiction," Pfeffer once told *SATA,* "which, in order to be successful, must be as compelling as fiction. Research is basic to nonfiction and interests me because I learn so much from it. Besides, as I research one topic, I always have a file going to add ideas for other topics."

Such research is evident, say critics, in her award-winning *From Tadpole to Frog,* part of the "Let's-Read-and-Find-Out Science" series of books. In this title, Pfeffer explores the metamorphosis from tadpole to frog, encouraging young children to read and look at full-color pictures of the process. Geared to preschool and kindergarten children, the book shows the life cycle of the frog, beginning with the frogs hibernating in the mud of a pond, and then progressing to the laying and hatching of eggs, and the slow growth of the tadpole until it matures into a full-grown frog. Reviewers responded warmly to this title. *Booklist*'s Carolyn Phelan found it to be an "attractive" choice for young readers, while Sandra Welzenbach, writing in *School Library Journal,* noted that most books on the topic were for older readers, a fact which made this title a "good starting point for beginning readers" looking to learn more about nature.

Further titles in the same series include *What's It Like to Be a Fish?* and *Sounds All Around.* The first title answers such questions as how a fish can live in water and not drown, and other queries that young children have about marine life. The text explains how the fish's body is perfectly adapted for its environment, just as the human body is adapted for life on land. Using the basic story of a boy buying some fish in a pet store and setting up a fish bowl, Pfeffer then introduces basic topics such as fish respiration and movement in this "lively" title, as *Booklist*'s Hazel Rochman described *What's It Like to Be a Fish?* Included in this interactive book are instructions for setting up a child's own goldfish bowl. *Horn Book*'s Margaret A. Bush called the same book "a sharply focused presentation for beginning readers," and Virginia Opocensky, writing in *School Library Journal,* found it to be a "useful addition to a subject area that has a paucity of material" for younger readers. *Sounds All Around* focuses on acoustics, ex-

plaining both sound production and hearing. Pfeffer uses snaps, claps, and whistles to illustrate how sound travels in waves through the air, ultimately making tiny bones in the ear vibrate upon contact. Additionally, she describes how other animals, such as bats and whales "hear." A critic for *Kirkus Reviews* found this an "appealing . . . title" that "provides a simple explanation" of sounds and hearing. Jackie Hechtkopf, reviewing the title in *School Library Journal,* praised the "many interesting tidbits about animals" included in Pfeffer's book, while *Booklist*'s Carolyn Phelan lauded the "clear and simple" text and illustrations.

Writing in Silver Burdett's "Creatures in White" series, Pfeffer penned a quartet of books, including *Mute Swans, Arctic Wolves, Snowy Owls,* and *Polar Bears.* The last-named title follows the life of these animals for two years, from the time the mother polar bear is about to give birth to the point where the young bears

Pfeffer humanizes her story about the great Midwest flood of 1993 by portraying young Patti, whose family farm is threatened by the rising waters of the nearby Mississippi River. (From The Big Flood, *illustrated by Vanessa Lubach.)*

are about to go out on their own. *Booklist*'s Phelan felt this title was "lively enough to be read aloud to a primary-grade class." Accompanied by full-color photographs, the brief text supplies basic information on growth, eating habits, and physiology of the polar bear. Susan Oliver, writing in *School Library Journal,* predicted "the story-like quality of the narration will appeal to new or reluctant readers." Similarly, *Bulletin of the Center for Children's Books* contributor Susan S. Verner dubbed the same title a "sunny tribute to the world's largest land-dwelling carnivore."

Mute Swans follows a similar pattern, detailing the life cycle of swans by focusing on one pair as they build a nest in the spring, lay and protect eggs, hatch the young cygnets, and rear them in time to migrate south once the cold weather sets in. Once again combining basic text with color photographs, Pfeffer creates an "attractive volume," according to Kathleen Odean, writing in *School Library Journal.*

Non-series titles, including *Popcorn Park Zoo: A Haven with a Heart* and *Marta's Magnets,* from Pfeffer have also been popular. Her 1992 *Popcorn Park Zoo* tells the story of a federally licensed New Jersey zoo that caters specifically to elderly, sick, abandoned, handicapped, and unwanted animals. Pfeffer personalizes her tale by telling how many of the animals arrived at the zoo, such as the story of an abandoned pet pig that had outgrown its small apartment. *Marta's Magnets* features a young girl with a penchant for collecting magnets. Though Marta's sister, Rosa, calls the collection junk, it comes in handy when the family moves to a new home and she is able to find a lost key for Rosa's new friend. In addition to the story at the heart of the book, Pfeffer also uses the tale to relate some basic science facts about magnets and also gives directions for making a refrigerator magnet. Reviewing this picture book in *School Library Journal,* Eunice Weech described the book as a "story about fitting in," though she did note that *Marta's Magnets* would also be appropriate "to introduce a unit on magnetism." Lolly Robinson, writing in *Horn Book Guide,* also praised "the ethnically diverse" cast of characters in the book.

With *A Log's Life,* Pfeffer explains what happens after an oak tree falls in the forest. Thereafter, it provides a new home for a host of other creatures such as porcupines, ants, salamanders, and even mushrooms. Finally, the oak rots into a mound of black earth. This award-winning volume was highly praised by reviewers. *Booklist*'s Phelan thought that "teachers . . . will welcome Pfeffer's simply explained depiction of the tree's cycle," and Patricia Manning, writing in *School Library Journal,* likewise called this book "an attractive introduction to the life, death, and decay of an oak tree."

From fallen trees, Pfeffer moves to rushing waters in *The Big Flood,* a picture book about the flood in the Midwest of the United States in 1993. Pfeffer tells this story through the experiences of one young survivor of the flood, Patti Brandon, who lives on a soybean farm near the Mississippi River. As the river swells and begins to flood the fields, Patti and her family realize they must pitch in together to try to stop the flooding, piling sandbags on the banks of the river. Patti helps out on the ham radio, as well, calling in a helicopter to rescue a man caught on the river. After the flood finally recedes and things return to normal, Patti has developed "a new respect for the mighty river," according to Anne Chapman Callaghan, writing in *School Library Journal.* Callaghan also felt that this "realistic story is softened" by the artwork. Christie Sarrazin, writing in *Horn Book Guide,* found Pfeffer's narrative to be a "heart-thumping story."

With her 2001 title *Mallard Duck at Meadow View Pond,* Pfeffer returns to series books, adding a title to the "Smithsonian Backyard" series. Here, she traces the first season of a newly-born mallard duck, looking at his first swim on the pond, the food he eats, and his encounters with other animals. Losing his first feathers in the summer, he prepares for the long migration flight as fall comes on. Writing in *School Library Journal,* Emily Herman praised this "realistic" tale which would put young readers "in touch with the natural world of mallard ducks and the wildlife that surrounds them." *Booklist*'s Gillian Engberg also called this book a "well-balanced read."

Pfeffer once concluded to *SATA:* "I enjoy working with children of all ages, leading creative writing workshops and speaking to school groups on writing, mine and theirs. My presentations vary depending on the ages and interests of the children. Even though I stopped teaching to have more time to write, now I feel I have the best of both worlds, working with children and writing. As I said before, I must write—so I do. For me, writing is a challenge and a joy."

Biographical and Critical Sources

PERIODICALS

Asbury Park Press, July 1, 1992.
Booklist, September 1, 1990, p. 62; June 1, 1992, p. 1760; August, 1994, Carolyn Phelan, review of *From Tadpole to Frog,* p. 2047; March 15, 1996, Hazel Rochman, review of *What's It Like to Be a Fish?,* pp. 1266-1267; August, 1996, Carolyn Phelan, review of *Polar Bears,* p. 1903; September 15, 1997, Carolyn Phelan, review of *A Log's Life,* p. 238; March 1, 1999, Carolyn Phelan, review of *Sounds All Around,* p. 1217; June 1, 2001, Lauren Peterson, review of *The Big Flood,* p. 1886; February 1, 2002, Gillian Engberg, review of *Mallard Duck at Meadow View Pond,* p. 946.
Bulletin of the Center for Children's Books, October, 1996, Susan S. Verner, review of *Polar Bears,* p. 72.
Horn Book, July-August, 1994, Margaret A. Bush, review of *From Tadpole to Frog,* p. 474; July-August, 1996, Margaret A. Bush, review of *What's It Like to Be a Fish?,* p. 482.

Horn Book Guide, spring, 1996, Lolly Robinson, review of *Marta's Magnets,* p. 41; spring, 1997, Daniel Brabander, review of *Mute Swans,* p. 125; fall, 2001, Christie Sarrazin, review of *The Big Flood,* p. 270.

Kirkus Reviews, June 15, 1992, review of *Popcorn Park Zoo: A Haven with a Heart,* p. 783; October 15, 1996, review of *Mute Swans,* p. 1605; December 1, 1998, review of *Sounds All Around,* p. 1738;

Library Talk, September-October, 1992.

NJEA Review, October, 1992, p. 50.

Reading Teacher, December, 1998, review of *A Log's Life,* p. 386.

Retirement Life, May, 1992, p. 38.

School Library Journal, November, 1990, p. 98; July, 1992, p. 87; November, 1994, Sandra Welzenbach, review of *From Tadpole to Frog,* p. 100; March, 1996, Eunice Weech, review of *Marta's Magnets,* p. 180; April, 1996, Virginia Opocensky, review of *What's It Like to Be a Fish?,* p. 127; September, 1996, Susan Oliver, review of *Polar Bears,* pp. 199-200; February, 1997, Kathleen Odean, review of *Mute Swans,* p. 95; September, 1997, Patricia Manning, review of *A Log's Life,* p. 207; January, 1999, Jackie Hechtkopf, review of *Sounds All Around,* p. 115; October, 2001, Anne Chapman Callaghan, review of *The Big Flood,* pp. 144-145; April, 2002, Emily Herman, review of *Mallard Duck at Meadow View Pond,* p. 90; June, 2002, Lynda Ritterman, review of *Hot Deserts,* p. 131.

Science Books and Films, October, 1992.

ONLINE

Author/Illustrator Source, http://www.author-illustr-source. com/ (June 29, 2003).

*   *   *

PIELICHATY, Helena 1955-

Personal

Surname is pronounced "Pierre-li-hatty"; born September 11, 1955, in Stockholm, Sweden; daughter of Boris and Joyce Rojinsky; married Peter Pielichaty; children: Hanya, Joe. *Education:* Breton Hall College, B.Ed. (with honors), 1978.

Addresses

Home—21 Dykes End, Collingham, Newark, Nottinghamshire NG23 7LD, England. *E-mail*—helena@ helena-pielichaty.com.

Career

Writer. Former teacher, 1978-2000. Chair of local history club.

Awards, Honors

Book Trust's Top 100 Books of 1998 selection, for *Vicious Circle;* Carnegie Medal nomination, for *Simone's Letters;* Sheffield Children's Book Award shortlist,

Helena Pielichaty

2000; third place in Askew's Children's Book Award, 2002; World Book Day Super Read nomination, 2002, for *Simone's Diary.*

Writings

Vicious Circle, Oxford University Press (London, England), 1998.

Simone's Letters, illustrated by Sue Heap, Oxford University Press (London, England), 1999.

Getting Rid of Karenna, Oxford University Press (London, England), 1999.

Simone's Diary, illustrated by Sue Heap, Oxford University Press (London, England), 2000.

Jade's Story, Oxford University Press (London, England), 2000.

There's Only One Danny Ogle, illustrated by Glyn Goodwin, Oxford University Press (London, England), 2001.

Never Ever, Oxford University Press (London, England), 2001.

Simone's Website, illustrated by Sue Heap, Oxford University Press (London, England), 2002.

Starring Sammie ("After School Club" series), Oxford University Press (London, England), 2003.

Starring Brody ("After School Club" series), Oxford University Press (London, England), 2003.

Pielichaty's work has been translated into German, Dutch, and Lithuanian.

Work in Progress

Other books in the "After School Club" series; researching the British education system in the 1950s for a novel called *The Diary Keepers*.

Sidelights

In Helena Pielichaty's young adult novels, her characters frequently confront problems that are familiar to many teenagers. Thus, in *There's Only One Danny Ogle*, a boy who loves soccer moves to a town that is so small it lacks a sports program.

In *Jade's Story*, the mental breakdown of a girl's father leads her into a more perceptive relationship with him. As Robert Dunbar noted in *Books for Keeps*, Pielichaty examines their evolving relationship "with subtlety and originality," aided by an effective use of setting and interesting secondary characters. For Alison A. Smith, writing in *School Librarian*, Pielichaty has done young people a service in presenting a realistic, carefully researched, fictional account of a scenario that is not uncommon among the families of contemporary young people.

Separated parents and a divided household are the issues at the heart of *Simone's Diary*, Pielichaty's first sequel to the successful *Simone's Letters*. Simone's young voice narrates the story of her life, aided by the questionnaires she completes for a researcher interested in young people's transition to secondary school. School life, friends, and quirky teachers are the subject of Simone's diary entries, "written in a lively style, with plenty of humour," according to Jan Cooper in *School Librarian*. Cooper concluded by appraising the likely popularity of Simone with young readers by describing Pielichaty's character as a more upbeat and realistic version of Adrian Mole, another popular young adult character in British literature.

Pielichaty told *SATA*: "I did not become a writer until after my first child was born in 1985. I gave up teaching full-time and wanted to do something stimulating so I attended a creative writing course. The course folded after a few weeks, but I was hooked. I attended a couple more weekend courses on how to write for children, but apart from those, I was on my own. Owing to the endeavours of my agent at the time, Oxford University Press accepted my first book, *Vicious Circle*, in 1998. They have been my sole publishers ever since.

"As I had several pieces of work already written, my second and third books were published quite rapidly after *Vicious Circle*, allowing a momentum to build up. My second book, *Simone's Letters*, took me by surprise by selling so well I was asked to write a sequel—*Simone's Diary*—and another one after that—*Simone's Website*! The "Simone" series is my most successful in terms of books sold.

"I write real-life stories, set in the present, similar to Paula Danziger, Judy Blume, and Beverly Cleary. I use a lot of humour to carry through some tough subjects, such as mental illness, poverty, and feeling different. Sometimes these are labelled as 'issues' books, which always sounds dreary but I must be doing something right as they have been translated into German, Dutch, and Lithuanian!

"I think teaching has definitely helped my writing. Reviewers often comment on my 'insight' into children's language and behaviour. This comes from many years of standing in a cold playground on playground duty observing children, counselling them, and so on. My teaching experience also helps when I meet children. I am often invited into schools and libraries to meet groups, and I know how to pace a session and how to fully engage them. I have performed at the Edinburgh Literary Festival three years in a row now, and I think the reason I am invited back is partly because I am not scared to perform and risk making a fool out of myself!

"Advice to aspiring children's writers? Don't make the mistake of thinking writing for children is easier than writing for adults. Read contemporary fiction. Be prepared to discuss the J. K. Rowling phenomenon with people ad infinitum!"

Biographical and Critical Sources

PERIODICALS

Books for Keeps, July, 2001, Robert Dunbar, review of *Jade's Story*, p. 25.
School Librarian, summer, 2001, Jan Cooper, review of *Simone's Diary*, p. 90; autumn, 2001, Alison A. Smith, review of *Jade's Story*, pp. 145-146; winter, 2001, Mary Crawford, review of *There's Only One Danny Ogle*, p. 192.

ONLINE

Helena Pielichaty's Web site, http://www.helena-pielichaty.com/ (May 19, 2003).

*   *   *

PROVENZO, Eugene (F., Jr.) 1949-

Personal

Born December 2, 1949, in Buffalo, NY; son of Eugene F. (a social studies teacher and high school principal) and Therese (an elementary school principal; maiden name, King) Provenzo; married Asterie Baker (a writer), December 24, 1973. *Education:* University of Rochester, B.A. (with honors), 1972; Washington University, M.A., 1974, Graduate Institute of Education, Ph.D., 1976. *Hobbies and other interests:* Designing toys, cooking, assemblage/sculpture, woodworking.

Eugene Provenzo

Addresses

Home—4921 Ponce de Leon Blvd., Coral Gables, FL 33146. *Office*—School of Education, P.O. Box 248065, University of Miami, Coral Gables, FL 33124. *E-mail*—provenzo@miami.edu.

Career

University of Miami, Coral Gables, FL, faculty member, 1976—, full professor of education, 1985—, research coordinator and associate dean for research of School of Education, 1986-88; writer.

Awards, Honors

Newbery Library fellow, 1978; Distinguished Young Leader in Education Award, Phi Delta Kappa, 1981; National Endowment for the Humanities fellow, 1984 and 1991; Professor of the Year Award, University of Miami, 1984; Man of the Year Award, University of Miami Chapter of Phi Delta Kappa, 1986; Freshman Outstanding Teaching Award, University of Miami, 1991; Outstanding Book on the Subject of Human Rights in the United States, Gustavus Meyers Center, 1992, for *Religious Fundamentalism and American Education: The Battle for the Public Schools;* Outstanding Book in the Field of State and Local History, American Association for State and Local History, 1993, for *Farm*

Security Administration Photographs of Florida; Portfolio Award Winner, 1998, for *Learning Online: The Voyage of Apollo 11: Mission to the Moon.*

Writings

WITH WIFE, ASTERIE BAKER PROVENZO

The Historian's Toybox: Children's Toys from the Past You Can Make Yourself (for children), illustrated by Peter A. Zorn, Jr., Prentice-Hall (Englewood Cliffs, NJ), 1979, reprinted as *Easy-to-Make Old-Fashioned Toys,* Dover (New York, NY), 1989.

Rediscovering Astronomy (for children), illustrated by Peter A. Zorn, Jr., Oak Tree (San Diego, CA), 1979.

Rediscovering Photography (for children), illustrated by Peter A. Zorn, Jr., Oak Tree (La Jolla, CA), 1980.

Play It Again: Historic Board Games You Can Make and Play Yourself (for children), illustrated by Peter A. Zorn, Jr., Prentice-Hall (Englewood Cliffs, NJ), 1981, reprinted as *Favorite Board Games You Can Make and Play,* Dover (New York, NY), 1990.

Pursuing the Past: Oral History, Photography, Family History, and Cemeteries, Volume 1, Addison-Wesley (Menlo Park, CA), 1983.

Forty-seven Easy-to-Do Science Experiments (for children), illustrated by Peter A. Zorn, Jr., Dover (New York, NY), 1989.

In the Eye of Hurricane Andrew, University Press of Florida (Gainesville, FL), 2002.

WITH PETER A. ZORN, JR., AND WIFE, ASTERIE BAKER PROVENZO

Spad XIII and Spad VII (for children), Crown (New York, NY), 1982.

Fokker Dr. 1 Triplanes (for children), Crown (New York, NY), 1982.

The Ford Trimotor 5-AT (for children), Crown (New York, NY), 1982.

The Spirit of Louis Ryan NYP (for children), Crown (New York, NY), 1982.

Education on the Forgotten Frontier: A Centennial History of the Founding of the Dade County Public Schools, Dade County Public Schools (Miami, FL), 1985.

OTHER

(With David A. Young) *The History of the St. Louis Car Company,* Howell-North Books (Berkeley, CA), 1978.

(With Betty Hall and others) *The Historian as Detective,* CEMREL, Inc., 1979.

(With Arlene Brett) *The Complete Block Book,* photographs by Michael Carlebach, Syracuse University Press (Syracuse, NY), 1983.

(With H. Warren Button) *History of Education and Culture in America,* Prentice-Hall (Englewood Cliffs, NJ), 1983, revised edition, 1989.

(Editor and author of introduction, with mother, Therese M. Provenzo) Mary H. Lewis, *An Adventure with Children,* University Press of America (Lanham, MD), 1985.

Beyond the Gutenberg Galaxy: Microcomputers and the Emergence of Post-Typographic Culture, Teachers College Press (New York, NY), 1986.

An Introduction to Education in American Society, C. E. Merrill (Columbus, OH), 1986.

(With Marilyn Cohn and Robert Kottkamp) *To Be a Teacher: Cases, Concepts, Observation Guides,* Random House (New York, NY), 1987.

Religious Fundamentalism and American Education: The Battle for the Public Schools, State University of New York Press (Albany, NY), 1990.

Video Kids: Making Sense of Nintendo, Harvard University Press (Cambridge, MA), 1991.

(With Arlene Brett and Robin Moore) *The Complete Playground Book,* Syracuse University Press (Syracuse, NY), 1993.

(With Michael Carlebach) *Farm Security Administration Photographs of Florida,* University Press of Florida (Gainesville, FL), 1993.

(Editor, with Paul Farber and Gunilla Holm) *Schooling in the Light of Popular Culture,* State University of New York Press (Albany, NY), 1994.

(With Arlene Brett) *Adaptive Technology for Special Human Needs,* State University of New York Press (Albany, NY), 1995.

(With Sandra H. Fradd) *Hurricane Andrew, the Public Schools, and the Rebuilding of Community,* State University of New York Press (Albany, NY), 1995.

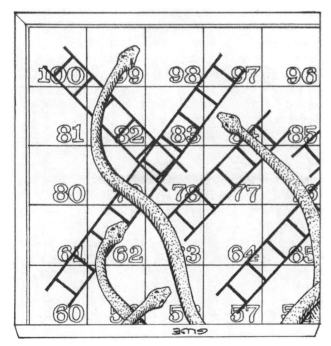

Along with historical background on numerous board games, Asterie Baker Provenzo and Eugene Provenzo provide detailed instructions for creating game boards and playing pieces from paper and cardboard. (From Favorite Board Games You Can Make and Play, *illustrated by Peter A. Zorn, Jr.)*

The Educator's Brief Guide to Computers in the Schools, Eye on Education (Princeton, NJ), 1996.

Schoolteachers and Schooling: Ethoses in Conflict, Ablex Pub. (Norwood, NJ), 1996.

(With Charles T. Mangrum and Mykel J. Mangrum) *Take Five: Daily Classroom Activities in Language Arts, Mathematics, Science, Social Studies, Humanities,* Curriculum Associates, Inc. (North Billerica, MA), 1996.

(With Charles T. Mangrum) *Learning Online: The Voyage of Apollo 11: Mission to the Moon,* Curriculum Associates, Inc. (North Billerica, MA), 1996.

(With Charles T. Mangrum) *Thinking Like a Mathematician: Learning How Mathematicians Think and Work,* Curriculum Associates, Inc. (North Billerica, MA), 1998.

(With Charles T. Mangrum) *Thinking Like a Writer: Learning How Writers Think and Work,* Curriculum Associates, Inc. (North Billerica, MA), 1998.

(With Charles T. Mangrum) *Thinking Like a Historian: Learning How Historians Think and Work,* Curriculum Associates, Inc. (North Billerica, MA), 1998.

(With Charles T. Mangrum) *Thinking Like a Scientist: Learning How Scientists Think and Work,* Curriculum Associates, Inc. (North Billerica, MA), 1998.

The Educator's Brief Guide to the Internet and the World Wide Web, Eye on Education (Larchmont, NY), 1998.

(With Arlene Brett and Gary N. McCloskey) *Computers, Curriculum, and Cultural Change: An Introduction for Teachers,* Erlbaum (Mahwah, NJ), 1999.

The Internet and the World Wide Web for Preservice Teachers, Allyn & Bacon (Boston, MA), 1999, revised edition published as *The Internet and the World Wide Web for Teachers,* 2002.

(With Doug Gotthoffer) *Quick Guide to the Internet for Education,* Allyn & Bacon (Boston, MA), 2000.

(With Doug Gotthoffer) *Allyn and Bacon Education on the Net,* Allyn and Bacon (Boston, MA), 2001.

(Editor) W. E. B. DuBois, *Du Bois on Education,* Rowman and Littlefield (Lanham, MD), 2002.

Teaching, Learning, and Schooling: A Twenty-first Century Perspective, Allyn & Bacon (Boston, MA), 2002.

Also editor, with Paul Farber and Gunilla Holm, of *Education and Popular Culture in the United States,* State University of New York Press (Albany, NY). Work represented in anthologies, including *Educational Equity: Integrating Equity into Perspective Teacher Education,* Eric Clearinghouse on Teacher Education (Washington, DC), 1981; *Allied in Educational Reform,* edited by Jerome M. Rosow and Robert Zager, Jossey-Bass (San Francisco, CA), 1989; and *Literacy Online: The Promise (and Peril) of Reading and Writing with Computers,* edited by Myron Tuman, University of Pittsburgh Press (Pittsburgh, PA), 1991. Coeditor, "Education and Culture Series," State University of New York Press (Albany, NY), 1990—. Contributor of articles and reviews to periodicals.

Work in Progress

At work on several titles dealing with computers, technology, and media, as well as the history of education, and cultural literacy.

In this work Provenzo offers a host of reasons for teachers to utilize the Internet, from curriculum development to creating an educational portfolio.

Sidelights

Eugene Provenzo is a professor at the University of Miami School of Education and the author of a wide variety of books on history, technology, culture, and education. He has specialized in the academic uses of computers and the Internet for online studying, publishing books such as *Beyond the Gutenberg Galaxy: Microcomputers and the Emergence of Post-Typographic Culture, Computers, Curriculum, and Cultural Change: An Introduction for Teachers, The Educator's Brief Guide to the Internet and the World Wide Web, Quick Guide to the Internet for Education,* and *The Internet and the World Wide Web for Preservice Teachers.* Working with his wife, Asterie Baker Provenzo, and with Peter A. Zorn, Provenzo has also written several how-to children's books, including *Play It Again: Historic Board Games You Can Make and Play Yourself, Forty-seven Easy-to-Do Science Experiments,* and *The Historian's Toybox: Children's Toys from the Past You Can Make Yourself.*

Born in 1949, in Buffalo, New York, Provenzo comes from a family of educators. His father was a social studies teacher and school principal, and his mother an elementary school principal. He attended the University of Rochester and later earned his doctorate from Washington University's Graduate Institute of Education with his thesis titled *Education and the Aesopic Tradition.*

Provenzo once commented: "While I was in graduate school, I focused primarily on historical and philosophical training, but I also received extensive background in ethnography and field-based research, as well as archival preservation and exhibit work. My career as a researcher has been interdisciplinary in nature."

Provenzo joined the faculty of the University of Miami in 1976, and became a full professor in the School of Education in 1985. "Throughout my work," Provenzo once said, "the primary focus has been on education as a social and cultural phenomenon. A particularly important concern has been the role of the teacher in American society. Cross-disciplinary methods, as well as philosophical questions related to the process of inquiry and the sociology of knowledge, are also of primary interest to me. In addition, I have followed personal interests related to the impact of computers on contemporary culture and education, local and regional history, and the history of toys, toy design, and evaluation."

Writing on academic affairs, Provenzo has also helped edit books, such as the 1994 *Schooling in the Light of Popular Culture,* an "excellent entry," as *Choice's* F. X. Russo put it, in the growing body of work that attempts to "sensitize educators and the public to the impact of cultural forces in the school." In a less academic vein, Provenzo coauthored *Farm Security Administration Photographs of Florida,* a "superbly crafted work," according to Augustus Burns in a *Social Forces* review. Burns went on to note that the authors "have produced a book that faithfully reflects both the achievement and the craftsmanship of the talented men and women who made these remarkable photographs." By cataloguing and contextualizing these Depression-age photos, Provenzo helped to save such images from becoming a "rural world lost," according to Burns. I. Wilmer Counts, reviewing the same title in *Journalism History,* felt that Provenzo and coauthor Michael Carlebach "make excellent use of their text along with the images to give us a solid words-and-pictures description of Florida during the Great Depression."

"As a professor and educational researcher," Provenzo once commented, "I am committed to relating theory to practice. I have worked closely with schools and teachers, and I consider myself a 'scholar-teacher,' working to advance the profession." In his educational works, Provenzo has been particularly interested in the impact of computers on learning. His *Adaptive Technology for Special Human Needs* examines the uses of new computer-based technologies for the learning needs of people with disabilities, introducing both hardware and software that educators might use. Additionally, he raises issues about affordability and equality in the use of such technologies in his study. K. Lam, writing in *Choice,* felt the book was "easy to read, with photographic inserts showing some of the devices mentioned in the text." Provenzo provides a basic introductory text with *Computers, Curriculum, and Cultural Change: An Introduction for Teachers.* Coauthored with Arlene Brett and Gary N. McCloskey, *Computers, Curriculum, and Cultural Change* is, according to B. Deever, writing in *Choice,* "a well-done introduction for undergraduates and/or educators." Deever also praised the book for its "explication of computing and educational technology."

With *The Internet and the World Wide Web for Preservice Teachers* and its second edition, *The Internet and the World Wide Web for Teachers,* Provenzo supplies not only an introduction to using such Web-related materials in the classroom, but also provides an extensive list of quality, educational links. He introduces the concept of the Internet and the World Wide Web, gives the basics of navigating online, and makes suggestion how the Web can be used in the classroom and blended with curriculum. His list of recommended sites for online work includes libraries, reference destinations, museums, and schools. Reviewing the first edition of this book in *Book Report,*, Donna Miller noted that it would "be helpful, not only for those entering the teaching field, but also for veteran educators."

Provenzo's interests have also led him into a critical social and cultural analysis of video games for children in *Video Kids: Making Sense of Nintendo.* In his capacity as an educator, he has testified before the U.S. Senate twice on the subject of video games and children. In a *People* interview with Don Sider, Provenzo noted that video games, good or bad, "are here to stay; they're increasingly as much a part of children's lives as TV." And like television, Provenzo recommends that such games be used in "moderation." Video games can be "powerful teaching tools" at their best, as he told Sider. The good games can, according to Provenzo, "fulfill a need for adventure and fantasy . . . [and] help kids role-play and problem-solve." The downside, of course, is that many games rely on violence and sexuality to attract young participants. Provenzo recommended that parents "know what game your children are playing." Parents might even play the game with their children at first. "If you have a problem with the game," he told Sider in his interview, "discuss what you like and don't like with your kids. It doesn't take a lot of time, and it's worth it."

Biographical and Critical Sources

PERIODICALS

Booklist, May 15, 1980, p. 1337.

Book Report, November, 1999, Donna Miller, review of *The Internet and the World Wide Web for Preservice Teachers,* p. 82.

Choice, January, 1995, F. X. Russo, review of *Schooling in the Light of Popular Culture,* p. 841; January, 1996, K. Lam, review of *Adaptive Technology for Special Human Needs,* p. 841; September, 1999, B. Deever, review of *Computers, Curriculum, and Cultural Change: An Introduction for Teachers,* p. 202.

Journalism History, spring, 1994, I. Wilmer Counts, review of *Farm Security Administration Photographs of Florida,* p. 38.

Journal of Popular Culture, fall, 1994, Ray Browne, review of *Schooling in the Light of Popular Culture,* pp. 234-235.

Library Journal, November 1, 1979, p. 2337.

New Statesman and Society, December 20, 1991, p. 49.

New York Times Book Review, December 22, 1991, p. 2.

People, October 16, 2002, Don Sider, "Virtual Vice? This Holiday Season, Some Video Games Come Wrapped in Sex, Gore, and Controversy," p. 79.

School Library Journal, October, 1981, p. 153.

Social Forces, September, 1995, Augustus Burns, review of *Farm Security Administration Photographs of Florida,* pp. 342-344.

Teachers College Record, winter, 1997, Susan Moore Johnson, review of *Schoolteachers and Schooling: Ethoses in Conflict,* pp. 426-428.

Times Educational Supplement, November 29, 1991.

ONLINE

University of Miami School of Education Web site http://www.education.miami.edu/ (March 20, 2003), faculty page of Eugene Provenzo.

R

REUTER, Bjarne (B.) 1950-

Personal

Born 1950, in Broenshoej, Denmark. *Education:* Graduated from teachers' college, 1975.

Addresses

Agent—International Children's Book Service, Skindergade 3 B, DK-1159 Copenhagen K, Denmark.

Career

Teacher, c. 1975-80; full-time writer, beginning 1980.

Awards, Honors

Children's Book Award, Danish Ministry of Culture, 1977, for *En dag i Hector Hansens liv;* Children's Book Award, Danish Bookseller Employees, 1981, for *Kys stjernerne;* Herman Bang grant, 1983; UNICEF Prize for best children's film, 1984, for *Buster's World;* named with Thoeger Birkeland as "The Children's Choice" by Danish School Librarians, 1985; Robert Prize, 1985, for screenplay of *Twist and Shout;* Copenhagen Association for Culture Prize, 1987; Roede Kro Prize, 1988; Golden Palm Award for best film, Cannes Film Festival, 1988, Golden Globe Award for best foreign-language film, Hollywood Foreign Press Association, 1989, and Academy Award for best foreign-language film, American Academy of Motion Picture Arts and Sciences, 1989, all for *Pelle the Conqueror;* Golden Laurels, Danish Booksellers, 1989; Culture Prize, Danish Labor Unions, 1989, for *Månen over Bella Bio;* Mildred Batchelder Award for best children's book in translation, Association for Library Service to Children, 1990, for *Buster's World;* "highly commended" citation for Hans Christian Andersen Medal, International Board on Books for Young People, 1990; Danish Library Associations Prize, 1990.

Writings

FOR YOUNG PEOPLE; IN ENGLISH TRANSLATION

Busters verden (novel; also see below), Branner and Korch (Copenhagen, Denmark), 1978, translation by Anthea Bell published as *Buster's World,* Andersen Press (London, England), 1988, Dutton (New York, NY), 1989.

Kys stjernerne (novel), Branner and Korch (Copenhagen, Denmark), 1980, translation by Anthea Bell published as *Buster, the Sheikh of Hope Street,* Dutton (New York, NY), 1991.

Da solen skulle saelges (retelling of a Chinese folktale), illustrated by Svend Otto S., Gyldendal (Copenhagen, Denmark), 1985, translation by Joan Tate published as *The Princess and the Sun, Moon, and Stars,* Pelham (London, England), 1986, Viking (New York, NY), 1987.

Drengene fra Sankt Petri, Gyldendal (Copenhagen, Denmark), 1991, translation by Anthea Bell published as *The Boys from St. Petri,* Dutton (New York, NY), 1994.

UNTRANSLATED BOOKS FOR YOUNG PEOPLE

Kidnapning, Branner and Korch (Copenhagen, Denmark), 1975.

Rent guld i Posen, Branner and Korch (Copenhagen, Denmark), 1975.

En dag i Hector Hansens liv, Branner and Korch (Copenhagen, Denmark), 1976.

Ridder af Skraldespanden, Branner and Korch (Copenhagen, Denmark), 1976.

Rottefaengeren fra Hameln, Branner and Korch (Copenhagen, Denmark), 1976.

Eventyret om den tapre Hugo, Branner and Korch (Copenhagen, Denmark), 1977.

Skoenheden og Udyret, Branner and Korch (Copenhagen, Denmark), 1977.

Det skoere land, Branner and Korch (Copenhagen, Denmark), 1977.

Den stoerste nar i verden, Branner and Korch (Copenhagen, Denmark), 1977.

Tre engle og fem loever, Branner and Korch (Copenhagen, Denmark), 1977.

Zappa (also see below), Branner and Korch (Copenhagen, Denmark), 1977.

Drengen der ikke kunne blive bange, Branner and Korch (Copenhagen, Denmark), 1978.

De seks tjenere, Branner and Korch (Copenhagen, Denmark), 1978.

Slusernes kejser, Branner and Korch (Copenhagen, Denmark), 1978.

Den utilfredse prins, Branner and Korch (Copenhagen, Denmark), 1978.

Boernenes julekalender, Branner and Korch (Copenhagen, Denmark), 1979.

Den fredag Osval blev usynlig, Branner and Korch (Copenhagen, Denmark), 1979.

Rejsen til morgensroedens hav, Branner and Korch (Copenhagen, Denmark), 1979.

Stoevet paa en sommerfugls vinge, Branner and Korch (Copenhagen, Denmark), 1979.

Kolumbine & Harlekin, Branner and Korch (Copenhagen, Denmark), 1980.

Suzanne & Leonard, Branner and Korch (Copenhagen, Denmark), 1980.

Knud, Otto & Carmen Rosita, Branner and Korch (Copenhagen, Denmark), 1981.

Skibene i skoven, Branner and Korch (Copenhagen, Denmark), 1981.

Det forkerte barn, Branner and Korch (Copenhagen, Denmark), 1982.

Hvor regnbuen ender, Branner and Korch (Copenhagen, Denmark), 1982.

Oesten for solen og vesten for maanen, Hernov (Copenhagen, Denmark), 1982.

Casanova, Branner and Korch (Copenhagen, Denmark), 1983.

Når snerlen blomstrer (also see below), part 1: *Efterår 1963,* part 2: *Forår 1964,* Gyldendal (Copenhagen, Denmark), 1983.

Maltepoes i den store vide verden, Gyldendal (Copenhagen, Denmark), 1984.

Tropicana, Branner and Korch (Copenhagen, Denmark), 1984.

Bundhu, FDF/FPF, 1985.

Shamran, Gyldendal (Copenhagen, Denmark), 1985.

Den dobbelte mand, Gyldendal (Copenhagen, Denmark), 1987.

Droemmenes bro, Gyldendal (Copenhagen, Denmark), 1987.

Os to Oskar . . . for evigt!, Branner and Korch (Copenhagen, Denmark), 1987.

Månen over Bella Bio, Gyldendal (Copenhagen, Denmark), 1988.

Vi der valgte mælkevejen, Gyldendal (Copenhagen, Denmark), 1989.

Mig og Albinoni, Gyldendal (Copenhagen, Denmark), 1990.

Den skæggede dame, Branner and Korch (Copenhagen, Denmark), 1990.

Tre til Bermudos, Gyldendal (Copenhagen, Denmark), 1990.

Lola, Gyldendal (Copenhagen, Denmark), 1991.

En Rem af Huden: Roman, Gyldendal (Copenhagen, Denmark), 1992.

Seven. A, Gyldendal (Copenhagen, Denmark), 1992.

Den korsikanske Bisp, Gyldendal (Copenhagen, Denmark), 1993.

Johnny & the Hurrycanes: Roman, Gyldendal (Copenhagen, Denmark), 1993.

Langebro med løbende figurer, Gyldendal (Copenhagen, Denmark), 1995.

Kaptajn Bimse & Kong Kylie, illustrated by Annette Reuter, Gyldendal (Copenhagen, Denmark), 1996.

Ved profetens skæg: Roman, Gyldendal (Copenhagen, Denmark), 1996.

Fakiren fra Bilbao, Gyldendal (Copenhagen, Denmark), 1997.

Mordet på Leon Culman: Roman, Gyldendal (Copenhagen, Denmark), 1999.

Under kometens hale, Gyldendal (Copenhagen, Denmark), 1999.

Prins Faisals ring, Gyldendal (Copenhagen, Denmark), 2000.

SCREENPLAYS FOR FILM AND TELEVISION

(With Bille August) *Zappa* (film; based on Reuter's novel of the same title), Kaerne, 1983, Spectrafilm, 1984.

Buster's World (film; based on his novel of the same title; originally broadcast in Denmark as a television miniseries), Metronome, 1984.

(With Bille August) *Tro, hab, og karlighed* (film; based on Reuter's novel sequence *Naar snerlen blomstrer*), Kaerne, 1984, released under English title *Twist and Shout,* Miramax, 1986.

(With Bille August and Per Olov Enquist) *Pelle erobreren* (film; based on Volume 1 of the novel by Martin Andersen Nexo), Kaerne, 1987, released under English title *Pelle the Conqueror,* Miramax, 1988.

OTHER

En dag i Hector Hansens liv [and] *Busters verden* [and] *Kom der lys i neonrøret, gutter?* (plays), Branner and Korch (Copenhagen, Denmark), 1984.

En tro kopi, Gyldendal (Copenhagen, Denmark), 1986.

Den cubanske kabale, Gyldendal (Copenhagen, Denmark), 1988.

Also author of additional plays and of radio programs for children. Reuter's works have been translated into Dutch, Finnish, French, German, Greenlandic, Icelandic, Japanese, Norwegian, Spanish, and Swedish.

Sidelights

Danish author Bjarne Reuter is one of that country's most beloved children's writers, creator of almost sixty titles, only four of which have been translated into English. Winner of the prestigious Mildred Batchelder Award in 1990 for the translated edition of his children's novel *Buster's World,* Reuter was also a recipient of an

Academy Award in 1989 for the script of the film *Pelle the Conqueror.* Other movie collaborations from Reuter include the 1983 *Zappa,* and its 1984 sequel, *Tro, hab, og karlighed,* released in English as *Twist and Shout.*

Born in Denmark in 1950, Reuter was trained as a teacher and worked in education until 1980 when his growing list of publications allowed him to pursue writing full time. He was already well-known in his native Denmark when he entered into a collaboration with the film director Bille August in the adaptation of several of his novels into the two films *Zappa* and *Twist and Shout.* These films deal with the lives of a pair of teenagers—Bjoern and Mulle—during the 1960s. The two are a good-natured pair but wind up getting in over their heads in a gang in *Zappa.* The leader of the gang, Sten, is a tyrant, bullying the members into committing crimes. Finally, however, Mulle and Bjoern break away from him. Bjoern is featured again in *Twist and Shout,*

In Bjarne Reuter's historical novel set in 1942, teenagers Lars and Gunnar and their colleagues take increasing risks in their opposition to the German soldiers occupying Denmark. (Cover illustration by Neal McPheeters.)

set some time after the action in *Zappa.* Here the teen undergoes typical experiences of his age, enjoying the music of the Beatles, and finding and then painfully losing a first love. In collaboration with the adult novelist Per Olov Enquist, Reuter and August next adapted a volume of the Danish classic *Pelle the Conqueror* for film, dealing with Pelle's impoverished youth in Denmark in the nineteenth century. Winner of the Cannes Golden Palm Award, *Pelle the Conqueror* also took home an Oscar for best foreign-language film.

At about this time, Reuter had his first juvenile novel translated into English and published by Dutton. *Buster's World,* originally appearing in Denmark as *Busters verden,* is "an episodic, seriocomic tale of a modern Danish schoolboy's trials and tribulations in a world no longer kind to performers," as a critic for *Kirkus Reviews* described the title. Buster is indeed a natural performer and buoys himself with a repertoire of magic tricks learned from his magician father. His teachers, however, do not appreciate his antics and are more interested that he should get a formal education. Equally unsympathetic, his classmates tease and taunt him because he is poor, with an alcoholic father and a mother who has grown increasingly dependent on her young son. Having to bring his father home from the bars is, unfortunately, not uncommon for Buster, and his family is always on the verge of dispossession. Despite this, however, Buster retains a positive attitude and a resilient spirit. He plots ways to get back at the school bullies and discovers love. While the *Kirkus Reviews* contributor asserted that "Buster's life and times stay with the reader," a *Horn Book* writer also lauded this title, dubbing it "a lively and effervescent story of the perils and raptures of a likable and amusing young boy."

More of Buster's adventures are presented in *Kys stjernerne,* published in English as *Buster, the Sheikh of Hope Street,* in which the hero hopes to play the lead in the school play. Again, Reuter uses telling details of Buster's life—fetching his dad from the pub, having to share a bed with his sister—to show the youth's difficult situation. Buster, however, meets life's hardships with determination if not plain mischief. Not chosen to play the part of the sheik in the school play, he seeks revenge by convincing the boy who did get the part to let him do his make-up. The result is that the new sheik—a privileged boy—goes on stage with a green face. Phyllis G. Sidorsky, writing in *School Library Journal,* was not as impressed with this title as she was with *Buster's World,* pronouncing the sequel "not a winner." However, a critic for *Kirkus Reviews* was more enthusiastic, writing that *Buster, the Sheikh of Hope Street* was "a moving story that captures childhood's essence in a rare blend of unblinking realistic detail, pathos, and rollicking, roguish humor."

Reuter turned his hand to a children's picture book with *Da solen skulle saelges,* published in English as *The Princess and the Sun, Moon, and Stars,* a "well-written folktale and a felicitous collaboration," according to

School Library Journal critic Judith Gloyer. In the tale, an emperor dreams that his daughter's suitor will offer her the most precious thing in the universe. His dream seems to come true as a succession of likely wealthy men offer the moon, the stars, and then the sun. Set in China, the story is based on a traditional tale in which the daughter, despite all the power of the wealthy suitors, finally finds the one man she loves. Though disapproving of the somewhat "pat" ending, Gloyer found the story's drama "builds well with lyrical passages." More praise came from a contributor for *Junior Bookshelf,* who termed the book "a really enjoyable story for reading aloud."

With the 1994 *Drengene fra Sankt Petri,* appearing in English as *The Boys from St. Petri,* Reuter returns to the novel form to tell a World War II story about a group of young men who find ways to thwart the German invaders in Denmark. These adolescents include Lars and his older brother, Gunnar, sons of Minister Balstrup. At first, the boys pull pranks on the Nazi invaders, such as stealing their license plates, but soon they escalate to more sophisticated and dangerous resistance activities. With the help of another youth, Otto—whose mother has a series of affairs with German soldiers—the group breaks into a train station to post anti-German flyers. Otto, during the raid, sets fire to the station, raising the stakes in their deadly game against the invading army. Increasingly, the boys become consumed with their resistance mission, limiting contact with friends and family, and plan to derail a German ammunition train. Difficulties also mount, including the threat to a Jewish friend who has been taken under the wing of the Balstrup clan. Meanwhile, their activities are being traced by a German soldier who gets closer and closer to their true identities just as the time draws near for the final attack on the train. *Horn Book*'s Maeve Visser Knoth commended the "pace and tension" of this tale, commenting favorably on the "dramatic, powerful conclusion." "The tension," according to Knoth, "is heart-stopping." *Booklist*'s Hazel Rochman felt that the novel "takes a while to get going," but "what will hold readers is the action." More laudable words came from a critic for *Kirkus Reviews,* who called the novel "tightly focused," and added that the last pages of the book "are suffused with the elation of victory and the success of their last defiant act." For Betsy Hearne, writing in the *Bulletin of the Center for Children's Books,* the novel is "involving," as well as "one that shows how courage changed . . . young lives."

Biographical and Critical Sources

BOOKS

St. James Guide to Children's Writers, 5th edition, edited by Sara Pendergast and Tom Pendergast, St. James Press (Detroit, MI), 1999.

PERIODICALS

Booklist, February 1, 1994, Hazel Rochman, review of *The Boys from St. Petri,* pp. 1001-1002.
Book Report, September-October, 1994, Daniel Harvey, review of *The Boys from St. Petri,* p. 44.
Bulletin of the Center for Children's Books, March, 1994, Betsy Hearne, review of *The Boys from St. Petri,* p. 232.
Horn Book, September, 1989, review of *Buster's World,* p. 623; March-April, 1994, Maeve Visser Knoth, review of *The Boys from St. Petri,* pp. 206-207.
Junior Bookshelf, October, 1986, review of *The Princess and the Sun, Moon, and Stars,* p. 183.
Kirkus Reviews, June 15, 1989, review of *Buster's World,* p. 919; November 1, 1991, review of *Buster, the Sheikh of Hope Street,* p. 1407; February 1, 1994, review of *The Boys from St. Petri,* p. 149.
New York Times, April 3, 1984; May 16, 1984; September 26, 1986; September 20, 1988; December 21, 1988.
School Library Journal, March, 1988, Judith Gloyer, review of *The Princess and the Sun, Moon, and Stars,* p. 184; September, 1989; February, 1992, Phyllis G. Sidorsky, review of *Buster, the Sheikh of Hope Street,* p. 89; February, 1994, Tim Rausch, review of *The Boys from St. Petri,* p. 120.
Variety, March 30, 1983; October 31, 1984; December 19, 1984; December 23, 1987.*

*   *   *

RICHMAN, Sophia 1941-

Personal

Original name, Zofia Reichman; born January 28, 1941, in Lwów, Poland (now Lviv, Ukraine); daughter of Leon (an accountant) and Dorothy (a teacher and seamstress; maiden name, Weiss) Richman; married Spyros D. Orfanos (a psychologist), November 25, 1976; children: Lina. *Education:* City College of the City University of New York, B.A., 1962, M.S., 1965; New York University, Ph.D., 1970, postdoctoral certificate in psychoanalysis and psychotherapy, 1975.

Addresses

Home—590 Highland Ave., Upper Montclair, NJ 07043. *Office*—303 Second Ave., Ste. 5, New York, NY 10003. *E-mail*—SophiaRichman@aol.com.

Career

Private practice of psychology in New York, NY, 1971—, and Upper Montclair, NJ, 1991—. American Board of Professional Psychology, diplomate. Member of supervising faculty, Institute for Contemporary Psychotherapy, New York, and Contemporary Center for Advanced Psychoanalytic Studies, New Jersey; lecturer at other institutions.

Member

American Psychological Association, Academy of Psychoanalysis (fellow).

Awards, Honors

Fellowship Grant, Memorial Foundation for Jewish Culture, 2000-01; Award for Scholarship winner, Jewish Women's Caucus of the Association for Women in Psychology, 2003.

Writings

A Wolf in the Attic: The Legacy of a Hidden Child of the Holocaust (memoir), Haworth Press (Binghamton, NY), 2002.

A Wolf in the Attic was translated into Greek.

Sidelights

Sophia Richman told *SATA:* "I have never thought of myself as a writer. I have been a psychologist for over thirty years and have found immense satisfaction in my profession. As I reached my middle years, however, I began to look back at my life and felt the need to write my story. Born into the Holocaust, a Jewish child marked for death, I survived against great odds with both of my parents. I spent the first four years of my life in hiding, in plain sight, with a false Christian identity. The life I created ultimately has been a successful and fulfilling one, but the early years have left their indelible mark.

"In my decision to tell the story of what happened to my family during the war years, I join the many other survivors who feel the responsibility to record the tragic events of the last century for posterity. For many years after the war, a wall of silence surrounded the Holocaust, and few survivors shared their experiences with the world. Now with the dwindling population of the last living witnesses, the climate has changed, the world is more receptive, and many of us are committed to record our stories. After reading many memoirs, I was inspired to write my own. This autobiography is somewhat unique in its perspective; it goes beyond the war years and focuses on the long-term psychological impact of a hidden childhood.

"Writing was an amazing experience for me. As a very young child survivor, my memories were few and fragmented. Creating a narrative has helped me achieve greater integration and a sense of continuity. The writing process was surprisingly effortless and gratifying. There was a driving force to express myself. Words came to me that I didn't even realize were in my vocabulary. Despite the painful subject, I didn't experience any emotional blocks. I felt empowered and free.

"The memoir has been well received by the general public as well as by a professional readership. It is a crossover book helpful to professionals working with survivors as well as survivors themselves. People who are interested in resilience after tragedy find it inspiring."

Biographical and Critical Sources

PERIODICALS

Booklist, December 15, 2001, George Cohen, review of *A Wolf in the Attic: The Legacy of a Hidden Child of the Holocaust,* p. 701.
Publishers Weekly, February 18, 2002, review of *A Wolf in the Attic,* p. 84.

*   *   *

ROPER, Robert 1946-

Personal

Born June 10, 1946, in New York; son of Burt W. (a lawyer) and Miriam (a teacher; maiden name, Wickner) Roper; married Summer Brenner (a writer); children: Michael, Doise, Caitlin. *Education:* Swarthmore College, B.A., 1968; University of California—Berkeley, M.A., 1969.

Addresses

Home—1321 Milvia St., Berkeley, CA 94709. *Agent*—Robbins Office, 866 Second Ave., 5th Fl., New York, NY 10019.

Career

Merchant seaman, 1970-71; guitarist and singer. Writer, 1972—.

Member

Sailors' International Union, Writers Guild of America, Phi Beta Kappa.

Awards, Honors

National Endowment for the Arts grant; Ingram Merril Award; Stegner Fellowship.

Writings

Royo County (novelized stories), Morrow (New York, NY), 1973.
On Spider Creek (novel), Simon & Schuster (New York, NY), 1978.

Mexico Days (novel), Weidenfeld & Nicolson (New York, NY), 1989.

In Caverns of Blue Ice (for young adults), Sierra Club Books (San Francisco, CA), 1991.

The Trespassers, Ticknor & Fields (New York, NY), 1992.

Cuervo Tales, Ticknor & Fields (New York, NY), 1993.

Fatal Mountaineer: The High-Altitude Life and Death of Willi Unsoeld, American Himalayan Legend, St. Martin's Press (New York, NY), 2002.

Victory to the Moth, Context Books (Berkeley, CA), 2003.

Contributor of stories to magazines.

Work in Progress

The Abode of Snows, a sequel to *In Caverns of Blue Ice.*

Sidelights

As a novelist, Robert Roper has received much attention for *Cuervo Tales* and *The Trespassers.* Also a specialist on mountaineering, Roper has used this sport as the basis for two books—one a fictionalized biography for children, the other an account of a climber's fateful assault on one of the world's highest peaks.

In Caverns of Blue Ice, a young-adult volume, covers the life of Louise DeMaistre, the first woman certified as an Alpine mountain guide. This was "a story I wanted

Mountain climber Willi Unsoeld is the subject of Fatal Mountaineer, *Robert Roper's account of a disastrous expedition to the top of the tallest peak in India. (Photo by Bob and Ira Spring.)*

kids to read," Roper once explained. "It originated in little bits of stories I would fold up and drop in my daughter's lunch bag each day. Finally, she demanded that I tell her the *whole* story of Louise DeMaistre . . . and so I began my book." A *Publishers Weekly* reviewer remarked favorably on the "detailed, breathtaking descriptions of various ascents" in the novel.

As *SF Gate* reviewer Floyd Skloot pointed out, "most mountaineering books are written by people who are mountaineers first and writers second." So it was with praise that Skloot welcomed *Fatal Mountaineer: The High-Altitude Life and Death of Willi Unsoeld, American Himalayan Legend.* What distinguishes this book, he noted, "is that Roper is a seasoned, talented novelist as well as an experienced climber. His book combines vivid characterization, gripping accounts of extreme mountaineering, as well as pertinent cultural, historical and philosophical reflection." The subject of this work, Willi Unsoeld, was considered one of the greatest climbers of the twentieth century.

Roper's book opens with Unsoeld's 1979 death in an avalanche on Washington's Mount Rainer, then goes on to chronicle the man's life and achievements, including his historic scaling of Mount Everest's West Ridge in 1963, "the hardest new route on the highest mountain in the world." Unsoeld dedicated his life to mountaineering, even naming his daughter Devi, after India's Nanda Devi mountain. In a tragic twist of fate, Unsoeld would be witness to his daughter's death on that very peak in 1976. The twenty-two-year-old Devi had fallen ill to altitude sickness, but no one in the expedition—not even her father—could convince her to curtail her climb. When Devi died, the other climbers could not carry her body down the mountain. So they wrapped her body in a sleeping bag, hurled it down a 10,000-foot cliff, and resumed the climb.

Beyond the story of one man's dedication to his goals, *Fatal Mountaineer* covers what Roper calls the "sea change" in mountaineering in the late twentieth century. The "ethos of camaraderie" that Roper says characterized Unsoeld's Everest quest had given way to a view of mountaineering as a more slick, commercial enterprise in the 1970s. Though "not the smoothest of narratives," said *Booklist*'s Gilbert Taylor, "Roper's story of the conflict will nevertheless gain purchase with fans of adventure books." Taking a more enthusiastic viewpoint, Skloot found the work "outdoor literature at its best," a "rich tapestry, a book for both the general reader and the climbing fanatic."

Biographical and Critical Sources

PERIODICALS

Booklist, February 15, 2002, Gilbert Taylor, review of *Fatal Mountaineer: The High-Altitude Life and Death of Willi Unsoeld, American Himalayan Legend,* p. 984.

Bulletin of the Center for Children's Books, April, 1991, p. 203.

Kirkus Reviews, May 1, 1993, p. 555.

Los Angeles Times Book Review, June 30, 1991, review of *In Caverns of Blue Ice,* p. 13.

New York Times Book Review, September 16, 1973, p. 4; November 8, 1992, p. 67.

Publishers Weekly, January 9, 1978, p. 72; June 16, 1989, p. 57; May 3, 1991, review of *In Caverns of Blue Ice,* p. 73; July 27, 1992, review of *The Trespassers,* p. 47; May 31, 1993, review of *Cuervo Tales,* p. 42; January 21, 2002, review of *Fatal Mountaineer,* p. 74.

School Library Journal, June, 1991, Joel Shoemaker, review of *In Caverns of Blue Ice,* p. 112.

Voice of Youth Advocates, June, 1991, Jane Van Wiemokly, review of *In Caverns of Blue Ice,* p. 101.

ONLINE

SF Gate, http://www.sfgate.com/ (April 2, 2002), Floyd Skloot, "Exhilarating Peaks and Devastating Slips."*

*   *   *

RUE, Leonard Lee III 1926-

Personal

Born February 20, 1926, in Paterson, NJ; son of Leonard Lee (a marine engineer) and Mae (Sellner) Rue; married Beth Castner, May 6, 1945 (divorced, 1976); children: Leonard Lee IV, Tim Lewis, James Keith. *Education:* Educated in Belvidere, New Jersey. *Religion:* Methodist.

Addresses

Office—Leonard Rue Enterprises, 138 Millbrook Rd., Blairstown, NJ 07825-9534.

Career

Freelance writer and photographer. Summer guide for canoe trips in Canada, gamekeeper for hunt club, teacher of outdoor subjects, lecturer, former camp ranger; founder of Leonard Rue Enterprises, purveyors of photographic equipment and accessories; consultant to Red Hawk Outdoors, Inc., producers of *Red Hawk Outdoors,* seen on The Outdoor Channel network, 2003; producer of outdoors and nature videos, Leonard Rue Video Productions, Inc.

Member

Society of American Mammalogists, National Parks Society, Wilderness Society, National Wildlife Federation, Audubon Society, Wildlife Society, Masons.

Awards, Honors

Received eleven book awards from New Jersey Institute State Association of English; New Jersey Institute of Technology Award, 1963, for *The World of the White-*

Leonard Lee Rue III

Tailed Deer, 1966, for *Cottontail: Children's Pet, Gardener's Pest, and Hunter's Favorite,* 1983, for *Meet the Opossum,* and 1988, for *Meet the Beaver;* New Jersey Institute of Technology Golden Award, 1979; inducted to New Jersey Literary Hall of Fame, 1979; Excellence in Craft Award, Outdoor Writers Association of America, 1987; D.Sc., Colorado State University, 1990; Lifetime Achievement Award, North American Nature Photography Association, 1997.

Writings

Animals in Motion, Doubleday (New York, NY), 1956.

Nature in Motion, prepared with the cooperation of the National Audubon Society, Doubleday (Garden City, NY), 1957, second edition, with Maurice Burton, 1966.

Tracks and Tracking, Doubleday (New York, NY), 1958.

(And photographer) *Cottontail: Children's Pet, Gardener's Pest, and Hunter's Favorite,* Crowell (New York, NY), 1961.

(And photographer) *The World of the White-Tailed Deer,* Lippincott (Philadelphia, PA), 1962.

The World Picture Guide to American Animals, Arco (New York, NY), 1962.

(And photographer) *The World of the Beaver,* Lippincott (Philadelphia, PA), 1964.

(And photographer) *The World of the Raccoon,* Lippincott (Philadelphia, PA), 1964.

(And photographer) *New Jersey Out-of-Doors: A History of Its Flora and Fauna,* Hicks Print Co. (Washington, NJ), 1964.

(Illustrator) John Bailey, *Our Wild Animals,* T. Nelson (London, England), 1965.

(Illustrator) *American Animals,* Ridge Press (New York, NY), 1965.

Tracks and Trails, Doubleday (Garden City, NY), 1965.

(And photographer) *Pictorial Guide to the Mammals of North America,* Crowell (New York, NY), 1967.

(And photographer) *Sportsman's Guide to Game Animals,* Outdoor Life (New York, NY), 1968, 2nd edition published as *Complete Guide to Game Animals: A Field Book of North American Species,* 1981.

(And photographer) *The World of the Red Fox,* Lippincott (Philadelphia, PA), 1969.

(And photographer) *Pictorial Guide to the Birds of North America,* Crowell (New York, NY), 1970.

(And photographer) *The World of the Ruffed Grouse,* Lippincott (Philadelphia, PA), 1973.

(And photographer) *Game Birds of North America,* illustrated by Douglas Allen, Jr., Outdoor Life (New York, NY), 1973.

The Deer of North America, Outdoor Life (New York, NY), 1978.

Furbearing Animals of North America, Crown (New York, NY), 1981.

(Photographer, and author with Joe Fischl) *After Your Deer Is Down: The Care and Handling of All Big Game,* Winchester Press (Tulsa, OK), 1981.

(Photographer, and author with William Owen) *Meet the Opossum,* (for children), Dodd, Mead (New York, NY), 1983.

How I Photograph Wildlife and Nature, W. W. Norton (New York, NY), 1984.

(Photographer, and author with William Owen) *Meet the Moose,* (for children), Dodd, Mead (New York, NY), 1985.

(Photographer, and author with William Owen) *Meet the Beaver,* (for children), Dodd, Mead (New York, NY), 1986.

(Photographer) Virginia Langley, *Babes in the Woods,* (for children), illustrated by Patrick Davis, G. Gannett Pub. (Portland, ME), 1987.

(Photographer with Len Rue, Jr.) Leslie McGuire, *Lions,* (for children), Atheneum (New York, NY), 1989.

(Photographer with Len Rue, Jr.) Miriam Schlein, *Hippos,* (for children), Atheneum (New York, NY), 1989.

(Photographer with Len Rue, Jr.) Miriam Schlein, *Elephants,* (for children), Atheneum (New York, NY), 1990.

Leonard Lee Rue III's Whitetails: Answers to All Your Questions on Life Cycle, Feeding Patterns, Antlers, Scrapes and Rubs, Behavior During the Rut, and Habitat, Stackpole Books (Harrisburg, PA), 1991.

Wolves: A Portrait of the Animal World, Magna (Leicester, England), 1993, Smithmark (New York, NY), 1994.

Birds of Prey: A Portrait of the Animal World, Magna (Leicester, England), 1993, Smithmark (New York, NY), 1994.

Alligators and Crocodiles, Smithmark (New York, NY), 1994.

(With Len Rue, Jr.) *How to Photograph Animals in the Wild,* Stackpole Books (Mechanicsburg, PA), 1996.

(Photographer with Len Rue, Jr.) Ann Mallard, *Bears,* Chartwell Books (Edison, NJ), 1998.

The Deer Hunter's Encyclopedia, Lyons Press (New York, NY), 2000.

Leonard Lee Rue III's Way of the Whitetail, Voyageur Press (Stillwater, MN), 2000.

The Deer Hunter's Illustrated Dictionary: Full Explanations of More Than Six Hundred Terms and Phrases Used by Deer Hunters Past and Present, Lyons Press (New York, NY), 2001.

(And photographer) *Beavers,* Voyageur Press (Stillwater, MN), 2002.

Contributor of articles and photographs to more than a thousand publications in thirty-three countries.

Sidelights

Noted as one of the most published wildlife photographers in the business, Leonard Lee Rue III is the author of and photographer for numerous books about nature. He has, according to Fred LeBrun, writing in *New York State Conservationist,* "always given us scientifically accurate but conversational prose in his popular wildlife books." Writing for both adults and juveniles, Rue has detailed the life cycle of the moose, the beaver, and the white-tailed deer, and has also provided valuable how-to advice for the budding photographer. Rue once commented, "I've often been asked how long it takes me to write a book. A lifetime! All of my life I have been preparing for this and every other book I've written or hope to write. All of my life I have been watching, studying, living with, and reading about wildlife, and my hope is that I can spend the rest of my life watching, studying, living with, and reading about wildlife."

Born in New Jersey, in 1926, Rue has his "roots in the soil," as he once commented. Raised on a farm, he became familiar at an early age to the cycle of nature and the importance of the mix of livestock, crops, soil, and water. Growing up during the Depression, Rue experienced hard times as a farm kid. "The life was a good one, though, and if I had my early life to live over I wouldn't change it at all," Rue once reported. He learned the value of hard work and of the pleasures to be found in roaming the countryside. His formal education happened much more outside than inside the classroom, for it was his love of nature that got him started reading and writing about animal life, especially deer.

Rue's first book, *Animals in Motion,* appeared in 1956, and since that time, he has written books about specific animals, such as the beaver, raccoon, deer, game birds, and the red fox. Rue has also contributed titles to the lore of hunting, how-to's of tracking animals or preparing the meat from game animals. His photography titles have also proven popular. Reviewing Rue's *How I Photograph Wildlife and Nature,* a contributor for *Kliatt* noted that for both the beginner and those experienced in photography, the book offers "a great deal of practical advice." A critic for *Modern Photography* also had praise for that title, commenting that "if wildlife photography has an old master, it is Leonard Lee Rue III." The same contributor noted that Rue "knows all the tricks," and in *How I Photograph Wildlife and Nature,* he provides "a real meat and potatoes guide."

Among his popular titles targeted specifically for younger readers are *Meet the Moose* and *Meet the Beaver.* In the former title, Rue weaves "personal insights throughout the factual narrative," according to a reviewer for *Booklist,* and illustrates the whole with his own photographs. The same contributor noted that Rue writes with "clarity" and that his black-and-white photos of these "awesome and seldom-seen creatures" are "well-labeled." Rue combines such physical facts as physiology, habits, and behavior in this book that should prove to be a "valuable resource . . . on an animal that is neglected in many animal collections," as Mavis D. Arizzi remarked in *School Library Journal.* Althea L. Phillips, writing in *Appraisal,* also lauded *Meet the Moose,* remarking that is was a book whose "excellent text" and plentiful photographs give it a "vital and alive tone." Richard A. Batwell, also reviewing the title in

Appraisal, recommended this "fine book . . . for anyone nine to ninety."

Rue follows the same formula in his *Meet the Beaver,* "a comprehensive summary of the life of beavers, including their enemies and interaction with humans," according to Mark S. Rich in a *Science Books and Films* review. Providing little-known facts, such as the existence of a 4,000-foot-long beaver dam in New Hampshire, Rue shows how the beaver has become well-suited to its environment. Patricia Manning, writing in *School Library Journal,* praised the "crisp black-and-white photographs [which] complement the text" in this "accurate and detailed introduction." Georgia L. Bartlett noted Rue's "obvious fondness for and enthusiasm about the species" in an *Appraisal* review, while Lynne Kroeger, also writing in *Appraisal,* called the same title an "informative book on the beaver," further noting that it was "packed full of interesting details."

Rue has long had a fondness for various deer species. As he once commented, "I've lived among deer all my life. I've watched them, studied them, photographed them, hunted them, eaten them." The fruits of much of this work is seen in his year 2000 title *Leonard Lee Rue III's Way of the Whitetail,* a book about one of the most

Using captivating photographs of the animal in its natural habitat, Rue offers a comprehensive study, month by month, of the behavior of the white-tailed deer. (From Leonard Lee Rue III's Way of the Whitetail.)

common mammals in North America. "Rue's narrative is intriguing and packed with information," wrote Fred LeBrun, who went on to note that the photographs separate Rue's title from "hundreds of other books on the subject." This book provides, according to LeBrun, "the essence of a lifetime of study." Nancy Bent, writing in *Booklist,* also had praise for the title, stating that it is "both scientifically accurate and eminently readable by the layperson." Similarly, in his 2002 title, *Beavers,* Rue once again returns to a favorite subject and one that he has explored before to explicate and educate about this second largest rodent. Rue explains not only physical facts about the beaver, but also how it builds its dams and lodges.

Biographical and Critical Sources

BOOKS

Ward, Martha E., et al, *Authors of Books for Young People,* 3rd edition, Scarecrow Press (Metuchen, NJ), 1990.

PERIODICALS

Appraisal, autumn, 1985, Althea L. Phillips and Richard A. Batwell, review of *Meet the Moose,* pp. 33-34; spring, 1987, Georgia L. Bartlett and Lynne Kroeger, review of *Meet the Beaver,* p. 52.

Booklist, July, 1985, review of *Meet the Moose,* p. 1560; September 1, 2000, Nancy Bent, review of *Leonard Lee Rue III's Way of the Whitetail,* p. 45; May 1, 2002, Nancy Bent, review of *Beavers,* p. 1494.

Field and Stream, November, 1991, David E. Petzal, review of *Leonard Lee Rue III's Whitetails,* p. 98.

Kliatt, winter, 1986, review of *How I Photograph Wildlife and Nature,* p. 67.

Modern Photography, October, 1985, review of *How I Photograph Wildlife and Nature,* p. 40.

New York State Conservationist, August, 2001, Fred LeBrun, review of *Leonard Lee Rue III's Way of the Whitetail,* p. 30.

School Library Journal, October, 1985, Mavis D. Arizzi, review of *Meet the Moose,* p. 176; January, 1987, Patricia Manning, review of *Meet the Beaver,* p. 78.

Science Books and Films, March, 1987, Mark S. Rich, review of *Meet the Beaver,* p. 242.

ONLINE

L. L. Rue Home Page, http://www.rue.com/ (March 23, 2003).*

S

SAVAGE, Candace (M.) 1949-

Personal

Born December 2, 1949, in Grande Prairie, Alberta, Canada; daughter of Harry G. (an educator) and Edna Elizabeth (a teacher; maiden name, Humphrey) Sherk; married Arthur D. Savage, August 22, 1970 (died, 1981); partner of Keith Bell (a historian), since 1992; children: (from marriage) Diana C. *Education:* University of Alberta, B.A. (with first class honors), 1971; attended University of Saskatchewan, 1975-77. *Hobbies and other interests:* Riding, pets, gardening, hiking, photography, singing.

Addresses

Agent—c/o Author Mail, Greystone Books, Suite 201, 2323 Quebec Ave., Vancouver, British Columbia V5T 4S7, Canada. *E-mail*—candace.savage@sk.sympatico.ca.

Career

News editor of *Sun Color Press;* editorial assistant for *Co-Operative Consumer;* curriculum development officer and audio-visual producer at Saskatchewan Indian Cultural College, 1975; freelance writer, editor, and consultant, 1975-84; Government of the Northwest Territories, Yellowknife, Northwest Territories, public affairs officer for culture and communications, 1984-86; Science Institute of the Northwest Territories, Yellowknife, Northwest Territories, coordinator of information and education, 1986-89. Saskatoon Public Library, Saskatoon, Saskatchewan, Canada, writer-in-residence, 1990-91; conductor of workshops and speaker at schools and libraries. Saskatoon Partnership for the Arts, steering committee member, 1997-99.

Member

Writers Union of Canada, Saskatoon Writers Co-op (president, 2001—), Saskatchewan Writers Guild, Native Plant Society of Saskatchewan, Saskatchewan Environment Society, Saskatoon Nature Society.

Candace Savage

Awards, Honors

Recipient of Rutherford Gold Medal in English and Governor-General's Medal for Scholarship; Honour Book Award, Children's Literature Roundtables of Canada, 1991, for *Trash Attack!: Garbage and What We Can Do About It;* Our Choice designation, Canadian Children's Book Centre (CCBC), 1991, for *Trash Attack!,* and 1992, for *Get Growing: How the Earth Feeds Us;* Honour Roll inductee, Rachel Carson Institute,

1994; Science in Society Book Award finalist, Canadian Science Writers Association (CSWA), 1994, for *Bird Brains: The Intelligence of Crows, Ravens, Magpies, and Jays,* and 1995, for *Aurora: The Mysterious Northern Lights;* Bull Duthie Award finalist, British Columbia Booksellers' Association, 1995, for *Bird Brains;* Book of the Year Award finalist and Nonfiction Award, Saskatchewan Book Awards, 1996, and Notable Book for Young Adults, American Library Association, 1997, all for *Cowgirls;* Nonfiction Award finalist, Saskatchewan Book Awards, 1997, for *Mother Nature: Animal Parents and Their Young,* 1998, for *Beauty Queens: A Playful History,* and 2000, for *Witch: The Wild Ride from Wicked to Wicca;* Association of Booksellers for Children Awards commendation, Book of the Year Award finalist and Saskatoon Book Award, Saskatchewan Book Awards, Norma Fleck Award finalist, CCBC, all 2001, and Our Choice selection, CCBC, 2002, all for *Born to Be a Cowgirl: A Spirited Ride Through the Old West;* Science in Society Award finalist, CSWA, and Children's Literature Award, Saskatchewan Book Awards, both 2003, both for *Wizards: An Amazing Journey Through the Last Great Age of Magic.*

Writings

CHILDREN'S BOOKS

Trash Attack!: Garbage and What We Can Do About It ("Earthcare" series), Groundwood Books (Toronto, Ontario, Canada), 1990.

Get Growing!: How the Earth Feeds Us ("Earthcare" series), Douglas and McIntyre (Toronto, Ontario, Canada), 1991.

Eat Up!: Health Food for a Healthy Earth ("Earthcare" series), Groundwood Books (Toronto, Ontario, Canada), 1992.

Born to Be a Cowgirl: A Spirited Ride Through the Old West (adapted from adult title *Cowgirls*), Greystone Books (Vancouver, British Columbia, Canada), Tricycle Press (Berkeley, CA), 2001.

Wizards: An Amazing Journey Through the Last Great Age of Magic, Greystone Books (Vancouver, British Columbia, Canada), 2002.

NATURAL HISTORY

(With husband, Arthur Savage) *Wild Mammals of Western Canada,* Western Producer Prairie Books (Saskatoon, Saskatchewan, Canada), 1981, published as *Wild Mammals of Northwest America,* Johns Hopkins University Press (Baltimore, MD), 1981.

Pelicans, Grolier (Toronto, Ontario, Canada), 1985.

The Wonder of Canadian Birds, Western Producer Prairie Books (Saskatoon, Saskatchewan, Canada), 1985, published as *Wings of the North: A Gallery of Favorite Birds,* University of Minnesota Press (Minneapolis, MN), 1985.

Eagles of North America, Western Producer Prairie Books (Saskatoon, Saskatchewan, Canada), 1987.

Wolves, Douglas and McIntyre (Toronto, Ontario, Canada), Sierra Club Books (San Francisco, CA), 1988, revised and updated as *The Nature of Wolves: An Intimate Portrait,* Greystone Books (Vancouver, British Columbia, Canada), 1996, published as *The World of the Wolf,* Sierra Club Books (San Francisco, CA), 1996.

Grizzly Bears, Douglas and McIntyre (Toronto, Ontario, Canada), Sierra Club Books (San Francisco, CA), 1990.

Peregrine Falcons, Douglas and McIntyre (Toronto, Ontario, Canada), Sierra Club Books (San Francisco, CA), 1992.

Wild Cats: Lynx, Bobcats, Mountain Lions, Douglas and McIntyre (Toronto, Ontario, Canada), Sierra Club Books (San Francisco, CA), 1993.

Aurora: The Mysterious Northern Lights, Greystone Books (Vancouver, British Columbia, Canada), Sierra Club Books (San Francisco, CA), 1994.

Bird Brains: The Intelligence of Crows, Ravens, Magpies, and Jays, Greystone Books (Vancouver, British Columbia, Canada), Sierra Club Books (San Francisco, CA), 1995.

Mother Nature: Animal Parents and Their Young, Greystone Books (Vancouver, British Columbia, Canada), Sierra Club Books (San Francisco, CA), 1997.

OTHER

(With Linda Rasmussen, Lorna Rasmussen, and Anne Wheeler) *A Harvest Yet to Reap: A History of Prairie Women,* Women's Press (Toronto, Ontario, Canada), 1976.

Our Nell: A Scrapbook Biography of Nellie L. McClung, Western Producer Prairie Books (Saskatoon, Saskatchewan, Canada), 1979.

Cowgirls (also see above), Greystone Books (Vancouver, British Columbia, Canada), Ten Speed Press (Berkeley, CA), 1996.

Beauty Queens: A Playful History, Greystone Books (Vancouver, British Columbia, Canada), Abbeville Press (New York, NY), 1998.

Witch: The Wild Ride from Wicked to Wicca, Greystone Books (Vancouver, British Columbia, Canada), 2000.

Columnist and contributor to *Canadian Geographic,* 1999-2003. *Wizards* has been published in Germany and France.

Work in Progress

Prairies: A Natural History, a book about the ecology of the central plains grasslands.

Sidelights

Candace Savage is a Canadian author of nature books, books about the environment, and women's and cultural history. While her many popular natural science titles—including *Wolves, Grizzly Bears, Peregrine Falcons, Wild Cats, Aurora: The Mysterious Northern Lights,* and *Bird Brains: The Intelligence of Crows, Ravens,*

Anecdotes and biographies blend together in Savage's portrait of the young women of the mid-nineteenth-century frontier who learned to drive cattle, ride broncos, and master the many challenges of being a cowgirl. (*From* Born to Be a Cowgirl.)

Magpies, and Jays—attract readers both young and adult, Savage has also written a clutch of books targeted toward the juvenile audience. These include "Earthcare" series titles such as *Trash Attack!: Garbage and What We Can Do About It, Get Growing!: How the Earth Feeds Us,* and *Eat Up!: Health Food for a Healthy Earth,* as well as books of a more pop history nature, including *Born to be a Cowgirl: A Spirited Ride Through the Old West,* adapted from her adult title, *Cowgirls,* and *Wizards: An Amazing Journey Through the Last Great Age of Magic.* Books dealing with cultural and women's history for adults, but which also appeal to a younger audience include *Beauty Queens: A Playful History* and *Witch: The Wild Ride from Wicked to Wicca.*

Savage is "a true Albertan," according to a contributor for *Kaleidoscope6.* Born in the Peace River county of the northwestern part of Alberta in 1949, she was brought up in small towns of the area as well as in Edmonton, Vermilion, and Pincher Creek. As a youth, she developed a love for reading and writing, as well as for nature and the outdoors. Such a duo of passions led her

naturally into writing about nature and the environment. She attended the University of Alberta, graduating with honors in 1971, and began her literary career in the mid-1970s as an editor and publishing consultant. Her first publication, *A Harvest Yet to Reap: A History of Prairie Women,* appeared in 1976 and was written in collaboration with three other writers. Another contribution to Canadian women's history, *Our Nell: A Scrapbook Biography of Nellie L. McClung,* came out in 1979. With *Wild Mammals of Western Canada,* published in the United States as *Wild Mammals of Northwest America,* coauthored with her husband and published in 1981, Savage began a long string of nature books. Thereafter, she spent many years in the Northwest Territories of Canada as a public affairs officer and a coordinator of information and education. A second publication, *Pelicans,* appeared in 1985.

With another 1985 title, *The Wonder of Canadian Birds,* published in the United States as *Wings of the North,* Savage began her solo efforts as nature writer and sometimes photographer. Concentrating on fifty-five of the best-known Canadian avian species, Savage targeted the book at the lay reader and filled the pages with "some surprising information about even well-known species," according to John Oughton, reviewing *The Wonder of Canadian Birds* for *Books in Canada.* Richard Perry, writing in *Quill and Quire,* found the same title to be an "entertaining and informative book," and one "studded with marvellous colour photographs culled from various sources." Laurie Bartolini, writing in *Library Journal,* also expressed praise for *Wings of the North,* pointing out that Savage "has an outstanding ability to dramatize avian environment . . ., physiology . . ., and behavior." And Syd Schoenwetter, reviewing the same title in *American Reference Books Annual,* claimed it "is certainly one of the best and most attractive books to introduce a favorite person to birds."

More avian subjects are presented in *Eagles of North America, Peregrine Falcons,* and *Bird Brains: The Intelligence of Crows, Ravens, Magpies, and Jays.* In the first title, Savage presents an overview to eagles. David M. Graber, reviewing *Eagles of North America* in the *Los Angeles Times Book Review,* termed the work "an attractive little book" that combines text and photography to detail the lives and precarious survival of golden eagles and bald eagles. *Peregrine Falcons* presents another bird whose survival is threatened. Savage combines color photos along with a text that gives a history of falcons, as well as their fight for survival in the light of insecticide and pesticide use, and also traces attempts to reintroduce the birds into the wild. *Booklist*'s Ray Olson observed that Savage discusses the pesticide "tragedy in detail." Avian, and more specifically, corvid, intelligence is examined in *Bird Brains,* "a book written with humor, style, and love for her subjects," according to Edna M. Boardman in *Kliatt.* Well-researched and illustrated, the book examines indicators of intelligence in jays, crows, ravens, and magpies, noting that such corvids live in social groups and are able to communicate with each other about food sources. Bonnie Smothers concluded in *Booklist* that Savage presents so many examples of the birds' "extraordinary feats of memory, calculation, foraging, and so forth" that readers must re-examine their use of the disparaging term "bird brain." Adding to the praise, Louis Lefebvre, writing in *Quarterly Review of Biology,* found the volume as "beautifully written and researched as it is illustrated."

Four-legged creatures take center stage in other nature books from Savage. Her *Wolves,* updated and revised as *The Nature of Wolves* and *The World of the Wolf,* blends "stunningly beautiful photographs and a laudatory text," as Gladys Hardcastle commented in her *Voice of Youth Advocates* review of *Wolves.* However, Hardcastle also felt that Savage's text, illuminating the lives of these often misunderstood animals, "is not as well focused as it could be." Writing in *Booklist,* Mary Carroll commented on the "new research and photographs" in *The World of the Wolf,* considering the work a good choice for "student research." Janet Arnett, reviewing *The Nature of Wolves* in *Canadian Book Review Annual,* lauded the "informative, well-researched, and conceptually strong nature of" Savage's text.

Grizzly Bears continues these animal studies in a book that "assembles[s] some of the best photographs ever taken of the great bear," according to John Murray in *Bloomsbury Review.* Murray went on to note that the "ultimate value of *Grizzly Bears* is that it contributes to the larger effort to educate people . . . and to dispel some of the myths and misconceptions that have accreted around the species." *Booklist*'s Olson also felt that Savage contributed "efficient, accessible chapters about the bear." Her 1993 title, *Wild Cats: Lynx, Bobcats, Mountain Lions,* also educates, combining photographs with "engaging natural history writing," according to a reviewer for *Petersen's Photographic. Booklist*'s Mary Carroll, noting that Savage's books on the peregrine falcon, the grizzly, and wolves were all best-sellers, further observed that *Wild Cats* "has a narrower but no less interesting focus," and offers an "intimate glimpse of the lives of these felines." *Kliatt*'s Celeste F. Klein had further praise for the title, noting that "these photos along with the excellent text, make this a worthwhile purchase."

Savage also deals with the amazing phenomenon of the aurora borealis in *Aurora: The Mysterious Northern Lights,* "a respectable explanation of northern (and southern) lights, along with the apocrypha and lore thereof," according to J. Baldwin in *Whole Earth Review.* Jeff Rennicke, writing in *Backpacker,* expressed relief that Savage did not try to describe the lights with any verbal pyrotechnics or by calling up "gushing, sappy prose." Instead, she presents "a clear, concise treatment" both of the science and of the many stories dealing with the northern lights, according to Rennicke. A reviewer for *Canadian Geographic* similarly found the book to be an "appreciative and thorough exploration into the aurora."

Savage turns to the softer aspects of nature in her *Mother Nature: Animal Parents and Their Young,* a blend of photos featuring mothers with their young and a discussion of recent research on parenting and reproductive patterns. Janet Arnett, writing in *Canadian Book Review Annual* warned that a "surfeit of cuteness threatens to take over this book."

Turning her hand to books more specifically geared to young readers, Savage deals with environmental concerns in three titles published in Canada. With *Trash Attack!,* she "tackle[s] the garbage crisis" in "a straightforward look," according to Pamela Hickman, writing in *Quill and Quire.* Savage presents an overview of the problem and then, importantly, provides many activities young readers can do themselves to help become part of the solution. Complete any six of her suggested projects, and the reader becomes an official Trash Attacker. Savage also introduces young readers to the basics of recycling and composting, and alerts them to the dangers of overly packaged products. Joan McGrath, writing in *Emergency Librarian,* thought this book offered "an amazing treasure trove of tips" on reducing trash. Much the same approach is used in *Eat Up!,* a book about healthy as opposed to unhealthy nutrition. "Throughout the book [Savage] continues to send a clear message that junk food is 'out' and natural food is 'in,'" wrote *Quill and Quire*'s Hickman, who concluded that "readers will come away with plenty of healthy food for thought." Adele Ashby, writing in *Emergency Librarian,* felt that Savage's book "aims to turn readers into good-food experts." Part of this task is done through her five Ns, guidelines for determining which foods are good. These include nutritional need, naturalness as determined by lack of processing and growing methods, the now-ness or freshness and seasonality of a food, how near the food is (which determines how much added shipping costs apply), and by a lack of packaging, what Savage refers to as "naked." Janet McNaughton, reviewing the title in *Books in Canada,* predicted that "parents . . . will welcome this book's approach to sensible nutrition." *Get Growing!* expands on the topic of food, working as an introduction to farming. Ashby, writing in *Emergency Librarian,* did not think this was as successful as other texts in the same series because it "is not well integrated." However, David C. Allison, writing in *Science Books and Films,* thought the book was "structured well" and also noted that Savage's "effort to inform children at an early age that planet earth has been and is being abused is laudable."

Perhaps her most popular book for young readers is *Born to Be a Cowgirl: A Spirited Ride through the Old West,* a book that "highlights the vigorous horsewomen who helped shape the West," as a contributor for *Publishers Weekly* reported. The same reviewer felt that the "historical context is unfortunately oversimplified," but also commented that it was a "browser's delight," full of tales and old photographs of women who rode the range. Employing diaries, interviews, and other original sources, Savage tells the stories of some of the lesser-known women of the West, from managers of vast ranches to rodeo stars. *Booklist*'s Linda Perkins deemed this an "enticing slice of western and women's history," while Nancy Collins-Warner, writing in *School Library Journal*, hailed the same book as "outstanding" and "an exemplary work." Similarly, Joan Marshall, writing in *Resource Links*, dubbed this an "amazing book about the exciting life of cowgirls on the western plains of North America," and a *Horn Book* contributor praised the "lively text" of this "handsome, well-rendered portrait of . . . impressive women and the frontier period."

Savage told *SATA* if she could turn herself into any animal, it would be the black-billed magpie. "More than anything, I am drawn to magpies by the glint of mischief in their round, black eyes. Magpies are always on the lookout for something, be it food, risk, novelty, or fun—anything that could possibly be of interest. I like to think that, in some small measure, I share this ability, as I scan my surroundings for curious new ideas and discarded titbits of information. For me, the fun and risk come from assembling these discoveries into books that, with luck, will bring some unexpected aspect of reality to the notice of other like-minded (magpie-minded?) people."

Biographical and Critical Sources

PERIODICALS

American Reference Books Annual, Volume 17, 1986, Syd Schoenwetter, review of *Wings of the North*, pp. 597-598.

Backpacker, April, 1995, Jeff Rennicke, review of *Aurora: The Mysterious Northern Lights*, p. 143.

Bloomsbury Review, March, 1991, John Murray, review of *Grizzly Bears*, p. 24.

Booklist, December 1, 1990, Ray Olson, review of *Grizzly Bears*, p. 701; November 1, 1992, Ray Olson, review of *Peregrine Falcons*, p. 475; November 1, 1993, Mary Carroll, review of *Wild Cats: Lynx, Bobcats, Mountain Lions*, p. 491; February 1, 1996, Bonnie Smothers, review of *Bird Brains: The Intelligence of Crows, Ravens, Magpies, and Jays*, p. 905; September 1, 1996, Donna Seaman, review of *Cowgirls*, p. 59; December 1, 1996, Mary Carroll, review of *The World of the Wolf*, p. 632A; September 15, 1997, Mary Carroll, review of *Mother Nature: Animal Parents and Their Young*, p. 189; May 15, 2001, Linda Perkins, review of *Born to Be a Cowgirl: A Spirited Ride Through the Old West*, p. 1742.

Books in Canada, December, 1985, John Oughton, review of *The Wonder of Canadian Birds*, p. 19; December, 1987, Paul Stuewe, review of *Eagles of North America*, pp. 15-16; March, 1993, Janet McNaughton, review of *Eat Up!*, p. 39; December, 1993, Lawrence Scanlan, review of *Wild Cats*, pp. 15-16.

Canadian Book Review Annual, 1997, Janet Arnett, review of *The Nature of Wolves*, pp. 425-426; 1998, Janet Arnett, review of *Mother Nature*, p. 431.

Canadian Geographic, February, 1986, Monty Brigham, review of *The Wonder of Canadian Birds*, p. 77; March-April, 1995, review of *Aurora*, pp. 82, 84.

Emergency Librarian, May, 1991, Joan McGrath, review of *Trash Attack!: Garbage and What We Can Do About It*, p. 57; March, 1993, Adele Ashby, review of *Eat Up!: Health Food for a Healthy Earth*, p. 60; May, 1993, Adele Ashby, review of *Get Growing!: How the Earth Feeds Us*, p. 61.

Horn Book, July-August, 2001, review of *Born to Be a Cowgirl*, p. 476.

Kliatt, September, 1997, Edna M. Boardman, review of *Bird Brains*, p. 43.

Library Journal, January, 1986, Laurie Bartolini, review of *Wings of the North*, p. 93; October 15, 1994, Gary Williams, review of *Aurora*, p. 85; July, 1996, Daniel D. Liestman, review of *Cowgirls*, p. 134.

Los Angeles Times Book Review, November 29, 1987, David M. Graber, review of *Eagles of North America*, p. 10.

Petersen's Photographic, March, 1994, review of *Wild Cats*, pp. 12-13.

Publishers Weekly, November 20, 2000, review of *Witch*, p. 61; May 7, 2001, review of *Born to Be a Cowgirl*, p. 248.

Quarterly Review of Biology, September, 1997, Louis Lefebvre, review of *Bird Brains*, pp. 354-355.

Quill and Quire, December, 1985, Richard Perry, review of *The Wonder of Canadian Birds*, p. 33; November, 1990, Pamela Hickman, review of *Trash Attack!*, p. 11; October, 1992, Ted Mumford, review of *Peregrine Falcons*, pp. 29-30; November, 1992, Pamela Hickman, review of *Eat Up!*, p. 34; April, 2001, review of *Born to Be a Cowgirl*, p. 35.

Resource Links, October, 1996, review of *Trash Attack!*, p. 38; June, 2001, Joan Marshall, review of *Born to Be a Cowgirl*, p. 30.

School Library Journal, July, 1993, review of *Peregrine Falcons*, p. 114; March, 1997, review of *The World of the Wolf*, p. 218; June, 2001, Nancy Collins-Warner, review of *Born to Be a Cowgirl*, p. 180.

Science Books and Films, April, 1992, David C. Allison, review of *Get Growing!*, p. 85.

Tribune Books (Chicago, IL), December 6, 1987, Peter Gorner, review of *Eagles of North America*, p. 8.

Voice of Youth Advocates, April, 1991, Gladys Hardcastle, review of *Wolves*, p. 63.

West Coast Review of Books, Volume 16, no. 1, 1991, review of *Grizzly Bears*, p. 68.

Whole Earth Review, summer, 1995, J. Baldwin, review of *Aurora*, pp. 28-29.

Wild West, August, 1997, review of *Cowgirls*, pp. 94-95.

ONLINE

Kaleidoscope6, http://www.ucalgary.ca/ (October, 1996), "K6 Biographies—Candace Savage."

*   *   *

SCHWARZ, Adele Aron
See GREENSPUN, Adele Aron

SHANBERG, Karen
See SHRAGG, Karen (I.)

*   *   *

SHIPPEY, T(homas) A(lan) 1943-

Personal
Born September 9, 1943, in Calcutta, India; son of Ernest (an engineer) and Christina Emily (Kjelgaard) Shippey; married Susan Veale, December 27, 1966 (marriage ended); married Catherine Elizabeth Barton, June 19, 1993; children: Louise Jane, Gillian Margaret, John Ernest. *Education:* Queens' College, Cambridge, B.A., 1964, M.A., 1968, Ph.D. 1990.

Addresses
Office—English Department, St. Louis University, 3800 Lindell Blvd., St. Louis, MO 63108. *Agent*—Maggie Noach, 22 Dorville Cr., London W6 OHJ, England. *E-mail*—shippey@slu.edu.

Career
University of Birmingham, Birmingham, England, lecturer in English, 1965-72; Oxford University, Oxford, England, fellow in English at St. John's College, 1972-79; University of Leeds, Leeds, England, professor of English language and medieval literature, 1979-1993; St. Louis University, St. Louis, MO, Walter J. Ong, S.J., Chair of Humanities, 1993—.

Writings

Old English Verse, Hutchinson (London, England), 1972.
(Editor and translator) *Poems of Wisdom and Learning in Old English,* D. S. Brewer (Cambridge, England), Rowman and Littlefield (Totowa, NJ), 1976.
Beowulf ("Arnold's Studies in English Literature" series), Edward Arnold (London, England), 1978.
The Road to Middle-earth, Allen and Unwin (London, England), 1982, Houghton Mifflin (Boston, MA), 1983, revised and expanded edition, 2003.
J. R. R. Tolkien: Author of the Century, HarperCollins (London, England), 2000, Houghton Mifflin (Boston, MA), 2001.

EDITOR

Fictional Space: Essays on Contemporary Science Fiction (1990 Volume of Essays and Studies for the English Association), Blackwell (Oxford, England), Humanities Press (Atlantic Highlands, NJ), 1991.
The Oxford Book of Science Fiction Stories, Oxford University Press (Oxford, England, and New York, NY), 1992.
(With George Slusser) *Fiction 2000: Cyberpunk and the Future of Narrative,* University of Georgia Press (Athens, GA), 1992.

For this work, editors T. A. Shippey and George Slusser chose essays that examine the past, present, and future of cyberpunk literature. *(Cover illustration by Lanny Webb.)*

The Oxford Book of Fantasy Stories, Oxford University Press (London, England, and New York, NY), 1994.
(With Andreas Haarder) *Beowulf: The Critical Heritage,* Routledge (London, England, and New York, NY), 1998.
(With Richard Utz) *Medievalism in the Modern World: Essays in Honour of Leslie Workman,* Brepols (Turnhout, Belgium), 1998.
(With Martin Arnold) *Appropriating the Middle Ages: Scholarship, Politics, Fraud,* D. S. Brewer (Cambridge, England), 2001.
Film and Fiction: Reviewing the Middle Ages, D. S. Brewer (Cambridge, England), 2002.
The Shadow-Walkers: Jacob Grimm's Mythology of the Monstrous, Arizona State University Press (Tempe, AZ), in press.

Work in Progress
How the Heroes Talk, a study of early Germanic poetry, and *Beowulf and the Origins of England,* a literary/historical study.

Sidelights

T. A. Shippey is a British academic and author of two studies on J. R. R. Tolkien, beloved creator of *The Lord of the Rings.* Shippey told *SATA:* "I have had two interests over the years: medieval studies, especially the early period c. 700-1000 A.D., and fantasy and science fiction. These interests came together in my two books on Tolkien, *The Road to Middle-earth* and *J. R. R. Tolkien: Author of the Century.*" In addition to the two works on Tolkien, Shippey has authored scholarly volumes on Old English verse and *Beowulf,* and has edited collections of fantasy and science fiction stories for Oxford University Press as well as numerous other volumes on mythology, film, and medieval studies.

Educated at Cambridge, Shippey was for a time a fellow at St. John's College, Oxford, teaching much the same syllabus as Tolkien decades before. Shippey explored this academic interest in Old English poetry in his 1972 title, *Old English Verse,* and in further volumes, such as *Poems of Wisdom and Learning in Old English* and his *Beowulf,* a critical study. In 1982, after moving on to the University of Leeds to the chair of English language and medieval literature, the same chair held by Tolkien fifty years before, Shippey published his first Tolkien book, *The Road to Middle-earth.* With this work, he attempted to establish a scholarly apparatus for the examination and appreciation of Tolkien's major works, including the *The Hobbit* and *The Lord of the Rings.* The major thrust of this book was to emphasize the importance of Tolkien the philologist in his writings. Shippey examined how Tolkien's knowledge of Anglo-Saxon and of Gothic languages and their literature helped to shape his own tales. Paula M. Strain, writing in *Library Journal,* felt that Shippey's "comments are learned and wide-ranging," while a reviewer for *Booklist* noted that Shippey's "arguments cannot be faulted," going on to claim the author "analyzes with delicacy and good sense" Tolkien's effects. Writing on the same title, a contributor for *Kirkus Reviews* found Shippey's work "erratically enlightening," and concluded it was "the most useful book on Tolkien since the [Humphrey] Carpenter biography."

Shippey next turned his hand to editing both *The Oxford Book of Science Fiction Stories* and *The Oxford Book of Fantasy Stories.* In the former volume, Shippey gathered thirty stories from masters of the genre such as Ursula K. Le Guin, H. G. Wells, Thomas M. Disch, and Frederick Pohl. However, a reviewer for *Publishers Weekly* also noted that some of the classic authors, such as Robert A. Heinlein and Isaac Asimov, were missing in this "wide and uneven range in the genre." For fantasy stories, Shippey collected tales from Tolkien, Theodore Sturgeon, H. P. Lovecraft, Lord Dunsany, and Peter Beagle in *The Oxford Book of Fantasy Stories.* A contributor for *Publishers Weekly* felt that Shippey did "an admirable job of collecting entertaining, exotic, and readable tales," and also that his selection "fairly represent[s] the varied trends in fantasy over the last century."

Shippey returned to Tolkien as a subject with his 2000 title, *J. R. R. Tolkien.* Teaching in the United States, at St. Louis University, Shippey furthered the arguments begun in his earlier *The Road to Middle-earth,* in particular that Tolkien's fantasy fiction was "fundamentally linguistic in inspiration," as the author writes in his book. Shippey examines *The Lord of the Rings* in light of Tolkien's deep knowledge and appreciation of Anglo-Saxon literature. Further, he takes to task those critics who have attacked Tolkien for his popularity. He also takes advantage of recent polls in England and the United States that indicate large numbers—if not a majority—place *The Lord of the Rings* at the top of the list of the greatest books of the twentieth century. In making such an assertion in his book, Shippey also risked rousing the same body of critics who regularly disparage Tolkien. However, on the whole, his critical study was well received.

Writing in *Harper's,* a contributor felt that Shippey's "commentary is the best so far in elucidating Tolkien's lovely myth." This same critic, however, questioned the appellation of 'author of the century,' requesting that "Tolkien stand beside such humbler mythmakers as Edgar Rice Burroughs and Georges Simenon." James E. Person, Jr., reviewing the title in *Insight on the News,* noted that Shippey "partly proves his thesis" that Tolkien was first in terms of book sales, in the development of a distinct new genre, and as writer of quality fiction. This contributor added that Shippey's central idea, "however, is that Tolkien told a cracking good story skillfully interwoven with a worldview reflecting the 'moral imagination' written of by Edmund Burke." Ralph Wood, writing in a lengthy *Christian Century* review, further explained Shippey's thesis of Tolkien being the "quintessential author of the twentieth century," by noting first that the former century was one of the bloodiest in history, but also one full of technological promise. Wood observed that "Tolkien, according to Shippey, offers what allegedly greater writers do not: a convincing narrative and mythological confrontation with the unprecedented violence and horror of late modern life, yet without despairing over the victory of the forces of goodness and life." Wood also noted that Shippey "is right to contend that Tolkien's intuition of this new all-pervasive evil gives his work a deep appeal to those for whom religious belief is no longer possible."

Aaron Belz, reviewing Shippey's second Tolkien title in *Books and Culture,* noted that "Shippey shares with his subject a deep, abiding passion for philology," and that it was "in no small part . . . this knowledge that made Tolkien's imaginative creations not merely believable but eerily resonant with modern imaginations." By an examination of many words in the text of *Lord of the Rings* as well as the names of characters in the book such as Frodo and Saruman, Shippey finds Tolkien's inspiration in Anglo-Saxon and Old English, according to Belz. The same critic concluded that "much more is contained in the pages of Tom Shippey's book, which is a thorough and highly readable study." Similarly, Martin Morse Wooster, writing in the *American Enterprise,* noted that "Shippey decisively demonstrates that Tolkien's exhaustive effort [in his fifteen years of writing *The Lord of the Rings*] produced one of the few twentieth-century novels likely to endure." Wooster also lauded Shippey's achievement, calling him a "crisp, forceful, and intelligent writer who has produced a highly readable appreciation" that is also "the ideal companion for readers." Richard Jenkyns also devoted a lengthy review to Shippey's book in the *New Republic,* in which he examined various aspects of the critical study, including fictional techniques. "Shippey skillfully analyzes the different registers of language used by different speakers in the story," according to Jenkyns, who also focuses on Shippey's discussion of Tolkien's critical reception, noting that "Shippey's assault on Tolkien's detractors is the most swashbuckling part of the book: he makes merry mischief and scores some hits." A reviewer for *Publishers Weekly* also commended Shippey's work, calling it a "wonderfully readable study . . . [which] makes an impressive, low-key case for why the creator of Middle-earth is deserving of acclaim." Likewise, Morris Hounion, writing in *Library Journal,* remarked that Shippey "convicningly argues that Tolkien deserves to be ranked as a major literary figure." And *Booklist*'s Ray Olson proclaimed Shippey's book "magisterial."

Shippey concluded to *SATA:* "What connects [an interest in medieval studies and fantasy and science fiction] to me is a sympathetic interest in strange and different cultures. My long-standing interest in science fiction meanwhile predisposes me to see technological reasons for cultural and literary differences in early societies; it is also an effective safeguard against what I call the 'Mark Twain fallacy,' the habit of seeing history as a progression leading fortunately and inevitably to ourselves."

Biographical and Critical Sources

BOOKS

Shippey, T. A., *J. R. R. Tolkien: Author of the Century,* HarperCollins (London, England), 2000, Houghton Mifflin (Boston, MA), 2001.

PERIODICALS

American Enterprise, January-February, 2002, Martin Morse Wooster, review of *J. R. R. Tolkien: Author of the Century,* p. 54.

Analog Science Fiction and Fact, March, 1993, Tom Easton, review of *The Oxford Book of Science Fiction Stories,* pp. 166-167.

Booklist, May 15, 1983, review of *The Road to Middle-earth,* p. 1184; September 15, 1992, Roland Green, review of *The Oxford Book of Science Fiction Stories,*

p. 130; March 15, 1994, John Mort, review of *The Oxford Book of Fantasy Stories,* p. 1333; May 15, 2001, Ray Olson, review of *J. R. R. Tolkien: Author of the Century,* p. 1724.

Books and Culture, January-February, 2002, Aaron Belz, review of *J. R. R. Tolkien: Author of the Century,* p. 27.

Christian Century, November 21, 2001, Ralph Wood, review of *J. R. R. Tolkien: Author of the Century,* pp. 24-29.

Harper's, September, 2001, review of *J. R. R. Tolkien: Author of the Century,* p. 81.

Insight on the News, October 29, 2001, James E. Person, Jr., review of *J. R. R. Tolkien: Author of the Century,* p. 27.

Kirkus Reviews, February 1, 1983, review of *The Road to Middle-earth,* p. 168.

Library Journal, April 15, 1983, Paula M. Strain, review of *The Road to Middle-earth,* p. 826; September 15, 1992, Jackie Cassada, review of *The Oxford Book of Science Fiction Stories,* p. 97; June 1, 2001, Morris Hounion, review of *J. R. R. Tolkien: Author of the Century,* p. 163.

Magazine of Fantasy and Science Fiction, April, 1994, John Kessel, review of *The Oxford Book of Science Fiction Stories,* pp. 18-28.

New Republic, January 28, 2002, Richard Jenkyns, review of *J. R. R. Tolkien: Author of the Century,* p. 26.

Publishers Weekly, August 17, 1992, review of *The Oxford Book of Science Fiction Stories,* pp. 491-492; February 28, 1994, review of *The Oxford Book of Fantasy Stories,* p. 76; May 7, 2001, review of *J. R. R. Tolkien: Author of the Century,* p. 234.

Science Fiction Studies, July, 1994, Jake Jakaitis, review of *The Oxford Book of Fantasy Stories,* pp. 252-253.

*   *   *

SHRAGG, Karen (I.) 1954-
(Karen Shanberg)

Personal

Surname is pronounced "Shrawg;" born May 29, 1954, in Minneapolis, MN; daughter of Robert I. (a physician and artist) and Sarah B. (a homemaker and artist) Shragg; companion of John S. Armstrong (in insurance sales). *Ethnicity:* "Jewish." *Education:* University of Minnesota, B.S. (elementary education), master's degree (outdoor education); University of St. Thomas (St. Paul, MN), doctorate degree (education). *Politics:* "Progressive." *Religion:* "Eco-humanist."

Addresses

Home—11307 Rich Circle, Bloomington, MN 55437. *E-mail*—ecoyenta@aol.com.

Career

Writer. Wood Lake Nature Center, Richfield, MN, director and interpretive naturalist.

Writings

(As Karen Shanberg; with Stan Tekiela) *Plantworks,* Adventure Publications (Cambridge, MN), 1992.

(As Karen Shanberg; with Stan Tekiela) *Start Mushrooming,* Adventure Publications (Cambridge, MN), 1993.

(As Karen Shanberg; with Stan Tekiela) *Nature Smart: A Family Guide to Nature,* illustrated by Julie Janke, Adventure Publications (Cambridge, MN), 1995.

A Solstice Tree for Jenny, illustrated by Heidi Schwabacher, Prometheus Books (Amherst, NY), 2001.

(Editor, with Warren David Jacobs) *Tree Stories: A Collection of Extraordinary Encounters,* Sunshine Press Publications (Hygiene, CO), 2002.

(With Lee Ann Landstrom) *Nature's Yucky: Gross Stuff that Helps Nature Work,* illustrated by Constance R. Bergum, Mountain Press (Missoula, MT), 2003.

Contributor to periodicals.

Sidelights

Karen Shragg told *SATA:* "I believe that children's literature is a wonderful medium for what I call 'message writing.' As a committed environmentalist, organic vegan cook, peace activist, organic gardener, and humanist, I have a lot to say. My activist personality would put me in jail, I'm afraid, if I didn't have writing as an outlet. I love to express myself in poetry, editorial columns, and children's literature because the written word is a long-lasting and powerful medium. Natalie Goldberg's books were a huge influence on me.

"As an interpretive naturalist who has worked at municipal nature centers for over eighteen years, I specialize in communicating to people of all ages about a wide variety of topics. Finding inviting ways to get out a message is the real challenge, particularly when the message is about a sensitive topic. Writing is an outlet that is still, thank goodness, a way to communicate about serious things. So much small talk is about topics I find too dull for my attention span. Writing indulges my change-the-world personality in the best of ways."

Biographical and Critical Sources

PERIODICALS

Booklist, December 15, 2001, Ilene Cooper, review of *A Solstice Tree for Jenny,* p. 740.

*   *   *

SINYKIN, Sheri(l Terri) Cooper 1950-

Personal

Surname is pronounced "*sin*-i-kin"; born May 3, 1950, in Chicago, IL; daughter of Norman (an optometrist) and Barbara (an elementary school teacher; maiden name, Kresteller) Cooper; married Daniel Sinykin (an attorney and land developer), August 18, 1974; children: Aaron Joel, Rudi Samuel, Joshua Paul. *Education:* Stanford University, B.A. (communications), 1972, Vermont College of Union Institute and University, M.F.A., 2003. *Politics:* Democrat. *Religion:* Jewish. *Hobbies and other interests:* Pottery, theater, collecting dolls and perfume bottles.

Addresses

Home—26 Lancaster Ct., Madison, WI 53719-1433; 9622 E. Sundune Dr., Sun Lakes, AZ 85248. *E-mail*—scsinykin@charter.net.

Career

Rockford Newspapers, Rockford, IL, reporter, 1972; Madison General Hospital, Madison, WI, public relations coordinator, 1972-75; Greater Madison Convention and Visitors Bureau, Madison, WI, assistant executive director, 1975-78; children's author.

Member

Society of Children's Book Writers and Illustrators (Wisconsin regional advisor, 1990-96), Authors Guild, Inc., Council for Wisconsin Writers.

Awards, Honors

Ed Press Award, Educational Press Association of America, 1986, for *Humpty Dumpty* story "Mostly I Share . . . but Sometimes I Don't"; Arthur Tofte Award for juvenile fiction, Council for Wisconsin Writers, 1994, for *Sirens;* Member of the Year award, Society of Children's Book Writers and Illustrators, 1995.

Writings

Shrimpboat and Gym Bags, Atheneum (New York, NY), 1990.

Come out, Come out, Wherever You Are!, Hazelden Educational, 1990.

Apart at the Seams, Hazelden Educational, 1991.

Next Thing to Strangers, Lothrop (New York, NY), 1991.

The Buddy Trap, Atheneum (New York, NY), 1991.

Slate Blues, Lothrop (New York, NY), 1993.

Sirens, Lothrop (New York, NY), 1993.

The Shorty Society, Viking (New York, NY), 1994.

A Matter of Time, Marshall Cavendish (New York, NY), 1998.

Contributor to reading textbooks published by C. E. Merrill; contributor of stories, including "Mostly I Share . . . but Sometimes I Don't," to periodicals, including *Jack and Jill, Humpty Dumpty, Child Life, Children's Playmate, Children's Digest, Redbook, Turtle,* and *Children's Album.* Stanford alumni magazine, "Class of '72" correspondent, 1972-97.

"MAGIC ATTIC CLUB" SERIES

The Secret of the Attic, Magic Attic Press (New York, NY), 1995.

Heather at the Barre, Magic Attic Press (Portland, ME), 1995.

Heather, Belle of the Ball, illustrated by Ed Tadiello, Magic Attic Press (Portland, ME), 1995.

Heather Takes the Reins, illustrated by Ed Tadiello, Magic Attic Press (Portland, ME), 1996.

Viva Heather!, illustrated by Richard Lauter, Magic Attic Press (Portland, ME), 1996.

Alison Walks the Wire, illustrated by Gabriel Picart, Magic Attic Press (Portland, ME), 1996.

Heather Goes to Hollywood, illustrated by Richard Lauter, Magic Attic Press (Portland, ME), 1997.

Trapped beyond the Magic Attic, illustrated by Gabriel Picart, Magic Attic Press (Portland, ME), 1997.

Work in Progress

Saving Adam and *Giving up the Ghost.*

Sidelights

Sheri Cooper Sinykin is the author of imaginative books for preteen readers that often combine recognizable adolescent difficulties with fantasy elements such as time travel and magic talismans. In *Slate Blues,* for example, thirteen-year-old Reina discovers that she has a rock-star relative, and she hopes popularizing this fact will provide her with a ticket to the in-crowd at school. *Sirens* introduces teen protagonist Chantal Lanier, whose wish that boys at school would like her comes true due to the power of a magic statue . . . until a chain of unforseen consequences causes her to question the price of popularity. *A Matter of Time* commences with eleven-year-old Jody being magically transported back into the 1950s when he steps inside an old television console. Through the use of distancing devices such as magic statues and time machines, Sinykin offers subtle lessons about growing up, facing down peer pressure, and coming to understand older generations. Praising *Slate Blues* as "a nicely delivered story with a wealth of carefully drawn characters," *Voice of Youth Advocates* contributor Kevin Kenny commended Sinykin for avoiding "the pedantry which a number of scenes invite" and penning "a story which delivers more complexity than the premise would seem to offer."

Among Sinykin's most popular books is *A Matter of Time.* After climbing into an old, boxy wooden television set on a lark, sixth grader Jody is surprised to find out he has actually been transported back a generation, to 1958. He meets up with his dad, who is a boy the same age as Jody, and gets to meet his now-deceased grandfather and his grandmother, whom he knows only from boring visits to the nursing home, as young, car-ing parents. Sharing their family experiences, he begins to understand why his father and grandparents view the world the way they do. Reviewing *A Matter of Time* for *Booklist,* Carolyn Phelan praised the novel's suspense and noted that readers "will enjoy this trip into the past."

Having raised three children of her own, Sinykin credits her family with being a source of support, as well as providing a host of ideas for her novels. Her first children's book, *Shrimpboat and Gym Bags,* was inspired by her son Aaron and his participation in the sport of gymnastics. *The Buddy Trap* was inspired by son Rudi's recollections of the games he played at summer camp. And *Next Thing to Strangers,* sprang from a family visit to Sinykin's parents at their senior citizen's trailer park in Arizona. Diane Roback in *Publishers Weekly* felt that young readers would enjoy the "Rocky-yesque flavor" of *Shrimpboat and Gym Bags.* Another *Publishers Weekly* reviewer wrote of *Next Thing to Strangers:* "The characters are well-intentioned and sympathetic, and merit applause."

"An adolescent stint with a junior ballet company in which I danced the only male role, a distorted body image, and my hesitance to express negative feelings conspired to push me into using food as a way to manage my emotions for many years," Sinykin once revealed in *SATA.* "My resulting eating disorder and my ongoing recovery have played a significant role in both my motivation for writing and in the themes that interest me. *Come out, Come out, Wherever You Are!,* my picture book on overeating and self-esteem, and *Apart at the Seams,* my young adult novel about a young dancer's struggle with bulimia, in particular were born of this pain."

Sharing her sons' frustrations over being shorter than other boys their age inspired several books by Sinykin. *The Shorty Society,* published in 1994, finds friends Kate, Drew, and Bo joining forces against seventh-grade bullies Grease and Scud when the "short" jokes get out of hand. Unfortunately, the tricks in which the three friends plan to avenge themselves result in counterattacks by the taller bullies, and the battle is propelled into a calamity at the school's Halloween dance. Praising the novel for its humor and energetic plot, *Voice of Youth Advocates* contributor Char Zoet noted that Sinykin's "characters are well drawn" and that the escalating pranks "are on the harmless side and are at time quite humorous."

In addition to her stand-alone novels, Sinykin has published several titles in the "Magic Attic Club" series, including the inaugural title, *The Secret of the Attic.* These works differ from Sinykin's other titles in that the "Magic Attic" books are formulaic and are written to support a collection of dolls and other collectibles. However, as she helped to create the "Magic Attic" series, Sinykin did have significant input into the characters' motivations and backgrounds—and it was Sinykin who suggested that the girls be multicultural and of different races.

Sinykin's fascination with the interplay between generations, "by the similarities and the differences of young readers and their older relatives," as she once remarked, causes her to incorporate such relationships into her work. "I write hopeful books," Sinykin added, "the kind I wished I had read in my youth. My goal is not to 'plant messages' but rather to entertain and connect with the reader's experience. Still, if young readers glean something meaningful that they can use in their lives long after they have closed my books, I will feel gratified."

Biographical and Critical Sources

PERIODICALS

Booklist, June 1, 1993, Sally Estes, review of *Slate Blues,* p. 1816; January 1, 1994, Jeanne Triner, review of *Sirens,* p. 816; May 15, 1998, Carolyn Phelan, review of *A Matter of Time,* p. 1627.

Book Report, March-April, 1994, Jo Clarke, review of *Sirens,* p. 38; January-February, 1995, Anne Marie Lilly, review of *The Short Society,* p. 49; May 15, 1998, Carolyn Phelan, review of *A Matter of Time,* p. 1627.

Kirkus Reviews, May 15, 1994, review of *Slate Blues,* p. 668.

Publishers Weekly, January 19, 1990, Diane Roback, review of *Shrimpboat and Gym Bags,* p. 110; October 11, 1991, review of *Next Thing to Strangers,* p. 143; May 31, 1993, review of *Slate Blues,* p. 56; July 11, 1994, review of *The Short Society,* p. 79; August 14, 1995, review of *The Secret of the Attic,* p. 85; February 23, 1998, review of *A Matter of Time,* p. 77.

School Library Journal, April, 1990, Susan Schuller, review of *Shrimpboat and Gym Bags,* p. 124; August, 1991, Carol A. Edwards, review of *Next Thing to Strangers,* p. 195; October, 1991, Jack Forman, review of *The Buddy Trap,* p. 130; April, 1993, Gail Richmond, review of *Slate Blues,* p. 143; January, 1994, Vanessa Elder, review of *Sirens,* p. 135; August, 1994, Melissa Yurechko, review of *The Short Society,* p. 158; February, 1996, Carolyn Jenks, reviews of *Heather at the Barre* and *The Secret of the Attic,* pp. 102-103; May, 1998, Lisa Dennis, review of *A Matter of Time,* p. 148.

Voice of Youth Advocates, October, 1993, Kevin Kenny, review of *Slate Blues,* p. 219; April, 1994, Cecilia Swanson, review of *Sirens,* p. 40; December, 1994, Char Zoet, review of *The Short Society,* pp. 280-281.

ONLINE

Sheri Cooper Sinykin's Place, http://www.sherisinykin. com/ (May 7, 2003).

Autobiography Feature

Sheri Cooper Sinykin

Fascinated by how one story can have many "truths" or points of view, I've always wanted to serve on a jury. But I've been called for duty only once, and because I had a nursing infant and two other children under five at the time, was excused. I've been waiting ever since to be called back. So far, though, it hasn't happened, and I am beginning to think that Justice, in her wisdom, has realized I might not make the best servant of Truth. My own lifelong struggle to figure out what is true even in my own life, plus my tendency to empathize with all people and have compassion for their respective points of view, might color my objectivity and ultimate ability to make a decision. Indeed, my mind tends to fill in unanswered questions with imaginings, until at some point, I don't know what "re-

ally happened" from what I came to *believe* happened. In my younger years, I might also have been easily swayed by others' opinions out of eagerness to please them. But now, as I cruise into my fifties more comfortable in my own skin, I am more apt to trust my intuition over my intellect. Were I asked to help determine Truth in the judicial process, I fear that my writer-self might sabotage my honest-citizen-self, without meaning to.

So, what is the truth of my life? Some facts are irrefutable. I was born Sheril Terri Cooper on May 3, 1950, at Michael Reese Hospital in Chicago, Illinois. At the time, my father, Norman Cooper, was in his last month of optometric training at Northern Illinois Col-

Sheri Cooper Sinykin

lege of Optometry. Raised on Faile Street in The Bronx, New York, to Jewish immigrant parents from Austria and Russia, my dad had a natural curiosity about people and a gift for conversation that he retains to this day. Both abilities helped win him instant friends on the train—all Jewish as it turned out—and a place to live at their fraternity house when he headed off after World War II to start at the University of California-Berkeley on the G.I. Bill. There he met my mother, Barbara Jane Kresteller, daughter of one of the first car dealers in San Francisco. A model and accomplished singer and dancer, she had enrolled at the university when she was only sixteen. Once she met Dad, though, she left her life of privilege and abandoned pursuit of an undergraduate degree in music performance. She married him six months later on September 13, 1947. At this writing, they have been together almost fifty-six years.

Mom would tell me of meeting my paternal grandparents for the first time in New York City, having driven cross-country with only her mother, Pauline Kuttner Kresteller Stulsaft; her father, Morton T. Kresteller, died when Mom was fifteen. I can imagine how she must have felt when Dad's parents questioned whether she was really Jewish and therefore "acceptable to marry" their only son. Years later when I met my prospective in-laws in Madison, WI, their friends questioned whether I too—a blue-eyed blonde—was really Jewish.

My father recalls that on the night I was born, he and Mom hailed a cab to get to the hospital. They lived on South Ellis Street on the South Side of Chicago, a

rough neighborhood even then, but what they could afford. Also on that street corner was a man clutching his stomach and bleeding profusely from an apparent knife wound. Dad pulled him into the cab. I don't know whether the man survived. I did, obviously, weighing in at a hefty nine pounds.

Soon after, Mom and I made the long trip to her mother's home in Burlingame, California, and Dad graduated a month later with only a few of his relatives present at the ceremony. I can imagine the mix of pride and sadness he must have felt on that day, his young family not there to share his joy and accomplishment.

Seeing herky-jerky home movie pictures of both Nanas diapering and powdering and swathing me in thick receiving blankets lets me know I was loved. And yet because of distance and finances, I rarely saw my Cooper grandparents, who lived in New York City and couldn't afford to visit often. Still, these distant grandparents—along with everything I didn't understand about them—would later influence my writing. In *Next Thing to Strangers* and *A Matter of Time*, for example, my characters struggle to understand grandparents who are strangers to them, as my Cooper grandparents were.

My paternal grandfather, Harry Cooper, immigrated from the Ukraine with his father Nehemiah and brother Ben as a youngster, and became a garment worker. He never saw his mother and sisters again. The Nazi invasion in Russia ended dreams of an eventual reunion in America. My Cooper grandparents retained many immigrant ways—thick accents, meals made with love but little seasoning and flavor, and an adherence to religious traditions that I and my siblings resisted. While my grandfather lived to be a hundred—he and Nana eventually followed her brother Max Cohen to Sacramento after I was out of high school—he never learned to read English and spoke it sparingly. His wife, Dora Cohen Cooper, was the brains and power in that union, and I always thought it a shame she was saddled at a young age with raising nine younger siblings rather than getting a formal education. I remember succumbing to her desire to plait my long blonde hair (which my mother never did), and squinting hard against the pull of the comb through my tangles and the firm tug of each section way down to the roots. At the time, I thought she was torturing me. One treasured gift from these grandparents was an "old world" music box, with metal disks of opera classics like *Carmen* and *The Merry Widow* and *Rigoletto* as well as nursery rhymes. Even when I was young, my parents trusted me with the precious polished-wood box—something I never did with my eldest son, to whom I bequeathed it on his birth. Despite the lack of my Cooper grandparents' physical presence in my life when I was growing up, their need for caretaking in later years would help me empathize with the older generation's desire to reconnect with their children and grandchildren.

After Dad began his first optometric practice in Sacramento, however, my Nana Pauline—Mom's mother—lived close enough to come for cherished visits. She'd drive up in her latest shiny Cadillac, honking from a block away, the sounds making my heart sing. She'd come bearing Dungeness crab from San Francisco, a treat that makes me think of her to this day. She'd bring Jewish rye breads and pastrami and lox—expensive delicacies that weren't priorities to my frugal, struggling parents. As much as I adored Nana and she me, I'm not sure we really knew each other at the deepest levels and I miss that, not knowing. At thirteen, she survived the Great San Francisco Fire and Earthquake, and I wish she'd been more of a storyteller, I more of a questioner then, so that together we could have brought those memories of hers to life for me. An equestrian as well as a high society woman who gave lavish parties at San Francisco's grand hotels, she was also an accomplished seamstress and knitter. I remember watching her create a slinky gold gown on the tiniest of needles, then hand-beading it with gold sequins. After her death in 1970, we found a dress she'd been knitting for me—two perfect shades of blue—which Mom finished so I could wear it as my going-away outfit after my wedding.

With Nana, I felt loved unconditionally, though I took great pains not to disappoint her by getting mud

The author, age five months, with her father, Norman

on her white carpets or touching the exquisite orchids she raised that called out to my curious fingers. We'd "lunch" at the St. Francis Hotel on Union Square, sharing Monte Cristo sandwiches, me wearing white gloves and in every way, acting the perfect little lady. She taught me never to order the most expensive thing on the menu, to make polite conversation with other adults, and to always be concerned about proper appearances. I was never one to receive a crack on the knuckles with her knife; that was reserved for my unfortunate brothers. I alone was chosen to accompany her to Disneyland soon after it opened in July, 1955.

Nana had an elaborate collection of antique perfume bottles, and I remember her trusting me to hold them gently, to admire how the light reflected off the cut-crystal surfaces. When she died, the latest of my uncle's several wives claimed them as her own, and it took years to track her down and persuade her to sell me the few she hadn't yet sold or given away to her own family members. I thank my husband for understanding how important those pieces of glass were to me—something that was surely foreign to his own understanding.

Nana loved to travel and she'd send back postcards of herself clinging to a camel in Egypt, riding in a rickshaw somewhere in East Asia, or climbing a Mayan pyramid in the Yucatan. She'd also send packages, each containing two dolls from the countries she visited. My sister (Merle, born in 1952) and I used to take turns having "first pick" of the dolls. I took special interest in tracing out Nana's journey with yarn on a large world map. When she returned, she'd show reel upon reel of movie pictures. Not fully understanding this new camera of hers, she'd often turn it on its side while filming—something she'd seen other photographers do using *still* cameras. And so we'd crank our heads whenever the Taj Mahal or some other wonder of the world suddenly went sideways.

Nana's journeys fed my own love of travel and of learning foreign languages—one thing Nana herself wished she had learned. I studied Spanish first, taking five years during high school plus commuting to a nearby college while still a senior for more courses. I also crammed three years of German and one year of French into my high school curriculum, adding a semester of Portuguese later in college. Each high school summer, I was fortunate to be able to travel with study abroad programs. At fifteen, I spent two months touring Spain and studying at the University of Barcelona on the island of Mallorca. The next summer I explored Germany, Switzerland, and Austria, with stops in Paris and in London for musicals and the then-famous Carnaby Street. Most painful for me was visiting Dachau concentration camp near Munich and hearing my "friends" in the tour group joke about visiting Jewish bakeries. I wondered how many of my relatives had perished there, whether I was gazing at their glasses in the mountain of frames on display.

The following summer a friend who knew no Spanish traveled by bus with me from Sacramento to Saltillo,

Age eight months, with mother, Barbara, and Nana Pauline

Mexico, to live with a family and study for three weeks at the Universidad de Jaime Balmes. This experience lit a fire under me. When I returned to Sacramento, I inspired the high school Spanish Club to plan a similar group trip the following summer, led by our advisor. At the last moment she refused to accompany us—no explanation given. The other students' parents, however, trusted me—an eighteen-year-old—to chaperone their kids and keep them safe on the bus trip, before turning them over to the care of their Mexican host families. It remains a mystery to me—especially now that I am a parent—that they would bestow this level of responsibility on me at such a young age. I suppose even then I must have struck them as a serious, old, and responsible soul. Still, while other teenagers spent their junior-and senior-year summer vacations listening to Top 40 hits on their transistor radios and ogling lifeguards at the neighborhood pool, I was serenaded in the middle of the night by mariachi bands and courted by a young matador.

This love of languages and foreign cultures had influence on my novel *Sirens,* where Spanish and German provide clues to a mystery set in motion when my character, Chantal, acquires a mysterious statue that she thinks gives her the power to attract any boy she wants. Even in the "Magic Attic Club" series, where most story ideas originated with the publisher/doll-creators themselves, I persuaded them to let me write *Viva Heather!*, which explores Heather's search for her Jewish Marrano relatives in the waning days of the Spanish Inquisition. The more I researched both Columbus's first voyage and the expulsion of the Jews—both "coincidently" on August 3, 1492—the more excited I became about links between the two events that to my knowledge had never before been explored in a children's book. The publishers' chief concern was that I might offend Catholic readers with this story. I assured them I could write the entire book without even

mentioning the religion, calling it only the "Queen's Faith." I had hoped *Viva Heather!* might add to the elementary school dialogue about Columbus and religious intolerance of any kind, but it was ignored by reviewers (as most series books are) and therefore largely undiscovered by teachers and librarians. Still, of the books I contributed to that series, *Viva Heather!* remains unique in that it grew out of my personal passions and my secret wish that my own Jewish ancestors—like my character Heather's—were Sephardic (from the Iberian Peninsula) rather than Ashkenazi (from Northern Europe) and spoke Ladino (a Jewish form of Spanish) rather than Yiddish (a Jewish form of German). That, I thought, would explain my feeling of connectedness with the Hispanic culture, language, and people.

I'd always hoped Nana and I would travel together, but it was never to be. One reason I chose to attend Stanford University was to be close to her, but the reality and demands of college life and the lack of transportation in the late sixties kept me reliant on boyfriends' generosity in taking me to visit her, which was never quite the same. On one such trip, my friend and I had become part of a multi-car accident on the Bayshore Freeway. When a policeman drove me to the front door of Nana's swanky high-rise apartment, eyebrows raised until a call went out for a doctor in the building to suture one small cut. Luckily, this was my only injury—except for a lifelong knee-jerk reaction to seeing sudden brake lights on freeways.

At the time, of course, I was blind to Nana's favoritism of me, something my parents did notice but felt powerless to change. My sister probably felt the sting—though she and I often made visits ourselves to see Nana during our school breaks. My brothers, however, must have suffered, since Nana made little secret of her intolerance for "little boys and everything about them." Ironically, by worshipping her own son despite his peccadilloes, pranks, and eventual banishment to military school, Nana succeeded in making my mother—her only daughter—feel like a second-class citizen.

As a child, however, I was unaware of all that. Between Nana's visits, I tried hard to be the good little girl my parents expected. (This "good little girl syndrome" I would later discover in graduate school can be a curse for a writer, who must thrive on conflict and rocking her characters' boats.) I and my siblings—I learned recently from my father—owe Mom our lives "twice": the first time for having borne and delivered us, and the second, because Dad admitted that he himself would have been happy to have had no children at all! He did confess, though, that I'd made him proud and that he was glad Mom had won *that* argument.

As I recall, I was delighted to have a sister born two years after me—and self-centered enough to assume that she adored me, since she followed me everywhere. We often dressed alike and played with our dolls together—me bossing her around, most likely.

Looking back now at photos of Merle's wide, pensive eyes, I wonder whether I overshadowed her, whether she felt she had to compete too hard, and whether adoration was the *least* of what she felt toward me.

When our brother Marc was born in 1954, however, we wondered what all the fuss was about. You'd have thought the Messiah had personally arrived in our modest redwood ranch house on La Goleta Way. A boy! Spread the word! Mom used to set Marc out barebottomed in a bassinet on the front porch, as if inviting the whole world to come admire the wonder of him—and all that Merle and I didn't have. We'd peer in at him, scratching our heads. Then he'd pee on us. The outrage! How dare he! Maybe it was a Jewish thing, finally having a boy in the family, someone to carry on the family name. But after Marc came along, I felt like yesterday's newspaper. I was Avis Rent-A-Car; now, being only a girl, I had to try harder.

I remember my father reading to us, Merle and me squeezed beside him in his red leather chair. He, more than Mom, loved words, reading, and educational shows on TV. Television came late to our family, and our parents were strict about how much and what we watched. No "Three Stooges," for example, and definitely no "Little Rascals," for fear we might get "bad ideas." Mom taught us to sew, and for many years, struggling

Age two

with what I then thought was "a weight problem," I made my own clothes. I felt that until I could maintain the "perfect weight," I didn't deserve more expensive store-bought ones.

Two years after Marc's birth, our brother Loren arrived. Six years younger than I, he grew up in another era it seemed, having his own car in high school and living a football-and-sports-centered social life quite foreign to his more bookish big sister. Always the cute, cuddly one, he became the family mascot who could make us all laugh. Mom encouraged us to play outside—for her own sanity, no doubt. We'd build strange forts of bikes and bricks and wooden beams in the middle of the driveway. When the four of us played horses, Merle and I were the relentless masters. We straightened paperclips into undoubtedly painful "bits" the boys would wear over their tongues. Then we tied on lengths of yarn that we used as "reins." Loren was sweet-tempered "Packy," and Marc, the more cantankerous "Kicker." Although I did not use these particular memories in writing *A Matter of Time*, I did explore the idea of how differently children of my generation—in the absence of TV and video games—and my children's generation played together. The gopher-catching and the pop-bottle "money" episodes in that time-travel novel came from my husband's childhood. Sadly, like my character Jody's grandmother, my mother-in-law has slipped into Alzheimer's in the years since the book's publication.

Unlike my husband's Wisconsin summers, ours in California were spent in and around our backyard pool, which Dad and Mom added when I was seven. Loren could swim almost before he could walk, and the competition began in earnest, with sister against sister against brother against brother, our Irish setter (creatively named Irish) barking his fool head off and chasing from one end of the pool to the other. Loren and Merle were the power swimmers, coached by Sherm Chavoor, Mark Spitz's Olympic coach; Marc and I opted out of the speed competition, turning to diving at which we excelled slightly. Fear kept me from moving beyond mediocre; Marc was fearless.

An unexpected gift from our parents helped Merle and me find privacy and create physical boundaries in our lives. I don't know where Mom and Dad got the idea to construct a playhouse out of wooden blocks from a pencil factory, let alone how they managed to pull it off as a surprise. Apparently, they would work on it at night after we were in bed, keeping the drapes in the back of the house drawn constantly. Since our living room was reserved for company only, we didn't notice and would have thought nothing of having the room darkened. Then one day they invited us into the special room and drew open the drapes, revealing something astonishing and new on our formerly bare patio: a kid-sized cottage with a door, windows, and a perfect slanted roof! We went for a tour and discovered immediately that a hook-lock on the inside would make it possible for us to lock our rowdy brothers *out*. Since our bedroom door had no lock—and we'd both learned

Sixth-grade school photo, 1961

to dress and undress with our backs up against it to guard against sudden intrusions—this degree of privacy was a special treat. We gaped at the sliding Plexiglass windows with curtains, at window boxes for our own flowers, and places for doll beds and even a kid-sized table and chairs. It was all ours; no brothers allowed, except by special invitation. My favorite memories revolve around listening to the rain on the roof while we created dyed eggshell mosaics.

Some years later, the little house disappeared as mysteriously as it had arrived—without warning, discussion, or apologies. Some things were like that in our family, untalked about.

Despite juggling these four rambunctious children, Mom found a way to go back to college and get that degree she'd let go of earlier. When I was thirteen, I recall watching her make the dress for her senior voice recital and hearing her sing in a clear strong soprano that shook the auditorium. Soon after she received her diploma, she began teaching school—music, kindergarten, and finally special education. Much responsibility fell on me to manage things at home when Mom couldn't be there. To her credit, though, she always had ingredients on hand for fully nutritious and home-cooked meals. TV dinners and McDonald's were dirty words in our house.

Once, however, on a night when I was rushing to get dinner made so we all could make it to temple for Jewish High Holy Day services—Mom was off picking up someone from swim practice—a police officer appeared at our front door. He asked if he could come in and look around, that someone in the neighborhood had reported "neglect." Why was I making dinner? Where was my mother? I told him and he said he'd wait. Frantic with worry, I'm sure I burned the hamburgers and maybe more than that. When Mom got home and talked to the officer, his concerns evaporated and he left. But I remember my parents conjecturing about which anti-Semitic neighbor might have picked this night to upset us all, especially Mom, before she had to sing in the choir.

It didn't take us long to earn our respective family labels. I was the good one, the smart and responsible one—also the peacekeeper. Merle was the beauty, the musician, and craftsperson like Mom. Marc, unfortunately, inherited the mantle of troublemaker from Mom's older brother Morton. He likely suffered from undiagnosed Attention Deficit Disorder. From my own experience raising three sons, I've also come to believe that his negative behaviors were inadvertently and unknowingly reinforced by spanking (which was how both of my parents were raised). Nevertheless, Marc seemed to make a career out of getting kicked out of one school after another until finally in desperation, my parents found a boarding school for him—a so-called school for "exceptional children." This fact of his being sent away from the family was something we never talked about, but it left an indelible mark on my soul. If I weren't perfect, I too could be banished from the family. And, because my father always maintained that I had a special ability to "get through" to Marc, it also became my personal failure that he was sent away. Once the focus was off Marc and his behavior, my eating and weight became the family focus—something new to work on and perfect. Unfortunately, such attention had the opposite effect.

Growing up, I was often told that I "felt things too deeply," that I "wore my feelings on my shirt sleeves." Both messages led to the conclusion that if I had nothing "nice to feel (or say)," I should feel (and say) nothing at all. This, of course, becomes a problem for someone who dreams of being a writer. If you silence your voice, you have nothing to write about. But if you speak your truth, you risk hurting the people you love. I solved this dilemma for many years by writing *privately*—letters to my parents I never gave them, attempts at poetry that released my deepest feelings. When that didn't work, I later realized, I turned to food—one way I could rebel against my mother's attempt to "perfect" me. As a result, I spent much of my life focused on the smoke screen of weight and negative body image. These obsessions masked and diverted me from facing pain and negative emotions in my life. Two of my early books, *Come Out, Come Out Wherever You Are!* and *Apart at the Seams* sprang from this struggle and inner journey. As a child I loved dancing—and still do, though now it takes other forms—but soon learned that my body was all wrong for ballet. The pain of having to dance the "male roles" in ballets also became part of *Apart at the Seams*, which graphically portrays a young dancer's descent into bulimia.

Having deep childhood friendships was something I craved, but never entirely trusted. Two neighborhood girls, Chrissy and Carol, were the closest I came to best friends, but I always retained the paranoid feeling that when the two of them were together, they were talking about me, making me the outsider. This theme of being the outsider persists to this day. Only when I am among other writers do I feel fully understood, as if I am home. Indeed, my best friends are fellow children's book writers. They understand that part of me is there with them in the moment, even as another part of me is splintered off, thinking of story or character or even standing back as an observer.

Being Jewish in an essentially Christian society provides another kind of distance, especially at Christmastime. For several years, my parents tried to quell feelings of disappointment by decorating a wooden three-dimensional Star of David with blue ornaments and lights. They also invented (I discovered years later, when comparing stories with other Jewish friends) the "Chanukah fairy," who would knock on our front door and leave presents. I am exploring this dichotomy—being American and Jewish, particularly in a small Midwestern city—in a work not yet published. *Calling Cobber*, I hope, will honor the Jewish immigrant generation and at the same time answer my own questions about what it means to be Jewish in America.

Moreover, other people's ideas of "fun" have never quite jibed with my own. I don't like speed, cold, and feeling dangerously out-of-control, for example, though each winter vacation I dutifully joined my family on ski trips to Sun Valley, Idaho. I knew I was finally a grown-up when I could decide for myself that skiing was *not* something I wanted to do anymore. A child's love of amusement park rides died for me when I was in the fifth grade and my sister fell out of the Octopus ride at the State Fair. Miraculously, she suffered only a broken leg from the thirty-five-foot fall onto asphalt. But I've never set foot on a ride since then. Neither have I found joy yet in following a little white ball around immaculate acres of green. Living part of the year now in Arizona (you can imagine *which* part, if you've ever wintered in Wisconsin!), I am fighting that outsider feeling even here, where playing golf ranks right up there with taking multi-vitamins. Pottery is something new, a discovery and a process that fills me with wonder, excitement, and a kind of in-the-moment meditation I also find in writing. Most of all, fun these days involves my growing family—I finally have a daughter, through my son's marriage!—and hanging out with our three Tonkinese cats, Oso, Joya, and Zuli. I look forward to discovering what else might be "fun" for me in the future.

High-school graduation, 1968

My "first fun," of course, has always been writing. When I stumbled on this discovery in third grade, a world of imagination and possibility opened for me. Unlike math, where there was a right and a wrong answer, writing gave me freedom, which felt exhilarating, living as I did in a family dependent on *shoulds* and *oughts* and *you'd betters*. I credit my teacher, Katharine Morten, for sparking my interest, not only in writing, but also in reading—though at the time, my book choices were more to please and impress her and other adults than myself. "Oh, look, Sheri's reading *David Copperfield*!" they'd exclaim, though I had little comprehension of what I was reading. Still, as I moved my Popsicle-stick book marker farther and farther through the huge volume, I warmed with their praise.

Though I recall going through "phases" in my reading—Nancy Drew mysteries, ballet books, horse books—the first book that personally spoke to me was Louisa May Alcott's *Little Women*. Jo became my earliest model of what I might do with my life—become a writer! Unlike children of today, however, I never met "a real live writer" until I was well into my thirties, and my dream remained an elusive one. I hadn't a clue what the writing life entailed, nor how to go about creating it. As long as I collected "A+ Very Goods" on my school assignments, I assumed (mistakenly) that I was a natural.

In fourth grade I discovered an alternative to the dreaded recess, where the popular kids paired up, excluding us outsiders. I'd help myself to a stack of writing paper from the back cupboard—in those days, schoolrooms were well stocked with supplies—staple the side together like a book and sit on the bench in the hall and write what amounted to daily soap operas about a continuing cast of characters that included my favorite TV stars mixed in with imaginary heroines with names like Carleen Carrigan. There was even a bit of the racy. I remember one chapter called "Shower Power" where hunks like Little Joe Cartwright from *Bonanza* soaped up Carleen's back. Only God knows where this inspiration came from. But soon, I realized, kids were clustered around me when I was writing, wanting to hear what happened next. It was a heady feeling, but also an activity I worried I must hide. What would the teachers say? Not to mention my parents! I imagined their faces as they flanked me into the principal's office to hear that their perfect, dutiful daughter was spinning out dirty little shower stories. The thought horrified me. I'm sure I destroyed the evidence and promised myself I'd "control my imagination" from then on.

One early "book" of this kind I called *Cabin Feud* and wrote out of love and longing for the Camp Fire Girls' summer camp I attended for many years. My second published novel, *The Buddy Trap*, set in a Wisconsin boys' summer camp, may well have unconsciously had its seeds in this fourth-grade work.

The early sixties—and 1963 in particular—affected me deeply. The Cuban missile crisis in the fall of 1962 marked a loss of childhood innocence with my realization that the world is not always a safe place. Closer attention to the news heightened my awareness of the unfair treatment of blacks in the South, though I had never met any African-Americans in my school or neighborhood. The only dark-skinned girl I knew claimed—rather defensively, I think in retrospect—to be Portuguese. Perhaps my being Jewish helped me empathize with the plight of Southern blacks; many of the Freedom Riders, I later learned, were also Jewish. Simon and Garfunkel's folk song about the death of such a civil rights activist, "He Was My Brother," still moves me to tears. Martin Luther King's march on Washington in August of 1963 was followed a month later by the Birmingham church bombing and death of four little girls, and when President John F. Kennedy was assassinated in November, I felt as if the world I knew had exploded before my eyes. I return to this painful, eye-opening period in *Saving Adam*, a yet-to-be-published "young" YA novel that became the creative thesis of my MFA program at Vermont College.

Whatever professional writing aspirations I had went into hiding during middle school and high school. Fiction skills were not taught, my teachers being more focused on book reports and proper grammar than on having us use story as a way to creatively and safely vent adolescent feelings and perhaps even attempt solu-

As a "Stanford dollie" at the 1972 Rose Bowl

tion of our problems. I wish I had had a teacher back then who had encouraged me to journal, as many teachers do these days; so many memories and emotions are lost to me now, and I would give anything to be able to access them. My private (or so I thought) poetry notebooks were the closest thing I had to a journal. I filled them during my teenage years with the pain of assassinations, of unrequited love, rage over the war in Vietnam, grief over the deaths of three astronauts, futility over the lack of control in my life, and finally budding sexual feelings over a first mutual attraction. They were meant for my eyes only. In the well-meaning but sometimes misguided way proud parents often have, however, mine published a collection of these poems as a high school graduation surprise. Imagine my complicated mix of feelings as I headed into a bookstore, ostensibly to retrieve an ordered book for my then-boyfriend, only to be met by family, friends, and total strangers, waving copies of a slim volume of poetry—*In Shining Amor*—written by . . . *me*! I remember that my first reaction was to cry, to hug all my loved ones, and then to wonder how in the world these poems went from under my mattress to the light of day. Only years later, when writing *Slate Blues* about the complicated relationship between popularity-seeking Reina Williams and her rock star Aunt "Slate" did I get in touch with the betrayal I felt over this act of parental pride and love. Some writers believe that we "write behind our own backs," which certainly proved true in this case.

To this day, my feelings about that poetry book are complicated, and it wounds my father, I'm sure, that I think of *Shrimpboat and Gym Bags* as my first book.

I did submit a few poems to contests, and remember winning $50 in the Greyhound Bus Company's "Amazing America" competition. An article on teens traveling abroad was purchased for $125, as I recall, but never published once then-President Lyndon Johnson urged Americans to "see the USA"—not necessarily in a Chevrolet, a popular ad jingle of the time.

Never a boat-rocker in high school, I did create something of a stir when I asked our gym teacher, who was giving us the old sex education talk, "If that's how you *get* pregnant, isn't there a way to *keep* from getting pregnant?" I didn't even know the word *birth control* at the time; I was so naïve and certainly not asking out of my own personal and immediate need-to-know. But I recall her turning on me, wide-eyed, as if I'd morphed into something distasteful on the spot. "Sheri Cooper," she spat, "why would you *ask* such a question?" She never answered it. My best friend turned up pregnant months later, too ashamed until we were in our twenties to tell me why she had graduated mid-semester and moved away. To this day, I've burned inside over that teacher's lack of information and wondered how many other young women's lives might have changed had she simply said, "Yes, there *is* a way." Even our high school valedictorian would have benefited from such a response. When creating Shelley Lewis, the main character in *Saving Adam*, I drew also on the naiveté of this time period, a time before "touching" had sexual connotations and only girls, we thought, were in danger from strangers.

My high school graduation in early June, 1968, was edged in sadness for me—and not because I'd missed being named valedictorian by getting a B+ in P.E. As salutatorian, I was charged with giving the invocation, a poem I'd written months before that began "Today, today, a troubled day, a dark and ominous hour." As it turned out, Presidential contender Robert F. Kennedy had been assassinated in our state only the day before. His death, along with Martin Luther King's two months earlier and President John F. Kennedy's in 1963, weighed heavy on my heart.

When I entered Stanford University in the fall of 1968, I was immediately seized by an overwhelming sense of gratitude to be there, as well as a paralyzing fear that I would soon be unmasked as undeserving of the honor. Not raised to offer my own opinion about anything, to argue, or to defend a position, I wished nothing more than to become invisible in classes where raising my voice was required. One class I looked forward to, however, was a freshman poetry colloquium, led by an exciting new female professor. She wanted to see everything we'd written and encouraged us to write more, more, more! And finally she issued her Judgment: My ideas were trite, my form and expression uninspired. In fact, she told me, I'd never be a writer. So impressionable was I as a lowly freshman that I took her words quite literally to be God's. For the many years I let her voice ring inside me as if it were my own, her Truth became my own. Who was I to think I could write, that I even had something worth saying? And so, it became a self-fulfilling prophecy. I could *not* write. Not poetry, not fiction. Perhaps all that was left was for me to write nothing but the literal truth—and so I chose the "safe" major of Communications-Journalism.

One of the most out-of-character experiences of my life occurred during my senior year at Stanford, when I got up the nerve to audition and was chosen to be one of five "pompon dollies" who danced at ball games, representing the then-Stanford Indians. Modest by nature and self-conscious about my body, I've never been one to relish the spotlight—I still have a terror of public speaking—but I adored the bawdy humor and music of the Stanford Band and thought, "What the heck? Why not at least try out? Odds are, I'll never be selected." The other four dollies were sophomores who at least pretended to be appalled by the band's off-color humor. But I loved trying to one-up the members' double-entendres. Our football team went to the Rose Bowl in 1972 for a second consecutive year, so I also had the thrill of riding on the parade float and dancing before millions at the half-time show—all with a fever of 102. Looking back on the experience, however, I still don't believe I had the nerve to perform in such skimpy outfits or to let myself be viewed as a sex-object. As I say, it was totally "out of character."

After one privileged summer as a Magazine Publishers' Association intern, working at *Cosmopolitan* and *Sales Management* magazines, I knew that I had no interest in living in New York City. Though it was a great place to visit, I could not imagine myself commuting daily or raising a family there. By graduating from Stanford a quarter early—in March, 1972, rather than in June—I had hoped to get a jump on the job market. The only jump I made was half-way across the country, sight unseen, to Rockford, Illinois, where I'd been offered a position as a general assignment reporter for an afternoon newspaper. Rockford and I were not a good fit; landlords looked with suspicion in those years on single women wanting to rent apartments. The newsroom itself was so dense with cigarette smoke that I hated going to work, and resented even more that the smoke came home with me to fill my $125-a-month furnished flat. Socially, because I wasn't married, I was ostracized from after-work get-togethers. Those were lonely months for me.

Though I learned I could work fast and on a tight deadline at the newspaper, I realized that all my hard work was ending up on the floor of a child's birdcage, not in her hands as I'd once dreamed. Still, I told myself I had to simply grow up and make it, somehow, in the "real world."

I moved to nearby Madison, Wisconsin, where a college roommate was starting graduate school. We'd room together, I thought, and I'd take some part-time

Sheri and Daniel on their wedding day, August 18, 1974

jobs until a professional position came along. I gave myself three months—until winter hit—and then if nothing came through, I figured I'd go back to California and admit defeat. After waiting tables by day and rewriting news for TV broadcasts at night, I landed a job as public relations director for what was then called Madison General Hospital. As editor of *In General* magazine, I had wide latitude in exploring subjects that were considered "before their time"—child abuse and stress, as well as access for and activism on behalf of the handicapped. This latter passion grew out of my friendship with two young quadriplegics forced to live in a nursing home for lack of other options. In another issue on alcoholism—due to the stigma still attached to it in the early seventies—I had to hire an actor to be photographed for the cover of the magazine.

The magazine won several writing awards in hospital PR circles, and, serendipitously, it brought me one step closer to writing children's books. The young photographer I hired, Parry Heide, mentioned that his mother, Florence Parry Heide, wrote children's books. Later, in the early eighties, after the birth of my third son, I would remember her name and write to her out of the blue. She became my first "real live author" and advisor, and we have maintained a correspondence for over twenty years.

But while at the hospital and still unmarried, I was charged with interviewing volunteers who had worked

there for a thousand hours. Ida Stein, one of these women, proved a tough interview. I finally trotted out my suspicion that she might be Jewish and asked whether she belonged to a temple, not a church as most interviewers would have inquired. "Are *you* Jewish?" she asked, and when I said I was, she suddenly became the most cooperative of subjects. At length she picked up my left hand and, noticing that I wasn't wearing a ring, asked whether I was seeing anyone seriously. When I said *no*, she told me about her nephew Daniel Sinykin, a young attorney in his father Gordon's law firm. Not being from Madison, I had no awareness of the Sinykin name, let alone its link with Progressive politics, the LaFollette family, and the *Progressive*.

It took some doing on my part to persuade Daniel that his aunt's dating referral might have some merit. But we finally met in January, 1974, and married on August 18 of the same year. My California roots did not transplant easily to Madison, however. I missed my family and hated the weather—winter with its unceasing cold and snow and summer with its humidity and mosquitoes reputed to be "the state bird." Daniel ingeniously convinced me to apply for a position as assistant executive director of the Greater Madison Convention and Visitors Bureau, and I soon realized that if I couldn't sell *myself* on Madison as a great place to be, I'd never convince a hiring committee, let alone prospective visitors and convention-goers.

Once I landed that job, however, my old dream of writing something substantive—a novel, I thought—reared its head. I'd spend my lunch hours hunched over my electric typewriter, turning out page after page of what I thought would be a novel for adults. Strangely, I found myself identifying more with the child characters than with the main character, their mother. At some level, I must have thought, "I'm grown up now; I *should* be writing for adults." Just who did I think children's books were written by, though? Children themselves?

Not until our eldest son, Aaron, was born in 1977 and I had sunk into a depression over working and leaving him at daycare did I take out my childhood dream, dust it off, and re-examine it. My husband supported this dream by enabling me to quit my "day job" and stay home to write and raise the boys. Reading picture books to Aaron and to his younger brother Rudi, born in 1979, re-immersed me in the world seen through *their* eyes, and I loved that space we shared together. Somewhere I had read the advice "write what you love to read," and it gradually dawned on me that, even as an adult, children's books were what I loved. I began to read more widely and discovered authors like Judy Blume, Lois Lowry, Robert Cormier, authors who wrote their Truth and treated children with respect, as if they were worthy of hearing it. Where were authors like *these* when I was growing up, I wondered. How I would have loved entering into their characters' worlds—realistic, contemporary worlds—instead of David Copperfield's!

By the time our third son, Josh, was born in 1982, I realized that no dream would come true without hard

The author's children, (left to right) Joshua, age six; Rudi, age eight; and Aaron, age ten; at the boys' camp used as the setting for The Buddy Trap

work and dedication on my part. I decided to make time to write when there really *was* no time—stolen minutes when the boys napped, an hour after they went to bed, another before they got up in the morning. At this point I contacted Florence Parry Heide and another generous Wisconsin author, Barbara Joosse, who had just begun her publishing career. Both steered me to the Society of Children's Book Writers and Illustrators, an organization that started with three members and had grown to over 10,000 worldwide by the time I was awarded "Member of the Year" in 1995. At SCBWI workshops and conferences I began to learn about craft and marketing, to meet other writers and hear editors and agents talk about the business of writing. I taught myself what I could, revised with the help of a critique group, and finally began submitting manuscripts. Between 1982 and 1988, I collected 156 rejection letters. I told myself that each one brought me closer to "success"—which I then defined as publication, as finally "being an author."

My earliest sales were to children's magazines, and I soon landed several assignments in the education market as well, writing to specifications and deadlines. Confident that I could produce regularly and swiftly, I doled out personal deadlines for the sheer discipline of

it and set regular writing hours once the boys started school. This dogged productivity would serve me well when the Magic Attic Club book creators called on me to get the series off the ground in 1995. I had no idea then, however, that it would eventually contribute to a five-year writer's block, from which I am only recently recovering.

My first novels, *Shrimpboat and Gym Bags, The Buddy Trap, The Shorty Society*, and *Next Thing to Strangers*, were stories that came to me "from the outside in." By empathizing strongly with my sons, their pain became my own and their life experiences (with permission) grist for my novels. In subsequent novels like *Sirens* and *Slate Blues*, I ventured more inside myself, creating characters that grappled with the same self-acceptance issues I did. How badly do I want to be popular? At what price? What if I were loved by any guy I wanted? *Then* would I love myself? The plot of *Sirens* proved especially challenging; at one point I literally wrote my character to the edge of a cliff and had no idea how I would save her. I searched the existing draft for seeds that might have been planted earlier and found to my amazement that the answer was there, as it often is when I trust the process and let go of trying to control everything.

For much of my adult life, despite my blessings of health and family, I fought depression, battling hard to stay on course through the discipline of daily writing I had developed. I eventually learned that I, like many people in northern states, suffered from Seasonal Affective Disorder (SAD), which was helped greatly by light therapy—not to mention spending winters now in Arizona. There also seemed to be a relationship between my creativity and depression, with manic writing "highs" often followed by lows.

Synchronicity played a role in my landing the job as lead author of the "Magic Attic Club" series. As I understand it, I was recommended by two different sources: the first, a book packager I had networked with at a national conference, and the second, a children's book marketer I had met in a public speaking class I took in an attempt to overcome my fears. By getting in at the ground level of the series, I had the privilege of re-envisioning the doll-creators' original concept for their characters Heather, Megan, and Alison. Discussions about the project began in earnest on Christmas Eve—lucky for them I am Jewish!—and continued by fax and phone during my family vacation in Arizona. The first book was to be a Christmas story, and I wondered whether one of the girls could be Jewish; in fact, why not add an African-American character—soon named Keisha—and introduce Kwanzaa in the same story? I asked them. The original girls all had two-parent traditional families; I introduced back stories for each character that more readily reflected the realities of today's readers. With the dolls, their costumes, and their accessories already in production, I—along with three other authors who chose to write under pseudonyms—was under great pressure to churn out manuscripts in less than a month's time to meet the already-announced release dates.

At first, the series excited me. I shared the creators' vision of empowering young girls to believe in themselves; "the real magic is in us" became part of the Magic Attic Club slogan. It certainly was in line with what my character Chantal discovers in *Sirens*. Soon frustrations and creative challenges crept in. Illustrations in *Heather at the Barre* inaccurately portrayed how toe shoes are tied. Readers notice; authors are blamed. *Heather Takes the Reins* featured a red riding jacket and was to be a story about dressage. I soon learned that *black* jackets are worn for dressage. Refusing to write an inaccurate story, I finally found a way around that problem, taking cues from Adagio, the horse, and Heather's character. The red jacket became a "red herring," throwing Heather off in her expectations of what she was to accomplish in her fantasy adventure, but ultimately leading her to some discoveries about "teamwork."

Although they were short chapter books, each one required much research into time period and setting in order to make the fantasy aspect of the story ring true. *Alison Walks the Wire*, in particular, required a Herculean effort for me to pull off a circus story about wire walking, when the regular author was unable to meet her deadline and the publisher called on me to step in at the last minute. Perhaps it would have been easier for me to use a pen name—that way if the book did not meet my own standards, I could essentially hide behind it. But I took a certain pride in being able to pull off what seemed impossible at the time, and stubbornly used my own name on the eight books I wrote before I declined other assignments. My hope was that with the huge marketing effort made by the publishers, young readers would know my name and look for my "own" novels. With sales of over one-and-a-half million copies (to my knowledge) this would have made sense. But at the same time The "Magic Attic Club" was finding its readership, my other novels were going out of print—often without even a warning from the publisher as

After Sheri's MFA graduate reading, 2003. Left to right: son Rudi, age twenty-three; Sheri; husband Daniel; daughter-in-law Debbie; son Aaron, age twenty-five

stipulated in my contracts. Each OP notice felt like the death of a child.

By the mid-nineties, these losses, coupled with the death of my nephew at age eighteen and my mother's Stage 4B endometrial cancer diagnosis in September, 1997, on her fiftieth wedding anniversary, cloaked me in grief. Even a little Russian Blue kitten I adopted, naming him Mikha in memory of Michael, died after a tragic accident, for which I blamed myself. What could I possibly have to say to children that would be hopeful, when I myself was sinking into a quagmire of sadness and cynicism? My agent of eight years dropped me, saying that I hadn't lived up to the promise she'd seen in me. Books under contract were cancelled; publishers went back on their word to me time and again. Editors kept manuscripts for months, even years, without responding—even editors I had worked with and considered friends. Everything in me screamed at the unfairness of the publishing life, and, more important, at the unfairness of life itself. But what were books next to the health and safety of my loved ones?

I haunted the Internet, looking for treatments and new, more hopeful doctors for my mother. All this kept my fear about her mortality at bay for a while. But eventually I forced myself to come face to face with it by signing up for training as a hospice volunteer. I stopped writing; what was there to say? I felt bankrupt emotionally and creatively. Maybe I'd learn to play Celtic harp and use it in my hospice work, I thought. But after two years of lessons, I finally had to admit that I lacked the coordination to do more than pluck with one hand. For the first time I tried wheel-throwing, and found refuge in pottery, in the meditative act of being one with the clay.

My long-time manuscript group members continued to love and support me through this period, which felt endless. They believed that the writer inside me was tired, beaten down, her creative well in need of refilling. One suggested that I was getting ready to write my "best book ever," that I just had to be patient and have faith.

I myself doubted that I really was a writer anymore. I felt like a fraud when schools called me to make author appearances. By this time, being an author, for me, had become a persona I put on for the public. It involved dressing up, venturing out of my writing study, and pretending I wasn't terrified of giving speeches. Even though teachers always praised my presentations after I'd given them—and I myself enjoyed my interaction with the children, once I got started—being an Author—as opposed to a writer—has always felt a bit foreign. Particularly during this fallow period, I had a hard time believing the hype that I was someone special, worthy of banners and walls filled with pictures dedicated to me. Inside, knowing the truth—that I wasn't actively writing—I felt ashamed and undeserving. I thought how foolish I'd been to covet being an Author, when it was really a *writer* I wanted to be, back in my study *writing*.

Letters from my Magic Attic Club fans managed to find me, no matter how many times the publishing company changed hands and ducked my own inquiries about sales. I answered each one personally and thoughtfully, always hoping that something I wrote might touch them, might mean something more than a class assignment to a "favorite author" whose only books they'd read were series books.

As my mother struggled back to a period of remission, I struggled to figure out the purpose of my life. With my sons leaving home for college—and marriage for one of them, so far—I had to acknowledge the double void in my life. No writing—and in an empty nest to boot. I felt as if I myself had one foot already in the grave. But how dare I be so self-pitying when Mom was fighting for her life? I had to *do* something, stare into the abyss, and admit that perhaps life as I had known it was over.

A well-meaning writer friend suggested that I enroll in Vermont College's MFA in Writing for Children and Young Adults Program. "That will impress editors," she said. The cynic in me cried out that I had impressed quite a few editors, thank you, and where had it gotten me? I was tired of pleasing others; I'd spent my whole lifetime doing it. The real question became "What exactly will please *me*?"

A still small voice inside whispered, "Writing again and loving it."

And so I applied to the Vermont College program with *that* goal—not publication or impressing editors—in mind, and started my graduate studies in January, 2001. I wanted to immerse myself in Process and totally let go of Results. At our class's first meeting, we introduced ourselves and shared our writing history, if we had one. Shame burned in my cheeks when I admitted that I'd published seventeen books, but most were out of print and I hadn't written a word in five years. One of the faculty members, Louise Hawes, approached me after the meeting. "Have you ever considered that writing series books might have something to do with your writer's block?" The question took me aback, but I was open to all explanations. She admitted that she had been blocked even longer than I, and had discovered a connection between her own series work and the loss of her voice.

Good fortune smiled on me when I was paired with Louise as my first program adviser. Rejecting all the "ideas" I presented for projects we might work on together, she said none of them came from my emotional core. I panicked. Surely she realized she was talking to a majorly blocked writer!

Instead, she asked me two questions about my childhood. The first was "If the Adult Sheri were to write a letter to the Child Sheri and tell her it's going to be okay, how old would the Child Sheri be?" I answered without hesitation: twelve. Then she asked me, "What happened when you were twelve?" I proceeded to tell her about how my younger brother had been sent away

Sheri, holding her MFA degree, with her parents, 2003

to this special school. But when my sister and I, waiting in the car, actually *saw* my brother's schoolmates, we were horrified. To make matters worse, my family never talked about it. (Recently, in finally discussing this event with my parents and siblings, I discovered that I was actually closer to sixteen than to twelve, but emotionally I felt twelve, and that became my Truth.)

"There's your novel," Louise said. I looked at her aghast and replied, "Oh, no. I can't write about *that!*" Louise smiled, as if she'd heard these words before, and said, "That's exactly why you *must*. That is where the power is."

I went at writing *Saving Adam* "with a certain fear and trembling," as James Baldwin says. "You know one thing. You know you will not be the same when this voyage is over. But you don't know what's going to happen to you. . . ." His words are among a wealth of comfort and courage I found in Ralph Keyes' *Courage to Write: How Writers Transcend Fear* (Holt, 1995). Coincidentally, this same book had sat on my coffee table for years. I just never had the courage to look inside! It helped to read that E. B. White was plagued with fears, as was Mark Twain, who described courage as "resistance to fear, mastery of fear—not absence of fear." When I told Louise I couldn't write about *that,* I had no idea, according to Keyes, that "*that* is what we write about with the greatest intensity. And *that* is what readers most want to read about."

"To touch their readers' feelings, writers must first improve reception of their *own* feelings, then set up loudspeakers so that others can listen in," Keyes writes. "Writing demands revelation. Reconciling this conflict puts writers in a literary-human bind: wanting to be open yet not wanting to offend those they care about. This is a fundamental courage point." If I really wanted to write again, and to write deeply, I would have to let go of my "family good girl" role and risk telling my Truth. By overprotecting myself or my family, I would produce weak fiction. And by writing quickly and doggedly as had long been my habit, I would skim the surface of what I really had to say.

Finally, I realized that my writer's block was actually "the ultimate triumph of fear," according to Keyes. "Rather than paddle boldly into the rapids of our fears, we search desperately for ways to portage around them."

In the program, I stopped paddling and went with the flow. Over the course of two years, I also worked with Ron Koertge, Carolyn Coman, and Marion Dane Bauer, writing not only *Saving Adam*, but also two drafts of another novel, *Giving Up the Ghost*. Set on a haunted Louisiana plantation, it explores my character Davia's fears about death while she and her parents tend an eccentric dying maiden aunt. At Davia's core—as at my own—is the fear that her mother's cancer may recur. While I worked on this novel with Carolyn Coman, my own mother's cancer did return. I spent almost three months with my parents in California, getting up before them at 5 A.M. in order to follow Davia's journey.

Writing then was my pain, my joy, and my salvation. Whatever the future may bring in my personal or professional life—with new books written by Sheri Sinykin, a subtle name change to mark this passage in my writing career—I know now that if I can hear my own voice and keep writing slowly and deeply with feeling, I will be blessed.

SMITH, Helene 1937-

Personal

Born March 14, 1937, in Manjimup, Western Australia, Australia; daughter of James (a wood craftsman and farmer) and Julia Petronella Delores (a teacher; maiden name, Brailey) Lee; married Thomas Latham Wallace (Pete) Smith (a teacher), December 29, 1956; children: Deirdre, Sari, Peta, Sally, Marais, Larry, Sean. *Education:* Edith Cowan University, B.A. (education and English), 1990. *Hobbies and other interests:* "Welfare of children and young adults. Equality for All. Environmental health-planet. World peace."

Addresses

Home—5 Barnes Ave., Australind, Western Australia 6230, Australia. *Agent*—Stephanie Green, Fremantle Arts Center Press, Box 158, North Fremantle, Western Australia. *E-mail*—helenes@iinet.net.au

Career

Writer. Has worked as a nurse, a swimming teacher, 1968-86, in community welfare, 1979-81, as a special needs teacher, 1984-85, as a writer in schools, 1995-2002, as a writer facilitator in schools, libraries, and the community, and as a teacher of creative writing, Curtin University, Western Australia, Australia, 2001.

Member

Victoria Federation of Australian Writers, West Australian Literature Centre, Fremantle Children's Literature Centre, Milligan House Community Centre, Millie-Millie Writers.

Writings

Operation Clancy (crime fiction), Fremantle Arts Centre Press (Fremantle, Western Australia, Australia), 1994.
Leaping the Tingles (adventure fantasy), Fremantle Arts Centre Press (Fremantle, Western Australia, Australia), 2001.
Children of Morwena (futuristic adventure), Fremantle Arts Centre Press (Fremantle, Western Australia, Australia), 2002.

Helene Smith

Work in Progress

A junior novel, *Dreamstone; Yes,* a novel for teenagers on the theme of friendship.

Sidelights

Helene Smith began her writing career with a crime novel, but then began to write the fantasy novels for which she is better known. Smith told *SATA,* "My love of literature and story was nurtured by my mother, Julia Lee. Along with my peers and siblings, I was spellbound by her tales and would beg for stories about her early childhood in South Africa and her family's pioneering days in the timber forests of Western Australia. She would also retell film scripts, novels, recite reams of poetry, and elaborate on our lives as they were lived in a way that was always dramatic and layered with meaning. Our relative isolation was offset by my parents' interest and consciousness of the wider world always. Reading was encouraged from an early age. We also enjoyed exceptional freedom, physical, intellectual, and artistic.

"My memories of those years are vivid and sensual. I remember running joyfully through flooded low-lying fields on our farm, swimming in fresh-water lakes, hunting for crustaceans and turtles, picking aromatic boronia for scent making. I remember the silent productiveness of my father in his workshop and always at the end of the day sitting around a wood fire telling stories and generally wondering about life and what it meant.

"My mother, though not religious in a conventional way, encouraged selfless service within one's profession. This probably influenced me to choose nursing as a profession. After a brief career, I married a school teacher and raised a large family. Once again, interaction with the natural environment became an important part of family life and the storytelling tradition continued in spite of television.

"When my children grew up, I attended university where I studied education and English. After graduation, my interest in the reading process and storytelling prompted me to write a fast moving, easy-to-read thriller for reluctant readers. *Operation Clancy* was subsequently published by Fremantle Arts Centre Press. In producing my first 'book,' I had been hooked by the sheer joy of invention, but I wanted to explore more serious themes."

Smith followed *Operation Clancy* with *Leaping the Tingles,* a story about Celia, a girl who knows she is different; her feet are so light that sometimes she is sure she can fly, but other times they are so heavy it hurts her to walk. Her parents seem to know the secret behind her differences, including the reason she feels an affinity for the tinglewood trees, but won't give her any answers. Neville Barnard, in a review for *Magpies,* explained that there is no real villain or "ultimate source of evil" in *Leaping the Tingles,* "just different creatures protecting their own kind. As such it is a gentle story about being different."

Smith told *SATA* about writing *Leaping the Tingles:* "I have long been concerned for the individual who is different, who feels misunderstood and isolated because of difference. I am also painfully aware of our separation from the world of nature, and in particular, our destruction of forests like the tinglewoods, unique to Western Australia. Put these together, and you have a person whose very life depends on the forest, a factor not recognized or known to those around her. This became the basis for *Leaping the Tingles.* It soon became a labor of love in which I was able to fuse the many images, memories, and imaginings derived from my own family

history with elements from tales told to my own children while camping under the tinglewood trees in the Normalup National Park at Walpole."

In Smith's next novel, *Children of Morwena,* she creates a post-apocalyptic world where a girl named Leila is separated from her family when the Technocrat political party uses their weapon, The Killer, to flood and destroy the town where Leila lived. In *Viewpoint,* Ronda Poultney commented, "All too often novels set in a post-apocalyptic world center on the horror of aftermath so it is refreshing to see in *Children of Morwena* a world beyond the aftermath, where humanity has attempted to re-establish itself."

Smith explained to *SATA,* "*Children of Morwena* has also been very much a labor of love for me. The images for this story came to me by the river near my home in Australind, Western Australia. I had been watching young people playing in and on the water. It was a picture of youth mastering the physical environment with joy and energy. It contrasted starkly with global forces destructive of youth which are ever present in my mind. Slowly and rather painfully, the story took shape. I knew it was about physical, psychological, and spiritual survival, but it didn't come easily. Instinctively, I used elements of epic and fairy tale which seemed to suit the metaphoric language I needed yet embrace all of those issues that are so real to young people in the present and into the future. As in my other novels, there is a great deal of myself in my work. I look upon fiction as something like a dream. Like our dreams, the raw material comes from our impressions, memories, desires, fears, and reflections in a more or less understandable whole. These are tempered then by the demands of literary conventions and the expectations of a young audience."

Biographical and Critical Sources

PERIODICALS

Magpies, November, 2001, Neville Barnard, review of *Leaping the Tingles,* p. 36.
Viewpoint, Volume 11, number 1, Ronda Poultney, review of *Children of Morwena.*

*   *   *

SPER, Emily 1957-

Personal

Born 1957, in New York, NY; daughter of Roy (in magazine publishing) and Rose (a book editor) Sper. *Education:* Rhode Island School of Design, B.F.A. (photography), 1978; New York University, M.A. (media ecology), 1986.

Addresses

Agent—c/o Author Mail, Scholastic, 555 Broadway, New York, NY 10012-3999.

Career

E. P. Dutton, New York, NY, junior designer of children's books, 1979-80; Studio Oron, Gil Goldfine Agency, Tel Aviv, Israel, graphic designer, 1980-83; Putnam & Grosset Group, New York, NY, Director of Marketing Services, 1986-90; writer, illustrator, children's book designer, graphic designer, and photographer, 1990—. Photographs are represented in solo and group exhibitions.

Writings

Hanukkah: A Counting Book in English, Hebrew, and Yiddish, Scholastic (New York, NY), 2001.
The Passover Seder: Touch, Turn, Open, and Learn!, Scholastic (New York, NY), 2003.

Sidelights

Emily Sper told *SATA:* "I grew up in a house full of books. Because my mother was an editor, our playroom was decorated with book jackets. *Whistle for Willie* by Ezra Jack Keats was one of my favorites. When I wasn't playing sports or wandering through the woods behind my house, I read books (for me, books were much more exciting than television!), drew pictures, and wrote stories. In middle school, when I learned how to develop and print photographs, photography became my new passion.

"It's magical to watch the book you are writing take on a life of its own. When I began to write my first book, *Hanukkah: A Counting Book in English, Hebrew, and Yiddish,* I didn't intend to include Hebrew and Yiddish, but it was impossible for me not to! Both languages are rich with vocabulary and expression, and I hope that the words in my book will serve as a springboard to learn more. By understanding language, we gain a greater understanding of tradition and culture. I still regret that there wasn't room to include Latino, French, Spanish, Russian, and Arabic!

"When you write books you write about what is closest to you, and the Jewish holidays are part of me. In the past I started books about both Hanukkah and Passover but never finished them. It was only when I decided to dedicate time to working on self-generated books and projects that I really concentrated on the ideas floating around my head. Advances in technology allowed me to develop my own style of illustration and to print color book dummies in my studio. Because I design my own books, I am able work on all aspects of a book at the same time and this gives me a lot of control.

"I have been asked what my goal was in making books that are so bright, colorful, and interactive. One goal is to create something that amuses ME. If I have fun, children will too! Another is to present information in a fun context. I also hope that my books will add meaning to children's lives and arouse curiosity."

Biographical and Critical Sources

PERIODICALS

Publishers Weekly, September 24, 2001, review of *Hanukkah: A Counting Book in English, Hebrew, and Yiddish,* p. 48; February 24, 2003, review of *The Passover Seder: Touch, Turn, Open, and Learn!,* p. 29.
School Library Journal, October, 2001, review of *Hanukkah,* p. 70.

ONLINE

Emily Sper Web site, http://www.emilysper.com/ (June 29, 2003).

* * *

STOOPS, Erik D(aniel) 1966-

Personal

Born November 18, 1966, in Cleveland, OH; son of Sherrie L. Stoops (an author). *Education:* Attended Scottsdale College and Phoenix College; Arizona State University, B.S., 1991, master's degree candidate. *Politics:* Republican. *Religion:* Jewish.

Addresses

Agent—c/o Author Mail, Sterling Publishing, 387 Park Ave. S., New York, NY 10016.

Career

Metro Discovery Center, Phoenix, AZ, Discover Living Treasures zoological center, vice president of education center, 1989-93, museum director and curator of reptiles, 1990-92. Public speaker at schools for outreach programs.

Member

American Zoological Parks and Aquariums, Society of Children's Book Writers and Illustrators.

Writings

FOR CHILDREN

(With Annette T. Wright) *Snakes,* Sterling Publishing (New York, NY), 1992.
(With mother, Sherrie L. Stoops) *Sharks,* illustrated by Jeffrey L. Martin, Sterling Publishing (New York, NY), 1994.

Facts about a variety of dolphin species, from their courting rituals to their eating habits, are found in the question-and-answer text of **Dolphins,** *written by Erik D. Stoops, Jeffrey L. Martin, and Debbie Lynne Stone. (Photo by Mari A. Smultea.).*

Penguins and Seals (CD-ROM), Emerging Technology Consultants, 1994.

(With Debbie Lynne Stone) *Alligators and Crocodiles,* Sterling Publishing (New York, NY), 1994.

(With Jeffrey L. Martin and Debbie Lynne Stone) *Whales,* Sterling Publishing (New York, NY), 1995.

(With Jeffrey L. Martin) *Scorpions and Venomous Insects of the Southwest,* Golden West Publishers (Phoenix, AZ), 1995.

(With Jeffrey L. Martin and Debbie Lynne Stone) *Dolphins,* Sterling Publishing (New York, NY), 1996.

(With Dagmar Fertl) *Wolves and Their Relatives,* Sterling Publishing (New York, NY), 1997.

The Teiidaes, Faulkner's Publishing (Benton Harbor, MI), 1997.

Skinks, Faulkner's Publishing (Benton Harbor, MI), 1997.

Geckos and Their Relatives, Faulkner's Publishing (Benton Harbor, MI), 1997.

Beaded and Monitor Lizards, Faulkner's Publishing (Benton Harbor, MI), 1997.

Chameleons and Agamids, Faulkner's Publishing (Benton Harbor, MI), 1997.

Iguanids and Their Relatives, Faulkner's Publishing (Benton Harbor, MI), 1997.

(With Dagmar Fertl and Michelle Reddy) *Bears,* Sterling Publishing (New York, NY), 2000.

FOR CHILDREN; WITH KIMBERLY JOAN WILLIAMS

The Banded Penguins, Faulkner's Publishing (Benton Harbor, MI), 2000.

Bat Basics, Faulkner's Publishing (Benton Harbor, MI), 2000.

Bat Conservation, Faulkner's Publishing (Benton Harbor, MI), 2000.

Bats That Drink Nectar, Faulkner's Publishing (Benton Harbor, MI), 2000.

Bats That Eat Fruit, Faulkner's Publishing (Benton Harbor, MI), 2000.

Bats That Eat Insects, Faulkner's Publishing (Benton Harbor, MI), 2000.

The Brush-Tailed Penguins, Faulkner's Publishing (Benton Harbor, MI), 2000.

The Crested Penguins, Faulkner's Publishing (Benton Harbor, MI), 2000.

The Little Blue Penguins, Faulkner's Publishing (Benton Harbor, MI), 2000.

Vampire Bats, Faulkner's Publishing (Benton Harbor, MI), 2000.

The Yellow-Eyed Penguins, Faulkner's Publishing (Benton Harbor, MI), 2000.

The Large Penguins, Faulkner's Publishing (Benton Harbor, MI), 2002.

OTHER

(With Annette T. Wright) *Snakes and Other Reptiles of the Southwest,* Golden West (Phoenix, AZ), 1992.

(With Annette T. Wright) *Boas & Pythons: Breeding and Care,* TFH Publications (Neptune City, NJ), 1993.

Sidelights

Author of thirty nonfiction books on animals and animal behavior for children and adults, Erik D. Stoops is a specialist in herpetology, the study of reptiles and amphibians. In addition to writing articles and books on snakes, he is an expert in the care of boas and pythons in captivity, and he has bred and raised them and many other species of reptiles. His book *Snakes and Other Reptiles of the Southwest,* coauthored with Annette T. Wright, was targeted at an adult audience, and has become a classic of its genre, already having gone through six editions. Working with Wright, Stoops thereafter helped pen *Snakes,* the first in a series of nature books examining many animal species and targeted for a juvenile audience. His books deal with species from bats to penguins, and blend photography with simple text—often in the form of questions and answers—to introduce young readers to the animal world.

Stoops was born in Cleveland, Ohio, in 1966. His mother, Sherrie L. Stoops, is an author, collaborating with her son on one title, *Sharks.* A graduate of Arizona State University, Stoops educates children about reptiles and their significance to the wildlife community. For several years, he worked at the Metro Discovery Center in Phoenix, Arizona, where he curated the "Discover Living Treasures" exhibit about reptiles and wrote articles for the museum's educational programs. In addition, he is involved with the Phoenix chapter of the Boy Scouts, helping youngsters earn merit badges by teaching them about wildlife conservation and proper care of neonates (newly born reptiles). Stoops has worked closely with registered nurse and coauthor Annette T. Wright in propagating certain reptiles that may be challenging to breed, especially endangered species. Together, they strive to protect wildlife, working with zoological agencies nationwide and even volunteering their own facilities as a holding or rehabilitation center.

Since the early 1990s, Stoops has also worked as a children's book writer. His first publication, *Snakes,* set the formula for many books to follow. Here, he and Wright ask direct questions—such as 'How do you know if a snake is asleep?'—to get young readers thinking about the subject. Working with his mother, Stoops next published *Sharks,* which follows the same basic formula of photos, but with longer text and more diagrams. The authors present chapters on "How Sharks Live," "Sharks and People," and "Shark Reproduction," among others. Stoops continues to follow the interrogative approach, leading readers through each chapter by a question-and-answer format. Eileen Egizi, reviewing *Sharks* in *Appraisal,* felt that "middle school students

This work by Stoops and Kimberly Joan Williams focuses on the banded penguins of South Africa. (From The Banded Penguins, *photo by Dr. Frank Todd and Shirley Todd.*)

should find this fascinating and informative to read." Also writing in *Appraisal,* James Knittle found the same title "concise and well written."

Teaming up with Jeffrey L. Martin and Debbie Lynne Stone, Stoops next wrote *Dolphins,* an introductory look at these intelligent and human-friendly animals and a work that *Booklist*'s Lauren Peterson praised for "its accessible format." The same formula of question-and-answer format paired with numerous photographs makes this an "attractive volume," according to Peterson. The information is once again arranged under subjects such as anatomy, eating habits, reproduction, and how the animal reacts to and relates with humans. Donald J. Nash, writing in *Science Activities,* called the book a "nice introduction to the world of dolphins." Nash further commended the thoroughness of the title and praised the authors for presenting scientific data "clearly and accurately." Lisa Wu Stowe, writing in *School Library Journal,* similarly lauded the "skillfully employed" question-and-answer format and the "well-organized text."

Whales is another collaborative effort with Martin and Stone, an "interesting book," according to *Appraisal*'s Melinda Cote. While *Booklist*'s Hazel Rochman praised the "chirpy question-and-answer format," Cote also noted that such a format allows the writers to "discuss many aspects of cetacean biology in a conversational style." Peg Ciszek, also writing in *Appraisal,* called the same title "a colorful, attractive book that provides some good information on whales." Writing in *School Library Journal,* Frances E. Millhouser found *Whales* "a clearly written and well-organized introduction to and overview of whales." Working with Stone, Stoops gives the same treatment to the favorite of Florida swamplands in *Alligators and Crocodiles,* a book that Susan Oliver, writing in *School Library Journal,* felt was a "compendium of trivia on crocodilians of all sorts."

Wolves and Their Relatives, written with Dagmar Fertl, is a "winner," according to *Appraisal*'s Augusta Malvagno. The book's eight chapters, once again employing the question-and-answer format, deal with life cycle, behavior, and related topics, and look at various types of wolf relatives, from the coyote to the dingo and jackal. Lisa Wu Stowe, however, reviewing the same title in *School Library Journal,* was less impressed with this work, suggesting that it "may confound more than clarify readers' knowledge." Patricia Braun, reviewing *Wolves and Their Relatives* in *Booklist,* was more positive in her evaluation, calling the book "a well-rounded view." Again in collaboration with Fertl and with Michelle Reddy, Stoops coauthored the year 2000 title, *Bears.* Arwen Marshall, writing in *School Library Journal,* lauded the "conversational and lively" tone of this overview.

Stoops has also worked solo and with Kimberly Joan Williams in the "Young Explorer" series for Faulkner's Publishing, offering numerous titles dealing with bats, penguins, and a wide variety of lizards. Stoops again uses a series of basic question and answers to make the information more appealing for young readers. Karey Wehner, in a review of *Bat Basics* for *School Library Journal,* found the text to be overall "clearly written."

Biographical and Critical Sources

BOOKS

Stoops, Erik D. and Annette T. Wright, *Snakes,* Sterling Publishing (New York, NY), 1992.

Stoops, Erik D. and Sherrie L. Stoops, *Sharks,* illustrated by Jeffrey L. Martin, Sterling Publishing (New York, NY), 1994.

PERIODICALS

Appraisal, winter-spring, 1996, Eileen Egizi and James Knittle, review of *Sharks,* p. 59; summer, 1996, Peg Ciszek and Melinda Cote, review of *Whales,* p. 35; fall, 1998, Deborah Lymer and Augusta Malvagno, review of *Wolves and Their Relatives,* p. 25.

Booklist, January 1, 1995, Mary Harris Veeder, review of *Alligators and Crocodiles,* p. 820; December 1, 1995, Hazel Rochman, review of *Whales,* p. 630; May 1, 1997, Lauren Peterson, review of *Dolphins,* p. 1492; November 1, 1997, Patricia Braun, review of *Wolves and Their Relatives,* p. 469.

Horn Book Guide, spring, 1997, Danielle J. Ford, review of *Dolphins,* p. 128.

School Library Journal, October, 1994, Frances E. Millhouser, review of *Sharks,* pp. 140-141; March, 1995, Susan Oliver, review of *Alligators and Crocodiles,* p. 220; January, 1996, Frances E. Millhouser, review of *Whales,* 126; July, 1997, Lisa Wu Stowe, review of *Dolphins,* p. 88; January, 1998, Lisa Wu Stowe, review of *Wolves and Their Relatives,* pp. 132-133; May, 2001, Arwen Marshall, review of *Bears,* p. 141; January, 2002, Karey Wehner, review of *Bat Basics,* pp. 127-128.

Science Activities, spring, 1997, Donald J. Nash, review of *Dolphins,* p. 45.*

*   *   *

STRICKLAND, (William) Brad(ley) 1947-
(Will Bradley)

Personal

Born October 27, 1947, in New Holland, GA; son of Silas Henry (a textile laborer) and Eavleen Hannah (a homemaker; maiden name, Watkins) Strickland; married Barbara Ann Justus (a teacher), June, 1969; children: Jonathan Bradley, Amy Elizabeth. *Education:* University of Georgia, A.B., 1969, M.A., 1971, Ph.D., 1977. *Politics:* Democrat. *Religion:* Baptist. *Hobbies and other interests:* Photography, travel, animated cartoons.

Addresses

Home—5044 Valley Ct., Oakwood, GA 30566. *Office*—Box 1358, Gainesville College, Gainesville, GA 30503. *Agent*—Richard Curtis Associates, 171 East 74th St., New York, NY 10021. *E-mail*—bstrickland@gc. peachnet.edu.

Career

Author, educator. Truett-McConnell Junior College, Cleveland, GA, chair of humanities department, 1976-85; Georgia Governor's Honors Program, Valdosta, GA, head of language arts department, 1981-85; Lakeview Academy, Gainesville, GA, head of secondary English department, 1985-87; Gainesville College, Gainesville, GA, associate professor of English, 1987—. Has acted in radio plays with the Atlanta Radio Theater.

Member

Horror Writers Association, Science Fiction and Fantasy Writers of America, Society of Children's Book Writers and Illustrators, American Association of University Professors.

Awards, Honors

Regents' Scholar, 1969-74; Northeast Georgia Writers Award for short fiction, 1974; Phoenix Award, Deep South Science Fiction Convention, 1992, for achieve-

Brad Strickland

ment in science fiction; Schaumburg Township Young Reader's Choice Award, 1996; Georgia Author of the Year (children's division), 1999, 2001.

Writings

To Stand beneath the Sun, Signet (New York, NY), 1986.

Shadowshow, Onyx (New York, NY), 1988.

Moon Dreams ("Jeremy Moon" series; fantasy) Signet (New York, NY), 1988.

Nul's Quest ("Jeremy Moon" series; fantasy), Signet (New York, NY), 1989.

Children of the Knife, Onyx (New York, NY), 1990.

Silver Eyes (thriller), New American Library, 1990.

Wizard's Mole ("Jeremy Moon" series; fantasy), Roc (New York, NY), 1991.

Dragon's Plunder (young adult fantasy), illustrated by Wayne D. Barlowe, Atheneum (New York, NY), 1992.

(As Will Bradley) *Ark Liberty* (science fiction), Penguin/Roc (New York, NY), 1992.

(With Todd Cameron Hamilton) *The Star Ghost* (based on the *Star Trek: Deep Space Nine* television series), Pocket Books (New York, NY), 1993.

(With Todd Cameron Hamilton) *Stowaways* (based on the *Star Trek: Deep Space Nine* television series), Pocket Books (New York, NY), 1994.

(With wife, Barbara Strickland) *The Tale of the Secret Mirror* (based on the *Are You Afraid of the Dark?* television series), Pocket Books (New York, NY), 1995.

(With Barbara Strickland and Todd Cameron Hamilton) *Nova Command* (based on the *Star Trek, the Next Generation* television series), Pocket Books (New York, NY), 1995.

(With Barbara Strickland) *Starfall* (based on the *Star Trek, the Next Generation* television series), Pocket Books (New York, NY), 1995.

(With Barbara Strickland and Todd Cameron Hamilton) *Crisis on Vulcan* (based on the *Star Trek* television series), Pocket Books (New York, NY), 1996.

The Hand of the Necromancer (young adult fantasy; based on the characters of John Bellairs), Dial (New York, NY), 1996.

(With Barbara Strickland) *The Tale of the Phantom School Bus* (based on the *Are You Afraid of the Dark?* television series), Pocket Books (New York, NY), 1996.

(With Barbara Strickland) *The Tale of the Deadly Diary* (based on the *Are You Afraid of the Dark?* television series), Pocket Books (New York, NY), 1996.

The Bell, the Book, and the Spellbinder (young adult fantasy; based on the characters of John Bellairs), Dial (New York, NY), 1997.

You're History (based on the *Sabrina, the Teenage Witch* television series), illustrated by Mark Dubowski, Pocket Books (New York, NY), 1998.

(With Barbara Strickland) *Frame-Up* (based on the *Mystery Files of Shelby Woo* television series), Pocket Books (New York, NY), 1998.

The Specter from the Magician's Museum (young adult fantasy; based on the characters of John Bellairs), Dial (New York, NY), 1998.

(With Barbara Strickland) *Man Overboard!* (based on the *Mystery Files of Shelby Woo* television series), Pocket (New York, NY), 1999.

The Wrath of the Grinning Ghost (based on the characters of John Bellairs), Dial (New York, NY), 1999.

The Beast under the Wizard's Bridge, Dial (New York, NY), 2000.

When Mack Came Back, Dial (New York, NY), 2000.

The Tower at the End of the World, Dial (New York, NY), 2001.

Survive! (based on the "Dinotopia" series by James Gurney), Random House (New York, NY), 2001.

(With Barbara Strickland) *No-Rules Weekend* (based on the *Full House* television series), Pocket (New York, NY), 2001.

Has written for radio with the Atlanta Radio Theater, adapting works by H. P. Lovecraft and others, as well as writing original scripts. Strickland's stories have appeared in *The Year's Best Horror,* Volumes 15 and 17.

CHILDREN'S NOVELS; BEGUN BY JOHN BELLAIRS; COMPLETED BY BRAD STRICKLAND

The Vengeance of the Witch-Finder, Dial (New York, NY), 1993.

The Ghost in the Mirror (also see below), Dial (New York, NY), 1994.

The Drum, the Doll, and the Zombie, Dial (New York, NY), 1994.

The Doom of the Haunted Opera, Dial (New York, NY), 1995.

The House with a Clock in Its Walls (contains *The Ghost in the Mirror* and John Bellairs' *The House with a Clock in Its Walls*), Puffin (New York, NY), 2002.

The Whistle, the Grave, and the Ghost, Dial (New York, NY), 2003.

"ADVENTURES OF WISHBONE" SERIES; BASED ON THE CHARACTER CREATED BY RICK DUFFIELD

Be a Wolf!, Big Red Chair (Allen, TX), 1997.

Salty Dog, Big Red Chair (Allen, TX), 1997.

(With Thomas E. Fuller) *Riddle of the Wayward Books,* Big Red Chair (Allen, TX), 1997.

(With Thomas E. Fuller) *The Treasure of Skeleton Reef,* Big Red Chair (Allen, TX), 1997.

(With Thomas E. Fuller) *The Disappearing Dinosaurs,* Big Red Chair (Allen, TX), 1998.

(With Thomas E. Fuller) *Disoriented Express,* Big Red Chair (Allen, TX), 1998.

(With Thomas E. Fuller) *Drive-In of Doom,* Big Red Chair (Allen, TX), 1998.

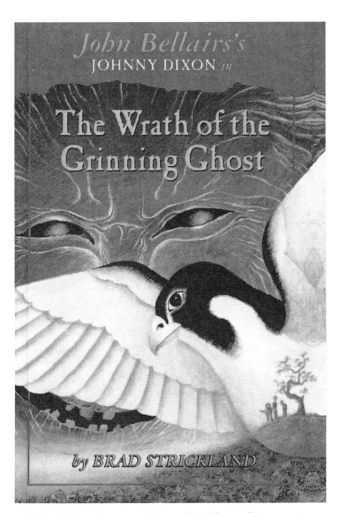

Assisted by a fortune teller and a falcon, thirteen-year-old Johnny discovers a devious plan by an evil spirit who must be stopped in order to save the world.

(With Barbara Strickland) *Gullifur's Travels,* Big Red Chair (Allen, TX), 1999.

(With Thomas E. Fuller) *Jack and the Beanstalk,* Little Red Chair (Allen, TX), 1999.

(With Thomas E. Fuller) *Terrier of the Lost Mines,* Little Red Chair (Allen, TX), 1999.

(With Anne Capeci and Carla Jablonski) *The Wishbone Halloween Adventure,* Lyrick (Allen, TX), 2000.

"PIRATE HUNTER" SERIES

(With Thomas E. Fuller) *Mutiny!,* Aladdin (New York, NY), 2002.

(With Thomas E. Fuller) *The Guns of Tortuga,* Aladdin (New York, NY), 2003.

(With Thomas E. Fuller) *Heart of Steele,* Aladdin (New York, NY), 2003.

PLAYS

(With Ed Cabell and Roy Forrester) *The Tale of the Rooster,* produced in Georgia, 1990.

C.O.'s D-Day, produced in Georgia, 1991.

(With Ed Cabell and Roy Forrester) *Farewell to Joe and Jackie,* produced in Georgia, 1991.

The House on Nowhere Road (radio play; part of "Horror House" series), broadcast on National Public Radio Theatre, 1993.

(With Thomas E. Fuller) *The Great Air Monopoly,* produced in Georgia, 1993.

Also author of *The Rats in the Walls* with Thomas E. Fuller, an adaptation of a story by H. P. Lovecraft, 1990.

Sidelights

Brad Strickland began as a writer with fantasy novels centered on the character of Jeremy Moon, an advertising executive who accidentally travels to a magical parallel universe where the power of words is quite literal. The books in this series, *Moon Dreams, Nul's Quest,* and *Wizard's Mole,* employ stock elements of fantasy novels enlightened by Strickland's puckish sense of humor. Other early novels include *Dragon's Plunder,* a pirate story described by Chris Sherman in *Booklist* as "a real page-turner, with cliff-hanging chapters that are perfect for reading aloud," and *Shadowshow,* a horror novel set in the author's native Georgia in the 1950s.

However, Strickland is perhaps best known for his collaboration with John Bellairs, an acknowledged master of horror novels for young adults. After Bellairs' death, Strickland finished some of his incomplete novels, beginning with *The Ghost in the Mirror,* featuring Bellairs regulars Rose Rita Pottinger and her neighbor Mrs. Zimmermann, a witch. Eventually, Strickland wrote several original novels that featured Bellairs' characters. Critical response to Strickland's assumption of Bellairs' mantle, along with his characters, was generally positive.

In *The Ghost in the Mirror,* Rose Rita and Mrs. Zimmermann wind up in 1828 Pennsylvania Dutch country when they go in search of Mrs. Zimmermann's lost powers. In *The Vengeance of the Witch-Finder,* featuring Lewis Barnavelt and his uncle Jonathan, an accidentally released ghost seeks revenge on his seventeenth-century murderer. A third Bellairs novel that Strickland completed, *The Doom of the Haunted Opera,* finds Lewis and Rose Rita staging an opera in an abandoned theater only to discover that the opera is a kind of spell that will allow the composer to take over the world. Critical response to these works was generally favorable, with reviewers assuring faithful readers that Strickland had seamlessly carried out the stories Bellairs started but failed to complete before his death. While *School Library Journal* contributor Ann W. Moore felt that *The Vengeance of the Witch-Finder* was not as successful as Bellairs' earlier novels featuring Lewis Barnavelt, a contributor to *Publishers Weekly* described this novel as "chock-full of deliciously spooky details and narrated in a voice that is as cozy as it is ornery," concluding, "this tale is utterly spellbinding."

With the publication of *The Drum, the Doll, and the Zombie,* Strickland began to receive accolades for his consistently high quality novels for young adults. Here, Johnny Dixon, Fergie Ferguson, Father Higgins, and Professor Childermass battle a legion of zombies unleashed by an evil sorceress. Unusual among the trappings of standard horror novel fare, however, are humor and well-rounded characters, critics noted. "This ably devised bit of supernatural fun . . . is perfect for the pre-Stephen King set," remarked Stephanie Zvirin in *Booklist.* Connie Tyrrell Burns made similar comments in *School Library Journal* about *The Hand of the Necromancer,* a novel that features some of Bellairs' characters in an original story by Strickland. Here Johnny Dixon becomes embroiled in a battle to save the world when an evil wizard arrives in town wanting to awaken the spirit of his powerful ancestor. Readers who enjoy traditional elements of horror fiction, such as haunted houses, bad weather, and the like, will appreciate *The Hand of the Necromancer,* noted Burns, concluding her review by claiming the story "is stylistically a treat as well, full of foreshadowing and figurative language."

"Strickland continues John Bellairs' series with great imagination," wrote Janet Mura in *Voice of Youth Advocates* in a review of *The Specter from the Magician's Museum.* In this story, Lewis and Rose Rita decide to perform a magic show for the school talent show and accidentally ensnare Rose Rita in the evil spell of an ancient sorceress. Krista Grosick, writing in *School Library Journal,* believed that while Strickland had managed to successfully imitate Bellairs' style, he "even improves upon the deceased author's well-rounded and dynamic characters." Strickland's imitation of Bellairs is so complete in *The Bell, the Book, and the Spellbinder,* in which Fergie's life is endangered via the agency of a magical library book, that Connie Tyrrell Burns quipped in *School Library Journal,* "could it be reincarnation or body snatching?" Likewise Kendra Nan Skellen, writing in a *School Library Journal* review of *The Wrath of the Grinning Ghost,* remarked

that this latest book "reads so much like Bellairs' books that [his fans] won't believe he didn't write it." In this story, Johnny Dixon's father is possessed, and only an ancient, chameleon-like book of magic can save him. The quest for the book takes Johnny and his friends all over the world and even into the underworld. "This is good reading for adventure enthusiasts as well as for series fans," remarked Kay Weisman in *Booklist.*

The Beast under the Wizard's Bridge is an effective mix of horror, mystery, and adventure story, according to reviewers. Here, Lewis Barnavelt and Rose Rita Pottinger are back, and along with Uncle Jonathan and Mrs. Zimmermann, they have a bad feeling about the town's plans to tear down an old (and evil) bridge. It turns out that the bridge is the only thing subduing a horrific monster capable of destroying everything it meets. "This entertaining page-turner . . . will captivate readers whether or not they are already familiar with Lewis and his friends," remarked Deborah L. DuBois in *Voice of Youth Advocates.* Strickland's next Bellairs novel, *The Tower at the End of the World,* is billed as a sequel to Bellairs' *The House with a Clock in Its Walls.* Although a contributor to *Kirkus Reviews* found this entry into the series, which takes place in Michigan's Upper Peninsula, a disappointing addition, Janet Gillen, writing in *School Library Journal,* called it "a wonderful blend of suspense, adventure, ghost story, and friendship that is a sure-to-please page-turner."

In a departure from his genre-fiction writing, which includes entries in the "Star Trek" and "Wishbone" series as well as the many supernatural novels inspired by John Bellairs, Strickland published a seemingly semi-autobiographical young-adult novel called *When Mack Came Back* in 2000. In this story, set in Georgia during the 1950s, a young boy rescues the dog his brother gave away when he left to serve in World War II. At odds with the wishes of his stern father, the boy nurses the dog back to health and refuses to relinquish him when his father tries to give the dog away again. "Strickland's strengths are vivid setting details and character development," remarked Kay Weisman in *Booklist,* commenting that the story lacks the fast pace or exciting action that some readers may desire. Like Weisman, Coop Renner, writing in *School Library Journal,* praised Strickland's period details about rural life during the World War II period, suggesting "*Mack* is a well-done novel aimed at a younger audience, most of whom will find the story satisfying and involving."

Strickland has also tried his hand at historical fiction for young readers, working with Thomas E. Fuller on the "Pirate Hunter" series. The first two books of the series, *Mutiny!* and *The Guns of the Tortuga,* feature an adolescent orphan boy named Danny Shea who travels to Jamaica in search of his only remaining relative, a surgeon. While not exactly pleased with his new charge, Dr. Patrick "Patch" Shea nonetheless takes the young lad on as his apprentice aboard a ship in the British

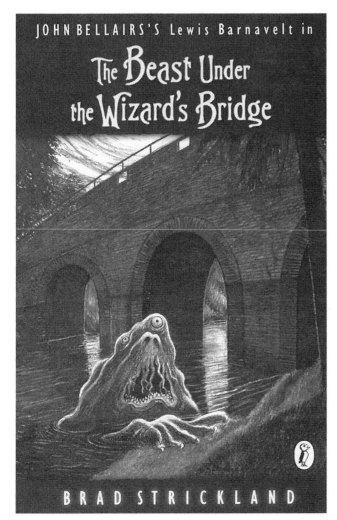

Lewis Barnavelt is pulled into a ferocious battle against evil when the destruction of a bridge unleashes a malicious force. (Cover illustration by Brett Helquist.)

Royal Navy. In *Mutiny!,* Danny and his uncle become involved in a dangerous mission to rid the Carribean of pirates by staging a mock rebellion on the *HMS Retribution,* while *The Guns of Tortuga* finds the duo on the trail of the particularly heinous pirate Jack Steele. Reviewing *Mutiny!* for *Publishers Weekly,* a critic claimed "if this rip-roaring adventure is any indication, it looks like smooth sailing ahead for an enjoyable new series." Referring to *The Guns of Tortuga, School Library Journal* contributor Kathleen A. Nester recommended the "fast-paced, action-packed tale" for "reluctant readers as well as adventure seekers."

Strickland once recalled, "Like many readers of fantasy and science fiction, I began early—in my teens. Like many of them, I tried my hand at writing a story early—at age sixteen. Unlike many, I actually sold my story, for one hundred dollars, to *Ellery Queen's Mystery Magazine.* The sale was unfortunate, for it gave me the mistaken impression that I had proved myself as a writer and need to write no more. However, after a lapse of seventeen years in my writing career, a friend talked me into reading some recent fantasy and science

fiction. I liked it, tried writing a story or two, and found modest success. That led to my first novel, and since then I have been writing constantly across the spectrum of fantasy literature, including science fiction, adventure fantasy, and horror. I don't intend to stop again until I have to."

Strickland once told *SATA:* "Coming from the South, I grew up in a family of storytellers. My aunts, uncles, and grandparents told tales of enchantment and terror involving vanishing hitchhikers, spirits of the dead wandering graveyards in the form of flickering flames, buried Confederate gold, indelible bloodstains at the site of murders . . . topics to make a child's flesh creep. However, I always wanted more and never failed to listen.

"So it was perhaps inevitable that my own stories, when I came to write them, were tales of enchantment and terror, all about flights to strange planets, wonder-working magicians, ghost-haunted mirrors, vengeful sorcerers, dragon gold and pirate booty, and resourceful young people. I'm still telling the kind of stories my relatives told, still writing books because I want to read them and they haven't been written by anyone else. Kindred spirits are important to a writer because writing can be a lonely business. My chance to work with the late John Bellairs was wonderful, exciting, and challenging, and my opportunity to write stories set in the Star Trek universe was both a joy and a fulfillment for a lifelong science-fiction fan like me. My chance to write in these series made at least one reader happy: myself.

"But, of course, no writer can write just to please himself or herself. The reading audience is very special, and it's always pleasant to discover these stories' appeal to others. I hope the young people who read my work will enjoy it half as much as I enjoy writing it, and it's good to hope that perhaps some of them will go on to become tellers of tales, masters of terror, workers of wonder."

Biographical and Critical Sources

BOOKS

St. James Guide to Fantasy Writers, St. James Press (Detroit, MI), 1996.

PERIODICALS

Booklist, January 15, 1993, Chris Sherman, review of *Dragon's Plunder,* p. 892; February 15, 1993, Kay Weisman, review of *Ghost in the Mirror,* p. 1059; July, 1994, Stephanie Zvirin, review of *The Drum, the Doll, and the Zombie,* p. 1942; August, 1995, Stephanie Zvirin, review of *Hand of the Necromancer,* p. 1946; September 1, 1997, Susan DeRonne, review of *The Bell, the Book, and the Spellbinder,* p. 127; October 1, 1998, John Peters, review of *The Specter from the Magician's Museum,* p. 330; September 15, 1999, Kay Weisman, review of *The Wrath of the Grinning Ghost,* p. 261; October 15, 2000, Kay Weisman, review of *When Mack Came Back,* p. 441; November 1, 2000, Carolyn Phelan, review of *The Beast under the Wizard's Bridge,* p. 542; September 1, 2001, Carolyn Phelan, review of *Tower at the End of the World,* p. 111: December 1, 2002, Todd Morning, review of *Mutiny!,* p. 668; February 1, 2003, Todd Morning, review of *The Guns of Tortuga,* p. 995.

Book Report, March-April, 1993, Sylvia Feicht, review of *Dragon's Plunder,* p. 44; November-December, 1993, Nancye Starkey, review of *Ghost in the Mirror,* p. 42; January-February, 1994, Patsy Launspach, review of *The Vengeance of the Witch-Finder,* p. 42; May-June, 1995, Norma Hunter, review of *The Drum, the Doll, and the Zombie,* p. 37; March-April, 1997, Charlotte Decker, review of *Hand of the Necromancer,* p. 42; May, 1999, Anne Sushko, review of *The Specter from the Magician's Museum,* p. 68.

Horn Book Guide, spring, 1997, Christine Heppermann, review of *The Bell, the Book, and the Spellbinder,* p. 76.

Journal and Constitution (Atlanta, GA), January 20, 1993.

Kirkus Reviews, July 1, 1996, review of *The Bell, the Book, and the Spellbinder,* p. 974; August 1, 2001, review of *Tower at the End of the World,* p. 1133.

Library Journal, May 15, 1988, Jackie Cassada, review of *Moondreams,* p. 96; February 15, 1989, Jackie Cassada, review of *Nul's Quest,* p. 180.

Publishers Weekly, November 4, 1988, review of *Shadowshow,* p. 77; January 6, 1989, review of *Nul's Quest,* p. 98; July, 1992, p. 81; July 12, 1993, review of *The Vengeance of the Witch-Finder,* p. 81; November 18, 2002, review of *Mutiny!,* p. 60.

School Library Journal, April, 1993, Susan L. Rogers, review of *Dragon's Plunder,* p. 125; September, 1993, Ann W. Moore, review of *The Vengeance of the Witch-Finder,* p. 228; September, 1995, Mary Jo Drungil, review of *Doom of the Haunted Opera,* p. 199; September, 1996, Connie Tyrrell Burns, review of *Hand of the Necromancer,* pp. 206, 208; August, 1997, Connie Tyrrell Burns, review of *The Bell, the Book, and the Spellbinder,* p. 160; January, 1998, John Sigwald, review of *Be a Wolf,* p. 116; November 1, 1998, Krista Grosick, review of *The Specter from the Magician's Museum,* p. 129; October, 1999, Kendra Nan Skellen, review of *The Wrath of the Grinning Ghost,* p. 160; January, 2000, John Sigwald, review of *Jack and the Beanstalk,* p. 112; June, 2000, Coop Renner, review of *When Mack Came Back,* p. 154; December, 2000, Lana Miles, review of *The Beast under the Wizard's Bridge,* p. 150; September, 2001, Janet Gillen, review of *Tower at the End of the World,* p. 234; November, 2002, Rita Soltan, review of *Mutiny!,* p. 176; March, 2003, Kathleen A. Nester, review of *The Guns of Tortuga,* p. 241.

Stone Soup, March, 2001, Austin Alvermann, review of *When Mack Came Back,* p. 32.

Voice of Youth Advocates, June, 1999, Janet Mura, review of *The Specter from the Magician's Museum,* p. 126; April, 2001, Deborah L. DuBois, review of *The Beast under the Wizard's Bridge,* p. 57.

*　　*　　*

STUTLEY, D(oris) J(ean) 1959-

Personal

Born April 14, 1959, in Enid, OK; daughter of Paul King (an electrical contractor) and Donna Rose (Starbuck) Anderson; married Chris Stutley (a construction electrician), October 15, 1977; children: Andrew, Belinda, Joanna, Samantha. *Religion:* Baptist. *Hobbies and other interests:* Family history, cross-stitch embroidery.

Addresses

Home—Australia. *Agent*—c/o Author Mail, Lothian Books, 11 Munro St., Port Melbourne, Victoria 3207, Australia. *E-mail*—djstutley@hotmail.com.

Career

Writer. Volunteer at local schools; also served as a missionary in Papua New Guinea.

Member

Australian Society of Authors, Children's Book Council of Australia, Western Australia State Literature Centre, Fremantle Children's Literature Centre.

Awards, Honors

Children's Book of the Year nomination, and Ned Kelly Crime Award shortlist, Crime Writers' Association of Australia, both for *Operation Foxtrot Five.*

Writings

YOUNG ADULT SUSPENSE NOVELS

Operation Foxtrot Five, Lothian Books (Port Melbourne, Victoria, Australia), 2001.
Operation Delta Bravo, Lothian Books (Port Melbourne, Victoria, Australia), 2002.
Operation Alpha Papa, Lothian Books (Port Melbourne, Victoria, Australia), 2003.

Work in Progress

Operation Tango Two-Two and *Operation Romeo Siera,* young adult suspense novels.

Sidelights

D. J. Stutley told *SATA:* "In 1998, I decided that I had done enough school duties in the kindergarten, library, canteen, and uniform shop. After all, I have been doing some form of school volunteer work for eighteen years as our four children progressed through the education system. Now I thought it was time to do what I'd always dreamed of doing—write a book.

"Once I got started, I was halfway through the book when I already had the next one going around in my head. By the time I was finished, three-and-a-half years had passed, and I was the proud owner of four manuscripts that I had no idea what to do with. Through an amazing series of events, the second publisher I approached took the first book in the series and also snapped up book two and book three as well. *Operation Foxtrot Five* was nominated for a children's book of the year award and short-listed for the Ned Kelly Crime Award. So far the royalty cheques from the sale of the book have been donated to our local Police and Citizens Youth Club. Because the series is based on the relationship between a police officer and a family of teenagers, I wanted to do something special with the proceeds of the first book. It has been a pleasure to support an existing program that encourages a good relationship between the police and teenagers in the local community.

"My writing style for the series is simple because I have a passion for the reluctant reader. I was one of those and really struggled to find something that was at my level. During my school years, I always received excellent grades for my English subjects. The projects and assignments that I completed came back covered in so much red ink that you would have thought someone had died over it because I was such a hopeless speller. Thankfully, my teachers could see my potential and didn't grade me according to my spelling.

"My husband and I have been married for twenty-five years, and we spent our first years living and working on farms. In the early 1980s, we joined Asia Pacific Christian Mission (now Pioneers) and went to Papua New Guinea with our two small children. For three of our four years there, we were hostel parents to the school-age children of other missionary families. The children, Australians and New Zealanders aged between eight and twelve, would fly from their outstations to Tari for their schooling and live with us. We had up to thirteen extra children in our care at a time, and through the years, we cared for a total of nineteen children. After we came back to Australia, my husband began a mature-age apprenticeship in the electrical construction industry, and we had two more children. I have never been in the workforce; I preferred to remain a stay-at-home mother raising the family.

"I love digging into our family history, and when time permits, I enjoy working on my latest cross-stitch project. I have become involved in a volunteer reading program with the local high school and go in for two hours a week."

T

TATHAM, Betty

Personal
Daughter of Julius and Elizabeth Theisz; married Winfield A. Tatham (an accountant), 1955; children: Richard, Susan Crotts. *Ethnicity:* "Caucasian." *Education:* Fairleigh Dickinson University, B.A. (sociology; cum laude); graduate study at Fordham University and University of Utah. *Hobbies and other interests:* Gardening, music, conducting scientific and historical research.

Addresses
Home—Holland, PA. *Agent*—c/o Author Mail, HarperCollins Children's Books, 1350 Avenue of the Americas, New York, NY 10019.

Career
Young Women's Christian Association of Hackensack, Hackensack, NJ, executive director, 1973-76; Young Women's Christian Association of Salt Lake City, Salt Lake City, UT, executive director, 1976-85; State of Utah, Salt Lake City, UT, assistant to the governor of Utah for health and social services and member of Cabinet Council, 1985-87; Utah Department of Human Services, Salt Lake City, UT, training specialist and executive assistant for programs, 1987-91; Young Women's Christian Association of Bucks County, Trevose, PA, executive director and chief administrative officer, 1992-2003. National Young Women's Christian Association Leadership Training Institute, faculty member, beginning 2001; also lecturer at local schools. Bucks County Review and Evaluation Committee, member, 1992; Bucks County Family Services System Reform Collaborative Board, member; Bucks County Opportunity Council, member of board of directors; Bucks County Wellness Partnership and Bucks County Violence Prevention Task Force, member; Bergen County Volunteers in Juvenile Corrections, charter board member; Utah Domestic Violence Council and Legislative Task Force,

past chair; Bergen County Committee for the Rehabilitation of Juvenile Offenders, past co-chair. HealthLink (clinic), member of advisory board.

Member
Society of Children's Book Writers and Illustrators, Association of United Way Executive Directors (president), National Association for the Advancement of Colored People (member of board of directors).

Awards, Honors
Jane Adams Agency Award (Utah chapter), National Association of Social Workers, 1983; Woman of Achievement Award, Utah Central Region of Business and Professional Women's Clubs, 1983; Area Community Service Award, American Association of Retired Persons, 1988; Spirit of American Woman Award, J. C. Penney and Co., 1989; Woman Who Makes a Difference Award, Health Partners, 1995; Community Service Award, National Association for the Advancement of Colored People (Bucks County branch), 1995; Bucks County Women's History Month Award, 2001; Woman of Distinction Award, Soroptimist International of Indian Rock, 2002.

Writings

Penguin Chick, illustrated by Helen K. Davie, HarperCollins Children's Books (New York, NY), 2002.
How Animals Shed Their Skin, F. Watts (New York, NY), 2002.
How Animals Communicate, F. Watts (New York, NY), 2003.
How Animals Play, F. Watts (New York, NY), 2003.

Work in Progress
Danger by the Delaware, a historical fiction picture book; *I Want to Go Home,* a picture book for preschoolers; *Humpback Whale* and *Amazing Hummingbirds,* science picture books.

Sidelights

Betty Tatham told *SATA:* "The Young Women's Christian Association of Bucks County, where I was the executive director for more than ten years, has tutoring programs in fifteen schools and in five other sites. I designed and implemented these programs where teachers supervise teen volunteers who work with younger students to help them improve reading, writing, and other academic skills. While purchasing several thousand dollars' worth of books in 1996 for these programs, I spent many weekend hours in bookstores, poring over children's books. Some were so beautiful that I wished I could write that well. I set out to find a teacher. I was fortunate that Wendy Pfeffer, a published author of children's books, was willing to give me private lessons in her home for the next three years. Writing became a passion and, while my full-time job was very demanding, I wrote as much as I could.

"In 1996, I researched and wrote *Penguin Chick*. I signed a contract with HarperCollins in early 1999, and my first book was published three years later. Doing science research is almost as much fun for me as writing. I love animals, and most of the books and manuscripts I have written are about animals. It is sad that many species are endangered, and I hope that my books will inspire children to love and respect animals so that they will work to protect them when they are older.

"While hiking with my husband, I found a snakeskin, and that led to my second book, *How Animals Shed Their Skin*. Researching this subject was especially challenging since I couldn't find any book by that title for children or adults, and I had to do much of the research at the Biology Library at Princeton University. An editor I had met at a conference suggested that I send the manuscript to the Grolier Division of Scholastic, and that led to three contracts with the publisher F. Watts.

"I recently completed my first historical fiction picture book manuscript. It is based on an event that took place on December 24, 1776, just a few miles from my home in Holland, Pennsylvania. There are several museums specializing in Revolutionary War history in the area, and General Washington crossed the Delaware River about five miles from where I live. I expect to keep writing science books, but I enjoy an occasional change to fiction.

"School visits are probably the most exciting aspect of being an author. I love sharing how I became a writer, why I chose each subject, where and how I do research, who edits my manuscripts before I submit them, what editors look for, the publishing process, et cetera. I also enjoy answering questions and sharing additional information about the animals I have written about, and I show students some spectacular pictures of Antarctica. I encourage children to 'read, read, read!,' and I recommend keeping a journal."

Biographical and Critical Sources

PERIODICALS

Booklist, March 1, 2002, Carolyn Phelan, review of *Penguin Chick,* p. 1138.
Horn Book, May-June, 2002, Danielle J. Ford, review of *Penguin Chick,* p. 347.
Kirkus Reviews, November 15, 2001, review of *Penguin Chick,* p. 1615.
School Library Journal, March, 2002, Nancy Call, review of *Penguin Chick,* p. 222.
Woman's Day, May 22, 1990, Grace W. Weinstein, "Volunteering for Success," p. 81.

ONLINE

Betty Tatham, http://www.bettytatham.com/ (May 21, 2003).

*   *   *

TESSENDORF, K(enneth) C(harles) 1925-2003

OBITUARY NOTICE—See index for *SATA* sketch: Born August 18, 1925, in Neenah, WI; died of amyotrophic lateral sclerosis March 6, 2003, in Falls Church, VA. Travel agent and author. Tessendorf wrote a number of books on popular history. He served in the U.S. Army Air Force during World War II before graduating with a B.S. from the University of Wisconsin in 1950. After college, he worked briefly as a reservationist with American Airlines before joining the U.S. State Department as a diplomatic courier for two years. Beginning in 1955, he worked as a travel counselor and agent, and later manager, at Enzor Travel Service in Arlington, Virginia, retiring in 1985. Tessendorf was the author of several books on various historical topics, including *Look Out! Here Comes the Stanley Steamer* (1984) and *Uncle Sam in Nicaragua: A History* (1987). Some of his books, including *Barnstormers and Daredevils* (1988) and *Over the Edge: Flying with the Arctic Heroes* (1998), were written for young readers, and the former was a Junior Literary Guild selection.

OBITUARIES AND OTHER SOURCES:

BOOKS

Writers Directory, 18th edition, St. James (Detroit, MI), 2003.

PERIODICALS

Washington Post, March 13, 2003, p. B7.

TOLAN, Stephanie S. 1942-

Personal

Born October 25, 1942, in Canton, OH; daughter of Joseph Edward and Mary (Schroy) Stein; married Robert W. Tolan (a theater director and producer), December 19, 1964; children: R. J.; stepchildren: Patrick, Andrew, Robert, Jr. *Education:* Purdue University, B.A., 1964, M.A., 1967.

Addresses

Home—4511 Eagle Lake Dr., Charlotte, NC 28217. *Agent*—Elaine Markson, Elaine Markson Literary Agency, 44 Greenwich Ave., New York, NY 10011. *E-mail*—StefT@carolina.rr.com.

Career

Purdue University, Fort Wayne, IN, instructor in continuing education, 1966-70; State University of New York—Buffalo, Buffalo, NY, faculty member in speech and theater, 1972; Franklin and Marshall College, Lancaster, PA, adjunct faculty member in English, 1973-75, coordinator of continuing education, 1974-75; writer, 1975—. Lecturer at Indiana University, 1966-70; participant, Artists-in-Education, Pennsylvania, 1974, Ohio, 1975, and North Carolina, 1984; faculty member, Institute of Children's Literature, 1988-93; senior fellow, Institute for Educational Advancement; consultant to parents and educators on the needs of highly gifted children and prodigies. Member of literature panel, Ohio Arts Council, 1978-80. Actress, performing with Curtain Call Co., 1970-71.

Member

Authors Guild, Authors League of America, Children's Book Guild of Washington, D.C.

Awards, Honors

Individual artist fellowships, Ohio Arts Council, 1978, 1981, and 1997; Post-Corbett Awards finalist, 1981; Ohioana Book Award for juvenile fiction, 1981, for *The Liberation of Tansy Warner;* Bread Loaf Writers' Conference Fellowship, 1981; Media Award for Best Book of 1983, American Psychological Association, for *Guiding the Gifted Child;* Best Book of 1988, *School Library Journal,* Dorothy Canfield Fisher Award nominee, and Books for the Teen Age selection, New York Public Library, all for *A Good Courage;* Sequoyah Children's Book Award nomination, and Georgia Children's Book Award nomination, both for *Grandpa—and Me;* Virginia Young Readers Best Choices winner, 1992-1993, Sequoyah Young Adult Book Award nominee, 1992-1993, Nevada Young Readers Award, 1993-1994, and Books for the Teen Age selection, New York Public Library, all for *Plague Year;* Sequoyah Young

Stephanie S. Tolan

Adult Book Award nominee, for *The Great Skinner Getaway;* South Carolina Children's Book Award nominee, for *The Great Skinner Homestead;* Mark Twain Award nominee, Rebecca Caudill Young Readers' Book Award nominee, 1992-1993, California Young Reader's Award nominee, and South Carolina Junior Book Award nominee, 1996-1997, all for *Who's There?;* Best Books for Young Adults, YALSA, 1994, Sequoyah Children's Book Award nominee, Land of Enchantment Children's Book Award nominee, and Editor's Choice selection, *Booklist,* all for *Save Halloween!;* Ohio Arts Council Summer Writing Residency, Fine Arts Work Center, Provincetown, MA, 1998; Dorothy Canfield Fisher nominee, and Books for the Teen Age selection, New York Public Library, both for *Welcome to the Ark;* Dorothy Canfield Fisher nominee, Best Books on Religion, American Library Association (ALA), and Sequoyah Young Adult Book Award nominee, all for *Ordinary Miracles;* Books for the Teen Age selection, New York Public Library, for *Flight of the Raven;* Best Book of 2002, *School Library Journal,* Notable Children's Books selection, *Smithsonian* magazine, 2002, Volunteer State Book Award nominee, Dorothy Canfield Fisher Award, Books for the Teenage selection, New York Public Library, and Newbery Honor Book, ALA, 2003, all for *Surviving the Applewhites.*

Writings

NOVELS FOR YOUNG READERS

Grandpa—and Me, Scribner (New York, NY), 1978.
The Last of Eden, Warne (New York, NY), 1980.
The Liberation of Tansy Warner, Scribner (New York, NY), 1980.
No Safe Harbors, Scribner (New York, NY), 1981.
The Great Skinner Strike, Macmillan (New York, NY), 1983.
A Time to Fly Free, Scribner (New York, NY), 1983.
Pride of the Peacock, Scribner (New York, NY), 1986.
The Great Skinner Enterprise, Four Winds, (New York), NY, 1986.
The Great Skinner Getaway, Macmillan (New York, NY), 1987.
A Good Courage, Morrow (New York, NY), 1988.
The Great Skinner Homestead, Macmillan (New York, NY), 1988.
Plague Year, Morrow (New York, NY), 1990.
Marcy Hooper and the Greatest Treasure in the World, Morrow (New York, NY), 1991.
Sophie and the Sidewalk Man, Macmillan (New York, NY), 1992.
The Witch of Maple Park, Morrow (New York, NY), 1993.
Save Halloween!, Morrow (New York, NY), 1993.
Who's There?, Morrow (New York, NY), 1994.
Welcome to the Ark, Morrow (New York, NY), 1996.
The Face in the Mirror, Morrow (New York, NY), 1998.
Ordinary Miracles, Morrow (New York, NY), 1999.
Flight of the Raven, HarperCollins (New York, NY), 2001.
Surviving the Applewhites, HarperCollins (New York, NY), 2002.
Bartholomew's Blessing, illustrated by Margie Moore, HarperCollins (New York, NY), 2003.

PLAYS

The Ledge (one-act), Samuel French (New York, NY), 1968.
Not I, Said the Little Red Hen (one-act), first produced in New York, NY, 1971.
(With Katherine Paterson) *Bridge to Terabithia* (based on Paterson's novel; first produced in Louisville, KY, 1990), music by Steven Liebman, Samuel French (New York, NY), 1992.
(With Katherine Paterson) *The Tale of the Mandarin Ducks: A Musical Play,* music by Steven Liebman, Samuel French (New York, NY), 1999.
(With Katherine Paterson) *The Tale of Jemima Puddle-Duck: A Musical Play Based on the Story by Beatrix Potter,* music by Steven Liebman, Dramatists Play Service (New York, NY), 2002.

OTHER

(With James T. Webb and Elizabeth Meckstroth) *Guiding the Gifted Child: A Practical Source for Parents and Teachers,* Ohio Psychology Publishing (Columbus, OH), 1982.

Contributor of poems to more than a dozen literary magazines, including *Roanoke Review, Descant,* and *Green River Review.*

Adaptations

The Great Skinner Strike was adapted as *Mom's on Strike,* a 1988 ABC-TV *After-School Special.*

Sidelights

The author of over twenty novels for children and young adults as well as several musical plays, Stephanie S. Tolan often writes of children who are, in some way or another, special if not exceptional. These include the outsiders, misfits, and misunderstood; there are also kids who are extraordinarily intelligent and intuitive, who are plagued by scandal, who find refuge in imaginary kingdoms, or who discover dangerous family secrets. Tolan's adolescent and teen protagonists have to learn to deal with the world as well as with their own special situations: surviving a personal fear of nuclear war, getting through the final years of boarding school, dealing with the life of a twin and with fundamentalism, contending with the violence of the larger world. Tolan is concerned about the rights of young people in a society that she feels cares less and less about children and their needs. Poverty, education, housing, the environment, violence, and abuse are some of the social issues that concern her, and she has dealt with some of these concerns in her books. She also raises these issues when she speaks to parents, educators, librarians, and other audiences.

According to Tolan's Web site, her earliest memories involve books, "those that were read to her and those she read to herself often late at night with a flashlight under the covers." Born in Ohio and raised in Wisconsin, she early on discovered the magic and joy to be found between the covers of a book. In the fourth grade, she wrote her first story, discovering for herself the magic of such creation, and from that time on she knew she would be a writer. By the time she was eleven, Tolan had already received her first rejection slips, but continued to write throughout her junior and senior high school years.

Majoring in creative writing at Purdue University, she went on to complete a master's degree in English. Married in 1964, she became an instant mother of three stepsons and then her own son; writing took second place to the concerns of family for a time, though she continued in fits and spurts even as she began instructing in English at the university level. Poetry and adult plays became Tolan's focus for a time; with her husband's career as a director in professional theater, the family was on the move frequently. When Tolan worked in a Poets-in-the-Schools program in Pennsylvania, she suddenly rediscovered her early connection to the magic of books. Her students were eager readers. "They brought back to me that special reading joy that most adults—even readers among us—have lost," Tolan noted on her Web site, "and I wanted to try my hand at writing for those kids, so like myself at their age and yet so different."

Tolan began writing about significant social problems with her first published work, *Grandpa—and Me,* which discusses the issue of dealing with aging family members. The central character, Kerry, grows to understand how age is affecting her grandfather's behavior and also comes to a new understanding of her place within her family. In *Plague Year,* Tolan writes about prejudice, ignorance, and hysteria, creating a compelling but frightening story about a maverick high school student whose appearance and personal background inspire hostility from the community.

In *Pride of the Peacock,* Tolan tells the story of Whitney and her fear of nuclear disaster. Whitney becomes preoccupied with the way the value and beauty of the Earth are threatened by people. She meets a sculptor, Theodora Bourke, who is trying to escape the violent atmosphere of New York, where her husband lost his life. They meet at an abandoned estate where the neglected garden has become overgrown with weeds. Together they clean out the garden and their friendship helps both Whitney and Theodora to cope in a troubled world. According to an *English Journal* reviewer, teens should relate to Whitney and her strong emotions, "her fear in grappling with unsolvable real-life problems, and her inability to own the solutions acceptable to her parents and peers."

Tolan deals with a number of social problems even in her "Skinner" series of books, which are lighter in tone and have much more humor than her other works. One of her Skinner stories, *The Great Skinner Strike,* deals with Eleanor Skinner's involvement in a nationally-publicized strike, while *The Great Skinner Enterprise* centers around running a home business. These books focus on issues about making a living that many middle-class people face in times of changing technology. Even *The Great Skinner Getaway* touches on the disillusionments of traveling, exploring, camping, and small-town American life. But despite their serious undertones, the "Skinner" series aim to fulfill Tolan's interest in writing stories that will bring joy and adventure to reading for children.

Marcy Hooper and the Greatest Treasure in the World, a chapter book for young readers, is a fairy tale story with nymphs and dragons, but it also shows how a little girl can gain courage and become self-reliant. Marcy is having trouble at school and runs off toward the hills near her house to forget spelling tests, two-wheeled bikes, and tripping on jump ropes. She feels like a failure. By the end of her adventure, during which she finds a treasure and encounters a dragon who would swallow her up if given the chance, Marcy finds the treasure of her own courage. Jana R. Fine, reviewing the book in *School Library Journal,* noted that Tolan's story "will attract those searching for mild adventure."

As with *Marcy Hooper and the Greatest Treasure in the World, The Witch of Maple Park* is "a semi-scary story with a happy ending," as Kathryn Jennings described it in the *Bulletin of the Center for Children's Books.* The story is told by Casey, but the central character is her friend Mackenzie, who is a psychic. Mackenzie is afraid that Barnaby, the little boy she is baby-sitting, is in danger of being kidnapped by a "witch" who seems to be following them. All ends well when the "witch" turns out to be an herbalist who helps Mackenzie's mother in her failing catering business. *School Library Journal* contributor Lisa Dennis called the book "a light, engaging read, jammed full of incidents and mild excitement, well blended into a pleasing whole." A *Kirkus Reviews* critic also wrote that "quick pacing makes this a prime candidate for readers, including reluctant ones, who enjoy a frothy mystery." And Carolyn Phelan concluded in *Booklist* that "this entertaining book is a cut above most middle-grade fare."

In *Sophie and the Sidewalk Man,* Tolan tells the story of an eight-year-old girl who is saving her allowance and collecting cans to buy Weldon, a stuffed hedgehog she sees in the window of a toy store. On one of her visits to see Weldon before she has enough money to buy him, Sophie encounters a ragged, dirty man sitting on the sidewalk holding a sign that asks for help because he is hungry. Buying Weldon is important to Sophie because her mother suffers from allergies and, consequently, pets are not allowed in the house. To help get the forty dollars she needs to buy Weldon, Sophie begins to skip lunch to add her lunch money to her savings. As Sophie experiences hunger, she becomes sympathetic to the "sidewalk man." Her sympathy for the man grows even stronger one day when she sees him giving half a sandwich to a stray cat. After having a discussion with her mother about giving handouts to the homeless, Sophie makes her difficult choice and helps the man.

Tolan has received praise from several reviewers for *Sophie and the Sidewalk Man.* One *Kirkus Reviews* critic called the story "a thoughtful, intelligent, and appealing book, with respect for its young readers and for the problem it explores." In *Horn Book Guide,* Elizabeth S. Watson commented that Sophie's progress toward growing up is admirable, and "no adult moralizing clouds the simple solution." Susannah Price, writing in *School Library Journal,* similarly found the story "a meaningful novel that is infused with the spirit of Christmas. . . . This story will really hit home, right where kids' feelings are." As *Booklist* contributor Deborah Abbott stated, "Tolan draws her characters carefully, making them believable and likable," and added that the story's theme is "a welcome change of pace."

Similarly, as in her books about the Skinner family, Tolan has also explored another family, the Filkins, in two novels, *Save Halloween!* and *Ordinary Miracles.* In the former, eleven-year-old Johnna is deeply involved in her school Halloween pageant, though her Evangelical

Christian family and preacher father consider it the devil's holiday. Johnna must soon choose between the two in this story with "no easy answers" and "no stock characters," according to a reviewer for *Publishers Weekly.* Maeve Visser Knoth, writing in *Horn Book Guide,* also praised Johnna as a "well-developed character," and further lauded the author for her thoughtful balance of "serious issues." Set about a year before this action, *Ordinary Miracles* focuses on two other members of the family: Mark and his twin brother, Matthew. Raised to become Evangelical preachers like other men in the family, Mark begins to find such a life claustrophobic. He begins pulling away from his brother and religion, and is befriended by a Nobel Prize-winning scientist whose genetic engineering work is anathema to Mark's family. "Tolan does not flinch from setting up a truly difficult dilemma for her character," wrote Susan Dove Lempke in a *Booklist* review. Lempke concluded, "Such well-written fiction exploring Christian themes is rare, and many libraries will want to snap this up." Writing in *Bulletin of the Center for Children's Books,* Elizabeth Bush noted that Tolan maintains a "deep respect of scientific and religious viewpoints and concludes that there are shadowy mysteries and miracles that, at last so far, elude our best attempts to illuminate them."

Chills are served up in *Who's There?,* a novel about fourteen-year-old Drew and her mute younger brother, both recently orphaned, who come to live with their deceased father's relatives. Here, they discover that the house is haunted by the ghosts of a potent family secret. Dubbed an "entertaining ghost story" by *Booklist*'s Stephanie Zvirin, the book produces "sufficiently creepy" ghostly encounters and characters "drawn with care," as Zvirin further commented. Reviewing the novel in *Book Report,* Charlotte Decker wrote, "Tolan is a skilled writer who manages to create a sense of terror in a story with a logical plot that flows smoothly to its suspenseful climax." Decker concluded, "Ideal for readers searching for a 'scary story.'"

"Sibling rivalry gets a pretty nasty portrayal" in the ghost tale *The Face in the Mirror,* according to Sally Margolis, writing in *School Library Journal.* Jared, the young son of two divorced and very much self-absorbed actors, has been living with his grandfather. But when this man becomes ill, Jared is sent to Michigan to live with the father he never met, a director who has started a Shakespearean company in a historical theater. Once there, Jared suddenly has to deal with his spoiled but very talented half-brother. Both are playing the children of Richard III, locked in the tower, but off-stage rivalries spill over on stage. A seemingly playful ghost befriends Jared, but soon the youth finds himself in over his head when this ghost of the nineteenth-century actor Garrick Marsden plots to involve him in the killing of his half-brother. Though a contributor for *Publishers Weekly* thought this "ghost yarn offers little in the way of thrills and chills," Kathleen Armstrong, writing in *Book Report,* felt that "lovers of mysteries will enjoy

this suspenseful story, a good choice for reluctant readers." Reviewing the same novel, *Booklist*'s Chris Sherman commented, "Tolan artfully weaves Shakespeare's Richard III, sibling rivalry, revenge, and a haunted theater with a vindictive ghost into a suspenseful story." Sherman further predicted that her incorporation of the Shakespeare play into the action of *The Face in the Mirror* might inspire readers to look into the original play.

Tolan's experiences with her own son and working with other gifted children have inspired several of her novels, including the 1996 *Welcome to the Ark* and its 2001 sequel, *Flight of the Raven.* Four child prodigies transfer from a center for research to an experimental group home, and thereby must learn a different way to connect with their new environment and the rest of the world. All the children's special gifts have to do with communication, from Elijah, who is empathic; to Taryn, the poet and healer; Doug, the musician and mathematician; and Miranda, master of many languages at fifteen. Together the four develop a telepathic link with themselves and other children around the world. But when the hospital director secretly sabotages this communication project, the children are disbanded and sent their individual ways. "Tolan blends elements of science fiction with nonstop suspense in a provocative, disturbingly real story set in a near future when violence is pandemic," wrote *Booklist*'s Sherman. Also reviewing *Welcome to the Ark,* Jacqueline Rose noted in *Voice of Youth Advocates* that the novel "will be best appreciated by sophisticated readers who understand its subtleties," and *Kliatt*'s Claire M. Dignan praised "Tolan's sense of urgency, combined with her beautiful imagery and use of metaphor [which] make this an enjoyable page-turner." The sequel, *Flight of the Raven* focuses on Elijah after the breakup of the home, or the Ark as it is referred to. The story also deals with twelve-year-old Amber and her father, the leader of a militia group that has just committed one devastating terrorist attack and is planning another. Elijah's empathic power is put to the test against this idealistic but misguided man who now plans to use biological weapons. A contributor for *Kirkus Reviews* felt this was "a slow-moving sequel" with "too much talk and not enough action." Hazel Rochman, however, writing in *Booklist,* felt that the "fear, the tenderness, and the evil seem very close to home," and Katie O'Dell, writing in *School Library Journal,* concluded that the novel will make "for a confrontational and thought-provoking read deserving much discussion."

A family of artistic geniuses is portrayed in *Surviving the Applewhites,* a "screwball comedy," according to *Booklist*'s Ilene Cooper, that takes a standard story about how a tough young kid is turned around by a new family and "pushes [it] to a whole new place." Juvenile delinquent Jake is given a final opportunity in his life, placed in the Creative Academy at the Applewhite farm, called Wit's End, along with the home-schooled siblings of that family who seem to set their own curriculum. Only the young daughter of the clan, E. D., is organized and decidedly non-artistic. The father is a theater director, the mother a mystery writer, and an uncle and aunt respectively carve wood and write poetry. Resistant at first to the new rural and creative environment, and "the outrageously eccentric Applewhite clan," as Faith Brautigam described the family in *School Library Journal,* Jake is ultimately turned around, even taking part in Mr. Applewhite's production of *The Sound of Music.* "Humor abounds in the ever-building chaos," wrote a reviewer for *Publishers Weekly,* who concluded, "In the end, it's the antics of the cast of characters that keep this show on the road." Similarly, a critic for *Kirkus Reviews* praised the madcap comedy, noting that the mixture of first- and third-person narration "result[s] in well-built characterizations held together in a structure that smoothly organizes the chaos that busy artistic geniuses create."

Tolan, who lives on a lake near Charlotte, North Carolina, with her husband and pets, is also a lecturer. In both her books and her speaking engagements, she is an outspoken proponent of children's rights and the development of positive self-awareness. "Most of the world is busy trying to tell children that they aren't good enough, aren't enough like other children, aren't really worthy of being loved," the author wrote on her Web site. "What every kid needs to know is that she is just exactly the person she is meant to be, and that—no matter what—she is absolutely and unconditionally worthy of love. If I could help even one boy or girl to begin to really believe that, I'd feel as if I'd done what I was meant to do."

Biographical and Critical Sources

BOOKS

Encyclopedia of Children's Literature, edited by Bernice E. Cullinan and Diane G. Person, Continuum (New York, NY), 2001, p. 779.

Helbig, Alethea K., and Agnes Regan Perkins, *Dictionary of American Children's Fiction, 1985-1989,* Greenwood Press (Westport, CT), 1993.

Writers for Young Adults, edited by Ted Hipple, Scribner (New York, NY), 2000, pp. 315-324.

PERIODICALS

Booklist, March 1, 1992, Deborah Abbott, review of *Sophie and the Sidewalk Man,* p. 1281; September 1, 1992, Carolyn Phelan, review of *The Witch of Maple Park,* p. 125; September 1, 1994, Stephanie Zvirin, review of *Who's There?,* p. 45; October 15, 1996, Chris Sherman, review of *Welcome to the Ark,* p. 414; September 1, 1998, Chris Sherman, review of *The Face in the Mirror,* p. 111; October 1, 1999, Susan Dove Lempke, review of *Ordinary Miracles,* p. 370; October 15, 2001, Hazel Rochman, review of *Flight of the Raven,* p. 396; November 1, 2002, Ilene Cooper, review of *Surviving the Applewhites,* p. 494.

Book Report, September-October, 1994, Charlotte Decker, review of *Who's There?,* p. 47; March-April, 1999, Kathleen Armstrong, review of *The Face in the Mirror,* p. 64.

Bulletin of the Center for Children's Books, December, 1992, Kathryn Jennings, review of *The Witch of Maple Park,* p. 125; October, 1993, pp. 59-60; December, 1994, Deborah Stevenson, review of *Who's There?,* p. 146; October, 1999, Elizabeth Bush, review of *Ordinary Miracles,* p. 72.

English Journal, October, 1987, review of *Pride of the Peacock,* p. 97.

Horn Book Guide, fall, 1992, Elizabeth S. Watson, review of *Sophie and the Sidewalk Man,* p. 259; spring, 1994, Maeve Visser Knoth, review of *Save Halloween!,* p. 83.

Kirkus Reviews, March 15, 1992, review of *Sophie and the Sidewalk Man,* p. 400; September 15, 1992, review of *The Witch of Maple Park,* p. 1194; September 15, 1998, review of *The Face in the Mirror,* p. 1391; October 1, 2001, review of *Flight of the Raven,* p. 1435; July 15, 2002, review of *Surviving the Applewhites,* p. 1046.

Kliatt, January, 1999, Claire M. Dignan, review of *Welcome to the Ark,* p. 20.

New York Times Book Review, April 30, 1978.

Publishers Weekly, September 20, 1993, review of *Save Halloween!,* p. 31; November 16, 1998, review of *The Face in the Mirror,* p. 76; August 5, 2002, review of *Surviving the Applewhites,* p. 73.

School Library Journal, January, 1992, Jana R. Fine, review of *Marcy Hooper and the Greatest Treasure in the World,* p. 99; May, 1992, Susannah Price, review of *Sophie and the Sidewalk Man,* p. 116; October, 1992, Lisa Dennis, review of *The Witch of Maple Park,* p. 122; October, 1993, p. 133; October, 1994, p. 150; October, 1996, p. 150; November, 1998, Sally Margolis, review of *The Face in the Mirror,* pp. 130-131; October, 1999, Elaine Fort Weischedel, review of *Ordinary Miracles,* p. 160; October, 2001, Katie O'Dell, review of *Flight of the Raven,* pp. 173-174; September, 2002, Faith Brautigam, review of *Suriving the Applewhites,* pp. 235-236.

Voice of Youth Advocates, April, 1997, Jacqueline Rose, review of *Welcome to the Ark,* p. 34.

Washington Post Book World, June 10, 1990.

ONLINE

Stephanie S. Tolan Home Page, http://www.stephanietolan.com/ (March 17, 2003).

U-V

U'REN, Andrea 1968-

Personal

Born August 16, 1968, in Palo Alto, CA; daughter of Richard C. (a psychiatrist) and Marjorie Jean (a professor of English) Burns; married Sean Healy (an artist), June, 2003; children: Sebastian. *Education:* Attended Rhode Island School of Design, 1986-87; Cooper Union, B.F.A., 1991; Whitney Museum of American Art, Independent Study Program, 1991-92.

Addresses

Home—4115 Northeast 11th Ave., Portland, OR 97211. *E-mail*—andreauren@yahoo.com.

Career

Author and illustrator.

Member

Society of Children's Book Writers and Illustrators.

Awards, Honors

Parents' Choice Award for *Pugdog.*

Writings

SELF-ILLUSTRATED

Pugdog, Farrar, Straus & Giroux (New York, NY), 2001.
Mary Smith, Farrar, Straus & Giroux (New York, NY), 2003.

Sidelights

Andrea U'Ren told *SATA:* "I wrote and illustrated my first full-length picture book at the age of twelve. It was about Mount St. Helens, the volcano in the Northwest

that—back in 1981—had just erupted. Amazingly enough, a local publisher wanted to purchase it for 2,000 dollars, but they also wanted to use an illustrator other than me. Meeting after meeting, they asked me to consider different illustrators; I turned each one down. The book never did get published.

"I went to art school first at the Rhode Island School of Design in Providence, than transferred to the Cooper Union in New York, New York. After receiving my degree in 1991, I attended the Whitney Museum of American Art Independent Study Program for artists. I began to feel the artwork I was making was speaking to and reaching a very small and exclusive audience. I needed a break from the fine arts.

"My latent desire to make children's books returned. I decided to finally publish a children's book. That was not as easy as I'd thought. Four years and *several* stories later, *Pugdog* was picked up by Farrar, Straus & Giroux.

"*Pugdog* is the story of a guy named Mike who assumes his dog is a male. After Mike discovers his boy-dog is actually a girl, he tries to get Pugdog to act more feminine—which means no more activities like digging, chasing squirrels, rolling on the ground, et cetera. Of course, Pugdog doesn't like this new life, and in the end Mike realizes the error of his ways. He loves his dog for being just who she is, male or female.

"Some people find it unbelievable that a grown man wouldn't know the gender of his pet. But, in fact, the story is based on a similar mistake my brother (a doctor!) made with a cat. When my brother first got his kitten, he was totally smitten with 'her.' Months later, I finally met the cat and hesitantly informed my brother that his little girl was in fact a little boy. My brother was floored—and he was never quite as smitten with his feline companion again.

"*Mary Smith* is about a woman in England who woke people (so they could make it to their jobs on time) by shooting dried peas at their windows. People who had this occupation were known as 'knocker-ups.'

"Writing is not an easy process for me—it's a serious struggle—and, for that matter, so is the process of illustrating. But, somehow, I can't keep myself from working on these succinct and intimate things known as picture books."

Biographical and Critical Sources

PERIODICALS

Booklist, March 1, 2001, Gillian Engberg, review of *Pugdog,* p. 1288.
Horn Book, March, 2001, Roger Sutton, review of *Pugdog,* p. 203.
Publishers Weekly, January 29, 2001, review of *Pugdog,* p. 88.
School Library Journal, June, 2001, Anne Parker, review of *Pugdog,* p. 131.

*   *   *

VAGIN, Vladimir (Vasilevich) 1937-

Personal

Born March 9, 1937, in Russia; son of Vasili Vagin (an engineer) and Alexandra Suranov (a school teacher); married Galina Markeev, June 19, 1962 (divorced); married Galina Smirnoff (a piano teacher), March 9, 1973; children: Anastasia. *Ethnicity:* Russian. *Education:* Moscow Polygraphic Institute, B.A., 1963. *Religion:* Christian. *Hobbies and other interests:* Painting.

Addresses

Home—191 Howard St., Burlington, VT 05401.

Career

Illustrator, 1990—. Perm Publishing House, Perm, Russia, art editor, 1964-1971; Moscow Publishing House, Sovremennik, Russia, art director, 1971-1990. Chairman of the annual Book Art Jury, Russia, 1985-1990.

Member

Artist Guild of Russia (1967-1990), Authors Guild.

Awards, Honors

Irma S. and James H. Black Award for Excellence in Children's Literature, Bank Street College, 1992, for *The King's Equal,* written by Katherine Paterson; Gold Best Book Award, Oppenheim Toy Portfolio, 2002, for *Firebird,* written by Jane Yolen.

Vladimir Vagin

Writings

SELF-ILLUSTRATED

(Coauthor with Frank Asch) *Insects from Outer Space,* Scholastic (New York, NY), 1994.
(Reteller) *The Nutcracker Ballet,* Scholastic (New York, NY), 1995.
(Reteller) *The Enormous Carrot,* Scholastic (New York, NY), 1998.
(Reteller) *The Twelve Days of Christmas,* HarperCollins (New York, NY), 1999.
(Reteller) *Peter and the Wolf,* Scholastic (New York, NY), 2000.

ILLUSTRATOR

Frank Asch, *Here Comes the Cat!/Siuda idet kot!,* Scholastic (New York, NY), 1989.
Frank Asch, *Dear Brother,* Scholastic (New York, NY), 1992.
Katherine Paterson, *The King's Equal,* HarperCollins (New York, NY), 1992.
Frank Asch, *The Flower Faerie,* Scholastic (New York, NY), 1993.
Katherine Paterson, *Celia and the Sweet, Sweet Water,* Clarion Books (New York, NY), 1998.
Katherine Paterson, *The Wide-Awake Princess,* Clarion Books (New York, NY), 2000.
Ralph J. Fletcher, *The Circus Surprise,* Clarion Books (New York, NY), 2001.
Jane Yolen, reteller, *Firebird,* HarperCollins (New York, NY), 2002.

Jane Yolen, *The Flying Witch,* HarperCollins (New York, NY), 2003.

Bethany Roberts, *Cookie Angel,* Henry Holt (New York, NY), 2003.

Adaptations

Here Comes the Cat was adapted for videocassette, Weston Woods, 1992.

Sidelights

Vladimir Vagin is a Russian-born illustrator of children's books whose detailed artwork reflects the influences of his heritage. He has teamed up with prominent authors such as Frank Asch, Katherine Paterson, and Jane Yolen in award-winning and highly commended fable-like picture books and retellings, and has also illustrated his own retellings of folktales and popular stories, including *The Nutcracker Ballet, Peter and the Wolf,* and *The Twelve Days of Christmas.* "I often draw my inspirations for images from my encounters in nature; sometimes as a participant and sometimes as a quiet observer," Vagin told *SATA.* "As far as my artistic influences, I have learned the most from looking at Russian folk art, paintings and frescos from the Renaissance, and Persian miniatures."

Born in 1937 Russia, Vagin grew up and passed much of his adult life in the Soviet system, but his memories deal more with folktales than with things political. "As a child growing up in Russia, I was fascinated by the Russian folktales," he told *SATA.* "They were read to me by my father and my teachers in kindergarten, and I spent hours on color pencil drawings of the characters as I envisioned them. Years later, my interest in storytelling along with my talent for drawing and painting led me to illustration." Starting in 1958, Vagin attended the Moscow Polygraphic Institute, where he received his art training. "I received my first job as an illustrator while I was studying design and illustration at the art institute in Moscow. My assignment was to illustrate a children's book about insects, and since I loved to observe their lives since I was a little boy, I enjoyed the project immensely. The book was a success, and I began working on my second book." Years later, after he had immigrated to the United States, he illustrated another book about such tiny creatures, *Insects from Outer Space,* coauthored with Frank Asch.

After graduation, Vagin worked first for the Perm Publishing House and then for Moscow Publishing House as art director. He also continued to illustrate children's books in Russia. In the mid-1980s, he began collaborating with American children's author Frank Asch on a project that would tell a story of fear that turns to trust. That neither spoke the other's language made this long-distance collaboration even more difficult; for three years, the pair communicated with sketches of the story. The result was the 1989 *Here Comes the Cat!,* written in both English and Russian, with Russian pronuncia-

An unpublished illustration by Vagin for the Russian folktale "Baba Yaga."

tion included. In the tale, a town of mice is frightened at the approach of a supposedly dreaded and fearful cat. The message spreads all over town and into the countryside, but when the cat finally arrives, it is carrying a gift of cheese for the mice. A reviewer for *Five Owls* suggested that young readers will receive the message that they "can't rely on stereotypes." *Here Comes the Cat!* was later adapted for video, using animation completed by a Moscow studio. It also cemented a friendship between Vagin and Asch that has taken them through several more collaborative efforts. When Vagin immigrated to the United States, he decided to settle in Vermont, where Asch lives.

Further works from the pair include *Dear Brother, The Flower Faerie,* and *Insects from Outer Space.* In the first title, "the spirit of glasnost lives on," according to a reviewer for *Publishers Weekly.* Two quarreling mouse brothers, Joey and Marvin, happen on a box full of letters when they are cleaning out the attic. In one box they find a packet of illustrated letters sent between their great-great-grand-uncles, Henry and Timothy, one who lived in the city, and the other who lived in the country. Reading the letters, they see that while these two men had their differences, brotherly love carried them through their life choices. Staying up all night to read these old messages, Joey and Marvin find a new respect and love for one another. Karen Litton, reviewing *Dear Brother* in *School Library Journal,* had praise for Vagin's illustrations, describing them as "dense with color and domestic details." *Booklist*'s Ilene Cooper also commended Vagin and Asch, claiming the pair once again "combine their talents in a gentle story," featuring Vagin's "bordered, deeply colored modern scenes." The critic for *Publishers Weekly* also lauded Vagin's "rich gouache and watercolor paintings [which] depict a verdant, hilly landscape and homey details."

The Flower Faerie is a more magical story for Asch and Vagin, about a faerie who is captured and thereafter loses her powers and will to live. The son of a mean-spirited emperor is shocked at his father when he intends to keep the faerie on display; she needs to run free in the woodlands to survive. Soon the kingdom has no flowers or crops because of the faerie's captivity, and the son determines to set her free. When he does, light and happiness once again return to the kingdom. A *Publishers Weekly* reviewer had more praise for how Vagin's "delicately graceful gouache and watercolor illustrations set the action in a feudal period of knights, kings and castles." Lisa Dennis, writing in *School Library Journal,* was less impressed with the book, noting that "despite attractive illustrations and a smooth, flowing text, this contemporary fable falls flat." *Booklist* reviewer Janice Del Negro, however, found more to like in the title, lauding Vagin's "intricately detailed paintings" which, she felt, gave the work "the romantic look of an old-fashioned fairy tale."

Another Vagin and Asch collaboration, this one coauthored by the two, is *Insects from Outer Space,* a book inspired by a nature outing Vagin took in his own backyard. "One day (since I still enjoy looking closely at insects that I find outdoors) I saw an unfamiliar insect that resembled a miniature hummingbird among the flowers in my garden," Vagin told *SATA.* "Hence came the idea of creating a book about insects as they have never been seen before but yet resemble our knowledge of what an insect looks like." The resulting book was *Insects from Outer Space,* about a friendly invasion of alien insects. Arriving at the Bug Ball, these insects are soon invited to take part in the annual festivities. Though Martha Sibert, writing in *Horn Book Guide,* thought the tale "lacks suspense," she did suggest that the illustrations "will attract readers' attention." *Booklist*'s Carolyn Phelan had similar comments, calling the plot "predictable" while praising Vagin's "delicately shaded and detailed" illustrations which offer "fascinating views of the robotic-looking space insects."

Vagin has teamed up with popular children's author Katherine Paterson on several other titles. *The King's Equal* is a chapter book that tells the story of an arrogant young prince who must find an equal for his bride, or risk his crown. In the event, he finds much more than he bargained for. Reviewers highly praised this award-winning title both for its text and its artwork. A reviewer for *Publishers Weekly* commented on Vagin's "elegantly detailed paintings, each featuring a smaller bordered scene laid atop a full-page illustration." *Horn Book*'s Maeve Visser Knoth praised Paterson's "remark-

able" original fairy tale and Vagin's "formal, detailed illustrations" that are as "equally elaborate" as the text. In an enthusiastic *School Library Journal* review, Martha Rosen noted that "Vagin's illustrations are exquisite, luminous in color, clarity, and precision." Rosen also commented that "finding a book equal in quality and brilliance to this one is an even more formidable task" than finding a princess who will be the equal to a future king.

Celia and the Sweet, Sweet Water and *The Wide-Awake Princess* are two further collaborations with Paterson. In the first quest tale, young Celia and her dog Brumble travel to find a cure for her mother's illness. On their way, they encounter three difficult people who present challenges for the young girl. *Booklist*'s GraceAnne A. DeCandido felt that Vagin's "hyperreal, densely patterned" illustrations "elegantly matched" Paterson's folktale. Similarly, Julie Cummins, writing in *School Library Journal,* felt that the "detailed watercolors are suited to the story," yet Cummins also complained of a page "design flaw" which has a "jarring effect." A reviewer for *Publishers Weekly* found no such problems, however, declaring that "Vagin . . . expertly navigates the thin line between the allegorical nature of the quest and the real world."

The Wide-Awake Princess provides another allegory from Paterson, the tale of a clever princess who—banished from the castle by three greedy nobles after her parents die—demonstrates to the peasants in her country how they can make better lives for themselves. *School Library Journal*'s Ronald Jobe found the people portrayed in Vagin's "expressionistic illustrations" to be "disturbing" with their "angular heads, long pointed noses, [and] unnatural sleeping positions." However, a critic for *Pubishers Weekly* commended the "portrait of a strong female protagonist" as well as the "uplifting ending," concluding that "readers will likely enjoy watching Vagin's trio of archetypal villains grovel."

Further collaborative efforts include work with Ralph J. Fletcher on *The Circus Surprise* and illustrations for two tales by Jane Yolen, *Firebird* and *The Flying Witch.* Nick is helped by a clown on stilts when he gets lost at the circus in *The Circus Surprise.* Reviewing that title in *School Library Journal,* Bina Williams found that Vagin's "pictures vividly portray the details of a circus." For Yolen's retelling of *Firebird,* the Russian folktale about Prince Ivan who encounters the magical bird that helps him defeat a foe, Vagin supplied "crisply rendered paintings [that] evoke czarist Russia," according to a critic for *Publishers Weekly.* A contributor for *Kirkus Reviews* felt that Vagin's illustrations for the same title "capture the Firebird's vibrant feathers, the ornate Russian costumes, and the fearful appearances of the wizard and demons."

Working solo, Vagin has also produced artwork for several retellings. *The Nutcracker Ballet* retells the E. T. A. Hoffmann tale of a little girl's Christmas Eve reverie with a wooden nutcracker that comes to life as a handsome prince in the Land of Sweets. Jane Marino, writing in *School Library Journal,* commented that the "real gift here" is Vagin's "stylized illustrations." The artist portrays hordes of army mice and a wealth of other detail. A contributor for *Dance Magazine* praised Vagin's "sharp-eyed attention to detail" in this "distinctive version." From the pattern in the parquet floor to the hydra-headed epaulettes on the shoulders of the mice, this is a rendition of which even Hoffmann "would surely have approved," stated the same critic. Similarly, *Booklist*'s Kathy Broderick predicted Vagin's "intricate period watercolors . . . will pull readers into this story." A contributor for *Publishers Weekly* concluded that the illustrator's artwork "take[s] playful liberties with perspective and echo the illusory nature of Tchaikovsky's ballet."

Vagin retells the old Russian folktale, "The Enormous Turnip," in *The Enormous Carrot,* a story in praise of teamwork as a group comes together to pull a giant carrot out of the ground. In Vagin's retelling, the group becomes a cast of farm animals and the carrot replaces the less well-known turnip. John Peters, writing in *Booklist,* called this "a classic tale about the value of cooperation, in a fresh, cheerful garb." A contributor for *Publishers Weekly* also enjoyed the title, noting that children "will enjoy the repetition of the growing chain of animals," and further commending how the "chipper . . . paintings pop out from shiny paper stock."

Vagin turns to the winter holidays in his rendition of the popular carol "The Twelve Days of Christmas" in a book of the same title which may take readers that many days to "fully appreciate Vagin's . . . striking watercolor paintings," according to a reviewer for *Publishers Weekly. Booklist*'s Shelley Townsend-Hudson found that Vagin illustrated this title using "visual allusions to both his native Russia and to his present home in Vermont." Vagin also retells an orchestral fairy tale in *Peter and the Wolf,* about the young boy who ignores his grandfather's warning to catch a wolf. Gillian Engberg, writing in *Booklist,* felt that this was "a crisp, appealing addition" to such retellings, and that Vagin's illustrations have a "gentle cast." A *Publishers Weekly* critic lauded this "faithful retelling" as well as remarking that the illustrations have a "distinctly Russian flavor." And a contributor for *Kirkus Reviews* also had praise for the work, noting that the "exciting illustrations give another context to a modern folktale."

Vagin told *SATA,* "In children's books, my interest is in the immediate and potentially powerful effect of visual experience. Beyond providing a visual accompaniment to a story, I think that illustrations can provide some of the first aesthetic experience for children. Chukovsky, a Russian writer of children's literature, was once asked: 'How should one write for children?' to which he answered: 'The same way one does for adults, only better.' In my work as an illustrator of children's books, I try to follow the same principle."

Biographical and Critical Sources

PERIODICALS

Booklist, June 15, 1992, Ilene Cooper, review of *Dear Brother,* p. 1844; July, 1992, Hazel Rochman, review of *The King's Equal,* p. 1944; January 1, 1993, Janice Del Negro, review of *The Flower Faerie,* p. 918; February 1, 1995, Carolyn Phelan, review of *Insects from Outer Space,* p. 1007; September 15, 1995, Kathy Broderick, review of *The Nutcracker Ballet,* pp. 173-174; March 1, 1998, John Peters, review of *The Enormous Carrot,* p. 1138; September 1, 1998, GraceAnne A. DeCandido, review of *Celia and the Sweet, Sweet Water,* p. 128; January 1, 2000, Shelley Townsend-Hudson, review of *The Twelve Days of Christmas,* p. 935; November 15, 2000, Gillian Engberg, review of *Peter and the Wolf,* p. 644.
Bulletin of the Center for Children's Books, June, 1998, Janice M. Del Negro, review of *The Enormous Carrot,* p. 377.
Dance Magazine, December, 1995, review of *The Nutcracker Ballet,* p. 9.
Five Owls, May-June, 1999, review of *Here Comes the Cat!,* p. 97.
Horn Book, September-October, 1992, Maeve Visser Knoth, review of *The King's Equal,* pp. 583-584.
Horn Book Guide, fall, 1995, Martha Sibert, review of *Insects from Outer Space,* pp. 284-285.
Kirkus Reviews, November 1, 2000, review of *Peter and the Wolf,* p. 1551; May 1, 2002, review of *Firebird,* p. 670.
Language Arts, September, 1989, Janet Hickman, review of *Here Comes the Cat!,* p. 568.
Life, July, 1989, Sue Allison, "Pen Pals," p. 14.
Publishers Weekly, April 28, 1989, review of *Here Comes the Cat!,* p. 75; January 1, 1992, review of *Dear Brother,* pp. 54-55; July 27, 1992, review of *The King's Equal,* p. 62; February 1, 1993, review of *The Flower Faerie,* p. 95; April 18, 1994, review of *Here Comes the Cat!* (videocassette), p. 32; September 18, 1995, review of *The Nutcracker Ballet,* p. 102; March 9, 1998, review of *The Enormous Carrot,* p. 66; July 20, 1998, review of *Celia and the Sweet, Sweet Water,* p. 218; September 27, 1999, review of *The Twelve Days of Christmas,* p. 53; March 13, 2000, review of *The Wide-Awake Princess,* p. 84; November 27, 2000, review of *Peter and the Wolf,* p. 78; April 23, 2001, review of *The Circus Surprise,* p. 77; April 29, 2002, review of *Firebird,* p. 68.
School Library Journal, April, 1989, Judith Gloyer, review of *Here Comes the Cat!,* p. 76; April, 1992, Karen Litton, review of *Dear Brother,* p. 86; September, 1992, Martha Rosen, review of *The King's Equal,* p. 255; April, 1993, Judith McMahon, review of *Here Comes the Cat!* (videocassette), p. 71, and Lisa Dennis, review of *The Flower Faerie,* p. 90; October, 1995, Jane Marino, review of *The Nutcracker Ballet,* pp. 42-43; September, 1998, Julie Cummins, review of *Celia and the Sweet, Sweet Water,* p. 178; July, 2000, Ronald Jobe, review of *The Wide-Awake Princess,* p. 85; November, 2000, Susan Scheps, review of *Peter and the Wolf,* p. 149; June, 2001, Bina Williams, review of *The Circus Surprise,* p. 112.*

W

WALDMAN, Neil 1947-

Personal

Born October 22, 1947, in Bronx, NY; son of Abraham (a businessman) and Jessie (Herstein) Waldman; married Jeri Socol (an elementary schoolteacher), December 20, 1972 (divorced, 1988); married, wife's name Kathy; children: Sarah, Jonathan. *Education:* Rochester Institute of Technology, B.F.A., 1969, M.S., 1970. *Politics:* Liberal. *Religion:* Jewish Reformed. *Hobbies and other interests:* Chess, guitar, classical music, travel, softball.

Addresses

Home—Greenburgh, NY. *Agent*—c/o Boyds Mill Press, 815 Church St., Honesdale, PA 18431.

Career

Painter, stamp designer, and freelance writer/illustrator, 1971—. Has worked as package designer, art teacher, and border guard. Olive farmer in Israel, 1970-73, 1975-76; Linbry Products, Yonkers, NY, art director, 1971; member of faculty, William Paterson College of New Jersey, 1980-81; art instructor at Westchester Art Workshop, State University of New York, 1994—; designer of postage stamps (for governments of Sierra Leone, Grenada, and Antigua), record album covers, book dust covers, and theater posters. Waldman's paintings can be found in the capitol buildings of more than a dozen nations, as well as in the United Nations building, and in the offices of several major corporations, including American Airlines, Merrill Lynch, and Sony. *Exhibitions:* Artwork exhibited at galleries in New York, Michigan, Massachusetts, Pennsylvania, and Connecticut.

Member

Graphic Artists Guild.

Neil Waldman

Awards, Honors

Desi Award, 1980, for a poster for Sylvania; Grammy Award nomination, National Academy of Recording Arts and Sciences, 1982 and 1983, for record cover designs; United Nations Poster Award for International Year of Peace, 1986; Parents' Choice Award, 1990, for *Nessa's Fish,* written by Nancy Luenn, and 1994, for *Nessa's Story,* written by Nancy Luenn; Washington Irving Award for illustration, 1990, for *Bring Back the Deer,* and 1992, for *The Highwayman;* Christopher

Award (ages 8-10), 1991, for *The Gold Coin*, written by Alma Flor Ada; Notable Book selection, American Library Association, and Children's Book of the Year selection, Bank Street College, both for *The Passover Journey: A Seder Companion*, written by Barbara Diamond Goldin; Best Book of the Year selection, *School Library Journal*, 1995, for *Bayou Lullaby*, written by Kathi Appelt; National Jewish Book Award, Jewish Book Council, for *Next Year in Jerusalem: 3000 Years of Jewish Stories*, retold by Howard Schwartz; American Storytellers Award, for *The Two Brothers: A Legend of Jerusalem;* Notable Book selection, *Smithsonian* magazine, 1998, for *Masada,* and 2000, for *Wounded Knee;* Sidney Taylor Honor Book for Younger Readers, Association of Jewish Libraries, 2000, for *The Wisdom Bird: A Tale of Solomon and Sheba*, written by Sheldon Oberman.

Writings

SELF-ILLUSTRATED

(With Jeri Waldman) *Pitcher in Left Field*, Prentice-Hall (New York, NY), 1981.

The Golden City: Jerusalem's 3000 Years, Atheneum (New York, NY), 1995.

The Never-Ending Greenness, Morrow (New York, NY), 1997.

(Reteller) *The Two Brothers: A Legend of Jerusalem*, Atheneum (New York, NY), 1997.

Masada, Morrow (New York, NY), 1998.

The Starry Night, Boyds Mills Press (Honesdale, PA), 1999.

Wounded Knee, Atheneum Books for Young Readers (New York, NY), 2001.

They Came from the Bronx: How the Buffalo Were Saved from Extinction, Boyds Mills Press (Honesdale, PA), 2001.

The Promised Land: The Birth of the Jewish People, Boyds Mills Press (Honesdale, PA), 2002.

The Snowflake: A Water Cycle Story, Millbrook Press (Brookfield, CT), 2003.

ILLUSTRATOR

Walter Harter, *Osceola's Head and Other Ghost Stories*, Prentice-Hall (New York, NY), 1974.

David C. Knight, *The Moving Coffins: Ghosts and Hauntings around the World*, Prentice-Hall (New York, NY), 1983.

Patricia T. Lowe, *The Runt*, Caedmon (New York, NY), 1984.

Michael Mark, *Toba*, Bradbury (New York, NY), 1984.

David C. Knight, editor, *Best True Ghost Stories of the Twentieth Century*, Prentice-Hall (New York, NY), 1984.

Lee P. Huntington, *Maybe a Miracle*, Coward (New York, NY), 1984.

(And editor) Edgar Allan Poe, *Tales of Terror: Ten Short Stories*, Prentice-Hall (New York, NY), 1985.

William Warren, *The Headless Ghost: True Tales of the Unexplained*, Prentice-Hall (New York, NY), 1986.

William Warren, *The Screaming Skull: True Tales of the Unexplained*, Prentice-Hall (New York, NY), 1987.

Jeffrey Prusski, *Bring Back the Deer*, Harcourt (San Diego, CA), 1988.

Margery Williams, *The Velveteen Rabbit: Or, How Toys Become Real*, Tom Doherty Associates (New York, NY), 1988.

(With Bryna Waldman) Sarah Leiberman, *A Trip to Mezuzah Land*, Merkos L'inyonei Chinuch (Brooklyn, NY), 1988.

Robert Orkand, Joyce Orkand, and Howard Bogot, *Gates of Wonder: A Prayerbook for Very Young Children*, Central Conference of American Rabbis (New York, NY), 1989.

Mark D. Shapiro, *Gates of Shabbat: Shaarei Shabbat: A New Shabbat Manual for the 1990s*, Central Conference of American Rabbis (New York, NY), 1990.

Alfred Noyes, *The Highwayman*, Harcourt (San Diego, CA), 1990.

Betty Boegehold, *A Horse Called Starfire*, Bantam (New York, NY), 1990.

Nancy Luenn, *Nessa's Fish*, Atheneum (New York, NY), 1990.

Robert Orkand, Howard Bogot, and Joyce Orkand, *Gates of Awe: Holy Day Prayers for Young Children*, Central Conference of American Rabbis (New York, NY), 1991.

Alma Flor Ada, *The Gold Coin*, Atheneum (New York, NY), 1991.

Ken Kesey, *The Sea Lion: A Story of the Sea Cliff People*, Viking (New York, NY), 1991.

Nancy Luenn, *Mother Earth*, Atheneum (New York, NY), 1992.

Ellen Blanker, *Down by the Seashore*, Silver Burdett and Ginn (New York, NY), 1992.

William Blake, *The Tyger*, Harcourt (San Diego, CA), 1993.

Katharine Lee Bates, *America the Beautiful*, Atheneum (New York, NY), 1993.

(Reteller) Sarah Waldman, *Light: The First Seven Days*, Harcourt (San Diego, CA), 1993.

Nancy Luenn, *Nessa's Story*, Atheneum (New York, NY), 1994.

Barbara Diamond Goldin, *The Passover Journey: A Seder Companion*, Viking (New York, NY), 1994.

Chaim Stern, editor, *On the Doorposts of Your House: A Mezuzot Beitecha—Prayers and Ceremonies for the Jewish Home, Hebrew Opening*, Central Conference of American Rabbis (New York, NY), 1994.

Kathi Appelt, *Bayou Lullaby*, Morrow (New York, NY), 1995.

Howard Schwartz, reteller, *Next Year in Jerusalem: 3000 Years of Jewish Stories*, Viking Penguin (New York, NY), 1996, reprinted as *Jerusalem of Gold: Jewish Stories of the Enchanted City*, Jewish Lights Publishing (Woodstock, VT), 2003.

Shulamith Levey Oppenheim, *And the Earth Trembled: The Creation of Adam and Eve*, Harcourt (San Diego, CA), 1996.

Dorothy Hinshaw Patent, *Quetzal: Sacred Bird of the Cloud Forest,* Morrow (New York, NY), 1996.

Sheldon Oberman, *By the Hanukkah Light,* Boyds Mill Press (Honesdale, PA), 1997.

Ellen Schecter, *The Family Haggadah,* Viking (New York, NY), 1999.

Sheldon Oberman, *The Wisdom Bird: A Tale of Solomon and Sheba,* Boyds Mill Press (Honesdale, PA), 2000.

Richard Michelson, *Too Young for Yiddish,* Talewinds (Watertown, MA), 2001.

OTHER

(Compiler and illustrator) *Dream Makers: The Hopes and Aspirations of Children,* Boyds Mills Press (Honesdale, PA), 2003.

Sidelights

Neil Waldman is a distinguished author and illustrator of children's books with several of his own self-illustrated titles and dozens of other books that he has illustrated for a myriad of authors. The author and illustrator of many books on the Jewish religion, tradition, and folklore, Waldman's solo efforts include the Holocaust tale *The Never-Ending Greenness* and explorations of Jewish history in *The Golden City: Jerusalem's 3000 Years, The Two Brothers: A Legend of Jerusalem, Masada,* and *The Promised Land: The Birth of the Jew-*

With rich paintings of New York in the style of Vincent Van Gogh, Waldman creates the backdrop for his story of a fictitious meeting in Central Park between the famous artist and a young boy. (From The Starry Night, *written and illustrated by Waldman.)*

ish People. In *Wounded Knee* and *They Came from the Bronx: How the Buffalo Were Saved from Extinction,* Waldman deals with Native-American and frontier history. Working with other authors, the illustrator has looked at similar themes, as in Jeffrey Prusski's *Bring Back the Deer* and Nancy Luenn's *Nessa's Story,* both of which deal with Native Americans, and Howard Schwartz's *Next Year in Jerusalem: 3000 Years of Jewish Stories* and *The Passover Story: A Seder Companion* by Barbara Diamond Goldin. Additionally, Waldman has proven an able illustrator for poems and stories by classic English and American authors, including Alfred Noyes' *The Highwayman,* William Blake's *The Tyger,* and a collection of horror stories by Edgar Allan Poe titled *Tales of Terror: Ten Short Stories.* After the publication of *Starry Night,* Waldman became involved with the Children's Aid Society, and his efforts for that organization include *Dream Makers: The Hopes and Aspirations of Children,* for which Waldman selected writings from children about their dreams and hopes for the future.

Waldman once told *SATA:* "I was raised in a house where all the arts were encouraged. I sensed, as a small child, that finger paints and coloring books were more than just fun. They were important tools that led to a road of joy, discovery, and fulfillment.

"When I entered first grade, I learned very quickly that, within the classroom walls, the arts were 'secondary subjects,' not nearly as important as reading, math and science. I resented this deeply, and unconsciously began to rebel. Through twelve years of school I was considered an 'underachiever.' In fact, I was doing the minimum possible to get by, while working on my art at home.

"When I graduated from high school (near the bottom of my class), I felt as though I had been liberated. I entered an art college, where I spent most of my time drawing and painting. Here, surrounded by other artists for the first time, I began to blossom. Though I'd always known that art was important too, now it was reinforced in my environment. Instead of struggling against the current, I was gliding freely, ever faster and deeper, to places I had never imagined."

Waldman studied illustration and painting at Rochester Institute of Technology. "During and after college there was never a plan for my life," the artist told John Dalmas in the *Sunday Journal-News.* "I wanted to travel since I was a kid, and I always wanted to draw and paint. It just never occurred to me I would end up doing what I like for a living." After graduation, Waldman added, "I began to work as an illustrator. This seemed a natural decision, because it would allow me to do what I love most, while earning a living. It was difficult at first, almost like learning a new language. But it was worth it."

Early in his illustration career, Waldman designed postage stamps for Sierra Leone, Granada, Antigua, and many other countries, and won the United Nations poster competition representing the International Year of Peace in 1986. He also designed book jackets and magazine covers, but never considered illustrating children's literature until an editor at Gulliver Books approached him about working on a book titled *Bring Back the Deer,* by Jeffrey Prusski. Illustrating that book changed Waldman's life. Erin Gathrid, the editor at Gulliver, chose Waldman because she had been drawn to his work and felt that it had the same mystical quality as the manuscript for *Bring Back the Deer.* Initially Waldman refused, but Gathrid talked him into reading the manuscript at least five times before he made a decision.

Bring Back the Deer is the story of a young Native American boy's search for identity. When his father goes to hunt for food and doesn't return, the boy follows after him, and in the process discovers the animal spirit inside himself. Waldman once recalled for *SATA:* "As I began to read, I felt like I was entering a dark, winding cave. By the time I finished reading, I was totally confused. The story left me feeling that I had missed something. If I hadn't promised to read it five times, I would never have looked at it again. But then a strange thing happened. On my second reading, a few things were revealed to me that had escaped me the first time. And when I read it again, I saw even more. By the fifth time, not only did I begin to appreciate it . . . I began to love it."

Though he had never worked on a children's picture book before, he agreed to handle the project. After weeks of difficulty finding the right images, Waldman arranged to meet with Gathrid and Prusski in New York City. Prusski told Waldman of his experience with Shamanism, and how a Native-American spirit had written the story through him. Waldman once told *SATA,* "As Jeff continued speaking, I felt myself being transported back . . . back . . . back into the story. Images began flooding my brain. I opened my napkin and began scribbling on it. When I got home later that afternoon, I unfolded the napkin and began to study it. One of my scribblings was the image of two rectangles, one inside the other. I envisioned the main subject of each page within the smaller rectangle, with secondary subjects floating around it. The larger rectangle became the frame for each page. The color within the smaller rectangle would be very bright, to focus the viewer's attention on the central image." After discovering the boy and the grandfather in the tale, "the paintings were flowing effortlessly. Each image was like a road sign, directing me to whatever came next. I created a tribe, with its own special clothing, dwellings, environment, and even its own language of pictographs. It was as if I was constructing an entire world, which I lived in as I continued to paint."

"I painted intensely for two months," Waldman continued, "and when I finished the book it was clear that my life had changed forever. I knew that I wouldn't be working for advertising agencies or design studios anymore. I wanted to do more picture books. I had tiptoed through the window, and my path lay clearly before me. Like a many colored fan, my life was unfolding before my eyes, revealing colors I had never even dreamed of." A *Publishers Weekly* critic praised Waldman's "splendid debut" in *Bring Back the Deer,* noting that his illustrations "have a lyrical quality that is haunting." Since 1988, when *Bring Back the Deer* was published, Waldman has worked exclusively on children's literature, having illustrated numerous picture books and dust jackets, including several Newbery or Newbery Honor winners. The book prompted changes in Waldman's personal life as well, as he decided to leave his marriage and embark on a journey of self-discovery.

In 1990, Waldman brought his artistic vision to Alfred Noyes' famous poem *The Highwayman,* which had recently been illustrated twice: once by Charles Mikolaycak and once by Charles Keeping. Unlike his predecessors, Waldman brought a broad palette to the poem, prompting Roger Sutton of the *Bulletin of the Center for Children's Books* to observe: "[Waldman's] colors are often unlikely—plenty of aqua and magenta—but surprisingly effective, as in a moody painting of the highwayman upon his horse, a study in blue and black and gray." A *Publishers Weekly* reviewer characterized Waldman's style in *The Highwayman* as "both abstract and realistic," adding that his watercolors "capture the haunting, tragic spirit of the text." Eleanor K. MacDonald, writing for *School Library Journal,* praised the effect of Waldman's artwork, stating that "the strong sense of atmosphere and dramatic use of design reinforce the melodrama of the story."

In 1993, Waldman illustrated another classic poem, this time William Blake's *The Tyger.* In her *School Library Journal* review, Ruth K. MacDonald described Waldman's acrylic artwork as "modern, highly painterly, and formal." The final picture is a fold-out spread of the "tyger" that covers four pages, with each of the pages leading up to it featuring a section of the larger picture, each reproduced in black and shades of gray. MacDonald stated that "the focus on individual portions of the whole gives readers an opportunity to study *The Tyger* carefully, and to discuss the artist's interpretation."

Nessa's Story, by Nancy Luenn, features the story of an Inuit girl who learns from her grandmother how to participate in the cultural tradition of storytelling. *Booklist* contributor Isabel Schon asserted that Waldman's "original, luminous watercolor paintings," which use a wide range of settings, "are the best part of this story." *School Library Journal* contributor Roz Goodman noted that the "soft, cool colors in a variety of pastel pinks, blues, purples, greens, and browns blend into scenes both realistic and imaginary."

In *Booklist,* Stephanie Zvirin described *The Passover Journey: A Seder Companion* as "a beautiful wedding of the work of two talented individuals" that is "exquisitely designed." Author Barbara Diamond Goldin describes the history behind the Jewish holiday of Passover, and the symbolism behind the Seder meal, eaten in remembrance of the Jews' freedom from slavery in Egypt. Waldman's interpretation of this text features the "geometric borders and pastels characteristic of [his] work," according to Zvirin, and are combined with "stylized classic Egyptian hieroglyphic figures and set against softly tinted pages that actually glow." Hanna B. Zeiger, writing for *Horn Book,* commented that "the page design and stylized illustrations, in pleasing soft pastel colors, help make this book a welcome addition to holiday literature."

Waldman followed his work on *The Passover Journey* with another Jewish-themed book the following year, writing and illustrating *The Golden City. School Library Journal* contributor Susan Scheps noted that the book "successfully introduces the panorama of religions and cultures that have formed the city's heritage and created its mystique." A *Kirkus Reviews* critic, on the other hand, maintained that the writing "often overly romanticizes and is entirely subjective about a topic few people can approach objectively." Both reviewers, however, praised Waldman's watercolor and pencil illustrations featuring architecturally accurate portraits of Jerusalem during various time periods in its three-thousand-year history.

In 1995, Waldman lent his talents to a story written by Kathi Appelt, *Bayou Lullaby.* Judy Constantinides, writing in *School Library Journal,* commented that while the verse of this Cajun lullaby is enjoyable, "the true merit of the book lies in Waldman's double-page acrylic paintings." Waldman's figures are stylized and his palette includes rich jewel tones set against a black background. A *Publishers Weekly* reviewer called *Bayou Lullaby* "an inspired pairing of author and artist."

Turning his attention once again to Jewish themes, Waldman teamed with reteller Howard Schwartz to create a collection of Jewish folktales titled *Next Year in Jerusalem.* The tales are taken in part from the Talmud and Midrash, some from folklore, and others from mystical or Hasidic sources. Marcia W. Posner wrote in *School Library Journal* that "Waldman has suffused the pages with the peach-colored dawns, golden sunlit days, and turquoise and lavender twilights of Jerusalem." In *Horn Book,* Hanna B. Zeiger observed that "Waldman's watercolor illustrations enhance the handsomely produced volume."

Two more books illustrated by Waldman and published in 1996 deal with ancient myth. *Quetzal: Sacred Bird of the Cloud Forest,* by Dorothy Hinshaw Patent, draws upon Mexican myths of the beautiful bird which inhabits the cloud forests of Mexico and Central America. Waldman employed colored pencil on tinted paper for his illustrations, which, according to *School Library Journal* contributor Pam Gosner, "are quite lovely, with

rich glowing tones." For Shulamith Levey Oppenheim's book *And the Earth Trembled: The Creation of Adam and Eve,* based on a traditional Islamic tale of creation, Waldman used the technique of pointillism, which Patricia Lothrop regarded in *School Library Journal* as "well suited to his subject." Lothrop continued: "The pages are brightly colored, the image of the Ibis is appropriately scary, and Paradise is a vision of order in green and blue."

In 1997, Waldman wrote and illustrated *The Never-Ending Greenness,* a story of holocaust survival. In this work, the Jewish narrator reflects on his childhood as he recalls being exiled to a ghetto along with his family at the hands of Nazi soldiers. The family escapes to the surrounding forest, and the boy later realizes his dream of planting trees in Israel. Waldman's story is told in simple language, and his illustrations feature his characteristic-stylized palette, using bright blue, orange, pink, and turquoise. A *Publishers Weekly* critic noted that the "reference to Tu b'Shvat . . . might commend the book to families who observe that holiday." Betsy Hearne of the *Bulletin of the Center for Children's Books* called *The Never-Ending Greenness* "perfectly paced as an unfolding of personalized history reflected in a life cycle like an unfolding of leaves." Hearne added that the "intensity of the boy's project is magnetic enough to build a bridge of identification with today's young listeners." Focusing on the artwork in the same book, a contributor for *Reading Teacher* lauded the "pointillistic" acrylic paintings which accent "the colorful beauty of new growth."

Waldman continues with Jewish themes in several more of his titles. *The Two Brothers,* a retelling of the legend of how Solomon selected the site of Jerusalem for his temple, is a "moving" tale, according to Maeve Visser Knoth in *Horn Book Guide.* The 1998 title *Masada* is a "tribute to the legendary citadel," according to a contributor for *Publishers Weekly,* following two millennia of history about the fortress built on a high plateau in the Negev desert, which became a final stronghold for the Jewish people in the Holy Land. Here the Zealots made the stand against the Romans, fighting to the last and committing suicide rather than surrendering. Waldman traces the history of the place from its founding by King Herod up to the 1960s when much of the current knowledge about it was revealed by an archaeological expedition. But it is the final battle against the Romans that takes center stage and is "most compelling," as the *Publishers Weekly* reviewer noted. Janice M. DelNegro, writing in *Bulletin of the Center for Children's Books,* spoke highly of Waldman's "thrillingly dramatic and admiring prose," adding that it has "strong nationalistic undertones." Susan Scheps, reviewing the same title in *School Library Journal,* observed that Waldman bases his tale on the account of Josephius Flavius, a young Jewish man who took an oath to serve the Romans in order to save his life. Waldman also uses dialogue in his account, "a tactic that gives a fictional quality to the otherwise carefully researched text," according to Scheps.

In 1907, a young Comanche boy awaits the return to Oklahoma of the buffalo which the American Bison Society has fought to keep from extinction in **They Came from the Bronx,** *written and illustrated by Waldman.*

A change of pace for Waldman is the 1999 *The Starry Night,* a "nifty little fantasy based on the life of painter Vincent Van Gogh," as *Booklist*'s GraceAnne DeCandido described the picture book. In Waldman's tale, the Dutch artist pops up in Manhattan, setting his easel in Central Park. A young boy makes his acquaintance and takes him on a tour of the city. Afterwards, Vincent takes the young boy to the Metropolitan Museum of Art and shows him the picture "Starry Night," which inspires the boy to sketch his own interpretation of the famous painting. Throughout, the artwork represents both Waldman's impression of what Van Gogh's colorful vision of the city might be as well as more realistic, sepia-toned illustrations. A reviewer for *Publishers Weekly* felt that "Waldman's paintings . . . cleverly imitate Van Gogh's feeling for color." Similarly, DeCandido praised the contrasting of "briliantly colored" paintings in Van Gogh's style with the "lively sepia-toned . . . sketches." Margaret A. Chang, writing in *School Library Journal,* similarly called the book a "showcase for Waldman's paintings of New York City."

Writing *The Starry Night* was a chance for Waldman to fulfill a childhood dream. Waldman explained on his website, "I first fell in love with Vincent's work when, as a young child, I came upon a book of his paintings. I was awestruck. I remember thinking that until I saw those amazing pictures, I'd never really seen the sky." After that experience, Waldman dreamed of bringing the artist to New York City, where he could leave the misery he experienced in Europe behind him. *The Starry Night* has also helped other children realize their dreams; the book was chosen by the Children's Aid Society of New York, an organization that provides adoption and foster care services, as well as health care and educational opportunities for underserved children in New York City. One focus of the Children's Aid Society is promoting arts to young people, and through a joint effort with Waldman, The Starry Night Fund was created to raise money to provide free copies of the book to underprivileged children. Waldman also contributes twenty-five percent of the book's royalties to the Children's Aid Society. In addition, 1,000 collector's edition copies were printed and sold for $100 per book, with the full proceeds going to the Children's Aid Society.

Waldman deals with Native American and Western themes in two further solo efforts, *Wounded Knee* and

They Came from the Bronx. In the former title—a "remarkable and well-written history," according to Linda Greengrass in *School Library Journal*—Waldman provides a "vivid description" of that Lakota Indian massacre in 1890. Waldman's book also details the history of the settlers and the Native Americans in the South Dakota region known as the Black Hills. Randy Meyer, writing in *Booklist,* found Waldman's account to be "balanced" and "succinct," accompanied by black-and-white and color portraits. Likewise, a reviewer for *Publishers Weekly* found Waldman's treatment a "moving yet balanced overview." A *Horn Book* critic also thought that Waldman "provides a clear and focused background" to the tragedy but complained that "the lack of documentation hampers readers who want to reconsider [Waldman's] opinions."

With *They Came from the Bronx,* Waldman presents something of a hybrid tale of the history of the American bison. This "articulate and informative volume," as a reviewer for *Publishers Weekly* described the picture book, begins with a Comanche boy in Oklahoma who asks his grandmother to tell him the story of the buffalo. The grandmother proceeds to tell the young boy of the amazing wild beast and its decimation at the hands of white settlers. Interspersed with this tale is a parallel one of how the herd was rebuilt from animals shipped west from the Bronx Zoo at the turn of the century. The same *Publishers Weekly* critic praised Waldman's "eloquent, sepia-tone watercolors." Mary L. Laub, reviewing the book in *Childhood Education,* found it "inspirational as well as informative," while Kate McDowell, writing in the *Bulletin of the Center for Children's Books,* reserved her praise for the illustrations, which, in her opinion, "provide some of the emotional appeal absent from the story."

Waldman returns to Jewish life and history with illustrations for Sheldon Oberman's *The Wisdom Bird: A Tale of Solomon and Sheba* and *Too Young for Yiddish,* by Richard Michelson. Patricia Pearl Dole of *School Library Journal* commended Waldman's illustrations for Oberman's book, noting that the artwork of "elegant abstract designs, the king and the queen, the city of Jerusalem, and the many beautiful birds shine forth in full splendor." A reviewer for *Publishers Weekly* also had kind words for Waldman's work on the intergenerational tale *Too Young for Yiddish,* noting that this volume was "handsomely illustrated . . . in a sepia-toned palette recalling old family albums."

In his self-illustrated *The Promised Land,* Waldman takes a look at the beginnings of the Jewish people, tracing the origins from the time of Abraham to Moses and Joshua. Waldman begins with an examination of the promise of the land that God made to Abraham, an act that seems to have sustained the people, according to Waldman, through their long and turbulent history, including the time in Egypt, the Exodus, and Diaspora. A *Kirkus Reviews* critic called this "a straightforward account that sticks to Biblical sources," while Amy

Lilien-Harper of *School Library Journal* felt it was "beautifully written but rather obscure." Lilien-Harper further noted that the writing is "lyrical and lovely," but that it is also often rather complex and "requires a certain amount of familiarity of Jewish history." A reviewer for *Publishers Weekly* also noted the demanding text, but found the artwork "consistently moving." Similarly, *Booklist*'s Stephanie Zvirin felt that Waldman's "densely packed text is not quite as successful as his art," which she described as "gorgeous."

In 2003, Waldman again teamed up with the Children's Aid Society on a book project, though this one was quite different from *The Starry Night.* Waldman was asked to create a book to commemorate the society's 150th anniversary. After they asked him, Waldman recalled an event that had happened a year earlier at a school in Alabama where he was speaking. He recounted the following to *SATA:* "I'd just finished speaking in a gymnasium packed with fifth graders in Birmingham, when a little blonde-haired girl began making her way up to the stage. She approached, lowered her head shyly, and handed me a folded piece of paper. Before I could say a word, she turned and ran from the gym. I glanced at the paper, recognizing that it was a poem, and stuffed it into my satchel, along with scores of other papers I'd received that day." After discussing the Children's Aid Society project, he found the poem and read it; it was to be the first piece he would include in the book, called *Dream Makers,* which became a collection of writings by children about their hopes, dreams, and aspirations. Waldman contacted schools throughout New York and around the United States; he received hundreds of submissions, eventually selecting forty-two that would appear alongside his illustrations in the book.

With *Dream Makers,* published in 2003, Waldman again dedicated a quarter of the royalties to the Children's Aid Society, and with a matching gift from his publisher, nearly one free copy of the book is given to a child for each copy that sells. The Children's Aid Society has also dedicated a portion of their web page to featuring submissions to the project that were not featured in the book.

Biographical and Critical Sources

PERIODICALS

Book Links, October-November, 2000, Neil Waldman, "City Kids and *The Starry Night,*" pp. 50-52.
Booklist, March 1, 1994, Stephanie Zvirin, review of *The Passover Journey: A Seder Companion,* p. 1260; February 1, 1995, Isabel Schon, review of *Nessa's Story,* p. 1012; November 1, 1999, GraceAnne DeCandido, review of *The Starry Night,* p. 541; March 15, 2001, Randy Meyer, review of *Wounded Knee,* p. 1389; March 1, 2002, Hazel Rochman, review of *Too Young*

for Yiddish, p. 1142; October 1, 2002, Stephanie Zvirin, review of *The Promised Land: The Birth of the Jewish People,* p. 344.

Bulletin of the Center for Children's Books, December, 1990, Roger Sutton, review of *The Highwayman,* pp. 95-96; June, 1997, Betsy Hearne, review of *The Never-Ending Greenness,* pp. 347-348; October, 1998, Janice M. DelNegro, review of *Masada,* p. 76; December, 2001, Kate McDowell, review of *They Came from the Bronx: How the Buffalo Were Saved from Extinction,* pp. 154-155.

Childhood Education, spring, 2002, Mary L. Laub, review of *They Came from the Bronx,* p. 172.

Horn Book, May-June, 1994, Hanna B. Zeiger, review of *The Passover Journey,* p. 334; July-August, 1996, Hanna B. Zeiger, review of *Next Year in Jerusalem: 3000 Years of Jewish Stories,* p. 472; July-August, 2001, review of *Wounded Knee,* p. 478.

Horn Book Guide, spring, 1998, Maeve Visser Knoth, review of *The Two Brothers: A Legend of Jerusalem,* p. 114; fall, 2001, Maeve Visser Knoth, review of *The Golden City: Jerusalem's 3000 Years,* p. 425.

Kirkus Reviews, August 1, 1995, review of *The Golden City,* p. 1118; January 15, 2002, review of *Too Young for Yiddish,* p. 106; September 1, 2002, review of *The Promised Land,* p. 1322.

New York Times, May 15, 1999, Donna Greene, "A Book First Written for Van Gogh"; October 14, 2001, Hilary S. Wolfson, "A Storyteller's Tale of the Buffalo and Their Ties to the Bronx."

Publishers Weekly, October 14, 1988, review of *Bring Back the Deer,* pp. 71-72; September 14, 1990, review of *The Highwayman,* p. 124; February 13, 1995, review of *Bayou Lullaby,* p. 77; February 3, 1997, review of *The Never-Ending Greenness,* p. 107; August 10, 1998, review of *Masada,* p. 390; February 22, 1999, review of *The Family Haggadah,* p. 86; October 18, 1999, review of *The Starry Night,* p. 80; August 28, 2000, review of *The Wisdom Bird: A Tale of Solomon and Sheba,* p. 78; May 14, 2001, review of *Wounded Knee,* p. 83; August 13, 2001, review of *They Came from the Bronx,* p. 312; January 14, 2002, review of *Too Young for Yiddish,* p. 60; September 9, 2002, review of *The Promised Land,* p. 65.

Reading Teacher, April, 1998, review of *The Never-Ending Greenness,* p. 589.

School Library Journal, December, 1990, Eleanor K. MacDonald, review of *The Highwayman,* p. 118; January, 1994, Ruth K. MacDonald, review of *The Tyger,* p. 118; April, 1994, Roz Goodman, review of *Nessa's Story,* p. 108; April, 1995, Judy Constantinides, review of *Bayou Lullaby,* p. 97; November, 1995, Susan Scheps, review of *The Golden City: Jerusalem's 3000 Years,* p. 94; January, 1996, Marcia W. Posner, review of *Next Year in Jerusalem,* p. 125; September, 1996, Patricia Lothrop, review of *And the Earth Trembled: The Creation of Adam and Eve,* p. 219; October, 1996, Pam Gosner, review of *Quetzal: Sacred Bird of the Cloud Forest,* p. 138; November, 1998, Susan Scheps, review of *Masada,* pp. 143-144; June, 1999, Yapha Nussbaum Mason, review of *The Family Haggadah,* p. 120; October, 1999, Margaret A. Chang, review of *The Starry Night,* p. 129; October, 2000, Patricia Pearl Dole, review of *The Wisdom Bird,* p. 132; May, 2001, Linda Greengrass, review of *Wounded Knee,* p. 172; September, 2002, Amy Lilien-Harper, review of *The Promised Land,* p. 255.

Sunday Journal-News (Rockland County, NY), December 30, 1984, Dalmas, John, "Neil Waldman: He Has Designs on Postage Stamps."

Teaching K-8, May, 2002, Neil Waldman, "Beyond the Green Darkness."

ONLINE

Children's Aid Society Web site, http://www.childrensaidsocitey.org/ (July 29, 2003).

Neil Waldman Paintings, http://www.neilwaldman.com/ (July 29, 2003).

The Starry Night *Web site,* http://www.thestarrynight.com/ (June 22, 2003).

*   *   *

WALKER, Pamela

Personal

Born in Scottsville, KY.

Addresses

Home—Brooklyn, NY. *Agent*—c/o Author Mail, Scholastic, 555 Broadway, New York, NY 10012-3999.

Career

Author, teacher, and librarian. Worked as a teacher and librarian for twelve years.

Writings

Pray Hard (young adult novel), Scholastic (New York, NY), 2001.

Sidelights

Pamela Walker's debut novel *Pray Hard* centers on twelve-year-old Amelia Forrest. It is one year after the sudden death of her father in a small-plane crash, a death for which Amelia secretly feels responsible, and Amelia and her mother have fallen apart in the interim. Her mother has gained fifty pounds and Amelia's grades in school have dropped. But on the morning that Amelia decides to regain control of their lives, sending her mother off to the beauty shop and herself sitting down to study, a mysterious stranger arrives at their door claiming to be a messenger from her father. This man, according to Sharon Grover in *School Library Journal,* "becomes the catalyst that allows Amelia and her mama to regain a sense of purpose in life, and more importantly, to regain their faith." Despite questioning the effectiveness of Walker's open-ended conclusion, *Booklist* reviewer Ilene Cooper called *Pray Hard* "a fine debut from a writer to watch." Writing in *Publishers Weekly,* a critic found Walker's ending "highly satisfying and accomplished in its deference to readers' imaginations."

Biographical and Critical Sources

PERIODICALS

Booklist, March 1, 2001, Ilene Cooper, review of *Pray Hard,* p. 1283.
Publishers Weekly, April 9, 2001, review of *Pray Hard,* p. 75.
School Library Journal, July, 2001, Sharon Grover, review of *Pray Hard,* p. 115.

ONLINE

Southern Kentucky Festival of Books, http://www. sokybookfest.org/Bookfest01/ (May 13, 2003).*

* * *

WATSON, Wendy (McLeod) 1942-

Personal

Born July 7, 1942, in Paterson, NJ; daughter of Aldren Auld (an art editor, illustrator, and writer) and Nancy (a writer; maiden name, Dingman) Watson; married Michael Donald Harrah (an actor and opera singer), December 19, 1970; children: Mary Cameron Harrah, one other child. *Education:* Bryn Mawr College, B.A. (magna cum laude; with honors; Latin literature), 1964; studied painting with Jerry Farnsworth, Cape Cod, MA, summers, 1961 and 1962, and drawing and painting at National Academy of Design, 1966 and 1967. *Religion:* Society of Friends (Quaker). *Hobbies and other interests:* Theater, music (plays the piano and cello), reading, gardening.

Addresses

Home—Southern Vermont. *Agent*—c/o Author Mail, Farrar Straus & Giroux, 19 Union Square W., New York, NY 10001.

Career

Hanover Press, Hanover, NH, compositor and designer, 1965-66; freelance illustrator of books, 1966—.

Member

Authors Guild, Authors League of America.

Awards, Honors

Fisherman Lullabies was included in the American Institute of Graphic Arts Children's Book Show, 1967-68; *When Noodlehead Went to the Fair* was included in the Printing Industries of America Graphic Arts Awards Competition, 1969; *New York Times* Outstanding Books citation, 1971, Children's Book Showcase award, Children's Book Council, 1972, and National Book Award finalist, Association of American Publishers, 1972, all for *Father Fox's Pennyrhymes,* which was also included in the American Institute of Graphic Arts Children's Book Show, 1972, and the Biennial of Illustrations, Bratislava, 1973.

Writings

FOR CHILDREN; SELF-ILLUSTRATED

Very Important Cat, Dodd (New York, NY), 1958.
(Editor) *Fisherman Lullabies,* music by sister Clyde Watson, World Publishing (Cleveland, OH), 1968.
(Adapter) Jacob Grimm and Wilhelm Grimm, *The Hedgehog and the Hare,* World Publishing (Cleveland, OH), 1969.
Lollipop, Crowell (New York, NY), 1976.
Moving, Crowell (New York, NY), 1978.
Has Winter Come?, Philomel (New York, NY), 1978.
Jamie's Story, Philomel (New York, NY), 1981.
The Bunnies' Christmas Eve, Philomel (New York, NY), 1983.
Christmas at Bunny's Inn: A Three Dimensional Advent Calendar with Twenty-four Windows and Doors to Open from December First to Christmas Eve, Philomel (New York, NY), 1984.
Little Brown Bear, Western Publishing (New York, NY), 1985.
Tales for a Winter's Eve (short stories), Farrar, Straus & Giroux (New York, NY), 1988.
Wendy Watson's Mother Goose, Lothrop, Lee & Shepard (New York, NY), 1989.
Wendy Watson's Frog Went A-Courting, Lothrop, Lee & Shepard (New York, NY), 1990.
Thanksgiving at Our House, Houghton (Boston, MA), 1991.
A Valentine for You, Houghton (Boston, MA), 1991.
Boo! It's Halloween, Clarion (New York, NY), 1992.
Hurray for the Fourth of July!, Clarion (New York, NY), 1992.
Happy Easter Day!, Clarion (New York, NY), 1993.
Fox Went Out on a Chilly Night, Lothrop, Lee & Shepard (New York, NY), 1994.
Holly's Christmas Eve, HarperCollins (New York, NY), 2002.

ILLUSTRATOR

Yeta Speevach, *The Spider Plant,* Atheneum (New York, NY), 1965.
A Comic Primer, Peter Pauper (Mount Vernon, NY), 1966.
Love Is a Laugh, Peter Pauper (Mount Vernon, NY), 1967.
The Country Mouse and the City Mouse, Stinehour Press (Lunenburg, VT), 1967.
Alice E. Christgau, *Rosabel's Secret,* W. R. Scott, 1967.
Paul Tripp, *The Strawman Who Smiled by Mistake,* Doubleday (New York, NY), 1967.

Edna Boutwell, *Daughter of Liberty,* World Publishing (Cleveland, OH), 1967.

Ogden Nash, *The Cruise of the Aardvark,* M. Evans (New York, NY), 1967.

Henry Wadsworth Longfellow, *Henry Wadsworth Longfellow: Selected Poems,* edited by Clarence Merton Babcock, Peter Pauper Press (Mount Vernon, VT), 1967.

Miska Miles, *Uncle Fonzo's Ford,* Little, Brown (Boston, MA), 1968.

The Best in Offbeat Humor, Peter Pauper (Mount Vernon, NY), 1968.

Kathryn Hitte, *When Noodlehead Went to the Fair,* Parents' Magazine Press (New York, NY), 1968.

Nancy Dingman Watson (mother), *Carol to a Child,* music by Clyde Watson, World Publishing (Cleveland, OH), 1969.

Louise Bachelder, compiler, *God Bless Us, Every One,* Peter Pauper (Mount Vernon, NY), 1969.

The Jack Book, Macmillan (New York, NY), 1969.

Margaret Davidson, *Helen Keller,* Scholastic (New York, NY), 1969.

Mary H. Calhoun, *Magic in the Alley,* Atheneum (New York, NY), 1970.

Mabel Harmer, *Lizzie, the Lost Toys Witch,* Macrae Smith (Philadelphia, PA), 1970.

Louise Bachelder, compiler, *Happy Thoughts,* Peter Pauper Press (Mount Vernon, VT), 1970.

How Dear to My Heart, Peter Pauper (Mount Vernon, NY), 1970.

Clyde Watson, *Father Fox's Pennyrhymes* (verse; also see below), Crowell (New York, NY), 1971, HarperCollins (New York, NY), 2001.

Life's Wondrous Ways, Peter Pauper (Mount Vernon, NY), 1971.

America! America!, Peter Pauper (Mount Vernon, NY), 1971.

A Gift of Mistletoe, Peter Pauper (Mount Vernon, NY), 1971.

Charles Linn, *Probability,* Crowell (New York, NY), 1972.

Clyde Watson, *Tom Fox and the Apple Pie,* Crowell (New York, NY), 1972.

Clyde R. Bulla, *Open the Door and See All the People,* Crowell (New York, NY), 1972.

Bobbie Katz, *Upside Down and Inside Out: Poems for All Your Pockets,* F. Watts (New York, NY), 1973.

Nancy Dingman Watson, *The Birthday Goat,* Crowell (New York, NY), 1974.

Paul Showers, *Sleep Is for Everyone,* Crowell (New York, NY), 1974.

Clyde Watson, *Quips and Quirks,* Crowell (New York, NY), 1975.

Michael Holt, *Maps, Tracks, and the Bridges of Königsberg,* Crowell (New York, NY), 1975.

Nancy Dingman Watson, *Muncus Agruncus: A Bad Little Mouse,* Golden Press (New York, NY), 1976.

Clyde Watson, *Hickory Stick Rag* (verse), Crowell (New York, NY), 1976.

Florence Pettit, *Christmas All around the House: Traditional Decorations You Can Make,* Crowell (New York, NY), 1976.

Clyde Watson, *Binary Numbers* (nonfiction), Crowell (New York, NY), 1977.

Clyde Watson, *Catch Me and Kiss Me and Say It Again* (verse; also see below), Philomel (New York, NY), 1978.

Miska Miles, *Jenny's Cat,* Dutton (New York, NY), 1979.

Clyde Watson, *How Brown Mouse Kept Christmas,* Farrar, Straus & Giroux (New York, NY), 1980.

Jan Wahl, *Button Eye's Orange,* Warne (New York, NY), 1980.

Anne Pellowski, *Stairstep Farm: Anna Rose's Story,* Philomel (New York, NY), 1981.

Anne Pellowski, *Willow Wind Farm: Betsy's Story,* Philomel (New York, NY), 1981.

Clyde Watson, *Applebet: An ABC,* Farrar, Straus & Giroux (New York, NY), 1982.

Anne Pellowski, *Winding Valley Farm: Annie's Story,* Philomel (New York, NY), 1982.

Anne Pellowski, *First Farm in the Valley: Anna's Story,* Philomel (New York, NY), 1982.

Rebecca C. Jones, *The Biggest, Meanest, Ugliest Dog in the Whole Wide World,* Macmillan (New York, NY), 1982.

Clyde Watson, *Father Fox's Feast of Songs* (musical adaptations of poems from *Father Fox's Pennyrhymes* and *Catch Me and Kiss Me and Say It Again*), Philomel (New York, NY), 1983.

Anne Pellowski, *Betsy's Up-and-Down Year,* Philomel (New York, NY), 1983.

Carolyn Haywood, *Happy Birthday from Carolyn Haywood,* Morrow (New York, NY), 1984.

Elaine Edelman, *I Love My Baby Sister (Most of the Time),* Lothrop, Lee & Shepard (New York, NY), 1984.

Elizabeth Winthrop, *Belinda's Hurricane,* Dutton (New York, NY), 1984.

John Bierhorst, *Doctor Coyote: A Native American Aesop's Fables,* Macmillan (New York, NY), 1987.

Marcia Leonard, *Angry,* Bantam (New York, NY), 1988.

Marcia Leonard, *Happy,* Bantam (New York, NY), 1988.

Marcia Leonard, *Scared,* Bantam (New York, NY), 1988.

Marcia Leonard, *Silly,* Bantam (New York, NY), 1988.

Clyde Watson, *Valentine Foxes,* Orchard Books (New York, NY), 1989.

B. G. Hennessy, *A, B, C, D, Tummy, Toes, Hands, Knees,* Viking Kestrel (New York, NY), 1989.

Clement Clarke Moore, *The Night before Christmas,* Clarion (New York, NY), 1990.

Clyde Watson, *Love's a Sweet,* Viking Penguin (New York, NY), 1998.

John Bierhorst, *Is My Friend at Home?: Pueblo Fireside Tales,* Farrar Straus & Giroux (New York, NY), 2001.

Patricia Hubbell, *Rabbit Moon: A Book of Holidays and Celebrations,* Marshall Cavendish (New York, NY), 2002.

Clyde Watson, *Father Fox's Christmas Rhymes,* Farrar Straus & Giroux (New York, NY), 2003.

Sidelights

An author and illustrator of books for children under the age of ten, Wendy Watson is most often recognized for her artistic work, especially when it accompanies stories written by her sister Clyde Watson. The sisters' award-winning collaboration *Father Fox's Pennyrhymes*

In soft, warm illustrations, Wendy Watson depicts a family's small-town Easter Sunday celebrations. (From Happy Easter Day!, *written and illustrated by Watson.)*

was widely praised by critics, including *New York Times Book Review* contributor George A. Woods, who called the book "an American original." Watson has gone on to produce many more titles for young readers, a score of which are her own self-illustrated works, and the rest done in collaboration with writers such as her sister, her mother—the writer Nancy Dingman Watson—and other notable authors from Ogden Nash to Anne Pellowski.

Watson once told *SATA,* "My parents provided, indirectly, a great deal of my basic training in drawing and books in general." Watson was born in New Jersey, but grew up on a farm in Putney, Vermont, with her seven siblings, her artist father, and writer mother. Surrounded by animals—goats, horses and chickens—Watson also grew up in the company of art, for her father, Aldren, had his studio on the third floor of the house. Books were present everywhere as well, including those published by her mother, Nancy. Watson's "cheerful, homey illustrations reflect this rural upbringing," according to a contributor for *Children's Books and Their Creators.*

Watson attended Bryn Mawr College, majoring in Latin literature and graduating in 1964. However, from the time she was a young child, she knew she wanted to become an illustrator; during her college summers and thereafter, she received formal training from Jerry Farnsworth, Helen Sawyer, and Daniel Greene both on Cape Cod and at the National Academy of Design in 1966

and 1967. Her father also helped in her art training. Following college graduation, Watson worked for a time at a small press in New Hampshire where she was a compositor and designer, learning much about typography and design that would be invaluable to her in her book-illustrating career. In 1970 Watson married the opera singer and actor, Michael Donald Harrah.

Watson's career as a professional author and illustrator got underway in 1958—when she was only sixteen—with the publication of the self-illustrated *Very Important Cat.* Throughout the 1960s, she went on to illustrate a score of titles by other authors, until she made her name with *Father Fox's Pennyrhymes,* written by her sister Clyde. This fox entertains his large family around the fire on wintry nights with rhymes, telling of love and family life, as well as topics including gluttony and the love of song. Watson's illustrations for her sister's title were warmly received by critics and helped win the book a nomination for a National Book Award as well as inclusion in the 1972 Children's Book Showcase. The contributor for *Children's Books and Their Creators* noted that "the pen-and-ink and watercolor illustrations" for this book "depict the changing seasons of rural New England life and the chaos and warmth of family life."

The drawings for *Father Fox's Pennyrhymes* are typical of the artist's style. Having spent most of her life in Vermont, Watson creates illustrations that exude a New England country charm—"cheerful, old-fashioned illustrations," as one *Publishers Weekly* contributor characterized them in a review of *A Valentine for You.* "Her colors have a real integrity that seems to derive from the New England light," Christina Olson observed of *Wendy Watson's Mother Goose* in a *New York Times Book Review* article.

Another quality of many of Watson's illustrations is their attention to small details. A picture by Watson is often filled with objects and bustling with activity that catches the reader's eye. This aspect of her work is especially evident in books like *Wendy Watson's Frog Went A-Courting.* But while a *Publishers Weekly* reviewer remarked that "youngsters will enjoy seeking out the many droll details" in the illustrations, Olson, writing in *New York Times Book Review,* felt in this case that the "frenetic" nature of the pictures does not mesh well with the "rhythms of the text." But, for Olson, this was a small complaint when compared to the quality of the artist's work in general. "Wendy Watson is, after all," the critic concluded, "an illustrator who knows what she is doing. There is a sweetness in her work that is unfailingly appealing, and she produces thoughtful and well-made books."

Other collaborative efforts with her sister include such titles as *Tom Fox and the Apple Pie, Catch Me and Kiss Me and Say It Again, How Brown Mouse Kept Christmas, Father Fox's Feast of Songs, Love's a Sweet,* and the 2003 *Father Fox's Christmas Rhymes.* Most of these have a simple rhyming text, easily memorized by young readers or listeners, accompanied by Watson's watercolor illustrations which reveal an appreciation for family life and the fine details of childhood. A reviewer for *Horn Book,* for example, praised her "jolly, decorative illustrations" for *Father Fox's Feast of Songs.* Teaming up on her sister's collection of poems showing the ups and downs of love, *Love's a Sweet,* Watson supplies "lively colored pencil drawing that skip across the pages," according to *Booklist*'s Kathy Broderick. A critic for *Publishes Weekly* found the artwork for that same title "sweetly misted but witty," as well as "serene and soothing."

Watson has also used her own rural background, growing up in a large, loving, and boisterous family, as inspiration for her illustrations for the works of Anne Pellowski about farm families in Wisconsin, including *First Farm in the Valley: Anna's Story, Stairstep Farm: Anna Rose's Story,* and *Willow Wind Farm: Betsy's Story.* With John Bierhorst, she has worked on a duet of books involving the Native American trickster, Coyote. The 1987 volume *Doctor Coyote: A Native American Aesop's Fables* presents a bevy of Aztec interpretations of Aesop's fables. Bierhorst returned to such Coyote tales with the 2001 title *Is My Friend At Home?: Pueblo Fireside Tales,* a compilation of seven trickster tales from the Hopi tradition. Rosalyn Pierini, writing in *School Library Journal,* felt that Watson's "child-centered, humorous illustrations enliven the text and lend a great deal of personality to these archetypal characters." Similarly, *Horn Book*'s Nell D. Beram noted that Watson's cartoon-like illustrations "capture the spirit of these disarmingly absurd, unexpectedly touching tales." Rabbits take center stage in a collaborative effort with writer Patricia Hubbell for the 2002 *Rabbit Moon: A Book of Holidays and Celebrations.* Piper L. Nyman wrote in *School Library Journal* that the "adorable characters cavort over the spreads."

Watson has also produced several books around the theme of holidays and celebrations. Christmas is featured in Clement Clarke Moore's traditional poem *The Night before Christmas,* an "utterly charming version," as a contributor for *Publishers Weekly* observed. Gathering several well-known rhymes and songs about love in *A Valentine for You,* Watson created "a fetching gift for a young Valentine," according to a reviewer for *Publishers Weekly.* In *Thanksgiving at Our House,* she presents an original story which contains traditional songs and rhymes, along with full-page artwork in "a pleasantly cluttered book," as another *Publishers Weekly* contributor described the book. The extended family featured in that book prepares for the big feast, and Watson's illustrations manage to "capture the high-spirited anticipation," according to the same critic. Independence Day receives the same treatment in *Hurray for the Fourth of July!,* featuring the family in a "heartening portrait of a holiday celebration in a small American town," as a contributor for *Publishers Weekly* commented. Watson once again peppers her original

tale with traditional rhymes and songs, as well as her own artwork. She reprises the same family in *Happy Easter Day,* as the clan prepares hot-cross buns and Easter eggs for the holiday. The birth of five kittens turns out to be the biggest Easter surprise of all. Virginia Opocensky, writing in *School Library Journal,* dubbed this effort "a delightful addition for holiday shelves," and further praised Watson's illustrations, which are "bustling with activity and details." An *Entertainment Weekly* contributor also lauded Watson's "jolly" illustrations in this same work.

Watson provides her own take on foxes in *Fox Went Out on a Chilly Night,* a retelling of an old folk song about the fox who manages to go out at night to provide food for its young brood of kits, evading and eluding all the townsfolk who are soon in hot pursuit. A contributor for *Kirkus Reviews* found Watson's adaptation a worthwhile addition, especially because of the artwork "that gives the classic a heft you can almost bite into." While *Booklist*'s Mary Harris Veeder commented that Watson's illustrations "supply the motivation that sends [fox] out" in the evening, a *Publishers Weekly* reviewer suggested that "Watson's timeless illustrations offer abundant particulars to pore over."

With the self-illustrated 2002 *Holly's Christmas Eve,* Watson returns to holiday themes in a tale of a painted wooden ornament on the Christmas tree who goes in search of her missing arm. Holly is the most recent addition to the ornaments, but when the family cat crawls up the tree, Holly is knocked down, losing her arm in the process. The vacuum cleaner proceeds to gobble it up, but Holly, joined by other ornaments, including the Tin Horse and Cloth Bear, make an expedition to retrieve the lost arm. She finds the missing appendage and, with the help of Santa, manages to repair it. Once again, Watson scored a winner, both in text and artwork, according to the critics. In a *School Library Journal* review, Maureen Wade praised the "vivid, full page . . . artwork [that] captures the drama and satisfying ending." *Booklist*'s Ilene Cooper also commended Watson's illustrations, which have "the exuberance and simplicity of children's own art." And a *Kirkus Reviews* critic focused on the text, noting that though the story is "simple," Watson blends "amusing characters" and a "folksy narrative voice . . . into a satisfying, if unusual, Christmas Eve tale."

From foxes to chaotic and happy families, Watson has portrayed a myriad of characters and activities in her warm, family-oriented tales and illustrations. Blending humor and traditional scenes, Watson has created a body of work praised by critics and honored by awards committees. Watson's "honest, often wise stories and detailed country illustrations are full of joy and life," concluded the contributor for *Children's Books and Their Creators.*

Biographical and Critical Sources

BOOKS

Children's Books and Their Creators, edited by Anita Silvey, Houghton Mifflin (Boston, MA), 1995, pp. 670-671.
Continuum Encyclopedia of Children's Literature, edited by Bernice E. Cullinan and Diane G. Person, Continuum (New York, NY), 2001, p. 808.
Kingman, Lee, et al, compilers, *Illustrators of Children's Books,* Horn Book (Boston, MA), 1978, p. 167.

PERIODICALS

Booklist, March 1, 1993, Deborah Abbott, review of *Happy Easter Day!,* p. 1233; September 1, 1994, Mary Harris Veeder, review of *Fox Went Out on a Chilly Night,* p. 47; August, 1997, Hazel Rochman, review of *Sleep Is for Everyone,* p. 1904; December 1, 1998, Kathy Broderick, review of *Love's a Sweet,* p. 668; September 15, 2002, Ilene Cooper, review of *Holly's Christmas Eve,* p. 247.
Entertainment Weekly, March 11, 1994, review of *Happy Easter Day!,* p. 72.
Horn Book, October, 1971, p. 474; January, 1989, p. 64; March-April, 1993, review of *Father Fox's Feast of Songs,* p. 232; September-October, 2001, Nell D. Beram, review of *Is My Friend Home?,* p. 600.
Kirkus Reviews, October 15, 1994, review of *Fox Went Out on a Chilly Night,* p. 1418; November 1, 2002, review of *Holly's Christmas Eve,* p. 1627.
New York Times Book Review, August 15, 1971, George A. Woods, review of *Father Fox's Pennyrhymes,* p. 8; May 27, 1990, Christina Olson, "Children's Books," p. 18.
Publishers Weekly, April 27, 1990, review of *Wendy Watson's Frog Went A-Courting,* p. 60; September 14, 1990, review of *The Night before Christmas,* p. 123; January 25, 1991, review of *A Valentine for You,* p. 56; July 25, 1991, review of *Thanksgiving at Our House,* pp. 52-53; March 9, 1992, review of *Hurray for the Fourth of July!,* p. 55; October 17, 1994, review of *Fox Went Out on a Chilly Night,* p. 80; October 26, 1998, review of *Love's a Sweet,* p. 65.
School Library Journal, April, 1993, Virginia Opocensky, review of *Happy Easter Day!,* p. 116; August, 1997, Marsha McGrath, review of *Sleep Is for Everyone,* pp. 150-151; October, 1994, Roseanne Cerny, review of *Fox Went Out on a Chilly Night,* p. 116; January, 1999, Marlene Gawron, review of *Love's a Sweet,* p. 122; September, 2001, Rosalyn Pierini, review of *Is My Friend Home?,* p. 211; June, 2002, Piper L. Nyman, review of *Rabbit Moon: A Book of Holidays and Celebrations,* pp. 97-98; October, 2002, Maureen Wade, review of *Holly's Christmas Eve,* pp. 64-65.

ONLINE

VisitingAuthors.com, http://www.visitingauthors.com/ (June 29, 2003), "Wendy Watson's Biography and Books."*

WILSON, Sarah 1934-

Personal

Born October 8, 1934, in Syracuse, NY; daughter of Homer Arthur (an engineer) and Elizabeth (an artist; maiden name, Remington) Turpin; married Herbert Eugene Wilson (an architect), September 30, 1956; children: Leslie Anne, Robert Murray. *Education:* University of Madrid, Diploma de estudios Hispanicos, 1955; Ohio University, B.A., 1956.

Addresses

Home—Danville, CA. *Agent*—c/o Author Mail, Henry Holt, 115 West 18th St., New York, NY 10011.

Career

Denver General Hospital, Denver, CO, medical social worker, 1963-64; Laguna Pre-School and Laguna Beach School of Art & Design, Laguna Beach, CA, and Newport Harbor Art Museum, Newport Beach, CA, art teacher, 1965-77; freelance artist and illustrator, 1977—. Co-owner of Art Workshop West, Los Angeles, CA, 1971-73; worked as a workshop leader and as a resource teacher in the public schools of Orange County, CA. Work exhibited at museums and galleries in southern California.

Member

Authors Guild, Society of Children's Book Writers and Illustrators (past regional adviser), Bay Area Illustrators for Children, Virginia Kittredge Crosley Society.

Awards, Honors

Don Freeman memorial grant, Society of Children's Book Writers and Illustrators, 1982.

Writings

FOR CHILDREN; SELF-ILLUSTRATED

I Can Do It! I Can Do It!, Quail Street (Newport Beach, CA), 1976.
Beware the Dragons!, Harper (New York, NY), 1985.
Muskrat, Muskrat, Eat Your Peas!, Simon & Schuster (New York, NY), 1989.
The Day That Henry Cleaned His Room, Simon & Schuster (New York, NY), 1990.
Three in a Balloon, Scholastic (New York, NY), 1990.
Uncle Albert's Flying Birthday, Simon & Schuster (New York, NY), 1991.
June Is a Tune That Jumps on a Stair, Simon & Schuster (New York, NY), 1992.

FOR CHILDREN

Garage Song, illustrated by Bernie Karlin, Simon & Schuster (New York, NY), 1991.

Christmas Cowboy, illustrated by Peter Palagonia, Simon & Schuster (New York, NY), 1993.

Good Zap, Little Grog, illustrated by Susan Meddaugh, Candlewick Press (Cambridge, MA), 1995.

Hats, illustrated by Mary Mayberry, Wright Group (Bothell, WA), 1996.

Disney Babies On the Go, layouts by Orlando de la Paz, illustrated by Ron Cohee and Adam Devaney, Mouse Works (New York, NY), 1997.

What Do People Do?: A Learn-About Book, illustrated by Josie Yee, Joshua Morris Publishing (Westport, CT), 1997.

The Guide Dog, illustrated by Graham Meadows, Wright Group (Bothell, WA), 1997.

Going to the Bank, illustrated by Damon McPhail, Wright Group (Bothell, WA), 1997.

Going to the Hairdresser, illustrated by Damon McPhail, Wright Group (Bothell, WA), 1997.

(With Susan Hood) *The Curious Little Lamb,* illustrated by Josie Yee, Reader's Digest (Pleasantville, NY), 1997.

Spotty Can't Sleep, illustrated by Thompson Brothers, Reader's Digest (Pleasantville, NY), 1997.

A Baby's Got to Grow, illustrated by Peter Panas, Simon & Schuster (New York, NY), 1997.

What Should Eddie Pack?, illustrated by Carolyn Bracken and Jim Durk, Joshua Morris Publishing (Westport, CT), 1998.

Sleepytime Farm, illustrated by Susan Calitri, Reader's Digest (Pleasantville, NY), 1999.

Love and Kisses, illustrated by Melissa Sweet, Candlewick Press (Cambridge, MA), 1999.

George Hogglesberry: Grade School Alien, illustrated by Chad Cameron, Tricycle Press (Berkeley, CA), 2002.

Big Day on the River, illustrated by Randy Cecil, Henry Holt (New York, NY), 2003.

A Nap in a Lap, illustrated by Akemi Gutierrez, Henry Holt (New York, NY), 2003.

ILLUSTRATOR

Elizabeth Rush, *The House at the End of the Lane,* Green Tiger (La Jolla, CA), 1982.

Phyllis Hoffman, *Baby's First Year,* Harper (New York, NY), 1988.

Elizabeth Winthrop, *Sledding,* Harper (New York, NY), 1989.

Phyllis Hoffman, *We Play,* Harper (New York, NY), 1990.

OTHER

Author and illustrator of "The World of Food," a weekly newspaper column for children in the *Valley Times,* 1981; illustrator of "The Letter Bear," a monthly subscription letter for children, 1982-86.

Sidelights

Author and illustrator Sarah Wilson is noted by critics for her children's books full of quirky characters and downright silly situations. "Humor is something I'm drawn toward in artwork and in the world in general," Wilson once told *SATA.* In her thirty books for children,

Wilson has had much opportunity to practice her particular blend of humor: from a little boy who finally cleans his room, to an alien facing his first day in school on Earth, she treats young readers to playful interpretations of everyday childhood events. Her use of a humorous perspective on topics such as eating peas and growing up allows children to view common situations from a reassuring distance, remark reviewers. In both narrative and verse, Wilson charts the daily lives of children and has proven herself an able illustrator, preparing the artwork for other authors, as well as illustrating seven of her own titles. She has also authored a score of titles illustrated by others.

Born in Syracuse, New York, in 1934, Wilson was an only child who early on discovered the joys of art. "I've always loved children's books and illustrations from the time my mother read to me as a small child," Wilson once told *SATA.* From the age of four, she began putting together her own self-illustrated booklets, held together by paper clips. She had her first art lesson at the age of seven, an experience that added to her fertile imagination. "There was something very appealing to me about being able to carry art around in my pockets and enjoy it in a compact form," Wilson once reported. By the time she was in the fifth grade, her output had increased so much that a teacher told her she should consider becoming a children's author and illustrator when she grew up.

With her father in the Navy, Wilson and her family moved frequently, attending several different elementary schools and three high schools. Far from being a liability, this constant moving aided Wilson's artistic growth, allowing her to see how color and expression changed with the varying climates and surroundings. A

A little girl kisses her cat and starts a chain of affection that ends with the girl receiving the gesture of love in Sarah Wilson's cumulative story **Love and Kisses,** *illustrated by Melissa Sweet.*

very special place for her, in the midst of all her moving, was her grandparents' rambling house in New York state which she often visited. Full of curios from around the world, an attic packed with old junk, and a massive basement, this house filled her with amazement and ideas.

Wilson spent a year abroad in college, studying at the University of Madrid in 1955. Returning to Ohio University, she graduated the following year and also married. Two children soon followed and then time spent as a social worker and art teacher. In 1976, she published her first picture book, *I Can Do It! I Can Do It!,* featuring her own illustrations. She also began writing and illustrating a weekly newspaper column and a monthly newsletter for children. Artwork for other authors occupied the early part of her career. Working with Phyllis Hoffman, she illustrated both *Baby's First Year* and *We Play.* Reviewing the first title, a miniature chronicle of a baby's first year of life, Anna Biagioni Hart, writing in *School Library Journal,* pronounced the work "pretty," further noting that the colorful cover to the book "will easily move this one off the shelves." A reviewer for *Publishers Weekly* also praised Wilson's "gently humorous and always affectionate" illustrations in this same work. A day at nursery school is portrayed in *We Play,* mostly as seen through Wilson's "action-filled pictures," according to *Horn Book*'s Carolyn K. Jenks. And working with author Elizabeth Winthrop, Wilson contributed artwork to *Sledding,* a verse celebration of sled riding. Ann Stell, reviewing the title in *School Library Journal,* drew attention to Wilson's "animated, cheerful watercolor illustrations" in this title.

Branching out on her own, Wilson has self-illustrated a variety of tales. *Muskrat, Muskrat, Eat Your Peas!* deals with the typical situation of a finicky eater. However, in Wilson's take on this subject, Muskrat feels badly that he does not want to eat peas at the Pea Picnic, and after friends and family encourage him to eat them, they finally relent and serve him up some spaghetti. "Peas are rarely treated with such charm and good humor as in Wilson's spirited tale," declared Jeanne Marie Clancy in *School Library Journal.* Clancy further lauded Wilson's "fresh" and "humorous illustrations," and felt that the book was "an excellent read-aloud choice." Beth Herbert, writing in *Booklist,* thought that parents might think twice about Wilson's solution to a finicky eater but still found the story "amusing" and the illustrations "bustling" as well as "packed with whimsical conversational balloons." A *Kirkus Reviews* critic concluded, "Simple problem, cheerfully presented, aptly solved."

Wilson presents a historical footnote in her *Three in a Balloon,* the true story of how a rooster, a sheep, and a duck were the first air passengers, sent up in a 1793 hot-air balloon experiment. Wilson retells the situation in "lilting verse with an enticing cadence," according to *Booklist*'s Phillis Wilson, as the animals look amazed down at Earth. Wilson also praised the "gracefully shaded watercolors," pronouncing the entire effort "a

delightful, high-flying trip." Likewise, May Lou Budd called the book "a glorious flight of fantasy (and fact!)," in a *School Library Journal* review. Budd commended Wilson's "irresistible" illustrations and the use of verbal imagery in the "engaging text" that would make "imaginations . . . soar." Less impressed with the text, Maeve Visser Knoth, writing in *Horn Book Guide,* still felt the illustrations allow young children "a real sense of this flight." More flight happens in *Uncle Albert's Flying Birthday,* in which a tired baker makes a silly mistake. When he uses soap powder instead of flour for Uncle Albert's birthday cake, he sends the party revelers on an air-born excursion, hoisted aloft by soap bubbles. Anne Irish dubbed this book a "slapstick fantasy" in *Horn Book Guide,* while a reviewer for *Publishers Weekly* called it a "Poppinesque romp," further praising the "gently humorous pictures."

More humor is served up in *The Day That Henry Cleaned His Room,* about a little boy who gives his room a good scrub for the first time in a year. So momentous is the event that television reporters gather for the breaking news, the army is on hand to help cart away the mess, and scientists abound, ready to help him sort out his various animals and study the strange growth on his walls. When all is done, Henry feels so lonely in his sterile room that he cannot go to sleep until his animal friends come back, carrying loads of junk with them. *Booklist*'s Stephanie Zvirin praised this "delightful narrative" for its "clever, bouncy text," and *Horn Book*'s Ethel R. Twichell found that "both pictures and text treat the messy-room problem with riotous exaggeration." Similarly, a reviewer for *Publishers Weekly* called the same title a "hilariously hyperbolic look at an all-too-familiar chore [that] is sure to be a favorite with kids."

Wilson presents thirty-one short verses about everyday events in *June Is a Tune That Jumps on a Stair,* a "sunny and appealing" book, according to a critic for *Publishers Weekly.* This self-illustrated title is both "gentle and playful," the same reviewer observed. A contributor for *Kirkus Reviews* was also favorably impressed with the collection of verse with its "deft phrasing and lilting cadences." Nancy Seiner of *School Library Journal* added to the positive reviews, applauding the "playful watercolors" and concluding that youngsters "may embrace poetry if they begin with a book like this one."

Increasingly, Wilson has collaborated with other illustrators on her books for young readers. She serves up more rhyming text in *Garage Song,* in which a young boy stops at a garage to fill up his bike tire and then sticks around to experience all the activity there. Juliann Tarsney commended "the energetic rhythm of Wilson's rhyming text" in *Booklist,* and *School Library Journal*'s Nancy A. Gifford commented that Wilson's text produces "all the sounds, sights, and well-orchestrated action of a bustling service station." The circular nature of love is presented in *Love and Kisses,* in which a young girl kisses her cat, who kisses a cow, who kisses a goose, and so on until the kiss comes back to the little girl who originated it. A contributor for *Kirkus Reviews* found this book "small, sweet, and silly," and Lisa Gangemi Krapp echoed the sentiment in *School Library Journal,* calling *Love and Kisses* a "lighthearted title." A *Publishers Weekly* reviewer further noted that Wilson's text "charts the travels of love unleashed."

Wilson has charted the world of aliens in a pair of other titles: *Good Zap, Little Grog* and *George Hogglesberry: Grade School Alien.* In the former book, she shows that children who live on other planets may well have the same sort of day as Earth children do. Employing rhyming verse with a wide array of made-up words for objects and animals on the alien planet, Wilson creates a "winsome fantasy," according to a reviewer for *Publishers Weekly. Booklist*'s April Judge urged readers to "join the fun as you learn all about these strange but lovable creatures." Judge also lauded Wilson's "silly rhyming text." Similarly, Deborah Stevenson commented on Wilson's "nonsense-tinged poem" in *Bulletin of the Center for Children's Books,* concluding that this bedtime story was "exotic but cozy." Another alien takes center stage in *George Hogglesberry,* a tale of the first day of school, with a twist. George has just arrived on Earth from the planet Frollop II and is afraid the kids at school will find his blue skin and absence of a nose weird. He tapes a nose on his face and hopes for the best; however, all the directions he gets before school become muddled in his head. He tells himself most definitely not to walk on the ceiling, as he does at home, or to turn himself into a tomato. But when he gets a part in the school play, his unusual talents come in handy. While a critic for *Kirkus Reviews* felt this story "doesn't ring true," Sally R. Dow, writing in *School Library Journal,* thought better of the book. Dubbing it an "offbeat" tale, Dow concluded that children experiencing something new "might find George's bizarre situation humorous and reassuring."

A further prose title from Wilson is the 2003 *Big Day on the River,* illustrated by Randy Cecil. Young Willie is anxious to be off on her own, rafting on the river. But when relatives intervene, loading her with absolutely essential material for her trip, the raft sinks. Pulling Willie out of the water and saving the raft, the relatives finally depart, leaving the young girl on her own, finally. Calling the story "sunny and silly," a reviewer for *Publishers Weekly* lauded this "lark of a tale" both for its "slapstick touches and Willie's independent spirit." Writing in *School Library Journal,* Kathleen Kelly MacMillan found *Big Day on the River* "a pitch-perfect picture book," adding that "Wilson's cheeky text sings."

"I feel very fortunate to be able to illustrate for children," Wilson once concluded to *SATA.* "It's the audience I would most like to work for in the world, one that I admire and enjoy and find full of resourcefulness, daring, and an open, gentle heart. Too, I'm pleased (and still surprised, sometimes!) to have the chance to try and return some of the great pleasure I've had—and still have—from the well-loved children's books and illustrations of others."

Biographical and Critical Sources

PERIODICALS

Booklist, June 15, 1989, Beth Herbert, review of *Muskrat, Muskrat, Eat Your Peas!,* p. 1830; March 15, 1990, Phillis Wilson, review of *Three in a Balloon,* p. 1462; October 15, 1990, Stephanie Zvirin, review of *The Day That Henry Cleaned His Room,* pp. 452-453; December 1, 1991, Juliann Tarsney, review of *Garage Song,* p. 708; October 15, 1995, April Judge, review of *Good Zap, Little Grog,* p. 413.

Bulletin of the Center for Children's Books, December, 1995, Deborah Stevenson, review of *Good Zap, Little Grog,* pp. 144-145.

Horn Book, May-June, 1990, Carolyn K. Jenks, review of *We Play,* p. 325; September-October, 1990, Ethel R. Twichell, review of *The Day That Henry Cleaned His Room,* pp. 595-596.

Horn Book Guide, fall, 1990, Maeve Visser Knoth, review of *Three in a Balloon,* p. 231; fall, 1991, Anne Irish, review of *Uncle Albert's Flying Birthday,* p. 247; fall, 1999, Sheila M. Geraty, review of *Love and Kisses,* p. 2424.

Kirkus Reviews, June 15, 1989, review of *Muskrat, Muskrat, Eat Your Peas!,* p. 922; June 15, 1992, review of *June Is a Tune That Jumps on a Stair,* p. 788; December 15, 1998, review of *Love and Kisses,* p. 1805; October 1, 2002, review of *George Hogglesberry: Grade School Alien,* pp. 1483-1484.

Magpies, March, 1996, Anne Hanzl, review of *Good Zap, Little Grog,* pp. 27-28.

Publishers Weekly, October 14, 1988, review of *Baby's First Year,* p. 70; May 11, 1990, review of *The Day That Henry Cleaned His Room,* p. 259; June 14, 1991, review of *Uncle Albert's Flying Birthday,* pp. 56-57; June 22, 1992, review of *June Is a Tune That Jumps on a Stair,* p. 61; September 20, 1993, review of *Christmas Cowboy,* pp. 34-35; September 4, 1995, review of *Good Zap, Little Grog,* pp. 68-69; December 3, 2001, review of *Love and Kisses,* pp. 62-63; January 13, 2003, review of *Big Day on the River,* p. 59.

School Library Journal, January, 1989, Anna Biagioni Hart, review of *Baby's First Year,* p. 64; August, 1989, Jeanne Marie Clancy, review of *Muskrat, Muskrat, Eat Your Peas!,* p. 134; November, 1989, Ann Stell, review of *Sledding,* p. 96; March, 1990, May Lou Budd, review of *Three in a Balloon,* p. 202; September, 1991, Marge Loch-Wouters, review of *Uncle Albert's Flying Birthday,* p. 244; January, 1992, Nancy A. Gifford, review of *Garage Song,* p. 101; July, 1992, Nancy Seiner, review of *June Is a Tune That Jumps on a Stair,* p. 71; October, 1993, Jane Marino, review of *Christmas Cowboy,* p. 49; January, 1996, Judith Constantinides, review of *Good Zap, Little Grog,* pp. 98-99; February, 1999, Lisa Gangemi Krapp, review of *Love and Kisses,* p. 94; December, 2002, Sally R. Dow, review of *George Hogglesberry,* pp. 112-113; April, 2003, Kathleen Kelly MacMillan, review of *Big Day on the River,* p. 144.*

Z

ZINDEL, Paul 1936-2003

OBITUARY NOTICE—See index for *SATA* sketch: Born March 15, 1936, in Tottenville, NY; died of cancer March 27, 2003, in Manhattan, NY. Author. Zindel was a Pulitzer Prize-winning playwright who was also famous for his novels for teenagers. Although his acclaim came from writing, in college he studied chemistry, earning a B.S. in 1958 and an M.S. in 1959 from Wagner College. After working as a technical writer for a year, he spent the 1960s as a high school chemistry teacher at Tottenville High School on Staten Island. While still teaching, in his spare time he wrote plays such as *Dimensions of Peacocks* (1959) and *A Dream of Swallows* (1962). His first big success came with the 1964 play *The Effect of Gamma Rays on Man-in-the-Moon Marigolds,* which was largely based on his own unhappy Staten Island childhood living with his manic-depressive, single mother. The play ran on Broadway and earned him an Obie Award and New York Drama Critics Circle award, both in 1970, and a Pulitzer Prize for Drama in 1971; he also adapted it into a 1966 film. In addition to his plays, Zindel became a critically acclaimed author of novels for teenagers, including *The Pigman* (1968), *The Undertaker's Gone Bananas* (1978), *The Pigman's Legacy* (1980), *The Doom Stone* (1995), and *Egyptian Mystery* (2002). He also wrote books for children and continued writing plays into the 1980s, such as *A Destiny on Half Moon Street* (1985) and *Amulets against Dragon Forces* (1989), screenplays such as *Mame* (1974), and teleplays such as *Alice in Wonderland* (1985), and *Babes in Toyland* (1986). In 1984, furthermore, he published a novel for adults, *When Darkness Falls,* and in 1992 released his memoirs, *The Pigman and Me.* For all his prolific years, however, Zindel will likely be best remembered for *The Effect of Gamma Rays* and *The Pigman.*

OBITUARIES AND OTHER SOURCES:

BOOKS

Writers Directory, 18th edition, St. James (Detroit, MI), 2003.

PERIODICALS

Chicago Tribune, March 31, 2003, Section 4, p. 8.
Los Angeles Times, March 29, 2003, p. B21.
New York Times, March 29, 2003, p. A23.
Washington Post, March 29, 2003, p. B7.